States at War

States at War

A Reference Guide for Michigan in the Civil War

RICHARD F. MILLER

UNIVERSITY OF MICHIGAN PRESS
Ann Arbor

For questions or permissions,
please contact um.press.perms@umich.edu

Published in the United States of America by the
University of Michigan Press
Manufactured in the United States of America
Printed on acid-free paper

First published April 2020

A CIP catalog record for this book is available from the British
Library.

Library of Congress Cataloging-in-Publication Data

Names: Miller, Richard F., 1951– author.
Title: States at war : a reference guide for Michigan in the Civil
    War / Richard F. Miller.
Other titles: States at war (University of Michigan Press)
Description: Ann Arbor : University of Michigan Press,
    2020. | Includes bibliographical references and index.
Identifiers: LCCN 2019053457 (print) | LCCN 2019053458
    (ebook) | ISBN 9780472131457 (hardcover) |
    ISBN 9780472125739 (ebook)
Subjects: LCSH: Michigan—History—Civil War, 1861–
    1865. | Michigan—History—Civil War, 1861–1865—Sources.
Classification: LCC F566 .M695 2020 (print) | LCC F566
    (ebook) | DDC 977.4/03—dc23
LC record available at https://lccn.loc.gov/2019053457
LC ebook record available at https://lccn.loc.gov/2019053458

To Nathaniel David Miller, "Blessed be he who comes!"

Acknowledgments

I would like to thank those who made this Michigan volume of *States at War* happen. Scott D. Ham, Associate Acquiring Editor for Michigan and the Great Lakes at the University of Michigan Press, saw value in a work of this kind and patiently shepherded *A Reference Guide for Michigan in the Civil War* through the publication process. Scott also facilitated my research needs along with Assistant Director and Archivist for University History Brian Williams and Director of the University Press Charles Watkinson. I am grateful for their confidence and hope that it is fulfilled in the finished book. The cheerful staff at the Bentley Historical Library was unfailingly helpful during my research visit to Ann Arbor. On the production side, editor Kevin Rennells and associate Daniel Otis copyedited the manuscript with great patience and precision. However, I am alone responsible for any errors that appear in this book.

In its beginnings, the *SAW* series was greatly improved by the criticism of Professor Emeritus James McPherson of Princeton University, Associate Professor of History Robert Bonner at Dartmouth College, and the dean of Vermont's Civil War historians, Mr. Howard Coffin. The late and very much lamented University Press of New England published *SAW*'s first six volumes, and I wish to thank my then editor Dr. Phyllis Deutsch, now a Lecturer at Dartmouth College, who oversaw the series from volumes 1 to 6.

Finally, although this latest addition to *SAW* is dedicated to our new grandson, Nathaniel David Miller, I lovingly acknowledge Alyson, my best friend, love and help mate for over four decades. A true *Eishet Chayil*, her influence can be found on every page and in each word that follows.

Contents

Digital materials related to this title can be found on the Fulcrum platform via the following citable URL: https://doi.org/10.3998/mpub.10196504

Abbreviations

Terms

AAG: Assistant Adjutant General
AAPMG: Acting Assistant Provost Marshal General
AC: Army Corps
ADC: Aide de Camp
AG: Adjutant General
AIG: Assistant Inspector General
AQM: Assistant Quartermaster
ASW: Assistant Secretary of War
AWOL: Away Without Leave
CSA: Confederate States Army
CSS: Confederate States Ship
DA: District Attorney
DFD: Discharged for Disability, i.e., wounds or disease
    incurred in active service
DOD: Died of Disease
DOW: Died of Wounds
EO: Enrollment Officer
GO: General Orders
IG: Inspector General
JAG: Judge Advocate General
JCCW: Joint Committee for the Conduct of the War
JR: Joint Resolution
KGC: Knights of the Golden Circle
KIA: Killed in Action
MIA: Missing in Action
NCO: Noncommissioned Officer
PG: Provost Guard
PM: Provost Marshal
PMG: Provost Marshal General
POW: Prisoner of War
QM: Quartermaster
QMG: Quartermaster General
SG: Surgeon General
UP: Upper Peninsula
USA: United States Army
USCT: United States Colored Troops
USDC: United States District Court
USG: United States Government

USMC: United States Marine Corps
USS: United States Ship
USSS: United States Sharpshooter
USV: United States Volunteers
VRC: Veterans Reserve Corps
WIA: Wounded in Action

Sources

AAC: *Appleton Annual Cyclopaedia*
AG: *Report of the Adjutant General of the State of Michigan*,
    followed by the year and page number
ALP: *Abraham Lincoln Papers, Library of Congress*
BD: *Biographical Directory*
CG: *Congressional Globe*
CIB: *Colonels in Blue—Michigan*
CQ: *Congressional Quarterly*
Dyer: *Dyer's Compendium*
EHM: *Early History of Michigan*
EMB: *Early Michigan Biographies*
FAC: *Father Abraham's Children*
GIB: *Generals in Blue*
HJ.37/38: U.S. House Journal, followed by Congress
JCC: *Journal of the Common Council*
JMH: *Journal of the Michigan House*
JMS: *Journal of the Michigan Senate*
MAP: *Michigan as Province*
MHM: *Michigan History Magazine*
MHR: *Michigan Historical Review*
MIW: *Michigan in the War*
MOG: *Messages of Governors*
MPL: *Michigan Public Laws*
MSSM: *Massachusetts Soldiers, Sailors and Marines in the
    Civil War*
OR: *The War of Rebellion: A Compilation of the Official Records
    of the Union and Confederate Armies*
ORN: *The War of Rebellion: A Compilation of the Official
    Records of the Union and Confederate Navies*
PH: *McPherson, Political History*
PR8: *Preliminary Report, Eighth Census*
RL: *Regimental Losses of the American Civil War, 1861–1865*

ROS: Roster of Service
SAL: Statutes at Large, U.S.
SAL-C: Statutes at Large, Confederate
SAW: States at War
SJ.37/38: U.S. Senate Journal, followed by Congress

Newspapers

AAA: Ann Arbor Argus
AG: Alexandria Gazette and Advertiser (Virginia)
AGZ: Allergan Gazette
BCT: Bay City Times
BCTr: Bay City Tribune
BJ: Boston Journal (Massachusetts)
CA: Crawford Avalanche
CAR: Critic and Record (Washington)
CCR: Cass County Republican
CDE: Cincinnati Daily Enquirer
CH: Cleveland Herald
CL: Cleveland Leader
CML: Cleveland Morning Leader
CNC: Charleston News & Courier (South Carolina)
CPD: Cleveland Plain Dealer
CT: Chicago Tribune
DA: Detroit Advertiser
DAT: Detroit Advertiser and Tribune
DDT: Detroit Daily Tribune
DFP: Detroit Free Press
DNI: Daily National Intelligencer
DSS: Daily State Sentinel
DT: Detroit Times
DWT: Detroit Weekly Tribune
ESC: East Saginaw Courier

FJ: Flint Journal
GHN: Grand Haven News
GRE: Grand Rapids Eagle
GREL: Grand Rapids Evening Leader
GRP: Grand Rapids Press
GRWL: Grand Rapids Weekly Leader
HDN: Hillsdale Daily News
HPG: Hudson Post Gazette
HS: Hillsdale Standard
HWS: Hillsdale Whig Standard
JC: Jackson Citizen
JCP: Jackson Citizen Patriot
JP: Jackson Patriot
KG: Kalamazoo Gazette
LSJ: Lansing State Journal
LSR: Lansing State Republican
MA: Michigan Argus
MC: Muskegon Chronicle
MSA: Michigan State Argus
MT: Milford Times
NR: National Republican
NYCA: New York Commercial Advertiser
NYT: New York Times
NYTr: New York Tribune
ODS: Ohio Daily Statesman
RIE: Riverside Independent Enterprise (California)
SH: Saginaw Herald
SJSH: St. Joseph Saturday Herald
SJT: St. Joseph Traveler
SN: Saginaw News
WE: Weekly Expositor (Brockway Center, Michigan)
WES: Washington Evening Star
WT: Washington Times
YC: Ypsilanti Commercial

Introduction

Organization of *States at War*

States at War: Michigan presents the period between January 1860 and December 1865 in chronological order. Preceding the chronology is an introductory section that provides Michigan's background as a state, a people, and an economy as well as a snapshot of Michigan in 1860. Introductory materials include Michigan's War Geography, Economy in 1860, Governance and Politicians, Slavery and Race, and Demography, each further divided into separate issues.

War Geography considers Michigan's geographic position not only as it influenced its economy (e.g., lakes for shipping, proximity to the war, and borders) but also as these affected the state's experience with territorial insecurities. Thus, Michigan's border with Canada and its vulnerability to Confederate and insurgent operations and hostile navies influenced how the state allocated resources to frontier troops, coastal fortifications, garrisons, and militias.

Economy in 1860 highlights state industries, commerce, finance, agriculture, and railroads on the eve of war.

Governance and Politicians summarizes Michigan's state constitutional provisions that are especially relevant to wartime matters. It lists congressional districts in the Thirty-Seventh Congress and delegations to the Thirty-Seventh and Thirty-Eighth Congresses, noting legislators' standing committee assignments. It also gives biographical information about Michigan's federal senators, representatives, and the most crucial "protagonists" of *SAW*, its governors and adjutant generals.

Slavery and Race sketches the history of Michigan's African American population and its history with racial discrimination. It also discusses its experience with the Fugitive Slave Act, abolition, and antislavery sentiment among its white and black populations.

Demography and **Immigrants and Immigration** sketches Michigan's 1860 population, the distribution of the population, and its ethnic groups. This section covers issues related to immigration, considering both the state's relatively inconsequential experience with the 1850s Know-Nothings and the far more consequential efforts to attract European immigrants.

Chronology

Following the brief introductory essay, the chapters present a detailed chronology outlining some major events and themes important to Michigan's involvement in the Civil War. A chronology is presented for each year between 1860 and 1865. Each year's chronology of key events is followed by sections on Selected Legislation and Military Affairs.

Key Events are "key" from Michigan's perspective and deal chiefly with in-state events. The actors whose doings matter are governors, lieutenant governors, adjutant generals, and also presidents, vice presidents, the secretary of state, secretaries of war, members of Congress, senior (and sometimes junior) War Department bureaucrats, and state political party officials. Occasionally, individual state legislators appear, as do state supreme court judges, general officers, newspaper editors, civic and religious leaders, and private citizens with something to say. This cast is occasionally leavened by the acts of Confederate raiders, POWs, racist mobs, peace men, genuinely disloyal citizens, social activists, philanthropic men and women, and a few spies. Together with the Chronology, Key Events hopes to provide a skeletal narrative of how Michigan responded to some of the war's challenges.

Selected Legislation sections are organized by date and include war-relevant statutes, resolutions, and committee reports. Each legislative session is introduced by a quotation from the governor's message to that session, which often set the agenda for the session. Readers should note that the summaries of statutes and resolutions have been substantially abridged.

Military Affairs concludes each year's entry. This section attempts to summarize the year's military events or trends, which can be difficult to place chronologically. "Military" is broadly defined: among other things, it includes state financing of military necessities and recruiting expenses; conscription, enrollment, and recruitment data; and Michigan operations supporting soldiers' health and morale, often a few miles from the battlefield. It is well to note here one aspect of the Civil War that bedeviled contemporaries as much as it has later historians: the utter irreconcilability of competing claims (between states and the War Department) about the number of men credited under various volunteer and draft calls. Michigan usually argued that they had sufficient *credits*, while the War Department confronted the reality of insufficient *men*; the answer depended on *when* one counted, *whom* one counted, and especially *how* one counted.

Editorial Considerations

Biographical notes generally are not given for federal executive-branch officials at the cabinet rank, or for senior federal army and navy officers (except those with strong state connections, such as Lewis Cass, Orlando Willcox, or Israel Richardson). Some minor figures are excluded, such as minor-party gubernatorial contenders and unsuccessful candidates for Congress, unless they were important contributors to Michigan's Civil War experience. One of *States at War*'s (*SAW*'s) objectives is to revive the narrative of state action during the war, which means providing biographical treatments of now-obscure figures. Some 195 men and women are presented. *SAW* aspires to a uniform presentation of these lives more often than it succeeds. Less is known about some now-obscure figures, and what is known is sometimes based on conflicting information. Moreover, the information that does exist is often gathered from many texts, and the editor asks readers' patience with what may appear to be excessive sourcing. The intention is to provide a bibliographic footprint that many readers may find useful.

What is true for less prominent state actors is also the case for many private soldiers' welfare organizations. While national organizations such as the Sanitary Commission and the Christian Commission are well documented, neighborhood (e.g., sewing circles), city (e.g., local auxiliaries of national organizations or other groups whose activities are confined to a particular town), and even statewide groups have left fewer tracks. Regrettably, this paucity also is reflected in *SAW*.

State General Orders and Special Orders could be issued or signed by the governor, the adjutant general, or another subordinate, in his own name or on behalf of the governor or adjutant general. With one exception, *SAW* attributes no special significance to particular signatories, and such orders may be attributed to the state, as in "Michigan issues GO No. 1." However, whether dealing with states or the War Department, personalities can matter, and where (in the opinion of the editor) they do, the actual signatory is identified and background information provided.

Annual election results for state legislatures are given by party. In weighing these, readers are cautioned that in many cases the "real" divisions might be less than implied by party labels. Readers should pay particular attention to the relationship between a given politician and the war. Unlike Ohio, which elected national "peace" candidates such as Clement Vallandigham and George Pendleton, Michigan politics were not conducive to peace candidates of any party. The state's Democrats were largely Unionists, and despite occasional rhetorical excesses driven by party competition, were in the main supportive of a vigorous prosecution of the war, despite harsh criticism of Lincoln's policies on civil liberties, war management, and especially, race and reconstruction.

Readers should be aware of an editing peculiarity present throughout Series III of the *Official Records*. Many of the letters sent by the War Department to state officials were copied to other recipients, or in some cases to all of the loyal governors or state adjutant generals. For reasons of economy, however, the *OR*'s editors chose to include only a single example of each letter; a list of other recipients appears nearby, or in a few instances, the statement "Copies sent to all loyal governors" or some such wording is included.

The federal and state statutes and resolutions selected for inclusion under each legislative session or in the Chronology are *not* the précis of statutes so beloved by law students; although every effort has been made to include original quoted material, the laws reproduced here have been doubly edited: first, statutory provisions that were purely procedural or irrelevant to a law's main purposes have been omitted; second, what has been included has been paraphrased from the language of legal contingency into something like ordinary prose. However, the original names of statutes and resolutions are retained and sourced; statutes are grouped by legislative sessions and, when available, the dates of passage are given. Statutes and resolutions appear in order by date of enactment and not by the statutory or other number later assigned. The section numbers within statutes are in numerical order but with omissions: only sections that embody the statute's main points are listed, while purely procedural provisions are omitted (with apologies to legal scholars who know that the line between "procedure" and "substance" is often blurry).

Reading *States at War: Michigan*

The streaming chronological structure invites two ways to read *States at War: Michigan*. The first reading is vertical, which considers Michigan solely as a state at war: its laws, elections, and federal relations; how it financed, recruited, organized, armed, and equipped its military units; its support programs for soldiers and their dependents; and many other matters. When integrated with the Chronology of Events, Battles, Laws, and General Or-

ders, the book might stand alone as a skeletal history of a Michigan's war years.

But *SAW* also can be read horizontally. In volumes 1 to 6 of *States at War*, similarly organized Civil War histories of thirteen states allow readers to scan the same month across other states, comparing reactions to the same event, or the different (or similar) solutions that states developed to solve the same problems (e.g., the welfare of soldiers' dependents), meet challenges (e.g., dissent, recruiting), or cope with frictions that occurred as the federal government intruded into areas previously under exclusive state control (e.g., conscription, and taxation).

What is different about *SAW* is not the facts it contains—these and the sources from which they derive have long been in the scholarly and public domains—but rather, its parallel presentments of states at war. The editor of *States at War* can hope for no more than that some future, better mind will read this material and, through the induction that such a presentation invites, discern previously unrecognized differences, similarities, and connections that eluded him.

Michigan
Upper Peninsula

Districts
circa 1860

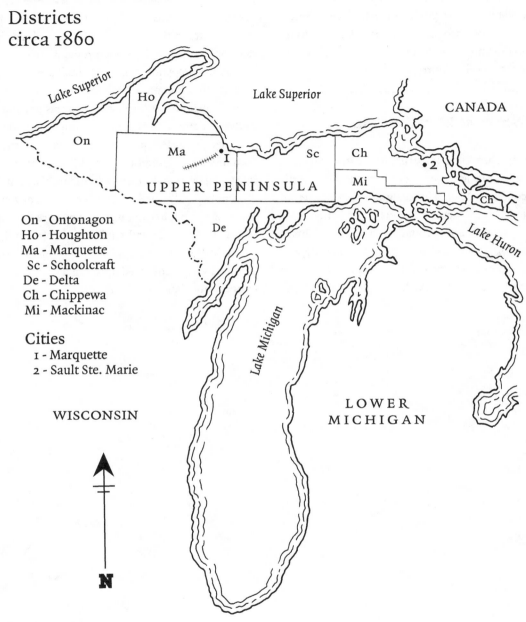

Lake Superior

Ho

Lake Superior

CANADA

On

Ma

Sc

Ch

•1

UPPER PENINSULA

Mi

•2

Ch

De

Lake Huron

On - Ontonagon
Ho - Houghton
Ma - Marquette
Sc - Schoolcraft
De - Delta
Ch - Chippewa
Mi - Mackinac

Cities
1 - Marquette
2 - Sault Ste. Marie

Lake Michigan

LOWER
MICHIGAN

WISCONSIN

N

Michigan

Districts circa 1860

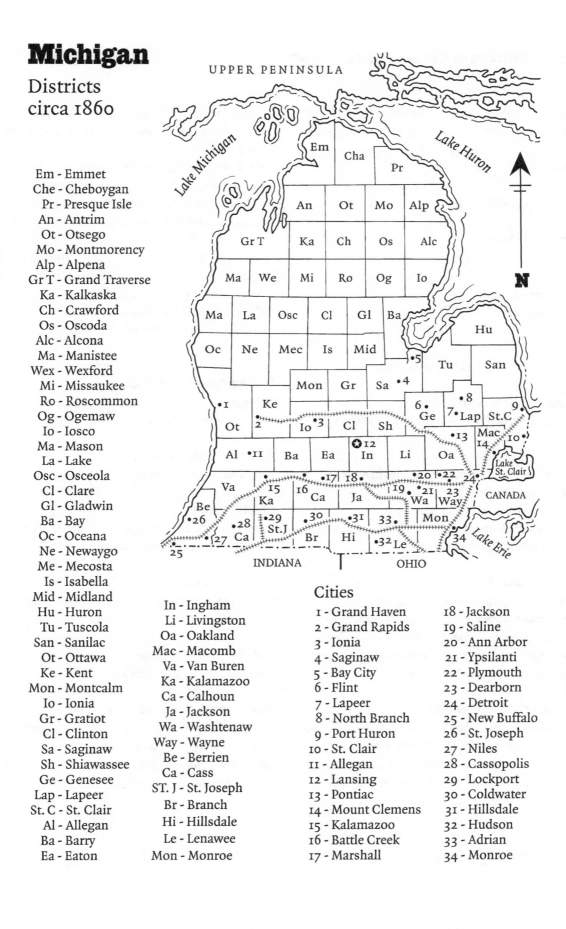

Em - Emmet
Che - Cheboygan
Pr - Presque Isle
An - Antrim
Ot - Otsego
Mo - Montmorency
Alp - Alpena
Gr T - Grand Traverse
Ka - Kalkaska
Ch - Crawford
Os - Oscoda
Alc - Alcona
Ma - Manistee
Wex - Wexford
Mi - Missaukee
Ro - Roscommon
Og - Ogemaw
Io - Iosco
Ma - Mason
La - Lake
Osc - Osceola
Cl - Clare
Gl - Gladwin
Ba - Bay
Oc - Oceana
Ne - Newaygo
Me - Mecosta
Is - Isabella
Mid - Midland
Hu - Huron
Tu - Tuscola
San - Sanilac
Ot - Ottawa
Ke - Kent
Mon - Montcalm
Io - Ionia
Gr - Gratiot
Cl - Clinton
Sa - Saginaw
Sh - Shiawassee
Ge - Genesee
Lap - Lapeer
St. C - St. Clair
Al - Allegan
Ba - Barry
Ea - Eaton

In - Ingham
Li - Livingston
Oa - Oakland
Mac - Macomb
Va - Van Buren
Ka - Kalamazoo
Ca - Calhoun
Ja - Jackson
Wa - Washtenaw
Way - Wayne
Be - Berrien
Ca - Cass
ST. J - St. Joseph
Br - Branch
Hi - Hillsdale
Le - Lenawee
Mon - Monroe

Cities

1 - Grand Haven
2 - Grand Rapids
3 - Ionia
4 - Saginaw
5 - Bay City
6 - Flint
7 - Lapeer
8 - North Branch
9 - Port Huron
10 - St. Clair
11 - Allegan
12 - Lansing
13 - Pontiac
14 - Mount Clemens
15 - Kalamazoo
16 - Battle Creek
17 - Marshall

18 - Jackson
19 - Saline
20 - Ann Arbor
21 - Ypsilanti
22 - Plymouth
23 - Dearborn
24 - Detroit
25 - New Buffalo
26 - St. Joseph
27 - Niles
28 - Cassopolis
29 - Lockport
30 - Coldwater
31 - Hillsdale
32 - Hudson
33 - Adrian
34 - Monroe

Principal Officers of the Department of War

During the war, the federal officials that states usually dealt with on matters of recruiting, organizing, equipping, arming, transporting, and conscripting recruits were employees of the Department of War. Biographical sketches for the following list of Principal Officers in the department can be found in *SAW.*5.

Secretaries of War

Joseph Holt, ad interim, December 31, 1860, appointed and confirmed by the Senate, January 18, 1861

Simon Cameron, March 5, 1861

Edwin M. Stanton, January 15, 1862

Chief Clerk

James Lesley, Jr., March to November 1861

Assistant Secretaries of War

Thomas A. Scott, appointment authorized August 3, 1861

Peter H. Watson, January 24, 1862, to July 31, 1864

Brigadier General Catharinus P. Buckingham, special duty, assistant to the secretary of war, July 16, 1862; resigned February 11, 1863

Christopher P. Wolcott, appointed June 12, 1862; resigned January 23, 1863

Adjutants General

Colonel Samuel Cooper, resigned March 7, 1861

Colonel Lorenzo Thomas, March 7, 1861, promoted to brigadier general, August 3, 1861 (From March 23, 1863, Thomas was on special duty and **Col. Edward D. Townsend** assumed his functions)

Assistant Adjutants General

Captain Absalom Baird, May 11 to July 2, 1861; assigned as adjutant general of Tyler's Division in Washington's defenses, and then during the Battle of First Bull Run, July 2 to July 25, 1861; afterwards, Baird returned to the War Department as AAG until November 21 when he was assigned as IG and Chief of Staff to the Fourth Corps.

Captain Thomas M. Vincent, August 3, 1861; promoted to colonel and lieutenant colonel, September 24, 1864; promoted to brigadier general, March 13, 1865

Captain Charles W. Foster, September 19, 1861; named chief of the Bureau of Colored Troops on May 22, 1863 (*see Chronology for this date,* GO Nos. 143 and 144); promoted to lieutenant colonel and colonel, September 24, 1864

Colonel Edward D. Townsend, November 1, 1861 to March 23, 1863, when promoted to Acting Adjutant General (*see above*)

Judge Advocate General

Colonel Joseph Holt, September 3, 1862, promoted to brigadier general, June 22, 1864

Quartermaster General

Brigadier General Montgomery C. Meigs, May 15, 1861

Chief of Engineers

Joseph G. Totten, died April 22, 1864, replaced by **Brigadier General Richard Delafield**

Chief of Ordnance

Brigadier General James W. Ripley, retired September 15, 1863

Provost Marshal General

Colonel James B. Fry, March 17, 1863

Assistants to the Provost Marshal General

Colonel George D. Ruggles, ADC, AAG, Brevet Brigadier General, to August 16, 1864

Colonel N. L. Jeffries, VRC, Brevet Brigadier General, USV, from August 17, 1864

Biographies

Russell A. Alger (1836–1907) was born in Lafayette, Ohio, and was educated publicly and privately. In 1857, Alger began to read law in Akron and was admitted to the bar in 1859. That year he moved to Grand Rapids and entered the lumber business. On September 2, 1861, he was commissioned a captain in the Second Michigan Cavalry and promoted to major on April 2, 1862. Taken POW at the Battle of Booneville in July 1862, he escaped the same day. On October 16, 1862, Alger became lieutenant colonel of the Sixth Michigan Cavalry, and colonel of the Fifth Michigan Cavalry on February 28, 1863. He was wounded at Boonsboro, Maryland, on July 8, 1863, and resigned on September 20, 1864. His battle itinerary included Corinth, Gettysburg, and the Overland Campaign, reportedly sixty-six battles or skirmishes. Postwar, Alger was double brevetted to brigadier and then major general for gallantry. Alger returned to Michigan and the lumber business. In 1884, he was elected governor of Michigan as a Republican, and in 1888 served as a presidential elector. In 1889, he was national commander of the Grand Army of the Republic. In 1897, President McKinley appointed Alger secretary of war, and he served throughout the Spanish-American War, resigning in 1899. In 1902, he was appointed to the United States Senate to fill an unexpired term, and served until his death. *BD*, 553; *Michigan in the War*, 769; "Death of Senator Russell A. Alger, Proceedings in the Senate," contained in *Russell Alexander Alger (Late a Senator from Michigan), Memorial Addresses, Fifty-Ninth Congress Second Session, Senate of the United States, February 23, 1907, House of Representatives, February 24, 1907* (Washington: Government Printing Office, 1907), 9–10, 12, 43, 48; as quoted, 74; 95–96; *WT*, January 24, 1907; *DT*, January 24, 1907.

Henry Jones Alvord (1811–1877) was born in Montague City, Massachusetts, graduated from medical school in 1832, and moved to Michigan soon thereafter. He practiced medicine, but also politics: he was a delegate to the 1835 statehood convention and the 1850 state constitutional convention. He also held local offices, including in the state Senate. Between 1859 and 1861, he was coeditor of the *Detroit Herald*, which closed in 1861. Postwar, Al-vord remained in Washington until his death. He is buried in Michigan. *A Genealogy of the Descendants of Alexander Alford, an Early Settler of Windsor, Conn. and Northampton, Mass.*, compiled by Samuel Morgan Alvord (Webster, NY: A. D. Andrews, 1908), 213–214; Farmer, *History of Detroit and Wayne County*, Vol. I, 91, 677.

Edwin V. Andress (1838–1884) was commissioned captain of Company K of the First Michigan Sharpshooters on July 22, 1863. On May 12, 1864, he was wounded at Spotsylvania (albeit under questionable circumstances) and discharged for disability on July 26, 1864. *Michigan in the War*, 762; see Raymond J. Herek, *These Men Have Seen Hard Service: The First Michigan Sharpshooters in the Civil War* (Detroit: Wayne State University Press, 1998), 157, 475n144–145, 35.

Walter O. Ashley (1835–1899) was born in Claremont, New Hampshire, and moved to Michigan in about 1850, eventually settling in Detroit. Postwar, Ashley eventually founded Ashley & Dustin, which owned a number of vessels offering service to Great Lakes destinations. *History of the Great Lakes, Illustrated*, in two volumes (Chicago: J. H. Beers, 1899), Vol. II, 335–336; *DFP*, September 28, 1899.

Electus Backus (1804–June 7, 1862) was born in New York. His father was a lieutenant colonel who was killed in action during the War of 1812. Backus graduated from West Point in 1824 and was stationed in Florida and Missouri. He served (1837–38) as an ADC to General Hugh Brady, then commanding Military District No. 7, headquartered in Detroit. Backus lived in Michigan for the rest of his life. He gained distinction in both the Seminole War (1838–40) and the Mexican War, and was brevetted major. During the 1850s, Backus was a recruiter in New York and also saw frontier service in New Mexico Territory, which included fighting Indians. By 1860, he was ranked lieutenant colonel. The attack on Fort Sumter found him in Texas; after General Twiggs's surrender, he returned north. Backus was appointed chief U.S. mustering and disbursing officer based in Detroit. He was on sick leave between March 8 and September 24, 1861; he returned to sick leave from March 6, 1862, until his death on June 7 in Detroit. *Biographical Register*, Vol. I (1868), 267; Farmer, *History of Detroit and Michigan*, 1078; DFP, June 8, 1862.

John S. Bagg (1809–1870) was born in Lanesborough, Massachusetts, and educated locally; afterwards he read law in Watertown, New York. While studying for the bar he also wrote for a cousin's newspaper, the Watertown *Freeman*. Bagg eventually became editor. In 1835, he moved to Detroit, and in 1836 became publisher and editor of the Detroit *Free Press*. After Michigan's admission to the Union, Bagg was chosen as state printer. He was a Jacksonian Democrat, and the *Free Press* often expressed his views. Polk appointed Bagg Detroit's postmaster. He sold the *Free Press* and retired to a farm in Hamtramck. Buchanan appointed Bagg U.S. marshal for the district of Michigan, and he served until 1861. Bagg returned to the *Free Press* and died in Detroit. *American Biographical History of Eminent and Self-Made Men, with Portrait Illustrations on Steel, Michigan Volume* (Cincinnati, OH: Western Biographical Publishing Co., 1878), 6–7.

Henry P. Baldwin (1814–1892) was born in Coventry, Rhode Island, and educated publicly and privately. By 1838, he had moved to Detroit and soon opened a retail shoe store before entering wholesaling, personally transporting dry goods to Michigan's interior. Baldwin became one of Michigan's most prominent businessmen and the state's foremost banker. He was also present "Under the Oaks" in Jackson. In 1860, he was a Michigan Republican senator and played a key role in restoring state finances after treasurer McKinney's defalcation. In 1864, Baldwin ran unsuccessfully against Henry H. Crapo for the Republican gubernatorial nomination, although he supported Crapo in the general election. In 1868, Baldwin won the nomination for governor and was elected for two terms. After Zachariah Chandler's death in November 1879, Baldwin was chosen to serve for the remainder of the term, but was not reelected. Afterward he returned to banking until his death in Detroit. Compiled from various eulogies to Baldwin contained in *Journal of the House of Representatives of the State of Michigan, 1893, in Three Volumes*, Vol. I (Lansing: Robert Smith & Co., State Printers, 1893), 834–857; BD, 601.

Kirkland C. Barker (1819–1875) was born in East Schuyler, New York, educated publicly, and worked as clerk in Utica, New York, and Cleveland, Ohio. He moved to Detroit in 1844 and sold tobacco, founding what was later named the American Eagle Tobacco Company. He was elected alderman in 1863 and mayor the next year. Postwar, he moved to Grosse Isle and became a devoted yachtsman. He drowned in a boating accident in the Detroit River. *Biographical Dictionary Mayors*, 16; DFP, May 22, 25, 1875.

Henry Barns (1815/16–1871) was born in England and immigrated to the United States, eventually settling in Detroit in 1836. He was trained as a printer, and in 1837 he purchased a share of the *Detroit Free Press*, sold it the following year, and then founded the *Niles Sentinel*. In 1851, he became a proprietor and editor of the *Detroit Daily Tribune*, a Whig sheet; in 1855 he became its sole publisher. Barns also published magazines, including the *Monthly Hersperian and Odd Fellows' Literary Magazine* and the *Michigan Journal of Education and Teachers' Magazine*. In February 1854, he chaired a conference of Whig newspaper editors (held in Austin Blair's office) to plot a course for a new party; soon he began publishing the Lansing *Republican*. Barns served as the clerk of the House of Representatives (1855) and in 1858 was elected to the state Senate. On July 8, 1862, the *Daily Tribune* was consolidated with the Detroit *Advertiser* to become the *Advertiser and Tribune*. Throughout the war years, Barns's paper became the nemesis of the Democratic organ, the *Detroit Free Press*. It was Barns who secured authorization for the First Michigan Colored Infantry. Postwar, Johnson appointed (1866) Barns postmaster; after 1869, he was a pension agent. In 1871, Barns committed suicide in Detroit. Farmer, *The History of Detroit and Michigan*, 683, 100, 883, 675, 226; 168; *Under the Oaks*, 26–28; William Stocking, "Prominent Newspaper Men in Michigan," in *Michigan Historical Collections*, Vol. XXXIX, 1915 (Lansing: Michigan Historical Commission, 1915), 160, 168; EMB, 70–71; DFP, July 22, 1871.

James J. Barns, Henry Barns's brother (also an *Advertiser* journalist) was born in New York. On May 1, 1861, he enlisted as a corporal in the three-months iteration of the First Michigan Regiment. He was captured at First Bull Run and not released until July 6, 1862. Barns was commissioned first lieutenant in the Twenty-Fourth on July 26, 1862, and remained with the regiment until October 25, 1862, when he took sick leave. He returned in early February 1863 and rejoined his unit, with combat at Fitzhugh Crossing, Chancellorsville, and on the Port Royal Expedition. He resigned for disability on May 9, 1863. *History of the Twenty-Fourth Michigan*, 321, 42, 359; *Michigan in the War*, 768.

John S. Barry (1802–1870) was born in Amherst, New Hampshire, and raised in Vermont. In 1824 he became headmaster of a Georgia academy, where he also read law. He was admitted to the bar and served as an ADC to Georgia's governor. He moved to White Pigeon, Michigan, in 1831 and then Constantine in 1834. Barry was a delegate to Michigan's 1835 constitutional convention, and afterward was elected to Michigan's Senate, serving several terms as a Democrat. Barry emerged as a party leader and was elected and reelected governor (1841 and 1843). He steered the state through a financial crisis, instituted bank reform, and oversaw the University of Michigan's founding and the chartering of Michigan railroads. Barry was constitutionally term-limited and left office in 1846, but returned in 1850 for one term, defeating the Whig and Free Soil nominees. Afterward, he returned to Constantine and business. His last public office was in 1864 as a Democratic presidential elector. *Biographical Directory of the Governors*, II, 743; *Portrait and Biographical Album of Oakland County, Michigan* (Chicago: Chapman Brothers, 1891), 113–114; *DFP*, January 16, 1870.

Robert J. Barry was appointed PM of the Third District on April 24, 1863, and was honorably discharged on October 15, 1865. A Republican and resident of Washtenaw County, Barry had served as county clerk (1855–1863).

Henry Baxter (1821–1873) was born in Sidney Plains, New York, and in 1831 moved to Michigan, ultimately settling in Jonesville. Baxter briefly attended the University of Michigan at White Pigeon, but left to enter the family milling business. In 1849 he crossed overland to California, but had returned to Jonesville by 1852. After the Civil War began, Baxter captained a local militia company, which became Company C of the Seventh Michigan. Within two years, Baxter, whose battle itinerary paralleled that of the Army of the Potomac, was promoted to brigadier general. Twice severely wounded, he earned a brevet to major general. Postwar, he was Grant's minister to Honduras (1869–1872), afterward returning to Jonesville. Jay C. Martin, *General Henry Baxter, 7th Michigan*

Volunteer Infantry, A Biography (Jefferson, NC: McFarland & Co., 2016), 6–7, 10–13; Ezra Warner, *Generals in Blue*, 25–26.

John Yates Beall (1835–February 24, 1865) was born in Jefferson County [West] Virginia, and attended the University of Virginia. He had prewar service in the Virginia militia; when the war began, his unit was folded into the Second Virginia and served with the Stonewall Brigade. In the fall of 1861 Beall was shot through the chest, ending his combat career. Having recovered by late 1862, he was in Canada seeking to rejoin the war effort. He conceived the plan to liberate Confederate POWs on Johnson's Island, and in January 1863, he was in Richmond, Virginia, to pitch that scheme and advocate for privateering on the Potomac River and Chesapeake Bay. He persuaded Secretary of the Navy Stephen Mallory, who commissioned Beall an acting master. Beall had some success, but in November 1863 was captured and in May 1864 exchanged. By August he was back in Canada, and by September, in Windsor, Ontario. The *Philo Parsons* plot, and Beall's role in it, are detailed in the 1864 chapter. Beall returned to the Confederate Secret Service. On December 16, 1864, Beall, in civilian dress, was captured in New York state during an attempt to seize a prison train thought to be carrying Confederate officer POWs. He was tried as a spy; Lincoln refused to pardon him, and he was executed at Fort Columbus, New York Harbor. *Memoir of John Yates Beall: His Life; Trial; Correspondence; Diary; including the account of the Raid on Lake Erie* (Montreal, Can.: John Lovell, 1865), 1, 4–5, 9–10, 18, 28, 30–31, 50–51; 63, 80–81; Amanda Foreman, *A World on Fire*, 530.

Alonzo F. Bidwell (1823–1870) was born in Livingston County, New York, and at some point moved to Tecumseh. In 1852, he moved to Coldwater, and held numerous local offices before the war. He was in hardware and banking, and suffered financial reverses during the Panic of 1857. After the Civil War began, Bidwell served as major in the three-months First Michigan, mustering out on August 7, 1861. On January 11, 1862, he was commissioned as captain of Battery D, First Michigan Light Artillery. On August 2, 1862, he resigned and was honorably discharged. He moved to Kansas in 1867, rebuilt his fortunes, and is buried in Kansas City. Rev. Henry P. Collin, *A Twentieth Century History and Biographical Record of Branch County, Michigan*, 322, 451, 125; *MIW*, 775; *State* of Michigan Gazetteer and Business Directory for 1856–57, 29; DAT, December 1, 1870.

James M. Birney (1817–1888; for James M's family background, see note for brother William in SAW.4.529.). Birney was born in Danville, Kentucky, and graduated from Miami College (Ohio) in 1836. He taught classical languages and later enrolled in Yale Law School, subsequently practicing in Cincinnati. Birney was the eldest son of James G., nationally prominent antislavery figure (and Liberty Party presidential candidate). James G. had earlier acquired substantial Michigan lands. When James G. died in 1857, James M. moved to Lower Saginaw to manage the assets. In 1858, Birney was elected to Michigan's Senate as a Republican. His service as lieutenant governor ended when he was appointed a state circuit judge. He served four years but was defeated for reelection. He returned to his law practice and founded the Bay City Chronicle in 1871. In 1875, Grant appointed Birney as U.S. Minister to the Hague, and he served until 1882. He died in Bay City. *History of Bay County Michigan and Representative Citizens*, edited and compiled by Captain Augustus H. Gansser (Chicago: Richmond & Arnold, 1905), 408–411; *History of Bay County, Michigan, with Illustrations and Biographical Sketches of some of its Prominent Men and Pioneers* (Chicago: H.H. Page, 1883), 72.

Levi Bishop (1815–1881) was born in Russell, Massachusetts, and moved to Michigan in 1835, settling in Detroit in 1837. He read law and was admitted to the bar in 1842. He was a director of the Detroit's Board of Education (1846–1858), and after 1851, its president. In 1858, he was elected a regent of the University of Michigan. A Democrat, Bishop was elected to the party's State Central Committee in 1863, and in 1864 ran unsuccessfully for state attorney general. In the debate leading to adoption of the Thirteenth Amendment, Bishop wrote on behalf of adoption. Remembered by peers for his temper and eccentricities, one obituarist wrote, "If [Bishop] can be said to have had a hobby that hobby was the restoration of capital punishment for murder in Michigan." Levi Bishop, *The Poetical Works of Levi Bishop*, Third Edition, with a sketch of the author (Detroit: E. B. Smith & Co., 1876), v–xvii; DFP, December 24, 25, 1881.

Anna Lorinda "Michigan Annie" Blair (1839 [and by some accounts, 1844] –1913) was born near Detroit and relocated with her family to Wisconsin. Before the attack on Fort Sumter, she married James Etheridge and was in Detroit when the war began. James enlisted in the Second Michigan and Annie followed him into the regiment, and deployed to Washington. After he deserted, Annie remained and eventually moved to the Third and later, the Fifth Michigan Infantry. She carried medical supplies but also a brace of pistols; she was especially remembered for sharing tough living conditions on the march, standing by the colors during battles, and providing nursing care near the line of battle. She was present at First Bull Run, on the Peninsula, at Second Bull Run, Antietam, Fredericksburg, Chancellorsville, Gettysburg, and at least through Spotsylvania. Her dresses were frequently ventilated with bullet holes and she was shot in the hand at Chancellorsville. In May 1863, Etheridge received the Kearny Cross. At Gettysburg she demonstrated (again) why she deserved it, rendering first aid services at the Peach Orchard. Although she preferred to remain on the battlefield, she also provided volunteer nursing services behind the lines and on hospital ships. Etheridge mustered out with the Fifth Michigan in July 1865. She was revered by her comrades and frequently mentioned by soldiers in letters home. Postwar, she clerked in the Pension Office in Washington, and in 1870 married Charles E. Hooks, who had served in the Seventh Connecticut. Congress awarded her a $25 monthly pension in 1886. She died impoverished in Georgetown and is buried in Arlington National Cemetery. *Women and War: A Historical Encyclopedia from Antiquity to the Present*, ed. Bernard A. Cook (Santa Barbara, CA: ABC-CLIO, 2006), 171–172; *Encyclopedia of the American Civil War: A Political, Social, and Military History*, ed. Heidler and Heidler, 658–659; *All the Daring of a Soldier*, 106–113.

Sarah Louisa Blair, nee Horton (1824–1897), was born in Waterloo, New York, and married Austin Blair in Jackson in 1849; the marriage produced four surviving sons. During the Civil War, she earned a legacy among Michigan's soldiers through her fundraising, relief efforts, and personal camp and hospital visits. When the Ninth Michigan deployed from Jackson, with no fanfare, she walked through the crowd ("quiet and unobtrusive") to distribute food to the soldiers. These acts were repeated many times, and soldiers reciprocated with their affection. The Twenty-Sixth Michigan's officers purchased a black horse, sliver-plated harness, side-saddle and blanket in recognition of her "untiring efforts . . . to relieve the wants of the sick of the Regiment"; and when that unit returned, it gratefully presented its battle-torn colors to her. She was buried in Jackson. JCP, July 5, 1897; JC, October 31, 1861; August 20, 1862; December 10, 1862.

In 1854, **John B. Bloss**, then living in Detroit, had been a signatory calling for what became "Under the Oaks" in Jackson that summer. A committed temperance man, he remained in Detroit as late as 1860, and was listed as "agent of Bloss & Co.'s seed store." His position in the land office was almost certainly a patronage position, although who appointed Bloss is unclear because he appears in a Washington city directory as a Land Office employee during the Buchanan administration. *Under the Oaks*, 40; *Johnston's Detroit City Directory and Advertising Gazetteer of Michigan* (Detroit: Fisher, Fleming & Co., 1857), 154; *DFP*, May 3, 1859; *Boyd's Washington and Georgetown Directory*, 1860, 42, 212; *MA*, December 27, 1861.

Charles E. Blunt (1823–1892) was born in New Hampshire, graduating third in his class from West Point in 1846. He was commissioned in the Corps of Engineers, and for the next fifteen years was assigned various construction projects, including in Boston, Hyannis, Provincetown, Fort Wayne, Detroit, and upstate New York. By 1861, Blunt was a captain of engineers. During the war years, he worked on defenses in Washington and vicinity, returned to Boston as supervisory engineer for the forts in Boston Harbor, and worked again in upstate New York. On March 3, 1863, he was promoted major of engineers. On June 30, 1866, Blunt was double brevetted, to lieutenant colonel and to colonel. In March 1866, he was promoted to full colonel of engineers. Postwar, he worked on East Coast harbor fortifications, with occasional postings in Pennsylvania and Ohio. He retired on January 10, 1887, and died in Boston. *Biographical Register*, Vol. II (1891), 255–256.

Elmina Brainard was born in New York, and in the 1860 census was listed as age forty-five, and the head of a household that included her sixteen-year-old daughter, a laborer, two maids, and a teacher. Aside from hosting boarders, Brainerd was a successful nurse. Her son Charles enlisted in the Seventh Michigan on June 19, 1861, and she followed him after deployment. Although Charles was discharged for disability four months later,

she remained with the unit at Camp Benton, Maryland. After it deployed to the Peninsula, she found work in Washington and eventually as an agent of the Michigan Relief Association, tasked with visiting hospitalized Michigan soldiers. She distributed necessaries to the patients, continuing this work through the end of the war. Postwar, Brainard remained active in veterans' affairs. In 1869, the Michigan legislature directed its congressional delegation to secure Brainard a pension. She also appeared at the state constitutional convention to ask for funding to complete the Detroit Soldiers' and Sailors' Monument. As quoted from *DAT*, November 25, 1862, in McTeer's article, 69n7. *Acts of the Legislature of the State of Michigan, passed at the Regular Session of 1869*, Vol. I (Lansing: W. S. George & Co., 1869), 410–411; *Collections of the Pioneer Society of the State of Michigan together with reports of county societies*, Vol. VI, reprint, 1907 (Lansing: Wynkoop Hallenbeck Crawford Company, 1907), 299; *ROS*, 7.17.

Jane W. Brent had strong federal connections: she was the daughter of U.S. judge for Michigan Ross Wilkins, and the sister of Colonel William D. Wilkins, who served on General Alpheus S. Williams' staff. She was the mother-in-law of General Orland M. Poe and the wife of Captain Thomas Lee Brent. Captain Brent was an artillery captain, a West Point graduate of 1835 who died at Leavenworth, Kansas, in 1858. After his death, Jane returned to Michigan. When the war began, Brent began hospital work, which she continued throughout the war. Brent and her daughter Winifred Lee Brent also wrote the lyrics for the state's war song, "Michigan, My Michigan." Set to the Christmas tune of "O Tanenbaum, O Tanenbaum," the song became immensely popular. Postwar, Brent lobbied the legislature for funds for the Detroit Soldiers' and Sailors' Monument, and in 1875, was appointed postmaster of Fort Union, New Mexico. Rev. Lemuel Moss, *Annals of the United States Christian Commission*, 348–349; Colonel Frederick Schneider, "Michigan, My Michigan," in *Historical Collections, Collections and Researches made by the Michigan Pioneer and Historical Society*, Vol. XXXV (Lansing: Wynkoop Hallenbeck Crawford Company, 1907), 155–168; Farmer, *The Michigan Book: A State Cyclopedia, with Sectional County Maps Alphabetically Arranged* (Detroit: Silas Farmer & Co., 1911), 155; *WES*, July 9, 1875.

Henry P. Bridge (1808–1884) was born in Littleton, Massachusetts, moved to Grand Rapids in 1836, and suffering "pecuniary reverses," eventually moved to Detroit. He served one term as a state senator (1840). He was a commission merchant, his firm becoming Michigan's largest in that business. In 1856, he was the Detroit Board of Trade's first president. He was a Democrat, although postwar, he served in municipal administrations of both parties. These included terms as Detroit city controller, in which he reportedly reduced municipal debt to almost zero. Philo Parsons, "Memorial of Henry P. Bridge," in *Pioneer Collections. Report of the Pioneer Society of the State of Michigan together with Reports of County, Town, and District Pioneer Societies*, Vol. VII (Lansing: Thorp & Godfrey, State Printers, 1886, reprint, 1904), 618; EHM, 120–121.

Thornton F. Brodhead (1820–September 2, 1862), a Congressman's son, was born in New Hampshire. He graduated from Harvard Law School in 1846 and moved to Pontiac, Michigan. He served with the Fifteenth U.S. Infantry in Mexico, and was assigned to General Winfield Scott for the war. He served under Scott throughout the war. Brodhead was brevetted captain for gallantry in December 1847, earned a captaincy in the Regulars. He mustered out in August 1848 and returned to Detroit. He purchased and edited the *Detroit Free Press* and was a delegate to the 1852 Democratic National Convention that nominated Franklin Pierce, a cousin. In 1853, Pierce appointed him postmaster of Detroit. In 1855, Brodhead was elected a state senator representing Wayne County. After the Civil War began, Brodhead became a War Democrat. He organized the First Michigan Cavalry in August 1861 at Detroit's Camp Lyon; it mustered into U.S. service on September 13. Now its colonel, Brodhead deployed for Washington in September and led his unit during Second Bull Run. On August 30, 1862, Brodhead was surrounded by enemy infantry and, refusing calls to surrender, was mortally wounded. He died on September 2 in Alexandria and his remains were transported to Detroit, where he is buried. He was posthumously brevetted brigadier general, USV, for gallantry. *The City of Detroit, Michigan, 1701–1922*, 600–603; *Landmarks of Wayne County and Detroit*, 652–654; *Brevet Brigadiers in Blue*, 78.

Christian H. Buhl (1812–1894) was born in Butler County, Pennsylvania, first working as a hatter before joining his brother in Detroit in 1833 to manufacture headwear. The brothers moved into fur and became a major regional dealer. In 1842, they merged with the former American Fur Company. In 1855, Christian left fur and entered wholesale hardware. He invested in railroads and served as president of several. Buhl was an early Republican who had earlier been a Detroit alderman. He was elected Detroit mayor in 1860 and 1861. When the Civil War began, Buhl contributed money to raise Michigan troops, serving as a draft commissioner for Wayne County in 1862 and on the Michigan Soldiers' Relief Committee. Postwar, he was a trustee of the Soldiers' and Sailors' Monument Association, and he prospered in Pennsylvania iron manufacturing, the Detroit Locomotive Works, and the Detroit Copper and Brass Rolling Mill Company. He was a philanthropist, donating the University of Michigan's law library and helping found the Detroit Art Museum. Farmer, *The History of Detroit and Michigan: or The Metropolis Illustrated*, 1043–1044; MIW, 20, 35, 131, 113.

Bennett G. Burley (1844–1914) was from Glasgow, Scotland. His father was a factory owner who had invented an underwater mine. In 1862 Bennett traveled to Richmond hoping to sell the device. He was first arrested as a spy, but Confederate authorities examined the designs and found them credible. Although his test of the device on an enemy ship was unsuccessful, he decided to stay. On August 13, 1863, he was commissioned an acting master in the Confederate Navy. He served with John Yeats Beall's Confederate Coast Guard. When the U.S. Navy captured Bennett's ship, he managed to escape; however, his freedom was short-lived. On May 12, 1864, Burley was captured and sent to Fort Delaware. But here too his incarceration was brief—he escaped and made his way to Canada. After the *Parsons* plot failed, Burley returned to Canada and another Jacob Thompson scheme: converting a steamer into a Great Lakes warship. However, Canadian governor-general Lord Monck's police were also active and Burley was arrested for violating neutrality laws. Bennett now faced extradition to the United States and a possible death sentence. On February 2, 1865, Burley was transferred to U.S. custody at Niagara Falls. Burley's influential father lobbied Parliament and prime minister Lord Russell, but it was mooted when in September 1865, Burley escaped from an Ohio jail and went to Canada through Detroit. Postwar, Burley changed his last name to Burleigh and became a foreign affairs writer for the London *Daily Telegraph*. Foreman, *A World on Fire*, 530–531, 559, 633, 716–717, 731, 790.

Isaiah Butler was an early settler and real estate investor in the village of North Branch. Following his release from prison for "disloyal" behavior, the *Grand Haven News* apparently interviewed Butler as he passed through Grand Haven on his return home; while he declared "the thousand and conflicting charges made against him were unqualifiedly false" he also said that he was "perfectly willing" not to aid the rebellion. *History of Lapeer County Michigan* (1884), 181; GHN, March 26, 1862.

William A. Butler (1813–1891) was born in Deposit, New York, and at fourteen left home to work. By 1836, he had moved to Detroit. He became a merchant and in 1847, a banker. By 1870, he was president of the Mechanics' Bank, remaining in that position until his death. He was a founder of the Detroit Fire and Marine Insurance Company, eventually becoming president. Other investments included Detroit real estate and the Mutual Life Insurance Company. During the Civil War, Butler was treasurer of the Michigan Soldiers' Aid Committee, and his wife served with its women's counterpart, the Michigan branch of the Sanitary Commission. Postwar, he reprised his treasurer's role on behalf of the Michigan Soldiers' and Sailors' Monument Association. Although not a politician, in 1864 and 1865, Butler served as a First Ward alderman on Detroit's City Council. *Detroit in History and Commerce*, 128; Farmer, *History of Detroit and Michigan*, 310–312, 757.

James V. Campbell (1823–1890) was born in Buffalo, New York, and relocated with his family to Detroit about 1826. Campbell attended Reverend William A. Muhlenberg's famed Flushing (New York) Institute, from which he graduated in 1841. He returned to Detroit, read law, and was admitted to the bar in 1844. He worked for the law firm Douglas & Walker, a fortunate choice. One partner had married his sister, and both partners edited Michigan Supreme Court or Chancery reports, conferring prestige and expertise on its partners. Campbell prospered, served as the University of Michigan's Board of Regents' secretary, sat on Detroit's Board of Education, and helped found Detroit's Young Men's Society. In 1857 he was elected to the state Supreme Court, and continued on that bench until his death in 1890. In 1858 the University of Michigan established its Law Department and appointed Campbell the Marshall Professor of Law. In 1876, Campbell wrote *Outlines of the Political History of Michigan*.

He was the brother of Valeria Campbell (see note). *Compendium of History and Biography of the City of Detroit and Wayne County, Michigan* (Chicago: Henry Taylor & Co., 1909), 300–301; *An Episcopal Dictionary of the Church: A User-Friendly Reference for Episcopalians*, ed. Don S. Armentrout and Robert Boak Slocum (New York: Church Publishing, 2000), 463.

Valeria Campbell (1815–1895) was born in Buffalo, New York, the daughter of a judge and sister of another judge, James V. Campbell of the Michigan Supreme Court. In 1826, Valeria moved with her family to Detroit and remained there for the next sixty-five years. For some twenty years before the war, she ran a private school from her home. She died in Ann Arbor and is buried in Detroit. "Local Brevities," MA, December 13, 1895. *Michigan Women in the Civil War*, 130n44.

John C. Carter (1810?–1870) was born in Virginia and appointed a midshipman from Kentucky on March 1, 1825. In 1827, he was assigned to the USS *Lexington* and afterward, the USS *Delaware*, Mediterranean Squadron. In 1831, he qualified as midshipman and six years later was promoted to lieutenant, on February 9, 1837. Later service included the USS *Macedonian*, West Indian Squadron. In 1855, he was promoted to commander. Carter commanded the USS *Michigan* between 1861 and 1862. He was commissioned commodore on July 16, 1862. He died in Brooklyn, New York. *Civil War High Commands*, 166; Bud Hannings, *Every Day of the Civil War: A Chronological Encyclopedia* (Jefferson, NC: MacFarland & Co., 2012), 552; "Commodore John C. Carter," *Philadelphia Ledger*, November 26, 1870.

Henry Laurens Chipman (1823–1910) was born in Canandaigua, New York, trained as a civil engineer, and before 1849 moved to Detroit. He left Michigan for California in 1849 and returned in 1851, working as a banker. Chipman was commissioned captain of the Eleventh U.S. Infantry on May 14, 1861, and appointed lieutenant colonel of the Second Michigan Regiment on May 25, 1861, from which he resigned on June 24 to continue with the Regular Army. He was brevetted major on May 3, 1863, for gallantry at Chancellorsville, and brevetted lieutenant colonel for gallantry at Gettysburg. During the war, Chipman served as AIG on the staff of Generals George Sykes and Romeyn B. Ayres. On April 15, 1864, Chipman assumed command of the First Michigan Colored Infantry, later renamed the One Hundred and Second USCT. Although elevated to brigade command in November, Chipman remained in technical command of the unit through the end of the war. Postwar, he was brevetted colonel and brigadier general for gallantry. He remained in the Regular Army and retired on February 1, 1887. He died in Detroit. *List of Army Officers of the United States from 1779–1900*, 242; *Michigan in the War*, 490; Bert Lee Chipman, *The Chipman Family: A Genealogy of the Chipmans in America, 1631–1920* (Winston-Salem, NC: Bert L. Chipman, Publisher, 1920), 190–191; *Civil War High Command*, 171; *Michigan State Gazetteer and Business Directory for 1856–'57*, 49.

Isaac P. Christiancy (1812–1890) was born at Johnstown, New York, educated publicly and privately, and afterward read law. In around 1836, Christiancy moved to Monroe, Michigan, and clerked for the federal Land Office. He was admitted to the bar in 1838 and held local offices, including county prosecutor. He was a lifelong antislavery man and moved from antislavery Whig to Free Soiler. He opposed the Mexican War and in 1848 was elected to Michigan's House on the Free Soil ticket. He was elected to Michigan's Senate in 1849 and was the Free Soil candidate for governor in 1852. He was present "Under the Oaks" and was a delegate to the 1856 Republican National Convention; in 1857 he was elected associate justice of the Michigan Supreme Court. He served until 1875, his last three years as chief justice. In 1875 he was elected to the United States Senate as a Republican until ill health forced his retirement in 1879. That year, Hayes appointed Christiancy minister to Peru, and he served until 1881. He died in Lansing. *Under the Oaks*, 11–13; *BD*, 819; *Proceedings of the twenty-first Annual Meeting of the Michigan State Bar Association, Battle Creek, Michigan, July 6 and 7, 1911* (Grand Rapids, MI: West Michigan Printing, no date), 29–33; *DFP*, September 9, 18, 1890.

Caleb Clark was from Michigan and had been working on soldiers' behalf in the field since May 1862. He was appointed a Soldiers' Relief Association agent on December 24, 1863. Clark seems to have functioned as a lawyer, helping soldiers "in collecting pay [and] in extricating them from all sorts of difficulties, in many cases resulting from ignorance of military rules." He also dealt with the common problem of soldiers in hospital erroneously classified as deserters.

Luke Howard, who worked under Edmunds at the Land Office, had more "hands on" duties. He dug wells for water for the wounded at Belle Plain, and followed the trail of casualties of Grant's Overland Campaign. In each location he established a "Government Kitchen" for "coffee, soup and tea and various other articles" for sick and wounded men. Both Clark and Howard wrote reports for the *Third Annual Report of the Michigan Soldiers' Relief Association for 1864*, 26–28.

Darius Clark (1814–1871) was born in Ovid, New York, and moved to Michigan in 1836. He settled in Marshall, and in 1839, ran an unsuccessful flax seed oil distillery. Sometime before 1850 the Michigan Central Railroad hired Clark as a detective. In 1850, he achieved fame when he infiltrated a group of arsonists who burned the Michigan Central Railroad's Detroit depot. He served one term as a Whig (and later Republican) in Michigan's House, but in 1852, he moved to New York City as Michigan Central's agent. He remained through the war and offered Governor Austin Blair his services gratis, as Michigan's New York state agent, asking only a colonel's commission. Postwar, Clark entered the wholesale drug business, but he failed. He appealed to Michigan (unsuccessfully) for relief, citing his wartime services. At his death in New York City, Clark held a minor position with the New York & Harlem Railroad. *EHM*, 173; *1830–1877, History of Calhoun County, Michigan* (Philadelphia: L.H. Everts & Co., 1877), 17, 52; *Historical Collections made by the Michigan Pioneer and Historical Society*, Vol. XXVI (Lansing: Robert Smith & Co., 1896), 77; General Friend Palmer, *Early Days in Detroit*, 347–350; *NYCA*, December 7, 1871.

Lewis Garrard Clarke (1812/1815–1897) was a fugitive slave from Kentucky and the basis for Harriet Beecher Stowe's character "George Harris" from *Uncle Tom's Cabin*. Clarke was born enslaved in Madison County, Kentucky, and eventually escaped across the Ohio River. In 1846, he published *Narratives of the Sufferings of Lewis and Milton Clarke*. By the time he spoke at "Under the Oaks," Clarke had become a popular lecturer as he promoted his book. In the early 1850s, Clarke went to Canada to avoid recapture under the Fugitive Slave Law; it is likely that the alias "Geo. Harris" was meant to protect him. According to one historian, Clarke's "appearance upon the stand created great excitement" among attendees at the "Under the Oaks" gathering at Jackson. Harriet Beecher Stowe,

Uncle Tom's Cabin: A Tale of Life Among the Lowly (London: George Routledge & Co., 1852), 20, 215–216, 457; Harriet Beecher Stowe, *A Key to Uncle Tom's Cabin: Presenting the Original Facts and Documents Upon which the Story Is Founded* (London: Sampson Low, Son, & Co., 1853), 21–28; *Narratives of the Sufferings of Lewis and Milton Clarke* (Boston: Bela Marsh, 1846); Fox, *History of Political Parties*, 175.

John/Johnny Lincoln Clem, born John Joseph Klem (1851–1937), was from Newark, Ohio, and reportedly the youngest soldier in federal service during the Civil War. After one or more unsuccessful attempts to enlist in an Ohio unit, he joined the Twenty-Second Michigan as a musician on May 1, 1863. He was known variously by the nicknames "Drummer Boy of Shiloh" (his presence is undocumented) and the much-better-founded "Drummer Boy of Chickamauga," where he was present and perhaps carried a musket. Klem was later attached to General Rosecrans and subsequently, General Thomas's headquarters. Postwar, Clem sought a West Point appointment, but failed his entrance examination. In 1871, President Grant commissioned him a second lieutenant. In 1915, Clem retired with the rank of major general, the last veteran of the Civil War still on active duty. He died in Texas. In 1959 Klem was featured in a historical novel and two films, *Johnny Shiloh* (Disney, 1963) and *Johnny: The True Story of a Civil War Legend* (Historical Productions, 2007.) *MIW*, 976, 428; Dyer, 1291; Aaron J. Keirns and Nathan J. Keirns, *Honoring the Veterans of Licking County, Ohio: An Illustrated History of Licking County's Military Heritage* (Howard, OH: Little River Publishing, 2009), 57–62; *Men of the Century, An Historical Work: Giving Portraits and Sketches of Eminent Citizens of the United States*, ed. Charles Morris (Philadelphia: L. R. Hamersly & Co., 1896), 157.

Charles W. Clisbee (1833–1889) was born in Cleveland, Ohio, and moved to Michigan in 1838. He attended Oberlin College in 1851, withdrawing because of finances. He spent three years at Williams College and afterward studied law, graduating from Hamilton College in 1856. He practiced briefly in Cleveland but returned to Cass County and was admitted to the bar in 1858, serving as a circuit court commissioner. Clisbee was an 1860 presidential elector for Lincoln, and Cass County prosecuting attorney in 1862. After the 1864 convention, Clisbee returned as a National Convention delegate in 1866. Postwar, he served in the state Senate and as the reading clerk for the

Fortieth Congress, and again in 1881. *History of Cass County, Michigan*, 93; *Collections and Researches made by the Michigan Pioneer and Historical Society, including Reports of Officers and Papers Read at the Annual Meeting of 1890*, Vol. 17, ed. M. Agnes Burton (Lansing: Wynkoop Hallenbeck Crawford Co., 1910), 77–80.

George A. Coe (1811–1869) was born in Rush, New York, read law in Rochester, New York, and moved to Coldwater, where he practiced after 1839. A Whig who served in Michigan's House (1840) and Senate (1846), he was the first Republican lieutenant governor, and a delegate to the 1856 Republican National Convention. He died in Coldwater. *EMB*, 181; *Under the Oaks*, 74, 122; *DFP*, October 23, 1869; *DAT*, reprint, *CT*, December 4, 1869.

Loren L. Comstock (1824/25–November 25, 1863) lived in Adrian. During the Mexican War, Comstock was commissioned a second lieutenant in the First Michigan Volunteers, but the unit arrived after most of the fighting was over, and Comstock mustered out in July 1848. On April 24, 1861, Comstock was commissioned lieutenant colonel of the "First Brigade Michigan Infantry," the three-months iteration of the First Michigan Regiment. On June 28, 1861, when the unit began to reorganize for three years' service, Blair directed Comstock to manage recruiting. When the Seventeenth Michigan was organized, he was commissioned captain on July 17, 1862, and promoted to lieutenant colonel on March 21, 1863. On November 25, 1863, near Knoxville, a Confederate sharpshooter mortally wounded him. *MIW*, 1035, 801, 174, 477; *DFP*, December 6, 1863.

James B. Crippen (d. 1869) served on the Coldwater Village Council in 1853 and owned J. B. Crippen & Co., a flour mill. Postwar, Crippen was an original subscriber to the Soldiers' and Sailors' Monument. *History of Branch County, Michigan, with Illustrations and Biographical Sketches of Prominent Men and Pioneers* (Philadelphia: Everts & Abbott, 1879), 153, 147, 159; *Michigan State Gazetteer for 1867–'8*, compiled by Chapin & Brother (Detroit: Detroit Post Company, 1867), 134; *Red Book of Michigan*, 219.

George Armstrong Custer (1839–1876) was born in New Rumley, Ohio, educated publicly, and later moved to Monroe, Michigan. After a brief teaching stint in Ohio, he was admitted to West Point in 1857. He graduated fifty-sixth out of sixty, and earned 196 demerits his last year, only 8 short of expulsion. The war shortened the class of 1861's term, and Custer graduated that May. He was commissioned a second lieutenant in the Second U.S. Cavalry and at First Bull Run carried dispatches. In August 1861 he transferred to the Fifth U.S. Cavalry and fought on the Peninsula. He served as an ADC to George B. McClellan, and afterward, to cavalry chief Alfred Pleasonton. Although Custer earned excellent reviews at Brandy Station and Aldie, his McClellan connections dissuaded Austin Blair from commissioning him in a Michigan cavalry regiment. However, governors did not appoint brigadiers, and on June 29, 1863, Custer skipped several ranks to brigadier general and was given command of the Michigan Brigade. For his actions at Gettysburg, he was brevetted major general, USV, to date from July 3, 1863. On September 13, 1863, he was wounded in the foot at Culpeper, and on March 14, 1864, injured in a carriage accident. However, he rode with great distinction in Grant's Overland Campaign. Custer ended the war with multiple brevets and mustered out of volunteer service on February 1, 1866. He returned to the Regular Army as colonel of the Seventh U.S. Cavalry, which he commanded until his death at Little Big Horn. Thom Hatch, *The Custer Companion: A Comprehensive Guide to the Life of George Armstrong Custer and the Plains Indians Wars* (Mechanicsburg, PA: Stackpole Books, 2002). As quoted, 1–4, 9–12, 14–15; *Civil War High Commands*, 196; *Generals in Blue*, 108–110.

James I. David (1822–1892) was born in Catskill, New York, and arrived in Michigan as a contractor for canals and bridges. In the early 1840s, he moved to Grosse Ile and engaged in the lumber business. A Democrat, between 1844 and 1859 he held local offices and in 1859 was elected to Michigan's House. He was commissioned a second lieutenant in the First Michigan Cavalry's Company K on August 22, 1861, but found his talents better utilized as QM. He advanced steadily in position to brigade QM. By autumn 1862 he had returned to Coldwater to organize the Ninth Michigan Cavalry, and was commissioned its colonel that November. After the unit's U.S. muster in May, 1863, it was deployed to Kentucky. The regiment's various detachments battled guerillas and John Hunt Morgan, and fought at the Battle of Buffington Island. David commanded the regiment until November 30, 1863, when he was honorably discharged for disability. He returned to Michigan, held local office,

and in 1875 was elected to Michigan's Senate. In 1886, he was appointed by Cleveland as Indian agent at the Osage agency (Pawhuska, Oklahoma.), *MIW*, 809, 706–710; *Early Michigan History*, 218; Farmer, *History of Detroit and Michigan*, 1322–1323; *CIB*, 148.

Samuel W. Day (1808–1881) was chaplain to the three-years Eighth Illinois Infantry, and later he would serve as "Military Agent for U.S. Sanitary Supplies." In fact, Day was an agent of the U.S. Sanitary Commission and by war's end was identified as commissioner, U.S. Sanitary Supplies, Michigan. Postwar, Day settled in Ann Arbor. Charles Lanman, *Michigan Red Book*, 202; *United States Sanitary Commission Bulletin*, Vol. III, nos. 25 to 40 (New York: 1866), 1260; T. M. Eddy, *The Patriotism of Illinois* (Chicago: Clarke & Co., Publishers, 1866), Vol. II, 87.

George DeBaptiste (1814–1875) was born free in Fredericksburg, Virginia, and in his teens, went to Richmond to learn barbering. He spent some years traveling throughout the South, and in 1836 settled in Madison, Indiana. He was deeply involved in that state's Underground Railroad, and in fact rescued and then married an enslaved woman whose freedom he eventually purchased. At some point he served William Henry Harrison as a valet and followed him to the White House. After Harrison's death, Baptiste returned to Madison, and in about 1848, moved to Detroit and found work as a clothing salesman and much later, a caterer. He joined the African-American Mysteries: The Order of the Men of Oppression and the Order of Emancipation, and his work for the Underground Railroad continued. He advised John Brown on the Harper's Ferry raid, and helped organize the First Michigan, Colored. Postwar, he worked with the Freedmen's Bureau and died in Detroit. His newspaper obituarist described him as "for years a leader of the colored people of Detroit and few of his race were better known in the nation fifteen years ago." Mary Ellen Snodgrass, *The Underground Railroad: An Encyclopedia of People, Places, and Operations*, vols. 1 and 2 (New York: Routledge, 2008), 154; *DFP*, February 23, 1875.

Samuel DeGolyer (1827–August 8, 1863) was born in Fondasbush, New York, living in Ohio and Illinois before moving to Hudson, Michigan, in 1858. He served as village council president. DeGolyer raised the Hudson Volunteers, a militia company, which under GO No. 24 (see

May 20, 1861) was incorporated into the Fourth Michigan Infantry. On June 20, the Hudson Volunteers, now Company F, was mustered into federal service at Camp Williams near Adrian. DeGolyer was captured at Bull Run and imprisoned at Richmond but escaped and rejoined the Fourth. He was promoted major on September 25, 1861, but on March 11, 1862, became captain of Battery H of the First Michigan Light Artillery. (The unit had mustered into U.S. service under Captain F. Lockwood, but DeGolyer replaced him before deployment.) Battery H left Michigan on March 13 to St. Louis, and then New Madrid, Island No. 10, and other points in western Tennessee and northern Mississippi. The battery had its baptismal fire at Thompson's Hill, Mississippi, on May 1, 1863. In the month remaining to DeGolyer, his battery earned plaudits; in the words of one historian, he was "the bravest artillerist in the 17th Corps." On May 12 under DeGolyer's command, Battery H was at the Battle of Raymond, later being singled out for high praise in Horace Greeley's *The American Conflict* and Frank Moore's *Rebellion Record*, quoting from the a *Cincinnati Commercial* account. He repeated this performance at Champion Hill on May 16. At Vicksburg on May 28 DeGolyer was directing counterbattery fire when a sharpshooter mortally wounded him. He was evacuated home, where he died. *Michigan in the War*, 222–223, 534–535, 811; Martin N. Bertera and Kim Crawford, *The Fourth Michigan Infantry in the Civil War* (East Lansing: Michigan State University Press, 2010), 33, 290–291; Dan Bokros, *The Battle of Raymond: The Untold Turning Point of the American Civil War* (Raleigh, NC: LuLu Press, 2007), 144; Hazel Pray Monahan, "Hudson Hero Samuel DeGolyer Is Still Remembered," *HPG*, January 5, 2011; *Rebellion Record*, ed. Frank Moore, VI, 612; Horace Greeley, *The American Conflict*, Vol. II, 304–305.

Charles V. DeLand (1826–1903) was born in North Brookfield, Massachusetts, and moved to Jackson, Michigan, at an early age. Attending public school only briefly, DeLand probably received most of his education on the job. In 1836, the Jacksonburg *Sentinel* hired him as a printer's devil. By 1840, the fourteen-year-old campaigned for the Whig ticket, continuing during the campaigns of 1844, 1848, and 1852, mostly writing party editorials. After Zachary Taylor's 1848 election, DeLand founded the pro-Whig *Jackson Citizen*. During the next six years, as national politics divided over the Fugitive Slave Act and the Kansas-Nebraska Act, DeLand became one of Michi-

gan's leading advocates for what became the Republican party. After Republicans carried the state legislature in 1854, DeLand, who sponsored and was present "Under the Oaks," became the legislative reporter, serving as Michigan's house clerk. In 1860, DeLand was elected to the state Senate. He was a leading Radical Republican, opposing any Michigan role in the February 1861 Peace Conference. When the war began DeLand sold the *Citizen* and was commissioned captain of the Ninth Michigan Regiment on October 12, 1861. On July 12, 1862, he was captured at Murfreesboro and exchanged that December. On January 1, 1863, he was commissioned colonel of the First Michigan Sharpshooters. He was wounded at Spotsylvania, Petersburg, and Poplar Springs, where he was also captured. DeLand was exchanged in February 1865 and honorably discharged that month for disability. On March 13, 1865, DeLand was brevetted brigadier general. Postwar, he moved to Saginaw and founded the Saginaw *Daily Express*, served in the state Senate, and later founded the Saginaw *Morning Herald*; he also served as U.S. Collector of Internal Revenue for the Sixth District. In 1882, DeLand retired and he returned to Jackson. *Michigan in the War*, 811; *Brevet Brigadiers in Blue*, 157; DeLand's *History of Jackson County, Michigan, embracing a Concise Review of its Early Settlement, Industrial Development and Present Conditions, together with Interesting Reminiscences*, compiled by Colonel Charles V. DeLand (no city, B. F. Bowen, 1903), 439–441; *Under the Oaks*, 26–28, 39, 41.

Martin Delany (1812–1885) was born in Charlestown, Virginia, the son of a free woman and an enslaved father. In 1822 he moved with his family to Chambersburg, and later to Pittsburgh. Around 1836, Delany became an antislavery activist and accomplished speaker as he trained in Pittsburg for medicine and dentistry. In 1843, he founded the antislavery sheet *Mystery* and in 1846 joined Frederick Douglass to publish the famed sheet *North Star*. In 1850 Delaney was admitted to Harvard Medical School but was dismissed on objections of white students; afterward, he advocated for American black emigration. In 1852 he wrote *The Condition, Emigration, and Destiny of the Colored People of the United States*, and in 1854, "The Destiny of the Colored Race in America." In 1856, he moved to Chatham, Canada, and practiced medicine. In 1859, he led the Niger Valley Exploring Party, sailing to Africa, and negotiated treaties with tribal leaders to advance a black homeland, returning to the U.S. the next year. Delany recruited on behalf of the Massachusetts Fifty-Fourth Infantry, for black units in Rhode Island, Ohio, and Connecticut, and for Michigan's First Colored Regiment. Near war's end he was commissioned a major, USCT. In August 1865, he was assigned to the Freedmen's Bureau. Although Delany mustered out in 1867, he continued as a civilian with the Bureau. In 1874, he ran unsuccessfully for South Carolina lieutenant governor. In 1876 he endorsed ex-Confederate cavalryman Wade Hampton for governor, believing he would advance black prospects. (He was mistaken.) Delany died in Wilberforce, Ohio. *Life and Public Services of Martin R. Delany, Sub-Assistant Commissioner Bureau Relief of Refugees, Freedmen, and of Abandoned Lands, and Late Major 104th U.S. Colored Troops* (Boston: Lee and Shepard, 1883), 15–16, 33–34, 36–39, 43, 48–49, 54–55, 69, 83–85, 141, 147–148, 164–179, 209–210, 297; Molefi Kete Asante, *100 Greatest Americans: A Biographical Encyclopedia* (Amherst, NY: Prometheus Books, 2002), 103–105; CNC, February 1, 1885.

Dorothea L. Dix (1802–1887) was born in Hampden, Maine, and raised in Worcester, Massachusetts. Her home was troubled, and in 1814, she began living with her grandmother. At age nineteen, she opened a school in Boston and successfully wrote children's books; in 1837, she traveled to Europe for her health, and was introduced to advances in the care of the mentally ill. After returning to the U.S. she devoted her life to improving treatment of the mentally ill, studying conditions from state to state and in Canada, and working toward reform. Postwar, she moved to Trenton, New Jersey, where she died. Recent biographies on Dix, popular and scholarly, include Thomas J. Brown, *Dorothea Dix: New England Reformer* (Cambridge, MA: Harvard University Press, 1998), 1–29 for Dix's early years; Margaret Muckenhoupt, *Dorothea Dix: Advocate for Mental Health Care* (New York: Oxford University Press, 2003); and Barbara Witteman, *Dorothy Dix, Social Reformer* (Mankato, MN: Bridgestone Books, 2003).

Charles C. Doolittle (1832–1903) was born in Burlington, Vermont, and in 1836 moved to Montreal, and later New York City. Doolittle moved to Hillsdale in the 1850s and on May 16, 1861, was commissioned first lieutenant in Michigan's Fourth Infantry, and then captain on August 20, 1861. He served with the Fourth throughout the Peninsula Campaign, and was wounded in the leg at Gaines's Mill. He was commissioned colonel of the Eighteenth Michigan on July 27, 1862, which was posted in Kentucky. In June 1864 the unit was assigned provost guard duty in Nashville; Doolittle commanded a brigade at the Battle of Nashville and was promoted brigadier, USV, on January 27, 1865. He also served in Louisiana. Postwar, he was brevetted major general and mustered out on November 30, 1865. He resettled in Toledo, Ohio, and became a banker. He died in Toledo. *MIW*, 814; *Generals in Blue*, 128–129; *Memoirs of Lucas County and the City of Toledo*, 357–358; CPD, February 21, 1903.

Edward Doyle was living in Detroit in 1860. He had represented the Seventh Ward on the Detroit City Council from 1852 to 1857. He was assigned to recruit an "Irish" regiment to rendezvous at Ypsilanti to be enumerated the Twenty-Eighth Infantry. Earlier, unrelated efforts had been made to raise the Twenty-Seventh Michigan, and recruiting for both regiments was slow. On February 1, 1863, the Twenty-Seventh was ordered to Ypsilanti to consolidate with companies of the Twenty-Eighth. On April 10, 1863, the combined unit—now called the Twenty-Seventh—was mustered into U.S. service. Afterward, Doyle ceased to have a military role in Michigan. *MIW*, 470; Farmer, *History of Detroit and Michigan*, 143–144.

Anthony M. Dudgeon (1818–1875) was born in Stewartstown, Ireland, and came to Detroit in about 1836. He worked for the American Fur Company, and later, became a shipping and commission merchant. Dudgeon helped found the Detroit Board of Trade in 1847, and in 1855 became its president. In 1848, he became a director of the Speed Line, one of the first telegraph lines in Michigan. In 1854, Dudgeon was a Detroit alderman, and by the mid-1850s, retired from business, although he remained active in politics. In 1859 he was elected to Michigan's Senate as a Democrat. During the war, he belonged to the Michigan Soldiers' Relief Committee. Postwar, Dudgeon's fortunes faltered. He died on Grosse Isle. *EHM*, 238; *Michigan in the War*, 131; "Michigan Contested Election," 45, in *The Miscellaneous Documents of the House of Representatives, printed during the first session of the Thirty-Sixth Congress, 1859–'60, in Seven Volumes* (Washington, DC: Thomas H. Ford, Printer, 1869); Farmer, *History of Detroit and Wayne County*, 100, 785, 884; DFP, December 23, 1875.

Divie Bethune Duffield (1821–1891) was born in Carlisle, Pennsylvania, son of Isabella Graham Duffield and Reverend George Duffield. He was educated privately and attended Yale College and Yale Law School, graduating from the latter in 1843. That year he was admitted to Michigan's bar, and held local office, notably, on Detroit's Board of Education, and was remembered as "the Father of the High School." He was an early Republican, fiercely antislavery, and after the war believed in enfranchising freed persons. He was also a poet of local note. He died in Detroit. *DFP*, March 13, 15, 1891; *Magazine of Western History*, ed. William W. Williams (Cleveland, np, 1886), Vol. 4, May 1886–October, 1886, 116–123; *DFP*, March 13, 15, 17, 1891.

Isabella Graham Duffield (1799–1871) was born in New York City to a wealthy merchant. Her grandmother and mother founded the New York Orphan's Asylum, and Isabella would uphold that philanthropic tradition. In 1817 she married Rev. George Duffield, and in 1838 they moved to Detroit where George was offered the pulpit of the First Presbyterian Church. Isabella was president of the Ladies' Soldiers' Aid Society of Detroit between November 6 and 20, 1861, but retired because of illness (the reason she cited) or because of her disdain for the limelight, as her obituary captured years later: "She had decided ideas in regard to the sphere within which she could work most appropriately and usefully, and her womanly activity was kept within such bounds as she conceived to be best." In 1861 Duffield became the indispensible woman because of her eastern social credentials. While she led Detroit's elite women, she remained personally connected with their New York counterparts, who were then establishing what later became the male-run United States Sanitary Commission. Her contacts included prominent women Mrs. R.N. Blatchford and Mrs. George Schuyler, who had signed the first call that led to the Sanitary Commission. Dorothy Dix had become a personal friend during her autumn 1860 tour of Detroit's prisons, poorhouse, and hospitals. (Duffield's husband and daughter belonged to the group that toured these facilities with Dix.) Duffield died in Detroit. *Michigan Women in the War*, 117n14, n15; 129; *The U.S. Sanitary Commission in the Valley of the Mississippi*, 242–243. *Funeral Address and Memorial Notices of Mrs. Isabella Graham Duffield, of Detroit, Mich.* (Detroit: Wm. Graham's Steam Presses, 1872), 19, 22–23, 17–18; see especially *DFP*, November 5, 1871.

William C. Duncan (1820–1877) was born in Lyons, New York, was educated publically, afterward working in Great Lakes shipping. In 1849, he moved to Detroit and became a successful brewer. Before the war, he was a Detroit alderman and later, the first president of the Common Council. In 1861, he was elected Detroit mayor as a War Democrat and served through 1863. Afterward, he was elected to the state Senate in later 1863 and 1864. After the war Duncan resumed his business career and held various Detroit offices. He died in Detroit. *The History of Detroit, or The Metropolis*, 1044; *General History of the State of Michigan, with Biographical Sketches, Portrait Engravings and numerous Illustrations*, compiled by Charles Richard Tuttle (Detroit: R. D. S. Tyler, & Co., 1874), 713–715.

Kin S. Dygert (1822–1894) organized Dygert's Independent Company of Sharpshooters in February 1862. Dygert advertised for "One Hundred Sharpshooters" for three years to be attached to Alpheus S. Williams Brigade. Dygert's unit was attached to the Sixteenth Michigan throughout the war. Dygert's men fought with the Sixteenth on Little Round Top at the Battle of Gettysburg on July 2, 1863; Dygert was taken "prisoner in action" and held until he escaped. He rejoined the Sixteenth on January 28, 1865, and mustered out on February 4. "Deaths," *Grand Rapids Press*, November 24, 1894; Dyer, 1281; an image of the recruiting poster may be found in B. Clay Shannon, *Still Casting Shadows: A Shared Mosaic of U.S. History, 1620–1913* (Lincoln, NE: iUniverse, 2006), Vol. I, 314; *Michigan in the War*, 360, 818; *The 1863–1864 Diary of Captain James Penfield, 5th New York Volunteer Cavalry, Company H*, edited by James Allen Penfield (Penfield Foundation, 1999), 85.

James M. Edmunds (1810–1879) was born and educated in Niagara County, New York. He taught school, afterward relocating to Ypsilanti. There he held numerous local offices, including school inspector. In 1839 he was elected to Michigan's Senate and in 1846, to its House. In 1840, he ran unsuccessfully as a Whig for governor. In 1851, he was a delegate to the state constitutional convention. Edmunds moved to Detroit in 1853 and became a lumber merchant. An early promoter of "Under the Oaks," between 1855 and 1861, Edmunds chaired Michigan's State Republican Committee, and between 1857 and 1861, he was Detroit's comptroller. In 1860, he was an unsuccessful nominee against Austin Blair for governor, but the next year, Lincoln appointed him commissioner of the General Land Office in Washington, and Edmunds served until 1866, when he was appointed postmaster of Washington. In 1862, he was appointed president of the National Council of the Union League of America, serving until 1869. Edmunds died in Washington. Charles Lanman, *Biographical Annals of the Government of the United States*, 154; "The Deceased Postmaster," WES, December 16, 1879; *Under the Oaks*, 23, 78, 80.

S. Dow Ellwood (1824–1898) was born and educated in New York, taught school, and afterward was appointed a clerk in the U.S. Post Office in Rochester. A lifelong Democrat, his patronage position ended with Zachary Taylor's election, and Ellwood joined the "Forty-Niners" in California. By 1851 or 1852 he had moved to Detroit, where he sold books and stationery. He rapidly ascended Democratic party ranks, and in 1863 was elected a Detroit alderman. Postwar, he served as president of the Wayne County Savings Bank and became an esteemed member of the Detroit's business community. Farmer, *History of Detroit and Wayne County*, Vol. 2, 1058–1059; DFP, July 10, 1898, and September 21, 1898.

Halmor H. Emmons (1817–1877) was born in Keesville, New York, and sometime before reaching twenty-one began to read law in his father's law office, demonstrating aptitude in legal writing. He practiced in New York and Ohio, eventually following his father to Detroit, where they practiced in the same office. Emmons built one of the largest railroad practices in the Old Northwest. A Whig, Emmons became a Republican in 1854, save for a brief flirtation with the Constitutional Union Party. He was strongly prowar, and personally contributed to Blair's first effort to equip troops. He was a leader of the July 22, 1862 (see date), Campus Martius war meeting. (From the lectern, Emmons recited the lyrics from the popular song, "We Are Coming Father Abraham." Postwar, Emmons practiced law. In 1870 Grant appointed him a Michigan U.S. district judge. He remained on the bench until shortly before his death. Fred. Carlisle, *Chronography of Notable Events*, 365–368; MIW, 19, 28–29; DFP, May 16, 1877.

Edmund Burke Fairfield (1821–1904) was born in Parkersburg, [West] Virginia, and attended several colleges before graduating from Oberlin College in 1842, and its

seminary in 1845. In 1849, he became president of Free Baptist College in Spring Harbor, Michigan, and after its move to Hillsdale, president of Hillsdale College. During his tenure as president, he was also politically engaged, serving as state senator (1857) and as Michigan's lieutenant governor (1859.) He left Hillsdale (and the Baptist Church) in 1869, became a Congregationalist, and held a pulpit in Ohio, later returning to academia as president of Pennsylvania's Normal School (Indiana County). In 1876, he became president of the University of Nebraska. He left in 1882 and returned to Michigan and another pulpit. In 1889 he was appointed U.S. consul to France, afterward returning to Oberlin, where he died. *West Virginia Biographical Dictionary* (St. Clair Shores, MI: Somerset Publishers, 1990), 71–73; "Lives of the Founders and Builders of Hillsdale College," *The Advance*, Hillsdale, Vol. 2, no. 19, 305–310.

Elon Farnsworth (1799–1877) was born in Woodstock, Vermont, educated locally, and in 1822 moved to Detroit. He read law, was admitted to the bar, and practiced in Detroit. He was elected to the Territorial Council in 1834. Between 1836 and 1842 he served as state chancellor, earned excellent reviews, and ran unsuccessfully as a Democratic candidate for governor in 1839. In 1843 he became state attorney general, serving until 1845. Farnsworth was a regent of the University of Michigan, a director of the Michigan Central Railroad, and president of the Detroit Savings Bank. *Early History with Biographies of State Officers*, 259; *Wayne County Historical and Pioneer Society: Chronography of Notable Events in the History of the Northwest Territory and Wayne County*, compiled by Fred. Carlisle (Detroit: O. S. Gulley, Bornman & Co., 1890), 114–115; DFP, March 25, 1877.

William M. Fenton (1808–1871) was born in Norwich, New York, and in 1826 graduated from Hamilton College. He served in the merchant marine, afterward moving to Pontiac (1835) and then Genesee County (1837), where he founded the village of Fenton. Admitted to the bar in 1842, he served in the state senate (1846) and in 1848 and 1850, as lieutenant governor. In 1852 Pierce appointed him register of the Land Office at Flint, and he later served as mayor. Fenton was a War Democrat. He personally offered Governor Blair $5,000 to equip recruits. On June 17, 1861, Blair appointed Fenton to the State Military Board. He was first commissioned major of the

Seventh Michigan, but before mustering, on September 23, 1861, Blair commissioned him colonel of the Eighth Michigan. Fenton deployed four days later. He fought at Port Royal, James Island, Second Bull Run, and Chantilly, earning excellent reviews; he was eventually promoted to brigade command. Fenton resigned in March 1863 for health reasons and returned to Flint, where he ran an unsuccessful governor's campaign against Blair. Fenton was later Chief Fire Marshal for Flint; he died from internal injuries suffered while fighting a fire. *Transactions of the Grand Lodge, of Free and Accepted Masons of the State of Michigan* (Grand Lodge F & A.M. Michigan, 1895), 33–35; CIB, 150; MIW, 5; DAT, May 18, 1871.

Thomas W. Ferry (1827–1896) was born on Mackinac Island, and moved with his family to Grand Haven. He was educated publicly and later delivered mail (sometimes by canoe) to remote Michigan settlements. Ferry served in Michigan's House as a Whig between 1850 and 1852. He joined Michigan's Republican Party at its inception and was elected to the state Senate in 1856. Ferry served for eight years on the Republican State Central Committee, and in 1864, was selected to represent Michigan on the Gettysburg Commission. After Lincoln's assassination, Ferry represented Michigan to accompany the president's remains to Springfield, Illinois. Postwar, he supported the Detroit Soldiers' and Sailors' Monument, and he was a delegate to the National (pro-Johnson) Convention in Philadelphia in 1866. He was elected as a Republican to the Thirty-Ninth Congress, and was reelected through the Forty-Second Congress. Ferry was elected U.S. senator in 1871, succeeding Jacob M. Howard. He was reelected in 1877 and served until 1883. He died in Grand Haven. BD, 1047; MIW, III, 20; *General History of the State of Michigan, with Biographical Sketches, Portrait Engravings, and numerous Illustrations*, compiled by Charles Richard Tuttle (Detroit: R. D. S. Tyler & Co., 1874), 530–533; DFP, October 15, 1896.

William M. Ferry (1796–1867), father of Thomas W. Ferry and Noah H. Ferry (the latter killed at Gettysburg on the third day), was born in Granby, Massachusetts, and clerked in Utica, New York. He attended Union College and seminary in New Brunswick, New Jersey, and was ordained a Presbyterian minister in 1822. He moved to Mackinaw Island as a missionary and worked for the next twelve years, notably in education, among indigenous

people. In 1834 he moved to Grand Haven and held a pulpit popular with recent settlers. Rev. Daniel H. Evans, *Funeral Obsequies on Occasion of the Death of Rev. William Montague Ferry* (Detroit: Tribune Job Printing, 1869), 8–13; DAT, January 10, 1868.

James Fields (d. 1868) was, according to one notice, "well-known as a self-styled 'Indian Doctor.'" He died in Adrian. DAT, May 22, 1868.

Mark Flanigan (1825–1886) was born in Antrim, Ireland, and worked as a butcher. He was elected a Detroit alderman in 1859 and reelected in 1860. That same year he also served as Wayne County sheriff, holding the office until August 15, 1862, when he was commissioned the Twenty-Fourth's lieutenant colonel. On July 1, 1863, at Gettysburg, he was wounded in the leg, which was amputated. This ended his combat command, and he was discharged on November 21, 1863. In recognition of his bravery, on March 13, 1865, he was double brevetted, USV: to colonel "For Gallantry in Action at Fredericksburg, Va.," and to brigadier general, "For Meritorious Conduct in the campaign of Gettysburg, Pa., and for service in that engagement." Flanigan returned to Detroit and on November 25, 1863, was appointed U.S. PM for the First District, serving until his honorable discharge on October 15, 1865. Postwar, Flanigan served as a school inspector between 1867 and 1874, and as president of the Detroit School Board in 1874. Between 1867 and 1873, he was a U.S. assessor, and from 1876 to 1883, a collector of Internal Revenue for the First District. *History of the Twenty-Fourth Michigan*, 476; *Michigan in the War*, 827; *Brevet Brigadiers in Blue*, 406; Farmer, *History of Detroit and Michigan*, 144, 757–758, 160, 752.

Charles C. Foote (1811–1891) was born in Olean, New York, and in 1840, graduated from Oberlin College. He was ordained as a Presbyterian minister, afterward attending medical school for two years intending to become a foreign missionary. He held pastorates in Ohio, New York, and Michigan, and in 1854, moved to Detroit. A fierce abolitionist, Foote was the Liberty Party's vice presidential candidate in 1848. He was a close friend to Sojourner Truth, and actively participated in Michigan's Underground Railroad. He was present "Under the Oaks" and spoke at the July 4, 1854, meeting. During the March 1863 riots, Foote's house was a refuge for terrified blacks. Postwar, Foote served as prison chaplain in Detroit. Abram William Foote, *Foote Family, comprising the Genealogy and History of Nathaniel Foote of Wethersfield, Conn.* (Rutland, VT: Marble City Press, 1907), 339; JC, July 5, 1854; Carol E. Mull, *The Underground Railroad in Michigan* (Jefferson, NC: McFarland & Company, 2010), 80, 91, 118, 119, 127; DFP, May 4, 1891.

Jabez H. Fountain (1819?–1901) was a prominent Manchester, Michigan, mill owner. In 1857, Fountain served as sergeant major in the Manchester Union Guards, a fifty-seven-man militia unit that eventually became Company D of the First Michigan Infantry. Between the start of the war and May 15, 1861, Fountain was the principal contractor for clothes, equipment, and subsistence for Michigan troops. After the creation of the State Military Board on May 15, 1861, he was relieved of this responsibility and afterward supervised the execution of Board contracts. Fountain remained QMG until replaced by William Hammond on March 25, 1863. He died in California. *History of Washtenaw County, Michigan, together with sketches of its cities*, 1321; MIW, 22–23; RJE, November 7, 1901.

Dorus Morton Fox (1817–1901) was born in Adams, New York, and in 1825 moved with his family to Pontiac. He was educated publicly and in 1841 moved to Lyons to open its first general store. He was Lyons's postmaster and also invested in steamboats and flour mills. Fox was commissioned major of the Ninth Michigan on September 10, 1861, and lost his son at Tyree Springs. On October 13, 1862, Fox was appointed colonel of the Twenty-Seventh Michigan, consolidated into the Twenty-Eighth in Ypsilanti. After its Detroit riot duty, Fox commanded the unit during the Vicksburg Campaign, at Jackson and at Knoxville. Here he lost another son, Oscar, from disease. Fox's unit went east and rendered distinguished service in the Overland Campaign. On June 17, 1864, Fox was shot in the right shoulder assaulting Petersburg, and he resigned on October 3, 1864, citing health and the reduced size of the regiment. Afterward, Fox returned to Lyons, and later lived in Chicago; New York City; Missouri; Rochester, NY; and Ottumwa and Des Moines, Iowa, usually working as a journalist. In 1889, he was named register of the United States Land Office. Fox published one work of historical interest, *History of Political Parties, National Reminiscences, and the Tippecanoe Movement* (Des Moines, 1895.) *Michigan in the War*, 470–473; Schenck, *History of Ionia and Montcalm Counties, Michigan*, 241, 242–243, 126, 239; CIB, 151–152; *Portrait and Biographical Album of Polk County, Iowa, containing full-page Portraits and Biographical Sketches of Prominent Representative Citizens of the County* (Chicago: Lake City Publishing Co., 1890), 509–510; Charles W. Bennett, *Historical Sketches of the Ninth Michigan Infantry (General Thomas' Headquarters Guards) with an Account of the Battle of Murfreesboro, Tennessee, Sunday, July 13, 1862* (Coldwater, MI: Daily Courier Print, 1913), 24.

Alfred Gibbs (1823–1868) was born on Long Island, New York, and graduated from West Point in 1846. His prewar army career included the Mexican War and extensive frontier service. Between December 1861 and August 1862, Gibbs commanded Fort Wayne; afterward, he became colonel of the One Hundred and Thirtieth New York Volunteers. After distinguished wartime service, he was brevetted major general, and served in the army until his death at Fort Leavenworth. *Biographical Register (1891) of the Officers and Graduates of the U.S. Military Academy at West Point*, 288–291.

William K. Gibson (d. 1901) graduated from Union College in 1852 and attended the University of Michigan. He was admitted to the bar in 1853 and practiced law, entering law partnership with Austin Blair; they practiced together until 1880. Gibson was present "Under the Oaks"; in 1858, he was elected circuit court commissioner, as a Republican. In 1860, he served as prosecuting attorney for Jackson County. Austin Blair appointed Gibson military secretary on May 15, 1861, and he served until September 13, 1862. In 1866, Gibson again served as county prosecutor. He moved from Jackson to Milwaukee in 1890 and entered the law firm of Winkler, Flanders, Smith, Bottum & Vilas. He remained until 1897, when for health reasons he moved to Riverside, California, where he died. Theodore R. Chase, *Michigan University Book, 1844–1880* (Detroit: Richmond, Backus & Co., 1881), 44; *Deland's History of Jackson County, Michigan*, 276, 174, 298, 408; MIW, 5; *Report of the Annual Meeting of the Wisconsin State Bar Association held at the City of Milwaukee, February 17 and 18, 1903* (Madison, WI: Taylor and Gleason, 1903), 208–209.

Marsh Giddings (1818–1875) was born in Sherman, Connecticut, and in 1830 moved with his family to Richland,

Michigan. He was educated publicly, attended Western Reserve College, afterward reading law; he was admitted to the bar in 1841. Giddings was elected to Michigan's House in 1849 and served as probate judge from 1861 to 1868. He was a delegate to the 1867 state constitutional convention, as well as the 1864 Republican National Convention, and was a state elector for Lincoln. In 1870 Grant appointed him as consul general for Calcutta, but Giddings declined; the next year, Grant appointed him territorial governor of New Mexico, which he accepted. He died in Santa Fe. H. G. Wells, "Law and the Legal Profession," *Report of the Pioneer Society of the State of Michigan*, Vol. III (Lansing: Robert Smith Printing, 1903), 137; *Early History of Michigan*, 288; DAT, July 14, 1870; JC, August 15, 1871, September 14, 1875.

Orrin N. Giddings (1814–1898) was born in Beekman, New York, and in 1836, married and moved to Charleston in Kalamazoo County. He farmed and operated a store until 1840, after which he focused on agriculture. In 1847 he moved to Augusta (Michigan), opened another store, and in 1849 leased the Augusta [flour] Mills. In 1853, he moved to Kalamazoo. Giddings was a fervent Whig, was present "Under the Oaks," afterward becoming a Republican. In 1847 Giddings represented Kalamazoo County in Michigan's House. In 1865, Crapo appointed him QMG, and subsequently he returned to Kalamazoo. *Portrait and Biographical Record of Kalamazoo, Allegan and Van Buren Counties, Michigan, containing Biographical Sketches of Prominent and Representative Citizens* (Chicago: Chapman Bros., 1892), 1061; EHM, 288–289; KG, November 15, 1898.

Thomas D. Gilbert (1815–1894) was born in Greenfield, Massachusetts, and moved to Grand Haven, Michigan, in 1835. He held local office, and in 1850 entered the lumber trade, moving to Grand Rapids in 1855. He became one of that city's wealthiest men, pioneering the gas company (1860) and serving in Michigan's House in 1861–62; in that year, he was also elected to the University of Michigan's Board of Regents. Postwar, he served as a Grand Rapids alderman, on the boards of public education and public works. He died in Grand Rapids. DFP, November 19, 1894.

John Briggs Gilman (1822–1881) was born in Sherburne, New York, and trained for the ministry at Oxford and Binghamton, both in New York. In 1844, he was licensed to preach, and for the next nine years held pulpits in Brooklyn, in Pennsylvania, and in Columbus, New York. In 1854 he moved to Manchester, Michigan, and between that year and his appointment as state military agent, preached there and at Tecumseh. Postwar, Gilman preached throughout Michigan; he also fundraised for Smithson College, Lombard University, and the Northwestern Conference. He died in Manchester. *The Universalist Register, Giving Statistics of the Church, Nov. 1, 1881, with the Usual Astronomical Tables, and a Counting House Almanac for 1882*, ed. Mrs. C. L. F. Skinner (Boston: Universalist Publishing House, 1882), 98–99.

Gordon Granger (1822–1876) was born in Joy, New York, graduated from West Point in 1841, and was assigned to the Detroit Barracks. After the Mexican War began, he fought in Mexico, earned two brevets, and spent his antebellum career in the West. After the attack on Fort Sumter, Granger mustered troops in Ohio and served on General George B. McClellan's staff. He saw action at the Battle of Wilson's Creek, after which he was offered the colonelcy of the Second Michigan Cavalry. He led the unit at New Madrid and Island No. 10, but soon moved to brigade command. Subsequent combat assignments included Kentucky, Tennessee, and notably Triune. He was promoted to major general, USV, to date from September 17, 1863. Granger fought with great distinction at Chickamauga and in the relief of Knoxville. He also contributed to the capture of Mobile in 1865. On March 13, 1865, he was double brevetted, USA, to brigadier and major general. After a brief hiatus as a civilian, he returned to the Regular Army for the rest of his career. *Civil War High Command*, 262–263; *Generals in Blue*, 181; *Biographical Register*, Vol. II (1891), 237–242.

Garrett A. Gravaraet (1840?–June 30 or July 10, 1864) was born on Mackinac Island; his father Henry (who would enlist in Company K as a sergeant) is described by Hauptman as a "Bear River band chief Mankewenan" of French and Indian descent, a merchant and trader. Garrett was a polymath: a musician, portraitist and landscape artist, fluent in Ottawa, Ojibwa, English, and French, who before his commission had taught at the Indian School at Little Traverse. On July 22, 1863, Gravaraet was commissioned second lieutenant in Company K. Six companies (apparently including K) of the

First Michigan Sharpshooters were mustered into U.S. service on July 7 and almost immediately deployed to Indiana to resist John Hunt Morgan's raid. They skirmished with Morgan at North Vernon (July 13) and Spencerville (July 14), and afterward were sent to Camp Douglas outside Chicago for prison guard duty. On March 17, 1864 they reported at Annapolis, Maryland, for assignment to the Second Brigade, Third Division of the Ninth (Burnside's) Army Corps. Here Gravaraet's war began in earnest. He crossed the Rapidan with his regiment on May 4/5 and afterward was engaged in most of the Overland Campaign's bloodiest battles. Both the regiment and Company K performed to excellent reviews but with major casualties. The regiment suffered thirty-four killed between the Wilderness and Spotsylvania, of whom thirteen were Company K Native Americans, including Garrett's father Henry. On the evening of June 17, 1864, at Petersburg, Garrett, sword in hand, led his company in repulsing a Confederate attack. Garrett was shot in the upper left arm, two Indian comrades were killed, and twelve others were taken prisoner; two would die at Andersonville. Garrett's arm was amputated in a field hospital and he was evacuated to Washington's Armory Hospital. Infection set in and Garrett died (according to Hauptman) on June 30, reportedly converting to Christianity before his death. He is buried on Mackinac Island. Hauptman, *Between Two Fires*, 129–130, 138–142; *MIW*, 838; Dyer, 1280.

George Gray (1824–1892) was born in County Tyrone, Ireland, graduated from Trinity College in Dublin, and immigrated to Michigan soon afterward. He moved to Grand Rapids in 1855, was admitted to the bar in 1856, and became a highly successful practitioner. Commissioned colonel of the Sixth Michigan Cavalry, he resigned in May 1864 due to injuries. Postwar, Gray was general counsel for the Northern Pacific Railroad. He died in Orange, New Jersey. *CIB*, 155; *History of the City of Grand Rapids*, 745–746; *Grand Rapids and the Civil War*, 35.

Neil Gray (1803–1868) was born in Ayrshire, Scotland, attended Glasgow University, and took a medical degree in 1830. The next year he immigrated to the United States, and by 1837 had settled in Romeo, Michigan. Afterward, he traded medicine for milling, and in 1851, built a flour mill in Clifton. A Republican, he served in the state Senate in 1843 and 1844. At his death he was president of the First National Bank of Romeo. EHM, 305; DAT, December 25, 1868; JCP, December 17, 1868.

Ann Eliza Gridley (1825–1909) was born in Cooperstown, New York, and moved to Tecumseh, Michigan as a young girl. About 1843 she married Frank Gridley and one year later, gave birth to Charles V. Gridley, later famous as the recipient of Admiral Dewey's command in Manila Bay, ("You may fire when ready, Gridley.") When Gridley's youngest son deployed as a drummer boy with the Twenty-Sixth Michigan, Ann turned to nursing. As she wrote, this "left me also at liberty to 'volunteer,' which I did, with the purpose of doing what I might for our sick and wounded patriots in camp and hospital," she recalled years later. The Ladies Hillsdale Aide Society paid her expenses, and on June 1, 1864, Gridley arrived at the front after the first battle of Cold Harbor. In 1885, the U.S. House Committee on Pensions recommended Mrs. Gridley ("now poor and in ill health") for a $20 monthly stipend. Her application was impressive and included endorsements (and wartime recollections) from six doctors and several congressional clerks who knew her in 1864. Her most impressive wartime work was done in Annapolis hospitals, treating patients just released from Andersonville. "She contracted a fever from the contagion brought from Andersonville," ex-Treasurer Moses remembered, "from the effects of which she may never fully recover." Postwar, Gridley relocated to Washington to live with her second son Lucius E. Gridley, later a prominent U.S. Treasury officer. After a brief stint working in the Patent Office, Ann Gridley was hired in the U.S. Land Office, where she reorganized the Office's files and was responsible for applying the official seal to all documents. She held that position for almost thirty years. Shortly before her death, Gridley was asked why, at 83 years old, she did not retire. "I have always worked, and when one is looking forward to her 83rd birthday it seems too late to form new habits." Gridley is buried in Hillsdale. "Report to accompany bill H.R. 7617," *Forty-Eighth Congress, Second Session, Report No. 1307*. Lucy B. Jerome, "Some Grand Old Women," *The World To-Day* (July 1911), 885–889; 693–695; Charles V. Gridley, "Mrs. Ann Eliza Gridley," *Historical Collections and Researches made by the Michigan Pioneer and Historical Society*, Vol. XXXVII (Lansing, MI: Wynkoop, Hallenbeck, Crawford Co., 1909–1910), 693–695.

G. Thompson Gridley (1816–1889) was born in Vernon, New York, probably educated privately, and then read law. In 1837, he moved to Ypsilanti, was admitted to the bar, and began his practice. In 1844, he relocated to Jackson, and two years later served as prosecuting attorney for Jackson County. In 1852, Gridley ran as a Democrat for probate judge and lost; he served two terms (1852 and 1853) as president of the village of Jackson. Postwar, Gridley continued practicing law but also served as U.S. assessor of internal revenue for Michigan's Third District from 1867 to 1873. In 1881 Gridley was elected judge of Michigan's Fourth Circuit. He remained on the bench until 1887 and died in Jackson. At Gridley's death, Austin Blair, then president of the Jackson County Bar Association, paid special tribute to Gridley's memory. *History of Jackson County, Michigan* (Chicago: Inter-State Publishing Co., 1881), 311, 335, 637; EMB, 312; JC, December 3, 1889.

Ira R. Grosvenor (1815–1899) was born in Paxton, Massachusetts, and clerked for a steamship line that took him to Monroe, Michigan, to oversee an insolvent land company. He remained for two years, moved to Detroit, and read law. After bar admission he practiced in Detroit. Before the war, Grosvenor joined the state militia; after Fort Sumter was attacked, Grosvenor organized and commanded the Seventh Michigan Regiment. He led the unit across the Peninsula Campaign; his health broken, Grosvenor resigned on July 7, 1862, and resumed practicing law. Postwar, he was elected as a Republican to Michigan's House, and in 1879 ran unsuccessfully for a state judgeship. In 1881 he was appointed a trustee of Michigan's Asylum for the Insane and served fourteen years. He named his farm in Monroe Fair Oaks, "on account of its resemblance to the battlefield of that name." *Bench and Bar of Michigan: A Volume of History and Biography*, edited by George Irving Reed (Chicago: Century Publishing and Engraving Company, 1897), 582–583; CIB, 156–157; DFP, April 9, 1899.

Frederick Hall (1816–1883) was born in Shelburne, Vermont, educated publicly, and in 1835 moved to Galena, Illinois. He chopped wood and held odd jobs across the Upper Mississippi Valley. In 1837, Hall settled in Lyons, Michigan, where he was appointed a deputy register of deeds, tasked with surveying some of the 500,000 acres transferred from the U.S. to Michigan. He became a Lyons justice of the peace in 1840, and in 1842 was hired to help locate developable parcels on former U.S. lands. Hall clerked in a store, returned to the deed registry, and in 1844 was elected register of deeds. He held this position until 1849, when he was sent to Michigan's House. Between that year and 1853, Hall began speculating in Michigan land (a lifetime habit), and his success, combined with equally successful investments in railroads and banks, reportedly made him Ionia County's wealthiest man. In 1853, President Pierce appointed Hall a receiver of public funds; he ran unsuccessfully as a Democrat for the Thirty-Ninth Congress. During the war, Hall became a War Democrat and helped with local recruiting. In 1873, he was elected the first mayor of Ionia, and the next year was the Democratic nominee for lieutenant governor, and a presidential elector in 1876. *History of Ionia and Montcalm Counties*, 173–174; EHM, 318; GREL, April 27, 1883.

Norman J. Hall (1837–1867) was born in Geneva, New York, and moved with his family to Monroe. In 1854 he was appointed to West Point and graduated in 1859 under the name Jonathan N. Hall. From December 26, 1860, to April 14, 1861, Hall was garrisoned in Fort Sumter (see SAW.6.279, 292, 318, 328). After its surrender, Hall participated in operations around the Shenandoah Valley and in Washington's defenses. He briefly served as chief of artillery for Hooker's division and was on McClellan's staff. On July 1862 Hall was commissioned colonel of the Seventh Michigan Volunteers, led it at Antietam, where he was wounded, and at Fredericksburg, earning brevets for gallantry to captain and major. He fought at Chancellorsville and Gettysburg and earned his third brevet to lieutenant colonel. After Gettysburg, severe dysentery ended his combat career. He commanded the Draft Rendezvous at Grand Rapids, but after March 1864 was back in hospital. He retired from volunteer service on June 4, 1864, for disability, and from active duty on February 22, 1865, with the Regular Army rank of captain. Hall died in Brooklyn and is buried at West Point. *Biographical Register*, Vol. II (1868), 726–727; FAC, 249–250; CIB, 157; NYH, May 28, 1867.

William Hammond of Tekonsha was appointed colonel and ADC to Blair on May 15, 1861, and by 1862 was a member of Michigan's State Military Board. Hammond also served on the commission that tested prospective marksmen for the First Regiment, United States Sharpshooters. With his promotion to state QMG came an elevation in rank to brigadier general. Hammond served as QMG until March 20, 1865. Referring to Hammond and his successor O. N. Giddings, Robertson wrote that "Both these officers served with marked ability and faithfulness." AG.62; MIW, 5, 744, 22, 23.

Henry A. Hayden (1817–1895) was born in Springfield, New York, and in 1829 moved to Buffalo to work as a sales clerk. About 1834, a lake schooner hired Hayden as a cabin boy. He was promoted to supercargo but later moved to Cleveland, Ohio, to pursue civil engineering. In 1837 he moved to Detroit, where the only job available was a surveying party's "axe man" for the Detroit-Jackson line of the Michigan Central Railroad. The route was completed in 1842, and in 1844 Hayden moved to Jackson and founded a successful flour mill. He also expanded into banking. Hayden was a Democrat, and before the war, held numerous local offices; after the Civil War began, he became a War Democrat, contributing $3,000 ($1,500 by another account) to arm Michigan troops. From 1863 to 1864 he served in Michigan's House, and unsuccessfully ran for Jackson's mayor (1860 and 1864). Postwar, he returned to railroading and was elected twice as Jackson mayor, in 1874 and 1887. Jabez Haskell Hayden, *Records of the Connecticut Line of the Hayden Family* (Windsor Locks, CT: Case, Lockwood & Brainard, 1888), 220–222; *Deland's History of Jackson County Michigan*, compiled by Colonel Charles V. Deland, 196–197, 151–152; MIW, EMB, 334; JCP, December 5, 1895.

Bennett H. Hill (1816–1886) was born in Washington, D.C., and graduated from West Point in 1837. He was commissioned in the First U.S. Artillery, served several stints in the Seminole Wars, "transferred" Cherokees west, and served in Maine during and after the Aroostook War. He was in Mexico at the Siege of Vera Cruz, and afterward was posted in the Pacific territories and then Texas. Hill refused to surrender his post at Brazos Santiago to Confederates but was forced to yield, then returned north. In 1861, he served at the Dry Tortugas, which commanded Key West. In August 1861 he was promoted to major, and between October 1862 and April 1863 he was the chief mustering and disbursing officer in West Virginia. He was promoted to lieutenant colonel and served as AAPMG for Michigan until July 31, 1865. From May 23 1864 until July 1865 he also served as commander of the Military District of Michigan. While the War Department held him in high regard, Michiganders did not always agree: see January 27, 1864. All AAPMGs were charged with intelligence collection, and Hill's interests (and network) ran deep into Canada. His efforts helped foil the attempt to liberate Confederate POWs on Johnson's Island. In January 31, 1865, Hill was double brevetted colonel and brigadier general. In postwar service he held the command of Fort Jefferson in the Tortugas and Key West, and he also served in Maine and Connecticut. He retired on December 15, 1870, and died in Washington, D.C. *Civil War High Command*, 296; *Biographical Register* (1891), Vol. I, 676; CAR, March 25, 1886.

Guy S. Hopkins, a practicing dentist, was also treasurer of the town of North Branch at the time of his arrest for "treasonable correspondence with parties in the rebel States," facilitating correspondence between rebels and "their friends in Europe," and with "propagating treasonable sentiments in the region of his residence." *History of Lapeer County Michigan* (1884), 186. The case file for this episode, including Hopkins's explanation to Seward, can be found in OR, II.2.1244–1267.

Joshua Howard (1793–1868) was born in Easton, Massachusetts, and had the distinction of serving in the War of 1812, the Mexican War, and the Civil War. During the first of these conflicts, he was commissioned an ensign with the Ninth U.S. Infantry; afterward, he remained in the Regular Army. Howard moved to Detroit in 1815, and in 1818, under a federal appropriation of $10,000, he built the Detroit Arsenal. Between 1819 and 1833 he was garrisoned throughout the East. In 1834, Howard returned to build the Dearborn Arsenal; he resigned from the service in 1835. Howard's home was Detroit, and from there he was elected to the state's House in 1838 and 1840 as a Whig. He was appointed U.S. marshal for Michigan in 1841, serving until 1844. During the Mexican War, Howard returned to service, recruiting the Fifteenth U.S. Infantry in Cincinnati, and on March 4, 1847, was commissioned its lieutenant colonel. The Fifteenth served in Mexico, and Howard was brevetted colonel for gallantry. After his return to Detroit, between 1855 and 1858, he served as sheriff of Wayne County and joined the Republicans. On June 1, 1861, Howard was appointed paymaster, United States Army, and served throughout the war. He died in Detroit. Heman Howard, *The Howard*

Genealogy: Descendants of John Howard of Bridgewater, Massachusetts from 1643 to 1903 (Brockton, MA: Standard Printing Company, 1903), 91–92; Early History of Michigan with Biographies of State Officers, 358.

William A. Howard (1813–1880) was born in Hinesburg, Vermont, and moved to New York in 1827. He was educated privately, apprenticed to a furniture maker, and graduated in 1839 from Middlebury College. In 1840 he moved to Detroit, read law, and was admitted to the bar in 1842. He practiced and also entered public life as city treasurer from 1848 to 1850. He was elected as a Republican to the Thirty-Fourth and the Thirty-Fifth Congresses. He lost for the Thirty-Sixth, but contested the election and was seated on May 15, 1860. He declined to run for the Thirty-Seventh. Howard remained a powerful figure in Michigan politics: chairman of the Republican State Central Committee (1860 and 1861), he was appointed by Lincoln as postmaster of Detroit (1861 to 1866), and he was a delegate to all Republican National Conventions between 1868 and 1876. In 1869, he moved to Grand Rapids and began a career in railroading. In 1871, Howard unsuccessfully lobbied for the U.S. Senate, and then joined the Republican National Committee, serving until 1876. In 1878, President Hayes appointed Howard territorial governor of Dakota, and he served until his death. Howard died in Washington, D.C. BD, 1285–1286; JC, April 23, 1880; DFP, April 14, 1880.

John E. Huff (1820–June 23, 1864) was born in Hamburg, New York, moving to Ohio, then to Canada, before settling near Armada in Macomb County. In 1861, Huff enlisted in Company B of the USSS; he fought across the Peninsula and was discharged for disability (disease) in January 1863. He joined the Fifth Michigan Cavalry on January 1864 and served in Virginia. Huff was a dead shot. But did he shoot J. E. B. Stuart? Huff's contemporaries had few doubts. Both the Fifth's colonel, Russell A. Alger, and A. G. Robertson vouched for Huff, and Alger later claimed that he specifically authorized Huff to shoot Stuart. But recent scholarship disputes this. Huff did not live long enough to report fully on the event. On May 31, 1864, he was mortally wounded at Hawes's Shop and died from pneumonia in Campbell Hospital in Washington. MIW, 596–597; Jeffry D. Wert, Cavalryman of the Lost Cause: A Biography of J. E. B. Stuart (New York: Simon & Schuster, 2008), 355–357; as quoted in FAC, 168–171, 176.

Erastus Hussey (1800–1889) was born in Scipio, New York, to a Quaker family and in 1824 moved to Detroit, then Plymouth, and in 1838, to Battle Creek, where he became a successful merchant. Hussey was a long-time antislavery Whig; in 1847, he became editor of the Michigan Liberty Press, the Michigan Liberty Party's sheet. He was a delegate to the 1848 Free Soil Convention in Buffalo. He controlled the Underground Railroad in the Battle Creek vicinity and was one of the Railroad's better-known conductors. In 1849, an antiabolitionist mob burned Liberty Press, but Hussey continued his antislavery activism; the same year he was elected to Michigan's House as a Free Soiler, and in 1852, ran for lieutenant governor on the Free Soil ticket. He represented Calhoun County at "Under the Oaks" and became a Republican; in 1854 he was elected to the state Senate, after which he held local office, including Battle Creek mayor in 1867. Hussey died in Battle Creek. Historical Collections. Collections and Researches made by the Michigan and Pioneer and Historical Society including reports of officers and papers read at the Annual Meeting of 1889, Vol. XIV (Lansing: Darius D. Thorp, 1890), 79–81; Early Michigan History, 370.

Many details of **Godfrey J. Hyams**'s life remain unclear. Probably from Arkansas and of Jewish descent, he moved to Toronto in 1863, and in May 1865 lived in Detroit. By some accounts, Hyams had been a politician, had been wounded multiple times during his Confederate army service, or he bore some grudge against Confederate Secretary of War Judah Benjamin. By other accounts, Hyams was shoemaker who was from Helena, Arkansas, who had fled to Canada as a war refugee. In June 1864, he reportedly joined Dr. Luke P. Blackburn (a postwar Kentucky governor) in what became known as the Yellow Fever Plot—a Confederate attempt (Blackburn's idea) to spread yellow fever in Washington, D.C., by distributing infected clothing. Hyams supposedly distributed some clothing, but (he claimed) he refused to make deliveries to the White House. According to one source, Hyams revealed this plot (whose details a Canadian court later thought credible) to the U.S. district attorney in Detroit in April 1865, in exchange for a pardon. Confederate secret service agent John W. Headley knew Hyams and blamed him for disrupting a number of Confederate operations, including the failed attempt to burn New York City. See the New York chapter in John W. Headley, Confederate Operations in Canada and New York (no city, Neale Publishing

Company, 1906), 281. "The Great Fever Plot," *New York Times*, May 26, 1865 (summary of *Toronto Globe* reports.); Andrew McIlwaine Bell, *Mosquito Soldiers: Malaria, Yellow Fever, and the Course of the American Civil War* (Baton Rouge: Louisiana State University Press, 2010), 103–106; FAC, 286–287; DAT, May 23 and June 6, 1865.

Mrs. Isaac W. Ingersoll's son Joseph enlisted in the three-months First Michigan Infantry and was taken prisoner First Bull Run. (His father, Isaac W. Ingersoll, a Detroit builder, would sponsor and captain Company B of the Twenty-Fourth Michigan.) Learning that Joseph was held in Charleston, South Carolina, Mrs. Ingersoll announced her intention to cross lines to deliver supplies and care for her son. Word spread rapidly, and other families in Detroit with POW relatives flocked to her home. She left for Charleston with 700 pounds of baggage, $4,000 in gold, and many instructions. After difficulties, Senator Zachariah Chandler helped her pass through via Fort Monroe. Returning to Detroit, she recounted her travails in a long January 19, 1862, letter to the *Detroit Free Press*. She reported generally kind treatment from Confederate soldiers and civilians. One exception was General Roswell S. Ripley, CSA. After he refused Ingersoll a pass, Charleston women at the same hotel lobbied their husbands and Ripley relented. Joseph returned to Detroit on May 24, 1862, but soon died of tuberculosis. Minnie Dubbs Millbrook, "A Mother Crosses the Rebel Lines," contained in *Twice Told Tales of Michigan and Her Soldiers in the Civil War*, ed. Minnie Dubbs Millbrook (published by the Michigan Civil War Centennial Observance Commission), 39–41; DFP, January 9, 1862; ROS, 1.69.

William P. Innes (1826–1893) was born in New York City and entered the workforce at an early age. When he was twenty, he was hired by the Erie Railroad for surveying and construction. He left in 1853 and moved to Grand Rapids, afterward finding employment by several major railroad companies. In 1857, he became chief engineer of the Grand Rapids & Northern Railroad and also continued surveying and constructing other Michigan lines. He was commissioned colonel of the First Engineers on September 12, 1861. The Engineers chiefly built and repaired roads, railroads, bridges, storehouses, forts, and field-works and also operated railroads across Kentucky, Tennessee, Alabama, Georgia, and North Carolina. Innes's combat commands included the defense of Lavergne, in

which he repulsed seven attacks and refused three offers of surrender ("I can't see it," he replied at one point, "so long as my ammunition holds out"). He later became military superintendent of railroads for the Department of the Cumberland. Innes honorably resigned on October 26, 1864. On March 13, 1865, he was brevetted brigadier general for gallantry. Postwar, Innes returned to railroading, and in 1867 to Grand Rapids. He served as Michigan's commissioner of railroads and died in Grand Rapids. Mark Hoffman, *"My Brave Mechanics": The First Michigan Engineers and Their Civil War* (Detroit: Wayne State University Press, 2007), 9–10, 308; Dwight Goss, *History of Grand Rapids and Its Industries* (Chicago: C. F. Cooper & Co., 1906), 617, 621; GRP, August 2, 1893; Dyer, 1280; *Brevet Brigadiers in Blue*, 308; MIW, 497, 858.

David H. Jerome (1829–1896), future Michigan governor, was born in Detroit but moved briefly to New York, returning in 1834 to a St. Clair County farm. Jerome was educated publicly and privately. He worked as a logger, held local and county offices, and later worked in the Great Lakes freight-hauling business. He moved to California in 1853, had mixed success, and in 1854 returned to Michigan, joining his brother in Saginaw in the lumber trade. Between 1855 and 1873 he prospered. Politically, Jerome was an early Republican, strongly antislavery, and in 1862, was a Saginaw alderman. That year, Governor Blair asked him to recruit what became the Twenty-Third Michigan; that fall, he was elected state senator. During his several senate terms, Jerome helped establish the Soldiers' Home and assisted the Harper Hospital. Between March 10, 1865, and May 10, 1867, Jerome served as Governor Crapo's ADC. He also served as president of the State Military Board for eight years. Postwar, Jerome became nationally prominent in Indian affairs; in 1876 he chaired the committee that negotiated with Chief Joseph, leader of the Nez Perce. In 1881, he was elected as Republican governor of Michigan and served one term. MIW, 5; *History of Saginaw County, Michigan*, 670–673; DFP, April 25, 1896; BCTr, April 30, 1896.

David Johnson (1809–1886) was born in Sangerfield, New York, read law, and was admitted to practice in Genesee County before moving to Michigan in 1837 finally settling in Jackson. A lifelong Democrat, Johnson held local office, including serving as prosecutor; he was elected to the statehouse and afterward became a circuit judge under the 1850 Constitution. He ran unsuccessfully for the Supreme Court in 1858 and for Congress in 1864, afterward returning to private practice. JCP, July 29, 1886; *Bench and Bar of Michigan: A Volume of History and Biography*, ed. George Irving Reed (Chicago: Century Publishing Company, 1897), 13.

Louise Johnson was from Royal Oak, Michigan, but lived in Washington, married to a government clerk. She served with the Michigan Soldiers' Relief Association until September 1, 1864, when she took a position with the United States Sanitary Commission. *Michigan Women in the Civil War*, 82n54.

DeGarmo Jones (1835–August 12, 1864) was born in Detroit. On June 15, 1861, he was appointed a captain and assistant adjutant general under state AG Robertson. He resigned on May 5, 1862, and died in Buffalo, New York. MIW, 5; AG, 61.2; *The City of Detroit Michigan, 1701–1922*, 1381.

Charles H. Lanphere (d. 1898) recruited Battery G at Coldwater, which on January 17, 1862, was mustered into U.S. service in Kalamazoo. Under Lanphere's command, the battery did excellent service in Kentucky, Ohio, western Virginia, and Tennessee. It was fully engaged at Chickasaw Bayou on December 28–29, firing some 2,160 rounds during the action; it was here that Lanphere was wounded, and his combat command ended. He resigned on September 1, 1863. *History of Branch County, Michigan, with Illustrations and Biographical Sketches, of Some of Its Prominent Men and Pioneers* (Philadelphia: Everts & Abbott, 1879), 94, 95; MIW, 869; KG, December 15, 1898.

Edward S. Lacy (1835–1916) was born in Chili, New York, and moved to Michigan in 1842. He attended public schools and Olivet College, afterward engaging in business and banking. Lacy lived in Kalamazoo (1853–1857), and during the war, Charlotte, serving as Eaton County register of deeds. Postwar, Lacy emerged as one of Michigan's most powerful Republicans, serving in the Forty-Seventh and Forty-Eighth Congresses, and as chairman of Michigan's Republican Central Committee. Harrison appointed him comptroller of currency (1889–1892); afterward, he moved to Chicago, where he died, although he is buried in Charlotte. BD, 1406.

DeWitt Clinton Leach (1822–1909) was born in Clarence, New York, moved to Michigan when young, was publicly educated, and later taught school. He was an antislavery Whig in Michigan's House, and a delegate to the 1850 constitutional convention. In 1854 he was present "Under the Oaks." Bingham appointed Leach state librarian and he also edited the *Lansing State Republican*. Leach served in the Thirty-Fifth and Thirty-Sixth Congresses, and between 1861 and 1865 served as Michigan's Indian agent. Postwar he moved to Traverse City and operated several newspapers. He died in Springfield, Missouri. BD, 1429; *Historical Collection and Researches, Michigan Pioneer Historical Society*, Vol. 37 (1909–1910), 698–699; DT, December 23, 1909.

George W. Lee (1812–1882) was born in Chenango County, New York, and moved with his family to a Marion, Michigan, farm in 1836. During the next twenty years, Lee held local offices and invested in plank road construction. Lee was present "Under the Oaks" in 1854 and served on the party's State Central Committee. He was an 1860 elector for Lincoln, and between 1859 and 1862, he started the Republican sheet, the *Livingston [County] Republican*. After the attack on Fort Sumter, Lee helped organize Livingston County for war and later was appointed a U.S. quartermaster. Based in Detroit, Lee was responsible for equipping and transporting Michigan troops. He mustered out as a colonel in June 1866 and was appointed Indian agent for the Mackinaw agency, which had jurisdiction over Michigan Indians. *History of Livingston County, Michigan*, 348, 162, 355, 177, 27, 55, 36, 58, 62; *History of Washtenaw County*, 1217–1218; *Under the Oaks*, 51; SH, June 15, 1882.

Peter Paul Lefevre (1804–1869) was born in Belgium, received a thorough Catholic education in Paris, and immigrated to the United States in 1828. He was ordained in St. Louis in 1831, and for the next decade he traveled throughout the then-western frontier of Missouri, Iowa, and Illinois, founding churches and attending to both Native Americans and settlers. Lefevre was appointed bishop of Zela in 1841 and tasked as administrator of the diocese of Detroit, a position he held until his death. Richard H. Clarke, *Lives of the Deceased Bishops of the Catholic Church in the United States* (New York: P. O'Shea, Publisher, 1872), Vol. 2, 191–202; DFP, March 10, 1869.

Edwin H. Lothrop (1806–1874) was born in Easton, Massachusetts, and in 1830 moved to Schoolcraft, Michigan. He was a prominent farmer, a member of the Democratic Party, an oft-elected town supervisor, many times a school inspector, and a local railroad promoter. He served in Michigan's House between 1835 and 1837, and again between 1842 and 1844, with his final term in 1848. In 1842 and 1843 he was speaker pro tem, and in 1844, House speaker. Lothrop also served as commissioner of railroads. In 1857 he moved to Three Rivers, where he lived until his death. EMB, 421–422; *History of Kalamazoo County Michigan*, 668, 515, 170.

George Van Ness Lothrop (1817–1897) was born in Easton, Massachusetts, graduated from Brown University in 1838, briefly attended Harvard Law School, and in 1843 moved to Detroit. He was admitted to the bar in 1844 and served as Michigan attorney general (1848–1851) and Detroit city recorder (1851). He twice ran unsuccessfully for Congress (1856 and 1860). Lothrop was a delegate to the Charleston Convention, a three-time nominee for the U.S. Senate, and minister to Russia, appointed by Grover Cleveland. He died in Detroit. NYT, July 13, 1897; *America's Successful Men of Affairs*, Vol. 2, 511.

Mrs. T. S. Mahan was the wife of Theodore S. Mahan (1834–1863), who was the son of prominent abolitionist and president of Adrian College Asa Mahan. Theodore was commissioned a first lieutenant in the Sixteenth Michigan and later captain; he was severely wounded at Fredericksburg and died in 1863. However, Mrs. Mahan makes no mention of this in her report and adds that in June 1864, she was residing at Hillsdale College. "Report of Mrs. T. S. Mahan," in the *Third Annual Report of the Michigan Soldiers' Relief Association for 1864*, 21; MIW, 878.

Thomas Jefferson Martin (1820–1912) was born in Shelbyville, Tennessee, to an enslaved mother and a white planter father. Martin was raised in Florence, Alabama, and became a barber who plied his trade on the Mississippi River boats of his era; by his account, customers included Abraham Lincoln and Stephen A. Douglas. In 1847, he moved to Madison, Indiana, married, and founded a free school for African Americans. He moved to Dowagiac in 1855 and operated a barbershop on Commercial Street. Martin was also an inventor, and key to Michigan African Americans, a leader. A senior Mason,

after the war, Martin frequently spoke during election seasons for the rest of his life. "No race movement was without his support and the young men gladly took counsel at his words," the *Michigan Manual of Freedmen's Progress* recalled in 1915. W. A. Norton's *Directory of Dowagiac, Cassopolis, and LaGrange, Pokagon, Silver Creek and Wayne Townships*, comp. Willard A. Norton (St. Joseph, MI: A. B. Morse Co., 1899), 230; *Michigan Manual of Freedmen's Progress* 278; SJSH, August 3, 1912.

Spencer J. Mather of Detroit sold Parker sewing machines before the war. On November 12, 1861, he was commissioned captain of K Company in the First Regiment, USSS. His company joined the regiment at Hampton, Virginia, in March 1862. Mather was discharged on July 7, 1862. Postwar, Mather returned to Detroit and in 1877 was granted a pair of U.S. patents, for a rotating brush and a mop handle. He later worked as a travel agent. Capt. C. A. Stevens, *Berdan's United States Sharpshooters*, 513, 4; MIW, 880; *Johnston's City Detroit Directory*, 1861, 222; *Detroit City Directory*, 1879, Vol. I, 544; *Official Gazette of the United States Patent Office*, Vol. 10, no. 6, August 8, 1876 (Washington, DC: Government Printing Office, 1877), 214.

Charles S. May (1830–1891) was born in Sandisfield, Massachusetts, and moved to Richland, Michigan, in about 1834. He was educated at the University of Michigan, Kalamazoo campus, and studied law in Vermont. He returned to Battle Creek and was admitted to the bar in 1854. May soon became the Detroit *Daily Tribune*'s associate political editor, and its Washington correspondent in 1855 and 1856. Afterward, he practiced law in Kalamazoo and Battle Creek. In 1860, he was elected prosecuting attorney for Kalamazoo. After the attack on Fort Sumter, May left office to recruit Kalamazoo volunteers, which became Company K of the Second Michigan. May was its captain, and fought at Blackburn's Ford and Bull Run with good reviews, but poor health compelled his return to Michigan. He was elected lieutenant governor in 1862 and presided over the state Senate. May became a Democrat in 1872, serving as a presidential elector for Horace Greeley. In 1877, he ran unsuccessfully for the U.S. Senate. He continued practicing law and retired in 1881. Postwar, he published a volume of his speeches, a five act play, and a citizens' textbook, *How We Are Governed in State and Nation* (1899). *Compendium of History and Biography of*

Kalamazoo County, Mich., Illustrated, ed. David Fisher and Frank Little (Chicago: A. W. Bowen & Co., no date), 522–523; *EMB,* 439.

Robert McClelland (1807–1880) was born in Greencastle, Pennsylvania, and graduated from Dickinson College in 1829. He read law, was admitted to the Pennsylvania bar in 1832, and moved to Monroe to practice in 1833. A delegate to the 1835 and 1867 state constitutional conventions, he served as Monroe's mayor (1841) and in Michigan's House (1838–1843), as speaker in his last term. A conservative Democrat, he served in the Twenty-Eighth through Thirtieth Congresses, was Michigan's governor (1851–1853), and afterward was appointed Secretary of the Interior by Franklin Pierce (1853–1857). During these years, McClelland was, next to Lewis Cass, Michigan's most powerful Democrat. He was a delegate to the national party's conventions in 1848, 1852, and 1868. In 1857, he moved to Detroit, where he practiced law until his death. *BD,* 1528–1529; *DFP,* August 31, 1880.

William B. McCreery (1836–1896) was born at Mt. Morris, New York, and moved to Michigan with his parents in 1839. He read law and in 1859 was admitted to the bar in Flint, where he practiced until after the attack on Fort Sumter. In May 1861 he enlisted as a sergeant in the Second Michigan Regiment and by September was a company captain. McCreery was thrice wounded at the Battle of Williamsburg. On November 20, 1862, he became the Twenty-First's lieutenant colonel, and full colonel on February 3, 1863. He saw hard action at Stone's River, throughout the Tullahoma Campaign, and at Chickamauga, where he was again thrice wounded, captured, and sent to Richmond's Libby Prison. McCreery belonged to the group that escaped from Libby. On September 14, 1864, he resigned due to disability on account of wounds. General George H. Thomas endorsed his resignation with deep regret and appreciation. Postwar, McCreery was Flint's mayor, Grant's appointee as collector of internal revenue, the elected state treasurer, and Harrison's choice as U.S. consul to Valparaiso, Chile. McCreery remained active in business and as a leader in Michigan's veterans' organizations. He died in Flint. McCreery wrote about his Libby days in "My Experience as a Prisoner of War, and Escape from Libby Prison," *A paper read before the Commandery of the State of Michigan, Military Order of the Loyal Legion of the U.S.* (Detroit: Winn & Hammond, 1893).

Society of the Army of the Cumberland: Twenty-Seventh Reunion, Columbus Ohio, 1897, Published by Order of the Society (Cincinnati: Robert Clarke Company, 1898), 104–105; *MIW,* 883; *CIB,* 167.

John McDermott (1826–1905) was born in Ireland and immigrated to New York. In 1844 he settled in Detroit and began constructing lake vessels. In 1859 he was elected to Michigan's House as a Democrat. After the attack on Fort Sumter, McDermott sold his business and organized the Jackson Guards, comprised of Irishmen recruited from his employees. But Michigan did not sponsor an Irish regiment, so McDermott led his unit to Illinois and on June 15, 1861, was commissioned first lieutenant of Company A, in Colonel James A. Mulligan's Twenty-Third Illinois. McDermott fought at Lexington, Missouri, with distinction, although McDermott was captured. Paroled weeks later, on January 1 1862, he was commissioned lieutenant colonel of the Fifteenth Michigan, and resigned honorably on September 16, 1863. He moved to Bay City in 1864, became a Republican, and was appointed deputy collector of that port in 1866, and also held local offices. *MIW,* 883, 743; *The City of Detroit, Michigan, 1701–1922,* 1083; *EHM, With Biographies,* 446–447; *Portrait and Biographical Record of Saginaw and Bay Counties, Michigan,* 837–838; *BCT,* November 18, 1905.

Thomas N. McEntee was from Westmoreland, New York, and graduated from Hamilton College in 1842. He attended Auburn Theological Seminary, but chose law, and moved to Michigan, where he practiced in Detroit. On November 1, 1861, McEntee was elected Detroit's city attorney, and he served until his resignation on September 1, 1863. During that time he also sat on the committee charged with recommending a bounty system to encourage enlistments. The committee's suggestions—$50 for single men and $100 for married men—were adopted by the Detroit City Council (see July 24, 1862.) Postwar, McEntee continued to practice law in Detroit but later moved to Marquette, Michigan; Omaha, Nebraska; San Francisco; and in 1888, San Jose, California. *Catalogue of the Sigma Phi with Thesaurus* (Printed for the Society, 1891), 143; *General Biographical Catalogue of Auburn Theological Seminary, 1818–1919* (Auburn, NY: Auburn Seminary Press, 1918), 107; Farmer, *History of Detroit and Michigan,* 141, 311; *A Daily Journal for the Use of Attorneys, Bankers and Business Men of Michigan, 1867* (Detroit: Wm. A. Throop & Co., nd), 51.

Phillip McKernan (1825?–September 26, 1861) of Mason served as a county supervisor in 1851 and as county clerk between 1853 and 1855. He belonged to the Curtinius Guards; after the attack on Fort Sumter, Governor Blair summoned the unit; its peacetime captain yielded the post to McKernan. When the Guard was folded into the Seventh Michigan, McKernan was commissioned captain of Company B on June 19, 1861, and was mustered into federal service on August 22, 1861, at Fort Wayne. McKernan deployed with his unit to Virginia on September 5, 1861. While the Seventh was encamped at Poolesville, Maryland, McKernan died of disease. He was buried in Mason. *ROS*, 7.68, 118; Samuel W. Durant, *History of Ingham and Eaton Counties, Michigan with Illustrations and Biographical Sketches of their Prominent Men and Pioneers* (Philadelphia: D. W. Ensign & Co., 1880), 100, 329, 261.

John McKinney (1803–1870) was born in Pennsylvania, moved to Michigan in 1837, and served in Michigan's House and Senate and as secretary of state before being elected state treasurer in 1858. In 1860, he embezzled thousands of dollars, which became a key issue in the 1860 state elections. McKinney was later prosecuted and convicted for the crime. See "The People v. John McKinney," in *Michigan Reports. Reports of Cases heard and decided in the Supreme Court of Michigan from the beginning of April Term, 1862, to November 13, 1862*, Thomas M. Cooley, Reporter, Vol. VI (Chicago: Callaghan & Co., 1880), 53–116; *Early History of Michigan with Biographies of State Officers, Members of Congress, Judges and Legislators* (Lansing: Thorp & Godfrey, 1888), 452.

David Edmond Millard was born in West Bloomfield, New Jersey, the son of a noted minister. Millard graduated from the Meadville Theological School in 1852, and the same year took his first pulpit at Fall River, Massachusetts. He later held pulpits in New Bedford, Massachusetts, and West Bloomfield, New York. An early Republican, he voted for Fremont in 1856 and moved to Michigan in about 1858. He held pulpits in Marshall, Belding, and Portland and eventually settled in Jackson. He was appointed State Agent by Governor Crapo, served in Washington until the end of the war, and was responsible for closing up the Michigan Soldiers' Relief Association in Washington. *MC*, March 18, 1909; "News from the Alumni and Former Students," *Meadville Theological School Quarterly Bulletin*, vol. II, no. 1 (October 1907): 21; 695 *Portrait and Biographical Album of Ionia and Montcalm Counties, Mich. Containing Full Page Portraits and Biographical Sketches of Prominent and Representative Citizens of the County Together with Portraits and Biographies of all the Presidents of the United States and Governors of the State* (Chicago: Chapman Brothers, 1891), 695.

Robert H. G. Minty (1831–1906) was born in County Mayo, Ireland, and in 1849 was commissioned ensign in the First West India Regiment. He spent five years at British garrisons in the Caribbean and on Africa's west coast. In 1853 he immigrated to the United States, settling in Michigan. After the attack on Fort Sumter, Minty was commissioned major in the Second Michigan Cavalry, and five days later, to lieutenant colonel of the Third Michigan Cavalry. Minty replaced Congressman Francis Kellogg as colonel when the unit deployed to Missouri. Minty compiled a distinguished service war record that included action at New Madrid, Island No. 10, Corinth, and elsewhere in Mississippi. On July 31, 1862, he was commissioned colonel of the Fourth Michigan Cavalry. In September, it deployed to Indiana and helped pursue John Hunt Morgan; by December, Minty had brigade command and occasionally engaged Confederate cavalrymen Joseph Wheeler and Nathan Bedford Forrest. Minty's later battles included Murfreesboro, Stone's River, Chattanooga, Chickamauga, and Atlanta. He was double brevetted to brigadier general and major general, and mustered out on August 15, 1865. Postwar, he worked as a railroad executive, dying in Jerome, Arizona. *MIW*, 615, 629; John Fitch, *Annals of the Army of the Cumberland: Comprising the Biographies, Descriptions of Departments, Accounts of Expeditions, Skirmishers, and Battles* (Philadelphia: J. B. Lippincott & Co., 1864), 205–209; *Brevet Brigadiers in Blue*, 417; *Civil War High Commands*, 391; *Officers of the Army and Navy (Volunteer) who served in the Civil War*, ed. Lieutenant Colonel William H. Powell (Philadelphia: L. R. Hamersly & Co., 1893), 313.

James Monroe was born in New York in 1816, and moved to Albion, Michigan, in 1838. In 1848 he founded a machine shop, remaining in the business until 1859. He lived in Calhoun County during the Civil War. A Republican, Monroe served as Calhoun County sheriff, and also as U.S. marshal for western Michigan. *EMB*, 468.

Frederick Morley (1821–1889) was born in Derby, England, and immigrated with his family to the United States in 1830, first settling in Seneca Falls, New York. At nineteen, Morley worked for the Wayne County (New York) *Whig*, and four years later (1845) moved to Palmyra and founded his own sheet, the *Courier*. He moved to Detroit in 1853 and the next year became editor of the Detroit *Inquirer*, an early booster of the Republican Party. The paper soon consolidated with the *Free Democrat* and Morley (temporarily) entered the book and stationary trade; however, by 1858, he was back in the newsroom, this time as editor and publisher of the *Daily Advertiser*, which he sold in 1861 to Henry Barns. On May 6, 1862, Morley was appointed AAG and captain in the state militia, and was promoted to lieutenant colonel on November 1, 1862. Morley's contribution to the war came in the form of record-keeping: for five years he organized the system whereby Michigan kept details on its men and units. He retired from state service and in April, 1867, acquired the Detroit *Post* and operated it until 1876. He supported Grant, who appointed him register of the U.S. Land Office in 1871. He also served as Michigan's commissioner for immigration in 1881 and 1882, and briefly as editor of the *Post and Tribune* between 1883 and 1884. *History of Detroit and Michigan: or, the Metropolis*, 1092–1093; *AG*, 64, 4; *Landmarks of Wayne County, New York, illustrated*, ed. George W. Cowles (Syracuse: D. Mason & Company, 1895), 176.

William V. Morrison (1817–1882) was born in Lansing, New York, and in 1837 relocated to Springport, Michigan. In 1839 he moved to Albion and taught school. He was a prominent Democratic Party official, although he never held public office, other than as a delegate to the 1850 constitutional convention. He was deeply partisan, outspoken, and aided by an exceptional intellect. Morrison was among the staunchest Copperheads in Michigan. John Perry Pritchett, "Michigan Democracy in the Civil War," contained in *MHM*, Vol. XI (Lansing: Michigan Historical Commission, 1927), 92.

Henry A. Morrow (1829–1891) was born in Warrenton, Virginia, and educated at Rittenhouse Academy in Washington, DC Afterward he became a U.S. Senate page and was mentored by Lewis Cass. Taking Cass's advice to move to Michigan, Morrow relocated in 1853. Before then, Morrow fought in Mexico with a unit recruited from Washington and Maryland. He fought at Monterrey and in the Tampico Campaign. Later, in Detroit, Morrow read law, and in 1854 was admitted to the bar. From January 13, 1858, to August 18, 1862, Morrow served as Detroit city recorder, and after 1857, became the first elected judge in the Recorder's Court. He was commissioned colonel of the Twenty-Fourth Michigan on August 15, 1862. He was wounded at Gettysburg, and the next year in the Wilderness. On August 1, 1864, he was brevetted brigadier general, USV, "For Gallant and Distinguished Service during the Present Campaign before Richmond." On February 6, 1865, he was wounded again at Petersburg, and on March 13, 1865, was brevetted major general, USV, for gallantry. He mustered out of volunteer service on July 19, 1865. Postwar, Morrow was briefly collector of the port of Detroit, but returned to the army. He was promoted to lieutenant colonel, USA, and assigned command of the Thirty-Sixth U.S. Infantry on July 28, 1866. On March 2, 1867, he was brevetted colonel, USA, for gallantry at Hatcher's Run, Virginia, February 6, 1865. He was on occupation duty in New Orleans and in 1869, transferred to the Thirteenth U.S. Infantry. In 1877, he was sent to suppress strikers during the railroad riots in Scranton, Pennsylvania. Morrow was promoted to full colonel of the Twenty-First U.S. Infantry in 1879. He died in Hot Springs Arkansas. *Brevet Brigadiers in Blue*, 433; Edward H. Moseley, and Paul C. Clark, Jr., *The A to Z of the United States–Mexican War* (Plymouth, UK: Scarecrow Press, 1997), 301; *MIW*, 892; Farmer, *History of Detroit and Michigan*, 137, 785, 196; *History of the Twenty-Fourth Michigan*, 41, 477–478.

Zebina Moses (1838–1918) was born in Marcellus, New York, and in about 1854 moved to Green Oak, Michigan, and was soon hired by the Detroit & Milwaukee Railroad Company. He helped establish the first line to Grand Rapids. In 1861, he moved to Washington and a clerkship at the General Land Office. Postwar, he remained in Washington and served in the U.S. Senate and House in several important administrative positions. He died in Washington. *WES*, January 24, 1918; Zabina Moses, *Historical Sketches of John Moses, of Plymouth, a Settler of 1633 to 1640; John Moses, of Windsor and Simsbury, a Settler Prior to 1647; and John Moses, of Portsmouth, a Settler Prior to 1640, also A Genealogical Record of some of their descendants* (Hartford, CT: Press of The Case, Lockwood & Brainard Company, 1890), 70, 150.

William Walton Murphy's biography can be found at SAW.2.381–382. Walton's Michigan connections included his role as one of few prominent Democrats calling for the meeting "Under the Oaks." Walton helped nominate Jacob M. Howard for the U.S. Senate. Murphy remained in Michigan until 1861, when Lincoln appointed him U.S. Consul in Frankfurt-am-Main. SAW.2 details Murphy's important work abroad during the war. *History of Hillsdale County, Michigan, with Illustrations and Biographical Sketches of Its Prominent Men and Pioneers* (Philadelphia: Everts & Abbott, 1879), 131–132, 85, 135; *Under the Oaks*, 35, 50; *History of Monroe County, Michigan*, 161.

John S. Newberry (1826–1887) was born in Waterville, New York, and when very young moved to Michigan. He lived in Detroit, Ann Arbor, and Romeo, and was educated privately. In 1847, Newberry graduated from the University of Michigan, and for the next two years worked as a civil engineer building railroads. In 1849, he decided to read for law in Detroit, and was admitted to the bar in 1853. He gained distinction by publishing admiralty cases arising on western rivers and the Great Lakes. While serving as PM, with the rank of cavalry captain, Newberry founded the Detroit-based Michigan Car Company, and later, the Detroit Car Wheel Company. Few of Draper's selections were retained as PMs after the passage of the March 3, 1863, Enrollment Act; Newberry was retained, reappointed on April 24, 1863, and served until he resigned on November 12, 1863. He returned to the manufacturing business. Postwar, he was elected as a Republican to the Forty-Sixth Congress, served one term, and did not run again. He died in Detroit. BD, 1651; OR, III.5.905.

David A. Noble (1802–1876) was born in Williamstown, Massachusetts, and graduated from Williams College in 1825. A talented classical linguist, he read law, practiced in New York City, and was admitted to the bar in 1831. That same year he moved to Monroe, Michigan, and as a Democrat, held local county, city, and state legislative offices. He was elected to the Thirty-Third Congress, and ran unsuccessfully for the Thirty-Fourth Congress, afterward managing the Louisville, Albany & Chicago Railroad. He was a delegate to the 1864 Democratic National Convention, and died in Monroe. *Michigan Biographies*, 167; DFP, October 14, 1876.

Lyman D. Norris (1825–1894) was born in Covington, New York, and when young moved with his father to Ypsilanti. Educated locally, he was the first student to enter (1841) the University of Michigan's first class; after three years, he transferred to Yale College, graduating in 1845. He returned to Michigan to read law in Detroit, and in 1848 moved to St. Louis, Missouri, to practice. In 1850, Norris attended Germany's Heidelberg University. He returned to St. Louis, resumed practice, and wrote occasionally for the St. Louis Times. Norris was involved in the early stages of the Dred Scott case, in which he represented Scott's owners in the Missouri state court proceedings. He returned to Ypsilanti in 1854 and continued his practice. Postwar (1871), he moved to Grand Rapids. Norris was a delegate to the 1867 constitutional convention, and in 1869 was elected to Michigan's Senate for Washtenaw County. In 1875, he was the unsuccessful Democratic candidate for the state Supreme Court. He later served as a regent of the University of Michigan. EMB, 494; Don E. Fehrenbacher, *Slavery, Law & Politics: The Dred Scott Case in Historical Perspective* (New York: Oxford University Press, 1981, abridged edition), 132; AAA, January 9, 1894.

John Owen (1809–1892) was born in Toronto, Canada, and in 1818, moved with his family to Detroit. At age twelve, Owen began running errands for a local druggist, eventually becoming a partner and expanding the enterprise into a successful wholesale drug supplier. During the 1850s, Owen invested in banks, insurance, and ships, and became president of the Detroit & Cleveland Steam Navigation Company. Earlier, he had served several terms as a Detroit alderman, and on the board of education as a regent of the University of Michigan. Owen was a signatory calling for Jackson's 1854 "Under the Oaks" meeting, and helped select the new party's first candidate slate. He was elected state treasurer in 1861 and held the post until 1867. His tenure as wartime treasurer was marked by his skillful handling of Michigan finances as well as his service as president of the Michigan Soldiers' Relief Society. EHM, 504; *Under the Oaks: Commemorating the Fiftieth Anniversary of the Founding of the Republican Party, at Jackson, Michigan, July 6, 1854*, ed. William Stocking (Detroit: Detroit Tribune, 1904), 40, 49; *The City of Detroit Michigan, 1701–1922* (Detroit: The S. J. Clarke Publishing Company, 1922), 125–126.

Malachi J. O'Donnell (1838?–July 1, 1863) was born in Ireland. By 1861 he had become a compositor for the *Detroit Free Press*. O'Donnell was commissioned a second lieutenant of the Twenty-Fourth Michigan's Company E on July 26, 1862, and promoted to captain on December 24 that year. He fought at Fredericksburg, was on Burnside's Mud March, and participated in the Port Royal and Westmoreland expeditions. O'Donnell was engaged at Chancellorsville and was killed in action at Gettysburg on July 1, 1861. *History of the Twenty-Fourth Michigan*, 331, 361, 371; MIW, 899.

Alonzo B. Palmer (1815–1887) was born in Richfield, New York, educated publicly and privately, and in 1839 graduated from the Western District of New York College of Physicians and Surgeons. He moved to Michigan soon thereafter and practiced in Tecumseh, while also attending medical lectures in Philadelphia and New York. In 1850, Palmer moved to Chicago and in 1852 was appointed city physician, which office also served as city health director. That year (1852) he also helped combat a cholera epidemic in Chicago; his report, *The Chicago Cholera Epidemic*, was highly regarded. Palmer accepted a professorship from the University of Michigan and there taught materia medica and therapeutics as well as the diseases of women and children. Palmer donated $100 to Blair's fund to equip Michigan troops and on April 25, 1861, was appointed surgeon of the Second Michigan Regiment. He resigned on September 23 and returned to the university. Postwar, he remained with the university, and in 1875 was named dean of the faculty, in which position he modernized the medical school. His professional writing included *A Treatise on the Science and Practice of Medicine* (1883), and he tirelessly lobbied for improved public sanitation and for abstinence from narcotics and alcohol. He died in Ann Arbor; his widow endowed the Palmer Ward in his memory. Burke Aaron Hinsdale, *History of the University of Michigan*, 226; MIW, 19, 21, 901; MC, December 30, 1887; Henry S. Frieze, *Memorial of Alonzo Benjamin Palmer, M.D., LL.D.* (Cambridge: Riverside Press, 1890), 16, 131–132.

Thomas W. Palmer (1830–1913) was born in Detroit, educated at Thompson's Academy (in present-day St. Clair), and attended the University of Michigan; after foreign travel, he returned to Michigan and entered the lumber and real estate business. Most of Palmer's distinguished career was postwar. In 1873, he was elected to Detroit's Board of Estimates; he served in the state Senate between 1879 and 1880, and was elected as a Republican to the U.S. Senate, serving from 1883 to 1889. Benjamin Harrison named him minister to Spain in 1889, and between 1890 and 1893, he was president of the World's Columbian Exposition at Chicago. He was a founder of the Detroit Museum of Art, and he died in Detroit. BD, 1696–1697; Theodore R. Chase, *Michigan University Book, 1844–1880* (Detroit: Richmond, Backus & Co., 1881), 39.

John G. Parkhurst (1824–1906) was born at Oneida Castle, New York, educated privately, read law, and was admitted to the New York bar in 1847. In 1849, he moved to Coldwater to practice law and also entered public life as county prosecutor. A Democrat, he was a delegate to the 1860 Charleston Convention and was among its note keepers. After the Civil War began, Parkhurst became a War Democrat, spoke at Coldwater's first war meeting, and in September was commissioned lieutenant colonel of the Ninth Michigan. Taken prisoner at Murfreesboro in July, 1863, he was exchanged in December and commissioned colonel in February, 1864. Parkhurst fought at Stone River and at Chickamauga, where his statue may be found. He next served as PM, Fourteenth AC between October 1863 and September 1865. In May 1865, Parkhurst was brevetted brigadier general, for gallantry. Postwar, Parkhurst returned to Coldwater. His public offices included the U.S. marshal for the East District of Michigan (1866), U.S. Treasury Department agent, and in 1886, U.S. minister to Belgium. ROS, 9.110; *Brevet Brigadiers in Blue*, 464; Collin, *History of Branch County*, 339–343; DFP, May 8, 1906.

Pay-baw-me (also known as **Joseph Pabawma/Pebawma**) appears as a signatory of the treaty with the Ottawa and Chippewa, 1855; in a later amendment he is one of thirteen native signatories, all described as "chiefs and headmen of the Grand River bands of the Ottawa and Chippewa Indians of Michigan." In 1855, Pay-baw-me was elected chief of his band, and that year moved to what became the town of Elbridge in Oceana County. At some point, he converted to Catholicism, and at one time served as town treasurer. *Indian Affairs. Laws and Treaties*, Vol. II, *Treaties*, compiled and edited by Charles J. Kappler (Washington: Government Printing Office, 1904), 730, 731; Virgil J. Vogel, *Indian Names in Michigan* (Ann Arbor: University of Michigan Press, 2005), 45.

George W. Peck (1818–1905) was born in New York City, educated at Yale, and then returned to New York to read law. In 1839, he moved to Michigan, was admitted to the bar in 1842, and practiced in Brighton. He was elected to Michigan's House in 1846, and the next year moved to Lansing, where he was the first postmaster. In 1848–49 he served as secretary of state. He bought the *Lansing Journal* and was state printer between 1852 and 1855. He served in the Thirty-Fourth Congress, but was defeated for another term. Peck was Lansing's mayor in 1864, and he practiced law there for another decade. Postwar, he lived in St. Louis, Hot Springs, and Bismarck, Missouri. He died in Saginaw. BD, 1715; EHM, 516; SN, July 1, 1905.

William Phelps (1816–1879) was born in Scipio, New York, and moved to Detroit in 1835. With little capital but considerable business acumen, he founded William Phelps & Company, wholesale grocers, which grew with the city. Phelps was "an active union man," and in 1861, expecting to be of service at the front, admitted longtime employee William H. Brace as partner (the firm was then styled Phelps, Brace & Co., by which name it operated for the next half century). In 1862, Phelps was named allotment commissioner; the next year, he was appointed an army paymaster, ranked major. By 1865, he was a lieutenant colonel, and would be known as "Colonel" Phelps for the rest of his life. Following his death in Detroit, wholesale grocers closed their businesses for a day. *Detroit in History and Commerce, Published under the direction of the Merchants' and Manufacturers' Exchange and Sanction of the Detroit Board of Trade* (Detroit: Rogers & Thorpe, 1891), 103; KG, July 27, 1879; DFP, September 9, 1862.

James E. Pittman (1826–1901) was born in Tecumseh, Michigan, and later accompanied his father, IG of Michigan militia, to Texas during its war of independence. Pittman graduated in 1843 from the University of Michigan's Tecumseh branch, entered business in Detroit, and in 1847 joined the Mexico War–bound First Michigan as Colonel Stockton's adjutant. He returned to Detroit and the shipping business in 1848. In 1855, Pittman helped convert the Grayson Guard militia into the Detroit Light Guard, and he remained active in the unit. When the war began, Pittman, a Republican, joined Alpheus Williams's staff to prepare Michigan volunteers for war. Pittman helped train the Fifth, Sixth, Seventh, Fourteenth, and Seventeenth Michigan infantries. On May 21, 1861, Blair

appointed Pittman colonel and state paymaster, and on November 1, 1862, IG of militia. He also served on the State Military Board. Postwar, Pittman held several state offices, and eventually became Detroit's police commissioner and later its superintendent. He died in Detroit. *Cyclopedia of Michigan: Historical and Biographical, comprising a Synopsis of General History of the State with Biographical Sketches of Men who have in their various spheres contributed towards its development* (New York: Western Publishing and Engraving Co., 1900), 216–217; AG, 64.4; DFP, November 12, 1901.

Emory M. Plimpton (1827–1888) was born in Ohio and at some point moved to Buchanan in Berrien County. Admitted to the bar in 1853, Plimpton became a prominent Republican and served as county prosecutor between 1857 and 1859. By 1862 Plimpton was residing in Niles, and from there was commissioned captain of Company M, Fourth Michigan Cavalry. He deployed with his unit in September 1862, and resigned on March 31, 1863, with an honorable discharge. Plimpton continued to serve the war effort. In May 1863, he was appointed a deputy marshal to supervise conscription for Niles and by October that year, had applied to raise a company for the First Michigan (colored). However, Plimpton was not among the First's officers. Postwar, Plimpton returned to Berrien County and resumed his law practice. In 1869, he served one term in the state legislature, and died in Benton Harbor. MT, April 7, 1888; Orville W. Coolidge, *A Twentieth Century History of Berrien County Michigan* (Chicago: Lewis Publishing, 1906), 218, 33, 36, 127; MIW, 639, 907; CCR, June 4, October 15, 1863; SJH, June 4, October 15, 1863.

Abner Pratt (1801–1863) was born in Springfield, New York, and although he received little formal education, he read law and was admitted to practice in New York, serving as a district attorney for Rochester. A lifelong Democrat, Pratt moved to Marshall, Michigan, in 1839, serving in the state Senate (1844–1845), as a justice on the state Supreme Court (1850–1852), as a circuit judge (1852–1857), and in 1858, as U.S. consul in Honolulu. In 1845, 1862, and 1863, he served in the House. He died in March. Washington Gardner, *History of Calhoun County, Michigan*, 276; DFP, March 29, 1863.

Eugene Pringle (1826–1908) was born in Richfield, New York, was educated publicly and privately, and read law;

in 1849 he was admitted to New York practice. He moved to Jackson in 1850 to practice law, and held local offices, including circuit court commissioner, prosecuting attorney, and city attorney. In 1860 he was elected to Michigan's House. Pringle was a Democrat, but he was alienated after the annexation of Texas; in 1854, he was "Under the Oaks." Postwar he served in Michigan's Senate (1866), as Jackson mayor (1885), and in other state offices. His private-sector activities included railroads and mining. He died in Jackson. *Men of Progress, embracing the Biographical Sketches of Representative Michigan Men with an Outline History of the State* (Detroit: The Evening News Association, 1900), 315; *Under the Oaks*, 41; AG, 64.4; *Deland's History of Jackson County, Michigan*, 499; GRP, June 16, 1908; FJ, June 18, 1908.

Benjamin D. Pritchard (1835–1907) was born in Wilson Township, Ohio, attended Hiram College, and in 1856 moved to Allegan, Michigan. He graduated from the University of Michigan Law Department in 1860 and was admitted to the bar that year. On August 13, 1862, Pritchard was commissioned captain of the Fourth Michigan Cavalry. He was wounded at Chickamauga, and on November 26, 1864, promoted to lieutenant colonel. He was brevetted brigadier general for his role in capturing Jefferson Davis. Pritchard mustered out on July 1, 1865. Postwar, he returned to Allegan and resumed his law practice; he also held state offices, including land commissioner and state treasurer, and he helped organize banks. "General Pritchard is Dead," AGZ, November 30, 1907, article contained in *Civil War Officers Union, Benjamin D. Pritchard, Excerpts from newspapers and other sources, from the files of the Lincoln Financial Foundation Collection*; MIW, 910.

Arthur Rankin (1816–1893) was born in Montreal, moved to Ontario in around 1830, and by 1836 was working as a government surveyor. In 1837, he was commissioned an ensign in the Queen's Light Infantry and distinguished himself in the Patriot War. Between 1855 and 1861, Rankin commanded the Ninth Upper Canadian Military District; between 1866 and 1868, he led the 23rd Essex Volunteer Light Infantry Battalion. Rankin was an entrepreneur: he organized an Ojibwa Indian troupe for a British tour, and in 1843 offered a forerunner of Buffalo Bill Cody's Wild West show. Other business interests included shipping, railroads, real estate, and mining. In 1854, he began the first of three terms in the Canadian Parliament. Patrick

Richard Carstens and Timothy L. Sanford, *The Republic of Canada Almost* (Xlibris Corporation, 2013), 161. More on Rankin's illegal recruiting in Canada may be found in William Francis Raney, *The Diplomatic and Military Activities in Canada, 1861–1865, as Affected by the American Civil War*, PhD diss., University of Wisconsin, 1918, 25–29.

Christian Rath was commissioned a second lieutenant in the Seventeenth Michigan on June 17, 1862. He was wounded at Antietam and later promoted to first lieutenant and captain. He served on the staff of Major General John Hartranft, who assigned him to supervise the executions of those who conspired to assassinate Lincoln. On July 8, 1865, Rath was double brevetted to major and lieutenant colonel "for special and efficient service during the confinement, trial, and execution of [the] conspirators." He was discharged on July 19, 1865. MIW, 912; Edward Steers, Jr., *The Lincoln Assassination Encyclopedia* (New York: Harper Perennial, 2010), 457.

Reuben N. Rice (1814–1885) was born in Boston, Massachusetts, educated publicly, and before 1840 moved to Concord (Massachusetts), where he operated a store. He knew Ralph Waldo Emerson; both men were directors of the Concord Atheneum. In 1844, Rice went to work for the Fitchburg Railroad Company, and two years later, moved to Detroit to become the disbursing officer for the Michigan Central Railroad. He remained with the line, advancing to master of transportation (assistant superintendent) in 1848, and in 1855 became general superintendent. He resigned in 1867. When Rice first worked for the Michigan Central, monthly receipts were $14,000 derived from 143 miles of track; when he left, they were $300,000 per month generated by 269 miles of track. Rice eventually returned to Concord, and is featured prominently in contemporary records after 1870. Lanman, *Red Book of Michigan*, 478; *Concord Massachusetts: Births, Marriages, and Deaths, 1635–1850* (Boston: Printed by the Town, Thomas Todd, Printer), 384; *Emerson in Concord: A Memoir*, 90; BJ, June 26, 1885.

John D. Richards, was, like George DeBaptiste, born free in Fredericksburg, Virginia, and moved with his family to Detroit in 1851. He was the brother of the famed Fannie Richards, a pioneer in Detroit and in African American education in Michigan. John D. Richards was a civil rights activist and later, a Republican, one of Michigan's indispensible men in organizing the First Michigan Colored. He continued championing black rights after the war. He was an inspector for the custom's service. One measure of John D.'s standing was his role in Michigan's celebration of the Fifteenth Amendment in 1870, where he delivered the keynote speech, along with Michigan governor Henry P. Baldwin and William A. Howard. It was at about this time that John D. joined with sister Fanny in a successful suit to desegregate Detroit public schools. *Manual of Freedmen's Progress*, 292; *Africana: The Encyclopedia of the African and African American Experience*, 576; DAT, April 14, 1870.

Israel B. Richardson (1815–November 3, 1862) was born in Fairfax, Vermont, and graduated from West Point in 1841. Afterward, he fought Seminoles in Florida and served in Louisiana and Texas. He fought in Mexico to excellent reviews, earning brevets to captain and major for gallantry. Postwar, Richardson was stationed in Mississippi, Texas, and New Mexico. He resigned from the army in 1855 to farm in Pontiac, Michigan. When the Civil War began, Austin Blair was quick to accept his services as a major in the Second Michigan. When the Second's proposed colonel, Henry L. Chipman, offered Richardson the command, Richardson demurred; his modesty matched his combat skills. But Blair insisted, and on May 25, 1861, he commissioned Richardson colonel of the Second Michigan; he was quickly elevated to brigade command, and soon promoted to brigadier general. Richardson fought at Blackburn's Ford, First Bull Run, and in 1862 across the Peninsula. Richardson's last command was during the 1862 Maryland Campaign, leading his division at South Mountain and Antietam, where he was mortally wounded; he died later from pneumonia. He was posthumously promoted to major general and is buried in Pontiac. *Biographical Register*, Vol. II (1879), 30–31; *Generals in Blue*, 402–403; *Civil War High Commands*, 452; MIW, 32, 46; HDN, November 18, 1862.

Henry H. Riley (1813–1888) was born in Great Barrington, Massachusetts, but raised in New Hartford, New York. Educated publicly, he was apprenticed to a printer and by 1837 edited the Democratic sheet, Seneca *Observer*. He remained in New York, read law, and in 1842 moved to Kalamazoo and was admitted to the bar. He practiced in Constantine, where he lived for the rest of his life. He was St. Joseph County prosecutor, and served as a Democrat

in the state Senate in 1850 and again in 1862. Riley was a delegate to the 1860 Charleston Convention, and supported Stephen A. Douglas. Postwar, Riley helped revise the Michigan constitution, but nationally and during his lifetime, Riley was known for the portraits of Michigan frontier life that he contributed to the *Knickerbocker Magazine* and that were later published in book form in *The Puddleford Papers; or Humors of the West* (1854). They remain in print. Riley died in Constantine. EHM, 555; *Appleton's Bio*, V. 255.

Erasmus D. Robinson was commissioned captain on October 29, 1862, mustered in on January 3, 1863, and discharged at Detroit, July 28, 1864. Allegations of political interference in Detroit's Tenth Ward during the 1863 elections required Robinson to testify in January 1864 (which testimony also contained additional information about the PG). ROS, 45.216; DFP, January 30, 1864.

Randolph Rogers (1825–1892) was born in Waterloo, New York, and was raised in Ann Arbor. Between 1840 and 1848, he cut woodblocks for the *Michigan Argus*, afterward moving to New York and ultimately Italy, where he studied under neoclassicist Lorenzo Bartolini. While he spent most of his professional life in Italy, his American commissions include the "Columbus Doors" for the U.S. Capitol building, and Civil War soldiers' memorials in Detroit, Gettysburg, Providence, Cincinnati, and Worcester (Massachusetts), as well as statues of statesmen and at the New York Metropolitan Museum of Art. Frank Cavaioli, "Randolph Rogers and the Columbus Doors," *Italian Americana* 17, no. 1 (Winter, 1999), 8–10; *Cyclopaedia of American Biography*, Vol. 5, 309.

James W. Romeyn (1839–1891) was born in Detroit and graduated from Columbia College (New York) in 1858. He studied law and was admitted to practice in 1860. On September 8, 1862, Romeyn was commissioned a first lieutenant and appointed as an ADC to Brigadier General Orlando Willcox (see his biographical note). He resigned honorably five weeks later. Postwar he was on the commission that built Detroit's Soldiers' and Sailors Monument. In 1869, he was elected to Michigan's House for one term and to the state Senate in 1871–1872, and again in 1888. Romeyn, a Democrat, was appointed by Grover Cleveland in 1886 as U.S. Consul to Chili. Returning to New York City in 1890, he died the next year from a cold contracted at the funeral of General William Tecumseh Sherman. *MIW*, 984, 112; *EMB*, 561; Robert B. Ross, *The Early Bench and Bar of Detroit: From 1805 to the end of 1850*, 174.

Alfred Russell (1830–1906) was born in Plymouth, New Hampshire, and graduated from Dartmouth College (1850) and Harvard Law School (1852). He moved to Detroit that year, joined the Republican Party in 1856, and was appointed Detroit's U.S. district attorney by Abraham Lincoln in 1861. He resigned in 1869 and practiced law in Detroit until his death. *DFP*, May 9, 1906; *American Biographical History of Eminent and Self-Made Men, Michigan Volume*, 1878, 123–124.

George P. Sanford was born in Byron, New York, in 1835 and moved to Saline in 1837. A farmer, carpenter, schoolteacher, and Republican, he graduated from Michigan's Normal School in 1856 and the University of Michigan in 1861. He was commissioned captain in the three-years iteration of the First Michigan on September, 1861, from Ann Arbor. He resigned on May 5, 1862, and on September 19, 1864, was commissioned a U.S. paymaster. On June 21, 1865, he was brevetted lieutenant colonel and mustered out on July 1, 1866. Postwar, Sanford became a Democrat in 1872, and from then until 1883 edited the *Lansing Journal*. *OR*, III.5.905; *History of Washtenaw County, Michigan*, 354; *EMB*, 468, 572.

Jacob K. Smalley (1831–1910) was born in New York and in 1834 moved with his family to Concord Township, Michigan. Smalley's father was antislavery in word and deed and the family house served as a stop on the "Underground Railroad." In 1854, Smalley and his brother George moved to Jackson. Succeeding his brother as Jackson County sheriff in 1860, Jacob would serve as a Republican until 1864. Postwar, Jacob joined his brother in the Michigan Bag and Paper Co. in Jackson and eventually became its president. He died in Jackson. State of Michigan, Department of State, Division of Vital Statistics—Death Certificate," July 6, 1910; DeLand, *History of Jackson County Michigan*, 344, 409; *Polk's Jackson City and County Directory, 1900–1901* (Detroit: R.L. Polk & Co., 1900), 55.

Joseph Rowe Smith (1802–1868) was born in present-day Hudson Falls, New York, and graduated from West Point in 1823. His first duty post was at Sault St. Marie in Michigan; he subsequently worked for the Topographical Department and in Maine, New York, and in the Black Hawk War. He also served at Forts Mackinac (1832–1833) and Brady (1833–1835), and saw service in the Seminole War at different times. Smith was frequently in action in Mexico and twice wounded. He was brevetted major and colonel for gallantry. Smith remained in service, although he was often on sick leave. He retired on September 25, 1861, for disability, but returned to active duty in 1862: between January 3 and June 11 that year he served as mustering and disbursing officer for the state of Michigan; between October, 1862, and June 11, 1864, as military commander of the District of Michigan; between June 11, 1864, and June 27, 1865, as assistant commissary of musters of the Northern Department (which included Michigan), and afterward, for the Department of the Ohio (which also included Michigan.). On April 9, 1865, Smith was double brevetted, to colonel and brigadier general. He is buried in Monroe. (See *SAW*.3.389, for information on son Joseph Rowe Smith, Jr.) *Brevet Brigadiers in Blue*, 568; *Biographical Register*, Vol. I (1868), 250; *DFP*, September 4, 1868.

Hestor Lockhart Stevens (1803–May 7, 1864) was born in Lima, New York, educated publicly, read law, and was admitted to the bar in Rochester, New York. Stevens joined the New York militia and advanced to general. He moved to Pontiac, Michigan, and was elected as a Democrat to the Thirty-Third Congress. He served one term but remained in Washington and practiced law. He died in Georgetown. *BD*, 1974.

Duncan Stewart (1818?–1897) was born in Fintry, Scotland, and received a classical education. Around 1835 he immigrated to Montreal to work for his uncle Dugard, reportedly one of Canada's wealthiest men. In 1837's Patriot War, Stewart earned distinction fighting the rebels. He moved to Detroit in 1842 and worked for the Michigan Central Railroad, but in 1850 became a grain exporter. He was the first to ship Michigan wheat to Europe. In 1859, Stewart became president of the Detroit Board of Trade. During the infamous July 15, 1862 (see date and July 22, 1862), recruitment meeting Stewart found himself a target of the mob's ire; he was a featured speaker at the July 22 meeting, offering $5 to the first company's volunteers, with $4 monthly stipends for the war to twenty-five families with four children and $2 each month to families with three children. Stewart was fervently free trade and a passionately antislavery Republican. He retired a wealthy man, but the Panic of 1877 ruined him. He died in Detroit. DFP, November 20, 1897; Farmer, *The History of Detroit and Michigan or the Metropolis Illustrated*, 792, 867, 788; *History of the Twenty-Fourth Michigan*, 26, 32, 73; *Charles F. Clark's Annual Directory of the Inhabitants, Incorporated Companies, Business Firms, etc., of the City of Detroit for 1864-'5*, compiled by Charles F. Clark (Detroit: Published by Charles F. Clark, 1864), 159; *Annual Report of the Chief of Engineers to the Secretary of War for the Year 1874, In Two Parts, Part I* (Washington, DC: Government Printing Office, 1874), 627.

Isabella Graham Duffield Stewart (1830–1888), the daughter of Isabella and George Duffield, was born in Carlisle, Pennsylvania. In 1838, she moved with her family to Detroit, and in 1852 married Dr. Morse Stewart. The marriage produced six children, five of whom survived Isabella. Like her mother, Isabella carried on the philanthropic tradition. In 1860, she helped organize Detroit's Home of the Friendless, and served on its board and as president. She became editor of the *Home Messenger*, a sheet that represented Detroit's Protestant charities. Other charities included the Thompson Home for Old Ladies, the Women's Christian Temperance Union, the Women's Christian Association, and postwar, based on a model she observed while in Europe, the formation of an umbrella organization, the Detroit Association of Charities. In 1879, hoping to combat prostitution, she successfully lobbied the legislature to establish a Reformatory for Girls; it was Isabella who first proposed to her father that one of his congregants, Harper, will his substantial property for the purpose of establishing a Protestant hospital, which ultimately became Harper Hospital. After the attack on Fort Sumter, Isabella devoted herself to the war. In its early days, she became a communication hub for different women's groups across Michigan, soliciting supplies and using her own home as a storage depot. (After its formal organization on November 6, 1861, the Ladies' Aid Society assumed these burdens.) *Memorial of Mrs. Morse Stewart*, edited by her husband, Morse Stewart, A.M., M.D. (Morse Stewart, 1889), 11–18.

John Stockton (1790–1878) was born in Lancaster, Pennsylvania, and was seventy-two when appointed the Eighth

Cavalry's commander. Stockton spent his boyhood in Chillicothe, Ohio, and held local office. He served in the War of 1812, and by war's end commanded Fort Malden (Amherst, Ontario) across the Detroit River. In 1815, he became Lewis Cass's private secretary, and in 1816 entered business in Detroit. In 1817, he helped pioneer Mount Clemens and over the years variously held most local offices. He sat on the Territorial Council (1824 to 1832, and 1834), served as village president (1855), and served several terms in Michigan's House. Stockton recruited the Eighth Cavalry with dual authorizations from Stanton and Blair. Stockton was commissioned colonel on October 3, 1862, and on May 2, 1863, the unit was deployed in detachments to Kentucky. The Eighth Cavalry would compile an excellent record, but not under Stockton. He was charged with filing false claims for government reimbursements, and he was cashiered on April 15, 1864; however, this action was rescinded on February 5, 1866, and an honorable discharge was issued to date from April 15, 1864. MIW, 37, 688, 940; *History of Macomb County Michigan* (Chicago: M. A. Leeson & Co., 1882), 312, 525, 919, 441, 523; EHM, 613–614; Robert F. Eldredge, *Past and Present of Macomb County Michigan* (Chicago: S. J. Clarke Publishing Co., 1905), 584, 585–586, 598; CIB, 174.

Thomas Baylis Whitmarsh Stockton (1805–1890) was born in Walton, New York, educated privately, and graduated West Point in 1827. He served in the West, including Detroit, often performing engineer duties. He resigned in 1834 to practice civil engineering, living in Indiana. He returned to the army during the Mexican War, commanding the First Michigan Infantry. Postwar, he moved to Flint, remaining until 1852, when he went to California, where he built telegraph lines and served as San Francisco collector of customs. In 1858 he returned to Flint and sponsored the militia unit the Flint Greys, serving as its first captain. In 1859, he served as major of the Saginaw Valley Battalion. When the Civil War began, Stockton raised the Stockton Independents, which became the Sixteenth Michigan. After deployment Stockton was promoted to brigade command. He fought on the Peninsula, was captured at Gaines's Mill, sent to Richmond's Libby Prison that June, and exchanged in August. Stockton also fought his brigade at Antietam, Shepherdstown, Fredericksburg, and Chancellorsville. He resigned on May 18, 1863. Postwar, Stockton became a commission merchant and died in Flint. *The Association of the Graduates of the United States Military Academy at West Point, New York, June 12th 1890* (Saginaw, MI: Evening News Printing and Binding House, 1890), 36–37; *CIB*, 174–175; *DFP*, December 11, 1890.

Wilbur F. Storey (1819–1884), a pioneer newspaperman, was born in Salisbury, Vermont, and at age twelve was apprenticed to the *Middlebury Free Press*. He briefly attended common school but received most of his education in the newspaper office. In 1836, he left Vermont to work as a compositor for the *New York Journal of Commerce*. Two years later, he moved to Indiana and founded the *LaPorte Herald*, an ultimately unsuccessful Democratic sheet; afterward, he moved to Chicago, and purchased a drug store, which was also unsuccessful. Determined to return to the newspaper business, in 1841, he moved to Mishawaka and founded the *Mishawaka Tocsin*, which he operated for some eighteen months, before moving to Jackson where, in 1844, he founded the *Jackson Patriot*. He also operated a store, sold books, and served as the Polk-appointed postmaster. Storey defeated Austin Blair to be a delegate to the 1850 constitutional convention. In 1853 he moved to Detroit and the *Free Press*, which was at that time in financial difficulty. The *Free Press* had always been a Democratic sheet; under Storey it became more so. And it also became one of the most innovative newspapers in the country, offering new features for readers. Storey widened margins, enlarged headline typeset and often published shocking stories that exploited as much human depravity as would sell. The writing was sharp and virulently racist concerning African Americans; Storey welcomed newspaper wars with Free Soil and Republican competitors. Under his management, the *Free Press* grew into Michigan's closest approximation to a national newspaper. In 1861, he sold the *Free Press* and moved to Chicago to publish the *Chicago Times*. General Ambrose Burnside briefly suppressed Storey's *Times* but the latter ignored the threat and proceeded to publish. At some point during his *Times*' tenure, he declared "It's a newspaper's duty to print the news and raise hell." Storey operated the *Times* until a stroke paralyzed him in 1878. He died in 1884. Frank Angelo, *On Guard: A History of the Detroit Free Press* (Detroit: Detroit Free Press, 1981), 59, 61–62, 63; 68–69; *CT*, October 28, 1884; *Biographical Sketches of the Leading Men of Chicago* (Chicago: Wilson & St. Clair, 1868), 134–140; David W. Bulla, "Palpable Injury: Abraham Lincoln and Press Suppression in the Civil War North," *An Indispensible Liberty: The Fight for Free Speech in Nineteenth Century America*, ed. Mary M. Cronin (Carbondale: Southern Illinois University Press, 2016), 52–54.

William L. Stoughton (1827–1888) was born in Bangor, New York, and educated privately in Ohio. In 1847, Stoughton read law, moving to Indiana and then to Centreville, Michigan. He was admitted to the bar in 1851, and in 1855 and 1859 was elected prosecutor. In 1854, Stoughton represented St. Joseph County, calling for what became Michigan's Republican Party. He supported Seward at the 1860 Republican Convention. Lincoln appointed Stoughton U.S. district attorney for Michigan in March 1861. On October 11, 1861, Stoughton was appointed lieutenant colonel of the Eleventh Michigan, and on April 1862, the unit's colonel. He earned excellent reviews in action battling Forrest and Morgan, and at Stone's River and Chickamauga. On July 3, 1864, Stoughton was wounded at the battle of Marietta and his leg was amputated. He mustered out on September 30, 1864. On March 13, 1865, Stoughton was double brevetted in the USVs, first to brigadier general and to major general for services rendered. Postwar, he was a delegate to the 1867 constitutional convention and served as Michigan's attorney general in 1867 and 1868. Stoughton was elected to the Forty-First and Forty-Second Congresses as a Republican. Afterward, he returned to Sturgis and his law practice. He died in Sturgis. *BD*, 1988; *Under the Oaks*, 41, 78; *Brevet Brigadiers in Blue*, 593; *MIW*, 941; *Society of the Army of Cumberland Nineteenth Reunion, Chicago, Illinois* (Cincinnati: Robert Clarke & Co., 1889), 195–198.

Byron G. Stout (1829–1896) was born in Richmond, New York, and in 1831 moved to Oakland County. Stout graduated from the University of Michigan in 1851, read law for a year, and served as superintendent of the Pontiac High School in 1853 and 1854. He had been a Democrat, but in 1854, outraged by the Kansas-Nebraska Act, was present "Under the Oaks." Stout was elected as a Republican to Michigan's House in 1854 and 1856, serving as House speaker. He was elected to Michigan's Senate in 1860, and entered the banking business in Pontiac. When the war began Stout supported it, but, increasingly uncomfortable with Radicals, he later shifted away from the party. In the fall of 1862, Stout joined the few remaining Know-Nothings, Constitutional Unionists, and Democrats to form the "Union Party," although he remained prowar. Postwar, he supported Andrew Johnson and was a delegate to the 1866 pro-Johnson National Convention in Philadelphia; thereafter, he was a delegate to several Democratic Party National Conventions and ran unsuccessfully for Congress in 1868 and 1870, and the U.S. Senate in 1883. He did serve in the Fifty-Second Congress, afterward returning to banking in Pontiac. *Under the Oaks*, 60, 127, 81–82; *MIW*, 20; *EHM*, 616; *Biographical Record: Biographical Sketches of Leading Citizens of Oakland County, Michigan* (Chicago: Biographical Publishing Company, 1903), 115–117; Dell, *Lincoln and War Democrats*, 193n126; 448; *CA*, July 2, 1896.

Charles E. Stuart (1810–1887) was born in Canaan Corners, New York, and reading law around 1829, he was admitted to the Seneca County bar. In 1835 he moved to Kalamazoo. A Democrat, he served in Michigan's House before being sent to Congress in 1847 to fill a vacancy. He was elected in his own right in 1850 and elected U.S. senator in 1852. Stuart served until March 3, 1859, and declined reelection. He supported Douglas at the Charleston Convention. When the war began, Stuart supported Lincoln's military measures and helped recruit, and was given command (January 17, 1862) of the Thirteenth Michigan Regiment. He resigned ten days later, citing poor health. His resignation was supposedly due to (probably spurious) connections with the subversive Knights of the Golden Circle. Postwar, Stuart was a delegate to the 1866 National (pro-Johnson) Convention in Philadelphia and to the Democratic National Convention in 1868. In 1873, Stuart retired for health reasons. Edward W. Barner, "Michigan Men in Congress: The Chosen of the People," in *Historical Collection, Collections and Researches made by the Michigan Pioneer and Historical Society*, Vol. XXXV (Lansing: Wynkoop Hallenbeck Crawford Company, State Printers, 1907), 473–475; *MIW*, 331; *CIB*, 175–176; *BD*, 1995; "Resigned," *GRE*, February 5, 1862, as reprinted in the *KG*, February 14, 21, 1862.

Thomas Swinyard (c. 1831–1915) was born in England, and entered the railroad business in 1850 as secretary to the general manager of the London & Northwest Railway Company; he proved a capable executive and in 1862 went to Canada at the request of British shareholders of the Great Western Railway. At the time of his death, he was president of the Dominion Telegraph Company. *NYT*,

February 26, 1915; *Telegraph and Telephone Age* (New York, March 16, 1915), No. 6, Thirty-Third Year, 128.

Henry P. Tappan (1805–1881) was born in Rhinebeck, New York, and graduated from Union College in 1825 and Auburn Theological Seminary in 1827. He held pulpits in New York and Massachusetts before he resigned for poor health. After foreign travel and recovery, he returned to the United States in 1832 and taught at City University of New York, later founding a private school. In 1852, Tappan accepted the post of chancellor of the University of Michigan. He increased total enrollment from 222 students to 652 by the time he left in 1863. He established four goals for the university: no insistence on a knowledge of classical languages for admission, as Michigan was deficient in secondary schools offering classics; the establishment of scientific training, including civil engineering, a scientific school, and an observatory; establishment of teacher education; and finally, public relations—"to keep the idea of a University constantly before the public mind." He also eliminated denominationalism as a requirement for teaching specialties, choosing to emphasize competence over ideology. He instituted assistant professorships; expanded the library; acquired scientific equipment; and built an astronomical observatory, a chemistry laboratory, and a museum for plant, animal, and mineral specimens. However, tensions over matters personal and professional ultimately led to Tappan's abrupt dismissal in 1863. Afterward he left for Europe, dying in Vevay, Switzerland. Tappan was also a prolific writer of influential works on philosophy and education. "Review by Rev. Dr. H. P. Tappan: Historic Statement of My Connection with the University," *University of Michigan Regents' Proceedings with Appendixes and Index* (Ann Arbor: Published by the University, October, 1915), 1121–1123, 1128, 1132–1133. *Appletons Biography*, VI.33; Burke Aaron Hinsdale, *History of the University of Michigan*, 49–51.

Charles H. Taylor (1813–1889) was born in Cooperstown, New York, educated privately, and in 1837, moved to Grand Rapids. A Democrat, he held local office and in 1847 was elected to Michigan's House. He was active in Michigan reform, serving on state commissions to establish asylums for the insane and the deaf. Beginning in 1847, he was the chief editor of the Grand Rapids *Enquirer*; afterward (1855) he became chief editor of the *Detroit*

Free Press. Taylor was the first secretary of state elected under the constitution of 1850, serving until 1853. Postwar, Johnson appointed him postmaster, and he served from 1867 to 1869. He died in Grand Rapids. *Early Michigan History*, 629; *Grand Rapids and Kent County Michigan: Historical Account of their Progress from First Settlement to the Present Time*, edited by Ernest B. Fisher (Chicago: Robert O. Law Company, 1918), Vol. 1 of 2, 506, 199, 190, 101; GRWL, January 16, 1889.

George W. Taylor (1810–1897) was admitted as a Methodist probationer in 1837 and received full ordination in 1839. He held several pulpits, including in Ypsilanti and in 1849, Detroit. During these early years, Taylor, a tireless temperance advocate, was friend and pastor to Lieutenant Ulysses Grant, stationed nearby. Around 1851, Taylor changed pulpits to the Trinity Methodist Episcopal Church. On October 9, 1862, Taylor joined the Eighth Michigan as regimental chaplain, credited to Ann Arbor; he resigned honorably on March 10, 1863, afterward joining the Christian Commission. He took a leading role in sponsoring receptions for homecoming soldiers in Detroit. He also served as the chief financial agent of the Detroit Soldiers' and Sailors' Monument. He died in Lansing. F. W. Conable, *History of the Genesee Annual Conference of the Methodist Episcopal Church, from its organization by Bishops Asbury and M'Kendree in 1810 to the year 1884* (New York: Phillips & Hunt, 1885), 412, 445; *The History of Washtenaw County*, 1176, 1383; Farmer, *History of Detroit and Michigan*, 840, 589, 706, 310–311; *The City of Detroit Michigan, 1701–1922*; 1190, 1264, 1100; ROS, 8.131; DFP, May 28, 1897.

Henry D. Terry (1812–1869) was born in Hartford, Connecticut, practiced law, and moved to Mt. Clemens, Michigan in 1842. In 1848 he was elected as a Whig to Michigan's House from Macomb County. In 1855, he moved to Detroit. After the attack on Fort Sumter, Terry helped recruit the Fifth Michigan Infantry, and on June 10, 1861, was commissioned its colonel. On August 28, 1861, the Fifth mustered into U.S. service and deployed to Washington, garrisoned its defenses, and fought on the Peninsula. At the Battle of Williamsburg a wounded Terry earned praise from the hard-to-please Philip Kearny, who also complimented Terry to Governor Blair. He was promoted to brigadier general to date July 17, 1862. In December 1862, Terry was assigned to brigade command in the Seventh Corps during the Suffolk Campaign

and reassigned to the VI Corps and the Army of the Potomac during the Bristoe Campaign. Between January 13, 1864, and May 11, 1864, he was in command of the POW camp on Ohio's Johnson's Island. Just before mustering out on February 7, 1865, Terry presided at the court martial of Maryland Congressman Benjamin G. Harris (see SAW.4.472–473). Later, he moved to Washington, D.C., where he practiced law until his death. *MIW*, 945, 238; *Early Biographies*, 632–633; *Generals in Blue*, 498–499; WES, June 23, 1869; *Civil War High Commands*, 524.

Franklin Thompson was in fact **Sarah Emma Edmonds** (1841–1898), who was born in New Brunswick, Canada, and raised on farm. In 1860, she entered the U.S., adopted male garb and roles, changed her name to Franklin Thompson, and worked for a Hartford, Connecticut, bible seller. According to Edmonds's memoir, she was at railroad station "returning from the far West" (probably Flint, Michigan) when word came that Lincoln called for 75,000 troops. Immediately after deployment, Thompson worked in noncombatant roles as a male nurse at the regimental hospital, and regimental postmaster while the Second Michigan was garrisoned in the Washington defenses. She received her baptism of fire along with her unit at First Bull Run. She successfully concealed her gender from all but one comrade, who kept the secret. By the spring of 1862, Thompson was a male nurse at several Washington military hospitals. Thompson deployed west with the Second Michigan in March 1863. In April, Thompson, posted in Kentucky, deserted, claiming later that having contracted malaria, she feared discovery of her gender. She went to Ohio and resumed her female identity. By June, she was nursing for the Christian Commission. Postwar, Edmonds returned to New Brunswick and married. In 1884 Congress granted her a pension under the name "Franklin Thompson" and expunged desertion from her record. She died in La Porte, Texas, and was buried with full military honors. Leonard, *All the Daring of a Soldier*, 169–185; S. Emma E. Edmonds, *Nurse and Spy in the Union Army: The Adventures and Experiences of a Woman in Hospitals, Camps, and Battlefields* (Hartford, CT: W. S. Williams & Co., 1865, reprint, Applewood Books), 17; Leonard describes this book as "melodramatic pseudofiction"; for one thing, it does not discuss Franklin Thompson. Dyer, 1282.

David Thurston (1818/19–d. after 1889) was born in Massachusetts and moved to Montreal during the 1850s, eventually settling in Toronto. He was a lumber trader and newspaper distributor, and unsuccessfully sought a municipal office. He often worked to facilitate good relations between Canada and the United States and in 1861 was named as consular agent in the new Toronto consular office. Thurston's intelligence on Confederate activities in Canada, enhanced by his local knowledge and good relations with Canadian authorities, was often reliable. Secretary of State Seward came to rely on Thurston for information. Seward appointed him as vice consul in Quebec and Montreal, and in 1865 named him Toronto consul. He retained office until 1869. Thurston remained in Canada and in 1878, Hayes appointed him vice consul in Toronto, where he served until 1882. J. G. Snell, "Thurston, David," *Dictionary of Canadian Biography*, Vol. XI (1881–1890) (Toronto: University of Toronto Press, 1982).

Charles A. Trowbridge (1817–1889) was born in Horseheads, New York, and moved with his family to Oakland County. At sixteen Trowbridge relocated to Detroit and his uncle Charles C. Trowbridge to learn business. His first investment was in a grain mill in Wacousta, which coincided with the Panic of 1837. Trowbridge was ruined; fortunately, there would be a second act. After clerking for a Detroit wholesale grocery business, Trowbridge began investing in the Upper Peninsula's (Marquette County) iron ore deposits. He organized the Collins Iron Company and built a furnace on the Dead River. Trowbridge was an early Michigan Republican and promoted a Pacific railroad; during the Civil War, he lobbied for federal authority to build a line. His mining interests also included silver on Lake Superior's north shore and in South America. He died in New York City. Francis Bacon Trowbridge, *The Trowbridge Genealogy: History of the Trowbridge Family in America* (New Haven, CT: Printed for the Compiler, 1908), 605–606; "The Late Charles A. Trowbridge," *Detroit Free Press*, April 18, 1889; *Under the Oaks*, 23.

Charles C. Trowbridge (1800–1883) was born in Albany, New York, and at age twelve was apprenticed to an Owego merchant; when that venture became insolvent, Trowbridge, now eighteen, was appointed by creditors to liquidate the business. He moved to Detroit in 1819, and in 1820 accompanied Lewis Cass to northern Michigan to pacify Chippewa tribes and for scientific purposes. Trowbridge had a facility for language; fluent in French, he mastered several Indian languages and acted as a government Indian agent until 1825; he also served as secretary to the University of Michigan Board of Regents, eventually becoming a regent. In 1825 he also became cashier of the Bank of Michigan, and eventually its president. He was a Detroit alderman in 1833 and mayor in 1834. Trowbridge ran unsuccessfully as a Whig for governor in 1837. In 1842 his bank failed, and the next year he was hired as the Michigan State Bank's president. After it closed in 1853, he turned to railroads with greater success. Trowbridge joined Michigan's Republican Party after it was established in 1854. During the Civil War, Trowbridge actively supported the war effort. In 1865 Trowbridge served on the committee to finance the reception of returning troops, and later was a sponsor of the Detroit Soldiers' and Sailors' Monument. James V. Campbell, "Biographical Sketch of Charles C. Trowbridge," contained in *Pioneer Collections. Report of the Pioneer Society of the State of Michigan*, Vol. VI (Lansing: W. S. George & Co., 1884), 478–491; 18–19, 85, 111.

Sojourner Truth (1797?–1883), birth name Isabella Baumfree, was born into slavery at Swartekill (Ulster County), New York. She would be sold and resold as a slave over the next thirty years, finally escaping bondage in 1826. She converted to Methodism and worked as a housekeeper in Kingston and New York City. Between 1832 and 1834, she lived in the utopian community of the Kingdom of Matthias (Robert Matthews). After the cult dissolved, Truth was accused of attempting to poison several members: she sued for slander and won a judgment of $125. She returned to housekeeping in New York City and Ossining. In 1843 she became an itinerant evangelical preacher in New York and southern New England and changed her name to Sojourner Truth. In the 1840s, she joined the Northampton Association, a Massachusetts utopian community. By 1850 she was a Northampton homeowner. That year, with the help of William Lloyd Garrison (who blurbed the book), she published the *Narrative of Sojourner Truth, A Northern Slave, Emancipated from Bodily Servitude by the State of New York in 1828* (Boston: Printed for the Author, 1850). She also began a remarkable speaking career devoted to antislavery and women's rights topics; both subjected Truth to occasional mob violence, arrest, and death threats. She lectured across New England, New York, Ohio, Pennsylvania, and in 1856–1857, Michigan and Indiana. She became a spiritualist and on July 28, 1857, purchased property in Harmonia, Michigan (west of Battle Creek), and affiliated with a spiritualist seminary. Her work continued during the war to include freedmen assistance. On October 29, 1864, she met with President Lincoln at the White House. In 1865, she boarded Washington streetcars to challenge segregation. Postwar, she continued her work with freed persons, and lectured for equality for African Americans and women. In 1867, she moved to Battle Creek and in 1870 visited President Grant at the White House. In 1872, she campaigned for Grant but was somehow denied the ballot in Battle Creek (although blacks had been technically enfranchised by the passage of the Fifteenth Amendment in 1870, the right remained unrealized in many jurisdictions). Truth died in Battle Creek. Carlton Mabee, *Sojourner Truth, Slave, Prophet, Legend* (New York: New York University Press, 1993), xiii–xvi, 1–5; *Encyclopedia of the American Civil War: A Political, Social, and Military History*, 1977.

Joseph Tunnicliffe, Jr. (also spelled "Tunnecliff"), (1818–1881) was born in Monroe County, Michigan, moved to New York in 1824, and returned to Michigan in 1834. He graduated from Castleton Medical College, Vermont, in 1841. He moved to Jackson and brought to Michigan innovative surgeries to correct strabismus and repair hernias and cataracts. In 1848, Tunnicliffe attended Philadelphia's prestigious Jefferson Medical College and was awarded an M.D. in 1849. On May 16, 1861, Tunnicliffe was appointed surgeon of the Fourth Michigan Infantry. He resigned that August to become the First Michigan Infantry's physician. Although Tunnicliffe resigned for disability on December 10, 1862, he remained in Washington as Michigan state agent through the war, with headquarters on the southeast corner of Seventh and E Streets. Postwar, he served as a surgeon for the Michigan Central Railroad and also as an examining physician for federal pensions. C. B. Burr, M.D., *Medical History of Michigan*, Michigan State Medical Society (Minneapolis: Bruce Publishing Company, 1930), 2 vols., Vol. II, 850; *MIW*, 223, 950; *DNI*, July 7, 1865; *History of Jackson County*, 741–742; *JCP*, March 21, 1881.

Daniel Upton (1818–1893) was born to a wealthy family in Newberg, New York, where he was publicly educated. In 1835 he moved to Jackson with his parents. A Republican, Upton had first been elected county clerk in 1857, and

was reelected throughout the war, only leaving in 1866 to assume a seat in the state legislature. The same year he moved to Muskegon, where he held local offices and became a successful real estate investor and merchandizer. *History of Jackson County, Michigan* (Chicago: Inter-State Publishing, 1881), 241–242, 336, 311, 493; *Portrait and Biographical Record of Muskegon and Ottawa Counties, Michigan* (Chicago: Biographical Publishing Company, 1893), 143–144.

John Thomas Van Stan was a Detroit housepainter before the war. He mustered with the Fourteenth Michigan as a second lieutenant in Company C on September 24, 1861. He resigned and joined the Provost Guard in late 1862, but was dismissed by the War Department on January 27, 1864, "for habitual drunkenness" and lost all pay and allowances. But something else caught the Democratic organ *Free Press*'s attention: Van Stan's alleged part in election interference in 1863. Van Stan was charged with escorting soldiers to the polls, and there was some testimony that he was acting on behalf of Republicans. Postwar, he was a Detroit constable in the Third Ward. *FAC*, 266; *ROS*, 14.1, 120; *Charles F. Clark's City Directory*, 1866–1867, 18; *DFP*, February 3, 4, 1864.

Benjamin Vernor (1820–1898) was born in Albany, New York, and educated privately. He moved to Detroit in 1840, and again to Marshall to manage a hardware store. In 1843, he moved to Jackson to produce stoneware and hollowware for a state prison. In 1846, Vernor returned to Detroit as a partner in that business, becoming active in manufacturing and merging with the Detroit Locomotive Works. In 1852 he left manufacturing for the insurance business. Politically, Vernor was a Whig and later a Republican, although he never held office. A talented manager, during the war he served as the hub for Michigan's state agents and managed Detroit supply depot with items for Michigan soldiers. Postwar, Vernor became one of Detroit's prominent bankers and manufacturers. His brother, James Vernor (late lieutenant of the Fourth Michigan Cavalry), was the founder of Vernor's Ginger Ale. *American Biographical History of Eminent and Self-Made Men with Portrait Illustrations on Steel, Michigan Volume* (Cincinnati: Western Biographical Publishing, 1878), 145–146.

David S. Walbridge (1802–1868) was a Vermont-born businessman and farmer who moved to Kalamazoo in

1842. He served in Michigan's House and twice in its Senate. Walbridge was the permanent chair of the "Under the Oaks" convention. He was sent to the Thirty-Fourth and Thirty-Fifth Congresses and died in Kalamazoo. BD, 2101; Durant, *History of Kalamazoo*, 225, 226, 253.

Hiram Walbridge (1821–1879) was a New York lawyer, merchant, and congressman, and an Ohio brigadier general of militia. BD, 2101.

Henry Waldron (1816–1880) was born in Albany, New York, graduated from Rutgers in 1836, moved to Michigan in 1837, worked as a civil engineer, and in 1839 moved to Hillsdale. A civil engineer active in railroads and banking, Waldron was sent to the Thirty-Fourth through Thirty-Sixth Congresses, as a Republican, and to the Chicago Convention in 1860. Postwar, he returned to the Forty-Second through Forty-Fourth Congresses. He died in Hillsdale. BD, 2103; YC, September 25, 1880; *Under the Oaks*, 85.

Charles I. Walker (1814–1895) was born at Butternuts, New York, and educated publicly and privately. He entered the mercantile business before moving to Grand Rapids in 1836 to sell real estate. In 1837, he represented Grand Rapids in the Second Convention of Assent. That year the panic ended his business, but he had funds enough to purchase the *Grand River Times*. It failed and he turned to law. In 1840 Walker was elected to Michigan's House, but in 1841 left for Vermont for more study and practiced there. In 1851 Walker returned to Michigan. He formed a Detroit law firm with his brother Edward, and retired in 1857. In 1858 he helped found the Historical Society of Michigan, and also wrote on local history. After the University of Michigan established its Law Department in 1859, Walker was appointed one of three professors. A Republican, he served in 1867 as Wayne County circuit court judge. Although he left his university chair in 1876, he returned as a "substitute" teacher in the years that followed. He also served on Detroit's Board of Education and was its president for two terms as well as an original member of the State Board of Corrections and Board of Charities when it was founded in 1871. *Early Bench and Bar of Detroit*, 208; Burke A. Hinsdale, *History of the University of Michigan, with Biographical Sketches of Regents and Members of the University Senate from 1837 to 1906*, ed. Isaac N. Demmon (Ann Arbor: Published by the University, 1906), 99, 102, 233–234; *Pioneer Collections. Report of the Pioneer Society of the State of Michigan, together with Reports of County, Town, and District Pioneer Societies* (Lansing: W. S. George & Co., Printers and Binders, 1883), Vol. IV, 406–407.

Edward C. Walker (1820–1894) was born in Butternuts, New York, and left school to help build the Chenango Canal. He trained as a civil engineer, but was disabled by a knee injury and in 1837 came to Detroit. He attended the University of Michigan (Detroit branch), then Yale, graduating with honors in 1842; afterward he went to Harvard Law School for one year and studied under Judge Joseph Story. Walker returned to Detroit to teach at the university and then read law in the office of Joy & Porter. Walker returned to Detroit, was admitted to the bar in 1845, and commenced practice. From 1850 to 1857, he partnered with his brother Charles I. Walker; after Charles retired, Edward continued the firm for many years. Walker specialized in business and real estate law and was an important source for out-of-state firms to verify Michigan land titles. In 1846, he served as secretary to one of Detroit's first temperance societies and in 1852 became the first president of Detroit's Young Men's Christian Association. Walker was an early signatory calling for the formation of a new party; although it is unclear whether he was present "Under the Oaks," he became a staunch Republican after the party was established. Between 1855 and 1858, Walker was alderman for Detroit's First Ward. Walker was chairman of the party's State Central Committee for four years. After the attack on Fort Sumter, Walker helped establish the Michigan Branch of the Christian Commission and served as its chairman. He raised and distributed some $30,000, and in the midst of Grant's Overland Campaign, traveled to the front and spent six weeks as a volunteer nurse to the wounded. Between 1863 and 1882, he served as a regent of the University of Michigan. Postwar, Walker continued to practice law and also helped found the Detroit Museum of Art. Farmer, *The History of Detroit and Michigan; or the Metropolis Illustrated*, 1129–1130; Farmer, *History of Michigan*, 756, 839, 362, 311, 732, 683, 638; EHM, 665; *Under the Oaks*, 40, 80, 82.

Henry N. Walker (1811–1886) was born in Fredonia, New York, was educated privately, and moved to Detroit in 1835. He read law, was admitted to the bar, and opened a successful practice. In 1837 he was master in chancery and in 1844 a state Supreme Court reporter. Between 1845 and 1847, Walker served as state attorney general. Buchanan appointed Walker postmaster of Detroit in 1859, and he remained until removed by the incoming Republicans. Walker was active in business: in 1836 he was Michigan agent for the Protection Insurance Company; in 1849 he founded and became president of the Detroit Savings Fund Institute; and between 1856 and 1863 he was president of the Detroit & Milwaukee Railroad and helped found the Great Western Railway of Canada. His most important wartime role began with his 1861 purchase of the *Detroit Free Press*. Walker, a Democrat, generally aligned his sheet with prosecuting the war while opposing the Lincoln administration's policies on press suppression and the suspension of habeas corpus. He virulently opposed emancipation and abolition, and continued Wilbur Storey's legacy of open and often crude racism. The *Free Press* was Michigan's Democratic party organ and Michigan's largest circulating daily. Walker continued with the sheet until his retirement in 1875. *Michigan Biographies*, 398–399; *Report of the Pioneer Society of the State of Michigan together with reports of County Pioneer Societies*, Vol. IX, 2nd ed. (Lansing: Wynkoop Hallenbeck Crawford Company, State Printers, 1908), 88–89; DFP, February 24, 1886.

Eber B. Ward (1811–1875) was born in Canada to Vermont parents. In 1818, the Wards moved to Ohio, and at age ten, Ward, a cabin boy on a Great Lakes ship, arrived in Detroit. He would prove to be an investor of remarkable vision, buying steam vessels, and then steam lines, building iron-hulled ships, manufacturing iron, acquiring iron-ore mines, and then acquiring vast tracts of timberland for charcoal. He was also a prominent investor in railroads, silver mines, smelting, and sand for plate glass. Ward was a fervently pro-Union Republican. Preceding the 1864 election, fears grew about an invasion from Confederate sympathizers; Ward famously converted his Detroit home into a barracks: eighty of his mill workers stood ready with 320 stand of arms and two six-pounder cannon. In his pocket (he claimed) was an appointment from Governor Blair as Detroit's PM, effective if an invasion took place. Farmer, *History of Detroit and Wayne County and Early Michigan*, 1234–1235; "Captain Eber B. Ward's Fortress: An Untold Chapter of Civil War Times in Detroit," in *Detroit Monthly* 1, no. 3 (May 1901), 20–21.

William Warner resigned as allotment commissioner in late February 1862. DFP, February 27, 1862.

David C. Wattles (1829–?) was born in Pennsylvania and moved to Lapeer County in 1837. He fought in Mexico with Company I, First U.S. Artillery. Wattles helped found the village of North Branch, having acquired large tracts of village land. Between 1859 and 1861, he served three terms as town supervisor. However, in October 1861, a letter supposedly written by Guy S. Hopkins seemed "to give assurance of the existence of an extensive league or conspiracy to overthrow the Government" and also claimed to facilitate communications between rebels and Europeans. Wattles' name was mentioned as a co-conspirator, and on November 25, 1861, he was arrested. Wattles was sent to Fort Lafayette, a site then used as a prison for political prisoners. Wattles was early offered a parole but declined to sign a loyalty oath, and remained in custody; however, he relented on April 9, 1862, signed the parole and was discharged. This episode did not deter voters from returning him to a fourth term as town supervisor in 1864. *History of Lapeer County Michigan* (1884), 185, 186, 190; close students of the arrest of Wattles, Butler, and Hopkins should consult the case file, found in OR.II.2.1244–1267, 240.

On August 6, 1861, **Jacob Webber** (d. 1876) of Lansing was commissioned as a first lieutenant of the Sixteenth Michigan, the successor to Stockton's Independent Regiment. (See note for Thomas Stockton.) Webber mustered into federal service on September 16, 1861, and resigned on January 19, 1863, honorably discharged. *MIW*, 959, 359; JCP, June 12, 1876; ROS, 16.168.

Hezekiah G. Wells (1812–1885) was born in Steubenville, Ohio, attended Kenyan College, and moved to Kalamazoo in 1833. He was a delegate to the 1835 state constitutional convention, served as a circuit court judge (1845–1850), and was a delegate to the 1850 constitutional convention. Among other wartime services, he raised the Twenty-Fifth Michigan. Postwar, Grant appointed him presiding judge on the Alabama Claims Commission. He died in Kalamazoo. Albert Welles, *History of the Welles Family in England and Normandy* (New York: Albert Welles, 1876), 258–259; DFP, April 5, 1885.

Luther B. Willard (1818–1877) was born in Cambridge, Massachusetts, and by 1832 was living in Rochester, New York. In 1835, Willard moved to Detroit and worked for the *Detroit Free Press*. The next year, he went to Toledo, Ohio, and founded the Toledo *Blade*; however, he eventually returned to Detroit and the *Free Press*. Willard was elected director of the city poor in 1850, and reelected six times through 1862, when Blair appointed him state agent. Willard was not alone in his wartime labors. In 1848 he married Electa L. Willard from Seneca County, New York; during the war, she worked as a nurse in Nashville hospitals. In 1904 Congress awarded her a pension of $12 per month in recognition of this work. Postwar, Willard returned to Detroit and served as director of the poor until his death. *Wayne County Historical and Pioneer Society: Chronography of Notable Events in the History of the Northwest Territory and Wayne County. Period Embraced, 1831–1890, together with Biographical Sketches of the early Explorers and Pioneers*, compiled by Fred. Carlisle (Detroit: O. S. Gulley, Bornman & Co., 1890), 232–233; *Statutes at Large, Fifty-Eighth Congress*, 2nd Session, chapter 1004.

Benjamin F. H. Witherell (1797–1867), born in Fair Haven, Vermont, was the son of Michigan's Territorial Supreme Court Judge James Witherell, appointed in 1807. The Witherells returned to Vermont during the War of 1812 and then returned to Michigan in 1817. Benjamin read law and was admitted to the bar in 1819. He practiced in Wayne County, held local office, and in 1830, was sponsored by Daniel Webster to United States Supreme Court practice. Witherell was a county probate judge and prosecuting attorney. He was a delegate to the 1836 statehood convention and the 1850 constitutional convention. He was elected to Michigan's Senate, and in 1843 was appointed state district judge. In 1848, he became a regent of the University of Michigan. Witherell returned to the district judgeship under the 1850 Constitution, and was reelected until his death. An historian (he served as historiographer to the city of Detroit between 1855 and 1867), Witherell served as president of the Detroit Soldiers' Monument Association. At different times, he was also JAG with the rank of brigadier general in the Michigan Militia, and a major general of militia. *Wayne County Historical Pioneer Society. Chronography of Notable Events in the History of the Northwest Territory and Wayne County*, compiled and arranged by Fred. Carlisle (Detroit: O. S. Gully, Bornman & Co., 1890), 277; Farmer, *The History of Detroit and Michigan*, 1133–1134; DFP, June 27, 1867.

William H. Withington (1835–1903) was born in Dorchester, Massachusetts, and educated publicly and at Andover's Phillips Academy. He worked for an agricultural toolmaker on whose behalf he moved to Jackson, Michigan, to manage the company's 125 workers and 6 salesmen. During the Panic of 1857, Withington reorganized the business. Later, he invested in banks, railroads, and tool and steel manufacturers. He was an early Republican and helped found the Jackson Greys militia. Before the war, Withington had already placed the Greys on a war footing. The unit became Company B of the three-months First Michigan. Withington was captured at First Bull Run, and later received a Medal of Honor for gallantry. He was exchanged on January 30, 1862, and given a warm welcome in Jackson. On August 11, 1862, he was commissioned colonel of the Seventeenth Michigan, which led with distinction at South Mountain and Antietam. He resigned on March 21, 1863, and was later brevetted brigadier general, for gallantry. Postwar, Withington held numerous Jackson municipal offices, served in Michigan's House and Senate, helped create Michigan's National Guard, and was a delegate to the Republican National Conventions in 1876 and 1892. He died in Jackson. Charles Moore, *History of Michigan, Illustrated* (Chicago: Lewis Publishing Company, 1915), 4 vols. Vol. II, 813–816; FAC, 258; JCP, June 30, 1903.

Julia Susan Wheelock (1833–1900) was born in Avon, Ohio, and moved to Michigan in 1854. She attended Kalamazoo College between 1858 and 1860, and afterward taught in Ionia. A devout Baptist, Julia was a fierce advocate for her patients. She confronted hidebound army medicine and exploited gender double standards to secure proper food and prompt treatment. She was beloved by her soldiers and the terror of underperforming doctors. On July 6, 1864, fever forced her to quit the field, and after nearly two months of hospitalization, she returned to Michigan. In her closing report, she noted that "I have always endeavored, in the distribution of goods, to give to those who needed, irrespective of RANK OR COLOR." Postwar, Michigan Congressman John F. Driggs arranged a position for Julia with the Counting Bureau of the United States Treasury in July 1865, in which she served until her 1873 marriage. She had two sons. In 1890, Congress awarded Julia, then living in Marshall, Michigan, a pension for "disease contracted while serving as a hospital nurse during the war of rebellion." As quoted in *Michigan*

Women in the Civil War, 65n2, 84n63, 75; readers should consult her wartime memoirs, *The Boys in White: The Experiences of a Hospital Agent in and around Washington* (New York: 1870).

Henry E. Whipple (c. 1816–1893) was born in Williston, Vermont, and graduated from Oberlin College in 1848. He taught at and later led Oberlin's preparatory school and graduated from Oberlin's Seminary in 1851. In 1853, he accepted a professorship at Hillsdale College. Whipple's son Francis had served with Berdan's Sharpshooters and later with the First Michigan Sharpshooters. Henry Whipple then volunteered for Christian Commission and followed Francis to war. Postwar, Whipple continued teaching at Hillsdale College until 1871, when an adultery scandal forced his resignation. After this episode, he moved to California, where a brother, publisher of the *Humboldt Times*, hired him as editor. He later worked for the U.S. Mint in San Francisco and died in that city. *History of Mendocino and Lake Counties, California, with Biographical Sketches of the Leading Men and Women of the Counties who have been identified with their Growth and Development from Early Days to the Present* (Historic Record Company, 1914), 297; *CDE*, April 30, 1871. *JC*, April 25, 1871; *Seventy Fifth Anniversary, General Colleague of Oberlin Colleague, 1833–1908, Including an Account of the Principal Events in the History of the College, with Illustrations of the College Buildings* (Oberlin, OH: April 1, 1909), 1046, 181; *Michigan in the War*, 130, 963, as quoted in Raymond J. Herek, *These Men Have Seen Hard Service: The First Michigan Sharpshooters in the Civil War* (Detroit: Wayne State University Press, 1998), 230; John F. Schmutz, *The Battle of the Crater: A Complete History* (Jefferson, NC: McFarland & Company, 2009), 315.

Henry Martyn Whittlesey (1821–1873) was born in Hartford, Connecticut, attended Yale's Law Department, and was admitted to the bar in 1845. Afterward, he worked for one of his mother's magazines, and in 1854 moved to Detroit. He was active in Detroit's volunteer fire department, the militia, and the Young Men's Society. By 1861, he was Wayne County's Registrar of Deeds. Whittlesey served on the State Military Board between March 11, 1859, and September 19, 1861. After Fort Sumter was attacked, Whittlesey volunteered his services to Blair and for six months helped organize Michigan for war. On April 24, 1861, Whittlesey was commissioned captain and AQM and assigned to Alpheus Williams's staff. He led a purchasing mission to New York City to acquire cloth for Detroit tailors for uniforms. Whittlesey assisted Williams in administering Fort Wayne as a camp of instruction, and followed him into U.S. service in October, 1861. He served as captain, AQM, and then division QM of the Twentieth Army Corps. By war's end, Whittlesey had been brevetted major, lieutenant colonel, colonel, and brigadier general. He remained in uniform, and in August, 1865, was appointed chief QM of the Army of Georgia, and in 1866, chief QM of the Department of Mississippi. He also served as chief QM of the Freedmen's Bureau and mustered out on July 16, 1867; however, as a civilian, he continued to serve as QM to the Freedmen's Bureau until 1870. That year, he was appointed comptroller of the District of Columbia, his place of death. *Brevet Brigadier in Blue*, 669; *MIW*, 6, 222, 166; *Genealogy of the Whittelsey-Whittlesey Family*, compiled by Charles Barney Whittelesey (Hartford, CT: Press of the Case, Lockwood & Brainard Company, 1898), 140–141; *Appletons Bio.* VI, 495; *FAC*, 31.

Ross Wilkins (1799–1872) was born in Pittsburgh and in 1816 graduated from present-day Dickinson College. He returned to Pittsburgh, read law, and was admitted to the bar. Between 1821 and 1823, he was Pittsburgh's prosecuting attorney and in 1829 was elected to Pennsylvania's House. In 1832 Andrew Jackson appointed Wilkins a Michigan territorial judge and he moved to Detroit. Wilkins served as a delegate to the 1835 and 1836 statehood convention, and as Detroit's city recorder. In 1837, Jackson nominated Wilkins as U.S. district judge for the state of Michigan. When Michigan was divided into two judicial districts in 1853, Wilkins held the eastern district bench. He retired in 1870. A War Democrat, Wilkins died in Detroit. *Bench and Bar of Michigan: A Volume of History and Biography*, ed. George Irving Reed (Chicago: Century Publishing and Engraving Company, 1897), 160–161; *EMB*, 693; Dell, *Lincoln and the War Democrats*, 453, 69; David Gardner Chardavoyne, *The United States District Court for the Eastern District of Michigan: People, Law, and Politics* (Detroit: Wayne State University Press, 2012), 17–19.

William D. Wilkins (1827–1882) was born in Pittsburgh, and in 1832 moved with his family to Detroit. Wilkins was publicly educated and pursued legal studies, although he yearned for a military career. He was a founder of the Detroit Light Guard and served as its first lieutenant under then-Captain Alpheus S. Williams. He joined Captain Alpheus Williams in the Mexican War–bound First Michigan Infantry. In 1850, Wilkins, a Democrat, was appointed USDC clerk, a position he held for the next twenty years. On April 24, 1861, Governor Blair appointed him a brigade inspector of Michigan troops garrisoned at Fort Wayne; he helped supply and transport state troops. On August 1861 General Williams appointed Wilkins to his staff. At Cedar Mountain, Wilkins was captured and held in Richmond's Libby Prison. He was paroled that September and returned to service. At Chancellorsville, Wilkins was captured again. He was again sent to Libby but paroled the next month. Wilkins's war ended on August 29, 1863, when he resigned for disability. His military résumé included brevets for gallantry to major, lieutenant colonel, and colonel. Wilkins became active in Detroit public education, helped send General Williams to Congress, and with less success in 1880, worked to send Winfield Scott to the White House. *Pioneer Collections. Report of the Pioneer Society of the State of Michigan, together with Reports of County, Town, and District Pioneer Societies* (Lansing: W. S. George & Co., Printers and Binders, 1883), Vol. IV, 438–444.

Orlando B. Willcox (1823–1907) was born in Detroit and graduated from West Point in 1847. Assigned to the Fourth U.S. Artillery, he arrived in Mexico too late to fight but was posted in Mexico City and Cuernavaca; afterward he twice fought Seminoles in Florida (1840s and 1850s) and later served in Missouri, Texas, Kansas, and at eastern harbor forts. During his Boston posting, Willcox participated in surrendering fugitive slave Anthony Burns. In 1857, Willcox left the army and returned to Detroit. He studied law, was admitted to the bar in 1858, and practiced law with his brother Eben. He also served in the state militia. Willcox was a Democrat, and in 1860, supported Stephen A. Douglas. Willcox also wrote *Shoepac Recollections: A Wayside Glimpse of American Life* (1856), and *Faca, an Army Memoir by Major March* (1857). Willcox's Michigan role after war began is discussed in the 1861 chronology. He commanded a brigade under General Heintzelman at First Bull Run, where he was wounded, taken prisoner, and held nearly thirteen months. Confederate authorities held Willcox as a hostage for the *Savannah* privateers. He was exchanged on August 15, 1862, commissioned a brigadier general, and assigned divisional command in the Ninth Corps. Occasionally leading the corps itself, Willcox fought at Antietam, Fredericksburg, and the siege of Knoxville, before returning east for Grant's Overland Campaign. Between June 5 and September 11, 1863, he commanded the districts of Indiana and Michigan, and was soon brevetted major general. Willcox mustered out of volunteer service on January 15, 1866. Postwar, Willcox returned to Detroit but six months later rejoined the regular army. He spent three years in occupation duty in Lynchburg, Virginia, and later in California and Arizona. On March 2, 1867, Willcox was double brevetted to brigadier general, USA, for his conduct at Spotsylvania, and to major general, USA, for service at Petersburg. He retired from service on April 16, 1887, and thereafter served as governor of the Soldiers' Home in Washington (1889–1892). On March 2, 1895, Willcox was awarded the Medal of Honor for First Bull Run. An important collection of Willcox's journals, letters, and memoirs were published in 1999; his published work includes coauthorship of *Famous Adventures and Prison Escapes of the Civil War* (1893). In 1905, he moved to Canada and wrote novels, under the nom de plume Major March. He died in Coburg, Ontario. *Forgotten Valor: The Memoirs, Journals, & Civil War Letters of Orlando B. Willcox*, ed. Robert Garth Scott (Kent, OH: Kent State University Press, 1999), 194–201; *Generals in Blue*, 558–559; *Appleton's Bio VI*, 516–517; *Civil War High Command*, 570; *Thirty-Eighth Annual Reunion of the Association of Graduates of the United States Military Academy at West Point, New York, June 13, 1907* (Saginaw, MI: Seemann & Peters, 1907), 102–111; *FAC*, 42, 262.

Floyd A. Willett of Kalamazoo was commissioned first lieutenant and adjutant of the First Regiment, USSS. He was later promoted to major on August 21, 1861, and discharged on July 7, 1862. Capt. C. A. Stevens, *Berdan's United States Sharpshooters in the Army of the Potomac, 1861–1865* (Dayton, OH: Morningside Bookshop, 1972, reprint, 1892), 513; *MIW*, 966.

Albert Williams (1817–1907) was born in Vermont and moved with his family to New York where he was privately educated. In 1844, he moved to Michigan, read law in Monroe, and was admitted to the bar in 1845. Eventually settling in Ionia, his Free Soil beliefs placed him in "Under the Oaks" in 1854, and he took an active role. He founded a Republican newspaper in Ionia, held county offices, and in 1862 and 1864 was elected state attorney general. Postwar, he practiced law and was affiliated with the National Prohibition Party, running for several offices. He remained a Republican until 1896, when he campaigned for William Jennings Bryan. *Bench and Bar of Michigan*, 184–187; *GRP*, April 9, 1907.

Alpheus S. Williams (1810–1878) was born in Saybrook, Connecticut, graduated from Yale College in 1831, and attended Yale's Law Department. Williams moved to Michigan in 1836, read law, and was admitted to the bar in 1837, practicing in Detroit. In 1838, Williams joined the Brady Guards, a Michigan militia unit mustered into U.S. service to watch the border during Canada's Patriot War (1837–1838). During the 1840s, Williams was a probate judge, editor of the Detroit *Daily Advertiser*, and held other municipal offices. During the Mexican War, he was commissioned first lieutenant in the First Michigan Infantry, but the conflict was almost over before the unit arrived. Postwar he was Detroit's postmaster, entered business, and served on Detroit's school board. When the Civil War began, Williams served as president of the State Military Board and as commander of Fort Wayne's camp of instruction. Williams was named brigadier general of the "First Brigade Michigan Infantry," which became the three-months iteration of the First Michigan Regiment; promotion to general, USV, followed on August 9, 1861. Williams commanded troops in the Shenandoah Valley and at Cedar Mountain. Williams's division became the Twelfth Corps, which he fought at Antietam, Chancellorsville, and Gettysburg, to good reviews. He moved west with his corps after the Battle of Chickamauga, and led a division of the Twentieth Corps to Atlanta and then to the sea. Postwar, he was brevetted major general, USV. Johnson appointed him minister to San Salvador. In 1870, he ran unsuccessfully for Michigan governor against Henry Crapo. He later represented Detroit in the Forty-Fourth and Forty-Fifth Congresses. He died in Washington during his second term. *BD*, 2165; *Memorial Addresses on the Life and Character of Alpheus S. Williams (A Representative from Michigan), delivered to the House of Representatives and in the Senate, Forty-Fifth Congress, Third Session, Published by Order of Congress* (Washington, DC: Government Printing Office, 1880), 20, 24, 29, 32, 38; *MIW*, 166; *GIB*, 559–560; Bak, *A Distant Thunder*, 176.

William B. Williams (1826–1905) was born in Pittsford, New York, educated at public and private schools, and graduated from the State and National Law School in

Ballston Spa in 1851. He practiced in Rochester and in 1855 moved to Allegan. During the war, Williams served as probate judge (1857–1865); during those same years, he enlisted as a private in the Nineteenth Michigan, but his company was soon attached to the Fifth Michigan Cavalry. Promoted to captain, Williams resigned for disability in 1863. Postwar, he served in Michigan's Senate (1866–1870) and other state offices. A Republican, he was elected to the Forty-Third and Forty-Fourth Congresses, afterward resuming his law practice and serving as state railroad commissioner. He died in Allegan. *BD*, 2173; *MIW*, 968; *History of Allegan County*, 74–75.

Moses Wisner (1815–January 5, 1863) was born in Springport, New York, educated publicly, and in around 1837, moved to Michigan. He struggled as a Lapeer County farmer, and by 1839, moved to Pontiac and read law. He was admitted to the bar in 1841 and returned to Lapeer to practice. Wisner was appointed as Lepeer County prosecutor but soon returned to Pontiac. He was an antislavery Whig, and his aloofness from politics changed after the Kansas-Nebraska Act passed. He was present "Under the Oaks" and that year ran unsuccessfully for Congress. He supported Fremont for president, and in 1857, lobbied unsuccessfully for the U.S. Senate. In 1858, he was elected as a Republican for governor and served between January 1859 and January 1861. His prospects for a second term were ended by treasurer John McKinney's defalcation. Wisner counseled Blair against sending peace commissioners to Washington, and suggested preparing for war. In July 1862, he organized the Twenty-Second Michigan Infantry and was appointed its colonel. He deployed to Kentucky on September 4. Once in Kentucky, Wisner caught typhoid fever; taken to a private residence, he died on January 5, 1863. He is buried in Pontiac. *MOG*, II, 345–348; *MIW*, 420–421; *Biographical Directory of the Governors of the United States*, 747–748; as quoted in Augustus C. Baldwin, "Oakland County—Its Bench and Bar Prior to 1840," in *Collections and Researches made by the Michigan Pioneer and Historical Society*, Vol. XXXI (Lansing: Wynkoop Hallenbeck Crawford Co., 1902), 168.

James C. Wood (1813–1897) was born in Decatur, New York, and educated privately, and at age twenty became editor of the Waterloo *Observer*. He also read law and was probably admitted to the bar there. He moved to White Pigeon, Michigan, in 1843, and the next year to Jackson, where he spent the next fifty-three years. Wood was admitted to the Jackson County bar in 1847 and practiced for over twenty years. He held local offices and was Jackson's first mayor. Wood was a prominent Michigan Democrat, and in 1860, supported Stephen A. Douglas. On April 15, 1861, he presided over Jackson's first war meeting at Jackson Hall. He remained a War Democrat for the rest of the conflict. Postwar, Wood was elected to Michigan's House in 1874 and reelected in 1876, and was a leader in defeating Zachariah Chandler's quest for another Senate term. He died in Jackson. *History of Jackson County, Michigan*, 240; JC, November 9, 1897; JP, November 6, 1897.

Obadiah C. Wood (1815–1886) was born in New York state, educated in Rochester, and in 1843 moved to Detroit. Wood organized Michigan's first black militia unit. Wood would have other firsts: postwar, he joined other black leaders in successfully suing the Detroit Board of Education to open its public schools to black children, and he was the first African American appointed to federal office in Michigan, and the first elected to municipal office. *Michigan's Manual of Freedman's Progress* (1915), 296–297.

Dwight Avery Woodbury (1827/8–July 1, 1862) was born in Adrian and worked as a conductor on the Michigan Southern Railroad; in 1859 he became owner of Adrian's main hotel. Woodbury was active in Michigan's prewar militia, and held a colonel's rank. He was commissioned colonel of the Fourth Michigan Regiment on May 16, 1861, and recruited men, mostly from St. Joseph's County. Deployed to the eastern theater, Woodbury and his unit earned exceptional reviews across Virginia's Peninsula. On July 1, 1862, Woodbury was killed in action at the Battle of Malvern Hill. Benjamin W. Dwight, *The History of the Descendants of John Dwight, of Dedham, Mass.* (New York: John F. Trow & Son, Printers, 1874), Vol. II, 972; John I. Knapp and R. I. Bonner, *Illustrated History and Biographical Record of Lenawee County, Mich, containing an Accurate Epitomized History from the First Settlement in 1824 to the Present Time* (Adrian, MI: Times Printing Company, 1903), 400–401; MIW, 961; as quoted in MIW, 227.

Grover S. Wormer (1821–1904) was born in Auburn, New York, and as a boy worked for the American Steamboat Line. Ten years later, he was overseeing steamboat ship construction. In 1851 he was hired by shipbuilder Isaac

Newton to build the *Western World* and *Plymouth Rock*, the two largest lake steamers then proposed. The ships connected the New York Central with the Michigan Central, and the latter soon hired Wormer, who moved to Detroit. By 1857, Wormer owned a Detroit-based wholesale machinery business, which prospered. Wormer, first a Whig and then a Republican, had been active in New York and in Detroit. In 1859, he joined the Lyon Guard. In April–May 1862, Wormer was commissioned captain and authorized to recruit a short-term unit to be known as the Stanton Guard. Its purpose was limited: to guard three Tennessee political prisoners at Fort Mackinac. When the prisoners were transferred, the Stanton Guard and Wormer were mustered out on September 25, 1862. On October 3, 1862, he was appointed lieutenant colonel of the Eighth Michigan Cavalry, and was appointed (but never mustered in) as colonel of the unit in April 1864. Wormer helped pursue John Hunt Morgan, fought at Buffington Island, and afterward battled Forrest. Wormer served to good reviews, afterward returning to Detroit. Blair appointed Wormer commander of the twelve-months' Thirtieth Michigan tasked with guarding "the line from [the] foot of Lake Huron to Malden." The Thirtieth's companies were posted between the Detroit and St. Clair Rivers: Fort Gratiot, St. Clair, Wyandotte, Jackson, Fenton, and Detroit. The Thirtieth mustered out on June 30, 1865. On March 13, Wormer was promoted brevet brigadier general, USV. Postwar, Wormer served as an ADC to Michigan governors Henry P. Baldwin, John J. Bagley, and Charles M. Croswell. *Civil War High Commands*, 693; *Michigan in the War*, 744, 971, 695, 487; *American Biographical History of Eminent and Self-Made Men, with Portrait Illustrations on Steel, Michigan Volume* (Cincinnati, OH: Western Biographical Publishing Company, 1878), 158–159; DFP, January 27, 1904.

Phineas C. Wright (1816–1890) was born in Rome, New York, married a Virginia widow and moved to New Orleans in 1850 to practice law. Wright, a Southern sympathizer, also became a slaveholder and city alderman. During the winter of 1857–58, he founded the Order of American Knights ("OAK"), not as a secret order but merely as a fraternal organization whose chief distinction was its principle of promoting "proper principles" of government, although these were vague. After the Panic of 1857, Wright moved to St. Louis to practice law and brought along his vision of OAK, which organization then existed only on paper. In February 1863 in the wake of Lincoln's Emancipation Proclamation, Wright began to recruit OAK members by transforming its doctrine to one of vehement opposition to the war and emancipation. He established a "temple" in St. Louis and in several Illinois and Indiana counties while Wright himself traveled as an OAK proselytizer throughout the region. Wright was the Order's Supreme Grand Commander, and in early 1864, moved to New York where he was hired as a deputy editor for the *New York News*, owned by Benjamin Wood, the brother of arch-Democrat Fernando Wood, famous mayor of New York. In the summer of 1864, Wright's name surfaced in federal investigations of subversive organizations. In a report summarizing these findings, Wright, together with Ohio Congressman Clement Vallandigham, were charged with organizing "a secret order intended to be general throughout the country," named the Order of the American Knights, or O.A.K." Federal authorities arrested Wright in Detroit on April 27, 1864, as he returned from Canada; he would not be released from federal custody until July 7, 1865. Postwar, Wright returned to New York and practiced railroad law. Mayo Fesler, "Secret Political Societies in the North during the Civil War," *Indiana Magazine of History* XIV, no. 3 (September 1918), 224–241; Lawrence S. Freund, "Prisoners of State," *New York History Review* 11, no. 1 (Elmira: New York History Review Press, 2017), 89–93; OR.II.7.645, 647, 658, 660; Frank Klement, *Dark Lanterns*, 64; as quoted, 65; 66–74; NYTr, January 29, 1890; Lawrence S. Freund, "The Wright Brothers of Rome," *New York History Review*, January 7, 2018 (online).

Michigan

Si quaeris peninsulam
amoenam circumspice.

If you seek a pleasant peninsula,
look about you.

War Geography

In 1860, Michigan's 56,243 square miles were divided into seventy-two counties,[1] which, for the Thirty-Seventh Congress (1861–1863), were grouped into four congressional districts. Michigan was bounded by four states: east to west, Ohio, Indiana, Illinois, and bordering the western edge of the Upper Peninsula, Wisconsin. Michigan consists of two peninsulas (Upper and Lower), which together were surrounded by four of the five Great Lakes: Erie, Huron, Superior, and Michigan, and one foreign country, Canada, then known as British America.[2]

The southern borders of Michigan's southern neighbor Ohio fronted slave states Virginia and Kentucky, while neighbors Indiana and Illinois also fronted Kentucky; during the Civil War, these states were subject to Confederate raids and costly defenses, but Michigan was too far north for anxiety about invasions from the south. Instead, it looked worriedly to its north. "We live upon the borders of the most powerful nation on the Globe," outgoing Governor Moses Wisner declared in January 1861, as he argued for strengthening the state militia. "Seven hundred miles of our coast form the boundary line between Great Britain and the United States. We are at peace with the whole world, but this peace may not last a year." He was almost right. (See November 8, 1861.) Not all was peril: Michigan's total coastline of 3,177 miles, including some 120 miles of harbors and inlets and 833 miles of island coast, had also offered critical economic advantages, and during the war, naval enlistments. (See Selected Summaries.)[3]

In the Lower Peninsula, potential geographic vulnerabilities included the Detroit River, Lake St. Clair, and the St. Clair River, all separating Michigan from Canada; in the Upper Peninsula, the border was St. Marys River. But it was memories of the War of 1812 that drove Michigan's concerns and freighted this geography with great insecurity. After a failed July 1812 invasion of Canada, General Isaac Hull had retreated to Detroit, where, following a brief siege, he surrendered to the British in August. Despite U.S. attempts to retake the Michigan Territory, it remained under British control for the next thirteen months until Oliver Hazard Perry swept its fleet from Lake Erie and compelled its army to evacuate Detroit. In 1861, these events remained well within living memory (for example, see the biographical notes for Lewis Cass and Colonel John Stockton); in many more cases, Michigan's leadership was only one generation removed from that war. Michigan's northern border was dotted with defenses—Forts Brady, Holmes (Mackinac), Shelby, Gratiot, and Wayne—that either figured in the War of 1812 or were constructed in its aftermath and reminded Michiganders of troublesome events not quite fifty years old.[4]

A British Canadian invasion across rivers was only one concern. Michigan's unique status bordering all but one of the Great Lakes, and the state's control of the American Lock at St. Mary's Falls[5] (which connected Lakes Superior, Michigan, and Huron), also heightened perceived vulnerabilities. (In 1860, an estimated $9,887,404 in goods passed through its locks, generating $24,460 in state revenue; by 1864, toll receipts had increased to $34,287.31.) Four times between 1862 and 1865 the Michigan legislature would ask the federal government to build a naval dockyard, or rearm and garrison Great Lakes' forts, or construct a harbor at the mouth of the Ontonagon River to protect lake shipping.[6]

Despite these anxieties, there was to be no British invasion. But during the Civil War Northern strategy expanded to include breaking Southern civilian as well as military morale, and the Confederacy responded in part by using Canada as a platform to mount covert operations into Northern states. These reached into Maine, Vermont, New York, Ohio, Illinois, Michigan, and indirectly, into Indiana and Kentucky. (See each state chapter for accounts of these operations; for threats and operations involving Michigan, see November 8, 1863; September 17, 1864; and November 3, 1864.)

Finally, Michigan, like its Old Northwest neighbors, believed that the existence of the Confederacy posed a potentially mortal threat to free navigation through the vital Ohio and Mississippi River valleys. When Governor Austin Blair addressed the importance of Union in his January 1861 inaugural, his argument of first resort was the need to keep the Mississippi under one-government control. (See introduction, 1861 Legislative Session.) While no rivers directly connected Michigan with the great river valleys, its 1861 rail network did. Considering only same-gauge rail lines, Port Huron, Grand Haven, Detroit, Jackson, Monroe, and Adrian enjoyed reasonably direct connections to Cincinnati, Jeffersonville, New Albany, and Evansville on the Ohio River and Cairo on the Mississippi; to the east, Toledo and Cleveland linked to canals connecting with the Ohio River; and to the west, rail lines connected to Terre Haute and Vincennes on the Wabash River, which flowed into the Ohio. At a May 3, 1861, meeting of governors, Blair declared, "We bought the mouth of the Mississippi, and we will hold it. The traitors may go into the Gulf, but they shall not take the territory with them." (See entry for that date.)[7]

Michigan's geography was not that of the Borderlands; it did not edge the Ohio and Mississippi River valleys, and thus had far fewer demographic and economic connections with the slave states across the great rivers. One result is that Michigan's early war politics were far less hospitable to making concessions to secessionists during the Secession Winter and afterward; Michigan had no Clement Vallandigham,[8] and its fears of internal subversion from pro-Southern secret organizations such as the Knights of the Golden Circle or the Sons of Liberty existed mostly in imaginations, and not, as in Ohio, Indiana, and Michigan, on the ground (although Detroit reportedly had a branch of the Knights). One cannot speak of a South-leaning "southern" Michigan as in Ohio, Indiana, and Illinois. In Michigan, there was a Republican-leaning south, and excepting a few settlements and mining operations, only the silence of semiwilderness to the north.[9]

Economy in 1860

In 1860, Michigan's $257,163,983 in combined real and personal property ranked twenty-second out of thirty-seven states, territories, and the District of Columbia; this placed Michigan just behind Wisconsin ($273,671,678) and ahead of Iowa ($247,338,265). Among states of the Old Northwest, Michigan was fifth ranked in aggregate value, preceded by Ohio ($1,193,898,422), Illinois ($871,860,282), and Indiana at $528,835,371. (Still frontier, Minnesota's 1860 valuation was only $52,294,413.) What five of the six Old Northwest states did share between 1850 and 1860 were triple-digit increases in the value of this property: Wisconsin topped the list at 550.72 percent, followed by Illinois (457.93 percent), Michigan (330.13 percent), Indiana (160.95 percent), and Ohio (136.54 percent) This growth reflected the region's rapidly developing, postfrontier status.[10]

In January 1865, Governor Henry H. Crapo pleaded, *"We want men—we want settlers."* While the frontier had moved west since the Michigan Territory was organized (1805) and statehood attained (1837), in 1860, vast portions of central and northern Michigan remained an internal wilderness. Pioneers were needed to settle the land, and Michigan aggressively sought them. In 1859 the state legislature offered settlers forty-acre parcels in exchange for a promise to reclaim and occupy the land. Within two years, some 1,700 "poor men" (of whom 1,500 were Germans) had acquired property through this program.

The 1859 legislature also appropriated $2,500 to hire two commissioners to encourage immigration, one based in New York City and the other in Detroit; both men were fluent in German, French, and English. (Governor Moses Wisner's chief regret was that the appropriation was insufficient to send a commissioner to Europe.) Seventy-five thousand dollars was authorized to subsidize swamp drainage and road construction: although 477 miles had been planned, by January 1861, only 179 miles of railroads had been completed under this program.[11]

Michigan's 1860 county populations depict sparse settlement. Of the state's counties, four had fewer than 100 inhabitants; three had fewer than 200; six had between 200 and 1,000; and seventeen had between 1,000 and 5,000. During the war and afterward, Michigan continued to organize internally: of the state's present-day eighty-three counties, forty-one were organized between 1850 and 1887, including ten during the 1860s. The location of "late" organizing counties also suggests another pattern of state settlement, and hence, economic development: the state grew from south to north, with the last ten counties organized (beginning with Keweenaw County in 1861 and ending with Luce County in 1887) on the Upper Peninsula or the north coast of the Lower Peninsula.[12]

In 1861, the state's northernmost railroad was in central Michigan, an unfinished twenty-mile line of the Saginaw-based Flint & and Pere Marquette railroad. The rest of the rail network covered the southern third of the state, with Detroit serving as the hub for Michigan's four principal lines: the one substantial north-south line, connecting Toledo to Detroit and Port Huron (south of Detroit, the road was named the Detroit, Monroe & Toledo, and north of Detroit, the Grand Trunk Railroad); the rest of the railroads ran east-west: Detroit-Owosso-Grand Haven (via the Detroit & Milwaukee); Detroit-Jackson-Michigan City (Indiana) (via the Michigan Central); and the Monroe-Adrian-White Pigeon (Indiana) via the Michigan Southern & Northern Indiana Railroad. Altogether, Michigan's 1860 track mileage was 799.3, more than double the 1850 number, yet small compared with other western states. For example, while Michigan was about the same size as Illinois and Wisconsin, the latter two had substantially more track mileage, at 2,867.9 and 922.61 respectively.[13]

In 1860, the farmer, the lumberjack, the miller, the shepherd, and to a lesser extent the miner defined Mich-

igan's economy. The war changed little of this. As Austin Blair declared in his 1865 valedictory, "Agriculture is the main pursuit of the great mass of our people, and must always so continue." In 1860, Michigan counted 62,722 occupied farms with a cash value of $163,279,087; since 1850, this amount had increased by $111,406,641. As with farms, so with farming implements: in 1860, Michigan farmers worked their properties with $5,855,642 in equipment, almost double the 1850 value. (However, it is highly likely that most of these tools were not made in Michigan, where 1860 agricultural implement production totaled only $412,192.) In the decade preceding the war, Michigan showed gains in almost every agricultural category measured. Although scale mattered (farm production should always be compared with agricultural behemoths New York, Pennsylvania, and Ohio), by 1860 Michigan had achieved fifth rank in the number of sheep (1,465,477 animals), ninth in wheat (8,313,185 bushels), eleventh in oats (4,073,098 bushels), fourth in wool (4,062,858 pounds), sixth in Irish potatoes (5,264,733 bushels), sixth in orchard products ($1,137,678), seventh in butter (14,60,384 pounds), and eighth in cheese, (2,009,064 pounds). In 1860, of some 236,987 Michiganders classified by occupation, the largest group (88,657) was farmers and the second-largest (35,884) was farm laborers, together 52.5 percent of the workers listed. Not coincidentally, in a postwar study that examined the occupations of Michigan volunteers and recruits, of 27,854 men sampled, 16,987, or 61 percent, were engaged in agricultural work.[14]

In 1860, Michigan ranked seventeenth nationally in the value ($35,200,000) of manufactured goods produced, based on $24,000,000 invested capital; among Old Northwest states, it was behind Ohio ($125,000,000/$58,000,000), Illinois ($56,750,000/$27,700,000), and Indiana ($43,250,000/$18,875,000). Altogether, Michigan manufactories employed 22,860 men and 1,260 women. (In contrast, Ohio employed a total of 81,210 of men and women.) However, Michigan's overall manufacturing rank masked several categories where the state had real strength. It led the Old Northwest (and was third ranked nationally) in the value ($7,033,427) of lumber produced; the Old Northwest was now the nation's lumberman, having surpassed the Middle Atlantic states since 1850. Michigan was eighth in the value ($8,663,288) of flour and meal milled; here also, the Old Northwest, led by Ohio, was now the nation's miller as well as granary, having surpassed the Middle Atlantic States in both categories since 1850. Michigan was also the nation's leader in 1860 copper production, mining 6,283 tons (much of it from Houghton and Ontonagon Counties) valued at $2,292,186; this represented 69 percent of the value mined nationally. In 1860, Michigan was also beginning to mine iron ore (138,800 tons) and salt (by 1864, 529,073 barrels), but at the time, output was small.[15]

In 1860, Michigan-built ships totaled 2,903 tons, and amounted to forty-six vessels; to be sure, these were dwarfed by the numbers from Maine, Massachusetts, New York, and Pennsylvania, but still large enough to rank Michigan fourteenth out of thirty-one states and territories listed.[16]

In 1860, Michigan was ranked near the bottom in the number of banks and the amount of bank capital. Of twenty-eight states listed, Michigan was twenty-sixth in the number (four) of bank branches; twenty-fifth in the amount of bank capital ($755,465); twenty-seventh in specie deposits ($24,175), and twenty-sixth in bank note circulation ($222,197). In the period after statehood, Michigan had experienced a banking bubble; when it ended, Michiganders were left with millions in worthless notes and tens of failed banks, many conceived in fraud. The result was a state economy that imported capital and combined it with human capital, thus enabling the state to export sizeable quantities of critical foodstuffs, lumber, and copper ore; refined copper was irreplaceable for electrical batteries and telegraph wire. The lack of domestic capital was a major impediment to Michigan's development.[17]

This absence of bank capital would have serious consequences during the war's first months. After the attack on Fort Sumter, Michigan faced a financial crisis: its cash had been embezzled by state treasurer John McKinney*,‡ Blair had no legislative authority to issue bonds, and banks were few and (unlike in some other states) apparently unwilling (or perhaps unable) to provide bridge financing for the war until the legislature convened. Blair was forced to raise $81,020 by private subscription from over 400 individuals and businesses in amounts ranging from $25 to $3,000. (State treasurer John Owen* personally guaranteed these funds.) In the war's critical first months, Michigan's bondholders were its private citizens. (See April 16, 1861.)[18]

Some indication of Michigan's economic status (and revenue contributions) during the war can be inferred from internal revenue reports. In the period between September 1, 1862, and June 30, 1863, Michigan had 3.757 percent of the national population (based on thirty-two loyal or nominally loyal states and territories) while paying 1.033 percent ($344,418.97) of national tax collections, thus ranking seventeenth in revenue generation. Meanwhile, the assets presumably generating these revenues constituted 2.634 percent of the "true value" of loyal states' property; thus, relative to population, Michigan appears to have "undercontributed" to national revenue.[19]

Finally Michigan's bounty and family aid expenses, which would consume much of state and local governments' wartime expenditures, should be understood in the context of 1860 wages. That year, the annual earnings of a Michigan day laborer averaged $379.60, exclusive of board. Carpenters fared much better, with an annual wage (exclusive of board) of $616.85, while average annual wage (with board) for a farmhand was $183.24. (For purposes of factoring board into any calculations, Michigan's average weekly board for laborers was $2.31.) Federal army compensation would begin at $13 per month or $156 annually; the value of federal "board"— that is, food and shelter (although given the frequent absence of both, soldiers might have ridiculed these as "compensation")—might be roughly calculated using a Michigan annualized board equivalent of $120.12. Thus, the amount that total federal army compensation was worth to a Michigander began at $276.12 (this was not distributed equally: the volunteer and not his family received "federal board," although the family was relieved of having to house or feed him). Added to any consideration of equivalents was the mitigating effect of state-offered family aid (see No. 2, May 10, 1861, infra). This law allowed soldiers' families up to $15 per month and gave counties the discretion to create the rules for distributing funds, although distributions had to be based on need. Although few families probably qualified for the maximum distribution (annualized at $180), hypothetically, a dependent family receiving the maximum aid distribution and whose private soldier allocated 100 percent of pay ($153) would receive $333 per annum—still less than a day laborer received exclusive of board. The result was want and sometimes destitution.[20]

‡An asterisk (*) appearing next to a name's first mention indicates that this person is listed in the Biography section.

Governance and Politicians

Constitution

During the Civil War, Michigan was governed by its 1850 Revised Constitution, which had replaced its charter of 1835. The revised charter featured a bicameral legislature with thirty-two senators (with two-year terms) and a requirement that the House "shall consist of not less than sixty-four, nor more than one hundred members," also with two-year terms. Apportionment was based on "the number of white inhabitants, and civilized persons of Indian descent not members of any tribe." There was no property requirement for office, but solons were required to be male U.S. citizens and "qualified electors"; besides certain residency requirements, this limited lawmakers to white and certain Indian males aged over twenty-one years. In 1861, Michigan's House consisted of seventy-seven members.[21]

Michigan was a "November state": elections for governor, the legislature, and other state officers paralleled the federal schedule: "the Tuesday succeeding the first Monday of November." The legislature convened biennially on the first Wednesday in January; however, Article V, Section 7, allowed the governor to "convene the Legislature on extraordinary occasions," and during the war, the biennial sessions of 1861, 1863, and 1865 were supplemented by Extra Sessions of 1861 (the emergency meeting after the attack on Fort Sumter), 1862, and 1864. Extra Sessions were limited to legislating only on matters "expressly stated in the Governor's proclamation, or submitted to them by special message."[22]

As noted, voters were limited by race (white and Indians not members of any tribe), gender (male), and age (a minimum of twenty-one years). Indians were required to be "a native of the United States and not a member of any tribe"; however, whether white or American, voters were subject to modest (relative to states more hostile to foreign immigration) residency requirements: three months' state residency and ten days preceding the election in the town or ward where the vote was to be cast. While U.S. citizenship was required to serve in the legislature, it was not required to vote: before January 1, 1850, noncitizens who declared their intention to become citizens six months before the next election were eligible to vote; after this date, an alien was eligible if he had lived in Michigan for two-and-a-half years, resided in the voting district at least six months prior to the election, and had declared his intention to become a citizen.[23]

Disenfranchised groups were not quiescent in the decades preceding the war. In 1846, 1849, 1855, and 1857, women petitioned the legislature for the vote; all requests were denied. However, Michigan's 1850 Constitution did declare that a woman's property, acquired both before and after marriage, remained hers; moreover, a woman was not liable for a husband's debts, and also had the absolute right to convey her property "as if she were unmarried." African American suffrage is discussed below, but before and after the 1850 plebiscite in which white voters denied blacks the right to vote, petitions to the legislature to permit African American suffrage "were regular features of Michigan politics during the 1840s and 1850s"—and numbered in the hundreds. And there was some progress. In 1855, blacks were enfranchised for local school elections, but in 1859, an effort to replicate New York state's black suffrage provisions (which included a property requirement—see *SAW*, Vol. III, New York) failed. Michigan's treatment of African Americans mattered for many reasons, one of which was that by limiting black freedoms, it discouraged black settlement; this shortage of black Americans was an impediment to recruiting black soldiers. (See September 16, 1863.) While Michigan tendered seventy-nine units of all arms during the war, only one was African American.[24]

The 1850 constitution also provided elections for governor, lieutenant governor, secretary of state, superintendent of public instruction, state treasurer, commissioner of the land office, auditor general, and attorney general, all for two-year terms. (Judges were also elected but for various terms.) The governor (or lieutenant governor) was required to be at least age thirty, a U.S. citizen for five years, and a resident of Michigan for two years preceding the election. The governor was designated commander-in-chief of the military and naval forces, and could call out this force "to execute the laws, to suppress insurrections and to repel invasions." While Michigan's 1850 charter had little else to say about the militia (it specified that all matters pertaining to "organizing, equipping and disciplining" armed forces be left to the legislature), a statute passed that year effectively exempted men from service by waiving all penalties for a failure to pay a nonappearance fine. Other than race and age, the only constitutional limitation (Article IX) for future laws was that they not be incompatible with federal law.[25]

The 1850 charter did specify the composition of the militia (such as it was), and here there was a change from the charter of 1835: the older compact had no racial test for militia service, while the 1850 charter limited membership to white males aged between eighteen and forty-five years; exempt were pacifist religious denominations and those who were otherwise exempt under state or federal law. The Constitution's "Miscellaneous Provisions" contained two measures relevant to the Civil War years: "Every person"—not just citizens, males, residents, or whites—had "a right to bear arms for the defence of himself and the State"; and, "The military shall, in all cases, and at all times, be in strict subordination to the civil power."[26]

During the Civil War, Governor Austin Blair issued draft calls to meet federal calls (as was his duty under the various federal militia acts) and also ordered troops to reinforce Michigan's side of the Canadian border. During this period, there was one major public disturbance (see July 15, 1862) and one race riot (see March 6, 1863). The governor did not mobilize militia for either, but the City of Detroit did call on existing militia to suppress the 1863 disturbance. The governor had no constitutional limitation on his ability to deploy troops out of state.

The 1850 constitution had no separate bill of rights; instead, declarations of rights were distributed in different sections, as the framers thought applicable. For example, under the judiciary article were those rights corresponding to the U.S. Bill of Rights' Fourth, Fifth, and Sixth Amendments; under the legislature article were provisions that corresponded to the First Amendment and the protections of Article I, Section 9 (prohibiting bills of attainder) and Section 10 (no impairment of contracts). In the 1850 Constitution, potentially relevant to the war was Article IV, Section 44, found under the legislative provision: "The privilege of the writ of habeas corpus remains and shall not be suspended by the Legislature, except in cases of rebellion, or invasion when the public safety requires it." Although Michigan was subject to several of Lincoln's various habeas corpus suspensions and was also included in the jurisdiction covered by Burnside's General Order No. 38 (see April 13, 1863), there was no state suspension of habeas corpus or state-ordered newspaper suppression. The 1850 charter did recognize a crime of treason against the state, defined as "levying war against, or in adhering to its enemies, giving them aid and comfort." Two witnesses to the same overt act were required for conviction. No evidence has been found that any Michigander was prosecuted under this provision; however, arrests were made under federal law. (See October 20 and 21 and February 22, 1862.)[27]

Finally, the 1850 constitution had several provisions governing state finance that would matter during the war. In peacetime, the state could borrow no more than $50,000 at any one time in order to remedy deficits in current accounts. However, if "to repel invasion, suppress insurrection, or defend the State in time of war," the state could borrow money and no limit was specified other than use of funds: proceeds must be "applied to the purposes for which it was raised, or to repay such debts," that is, for military expenses or to repay debts incurred for the same. (See April 17, 1861.)[28]

Slavery and Race

Slavery existed in the future state of Michigan and long predated the Revolutionary War, although enslaved persons were relatively few, limited by geographical remoteness, a small white population, and a short growing season. But slavery grew throughout the eighteenth century. In 1706, Detroit hosted 45 enslaved persons; by 1779, there were 141 enslaved, and in 1782, 180; as late as 1796, there were some 300 enslaved persons.[29] The 1787 Northwest Ordinance had declared in Article VI that "There shall be neither slavery nor involuntary servitude in the Said Territory."; this put Michigan slavery "on the road to extinction" but did not extinguish it, chiefly because the Northwest Territory's Arthur St. Clair interpreted Article IV as applying to slavery's extension and not enslaved persons preexisting the ordinance. Because a portion of Michigan remained part of Canada until the 1794 Jay Treaty, slave owners could exploit this dual status; the treaty itself allowed British subjects to retain their slaves (Canada as part of Great Britain would not abolish slavery until the 1833 Imperial Act); however the institution was forbidden to American residents. The Michigan District taxed slaves as late as 1818; the 1810 census counted 24 slaves; in 1820, none; in 1830, there were 32 slaves; finally, Article XI of the 1835 constitution banned slavery altogether.[30]

In addition to restrictions on black suffrage and militia service, Michigan had at least two statutes that entrenched legal discrimination in the antebellum decades. One provision imposed residency restrictions on blacks. On April 13, 1827, the territorial legislature passed "An

Act to regulate Blacks and Mulattoes, and to punish the Kidnapping of such persons." It prohibited blacks and mulattoes from residing in Michigan unless they could produce "a fair certificate" issued by a court attesting to their "actual freedom." (Certificates of freedom were available for 12.5 cents after registering with the county clerk.) Persons secreting fugitives were subject to modest fines, and those employing noncompliant blacks were fined $100; state officials were required to comply with the 1793 Fugitive Slave Act, and blacks first entering Michigan were required to post a $500 bond for "good behavior" and against pauperism. But the law also provided some legal protection against slave catchers: persons who "by violence, fraud or deception seize upon any free black or mulatto person" for out-of-state transport faced imprisonment of up to ten years at hard labor. Although it may have had a chilling effect, enforcement of the restrictions on black residency was probably lax, and despite the law, between 1820 and 1830 Michigan's free black population increased from 174 to 261.[31]

The 1827 law was dropped from the 1838 revised code. That same code revision, however, prohibited interracial marriage, even though whites and Indians could marry. With one 1859 exception, the law against interracial marriage also appears to have been largely unenforced. During the next two decades, Michigan's black population (see Demography) and white allies grew in number, as did antislavery organizations, the first being organized in Lenawee County in 1832. In 1836 the Michigan State Anti-slavery Society was founded, maintaining a newspaper for ten years until it was destroyed by antiabolitionists in 1849. In the meantime, African American Michiganders began to organize, one of the first efforts being the 1843 Detroit meeting of the State Convention of Colored Citizens of Michigan. However, as suggested by the abolition newspaper's destruction, there was resistance, sometimes violent. But Michigan's African Americans also pushed back against existential threats. By 1840, black Detroiters organized the Colored Vigilant Committee, which helped thousands of fugitives escape to Canada.

During the 1840s and 1850s, petitions to the legislature to expand African American suffrage were routinely denied. Blacks struggled not just for "equal access" to public education, but just as often for any access. In Detroit there were no schools for black children until 1836, and then it was a private school; in 1842, the legislature permitted free public schools in Detroit but permitted segregation by race; colored schools there were perpetually underfunded and their locations constantly changed. During the Civil War, white Michigan's anxieties about black emancipation were pervasive. Among Democrats, fear was policy, and anxieties often took form in economics. "[If] abolitionism should succeed in its designs, four millions of a barbarous race would be let loose upon the country, nineteen-twentieths of whom would have to be supported at the public expense as vagrants or criminals," the *Free Press* fretted. But Republicans, too, were concerned. In the U.S. Senate, when Kentucky's Garrett Davis explained that post-emancipation, Michigan's "share" of freed persons would be 121,301, Jacob Howard, who would later have a hand in drafting the Thirteenth and Fourteenth Amendments, answered, "Canada is very near us, and affords a fine market for 'wool' [a racist term indicating black people]."[32]

Yet despite this discrimination, in the years preceding the war Michigan was seen "as a beacon of liberty on the Great Lakes." In the antebellum years, its white population grew increasingly antislavery (not to be confused with favoring racial equality); as noted above, unlike Ohio, Indiana, and Illinois, Michigan had no "river counties" bordering slave states, and there were far fewer ties of commerce and kinship with slave economies and culture.

Fugitive repatriations met with real resistance in Michigan while the Underground Railroad became active. Fugitive slaves were often from Missouri and Kentucky, and depending on point of entry, might choose two routes through Michigan. The first led from southwest Michigan to Detroit, began in Cassopolis and led to Schoolcraft, Climax, Battle Creek, Marshall, Albion, Parma, Jackson, Michigan Center, Dexter, Ann Arbor, Plymouth, and Detroit. The second line accommodated fugitives entering from the southeast and ran from Adrian through Ann Arbor and Ypsilanti. Nevertheless, it is important to remember that the Michigan electorate voted down African American suffrage in 1850, 12,840 (28.6 percent) to 32,026, (71.4 percent). Three years after the Civil War, it would be voted down again, albeit by smaller margins.[33]

In 1849, the Michigan Legislature found that "slavery is a mere local institution which cannot exist without positive laws authorizing its existence" and that "Congress has the power, and that it is their duty to prohibit by legislative enactment, the introduction or existence of slavery within any of the territories of the United States, now, or hereafter to be acquired." Michigan's congressional delegation was effectively instructed to support the Wilmot Proviso. The House passed this resolution 46 to 17 and the Senate 14 to 7. In 1855 the legislature adopted a joint resolution declaring that "Slavery is regarded by the people of this State as a great moral, social and political evil, at war with the Declaration of Independence; an impediment to the prosperity of our common country, and an element of domestic weakness and discord." It denounced its U.S. senators and two congressmen who had supported Kansas-Nebraska against the wishes of Michigan's people and in violation of the Compromise of 1820, demanded repeal of the Kansas-Nebraska with no further extension of territorial slavery, the abolition of slavery in Washington and the domestic slave trade anywhere, and so instructed its congressional delegation. The House passed this resolution 49 to 22 and the Senate 23 to 5. But U.S. Senator Lewis Cass, who was opposed to the Wilmot Proviso, threatened to resign unless the legislature rescinded its instruction. On March 28, the Michigan legislature complied, rescinding its January approval by 11 to 11 in the Senate and 27 to 20 in the House. Yet even here, the contours of Michigan's antislavery sentiment are clear: the rescinding resolution noted that "The people of this State are opposed to the extension of slavery," but believe that a "crisis in our national affairs has arrived which demands an expression of their deep, devoted, and unalterable attachment to the Union."[34]

In January 1855, Republican state senator (and Underground Railroad conductor) Erastus Hussey* of Battle Creek introduced, and on February 13, 1855, Republican Governor Kinsley S. Bingham signed, "An Act to protect the rights and liberties of the inhabitants of this State." This measure was as comprehensive as any single personal liberty act in the country. It mandated county prosecutors to defend "every such person so arrested or claimed as a fugitive slave"; it claimed fugitives were entitled to the writ of habeas corpus and a jury trial; if the writ were vacated, the fugitive was entitled to appeal on that question; the fugitive would be entitled to trial on all facts; fugitives could not be detained in state or local prisons, and public officials violating these provisions were subject to large fines; any person falsely charging fugitives was liable to up to five years' incarceration; kidnappers of free persons were likewise liable to five years' imprisonment; moreover, any proof presented by an owner (or

his agent) asserting fugitive status "shall not be deemed proved except by the testimony of two credible witnesses, testifying to facts directly tending to establish the truth of such declaration"—that is, the witnesses must have first-hand knowledge of the fact of bondage.[35]

South Carolina would name (see December 24, 1860) Michigan as one of thirteen Northern states that enacted laws "which either nullify the acts of Congress or render useless any attempt to execute them"; powerful Northern governors would insist (see entry for December 21, 1860) that repealing personal liberty laws was essential to conciliating the South. For similar reasons, Michigan Democrats also demanded (see February 8, 1861) repeal of personal liberty laws. But Michigan retained its personal liberty statutes throughout the Secession Winter.[36]

Many Michigan African American males did not abide their own state's delay in organizing colored units. The first real organized opportunity for Michigan's black men to serve came from Massachusetts in early 1863. At least sixty Michigan men served in the Fifty-Fourth Massachusetts, ten in the Fifty-Fifth, and five in the Fifth Massachusetts Cavalry.[37]

While Michigan's African American community was small, it was vocal in advocating for equality of rights. In October, 1843, the Michigan State Colored Convention met in Detroit and declared, "we find ourselves the subjects and not the objects of legislation, because we are prevented from giving an assenting or opposing voice in the periodic appointments of those who rule us." Adopted resolutions included a demand that the word "white" be stricken from Michigan's constitution; a statement that Michigan's refusal to grant black suffrage violated the Declaration of Independence and the U.S. Constitution; and a commitment "to continue to write, publish, cry aloud, and spare not, in opposition to all political injustice, and all legislation, violating the spirit of equality until" the Michigan's constitution's first and second articles were reconciled. The two most important black conventions during the Civil War period were convened in Detroit in 1865, and will be found in this chapter.[38]

"Under the Oaks": Republicans in Michigan

Throughout this chapter the words "Under the Oaks" (a phrase familiar to contemporaries) are used to describe what was probably antebellum Michigan's second most important political gathering, after its statehood convention. On May 30, 1854, President Franklin Pierce signed the Kansas-Nebraska Act, which repealed the Missouri Compromises of 1820 and 1850, incorporated the doctrine of "popular sovereignty," and thus potentially opened federal territories to slavery. The Act ignited a firestorm in Michigan and throughout the North. On June 21 in Kalamazoo an Anti-Nebraska convention gathered and issued a call for a statewide convention in Jackson on July 6. "A great wrong has been perpetrated," the invitation began. "The slave power of the Country has triumphed. Liberty is trampled under foot." It declared that the Act threatened Northern rights, free labor, humanity, and the Union itself, and it placed the blame squarely on Northern politicians who, "Judas-like, betrayed the cause of liberty" by supporting the Kansas-Nebraska Act. The Kalamazoo call concluded by inviting "all our fellow-citizens, without reference to former political associations who think the time has arrived for a union at the North to protect liberty from being overthrown and downtrodden . . . [and] to take such measures as shall be thought best to concentrate the popular sentiment in this State against the aggression of the slave power." Sympathetic newspaper editors provided publicity, and within two weeks 10,000 Michiganders had signed the call.

On the appointed day the convention opened in Jackson's City Hall. The crowd grew to an estimated 3,000 to 5,000 and included prominent Whigs, Democrats, Free-Soil Democrats, abolitionists, Prohibitionists (temperance), and others intent on fusion. (The movement would eventually absorb the few Michigan Know-Nothings.) As City Hall was not large enough, the convention reassembled in an oak grove on the outskirts of town. A brass band played; speeches were made, including one by George Harris*, identified as a "mulattoe"; resolutions were passed; and "Republican" was adopted as the new party's name. Present at the creation were many who would guide Michigan's political fortunes for the next decade, including future U.S. senators Jacob M. Howard and Zachariah Chandler; future congressmen Fernando C. Beaman and David S. Walbridge; future governors Kinsley S. Bingham, Moses Wisner, and Austin Blair; future state treasurer and defalcator John McKinney; and McKinney's remediating successor, John Owen. This event soon became iconic, and to have been "Under the Oaks" was to have witnessed history, and it also connected a generation of Republican leaders whose legacies became for many Michiganders entwined with that of the state's civil war.[39]

Democrats in Michigan

By 1860, the Democrat party (the "Democracy") was centered in two regions: Detroit and the Upper Peninsula (UP).[40]

Congressional Districts: Thirty-Seventh Congress

[NB: *The counties shown below were based on the Seventh Decennial Census, and do not reflect new counties as of 1860. The population density per square mile, racial, religious, and nativity percentages are based on constituent counties, where available.*]

First: Jackson, Livingston, Washtenaw, and Wayne counties (39.8; 1.0 percent black, 20.8 percent foreign-born, 9 percent Catholic)

Second: Branch, Cass, Hillsdale, Lenawee, Monroe, and St. Joseph counties (27; 0.6 percent black, 7.8 percent foreign-born, 2 percent Catholic)

Third: Allegan, Barry, Berrien, Calhoun, Clinton, Eaton, Ionia, Gratiot, Kalamazoo, Kent, Lake, Mason, Montcalm, Newaygo, Oceana, Ottawa, and Van Buren (10.9; 0.6 percent black, 11.3 percent foreign-born, 2.5 percent Catholic)

Fourth: Chippewa, Genesee, Ingham, Lapeer, Macomb, Midland, Oakland, Saginaw, Sanilac, Arenac, Shiawassee, St. Clair, Tuscola, Huron, Isabella, Mecosta, Manistee, Wexford, Missaukee, Osceola, Clare, Gladwin, Iosco, Ogemaw, Roscommon, Leelanau, Grand Traverse, Kalkaska, Crawford, Oscoda, Alcona, Antrim, Otsego, Montmorency, Alpena, Presque Isle, Cheboygan, Charlevoix, Emmet, Mackinac, Schoolcraft, Marquette, Delta, Houghton, and Ontonagon counties (9.5; 0.1 percent black, 13 percent foreign-born, 3.2 percent Catholic)[41]

Senate

Zachariah Chandler, Republican, elected 1857 and reelected January 8, 1863, and 1869; he failed to be reelected in 1874, but was returned to the Senate in February 1879 to fill an unexpired term, and served until his death on November 1, 1879.

• **Zachariah Chandler** (1813–1879) was born in Bedford, New Hampshire, the nephew of Maine's U.S. senator John Chandler and also of New Hampshire congressman Thomas Chandler. He was educated publicly, taught school, and in 1833 moved to Detroit.

(Reportedly, Chandler's father offered him a choice of college or $1,000; the young man took the cash.) Within several years, he became one of Michigan's most successful wholesale dry goods merchants. Chandler was a passionately antislavery Whig and eventually entered politics. In 1851 he was elected Detroit's mayor, and the next year, unsuccessfully ran for governor, the state's last Whig gubernatorial candidate. In 1854, Chandler was among the first to call for a new party and was present "Under the Oaks"; after the formation of the Republican party, he became its "traveling agent," gave almost 100 speeches, and was influential in converting many Michigan Whigs into Republicans. In 1860, Chandler served on the Republican National Committee.

In 1857 Chandler was elected to the U.S. Senate to replace Lewis Cass. A newspaper editor commented that "Chandler will never bow the knee to the behests of the slave power, will never *cringe* to the threats of the Southern fire-eaters [and] will never brook the sneers and insults of slavedom's bullies"; a few days later the editor added, "If [Chandler's] speeches prove *not to be* replete with eloquence, elegant diction, rounded periods, logical arguments and cogent reasonings, his acts and *votes* will be *eloquent* and on the right side." Chandler's lack of classical polish, his blunt manner and plain speaking, appealed to postfrontier Michigan, and the editor accurately predicted the traits Chandler brought to Washington.

During the Thirty-Fifth and Thirty-Sixth Congresses, Chandler took his place with other Senate Radicals. Often harshly attacking President Buchanan and Northern and Southern Democrats, Chandler became one of the most divisive, and in some quarters hated, Republicans in Washington. (After Missouri Senator James S. Green threatened Chandler, the Michigander entered into a written agreement with Ohio's Benjamin Wade[42] and Pennsylvania's Simon Cameron[43] to accept any challenge to duel and "to carry the quarrel into a coffin.") On February 11, 1861 (see date), Chandler wrote his famous Blood Letter to Austin Blair, lobbying against Michigan sending commissioners to the ill-fated Washington Peace Conference (see February 14, 1861), declaring that "Without a little blood-letting this Union, will not, in my estimation, be worth a rush." (The printed letter caused a furor.) In Congress on March 2, he voted against the Corwin Amendment (prohibiting Congress from legislating on slavery). Chandler greeted the attack on Fort Sumter with enthusiasm; three months later, at the Battle of Bull Run, Chandler was with Wade and Ohio congressman Albert G. Riddle,[44] waving pistols in a vain effort to stem the Union rout.

Chandler voted consistently Radical during the periods analyzed by Allan G. Bogue.[45] On December 5, 1861, Chandler sponsored a Senate resolution that authorized the Joint Committee on the Conduct of the War. As sponsor he was entitled to chair the Joint Committee; however, he waived the privilege in favor of lawyer Benjamin Wade. As the Joint Committee transcripts reveal, Chandler was a powerful force who carried his attitudes (and lack of judicial temperament) with him: he distrusted West Pointers, disliked Democratic generals, and was especially venomous toward McClellan and Fitz John Porter; he merely disliked George Meade. Chandler's lens was ideological: defeats suffered by Democratic generals were treason; presumably radical officers such as John C. Fremont, Benjamin Butler,[46] and Joseph Hooker might be unsuccessful but were presumed competent. In one telling anecdote, after listening to McClellan explain that as an army advanced it had to consider lines of retreat, Benjamin Wade asked Chandler's opinion. "I don't know much about war," Chandler replied, "but this is infernal, unmitigated cowardice."

Chandler lobbied Lincoln to accept the Wade-Davis Bill, but supported the president in his 1864 bid for reelection. Postwar, Chandler opposed Andrew Johnson, damning those who refused to convict him after impeachment. He remained a proponent of harsh terms for the South. By 1875, Chandler's Michigan enemies were finally powerful enough to deny him a fourth term, and sent Isaac Christiancy* in his place. President Grant rescued Chandler that year by appointing him secretary of the interior. Chandler chaired the Republican National Convention in 1876. In February 1879, after Christiancy resigned, Chandler maneuvered his way back into the vacancy for the unexpired term. He died in office nine months later.[47]

Kinsley S. Bingham, Republican, elected 1859 and served until his death on October 5, 1861.

- **Kinsley Scott Bingham** (1808–1861), the son of a farmer, was born in Camillus, New York, educated publicly, and later read law under General James R.

Lawrence in Syracuse, New York. In 1833, he moved to Green Oak, Michigan, where he was admitted to the bar although he never practiced law. But he was best known as a farmer; his 440 acres would yield abundant wheat and livestock. In the 1830s, Bingham also served as justice of the peace, postmaster, and county probate judge. He was elected to Michigan's House as a Democrat in 1836 and was reelected four times; in his last three terms he served as speaker. Bingham was a Radical Democrat, a Jacksonian champion of the common man, fiercely opposed to monopolies, chartered banks, and unlike Jackson, slavery. He was sent as a Democrat to the Thirtieth and Thirty-First Congresses, and in his last term, chaired the Committee on Expenditures in the Department of State.

During his congressional years, Bingham supported the Wilmot Proviso (as instructed by Michigan's legislature, although it later reversed itself), opposed Lewis Cass on popular sovereignty, denounced the Slave Power, and in 1850 alone, submitted sixty-three antislavery petitions to Congress. He opposed the Compromise of 1850, and he was expelled from the Michigan Democracy, which supported the Compromise. Bingham returned to his Green Oak farm.

Although out of office, Bingham became a Free [Soil] Democrat. The passage of the Kansas-Nebraska Act returned slavery to the fore, and the Free Democrats led the opposition. In 1854, Bingham was a founder of Michigan's Republican Party "Under the Oaks."

In 1854 Bingham was elected as Michigan's first Republican governor, and was reelected in 1856. Known as the "Farmer Governor," Bingham helped pass Michigan's first personal liberty law (see above). He was an education reformer and helped establish the Michigan Agricultural College and the state reform school. A friend of the lumber industry, Bingham also eased the incorporation of lumber companies and provided for lumber inspection. But he continued his antislavery work, and in his first inaugural called for abolition of territorial and District of Columbia slavery, repeal of the Fugitive Slave Act, and prohibition of both slave auctions and the use of American ships in the slave trade.

In 1859 Bingham was elected to the U.S. Senate. In the first session of the Thirty-Seventh Congress (his last), he was chairman of the Committee on Enrolled Bills, and first ranking member of both the Committee on Public Lands and the Committee on Pensions. On March 2, 1861, Bingham voted to amend the Constitution to prohibit secession (it lost), proposed a resolution declaring that the existing Constitution was sufficient to resolve sectional differences (it also lost), voted against the first Crittenden Resolution (see July 25, 1861), and supported the First Confiscation Act, as well as most war measures during the July 1861 Special Session of the Congress. Bingham died unexpectedly that October.[48] Bingham's seat was vacant from October 5, 1861, to January 17, 1862.

Jacob M. Howard, Republican, elected January 17, 1862, to fill the unexpired term of Senator Kinsley S. Bingham; reelected January 5, 1865, and served to March 3, 1871.

- **Jacob Merritt Howard** (1805–1871) was born in Shaftesbury, Vermont, worked on a farm, and was educated in the common schools. He attended Bennington Academy and afterward, Brattleboro Academy, graduating from Williams College in 1830. He then read law, moved to Detroit in 1832, and was admitted to the bar in 1833. The next year he was appointed city attorney for Detroit, and in 1838, was elected to Michigan's House as a Whig. During his state House tenure, Howard helped revise Michigan statutes, draft laws governing railroads, and investigate abuses under the state banking statutes. He canvassed for Whig presidential candidates in 1844, 1848, and 1852. (In 1847, Howard somehow found time to produce the *Translation from the French of the Secret Memoirs of the Empress Josephine*.) He was sent to the Twenty-Seventh Congress as a Whig but did not run for reelection. Like many antislavery Whigs, Howard was infuriated by the 1854 Kansas-Nebraska Bill; in response, he helped found the Michigan Republican Party "Under the Oaks." He wrote the first Republican platform. In 1855 he was elected state attorney general as a Republican, serving until 1861. During his tenure as attorney general, he drafted the state's first voter registration law.

By the third term of the Thirty-Seventh Congress, he was fourth ranking member of the Committee on Military Affairs and the Militia, fourth ranked on the Judiciary Committee, and third ranked on Private Land Claims, important committee assignments for a first termer and evidence of his peers' esteem. (His nickname was "Honest Jake," and he was often consulted on constitutional questions.) In the first session of the Thirty-Eighth Congress, Howard had advanced to second rank on the Military Affairs and the Militia, remaining at fourth rank on Judiciary and third rank on Private Land Claims. In the second session of the Thirty-Eighth Congress, Howard retained his second rank on Military Affairs and Militia, left Judiciary, advanced to second rank on Private Lands Claims, served on the Committee on the Library, and became chairman of the Committee on the Pacific Railroad. He held this chairmanship through the Forty-First Congress. Postwar, Howard insisted on Congress's exclusive right to set reconstruction policy and in 1865–1866 served on the Joint Committee on Reconstruction.

Bogue describes Howard during his Civil War years as a "constitutional radical" and so classifies him in his vote analysis for the second session of the Thirty-Seventh Congress through the first session of the Thirty-Ninth; the constitutional qualifier was based on Howard's arguments, which often rationalized support or opposition to a measure in constitutional terms. Howard died in Detroit of a heart attack one month after he left office.[49]

Lewis Cass, civil governor, Territory of Michigan, 1813–1831; secretary of war, 1831–1836; United States senator, 1845 to 1848 and 1849 to 1857; secretary of state from 1857 to December 12, 1860.

- It would be difficult to overstate the role of Lewis Cass (1782–1866) in Michigan's early history. Although retired from public life by the time Fort Sumter was attacked, Cass's influence continued during the Civil War. He was a staunch Unionist and among the first of Buchanan's inner circle to break with his policy for dealing with secession (see December 12, 1860). When the war began, Cass lent his name and prestige to support the war (see July 15, 1862) and privately gave sound counsel to Secretary of State Seward during the *Trent* Affair (see December 18 and 19, 1861).

Cass was born in Exeter, New Hampshire, the son of a Revolutionary War soldier who had previous service in what became the Northwest Territory. Lewis Cass attended Phillips Exeter Academy and in 1799 moved with his parents to Wilmington, Delaware. He taught school there for several years, and in 1801 moved again with his parents to the Northwest Territory and a farm near Zanesville, Ohio. He read law under future Ohio Supreme Court Justice, governor, U.S. senator, and postmaster general Return J. Meigs, Jr., and was admitted to the bar in 1802. In 1806, he was elected to Ohio's territorial legislature. The next year, Thomas Jefferson appointed Cass U.S. marshal for the district of Ohio, a position he held until the War of 1812, when he resigned to take command of the Third Ohio Volunteers. Assigned to General William Hull, Cass participated in the invasion of Canada, which met with initial success; however, U.S. forces were ultimately defeated, and Detroit was surrendered to the British. After exchange, Cass returned to the service, and by war's end, held a brigadier's rank and had military command of Michigan Territory.

In 1813, Cass was appointed Michigan territorial governor and lived in Detroit. During his eighteen-year term, Cass negotiated some twenty-two treaties with Indian tribes, authorized vast surveys, established towns and counties, built lighthouses along the lake shores, and led several important scientific expeditions. In 1831 Andrew Jackson appointed Cass secretary of war. During the next five years, he oversaw the suppression of the Sauk band under Chief Black Hawk and the forcible Cherokee migration (Trail of Tears) from Georgia and Mississippi; he supported Jackson during the Nullification Crisis. In 1836, Cass resigned to become minister to France. In 1842, he returned to the United States, and in 1845 was elected to the United States Senate from Michigan as a Democrat. In 1848 Cass was nominated as the Democratic candidate for president, and he resigned his Senate seat to campaign. After losing to Zachary Taylor, the next year, Cass returned to the Senate (to fill his own unexpired term); he was reelected in 1851 and served until 1857. During the Thirty-Third Congress, he was president pro tempore of the Senate. During these Senate years, Cass opposed both secession and the Wilmot Proviso, and he was among the first (1847) to propose popular sovereignty. President Buchanan appointed him secretary of state in 1857.

During his term as secretary of state, Cass tried to balance conciliation toward the South with a determination to preserve the Union. When Buchanan read to his cabinet a draft of his December 1860 message denying that the federal government had authority to prevent secession, Cass remained silent, but eight days later, when Buchanan initially declined to reinforce Robert Anderson, Cass resigned. (Several weeks later Buchanan changed his mind.) After the attack on Fort Sumter he predicted that he would die before the Union was restored; he took great comfort in having been wrong. Cass died in Detroit.[50]

House Delegations

Thirty-Seventh Congress by District[51]

First District: Bradley F. Granger, Republican; Committee on Revolutionary Pensions, sixth member; Joint Committee on Enrolled Bills

- **Bradley F. Granger** (1825–1882) was born in Lewis County, New York. He was educated in the public schools and afterward read law. Following admission to the bar in 1847, Granger practiced in Manchester, Michigan (where he served as a justice of the peace in 1849), and later moved to Ann Arbor, where he practiced law. In 1856 he was elected a probate judge as a Republican, and on that party's ticket he was elected to the Thirty-Seventh Congress. He was denied renomination for "not having kept pace with his party"; this may have referred to Granger's votes against compensated emancipation in Missouri and Maryland and against supporting the Preliminary Emancipation Proclamation. Granger afterward returned to Ann Arbor and the law. In 1865, he served as an alderman for Ann Arbor. Andrew Johnson appointed Granger a deputy collector of internal revenue for the Third District, and Grant nominated him for chief collector in 1872. He also served as a justice of the peace. He died in Ann Arbor.[52]

Second District: Fernando C. Beaman, Republican; Committee on the Territories, fourth member; Committee on Roads and Canals, eighth member

- **Fernando C. Beaman** (1814–1882) was born in Chester, Vermont, and in 1819, relocated with his family to a New York farm. He was educated publicly and privately, subsequently teaching briefly before moving to Rochester, New York, in 1836. He read law, and in 1838 moved to Manchester, Michigan. He was admitted to the bar in 1839 and practiced in Manchester and Clinton. In 1843, Beaman was appointed Lenawee County district attorney, and he moved to Adrian and served for the next seven years. During these years, Beaman also served as Adrian city attorney. He had been a Democrat until 1848; that year he became a Free Soiler and campaigned for the Van Buren-Adams ticket. In 1854, Beaman was a vice president at "Under the Oaks" representing Lenawee County. He was a delegate to the 1856 Republican National Convention that nominated John C. Fremont, and later served as a presidential elector. That year he was also elected mayor of Adrian. Between 1856 and 1860, he served as Lenawee County probate judge. Beaman was elected as a Republican to the Thirty-Seventh Congress and served through the Forty-First Congress. In the Thirty-Ninth Congress, he chaired the Committee on Roads and Canals. He did not run for the Forty-Second Congress, returning to Adrian and his law practice. In 1871, he was reappointed to the Lenawee County probate bench; he was elected in his own right in 1872 and reelected in 1876. When Zachariah Chandler died in 1879, the vacancy was offered to Beaman, as were appointments to the state Supreme Court and as a U.S. commissioner of Indian affairs. For health reasons, Beaman declined them all. He died in Adrian.[53]

Third District: Francis W. Kellogg, Republican; Committee on Public Lands, sixth member; Committee on Expenditures in the Post Office Department, third member

- **Francis W. Kellogg** (1810–1879) was born in Worthington, Massachusetts, educated publicly, and in 1833 moved to Columbus, Ohio. In 1845 he moved to near Grand Rapids. He founded Kelloggsville (since absorbed by Grand Rapids), where he established the lumbering firm of Kellogg, White & Company. He was elected to Michigan's House as a Republican in 1857 and 1858, and then elected to the Thirty-Sixth through the Thirty-Eighth Congresses. Kellogg was arguably the founding father of Michigan's Civil War cavalry. He secured War Department approval or otherwise helped establish the Second, Third, Sixth, and Seventh Michigan cavalry. Governor Blair commissioned him colonel of the Third Michigan Cavalry on December 6, 1861; however, Kellogg yielded command to more experienced leadership once the unit was complete. On April 30, 1866, Andrew Johnson appointed Kellogg collector of internal revenue for the southern district of Alabama. He served until July 1868, residing in Mobile. When Alabama was readmitted to the Union, Kellogg was elected as a Republican to the Fortieth Congress and served until March 3, 1869. (Referring to Kellogg among others, a 1921 Alabama history characterized his constituents as "aliens, scalawags, and negroes.") Afterward, Kellogg moved to New York City, and later, Alliance, Ohio. He is buried in Grand Rapids.[54]

Fourth District: Rowland E. Trowbridge, Republican; Committee on the Post Office and Post Roads, seventh member

- **Rowland E. Trowbridge** (1821–1881) was born in Chemung County, New York, and before his first birthday, relocated with his parents to a farm in Troy, Michigan. He graduated from Ohio's Kenyon College in 1841, and while there became lifetime friends with future president Rutherford B. Hayes and future U.S. Supreme Court justice Stanley Matthews.[55] After graduation, Trowbridge wanted to study law, but eye trouble compelled his return to farming. By 1848, he had returned to Michigan and a farm in Thorndale, and in 1851 to a farm in Bloomfield. Before Michigan had a Republican Party, Trowbridge was a Whig, although it is unclear on what ticket he ran when he was elected Bloomfield's supervisor in 1855. The next year, he was elected to Michigan's Senate and then to the Thirty-Seventh Congress as a Republican. Although he was defeated for the Thirty-Eighth Congress, he returned to the Thirty-Ninth and Fortieth. Trowbridge was a delegate to the 1866 National (pro-Johnson) Convention in Philadelphia. In his final term he served as chairman of the Committee on Agriculture, Trowbridge was defeated for the Forty-First Congress, afterward returning to farming in Lansing. In 1880, President Hayes appointed Trowbridge U.S. commissioner of Indian affairs and he held the office until his death in Birmingham, Michigan.

Thirty-Eighth Congress by District[56]

First: Fernando C. Beaman, Republican; Committee on the Territories, first member; Committee on Roads and Canals, third member

Second: Charles Upson, Republican; Committee on Elections, seventh member; Committee on Revisal and Unfinished Business, third member

- **Charles Upson** (1821–1885) was born in Southington, Connecticut, and educated publicly and privately, in the hope of preparing for college. To earn tuition, he taught school, and entered Meriden Academy in 1842. He withdrew for lack of funds, and never attended college. Upson resumed teaching; sometime before 1844 after reading Blackstone's *Commentaries*, he decided to study law. In early 1844 he enrolled in Yale's Law Department, and that December, moved to Constantine, Michigan. He taught while he read law and in 1847 became deputy county clerk of St. Joseph County. The same year he was admitted to the bar and practiced in Kalamazoo, thereafter starting his ascent in local and state politics: he was county clerk in 1848 and 1849, was elected prosecutor in 1852 (after an unsuccessful 1850 run), and was elected on the Whig ticket to Michigan's Senate in 1854. In 1856, Upson moved to Coldwater and formed a law partnership with lieutenant governor George A. Coe*, and in 1857 joined Michigan's Board of Railroad Commissioners. He was elected state attorney general as a Republican in 1861. As a Republican, Upson served in the Thirty-Eighth through Fortieth Congresses, in his last term chairing the Committee on Expenditures in the Department of the Navy. He did not run for the Forty-First Congress and returned to Michigan. In 1869 he became a judge on Michigan's Fifteenth Circuit, resigning in 1872. The following year, he joined the Commission to Revise the State Constitution. After declining an appointment as U.S. commissioner of Indian affairs, he became mayor of Coldwater in 1877. He returned to Michigan's Senate in 1880, afterward returning to the law. He died in Coldwater.[57]

Third: John W. Longyear, Republican; Committee on Commerce, seventh member; chairman, Committee on Expenditures on Public Buildings.

- **John W. Longyear** (1820–1875) was born in Ulster County, New York, received a classical education, afterward teaching school. In 1844 he moved to Mason, Michigan, kept school, and read law. He was admitted to the bar in 1846 and the next year moved to Lansing to practice. Longyear was successful, and according to contemporaries had the second-largest practice in the county. "He never made a mistake," one biographer wrote, and he had such a reputation for rectitude that once, Longyear's stern gaze alone (it "convey[ed] the idea of endless perdition") compelled an adversary to withdraw a remark at the bar. He was elected as a Republican to the Thirty-Eighth and Thirty-Ninth Congresses, but declined to run for the Fortieth. Longyear was a delegate to the pro-Johnson National Convention in Philadelphia in 1866 and in 1867 attended the Michigan Constitutional Convention. In 1870, Grant appointed him judge of U.S. District Court for the Eastern District of Michigan, and the following year he moved to Detroit. Longyear held office until his death.[58]

Fourth: Francis W. Kellogg, Republican; Committee on Military Affairs, seventh member

Fifth: Augustus C. Baldwin, Democrat; Committee on Agriculture, seventh member; Committee on Expenditures in the Interior Department, fourth member

- **Augustus C. Baldwin** (1817–1903) was born in Onondaga County, New York, educated publicly, and relocated to Oakland County, Michigan, in 1837. He taught school, read law, and was admitted to the bar in 1842. He practiced in Milford. He was elected to Michigan's House in 1844 and served through 1846, in his last term as speaker pro tempore. A brigadier general of militia, in 1849 he moved to Pontiac and in 1853 became Oakland County prosecuting attorney. Baldwin was a delegate to the 1860 Democratic National Convention in Charleston, supporting Stephen A. Douglas for president. He was elected to the Thirty-Eighth Congress as a "Union" Democrat. He voted against peace conventions with the South, in particular those proposed by Ohio Congressman Alexander Long.[59] Perhaps the high point of his congressional career occurred toward its close: Baldwin was one of 15 Democrats to vote in favor of the Thirteenth Amendment. He was defeated for the Thirty-Ninth Congress, and in 1866, was a delegate to the pro-Johnson National Convention in Philadelphia. Postwar, Baldwin continued to live in Pontiac, serving on its school board (1868–1886) and as its mayor in 1874. He also served as a judge on Michigan's sixth

judicial circuit from 1875 to 1880, afterward resuming his law practice. He died in Pontiac.[60]

Sixth: John F. Driggs, Republican; Committee on Public Lands, seventh member

- **John F. Driggs** (1813–1877) was born in Kinderhook, New York, was educated there, and moved to Tarrytown in 1825. Two years later, he moved to New York City, where he apprenticed as a sash, door, and blinds maker. Between the years 1829 and 1856, Driggs achieved journeyman and master status. He also managed prisons, and in 1844 was appointed superintendent of Blackwell Island's penitentiary. He moved to East Saginaw in 1856, attracted by opportunities in real estate and the salt-mining industry, where he established himself as an industry pioneer, helping to found the East Saginaw Salt Company, the first in the Saginaw Valley. In 1858, he was elected to that city's common council, and the next year was sent to Michigan's House, where he served through 1860. In 1861, Lincoln appointed Driggs register of the United States Land Office in East Saginaw. He was elected as a Republican to the Thirty-Eighth Congress and served through the Fortieth Congress. During the war, Driggs was actively engaged in recruitment. Under Lincoln's July 18, 1864, call, Governor Blair arranged to have one infantry regiment raised for each of the state's six congressional districts, and Driggs organized the Twenty-Ninth Michigan in his Sixth District. He belonged to the House committee chosen to accompany Lincoln's remains to Springfield. Driggs died in East Saginaw.[61]

War Governors
Austin Blair (1818–1894), Republican, served two consecutive terms as governor from January 1, 1861, until January 1, 1865.

- Austin Blair was born in Caroline, New York, to a farming family, and to abolitionist parents. His early education reflected the seasons: winter in Caroline's common school, summers on the farm. At age sixteen Blair was sent to a private school in Tioga County, where he was taught Latin and science; in autumn, 1834, he enrolled in the Cazenovia Seminary (present-day Cazenovia College) to prepare for college; dissent over religious doctrine probably expedited his early departure. In 1836 he enrolled for about eighteen months as a sophomore in Hamilton College, and in 1837, transferred to Union College. Here Blair continued to demonstrate a willingness to challenge the status quo, organizing a student association against unfair privileges enjoyed by private fraternities. After graduating in 1839, he moved to Oswego to read law in the offices of Sweet and Davis.

Blair was admitted to the Tioga (New York) County bar in 1841, and that June moved to Jackson, Michigan, where he was admitted to the state bar. Poor health compelled a move to Eaton Rapids in 1842 and Blair was elected Eaton county clerk, presumably as a Whig. In 1844 he returned to Jackson and campaigned for Henry Clay for president, and also proved his talent for public speaking. In 1845, Blair was elected as a Whig to Michigan's House. The 1846 session (the last to convene in Detroit) was charged with revising state law, and Blair served on the judiciary committee. Blair's reformist instincts were manifest in the resulting revision: he urged the abolition of capital punishment (it was abolished) and fought hard and publicly to remove the word "white" as a requirement to vote (he was unsuccessful). However, Blair's efforts did capture the unfavorable attention of his Jackson constituents, and in the next election he was replaced by a Democrat. In 1848 Blair left the Whigs and embraced the Free Soil Party, serving as a delegate to its national convention in Buffalo. (He was on the committee that nominated Martin Van Buren and Charles Francis Adams[62] for president and vice president). In the ensuing election, the Free Soil Party showed unexpected strength in Michigan, attracting 10,395 votes from 65,083 votes cast. By 1852, Blair had returned to the Whigs, and as he campaigned for Winfield Scott he was himself elected Jackson County prosecuting attorney.

Eighteen fifty-four was a pivotal year for Michigan's politics and Austin Blair: as the Kansas-Nebraska Bill became law, Blair promoted the call for "Under the Oaks" and served on the first Republican Party platform committee. He supported the party's Radical ticket (Kinsley S. Bingham for governor and Jacob M. Howard for U.S. senator) and was himself elected to Michigan's Senate as a Republican. In the legislature's next (1855) session, Blair and abolitionist Erastus Hussey cosponsored the state's first Personal Liberty Law, and although opposed by some Republicans, the two men shepherded the measure to enactment. In 1856, Blair supported Fremont, and the Michigan Republican Party's future seemed assured by the result: Fremont carried the state. In 1860, Blair chaired the Michigan delegation to the Republican National Convention in Chicago. He was a staunch Seward supporter, but eventually conceded the state's delegates to Abraham Lincoln. He closed Michigan's ranks around the Illinoisan with a concession famous among his contemporaries: "We marshal now behind [Seward] in the grand column which shall go out to battle for Abraham Lincoln, of Illinois." At the 1860 state convention, Blair was nominated for governor (his predecessor Wisner being too mired in scandal because of the defalcating state treasurer) and was reelected in 1863.

Blair's wartime story is extensively detailed in this volume. Postwar, Blair left office a poor man. His law practice had dissipated and the exhausted Blair lacked his prewar energy. After several years his health returned, and Blair was elected to the Fortieth, Forty-First, and Forty-Second Congresses as a Republican, serving in the last two as chair of the House Committee on Private Land Claims. While he supported Andrew Johnson's impeachment, he often voted with Republican moderates. He fell out with the Grant administration, and after he left Congress ran (unsuccessfully in 1872) for Michigan governor on the Liberal Republican ticket. Blair returned with mixed success to his law practice. In 1881, he was elected a regent of the University of Michigan, and in 1885, returned as Jackson County prosecutor. In 1887, he was nominated for Michigan' Supreme Court, but lost with the rest of the Republican ticket. He returned to his law practice and died in Jackson. A statue of Blair stands at the entrance of Michigan's Capitol Building in Lansing.[63]

Henry H. Crapo (1804–1869) served two consecutive terms as governor, from January 1, 1865, until January 1, 1869.

- Henry H. Crapo was born in Dartmouth, Massachusetts, his father a subsistence farmer. Crapo's early education was limited; he was a passionate autodidact who compiled his own dictionary because he lacked the money to buy one. He copied into this book every word whose meaning he did not understand; encountering the same words in newspapers or borrowed books, he slowly ciphered definitions.

(Reportedly, he kept that dictionary for the rest of his life.) One of the books he mastered was on surveying; he learned enough to practice, and with the help of a local blacksmith, hand-forged his own surveyor's instruments. He earned his living surveying, but also teaching in the Dartmouth common schools. When the State of Massachusetts required a teaching certificate (and Dartmouth established a high school), Crapo passed the examination and became principal. In 1832, he moved to New Bedford, continued surveying, and entered public life as town clerk and treasurer (1835), tax collector, and justice of the peace; after New Bedford was incorporated in 1847, he served as alderman, chairman of its board of education, and trustee of the public library. He joined the Massachusetts Militia and eventually became a colonel in the Fifth Division. Between 1836 and 1845, he published the *New Bedford Directory*.

Given New Bedford's importance as a whaling port, it was fitting that Crapo also became part owner of a whaling ship, the *H. H. Crapo*. The New Bedford maritime economy presented other opportunities: after losing an election in 1849, Crapo became secretary of Bedford Commercial Fire Insurance Company and eventually president of the Bristol County (Massachusetts) Mutual Fire Insurance Company, both specializing in marine insurance.

As early as 1836, Crapo was speculating in vast tracts of Michigan pine forests. This continued over the years, and in 1854 culminated in the acquisition of the 12,000-acre Driggs Tract near Flint. He moved to Flint and began harvesting his lands, sawing and selling lumber there and in Feltonville, Holly, and Detroit. By 1860, in a lumbermen's state, he was largest of them all. Crapo was an active railroad investor, having been the prime mover and president of the Flint & Holly Railroad. His rise in Michigan politics was remarkable. A longtime Whig, Crapo became an early Republican. He was elected mayor of Flint as a Republican in 1860, then state senator in 1862. He was elected governor in 1864, and reelected in 1866.

Crapo was a Radical Republican and eagerly oversaw the state's adoption of the Thirteenth Amendment. He opposed Andrew Johnson's Reconstruction policy as well as state borrowings in support of private enterprise. He died in Flint.[64]

Adjutant Generals
Frederick W. Curtenius, March 31, 1855, to March 1861.

- Frederick W. Curtenius (1806–1883) was born in New York City, the son of a War of 1812 general officer who later, as a U.S. marshal, arrested Aaron Burr for treason. Curtenius graduated from Hamilton College in 1823 and intended to study law. However, after three months, he exchanged his books for service under Simon Bolivar in South America. Arriving (probably in Peru) in 1824, Curtenius joined the New Granadian Army as a lieutenant. He fought with distinction, was slightly wounded, and returned to New York. In 1831, he was appointed colonel of a regiment in the New York State Militia. Curtenius moved to Michigan in 1835 to start the very different life of a farmer on the Grand Prairie. But military matters were never far off, and in 1847 he was appointed to West Point's Visiting Board. By this time, Curtenius was deeply involved in the growth of Kalamazoo, serving as a director of the Kalamazoo Mutual Insurance Company, and in the 1850s, as president of Kalamazoo Village. In 1844, he backed Henry Clay for president. With the war in Mexico, Curtenius raised a company at Kalamazoo, which was folded into Colonel Thomas B.W. Stockton's* First Michigan as Company A. It served between November 1847 and July 1848, and was led by Captain Curtenius during its Mexico deployment. In 1855, Republican Governor Kingsley S. Bingham appointed Curtenius state adjutant general, a position he held until replaced by John Robertson in 1861. (Being state AG did not preclude his 1856 election to the state Senate or his election as president of the Kalamazoo City Bank the same year.) He immediately devoted himself to recruiting what became the three-year Sixth Michigan Infantry, and on August 20, 1861, was commissioned its colonel. Curtenius and the Sixth deployed to Baltimore on August 30, 1861, and remained in Maryland until February 22, 1862. It then joined Butler's expedition to New Orleans, and later, Baton Rouge. On June 20, 1862, Curtenius resigned, citing his and his wife's poor health. However, there may have been another factor. Curtenius, by then commanding a brigade, willingly sheltered fugitive slaves. When ordered to return them to their owners, Curtenius refused, was arrested, and left the army. (Nothing about Curtenius's actions would harm him with Blair or most Michiganders; after returning home, the governor issued a rebuke to Curtenius's commander.) Postwar, Curtenius was returned to the state Senate in 1867, and the following year, President Johnson appointed him as the U.S. collector for internal revenue for the Fourth Congressional District, a position he held until 1870. Curtenius died in Kalamazoo.[65]

John Robertson, March 15, 1861, to April, 1887.

- John Robertson (1814–1887) was born in Portsoy, Banffshire, Scotland, and while educated for a profession, he sought the life of a professional soldier. But after he completed school in 1829, his family sent him to clerk in Edinburgh's General Post Office. Unhappy, in about 1833, Robertson moved to Canada, and from there to Burlington, Vermont, arriving on July 2, 1833. He immediately enlisted as a private in the United States Army. In the spring of 1834, he was assigned to the Fifth U.S. Infantry, then at Fort Howard in Green Bay, Wisconsin. He was appointed quartermaster sergeant and afterward, a sergeant major. He served six years, including a stint working as division commissary at Prairie du Chen. He left the army in 1840 and settled in Detroit, clerking for a mercantile firm specializing in shipping and in supplying Lake Superior iron and copper mines. Robertson was successful, and within several years, was sent to Mexico on company business, spending eighteen months in trading operations. After he returned to Detroit he became a partner in the firm. In 1850 the Grayson Light Guard was organized, and Robertson became a sergeant. (A December 21, 1850, newspaper account placed Robertson at a Guards' dinner along with one Lieutenant Ulysses Grant, Fourth U.S. Infantry, then posted in Detroit.) In 1855 the Grayson Light Guard became the Detroit Light Guard and Governor Kingsley S. Bingham commissioned Robertson a lieutenant in the renamed organization. Bingham may have found this appointment congenial for other reasons, as Robertson was by then a Republican. At the time of his appointment as state AG, Robertson was serving as a first lieutenant in the Guard.[66]

Robertson's wartime service is chronicled in this volume. Postwar, he wrote two important books, *The Flags*

of Michigan (1877), which contains essay material on Michigan's historical flags and also a summary of the state's Civil War units' battle itineraries. *The Flags* was similar to a guidebook, written in preparation for the deposit of the regimental colors that were to be placed in the capitol building in Lansing. Robertson's second book was *Michigan in the War* (1882), an indispensable reference work for Michigan's regimental histories and a repository for countless general and special orders, speech excerpts, proclamations, and pieces of information about private aid organizations, officers' service records, and anecdotes that from this distance would be difficult replicate. Robertson remained state AG until his death.[67]

Federal Military Department
January 1 to April 13, 1861, Department of the East.
April 13 to November 9, 1861, in no department.
November 9 to March 11, 1862, Department of the Ohio.
March 11 to June 26, 1862, divided by "an indefinitely drawn" north-south line running through Knoxville, Tennessee. East of the line is in the Mountain Department; west of the line, in the Department of the Mississippi.
June 26 to August 19, 1862, east of the aforementioned line in no department; west of the line continues in the Department of the Mississippi.
August 19 to November 16, 1863, all Michigan returned to the Department of the Ohio.
November 16, to January 12, 1864, in no department.
January 12 to the end of the war, all Michigan is in the Northern Department.[68]

Important State Forts, Barracks, and Arsenals
Camp Backus was built on land leased by the government in January 1862, and named after Electus Backus*; by June, barracks were built that could accommodate 10,000 troops.[69]

Camp Ward in Detroit was the rendezvous for the First Michigan Regiment (colored). Located on Macomb Street near Chene, Camp Ward was named after Detroit Republican Eber B. Ward*. Camp Ward, conceded the racist *Free Press*, "presents quite a military aspect"; on site were five barracks for enlisted quarters (each with a kitchen, and separate buildings for officer quarters, quartermaster, and commissary stores.[70]

Detroit Arsenal was located on a 232-acre Dearbornville parcel some ten miles from Detroit; construction of the "new" Detroit Arsenal began in 1833. Both experience and safety dictated its location—Detroiters wanted explosive ordnance kept outside city limits, and the British had occupied Detroit and that arsenal during the War of 1812. Never intended as a garrison, during the Civil War, the arsenal became a troop rendezvous.

Completed in 1837, the original facility consisted of eleven brick buildings that fronted a square whose sides measured 360 feet each. The arsenal itself was a three-story building 120 feet long and 30 wide, used for arms storage. A twelve-foot-tall wall of "heavy masonry" surrounded the square and connected most buildings, "all calculated as a defence against an invading or insurrectionary foe." In peacetime, the Arsenal hosted fifty workers and two army officers, but in emergencies, that number could double. "The whole object of this institution is, not a military station of soldiers, but for the mounting and equipping of artillery; repairing small arms, and the preparation of all the other numerous munitions of war. It is intended more particularly for the supply of Michigan and Wisconsin."[71]

Detroit Barracks was built in September 1830 on federal land located on Gratiot Road near the intersection with Russell Avenue. A structure was erected almost immediately. It was under active federal control through 1851, and between June 5 and 11 that year was commanded by Lieutenant U. S. Grant. The barracks served as a rendezvous and depot for troops and supplies during the Mexican War and afterward. The barracks was unoccupied beginning shortly after Grant's 1851 command and remained so through the Civil War's eve.[72]

Fort Wayne, named after Revolutionary War General Anthony Wayne, was located in Springwells Township, three and one-half miles from Detroit City Hall. In 1841, the United States appropriated $50,000 for the fort's construction; previously, the site of Fort Wayne had served as a troop rendezvous, during the Patriot War in 1837 and in the Black Hawk War the following year. In 1842, the federal government purchased twenty-three acres of land, followed by an additional forty-three acres in 1844. Construction was overseen by future U.S. QMG Montgomery Meigs, and was completed in 1851 at a cost of $150,000. The fort was strategically sited on the first

bend of the Detroit River and 1,000 yards from Canada, which showed its original purpose: to defend against British invasion. From this site Wayne's guns could be brought to bear on the city and across or on the mouth of the Detroit River, protecting the channel. (Across the river sat the British-Canadian Fort Malden at Amherstburg.) However, by the time Wayne was complete, improvements in Anglo-American relations justified keeping the garrison almost empty. The attack on Fort Sumter renewed concerns about potential British hostility, and later, Confederate activity in Canada. Fort Wayne was built as a square bastioned star fort with sand embankments escarped in thick cedar. During 1861, it was used as a camp of instruction to train officers and NCOs of the Fifth, Sixth, and Seventh Michigan Volunteers. In 1864, a seven-and-a-half-foot-thick and twenty-foot-tall masonry wall replaced the cedar at a cost of $250,000.[73]

Fort Gratiot was located on the west bank of the St. Clair River one mile north of Port Huron. Named after Charles Gratiot for his War of 1812 service, it was originally established by France in 1686 as little more than a reinforced trading post to deter English expansion. Abandoned in 1701 in favor of Detroit, Fort Gratiot was reestablished in 1763 during the French-Indian War. In 1807, the fort was occupied by General William Hull and abandoned after 1813. In 1814, U.S. forces (including Captain Gratiot, after whom the fort was named) reoccupied the site. In 1828, the site was rebuilt along the lines that remained in 1861.[74]

Fort Mackinac was located on the southeastern side of Mackinac Island, overlooking the Mackinac Straits that join Lakes Huron and Michigan. It is sixty miles southwest of Fort Brady. (At the time of the Civil War, the closest major town was Sheboygan, located eighteen miles south.) The British had occupied the island and the post in 1763 after the French destroyed former Fort Mackinac on the mainland. In 1795, the fort was given to the United States via the Treaty of Paris that settled the Revolutionary War. The British held it during the War of 1812 and renamed it Fort George. In 1814 (the Battle of Mackinac Island), the United States unsuccessfully tried to recapture the fort. It finally reverted to U.S. control after the Treaty of Ghent that settled the War of 1812. The fort was renamed Fort Holmes after Major Andrew Hunter Holmes, who was killed during the Battle of Mackinac. Between the War of 1812 and the Civil War, the fort was periodically occupied by small U.S. forces and then abandoned. It was evacuated on April 28, 1861, and then reoccupied in May 1862, holding three Tennessee political prisoners who remained until that September. Afterward, the fort stood idle until 1866.[75]

Fort Brady was located on the southern bank of the Sault Ste. Marie River. It originated in 1750 as a small French outpost. In 1762 the French abandoned the site after Quebec fell to the British, who soon burned the fort. Afterward, the British had a small presence until 1802; however, the general area was actually under the control of local Indian tribes. During his 1820 expedition, General Lewis Cass discovered that the British presence was little more than a Union Jack flying above the fort's location. In a tense scene, Cass personally lowered the flag and raised the Stars and Stripes: it nearly started a war with local inhabitants, but cooler heads prevailed, and in June 1820 a treaty was negotiated (assisted by Chippewa-fluent Charles C. Trowbridge) that gave the site to the United States. In 1822, the fort's namesake, General Hugh Brady, built a stockade. The fort was in continuous occupation except briefly during the Mexican War and again after 1857, when the garrison was transferred to Fort Snelling, Minnesota. It remained unoccupied until 1866.[76]

Demography

Among the states in 1860, Michigan ranked sixteenth in population (749,113) and twenty-sixth in density per square mile at 13.32. By comparison, the most densely populated state, Massachusetts, was at 157.83, while the least was Oregon, with 0.55 persons per square mile.[77] Detroit was Michigan's largest city (with 45,619 residents, ranked nineteenth in the nation), but contained only 6.1 percent of the state's population. By comparison, Philadelphia contained 19.46 percent of Pennsylvanians and New York and Brooklyn contained 27.63 percent of New York state residents. In this overwhelmingly rural state, only Detroit's population exceeded 10,000; another 25,465 Michiganders (or 3.4 percent of the population) lived in cities with between 5,000 and 10,000 residents; of some 695 Michigan cities, towns, and villages listed in the 1860 census, two had populations between 4,000 and

5,000, six were between 3,000 and 4,000, and 391 had fewer than 1,000 inhabitants. Between 1850 and 1860, the state population grew by 351,459, or 88.38 percent. This growth rate mirrored those of other states formed from the Old Northwest; while "mature" Ohio grew by 18.14 percent during the same period, Illinois grew by 101.06 percent, Indiana by 36.63 percent, Iowa by 251.14 percent, and Wisconsin by 154.06 percent.[78]

This new population overwhelmingly resided on farms or in villages. In 1860, Michigan's nine largest cities after Detroit were Grand Rapids (8,085), Adrian (6,213), Kalamazoo (6,070), Ann Arbor (5,097), Jackson (4,799), Port Huron (4,371), Ypsilanti (3,955), Monroe (3,892), and Marshall (3,736). The combined population (46,218) of these nine cities exceeded that of Detroit by only 599 persons. Between 1850 and 1860, Detroit's population more than doubled, increasing by 24,600. But despite its bank capital ($2,897,390), its manufacturing output ($3,620,387), and its place as a railroad hub and major Great Lakes port, only 6.9 percent of people who had moved to Michigan since 1850 had settled in Detroit. Thus, the state's chief attractions were rural.[79]

Michigan's population clustered in the southern third of the state. Contained in twenty-one counties (a line from Allegan to St. Clair Counties) lived 543,473 inhabitants, or 72.5 percent of the state population. If one adds the population (124,130) of the next northern tier of seven counties (Ottawa to Lapeer), which occupy central Michigan, the twenty-eight combined counties held 89.1 percent of the state population. The other 10.9 percent of Michigan's population resided in the rest of the state, with 20,328 (2.7 percent of the state total) on the Upper Peninsula.[80]

In common with every state of the Old Northwest (and unlike many eastern states), Michigan's gender balance favored men over women across all measured subgroups (white, black, foreign-born, and "civilized Indians"). This totaled 394,694 men and 354,419 women, an imbalance of men by 40,275. Gender gaps mattered during the Civil War, because until the March 3, 1863, Enrollment Act, federal troop quotas were based on a state's general population and not the number of eligible males.[81]

As to age eligibility in 1860, some 203,371 white and 1,455 Indian males[82] were aged between fifteen and fifty, which included the military range of eighteen to forty-five. This amounted to 52.3 percent of the combined white and Indian male population of 391,127. African

American males in the same age cohort totaled 1,922, or 53.8 percent of Michigan's total black male population of 3,567. These figures do not account for a variety of subtractions from this force, which included those for physical disability, legal exemption, and draft evasion.[83]

In 1860, 736,142 Michiganders were white, 6,799 were African American (0.9 percent of the total population), and 6,172[84] were Indian. The four counties hosting the largest black populations (with the principal city and the number of black residents in parenthesis) were 1,673 in Wayne County (Detroit/1,403, with the largest concentrations in Ward Four, 373; Ward Two, 326; and Ward Seven, 267); 1,368 in Cass County (Calvin/795), 634 in Washtenaw County (Ann Arbor/106), and 410 in Berrien County (Niles/127). Calhoun County's Battle Creek, home to Sojourner Truth* since 1857, counted 155 African Americans. The largest concentration of Native Americans was in the counties of Emmet (1,149), Mackinac (907), Isabella (818), Leelanau (628), and Oceana (570). In 1863, the federal government studied state African American populations and estimated the number of black men eligible for military service. (See February 11, 1863.) Native Americans living in Michigan made a distinct contribution to the war effort, which is discussed in the Selected Summaries.[85]

In 1860, 294,828 Michigan residents (39.35 percent) were born in Michigan before or after statehood (1837); 303,582 (40.52 percent) were born in other states; and 149,092 (19.9 percent) were born in other countries, with the balance being of unknown nativity or born at sea. As noted above, Michigan did not resemble border slave states, and unlike Ohio, Indiana, and Illinois, did not count large numbers of Southerners among its early settlers.

Michigan had been a state for thirteen years when the Seventh Census (1850) began including state-by-state nativities, thus helping to quantify the origins of Michigan residents born in the United States but outside the state. Of 341,591 American-born inhabitants residing in the state in 1850, fewer than half (41 percent or 140,648) had been born in Michigan. Of the remaining 200,943 residents, nativities included 133,756 from New York, 14,677 from Ohio, 11,113 from Vermont, 9,452 from Pennsylvania, 8,167 from Massachusetts, and 5,572 from New Jersey. For the Seventh Census, nativities from the fifteen slave states and the District of Columbia totaled 3,634, or 1.8 percent of out-of-staters. Michigan in 1860 was no

more attractive to slave states than in 1850: slave states and the District of Columbia had contributed 5,822 residents, or 1.9 percent of all out-of-staters. Unlike the states on the north bank of the Ohio River, white Michigan was a northern state settled chiefly by northerners. Insofar as this produced a certain ideological uniformity, Michigan was largely (but not entirely) spared some of the extreme political tensions found in southern New York, Pennsylvania's coal mining regions, and Ohio's small but influential clique of antiwar Democrats.[86]

Of the foreign-born, Ireland supplied 30,049 (20.1 percent) of the state's foreign born, followed by (among others) the German states (38,787/26 percent), England 25,743/17.3 percent), British America, (36,482/24.45 percent), Scotland (5,705/3.8 percent), France (2,446/1.6 percent), Wales (348/0.23 percent), and Switzerland (1,269/0.85 percent). Almost half (48.28 percent or 71,988) settled in one of seven counties (principal city/ number in parenthesis): Wayne County (29,298/Detroit), St. Clair County (11,640/Port Huron), Washtenaw County (6,994/Ann Arbor), Kent County (6,520/Grand Rapids), Houghton County (6,192/Houghton, area of mining operations), Oakland County (5,859/Pontiac), and Macomb County (5,485/Clinton).[87]

Immigrants and Immigration

During the mid- to late 1850s in some New England and Mid-Atlantic states, the nativist movement damaged legal and social relations between the foreign-born and white native communities. In many states this required remediation during the Civil War. But Michigan was not among these states. "The Know-Nothing Party in Michigan was comparatively weak and short-lived," noted one historian. In the 1855 Detroit charter election, the Know-Nothing ticket was defeated (local Germans had organized the Anti-Know-Nothing Association); that year, the nativist American Party did win local elections in Marshall, Battle Creek, Pontiac, Mt. Clemens, Kalamazoo, and Grand Rapids. A Know-Nothing National Council had convened in Philadelphia in 1855, but when a majority of delegates urged Congress not to legislate on territorial slavery, Michigan's representatives (together with those of other free states) walked out. In 1856, Michiganders had an opportunity to vote for the nativist American Party ticket, topped by ex-president Millard Fillmore; of some 125,561 ballots cast, Fillmore received 1,660, or 1.32 percent. (In contrast, Fillmore carried Maryland with 54.63 percent of the vote, and he received 20.89 percent in New York and 11.54 percent in Massachusetts.) In Michigan, the movement virtually disappeared after 1856, its constituents absorbed into the growing Republican Party. It left few traces.[88]

Michigan avidly sought white European immigrants. In 1845, its legislature created the Office of Foreign Immigration, appointing an agent who wrote a promotional pamphlet, "State of Michigan—1845—To Emigrants." In mid-April, 1859, Rudolph Diepenbeck, Michigan's state commissioner of emigration, opened a New York City office; in the ensuing eleven months, of 27,070 Germans entering New York, he claimed to have steered 562 to Michigan, with an estimated per capita wealth of $100. Among the several factors he cited to explain the steep drop in German immigration to the United States between 1854 and 1859 was the "many deplorable facts relative to the American social and political life," a reference to the Nativism movement, which had become prominent in many states earlier in the decade. Diepenbeck noted that Michigan was different. It had appointed state agents to stimulate immigration, had passed its own Homestead Law, and circulated "all over Germany Diepenbeck's pamphlet promoting Michigan."[89]

The fiercely Democratic *Detroit Free Press* declared that "The Germans at this day are the mainstay of the black republicans," and blamed them for the 1859 election of Detroit's Republican mayor Christian Buhl. (The *Free Press* neglected to mention that while Buhl was born in the United States, his father had emigrated from Germany, an affinity probably not lost on Detroit's Germans.) The editors pointed to the different nature of pre- and post-1848 German immigrants. While the former were largely "Lutherans or Catholics . . . mostly believers in religion, and live in strict accordance with their professions," those Germans forced to immigrate by the 1848 Revolution were different, as the *Free Press* italics were wont to show: they were "EXTREME, RADICAL, REVOLUTIONARY, SECTIONAL, FANATICAL, SOCIALISTIC, AND TRANSITORY."[90]

1860

Key Events

February

1: After eight weeks and forty-four ballots in a contest rife with sectional division, New Jersey Republican William Pennington[1] is elected speaker of the U.S. House of Representatives. The moderate Democrat *Michigan Argus* welcomes the result, declaring that "Mr. Pennington is a national man," while the Republican *Lansing State Journal* agrees, but with a party tilt: it denounced Democrats as the party of "fire-eaters" making "empty threats of disunion"; it was "the Republican members of Congress who have thus held themselves at the service of the country, amid threats, provocations, and affronts, undisturbed and unintimidated." The *Detroit Weekly Tribune* finds evidence that Pennington's election "is also important as an expression and triumph of the conservative Union anti-slavery extension sentiment of the country preliminary to the great contest of 1860."[2]

14: The *Lansing State Republican* speaks for most Michigan Republicans when it declares today "That the delegates from Michigan to the Chicago Convention will cast their votes for William H. Seward, we are certain. That the Chicago Convention will tender him the nomination, we have little doubt," and if Seward accepts, "his election may be considered sure."[3] (See May 2.)

22: **The Democratic State Convention** convenes in Detroit's Firemen's Hall to pass resolutions and choose delegates for the April 23 Charleston Convention. Charles H. Taylor[*] presides as twelve delegates are chosen: four at-large, George V. N. Lathrop[*], H. H. Riley[*], Charles E. Stuart[*], George W. Peck[*], and eight others.[4] Thirteen resolutions are adopted, which include an affirmation of the Democratic platform from the 1856 Cincinnati Convention; reaffirmation of U.S. Supreme Court decisions, (unnamed but understood was one decision in particular: *Dred Scott*); condemnation of John Brown's Harper's Ferry raid and holding Republicans responsible; the declaration that national unity could only be achieved under Democrats, and that only with Stephen A. Douglas as nominee for president; condemnation of the defalcating Republican state treasurer; condemnation of excessive state expenditures by the current Republican governor and fears of "bankruptcy and disgrace"; and a demand for an accounting and retrenchment of state expenditures.[5]

The Republican sheet *Detroit Weekly Tribune* later comments that the "show of enthusiasm" for Douglas "was all forced work.—There is no deep popular enthusiasm for Senator Douglas in Michigan." As the *Tribune* understands matters, convention Democrats were only genuinely united "when the Republicans were denounced as pirates, negro-thieves, robbers and villains generally." Next week, the *Tribune* denounces the Democratic state convention as "treasonable."[6]

23: Wilbur Storey's[*] fiercely Democratic *Detroit Free Press*[7] reflects on yesterday's convention. "We confess that we have never witnessed such deep, devoted, irrepressible popular feeling in favor of any man as that which we witnessed yesterday in favor of Douglas. . . . And the testimony was unanimous that with Douglas [Michigan] can be redeemed."[8]

March

2: The *Free Press*, appraising the net effect of both Democratic and Republican national conventions, declares, "The contest is to be over the very existence of the Union itself, and the issue is to be Union or disunion." State sovereignty is the issue, "and involves the very perpetuity of the Union."[9]

April

23: Charleston Convention: Democrats convene in Charleston to select a president. Charles E. Stuart leads the Michigan delegation, and two members are assigned to committees: Benjamin Follett to the

Committee on Credentials and August C. Baldwin to the Committee on Permanent Organization.[10]

24: Charleston Convention: Each state chooses one delegate to serve as vice president of the convention and one secretary. Michigan chooses H. H. Riley, and John G. Parkhurst*, who the next day will be chosen as the convention's recording secretary and later publishes its official proceedings. George V. N. Lothrop is chosen as Michigan's representative on the all-important Committee on Resolutions and Platform. A far-reaching decision is also made: "this Convention will not proceed to ballot for a candidate for Presidency, until the Platform shall have been adopted." This means that explosive positions on territorial slavery must be decided before selecting a nominee.

Meanwhile, the Republican *Detroit Advertiser* presciently suggests that the Charleston Democrats (the "standard bearer of the black of slavery during the coming campaign") will fracture at Charleston and provide the spectacle of "the last dying spasm of the slave Democracy."[11]

27: Charleston Convention: The Platform Committee issues two reports. The Majority Report declares that neither Congress nor territorial governments can abolish, exclude, or regulate slavery; that the free states' efforts to obstruct Fugitive Slave Act enforcement are "hostile in character, subversive of the Constitution, and revolutionary in their effect"; and that the federal government is required to protect such property on "the high seas, in the Territories, or wherever else its constitutional authority extends." Finally, it calls for protecting naturalized citizens, acquiring Cuba, and building a Pacific railroad. In sum, the Majority Report rejects Stephen A. Douglas's Freeport Doctrine (popular sovereignty) and presents a slave code platform, which most Northern Democrats cannot accept.

But a Minority Report is also issued. Northern free-state delegates, including Michigan's Lothrop, affirm the 1856 Cincinnati platform; recommend that the Supreme Court should decide state and territorial questions of property (slaves); affirms the rights of naturalized citizens; urges the construction of a Pacific railroad; seeks the acquisition of Cuba; and claims that state efforts to stymie the Fugitive Slave Law are "hostile . . . subversive . . . and revolution-

ary." The Minority Report seeks a platform on which Northern Democrats can campaign.[12]

28: Charleston Convention: Efforts are made to reconcile the Majority and Minority Reports in such a way as to allow Northern Democrats an acceptable platform. On the issue of slavery, a reconciliation proposal reads, "Inasmuch as differences of opinion exist in the Democratic party as to the nature and extent of the powers of a Territorial Legislature, and as to the powers and duties of Congress, under the Constitution of the United States, over the institution of slavery within the Territories: . . . Resolved, That the Democratic party will abide by the decision of the Supreme Court of the United States on questions of constitutional law."

A vote is scheduled for the April 30.[13]

30: Charleston Convention: A vote is taken on adopting the Minority Report—favorable to Northern Democrats—as the Democratic party platform. It passes by 165 to 138, with Michigan unanimously voting to adopt the Minority Platform. In separate votes, Michigan also unanimously supports adoption of the 1856 Cincinnati Platform, protection of naturalized citizens, building a Pacific Railroad, acquiring Cuba, and denouncing state obstruction of the Fugitive Slave Law. But it is not enough; by evening Alabama, Mississippi, Louisiana, most of South Carolina, Texas, Florida, and Arkansas delegations withdraw from the convention. These states are referred to as "Bolters" and will meet later that night.[14]

May

1: Charleston Convention: Georgia withdraws from the convention. Voting commences for president: twelve indecisive ballots are taken. In each, Michigan votes unanimously for Douglas. The Bolters continue to separately organize.[15]

2: Charleston Convention: Ballots thirteen through fifty-seven are cast today: in each, Michigan votes unanimously for Douglas; however, in the final ballot, Douglas remains some fifty votes short of the nomination. The *Detroit Weekly Advertiser* concludes, "[The] Democracy is National no more."[16]

Detroit Republican State Convention: Meanwhile, the Republican State Convention convenes in Detroit's Merrill Hall, with Kalamazoo's David S. Walbridge* presiding. Austin Blair delivers an antislavery keynote speech, including "The first choice of Michigan is undoubtedly the tried and wise statesman of New York, William H. Seward." (The reporter notes that "Here the applause was overpowering, and it was some time before silence permitted the speaker to resume.") Blair's concluding remarks capture the spirit of this convention. "[T]he Republicans of this State were all on fire with truth, they 'sniffed the battle afar off,' and hoped to meet the hosts of slavery in solid column, and not in broken ranks, for they wanted to overthrow them horse, foot and dragoons."

The convention then unanimously adopts eleven resolutions, including comparing themselves to "an infant Hercules, which in its very cradle, is strangling the twin-serpents of polygamy and slavery"; denunciation of the Buchanan administration for a variety of sins, including its being "subservient to behests of the slave power" and "so treacherous in all its actions and movements—in regard to the admission of Kansas"; reaffirmation of the 1856 Philadelphia Platform; demands for a Pacific railroad, the admission of Kansas, river and harbor improvement, a homestead law, an affirmation of the "power of Congress to maintain the rights of freedom, free soil, and free labor in the Territories of the Union"; most importantly, endorsement of William H. Seward for president: a "life-long supporter of Republican principles, the statesmen of his time, eminently conservative and national in his views, commanding in private and in public life, the respect of all men of all parties, North and South[; he] is our *first* choice as a candidate for the Presidency."

The state convention chooses delegates to the Chicago convention, including delegates at large Austin Blair, Walter Walton Murphy*, Thomas W. Ferry*, and J. J. St. Clair; district delegates who appear in Chicago and participate in the proceedings include William L. Stoughton*, D. C. Buckland, and Francis Quinn. Michigan will have six votes. (See May 16–18.)[17]

3: Charleston Convention: The Democrats adjourn without selecting a nominee and agree to reconvene in Baltimore on June 18. Meanwhile, the Bolters agree to reconvene in Richmond on June 11. (See date.)[18]

9: National Convention of the Constitutional Union

Party convenes in Baltimore. Michigan sends no delegates.[19]

16: Republican National Convention convenes in Chicago. As the roll of states present is called, there are no delegates, and thus no responses, from Tennessee, Arkansas, Mississippi, Louisiana, Alabama, Georgia, and South and North Carolina. Massachusetts's George Ashmun is chosen as convention president, Michigan's Thomas W. Ferry is chosen as one of twenty-seven vice presidents, and William L. Stoughton as one of twenty-six secretaries. Austin Blair will serve on the all-important Committee on Resolutions.[20]

17: Republican National Convention resumes with the adoption of the party platform. It consists of seventeen planks, including an assertion that "the rights of the states, and the union of the states must and shall be preserved"; a stern denunciation of "all schemes for disunion" as "an avowal of contemplated treason" that should be rebuked and silenced. Simultaneously, it denounces "the lawless invasion, by armed force, of the soil of any state or territory" as the "gravest of crimes"; states that the Buchanan administration is in "measureless subserviency to the exactions of a sectional interest" (that is, the Slave Power); denounces the Buchanan administration's corruption and waste; appeals to Congress to close the slave trade; condemns federal governors in Kansas and Nebraska Territories for vetoing antislavery bills from the legislature; urges the admission of Kansas as a state; makes a vague statement supporting tariffs; demands a homestead bill; favors an antinativist plank opposing state law changes in naturalization; and supports internal improvements and a Pacific railroad.

However, the three most important planks dealt with slavery:

"4. That the maintenance inviolate of the rights of the states, and especially the right of each state to order and control its own domestic institutions [i.e., slavery], according to its own judgment exclusively, is essential. . . .

"7. That the new dogma [i.e., *Dred Scott*], that the Constitution of its own force carries slavery into any or all of the territories of the United States, is a dangerous political heresy. . . .

"8. That the normal condition of all the territory

of the United States is that of freedom." That the founders had abolished slavery in the territories and applied Fifth Amendment protections to all inhabitants, "and we deny the authority of Congress, of territorial legislature, or of any individuals, to give legal existence to slavery in any territory of the United States."[21]

18: Republican National Convention resumes. Nominations for president are made for a variety of men, but the most likely contenders are William H. Seward, Abraham Lincoln, William L. Dayton, Simon Cameron, and Salmon P. Chase. Austin Blair seconds Seward's nomination, and the first ballot is taken: 173.5 votes for Seward 102 for Lincoln, 50.5 for Cameron, 49 for Chase, and 48 for Bates. Michigan votes unanimously for Seward, but no candidate receives a "majority of the whole number of votes cast," so a second ballot is taken: the top three candidates are Seward with 184.5 votes, Lincoln with 181, and Chase with 42.5. Again, Michigan votes unanimously for Seward. On the third ballot, Lincoln polls 231.5 votes and Seward 180, with Michigan supporting the latter.

As the Lincoln triumph is clear and the party seeks unanimity, different states announce they are recasting their votes to Lincoln. The most important endorsement of Lincoln comes from the New York delegation, which at Seward's urging recasts its votes unanimously for Lincoln. But Austin Blair gives one of the most famous convention speeches. He is disappointed: "the State of Michigan, from first to last, has cast her vote for the great statesman of New York." "We stand by him still," Blair states; but believing that Seward's legacy of statesmanship is secure, Blair also announces that "We marshal behind [Seward] in the grand column which shall go out to battle for Abraham Lincoln of Illinois" and closes on a stirring note: "I promise you that in the State of Michigan . . . where the Republican party from the days of its organization to this hour has never suffered a single defeat . . . we will give you for the gallant son of Illinois, and glorious standard-bearer of the West, a round twenty-five thousand majority." Later on this day, Maine's Hannibal Hamlin[22] is nominated as vice president, and that night the Republican National Committee reconstitutes itself with Austin Blair replacing Zachariah Chandler. (See June 11.)

Michigan's Republican newspapers endorse Lincoln's nomination. Under the headline, "Republicans of Michigan! To your Duty," the *Detroit Weekly Tribune* endorses Lincoln, while acknowledging that "Mr. Lincoln was not . . . our, first choice" it declares that he has "everything to commend him, as a man of ability, integrity, firmness and steadfast to principle." It attributes Seward's loss to "the envy and malice of Senatorial rivals, and base, ungrateful, dastardly Greeleyism," referring to a bitter dispute between Seward and *New York Tribune* publisher Horace Greeley.[23]

The *Hillsdale Standard* declares that Lincoln and Hamlin "are no new recruits but long working and well tried veterans in the Republican service"; they "are representative men," and the sheet declares that Hillsdale will contribute 2,500 of the 25,000 thousand majority votes Blair promised. The *Lansing State Republican* declares, "To-day we fling to the breeze the Republican banner of 1860, inscribed with LINCOLN, HAMLIN, UNION AND VICTORY!" "He has sprung from the laboring classes," the sheet notes, "and is emphatically the people's candidate."[24]

June

7: In Detroit the State Republican Convention nominates Blair for governor and James M. Birney* for lieutenant governor.[25]

8: Tennessee voters approve secession.

11: In Detroit, a meeting convenes to ratify the national and state Republican tickets. A reported 8,000 persons participate.[26]

Meanwhile, in Richmond, the "Bolters Convention" reconvenes as the Southern Rights Convention. Ten slave states are represented.[27]

18–23: Democratic National Convention is reconvened. The Convention opens in Baltimore at the Front Street Theater and Michigan attends with the same delegates as in Charleston. South Carolina, Florida, Alabama, Mississippi, and Texas do not attend. The next several days are spent on procedural matters and credentials, in which Michigan's chair, Charles Stuart, is active. However, he is not among the principal speakers.[28]

21: In Dowagiac, Republicans dedicate a wigwam and raise flagpoles to promote the Lincoln-Hamlin ticket. The featured speaker is Austin Blair (who repeatedly refers to Lincoln as "the Rail Splitter"). Festivities include choral and band music.[29]

23: In the **reconvened Democratic National Convention**, balloting resumes for a presidential nominee. In casting Michigan's six votes for Douglas, Charles Stuart, in a swipe at the Bolters, declares that Michigan will not give "arguments in favor of her devotion to the party and the Union. She will manifest it by conforming to the usages of the Democratic party, and abiding by the result of all Conventions in which she takes part." Douglas wins on the second ballot, 181 1/2 votes of 194 1/2 cast.[30]

Meanwhile, Democratic delegates who abandoned (or were refused seats to) the reconvened Democratic National Convention meet briefly at the Maryland Institute in Baltimore. Michigan is one of ten Northern states that send no delegates. This largely Southern gathering nominates John C. Breckinridge of Kentucky and Joseph Lane of Oregon for president and vice president. Delegates also agree to reconvene on June 26 in Richmond, Virginia.[31]

26: The *Detroit Weekly Tribune* offers a flavor of the 1860 campaign. Its lead editorial, "Republicans! To Action!," asks, "Republican Reader, is your township organized? is every school-district canvassed? is every voter properly enrolled and classified? have you organized clubs and made arrangements to supply the needy and doubtful with Campaign Papers and Documents?" It concludes, "*Let every Republican do his duty, remembering that Every Man is Personally Responsible to his God and his Country for the manner in which that duty is performed.*"[32]

26–28: In Richmond, the Breckinridge wing of the Democratic Party convenes, renominates Breckinridge, and adjourns. Although free states Massachusetts, Pennsylvania, California, and Oregon are represented, Michigan sends no delegates.[33]

28: In Detroit, the State Democratic Convention nominates former three-term governor John S. Barry* for governor, and former lieutenant governor William M. Fenton* for lieutenant governor. Reacting to the nomination of Breckenridge, six resolutions are adopted, including opposition to congressional interference "in the affairs of the Territories," which it claims is embraced by both Republicans and Breckenridge (i.e., both oppose the Freeport Doctrine); with "hopeful zeal," Douglas's nomination is

affirmed; confidence is expressed that the "final decision of the South will put forever to rest the efforts of those politicians in their section whose action must inevitably lead to the eventual disruption of the union"; denunciation of the corruption of governors Wisner and Bingham, evidenced by defalcating treasurer John McKinney; and other matters.[34]

July

2: The *Free Press*, speaking for Michigan's Democratic Party, offers the past words of Breckinridge and Lane in support of popular sovereignty, thus implying that the two men are hypocrites. Popular sovereignty, the *Free Press* concludes, is something that "the democracy of the North will insist upon to the end of time." The *Free Press* also claims that reports of pro-Breckinridge demonstrations are actually plants by "black republicans."[35]

6: In Lansing, Ingham County African Americans meet to appoint delegates to a Battle Creek convention planned for October 9. The purpose of the Battle Creek meeting "is to devise ways and means, by which the colored inhabitants of Michigan may obtain and enjoy those political rights to which they are justly entitled as tax payers, and industrious, quiet, orderly citizens."[36] (See October 9.)

12: Nine signatories, led by Levi Bishop*, issue a circular calling for a July 24 meeting in Detroit to form a Breckinridge and Lane organization. Somewhat enigmatic, it states that, "It has been urged by many National Democrats, that a consultation be had to the end that they act in concert in the present crisis. The propriety of an independent organization cannot be fully discussed by correspondence."[37] (See July 24.)

24: An estimated fifty persons meet to support the Breckinridge-Lane ticket. Noted is a divided Democratic Party, an assertion that the Baltimore Convention was "without precedent and without authority," that the divisions were produced by "the personal interests of Mr. Douglas and his particular friends, at the expense of the party," and that as a result, "we feel at liberty, consistent with party allegiance . . . to vote for whichever of the Democratic candidates we please." Nine resolutions are adopted, including the observation that Douglas has failed to unify the national Democratic Party; an endorsement of

Breckinridge-Lane ticket as truly national; and calls for a state convention and a state central committee.[38]

30: Kalamazoo's Douglas Club opens its campaign in a filled Humphrey Hall.[39]

31: In Port Huron, Republicans have constructed a wigwam with a capacity of 1,000 people. It is dedicated this night to "the cause of Republican Freedom, Free Soil, and Free Homes." Seventy-five Wide-Awakes parade, and Congressman William A. Howard speaks. Meanwhile, in Ann Arbor, the Douglas Democrat Club meets, with E. B. Pond as temporary chairman and Alpheus Felch elected president.[40]

August

1: In Detroit, the Douglas or Democratic "Ranche" is dedicated, capacity 2,000 persons; presumably this is the party's answer to Republican wigwams. Those speaking for Douglas include Clement Vallandigham, Charles E. Stuart, and George V.N. Lothrop.[41]

10: In Jackson, Republicans dedicate a wigwam, built of wood and measuring 45 by 80 by 30 feet; supported by thirty-three posts (one for each state). The interior is festooned with state flags and evergreens forming the words "Our Blair." Some 100 Jackson Wide-Awakes demonstrate, together with the Jackson Guard Band. Speakers include Bradley F. Granger, Francis W. Kellogg, Henry Waldron★, and Ohio Congressman James M. Ashley.[42] Estimated attendance is 4,000 persons.[43]

13: On this night Detroit Republicans dedicate a wigwam to "Lincoln and Freedom." The crowd is claimed to be "not less" than 10,000 persons; featured speakers include former Ohio governor Salmon P. Chase[44] and James M. Ashley, and familiar Michiganders Bradley F. Granger and William A. Howard. Detroit Wide-Awakes mount a torchlight procession, and the evening is enlivened with bands, bonfire, and fireworks.[45]

17: In Ypsilanti, a Republican mass meeting convenes, with attendees estimated at 15,000. Featured speakers include Ohioan Salmon P. Chase and familiar Michiganders Jacob and William A. Howard, Kinsley Bingham, and Senator Chandler. There are torchlight demonstrations and Wide-Awakes from Detroit, Ann Arbor, Jackson, and Dexter. Meanwhile, in Kalamazoo, the *Gazette* announces that 500 Douglas badges have just been received.[46]

18: In Detroit's Second Ward, Germans organize a German Republican Club. Separately, in East Saginaw, a Mr. Strasburg ("a worthy, staunch, and ever reliable German Democrat") raised a pole and hosted a "Douglas & Johnson" banner across from his hotel. Over the ensuing days, East Saginaw Democrats will raise poles and organize campaign meetings. "Let the ball roll on," the editor notes. "Saginaw county never yet surrendered . . . [and] she is good for a clean five hundred Democratic majority next November." Meanwhile, in Kalamazoo County, some 1,500 Democrats gather to ratify the state party's vote for Douglas-Johnson and to list featured speakers, including Charles E. Stuart. At night, nearly 500 lamp-carrying "Douglas Invincibles" demonstrate.[47]

22: In Kalamazoo, Republicans dedicate a wigwam. An estimated crowd of 3,000 hears speakers, including William A. Howard and Joseph W. Huston, the latter a convert from Douglas and local attorney, and later an officer in the Fourth and Third Michigan Cavalry.[48]

23: In Grand Haven, African Americans from Muskegon and Ottawa Counties meet to name delegates to the October 9 Battle Creek convention to petition for the elective franchise.[49]

28: In Jackson, in a field between East Main and Granson Streets, a three-day encampment of the Michigan militia begins. It is the first statewide gathering of its kind. There are twenty-eight companies in the state, and at least nine appear at Jackson: Jackson Greys, Detroit Light Guard, Adrian Guard, Ypsilanti Light Guard, Steuben Guard, Union Guard, Williams' Rifles, Curtenius Guards, and Williams' German Light Artillery, with the Hudson Artillery and the Coldwater Light Artillery expected later in the day. The encampment is commanded by Alpheus S. Williams★. Also present are James E. Pittman★, Eugene Pringle★, H. M. Whittlesey★, James W. Romeyn★, Henry L. Chipman★, Loren L. Comstock★, Phillip McKernan★, Jacob Webber★, and Orlando B. Willcox★, "an unofficial inspector and critic." At the encampment during the afternoon, the Jackson Break-of-Day Base Ball Club plays Detroit's Early Risers. These units and their commanders will be the nucleus of Michigan's military Civil War.[50]

September

1: In Meridian, a ninety-five-foot pole is raised bearing a banner inscribed "Lincoln and Hamlin." A Wide-Awake demonstration occurs in the evening.[51]

4: In Detroit, William Henry Seward delivers a speech ("The National Divergence and Return") to an audience estimated (by the Republican *Detroit Tribune*) at 50,000. It is a day of speeches, including from Senators Wade and Chandler, Governor Wisner, Jacob M. Howard, DeWitt Clinton Leach*, and Kansas newspaper editor T. Dwight Thatcher. New York newspapers consider Seward's speech important, and it will appear in the *New York Times*, *New York Tribune*, the *New York World*, and the *New York Herald*.

There is little in Seward's speech about Michigan; instead, he presents a picture of chaos at home and abroad under the Buchanan administration. He offers a history of the territorial slavery question and presents Republican policy as consistent with the past. But while arguing against legalizing territorial slavery, his condemnation is chiefly moral: "Slavery, however it may be at any time or in any place excused, is at all times and everywhere unjust and inhuman."[52]

6: William H. Seward speaks in Lansing to an estimated 20,000 persons; happy to be there ("the newly formed capital of an embryo State"), he estimates his audience at "15,000 freemen" and delivers a fiercely antislavery speech. He denounces "Popular Sovereignty" and repeatedly uses the phrase he made famous, "irrepressible conflict." Others present include Benjamin Wade, Jacob and William Howard, and Austin Blair. Festivities include 100 mounted Wide-Awakes, several bands, fireworks, and a torchlight parade. Seward is scheduled to speak at Kalamazoo on September 8.[53]

8: William H. Seward speaks in Kalamazoo with Austin Blair and Senator Chandler, among other speakers.[54]

12: In Cassopolis, amid bands and Wide-Awake demonstrations, a reported 8,000 "Freemen in Council" gather in a wigwam to hear featured speakers Senator Chandler and Congressman William A. Howard.[55]

17: In a Republican rally in Allegan, an estimated 3,000 listen to speeches by Francis W. Kellogg and Austin Blair.[56]

20: In Hudson, Austin Blair and Henry Waldron speak for Lincoln, followed by a torchlight Wide-Awake procession.[57]

21: In Monroe, an estimated 4,000 people listen to speeches by Senator Chandler, and others; tonight, Wide-Awakes mount a torchlight procession.[58]

24: As the election draws near, Republican speakers canvass the state. Mass meetings are scheduled for Lapeer, Flint, East Saginaw, Bay City, Allegan, Grand Rapids, Grand Haven, Ionia, and Corunna; speakers include Senators Chandler and Bingham, gubernatorial hopeful Austin Blair, Ohio's Benjamin Wade, state attorney general Charles Upson, and Congressman Henry Waldron. Kentucky Abolitionist Cassius M. Clay has a separate speaking schedule, which includes Niles, Three Rivers, Jackson, Battle Creek, Howell, and Ann Arbor.[59]

27: It is probably on this day that nationally prominent philanthropist Dorothea Dix arrives at Detroit's Russell House Hotel, from Kalamazoo. Described by a *Free Press* reporter as "a quiet, unassuming lady, of about forty years of age, of intelligent appearance, interesting demeanor, and plain address," Dix will visit Detroit's jail, hospitals, poorhouse, and different charitable institutions. During her Michigan visit, Dix establishes relationships with Detroit women, including Isabelle B. Duffield and her daughter, Isabella Duffield Stewart, which later helps connect Michigan with national relief efforts.[60] (See April 23.)

October

3: In Firemen's Hall in Detroit, some fifty delegates from sixteen Michigan counties assemble, Henry Chipman presiding, to pledge support for the Constitutional Union ticket. No state nominations are made.[61]

8–9: In Battle Creek, a convention[62] of African Americans, chaired by Thomas Jefferson Martin of Dowagiac, petitions Michigan's legislature to strike the word "white" from Michigan's constitution, thereby allowing black men to vote. It also names a permanent committee with representatives from fifteen Michigan counties that has the power to convene future conventions at any time.[63]

9: At a Republican rally in Grand Rapids, a crowd estimated at 15,000 listens to speeches from Zachariah Chandler and Austin Blair; 600 Wide-Awakes march in procession.[64]

15: Beginning the previous night and through the following morning, a train carrying Democratic presidential nominee Steven A. Douglas wends through Michigan en route to Detroit. Even in the dark, it passes cheering crowds of supporters in Jackson, Ann Arbor, Ypsilanti, Dexter, and Dearborn. Arriving in Detroit at 7:30 a.m., Douglas is escorted to the Michigan Exchange Hotel; from its balcony, he addresses, impromptu, thousands of supporters in the street. During the day, trains and steamers arrive carrying more supporters. In the afternoon, a crowd assembles before a speaking stand on the Campus Martius to hear Douglas speak.

Douglas opens by criticizing Seward's September 4 speech. He accuses Seward of exaggerating: secession is not "the whole South" nor is Lincoln "the whole North." He challenges Seward's history of territorial slavery ("Just so long as Congress left that subject alone, just so long as there was peace, harmony and fraternity in this country."). Dangerous divisions happened only after Congress began to meddle. He then offers another history: how federal efforts to regulate territorial slavery have produced near-disasters. The only extremists in this contest are secessionists under Breckinridge and Republicans under Lincoln; the former want Congress to permit all slavery in the territories and the latter to prohibit slavery there—both demand Congressional interference. He defends popular sovereignty and praises Congressional candidate Lothrop for defending it. Douglas denies that he seeks to deprive blacks of their civil rights, but adds this: "It may be entirely safe and prudent to extend to the negroes in Michigan, where you have very few, rights and privileges which it would be unsafe and dangerous to give them in South Carolina, where slaves outnumber whites two to one." This evening Douglas is honored by a torchlight parade estimated to be three miles long.[65]

November

6: Presidential and State Elections (*see State Affairs—1860 for further details*):

For President (6 Electoral Votes):

Abraham Lincoln/Hannibal Hamlin, *Republican*, 88,481 (57.2 percent)

Stephen A. Douglas/Herschel V. Johnson, Douglas Democrat, 65,057 (42 percent)

John C. Breckinridge/Joseph Lane, Southern Democrat, 805 (0.5 percent)

John Bell/Edward Everett, Constitutional Union, 415 (0.3 percent)[66]

For Congress:

First District: *Bradley F. Granger, Republican,* 16,987 *(52.51 percent)*; George V. N. Lathrop,

Democrat, 15,216 (47.03 percent); John Conley, 145 (0.45 percent)

Second District: *Fernando C. Beaman, Republican,* 19,173 *(60.16 percent)*; Salathiel C. Coffenberry, Democrat, 12,699 (39.84 percent)

Third District: *Francis W. Kellogg, Republican,* 29,042 *(59.04 percent)*; Thomas B. Church, Democrat, 19,970 (40.59 percent); John Bell, 182 (0.37 percent)

Fourth District: *Rowland E. Trowbridge, Republican,* 23,078 *(55.79 percent)*; Edward Thompson, Democrat, 18,287, (44.21)[67]

For Governor:

Austin Blair, *Republican*, 87,780 *(65.7 percent)*

John S. Barry, Democrat, 67,053 (43.3 percent)[68]

State House

Senate: 2 Democrats, 30 Republicans

House: 11 Democrats, 72 Republicans[69]

Michigan's Republican press is ecstatic about Lincoln's victory and the Republican triumph in the state. The *Detroit Tribune* is overjoyed and optimistic: "We have now returned from a tortuous and dangerous line of national error and iniquity," it observes, "and are again on a safe course." And Michigan's almost vote redeemed Blair's convention pledge of 25,000 votes. The *Hillsdale Standard* is more concerned with healing divisions than with crowing: "To the Democracy we can say, now that victory is ours— 'enemies in war, friends in peace.'" In contrast, the *Cass County Republican* is far less concerned with conciliation. Referring to the fact that Douglas's defeat had been ensured by Breckinridge's Southern Democratic wing, it gloated, "There is a large measure of poetic justice in the fact that the traitor has been scourged on his way to the political grave by the *cat-o'-nine tails* of the Slave Power."[70]

Michigan's Democratic reaction ranges from the crudely racist, with the *East Saginaw Courier* running racially charged cartoons captioned "Lincoln Elected! Sambo Jubilant!!" to the *Detroit Free Press*, which, like many sheets of both parties, placed Lincoln's election in the context of potential secession. "Until the government which Lincoln will administer shall commit wrongs to a State or section the only remedy for which is revolution, secession will be inexcusable rebellion"; it added that, "We would prefer that there should be a twenty years' war rather than a State should be permitted to secede" and predicted that "The ensuing few weeks will perhaps give birth to events which will mark the most extraordinary epoch in the history of free government." The *Kalamazoo Gazette* took comfort in "Assurances from high Republican sources" that "Mr. Lincoln will administer the Government on recognized constitutional principles"; the sheet promises to be fair: "For ourselves, we intend to maintain a hopeful, indulgent and charitable spirit until we see evidence that Mr. Lincoln is departing from the established interpretation of the Constitution."[71]

December

4: The U.S. House establishes the Committee of Thirty-Three[72] intended to settle the secession crisis. Michigan's representative is retiring Republican Congressman William A. Howard. (See January 14, 1861.)[73]

12: Lewis Cass resigns as secretary of state. He writes Buchanan that "In some points, which I deem of vital importance, it has been my misfortune to differ from you. It has been my decided opinion, which for sometime past, I have urged at various meetings of the Cabinet that additional troops should be sent to reinforce the forts in the harbor of Charleston. . . . I have likewise urged the expedience of immediately removing from the Custom House at Charleston to one of the forts in the port, and of making arrangements for the collection of duties there" by having an officer posted at this fort. By one account, Cass' action meets with "universal approval" in Michigan.[74]

17: Auction of U.S. Treasury notes fails, with no bidders below 12 percent interest.[75]

18: The Senate appoints a Committee of Thirteen to attempt to resolve the sectional crisis. No Michigan senators are appointed. (See December 28.)

Separately, Kentucky senator John J. Crittenden proposes six constitutional amendments. First, that the 36° 30□ line be recognized, with slave states south of that line and free states north of it. Second, that "Congress shall have no power to abolish Slavery in States permitting Slavery." Third, that Congress would not abolish slavery in the District of Columbia or prohibit federal officers and employees required to work in the District from bringing slaves there. Fourth, that Congress would not "hinder the transportation of slaves from one State to another,

whether by land, navigable rivers or sea." Fifth, if fugitive slaves are "rescued" by violence or otherwise, Congress will compensate the owner and sue the county where the rescue occurred for damages. Finally, "Congress shall never have power to interfere with Slavery in the States where it is now permitted."[76]

20: South Carolina secedes. The state convention declaring secession issues the "Declaration of the Immediate Causes which Induce and Justify the Secession of South Carolina from the Federal Union," and it will name Michigan and fourteen other states which "have enacted laws which either nullify the Acts of Congress [i.e., in particular the Fugitive Slave Act] or render useless any attempt to execute them."[77]

21: In New York City at Governor Edwin D. Morgan's request, five other Northern governors (but not outgoing Michigan Governor Moses Wisner) meet in a private conference arranged by Thurlow Weed. "No persons except Governors will be present," Morgan writes Maine governor Israel Washburn. At this conference, Morgan urges conciliation, including repeal of the Northern states' personal liberty laws. Unlike many Northern states, the Michigan legislature will not comply.[78]

24: South Carolina's Declaration of Independence includes Michigan as one of fourteen states refusing to enforce the Fugitive Slave Law.[79]

26: Major Robert Anderson transfers command from Fort Moultrie to Fort Sumter, Charleston Harbor, South Carolina. From Washington, Senator Kinsley Bingham encourages Lincoln to nominate Jacob M. Howard for U.S. AG. He has not only served as Michigan's AG for six years, but "is a lawyer of great ability and distinction" and "a man of industry, and application, of Courage and nerve and patriotism."[80]

28: The Senate Committee of Thirteen fails to agree on compromise measures.[81]

29: As the year winds down, the news depresses friends of the Union of both parties. The *Detroit Free Press* pleads with Republican legislators to compromise their position on territorial slavery for the sake of Union. But the headlines describe confrontations, not compromise: "The South Carolina Commissioners Demand Major Anderson's Return to Fort Moultrie . . . The Florida Delegates for Immediate Secession . . . A Conflict Considered Inevitable."[82]

31: John B. Floyd, former Virginia governor and future

Confederate general, is replaced as secretary of war by Joseph Holt[83] ad interim. (See January 3 and 18, 1861.)[84]

State Affairs

1860 Election: Detroit, long a Democratic pocket, gave Republicans a virtual sweep of federal, state, and local offices. Lincoln garnered 4,407 votes to Douglas's 3,893; Austin Blair triumphed over John Barry, 4,406 to 4,046. Republican Bradley F. Granger★ was sent to Congress and Republican Mark Flanigan to the sheriff's office Detroit also elected Republicans to the probate court and as county clerk, register of deeds, country treasurer, county surveyor, coroner, and prosecuting attorney. Republicans also won three of four state senator races and three of four state house races.[85]

On February 14, 1859, "An Act to provide a military fund in aid of the volunteer uniformed militia" was passed that appropriated $3,000 annually "for military purposes." This money was to be distributed among the small number of volunteer, uniformed militia (as distinct from enrolled militia, that is, all Michigan men between the ages of eighteen and forty-five deemed "militia" by the legally required enrollment). But this appropriation was minute compared to actual militia requirements. The funds were appropriated for a maximum of forty companies—the equivalent of four full regiments. When war came, the estimated cost to stand up *one* regiment would be $69,020 (see State Military Affairs—1861).[86]

By early 1861, departing Governor Moses Wisner declared that "This law has had good effect," and certainly misspoke when he noted that in January 1861, Michigan could boast of forty companies. In fact, the number was twenty-eight, and the aggregate forces were 1,241 men. State AG Frederick W. Curtenius estimated that Michigan's "enrolled militia"—able-bodied civilian males eighteen to forty-five years old—numbered approximately 110,000.[87]

In November 1859, the Detroit Arsenal inventory claimed 346 .69-caliber smooth and 100 .58-caliber rifled muskets, for a total of 446 long arms. Of the twenty-one federal arsenals listed, Detroit's accounted for 0.007 percent of the nation's 610,262 rifles and muskets in federal storage.[88]

On February 25, 1862, as required by U.S. law (Act of March 2, 1803), Secretary of War Stanton reported to the U.S. House that militia strength for all states and territories—on paper—was 3,214,310 males. Michigan's last militia report was on December 1, 1858, and claimed 112,632 enrolled men consisting of 111,773 NCOs and privates and 859 officers. By service arm, this number presumably included a claimed 1,787 cavalrymen, 580 artillerymen, and 2,714 infantry. Michigan's total enrollment was 3.5 percent of the national total.[89]

During 1860, Michigan received from all sources $692,482.23; added to 1859's cash surplus ($163,577.22), the state had $856,059.45 in available cash. The total amount expended was $721,437.57, which left a surplus of $125,618.02; when added to miscellaneous income, this provided a cash surplus at the start of 1861 of $134,621.88. State debt as of December 10, 1860, was $2,006,177.63. Converted into 2019 dollars, the equivalent debt today would be $60,919,590.[90]

1861

Key Events

January

1: Outgoing Governor Moses Wisner delivers valedictory speech (see Selected Legislation—1861). Meanwhile, Michigan newspapers weigh in on the New Year's prospects. The Republican sheet *Hillsdale Standard* seems to dismiss South Carolina's secession. "If then Carolina has made up her mind she *must and will* secede from the Union, *let her go, and let her rip!* Shut the door." The state's chief Democratic organ, the *Detroit Free Press*, adopts a graver tone: "Revolution is now a FACT," its editorial opens, and it predicts that "The Union cannot fall without a great struggle." The *Free Press* reminds its readers that "We are now, as we have always been, opposed to secession." But hope remains: "We wish to arouse [the people]—to induce them to discussion—to survey of the causes of difficulty—to action—peaceful, manly patriotic action, for the preservation of their own property and the integrity of their native land." But the next day's *St. Joseph Traveler* understands the case differently: South Carolina has acted alone and alone will bear the consequences; the editor warns, "when the curtain falls, it will be rung down by the hand of Union, and upon a scene such as the world will not care often to witness." To Ann Arbor's Republican sheet, *Michigan State News*, the news is even less hopeful: "look for a civil war."[1]

2: Blair is inaugurated as governor. His inaugural speech includes remarks on secession. "If South Carolina may of right secede, then may also New York and Louisiana, thus cutting off the free right of way, of the entire North-west to the ocean, in both directions. The doctrine cannot be admitted. Self-preservation, if no other reason, would compel us to resist it. . . . The Union must be preserved and the laws must be enforced in all parts of [the Union] at whatever cost."[2]

3: Meanwhile, in Washington, secretary of war ad interim Joseph Holt discloses what ordnance has been sent Michigan since January 1, 1860. Distributions from federal arsenals include 160 .58-caliber muskets and 50 cavalry sabers.[3]

4: On December 14, 1860, President James Buchanan had declared today a national day of fasting, and his reasons included the sharp economic decline being caused by secession. "The Union of the States is at the present moment threatened with alarming immediate danger" and "panic and distress of fearful character prevail throughout the land—our laboring population are without employment," and "All classes are in a state of confusion and dismay."[4]

8: President Buchanan delivers a gloomy message to Congress, asserting that secession is illegal but denying that he has any constitutional power to avert it. The matter is for Congress to decide. He urges constitutional amendments to resolve sectional differences and reserves the use of force to protect federal property and defend federal officers executing their duties. Buchanan's message finds little support in Michigan. "There is no such thing as secession," the Democratic-leaning *Michigan Argus* declared. "No one State can go out of the Union without the consent of the other, and disunion must be accomplished by means awful to contemplate," adding that the message "failed to satisfy anybody in Congress or out." The *Lansing State Republican* was more generous, crediting Buchanan with a "moderate amount of good intentions."

In a rebuke to the president, the next day Michigan congressman William A. Howard would offer a resolution referring Buchanan's message to a special five-member committee tasked with learning whether Buchanan has any undisclosed communications or negotiations about the status of Fort Sumter, other public properties, the decision to send/withhold reinforcements to any fort, and other matters. Howard's resolution carries, 133 to 62.[5]

9: *Star of the West*, bearing supplies for Fort Sumter, is fired on as it approaches Charleston Harbor.

Meanwhile, the Mississippi state convention votes to secede and part of the southeastern bank of the Mississippi River takes itself out of the Union.[6]

10: Florida secedes. In Louisiana, troops seize Fort Jackson and Fort St. Philip below New Orleans. Meanwhile, Colonel Dwight Avery Woodbury* writes Blair to offer the services of the Third Regiment, Michigan Militia "to aid in enforcing the laws and suppressing rebellion."[7]

11: Alabama secedes.

13: Vicksburg's bluff battery fires on the civilian steamer *A. O. Tyler* of Cincinnati as it rounds a bend on the Mississippi River. (See February 21.)

14: The Committee of Thirty-Three submits its report. Fourteen congressmen file separate, dissenting reports or join other dissenters, and there is no consensus save for one amendment: what will become a proposal for Article Thirteen (nicknamed, "the Corwin Amendment") to the United States Constitution. (See February 27 and March 1 and 2.)[8]

18: Buchanan names Kentucky's Joseph Holt as permanent secretary of war. In a report by U.S. engineer Joseph Totten, Detroit's Fort Wayne is described as "In a condition to mount its entire armament but deficient in quarters."[9]

19: Georgia secedes.

20: With fewer Southerners left in Congress, Republicans pass the Morrill Tariff Act.

21: Secretary of War Joseph Holt gives Congress an inventory of weapons and garrison strength for U.S. forts and arsenals for most states. The Detroit Arsenal is listed with a six-man garrison. Separately, U.S. senators from Florida and Alabama and Mississippi's Jefferson Davis resign from the Senate. The Senate votes 36 to 16 to admit Kansas as a free state.[10]

22: In Michigan's House, a petition is presented asking that "your Honorable Body pass a law granting the colored people the elective franchise in common with the white citizens of this State." It is referred to the Judiciary Committee without result.[11]

25: The Louisiana Convention votes to secede and the lower eastern bank of the Mississippi River is lost to the Union.

26: Blair sends to Michigan's Senate the resolutions of Virginia's General Assembly inviting all states to a peace conference to convene in Washington on February 4. (See January 31 and February 1.) The resolutions are referred to a special committee. Separately, Louisiana secedes and the Mississippi River's lower east and west banks leave the Union.

Separately, the *Free Press* ponders the implications of Republican control of the state legislature, dwelling on what it sees as the contradiction between resolutions asking for preservation of the Union while it refuses to repeal the state's personal liberty law. The *Free Press* issues a warning that it will soon have reason to regret: "if troops shall be raised in the North to march against the people of the South, *a fire in the rear shall be opened upon such troops which will either stop their march altogether or wonderfully accelerate it.*"[12]

In Ann Arbor a colored convention convenes for two days. Among its actions is a petition to Michigan's legislature "praying for the preservation, in full force, of whatever laws for the protection of personal liberty, that are now found on the statue books of this State."[13]

31: The Michigan Senate's special committee reports on Virginia's resolution for a peace conference. Among its conclusions is that the committee should "unhesitatingly express their belief that the people of this State should not and would not consent to any compromise with the slave States which allowed or favored the extension of African slavery into any of the common territories of the nation, to say nothing of granting the further compromises and demands therein contained." (See February 1.)[14]

February

1: By a 16 to 15 vote, Michigan's Senate refuses to approve a resolution authorizing peace commissioners to the February 4 Peace Conference. Also, Blair signs a resolution "That Michigan adheres to the government as ordained by the Constitution, and for sustaining it intact hereby pledges and tenders to the general government all its military power and material resources." (See February 2 and Selected Legislation—1861.)[15]

Separately, Texas secedes.

2: By a vote of 35 to 26, Michigan's House votes to postpone indefinitely consideration of a measure to send peace commissioners to the Peace Conference.[16]

4: The Peace Conference convenes at Willard's Hotel in Washington. (See February 11 and 14.) Separately, seceded state delegates meet in Montgomery, Alabama.

7: Michigan's State Democratic Convention meets in Detroit to nominate a candidate for the state supreme court, the only statewide office on 1861's ballot. The resolutions adopted include the party's pledge of loyalty to the Constitution; a call to set aside sectarian differences and unite to conciliate all sections; a call for mutual respect among the sections; that secession is unconstitutional and that all sections should remove any grievances felt by others; that coercion means "civil war," and urges conciliation; an endorsement of the Crittenden proposals;[17] a call to repeal all personal liberty bills ("unworthy of ourselves or our State"); and an endorsement of the Peace Conference.[18]

8: In a lengthy report argued almost entirely from current statutes, state and federal constitutions, and case law, a majority of the House Judiciary Committee recommend against repealing any section of the state's personal liberty laws.[19]

Tennessee voters reject secession, 67,360 to 54,156. But in Montgomery, a Confederate Provisional Constitution is approved.[20]

9: From Washington, Senators Chandler and Bingham, at the request of "Massachusetts and New York" (persons not specified), wire Blair, urging him to send delegates to the Peace Conference. (See February 11 and 15.) In Montgomery, Jefferson Davis is elected president and Alexander Stephens vice president of the provisional Confederate government.

11: Senator Chandler writes again to Blair and urges him to send peace commissioners to the Peace Conference. But his motives have little to with compromising with slave states; instead, Chandler believes that any compromise on territorial slavery will damage Republicans. With a sense of vindication, he informs Blair that other Northern commissioners "admit that we were right and they were wrong; that no Republican State should have sent delegates," adding, "but they are here and cannot get away." He notes with alarm that "Ohio, Indiana and Rhode Island are caving in, and there is danger of Illinois; and now [Massachusetts and New York] beg of us for God's sake to come to their rescue, and save the Republican Party from rupture." Chandler had always opposed the conference, but now, hoping to sabotage any compromise, offers some advice ("I hope you will send *stiff-backed* men or none") followed by

a postscript soon to become famous: "Some of the manufacturing states think a fight would be awful. Without a little blood-letting, this Union will not, in my estimation, be worth a rush." (See February 14, 15, and 27.) The letter earns Chandler a nickname: "The Blood-letter."[21]

14: Convinced by Chandler, Blair (who receives another wire from Michigan's two senators) sends a message to the legislature to name commissioners to the Peace Conference. He transmits the resolutions from New York and Indiana appointing commissioners, and asserts that "it has seemed to me that the circumstances affecting the propriety of sending the commissioners are so far changed as to justify a further consideration of the question." He also discloses that several Michigan congressmen have told him to send commissioners, "with credit to herself and benefit to the whole country." If the commissioners arrive in Washington by February 20 there would still be time to participate in the conference.[22]

15: From Washington, Senator Bingham writes Blair, notes his initial opposition to the Peace Conference, and is pleased that Michigan's legislature refused to send commissioners. But his views have changed, and for reasons similar to those noted in Chandler's February 11 letter. Commissioners should be sent to prevent any compromise "to avert the lasting disgrace which will attach to a free people who, by the peaceful exercise of the ballot, have just released themselves from the tyranny of slavery, if they should now succumb to treasonable threats, and again submit to a degrading thralldom."[23]

21: Meanwhile, the Michigan Republican State Convention meets in Detroit, and the resolutions include one "favoring the maintenance of the Constitution without compromise."[24]

Separately, the Confederate Congress passes an act promising that "the peaceful navigation of the Mississippi River is hereby declared free to the citizens of any of the States upon its borders, or upon the borders of its navigable tributaries." This law is an effort to reassure Northern states that bordered either the Mississippi River (Minnesota, Wisconsin, Iowa, Illinois, Tennessee, and Missouri) or its important tributaries: Ohio (the Ohio River), Indiana (the Ohio and the Wabash Rivers), Iowa (the Iowa and Des Moines Rivers), and Wisconsin (the Wisconsin River).[25]

27: Michigan's Committee of Thirty-Three representative, William A. Howard, votes in favor of the committee's declaratory resolutions, which include denouncing state attempts to frustrate the Fugitive Slave Act; asking states to revise conflicting laws, and affirming that Congress has no authority to interfere with slavery in the states. Howard also favors the Corwin Amendment (introduced by Ohio Congressman Thomas Corwin[26]) and votes against calling a constitutional convention. (See February 28 and March 2.) Separately, in the Senate, colorful Kentucky senator Lazarus W. Powell, a staunch Democrat, has obtained copies of Chandler's correspondence with Blair on the subject of the Peace Conference. (See February 11.) They are read in the Senate, and Powell accuses Chandler of wanting the Peace Conference to fail. Chandler initially dismisses the letters, but then declares that their sentiment reflects the will of Michigan's people, and promises a reply. (See March 2.)[27]

The Peace Conference, to which Michigan sent no representatives, adjourns. It adopts a proposed Amendment XIII to the U.S. Constitution, which includes the prohibition of slavery north of 36°30□. It prohibits the future acquisition of territory without the agreement of a majority of senators from states permitting slavery. Congress is prohibited from legislating on slavery in any territory. Article IV, Section 2 (Fugitive Slave Clause), is reaffirmed. Foreign slave trade is prohibited, and there can be no amendment of this amendment without unanimous acceptance of the states. Finally, Congress promises to compensate slave owners obstructed from recapturing fugitive slaves.[28]

28: With W. A. Howard's approval, the Corwin Amendment passes the U.S. House and will be sent to the states for ratification as Article XIII. It reads, "No amendment shall be made to the Constitution which will authorize or give Congress the power to abolish or interfere, with any State, with the domestic institutions thereof, including that of persons held to labor or service by the laws of said State." Francis Kellogg, Henry Waldron, and Dewitt C. Leach vote against, with George B. Cooper not voting; see March 2.[29]

Meanwhile, in Jefferson City, Missouri, a state convention convenes to debate secession.

March

1: Michigan's Committee of Thirty-Three representative Howard votes to table a bill admitting a new state of New Mexico "with or without slavery"; he supports amending the Fugitive Slave Act to heighten due process in determining if fugitive slaves are in fact slaves (with the right of appeal) and to excuse citizens from any duty to assist in apprehending fugitive slaves; and he votes against allowing the extradition of persons charged by a state with treason.[30]

2: The Corwin Amendment passes the U.S. Senate and will be sent to the states for ratification as Article XIII. It reads: "no amendment shall be made to the Constitution which will authorize or give Congress the power to abolish or interfere, with any State, with the domestic institutions thereof, including that of persons held to labor or service by the laws of said State." It passed the House on February 28 (with Howard voting yes; Francis Kellogg, Henry Waldron, and Dewitt C. Leach voting no; and George B. Cooper with no recorded vote); on this day it passes the Senate (with both Chandler and Bingham voting no).[31]

Meanwhile, in the U.S. Senate Chandler spars with Kentucky's Lazarus W. Powell about his February 11 correspondence with Blair. Chandler defends his remark ("a little blood-letting") by quoting Jefferson on refreshing the tree of liberty with patriots' blood[32]; Chandler then delivers a thundering speech invoking Washington and Jackson, denouncing corruption in the Buchanan administration and the Democratic Party, and concluding with this judgment on the Peace Conference: "when traitorous States come here and say, unless you yield this or that established principle of right, we will dissolve the Union, I would answer, in brief words: no concession, no compromise—ay, give us strife even to blood—before yielding to the demands of traitorous insolence."[33]

4: Lincoln inaugurated. The U.S. Senate briefly convenes. In Michigan, the *Detroit Free Press* is critical of Lincoln's Inaugural Address, concluding that from "the temper" of the speech, "We shall have the secession of the border slave States and war." But after several days' reflection, the sheet softens its views. The speech was, it later believes, "a war paper or a peace paper, as the reader shall construe it," and it hopes that the "border slave States" will "be able to make a peace paper of it." From Ann Arbor, the Democratic *Michigan Argus* is more favorable. While not endorsing all of Lincoln's suggestions, it declares "The Inaugural appeals to all Union loving men, North and South, to stand by the Union, and we hope, sincerely hope, that this appeal will meet a proper response." To the *Cass County Republican*, the speech "meets the highest expectations of all parties both in point of statesmanship and patriotism." The *East Saginaw Courier* seems to split all differences. The address was "a peculiar document and is applauded, condemned, denominated manly, statesman-like, firm, wishy-washy, warlike, judicious, silly, sensible, or flat, according to the temper of those who critisise [sic] it."[34]

5: Lincoln's Inaugural Address reaches Lansing during the afternoon. "It had been looked for by all parties with intense anxiety," the *Lansing State Republican* reports, reflecting concern that the inauguration risked being disrupted by a riot or coup. In Capitol Square, the German Artillery Corps fired off thirty-four salutes as the address was read in Michigan's Republican-dominated House and Senate. "Senators and Representatives rejoiced with great joy at the glad tidings of the peaceful inauguration," and the sheet assured its readers that "The people will rally around the leader of their choice, and will aid him in enforcing the laws, maintaining the plighted faith of the States and the binding authority of the Constitution."

In Washington, Zachariah Chandler leads a "150-strong" Michigan delegation to pay "a visit of respect" to President Lincoln.[35]

15: Blair appoints John Robertson as state adjutant general, with the rank of brigadier general.[36]

16: The regular session of the Michigan legislature adjourns.[37]

April

1: Blair appoints Jabez H. Fountain* Michigan's Quartermaster General. (See November 1, 1862.)[38]

3: Lieutenant Governor James Birney resigns.[39]

12: Fort Sumter attacked; among its defenders is Michigander and second lieutenant Norman J. Hall*, future colonel of the Seventh Michigan.

Meanwhile, back in Detroit at around midnight, a volunteer black militia "armed with muskets and bayonets and fully uniformed, paraded the streets . . . preceded by a full brass band." The *Detroit Free Press*

declares that "It is the first time in our knowledge than an armed organization of such a character was ever seen in the streets of Detroit." In fact, in May 1860, led by Obadiah C. Wood*, thirty-five black Detroit men had founded the unit. Because Michigan prohibited blacks in militia service, the Guards was independent, armed, and uniformed at its own expense. The Guards pledged to fight for the Union, "relying on the magnanimity of the American people to render us those rights, privileges, and protections which the Declaration of Independence, the Constitution, and the laws of the government extend to, and should be extended to all men!" Within several days, Blair would refuse the offer of its service.[40]

13: This morning in Detroit, readers of the *Free Press* awake to the headlines, "War! War! War!" and "The Blow At Last Fallen."

In Hillsdale, the *Hillsdale Democrat* speaks for most Michigan Democrats when it predicts "every democrat will feel his imperative duty, as an American citizen and patriot, to help sustain our present Government against its common enemy."[41]

14: Surrender ceremonies at Fort Sumter.

15: Lincoln calls for 75,000 state militia. In a separate message, Secretary of War Simon Cameron informs Blair that Michigan's quota will be one regiment with 37 officers and 743 men for a total of 780. Detroit is designated as the rendezvous for Michigan's troops. Blair receives Lincoln's telegram tonight.[42] AG Lorenzo Thomas issues SO No. 106, assigning Regular Army officers to the different states to muster troops into service. Colonel Electus Backus will be assigned under this order as chief mustering and disbursing officer.

Meanwhile, at the Detroit Board of Trade, "no business [is] transacted" because of "the high state of feeling and excitement at the threatening aspect of national affairs," but a resolution is adopted, declaring "That it is the duty of all citizens of the Federal government to give the administration their united support in maintaining the supremacy of the American flag and repelling the insults upon the same."[43]

Today and in the days that follow, patriotic, prowar rallies occur across Michigan. In Jackson Hall in Jackson, "a large Union meeting" assembles with James C. Wood* presiding, Blair attending, and an estimated 3,000 people gathered. After some speeches, "a tramping was heard upon the stairs and the Jackson Grays, some fifty men led by Captain William H. Withington*, pushed their way through the dense crowd and formed in front of the platform." Withington offers Blair the unit's services, to which the governor replies by reading Cameron's telegram requisitioning troops; he then accepts Withington's offer on the spot.

Luce Hall in Grand Rapids, which could accommodate 1,000 people, is filled beyond capacity as patriotic speeches are given expressing outrage at secessionists, promising vengeance and pledging loyalty to the Constitution and Lincoln.

In Adrian, Democrats and Republicans unite in Bidwell Hall to hear town founder Addison Comstock urge defending the country; Bidwell is filled to capacity with "hundreds of people outside . . . wanting to hear the speeches"; the meeting adjourns to an outside balcony, where Dwight A. Woodbury promises to lead local militia and crush the rebellion. In Ann Arbor, the courthouse bell rings, signaling important news, as the events in Charleston Harbor are announced; this afternoon, the bell rings again, a crowd assembles, and a meeting takes place, chaired by University of Michigan President Henry Tappan and Elihu B. Pond, editor of the Democratic-leaning *Michigan Argus*. A committee is formed to begin drilling males of military age into military units. In St. Joseph, news of Sumter is only received tonight. The *St. Joseph's Traveler* remarks, "We are not advocates of war. We hate and loathe the principle"; yet the sheet adds that if war is the only way to preserve the government's integrity, rebuke "treason and rebellion," and preserve national peace and prosperity, "then let it come."

At some point on this night or early the next day, Blair departs for Detroit.[44]

16: Governor Blair arrives in Detroit and immediately receives "a large number of . . . citizens" at H. M. Whittelsey's (of the Detroit Light Guard) offices in the Michigan Exchange Building. A formal meeting is quickly organized by Henry P. Bridge*, chair, with James E. Pittman as secretary. Because the legislature has not appropriated funds to equip troops, the money must be raised privately. The meeting endorses a resolution that "a loan of $100,000 to the State of Michigan will be necessary for military purposes;

that the citizens of Detroit pledge one half of that amount, and ask their fellow-citizens in other towns of the State to take immediate steps for raising the balance." Two committees are then appointed. The first consists of Bridge, Duncan Stewart*, Henry P. Baldwin*, John Owen, Anthony Dudgeon*, Charles I. Walker*, and Detroit mayor Christian H. Buhl.* It raises $15,000 in pledges on the spot. The second committee is mostly military men and is intended to produce the regiment requisitioned yesterday. Besides Pittman, its members include men destined for state or national service: state AG Robertson, future colonel USV William D. Wilkins*, future brevet brigadier generals Henry L. Chipman and Henry M. Whittelsey, and future generals Alpheus S. Williams and Orlando B. Willcox. The two largest individual contributions are $3,000 each from Lewis Cass and Henry A. Hayden* of Jackson.[45]

Just after the meeting adjourns, Governor Blair issues his first proclamation of the war. He notes both Lincoln's proclamation and that existing Michigan law authorizes up to two regiments for federal service; the law also requires that the first recruits be drawn from existing uniformed volunteer companies. Blair invites these companies to apply to Robertson and authorizes the AG to select ten from the applicants, all for U.S. muster for three months. (See April 24.) Companies will include one captain, one first and one second lieutenant, four sergeants, four corporals, two musicians, and sixty-five privates. Hardee's *Tactics* will govern instruction. Companies "not immediately required will be formed into one or more additional regiments, as the exigencies of the service may demand." Finally, Blair declares that "It is confidently expected that the patriotic citizen-soldiery of Michigan will promptly come forward to enlist in the cause of the Union, against which an extensive rebellion in arms exists, threatening the integrity and perpetuity of the government."[46]

On this or the previous night, Detroit's African Americans meet at the Second Baptist Church, pledge support for the Union, and resolve "to sacrifice and repel any invasion 'at all hazards and to the last extremity.'" (See July 24, 1863.)[47]

At night, pro-Union rallies occur in Kalamazoo, Adrian, and elsewhere.[48]

Meanwhile, Cameron wires Blair an important

addition to yesterday's note: Michigan does not have to produce its quota until May 20.[49]

17: In Detroit this morning, "a large crowd, who blocked up the street on both sides," witnesses the president of the Detroit Board of Trade raise the Stars and Stripes (also inscribed with the words, "Detroit Board of Trade—the Stars and Stripes Forever") over the Board of Trade. Speakers include future Mayor Duncan, Zachariah Chandler, and Lewis Cass ("I was born under [the national flag], and have lived under it, and I hope that the last hour that comes to all may come to me before its stars are diminished in number."). Militia units offer their services and money is raised for volunteers.[50]

Meanwhile, Senator Chandler offers Cameron advice and reassurance. The advice is from "One of the most distinguished Democrats in the country" (which just happens to align with Chandler's own hard war policy that he will hold throughout the war): "Don't defend Washington. Don't establish batteries on Georgetown Heights. March your troops into Virginia. Quarter them there. Stand by the Union men there, and you will find plenty of them. By this bold policy you will save the border States." Chandler is also certain about Michigan's commitment. "We will furnish you with the regiments in thirty days if you want them and 50,000 men if you need them." He adds that General Lewis Cass has personally contributed $3,000 to equip units, and as for the state's morale, "There are no [Southern] sympathizers here worth hunting, and if there were, our population would diminish to the extent of their numbers forthwith."

While Chandler talks of men, the *Lansing State Republican* addresses available means and hard realities: "Michigan has no money. She has no arms—hardly a musket, no accouterments . . . no blankets, tents, powder or ball." The answer, according the sheet, lies in finances: $100,000 is required to stand up the one regiment called, and this sum must be found. Issuing warrants is impractical because the treasury has no money. But the sheet makes a novel legal argument: the legislature is not in session but the state should issue the bonds: "If the President has the power to call for a force from the State of Michigan . . . [Michigan's] power to raise money to put that force in the field is one of direct and irresistible implication."[51]

Separately, the Virginia state convention votes to secede subject to voter approval. (See May 23.) From Montgomery, Jefferson Davis invites applications for letters of marque.[52]

Meanwhile, the Virginia state convention endorses secession.

18: In Dowagiac at Larzelere's Hall tonight, "a large and enthusiastic Union Meeting, without distinction of party" convenes. Thirty men enroll in a volunteer company; in two days, the company will be full.[53]

19: Blair writes Cameron to offer more men than required under Michigan's federal call. (See April 26.) The three-month First Michigan is armed, equipped, and prepared for federal muster. (See May 1 and 13.) In Ann Arbor, another meeting is held where $4,500 is raised to redeem Governor Blair's April 17 call for $100,000.[54]

The Sixth Massachusetts is attacked in Baltimore by a prosecessionist mob. (See SAW.4.290–296.) Separately, Lincoln proclaims a blockade of Southern ports.[55]

Meanwhile, tonight in Lansing, "an enthusiastic meeting" is held in Representative Hall, Dewitt Clinton Leach presiding. Resolutions are adopted declaring unity ("irrespective of party") to support the government, and that "we will support the families of those among us who may enlist in the service of their country." (See April 23.) Talk of setting party aside is mentioned here and in other speeches. But there are limits; a staunch Republican, Leach declares tonight that "there will be but one party in the North, and that will be a Union party.—If there is any other party it will be a Tory party."[56]

20: AG Robertson informs Senator Chandler (now in Detroit) that Blair has ordered out two regiments although the April 15 call only requisitioned one. "Will you please use your influence with the War Department, so that both regiments may be received as a brigade, and to have the necessary instructions issued to the Governor to that effect?" Robertson asks. (See the next day.) Meanwhile, Robertson publicly assures the state that the two regiments called by Blair "will be enrolled and ready for orders in a few days," and that "The volunteer uniformed militia of the State have responded nobly to the call"; based on information received in Detroit, "Michigan is good for the fulfillment of any requisition to support the Federal Government."[57]

Meanwhile at a mass meeting in Detroit, Judge Ross Wilkins* administers a loyalty oath to federal, state, and local government employees as well as military personnel.[58]

In Hillsdale, what is claimed to be the largest meeting in county history convenes; a committee is formed to draft resolutions, one of which pledges that Hillsdale County "tenders to the State authorities its full quota of men and money"; former congressman Henry Waldron then speaks. "He said he knew no party but a Union party, no platform but the Constitution." In Grand Haven, a Union meeting convenes tonight at the courthouse; chaired by Rev. William M. Ferry, the father of Congressman Thomas W. Ferry (who also is present); funds are raised to equip local volunteers, and the "Star-Spangled Banner" is sung. Rallies at Northville, Eaton Rapids, Pontiac, Mt. Clemens, and Hudson are also reported. In Detroit, AG Robertson has already established his headquarters "over the store of Oliver Bourke, 122 Jefferson Avenue"; the *Free Press* reports that, "His office is thronged daily with military men from all parts of the State."[59]

21: Chandler forwards to Cameron the previous day's wire from Robertson, and adds some details. Of the two units called, "One is full and ready to march at a moment's notice," but it requires uniforms and equipments. The other regiment will be ready "in two or three days." Moreover, "a large number of full companies not yet organized into regiments" exist, and Chandler makes his pitch: "I will esteem it a very great favor if you will officially call for at least four more regiments immediately from this State." He adds that $100,000 has been raised privately and offered as a loan to the state of Michigan to facilitate equipment purchases. (See entry for April 29 for Cameron's reply.)[60]

Illinois troops occupy Cairo, Illinois.

22: A letter signed, "A Soldier's Wife" appears in a Detroit newspaper. While the writer notes that "Our prayers and our hearts go with our brave volunteers," she also asks some questions: "[C]an we not at the same time add our works to their comfort? . . . . Cannot we, the women of Detroit concert some plan by which lint and surgeon's bandages can be prepared by us?" (See May 12.)

This afternoon in East Saginaw, an "Immense Union Demonstration" gathers whose purpose is to "co-operate with other portions of the State in furnishing men and means to sustain the Government in its present emergency." A meeting is organized, chaired by Colonel W. L. P. Little, and resolutions are unanimously adopted: Although the meeting convenes in the name of "we the People of Saginaw county, without distinction of party," another resolution retains the right to "political divisions among the people [that] are solely with reference to the policy by which the government should shape its actions" (see April 24); secession is denounced as "a dangerous heresy"; and pledges are made "to sustain the families of such as go forth to maintain the flag of our country"; $2,000 is pledged on this day.[61]

23: Blair issues a proclamation convoking an Extra Session of the Legislature at Lansing on May 7. It is necessary because, "in order that the whole military power of the State may be made available and sufficient means furnished for arming and equipping the force to be used in defence of the constitutional rights and liberties of the people, and in the preservation of the government of the United States from destruction, and that the insulted majesty of the nation may be fully vindicated."[62] Meanwhile, in a move that will have profound consequences for some Michigan women, Simon Cameron declares that the War Department will accept "the free services" of "Miss D. L. Dix" and that "she will give at all times all necessary aid in organizing military hospitals for the care of all sick or wounded soldiers, aiding the chief surgeons by providing nurses and substantial means for the comfort and relief of the suffering." Dix is also authorized "to receive, control and disburse special supplies" given her by private parties for "the comfort of their friends or the citizen soldiers from all parts of the United States." (See May 12 and 20.)[63]

In Lansing, a second Union meeting convenes at night, with A. N. Hart presiding. Speakers include Kingsley Bingham, George W. Peck, H. H. Smith, and Colonel Alpheus Williams. The resolution pledging family aid is reaffirmed and a committee appointed to solicit subscriptions.[64]

24: AG Robertson issues GO No. 5 to organize Michigan's first contribution to the war. Alpheus S. Williams is appointed state brigadier general of the First Brigade Michigan Infantry and officers are appointed to the First Michigan Regiment (ninety days): Willcox is colonel, Lorin L. Comstock is lieutenant colonel, and Alonzo F. Bidwell* is major. Selected for the First's ten companies are the Detroit Light Guard, Jackson Greys, Coldwater Cadets, Manchester Union Guard, Steuben Guard, Michigan Hussars, Burr Oak Guard, Ypsilanti Light Guard, Marshall Light Guard, and the Hardee Cadets. All companies will report at Detroit, and the state QMG is directed to obtain their uniforms and to order "the necessary guns, caissons, harness, sabres, and other equipments"; railroads have agreed to transport troops, arms, horses, and ammunition free of charge. Once enough companies have reported for the First, a second infantry regiment will be formed.

Meanwhile, the *Free Press* runs two editorials, the first of which declares, *"Whatever is necessary to conduct the war expeditiously and successfully must be done"*; but a second column suggests that necessity will not include cooperating with "black republicanism" in every event. "The democratic party are not willing to see the flag of Union trailed in the dust. But in thus standing by and protecting that flag, we by no means, nor does the democratic party, approve of the administration of Mr. Lincoln."[65]

25: AG Robertson issues GO No. 6, organizing the Second Michigan as a three-month unit whose companies consist of the Scott Guard, Adrian Guard, Hudson Artillery (now infantry), Flint Union Guard, Battle Creek Artillery (also infantry), Constantine Union Guard, East Saginaw Guard, Kalamazoo Light Guard, Kalamazoo No. 2, and the Niles Company. Colonel Israel B. Richardson* commands the regiment. (But see May 25.)

The fiercely Democratic *East Saginaw Courier*, echoing the political unanimity across Michigan, declares "there is no middle ground in the contest" and that "there is but one course and that is to stand by the flag of our country, the glorious 'stars and stripes' 'without a why or wherefore,' and that is where we stand."[66]

In the midst of this patriotic sentiment, suspicion also grows. In a column entitled "Traitors in Cass County," the *Cass County Republican* reports that one unnamed man has declared "that he would do nothing to sustain an Abolition government; that the war belonged to Republicans and they might fight it out."

Another is quoted that he hopes that every volunteer from the county "would be the first to meet his death at the hands of the South." While the sheet does not "wish these persons any harm," it adds that "it is high time that no avowed and active sympathizer with treason should be allowed to corrupt the air of our loyal county with their pestiferous breath."[67]

26: Cameron replies to Blair's April 19 offer of additional troops: he gives "the thanks of the President and myself for your very prompt and speedy action," but "At present no further troops than those called for are needed"; however, because units are legally limited to three months under the April 15 call, "it is quite probable that a further demand may be made upon the patriotism of your people."[68]

27: George B. McClellan proposes to General Winfield Scott his strategy for the western war: centralize western command, and mount seize-and-hold operations until the northwestern states are ready to fight. This prompts Scott to do some strategic thinking of his own. (See May 2, 3, and 21.) In Ann Arbor, a taxpayer's meeting votes $5,000 in additional taxes "to aid in fitting out the volunteer Companies enrolled here, and for the support of the families of those husbands and fathers who have gone into the service of their country."[69]

29: Cameron replies to Chandler's April 21 letter asking that Washington take four more regiments. The president has decided that no more three-month regiments will be accepted; however, Lincoln has decided "to add to the Regular Army twenty-five volunteer regiments, whose members shall agree to serve for two years, unless sooner discharged." Washington is willing to accept more units if Michigan agrees to these terms.[70]

Meanwhile, the three-year Second Michigan is ready for muster. (See May 25.)[71]

May

1: At Fort Wayne, Colonel Backus musters into U.S. service the three-month 798-man First Michigan, which has been recruited from Detroit, Jackson, Coldwater, Manchester, Ann Arbor, Marshall, Adrian, and Ypsilanti. (See July 21 and August 7 for casualties.)[72]

Tennessee's legislature authorizes Governor Isham Harris to negotiate a military alliance with the Confederacy. (See May 6.)[73]

2: General Winfield Scott criticizes McClellan's April 27 plan, and proposes his own: "enveloping [seceded states] (nearly) at once by a cordon of posts on the Mississippi to its mouth from its junction with the Ohio, and by blockading ships of war on the [eastern] seaboard."[74]

3: Abraham Lincoln issues a proclamation requesting 42,034 volunteers to serve three years or the war. Separately, New York's Union Defence Committee (see SAW.2) informs the War Department that AG Robertson has reported Michigan's status as "1 regiment ready; 1 field battery, 4 guns, ready in four days; 2 regiments armed and nearly equipped; 3 regiments ready to be called—enrolled, waiting arms."[75]

Meanwhile, Blair, at Ohio governor William Dennison's invitation, is at Cleveland's Angier House Hotel for a conference of all western governors. Also attending are Pennsylvania governor Andrew G. Curtin, Indiana's Oliver P. Morton, Wisconsin's Alexander W. Randall, and Ohio militia commander General George B. McClellan. (Unable to attend are Minnesota governor Alexander Ramsey, New York governor Edwin D. Morgan, and Illinois's Richard Yates; however, the last two send representatives.)

Afterward, brief public remarks are made. Blair speaks to a crowd. "We are in the midst of war—a war of which we cannot stop to count the cost," he declares. "In the name of Michigan I promise to stand by you shoulder to shoulder, and to march beside you of Ohio, and beside them of Pennsylvania, and beside brave old Massachusetts. . . ." Blair emphasizes western states' geopolitical concerns. "We bought the mouth of the Mississippi, and we will hold it. The traitors may go into the Gulf, but they shall not take the territory with them."[76] (See May 6.)

Wisconsin's Governor Randall is delegated to convey the governors' sentiments to the Lincoln, which he will do on May 6. (See May 6 and May 7.)[77]

4: The War Department issues GO Nos. 15 and 16, specifying the size and organization of state-proffered regiments and that each regiment's company and field officers "will be appointed by the Governor of the State furnishing it." The president will appoint all general officers of the volunteer force. (See May 22.)[78]

6: Cameron notifies Blair that hereafter all enlistments should be for three years.

Arkansas secedes. In Tennessee, Governor Harris presents his legislature with the agreement to join the Confederacy. Tomorrow the legislature will vote to approve the agreement: Tennessee militia are placed under Confederate control, and on June 8 the question of secession will be submitted to a popular vote. In Knoxville, riots between pro- and antisecession factions erupt; in Kentucky, Lincoln orders "hero of Fort Sumter" Robert Anderson to begin recruiting.

Separately, Governor Randall of Wisconsin explains western governors' concerns to President Lincoln: there has been insufficient emphasis on the western theater. Washington now being safe, the federal government should shift focus. "From Pittsburg and Cincinnati to the mouth of the Ohio, on the northern side of the river, the country is almost entirely defenseless against an armed enemy." Randall declares "It is a matter of absolute necessity, not only for the Northern Border States but for all the Northwestern States, to be able to control the business and commerce of the Ohio River and the Upper Mississippi in order to reach a vital part of this rebellion." The North must hold Cairo, and the Mississippi and Ohio Rivers must be secured for Northern commerce. The war needs men and the northwest "needs a better military organization . . . without tedious and mischievous delays." This cannot wait; "immediate action" is necessary. The western region will idle as its cities are destroyed, content only with retaliation; such disasters must be prevented. The governors are dissatisfied with only "a small call of raw troops"; they want arms, training, and the recruiting of larger armies. The War Department has been particularly unresponsive to the governors on these points.[79]

7: The Extra Session of the Michigan Legislature called on April 23 convenes in Lansing.[80]

Separately, a committee from the May 3 governors' conference meets with Lincoln and "renews [their] pledge of resources and men." But Austin Blair is in Lansing, not Washington.[81]

8: In Michigan's Senate, a bill is introduced "to provide for the punishment of certain offenses against the public safety, and to define treason and sedition." (See Selected Legislation—1861 for excerpts.) The bill is referred to the Judiciary Committee, which later on this day recommends passage. Nevertheless, the next day the bill will be handily defeated, 7 yeas to 24 nays. (But see May 11.)[82]

10: The Extra Session adjourns. (See Legislative Session—1861.)[83]

Meanwhile, in St. Louis, pro-Union forces led by Nathanial Lyon[84] and Francis P. Blair, Jr., clash with prosecessionist state militia. The violence will continue for several days.

11: Cameron writes Blair to "earnestly recommend to you to call for no more than four regiments, of which only three are to serve for three years or during the war. And if more are already called for to reduce the number by discharge." (But see May 21.) Replying for Blair, Robertson informs Cameron that four Michigan regiments—a brigade, he emphasizes—are ready for U.S. muster for three years. "The Governor desires that they may be accepted as a brigade and move together, if the interests of the service will permit." Two regiments are fully equipped and two lack arms and accouterments. (See May 14 and 21.)

Separately, the *Free Press*, certainly speaking for many Michigan Democrats, praises the state legislature for having "done their duty," and declares, "Every State, so well as every man, must do their duty. No half measures now."[85]

Meanwhile, the First Michigan receives its colors on Detroit's Campus Martius.[86]

12: Cameron's April 23 order authorizing Dorothea Dix to work with army surgeons and to control privately gifted supplies is published in Detroit. Area women begin to organize: circulars containing patterns and instructions for making hospital shirts and socks are distributed to women in twenty nearby towns. Isabella Graham Duffield★ and Isabella Duffield Stewart★ take the lead in this effort. (See May 20 and June 30.)[87]

13–15: What will later be known as the First Wheeling Convention, representing some twenty-six counties whose delegates are ardently opposed to secession, convenes in Wheeling, which will later become the capital of the not-yet-formed state of West Virginia. The Convention pledges to reconvene in Wheeling on June 11 (see entry for that date) and concludes by singing the Star Spangled Banner.[88]

13: Major General George B. McClellan, Ohio Volunteer Militia, now commands the Department of the Ohio, with headquarters in Cincinnati. Separately, the three-month First Michigan departs for Washington. It will become the first regiment west of the Allegha-ny Mountains to report at the capital. Before leaving, the First forms on the Campus Martius to receive a flag from the ladies of Detroit. Each soldier is given a cockade, and Orlando B. Willcox accepts the flag. "Ever since the first drum beat of war," Willcox declares, "the ladies of Detroit have been busy contriving comforts for the soldiers." At 5:00 p.m., the steamers *Illinois* and *Mary Queen* load the unit while a band on one ship plays "The Girl I Left Behind Me." As the ships pass Detroit the sky is lit by a fireworks display.[89]

16: Cameron supplies Michigan with its quota under Lincoln's May 3 call: "Three regiments [for three years] in addition to one three-months regiment." Cameron adds this plea: "It is important to reduce rather than enlarge this number, and in no event exceed it." (Cameron is concerned about the absence of Congressional authorization and funds. See May 21.)[90]

Separately, Tennessee is admitted to the Confederacy.

Meanwhile, the First Michigan has passed through Baltimore, to the approbation of the *Baltimore Sun*. "The Michigan regiment attracted general attention and commendation by their solid appearance and well disciplined movements. It was composed almost wholly of young, steady, and intelligent looking men, and it appeared capitally officered . . . [and] exceedingly well equipped." On this night the unit arrives in Washington.[91]

17: At the White House President Lincoln and several cabinet members receive First Michigan's officers and band after the unit parades down Pennsylvania Avenue. It greatly impresses Washington journalists. "No regiment that has yet arrived has created such excitement as the Michigan First," a reporter for the *New York Tribune* notes, commenting on the men's "great pride in their appearance" and that "Michigan may well feel honored in such representatives." The *National Intelligencer* declares that "The display was a very imposing one." The band serenaded the president, who afterward commented to bandleader Professor [Henry] Kern (a "figure of conspicuous rotundity"), "Professor," he said, "you must be the biggest blower in the service."[92]

Separately, caught up in the general *rage militaire* is a Canadian-born recruit, one Franklin Thompson, who signs the rolls of Company F, Second Michigan Infantry*.

20: North Carolina secedes. In Kentucky, Governor Magoffin issues a proclamation of neutrality. Meanwhile, Acting U.S. SG Robert C. Wood,[93] noting "the national reputation of Miss [Dorothea] Dix as connected with objects of philanthropy and usefulness," authorizes her "to exercise a general supervision of the assignment of nurses to hospitals, general and regimental, occupied by the troops at Washington and its vicinity." (See June 30.)[94]

21: Cameron refuses Robertson's May 11 request that Michigan units be brigaded together. "However desirable and gratifying it would be to the regiments mustered into the U.S. service from Michigan to serve together as a brigade, the interest of the service will not permit it." The secretary encloses a copy of War Department GO No. 15 (see May 4, 1861), which controls how regiments will be organized.

Meanwhile, AG Robertson, reacting to Cameron's May 16 instructions to "reduce rather than enlarge" the number of regiments, issues GO No. 25: "the [Governor] feels obliged to decline the rendezvous of any more State troops by regiments." However, Blair will not allow Cameron's short-term concerns to overrule his sense of the war that looms, and adds that "In order, however, to prepare for any future call, and to insure at the least expense to the State an efficient corps of officers and non-commissioned officers, two additional regiments will be formed." The two regiments will eventually be enumerated the Fifth and Sixth Michigan. (See June 10.)[95]

Separately, in a letter to McClellan, Winfield Scott makes his final iteration of the Anaconda Plan. Finally, James E. Pittman is appointed paymaster of the Michigan Militia, ranked colonel.[96]

22: Cameron asks Blair to consider moral character and age in commissioning the officers under War Department GO No. 15. No one "of doubtful morals or patriotism and not of sound health should be appointed." No lieutenants older than twenty-two years should be commissioned; no captains over the age of thirty; no field officer unless a West Point graduate or "known to possess military knowledge and experience"; no major over thirty-five; no lieutenant colonel over forty and no colonel over forty-five. In general, Cameron advises, "the higher the moral character and general intelligence of the officers so appointed, the greater the efficiency of the troops and the resulting glory to their respective states."[97]

23: Virginians vote to secede. Meanwhile, Colonel Thomas A. Scott,[98] formerly of the Pennsylvania Railroad, "has been appointed to take charge of all Government railways and telegraphs or those appropriated for Government use."[99]

24: The War Department recommends that Blair choose campsites and asks that after Michigan fills its quota of three-year volunteers, the campsites be converted to camps of instruction.[100] Meanwhile at 2:00 a.m., Michigan soldiers enter enemy territory for the first time: the First Michigan crosses the Long Bridge to Alexandria and occupation duty.[101]

Separately, in Indianapolis, Governors Yates of Illinois, Morton of Indiana, and Dennison of Ohio meet and sign a memorial to Washington urging more aggressive action in Kentucky and elsewhere. Loyal Kentuckians should try to secure their state for the Union. If they cannot, then Regulars should be deployed. If Regulars cannot or will not be sent, then Indiana, Illinois, and Ohio should send troops. The governors insist on a campaign plan for the western theater and demand a unified command to implement it. They argue that McClellan's forces should be expanded; moreover, each of the three state legislatures is appropriating money for the cause and "we desire it to be understood that these appropriations will be promptly available to the [U.S.] as its necessities . . . shall require." The three governors also suggest that authority be granted for preemptive occupation of strategic points in Tennessee and Missouri.[102] (See May 29.)

25: At Fort Wayne, Colonel Backus musters into U.S. service the Second Michigan for three years. The Second will initially deploy east, serve briefly west, before returning east and reenlisting as Veteran Volunteers in December 1863. (See June 6, 1861 and June 28, 1865.) In Coldwater, Battery A of the First Michigan Light Artillery musters into U.S. service. The unit will deploy west.[103] (See June 28, 1865.)

29: General Winfield Scott responds to the Ohio, Indiana, and Illinois governors' May 6 message: first, some of the recommended steps in Kentucky have already been taken. However, Kentucky Unionists believe "that thrusting protection upon their people is likely to do more harm than good." Scott insists that the Kentuckians should be heeded. Scott also believes Regulars will not be needed because Robert Anderson is successfully raising Kentucky volunteers. As for a western plan of action, Scott refers the governors to his May 3 and May 21 letters to McClellan. (See dates.) Finally, Scott refers to a recent meeting with Yates and several senators urging the preemptive occupation of Memphis. Scott discourages this because U.S. forces are not ready and the season is not right. He also implies that the same hesitation should apply to the governors' suggestion to occupy points in Missouri.[104]

June

3: Cameron presses Blair for Michigan's requisition: "Send to [Washington] your three years' regiments as soon as organized. Report when." (See June 13.)[105]

In Western Virginia, the Battle of Philippi scatters Confederate forces.

4: Word reaches Detroit that Stephen A. Douglas is dead.

6: The Second Michigan deploys. Accompanying them is seventeen-year-old Annie Etheridge★ (nicknamed "Michigan Annie"), who will become one of the most famous nurses in the army.[106]

7: A group of Michiganders, many from Paw Paw, leave that place for New York City to enlist in what will become Company C of the Seventieth New York Infantry. The unit serves in the east.[107] (See July 7, 1864.)

8: The popular vote in Kentucky favors secession, 104,019 against 47,238. (See June 24.)[108]

10: In Grand Rapids, 1,040 Third Michigan Infantry men muster into U.S. service for three years; recruits are drawn from Grand Rapids, Saranac, Lyons, Lansing, Muskegon, and Georgetown. The unit will deploy and serve east. By war's end, total enrollment will be 1,432, including 110 KIA, 65 DOW, 15 died as POWs, 81 DOD, and 404 DFD. (See October 15, 1864.)[109]

AG Robertson issues GO No. 30, appointing officers for the Fifth and Sixth Michigan (the latter commanded by former state AG Curtenius), and appointing Ira R. Grosvenor★ as colonel of the Seventh Michigan. Officers and NCOs are ordered to Fort Wayne, designated a camp of instruction, where they will be examined by a military board. Brigadier General Alpheus Williams commands the camp.[110]

11: Delegates reconvene at Wheeling, West Virginia, for what will be called the Second Wheeling Convention; a pro-Union government is formed. (See June 19.) Meanwhile, the Battle of Rich Mountain is fought.[111]

13: Robertson informs Cameron that the Third Michigan Regiment departs on this day for Washington by rail via Cleveland, Harrisburg, and Baltimore. It is fully armed and equipped. (See June 18.) Meanwhile, almost certainly reflecting someone's influence, Lincoln informs Cameron that "I think it is entirely safe to accept a fifth regiment from Michigan"; moreover, with Cameron's approval the president declares that "a regiment presented by Col. T[homas] B. W. Stockton ready for service within two weeks from now, will be received." The president urges Cameron to "Look at Stockton's testimonials."[112]

14: Given Cameron's penchant for accepting regiments outside of governors' authority, he sends an unusual message to Blair. A regiment commanded by Stockton "has been offered to this Department for acceptance for three years or during the war." Lincoln is prepared to accept this unit "if it meets with your approbation, and if it can be got ready for service, full, thoroughly organized and uniformed within two weeks from this date." Apparently, Blair does not approve, but it makes no difference: Cameron authorizes Stockton to form a regiment. (See entry for August 24.)[113]

15: Blair writes Hiram Walbridge for assistance to lobby the War Department. "Now what I want is to be allowed to furnish four more regiments just as soon as the Government please if they will furnish the arms and if they cannot, then as soon as I can get them, which I imagine can be done in a reasonable time." (See June 20.) In Washington, Senator Chandler writes Lincoln about rebel depredations in Missouri and closes with a suggestion: "Pardon me when I say, the People of Michigan think the time has arrived to commence hanging & so think I."[114]

Meanwhile, Secretary Cameron accepts Hiram Berdan's[115] proposal to form a regiment of sharpshooters, eventually designated as the First United States Sharpshooters. Of the unit's ten companies, three will be recruited from Michigan and serve under Michigan captains. (See September 12 and 28, 1861.)[116]

Separately, in Chicago, the Twenty-Third Illinois musters into U.S. service. Raised as an Irish regiment, Company A was recruited in Detroit by fellow resident John McDermott★. (See September 20.)[117]

18: Continuing to comply with Cameron's June 3 request, Blair informs the Secretary that the Fourth Michigan is mustered into U.S. service, [*sic*, muster is June 20] "and ready to march if it has arms and accouterments. Can they be forwarded to it immediately?" (See June 20.)[118]

19: The Second Wheeling Convention unanimously adopts "An Ordinance for the Reorganization of the State Government" and names Francis H. Pierpoint governor of Virginia. The state of West Virginia will be admitted to the Union on June 20, 1863.[119]

20: In Adrian, the Fourth Infantry, which will number 1,025 in several days, musters into U.S. service; recruits are drawn from Sturgis, Adrian, Ann Arbor, Monroe, Trenton, Dexter, Hudson, Hillsdale, Jonesville, and Tecumseh. The unit will deploy and serve east. When the unit's term expires, total enrollment will be 1,399, including 124 KIA, 68 DOW, 16 died as POWs, 99 DOD, and 385 DFD.[120] (See October 14, 1864.)

Walbridge lobbies Cameron on behalf of Blair, quoting the latter's desire to provide four more regiments. He vouches for Michigan, declaring that, "Should you believe the public interest promoted by the acceptance of the regiments to which [Blair] refers, I am confident that they would be inferior to no troops in the field, and would be regarded with pleasure by him and the worthy and gallant people he represents." Meanwhile, Cameron replies to Blair's query about arms for the Fourth Michigan: he should send them to Washington via Elmira and Harrisburg. "They can be furnished with arms, &c., here or, if necessary, at Harrisburg."[121]

21: Cameron asks Blair to furnish him with a statement of "the number of regiments organized . . . in your State . . . and the number accepted by this Department not yet mustered . . . and when these will be ready to muster." Blair, through his military secretary William K. Gibson★, replies at once. Four infantry regiments have been organized and are mustered into three-year U.S. service: the First, Second, and Third are already at or en route to Washington. The Fourth will leave on June 24. In addition, Blair has raised

three regiments whose officers and NCOs are at the camp of instruction at Fort Wayne. "They are not uniformed or equipped," Gibson concedes, "but can be on short notice."[122]

24: Governor Isham Harris officially declares Tennessee out of the Union.[123]

30: In Detroit the informally organized ladies' group, led by Isabella Graham Bethune Duffield, is now organized as the Committee on Havelocks and Hospital Supplies, and makes its first report. Besides contributions from Detroit, the Committee lists supplies sent by women in Jackson, Marshall, Clinton, Pontiac, Grand Rapids, Adrian, Monroe, Niles, St. Clair, Port Huron, Clarkston, Rochester, and Troy, Michigan. (See August 20.) Mrs. Duffield publishes a letter to her from Dorothy Dix, specifying flannel shirts, yarn socks, and havelocks as being in special demand. Seventy-two shirts, twelve pair of socks, and 1,050 havelocks have been sent to the Second Michigan; 127 shirts and 47 pair of sox have been sent to Dix for the First and Third Michigan; Adrian women have sent sixty shirts and twenty-two pair of socks to the Fourth Michigan.[124]

July

4: Congress convenes. Lincoln delivers his war message. "This is essentially a People's contest," Lincoln declares, adding later that "It is now for [the people] to demonstrate to the world, that those who can fairly carry an election, can also suppress a rebellion—that ballots are the rightful, and peace, successors of bullets."[125]

5: Missouri governor Jackson's militia clash with Union forces at Carthage.

10: Battle of Big Bethel, Virginia.

11: Confederates are defeated at Rich Mountain, western Virginia.

13: Cameron issues a circular that declares, "No more troops will be received by this Department till authorized by Congress."[126]

Confederates are defeated at Corrick's Ford, western Virginia.

17: Governor Blair, in Washington to visit the state's troops, is welcomed by a fifteen-gun salute. Blair reviews the troops who "formed in columns and went through various evolutions," all to apparent satisfaction. Blair will continue visiting Michigan units before and after First Bull Run, always speaking and occasionally joined by Senator Chandler and Congressman Kellogg. Blair is less happy with Washington. "The appearance of decay is everywhere in this southern country" and of his stay at the National Hotel, he noted it was "low mean [and] dirty . . . and on the pattern of everything in Niggerdom."[127]

18: Action at Blackburn's Ford. The Second and Third Michigan are engaged and the state takes its first casualties: one enlisted man wounded from each regiment.[128]

19: War Department GO No. 45 affirms governors' appointment powers for officer vacancies. Of interest to states with large foreign-born populations (19.9 percent of Michigan's population was born outside of the U.S.), GO 45 also stipulates that "no volunteer will be mustered into the service who is unable to speak the English language."[129] (But see August 8.)

21: Battle of First Bull Run. Michigan has four units on the field. Michigan units include the First, Second, and Third Infantries. In the First Division, Colonel Israel B. Richardson commands the Fourth Brigade, which includes the Second and Third Michigan; in the Third Division, Orlando Willcox commands the Second Brigade, which includes the First and Fourth Michigan. The First Michigan suffers six dead, thirty-seven wounded, and seventy missing, most of whom are POWs, including Colonel Willcox (about whom, see August 27, 1862).[130]

On this morning in Detroit, first reports of a battle are received, heralding a victory, throwing Detroiters "into a state of the deepest excitement." But after 12:00 p.m., the news slowly changes to reflect the Federal defeat, which "for a time seemed absolutely to paralyze the thoughts of all, and as further intelligence came, each bit more sad than that preceding it, it fell like a funeral pall upon the community." Throughout the day, relatives of the First Michigan crowd into newspaper and telegraph offices. It is much the same across Michigan. "Universal gloom overspreads our community," the *Lansing State Republican* states, although it rationalizes defeat and urges those without military expertise to avoid commenting. In Dowagiac, the *Cass County Republican*'s editors declare, "That it is with deep regret that we are called upon to record the disastrous and overwhelming defeat" of Bull Run. The *East Saginaw Courier* was the

most clear-eyed. "The recent disaster to our army in Virginia, settles some fact, if they had been considered at the outset, instead of giving credence to the thousand lies in circulation," among which were "the demoralization of the Southern army, scarcity of arms and provisions, imperfect discipline, [and the] danger of negro insurrections." "War is stern, serious business, and no amount of deception or braggadocio is sufficient to weaken or damage the enemy."[131]

22: Congress enacts Chapter 9: "An Act to authorize the Employment of Volunteers to aid in enforcing the Laws and protecting Public Property," which authorizes a 500,000-man call (repeated on July 25). Chapter 9 also has provisions important to Michigan's home front: it extends to volunteers Regular army pensions (see July, 14, 1862) for wounds or disabilities incurred in service; when a soldier is killed, $100 is paid to his family. Chapter 9 also authorizes an "allotment ticket . . . by which the family of the volunteer may draw such portions of his pay as he may request."[132]

Meanwhile, at Decatur, Illinois, the Forty-Second Infantry musters into U.S. service. The unit serves west and will muster out in January, 1866. By war's end, 220 Michiganders will enroll in several companies; these include 16 KIA, 17 DOW, 3 died as POWs, 25 DOD, and 53 DFD.[133]

23: General William Rosecrans[134] assumes command of the Department of the Ohio.

25: Austin Blair is in Washington. At night, Professor Kern's First Michigan band serenades the governor, Zachariah Chandler, and Francis Kellogg of Michigan and New York congressman Charles H. Van Wyck[135] at the National Hotel. Afterward, Blair addresses "the large and enthusiastic crowd" and tries to explain recent events to Michigan's troops: "our forces were checked, not defeated at the late battle" and "they will soon be prepared for a renewal of the fight in defense of all that is dear to American freemen—the preservation of constitutional liberty." He offers praise for the new commander: "We have now here a young soldier of the West—Gen. McClellan—under whose lead our army cannot fail of victory," and speaks of the need for determination: "Till now it was supposed that the rebellion would soon be suppressed but the facts show that a more extended effort is necessary for the restoration of peace. . . . The war must be vigorously prosecuted." He declares that he obtained this day "authority to send five additional regiments into the field." The reporter noted that Blair "retired amid cheers from the delighted multitude."[136]

Earlier in the day, War Department Chief Clerk James Lesley, Jr.,[137] informs Blair that it will accept five new Michigan infantry regiments for three years, on condition that three be ready to march by August 15 and the remaining two by September 1. Lesley also includes the now-standard condition that "this Department will revoke the commissions of all officers who may be found incompetent for the proper discharge of their duties." Blair is to notify AG Lorenzo Thomas when the regiments are expected to be ready. Separately, in GO 47, the War Department will subject officers of volunteer regiments to fitness examination boards.[138]

Meanwhile, Congress adopts the Crittenden-Johnson Resolution, which blames the South for starting the war and adds "that this war is not waged, on our part, in any spirit of oppression, nor for any purpose of conquest or subjugation, nor purpose of overthrowing or interfering with the rights or established institutions [i.e., slavery] of those States; but to defend and maintain the supremacy of the Constitution, and to preserve the Union . . . and as soon as these objects are accomplished, the war ought to cease."

Congress also enacts Chapter 17: "An Act in addition to the 'Act to authorize the Employment of Volunteers to aid in enforcing the Laws and protecting Public Property,' approved July twenty-second, eighteen hundred and sixty-one," which repeats the 500,000-man call.[139]

Major General John C. Fremont takes command of the Western Department, headquartered in St. Louis.[140]

27: Crucial to cash-strapped Michigan, Congress passes Chapter 21, "An Act to indemnify the States for Expenses incurred by them in Defence of the United States." It directs the treasury secretary "to pay to the Governor of any State . . . the costs, charges, and expenses properly incurred by such State for enrolling, subsisting, clothing, supplying, arming, equipping, paying, and transporting its troops in aiding to suppress the present insurrection against the United States, to be settled upon proper vouchers, to be filed

and passed upon by the proper accounting officers of the United States." Lincoln appoints George B. McClellan to command the Federal Division of the Potomac, which includes all troops in the Washington vicinity.[141]

29: Federal enforcement of militia calls is expanded in Chapter 25: "An Act to provide for the Suppression of the Rebellion against and Resistance to the Laws of the United States, and to amend the [1795 Militia Act]."[142]

30: With the Battle of Bull Run over and the return of the ninety-day First Michigan imminent, the *Detroit Free Press* prints a letter from future Michigan U.S. senator Thomas W. Palmer*: "With what renewed ardor our men would fight, content to suffer, knowing that, instead of being forgotten in a nameless grave on some battle field, a grateful people were erecting monuments to commemorate their heroic deeds." On August 6, committees will be formed and plans made to raise money. (See July 20, 1865.)[143]

31: Congress expands federal authority over threats to the USG with Chapter 33: "An Act to define and punish certain conspiracies."[144]

The pro-Union Missouri State Convention elects Hamilton R. Gamble governor.

August

3: The War Department issues GO No. 49 that excerpts U.S. Chapters 9 and 17. Under these calls (which incorporated the May 3 call), Michigan will be requisitioned for 21,357 men; it will furnish 23,546.[145]

Meanwhile, the War Department reports that from July 8 to today, it has accepted six infantry regiments from Michigan.[146]

5: Congress passes Chapter 45: "An Act to provide Increased Revenue from Imports, to pay Interest on the Public Debt, and for other purposes." Section 8 provides for "a direct tax of twenty millions" of which Michigan's share is $501,763.33.

Congress also passes a bill of great interest to the western "river" states, such as Ohio, Indiana, Illinois, and southward: Chapter 51, "An Act making further Appropriation for the Support of the Naval Service for the Year ending June thirtieth, eighteen hundred and sixty-two, and for other Purposes." Section 1 authorizes the president to accept 500,000 men for naval service and spend $20,000,000; Section 3 appropriates "the sum of one hundred thousand dollars, for the construction and equipment of gunboats for service on the Western rivers."[147]

6: Congress enacts Chapter 63 ratifying Lincoln's May 3 call and increasing private's pay to $13 per month. Meanwhile, in Richmond, the Confederate Congress appropriates $1,000,000 "to supply clothing, subsistence, arms and ammunition to the troops of Missouri" who cooperate with Confederate forces. (See August 20.) Of perhaps greater importance, Lincoln signs into law Chapter 60: "An Act to confiscate Property used for Insurrectionary Purposes," better known as the First Confiscation Act.[148]

Separately, delegates reassemble in Wheeling and vote to form a new state, hereafter called the State of Kanawha. (See October 24.)[149]

7: The ninety-day First Michigan musters out of service in Detroit. (See September 16.)[150]

8: The War Department issues GO No. 53 repealing paragraph 3 of GO No. 45 (see July 19): the ban on mustering any volunteer who is unable to speak the English language has been "misunderstood." The new rule is that volunteers should "enlist under officers whose language they speak and understand."[151]

9: At White Pigeon, Chandler Horse Guard Companies A and B muster into U.S. service. The unit will have 189 men enrolled but will muster out on November 22 owing to "some irregularity" in complying with War Department regulations.[152]

10: Federals are defeated at Wilson's Creek, Missouri. Among the killed is soon-to-be Northern martyr General Nathaniel Lyon.

12: In Grand Rapids, Michigan men, in response to Carl Schurz's call, muster into U.S. service as Company K, First New York Cavalry. Drawn from Grand Rapids and vicinity, the unit serves east.[153] (See June 27, 1865.)

Meanwhile, Cameron asks Blair "What number of regiments have you now organized and what number can be organized ready for marching orders this week?" The governor replies immediately. "The First Regiment, reorganized [i.e., from ninety-day to three-year service], the Fifth, Sixth, Seventh, and Eighth Regiments of the new levy . . . will all be in rendezvous and ready to be mustered into the service of the United States within the next ten days." However, Colonel Backus's health prevents him from efficiently mustering troops, and Blair recommends that Cameron authorize Alpheus S. Williams to process recruits; better yet, Williams wants the War Department to assign him to Michigan and place him in command of these regiments. The First will be sent when ready "and the others as the Department may desire. I think this would be well. It would be agreeable to [the] regiments themselves to be brigaded under his command, and I trust it may be so."[154]

13: Following up yesterday's note, Blair offers Cameron more details about Michigan's status. The First will be ready to muster once uniforms arrive; the Fifth, Sixth, and Seventh are organized and arriving at their rendezvous. Blair estimates that these units will be ready for muster during the upcoming week, "but another week will be necessary to complete their uniforms."[155]

19: Cameron sends Blair two dispatches. First, "The Government desires to know immediately whether a requisition for the whole or a part of the uniformed militia or home guards of your State for temporary service would seriously retard or embarrass the enrollment and organization of the volunteer forces now being enrolled for three years. . . ." The second message is more urgent, probably reflecting pressure by the newly appointed General G. B. McClellan: Blair should forward "immediately to the city of Washington all volunteer regiments, or parts of regiments, at the expense of the United States Government." Supplies will be furnished in Washington, and he asks that Blair "please confer with and aid all officers of independent regiments [i.e., those authorized by Cameron without consulting governors] in such manner as may be necessary to effect the object in view."[156]

From Jackson, Blair immediately replies to Cameron's two dispatches. To the first, he informs Cameron that "We have no military organization in the State of any consequence now [i.e., militia], except the three-years' regiment." It would be "useless" to call up militia presently as "We can furnish three-years' men just as easily, and prefer it." In fact, Blair can do even better and "can furnish more regiments than have been required if you wish on pretty short notice." In a separate response to Cameron's second request, Blair promises to obey it "at once" and will keep Cameron apprised of developments as troops deploy. (See entry for August 24.) "Hope to send 5,000 men within six days," Blair states, and then repeats his August 12 request: "Can Brig. Gen. A. S. Williams be detailed to aid in mustering?" Cameron manages a brief reply on this day. He is silent on Blair's request for Williams, but does accept the governor's offer to raise more troops. "Fill up all regiments authorized as rapidly as possible," he instructs Blair, "and hold yourself in readiness for more. We may require them."

But if Blair is being asked for something, perhaps Cameron must give something, and here, Michigan's governor joins the ranks of other state executives frustrated with Cameron's circumvention of state authority. "I desire to say a word which is not appropriate for the telegraph," Blair replies to Cameron. "It is to make an earnest appeal to you to recognize no more independent regiments in this State. They are introducing confusion and discord into all our affairs. Companies are divided and officers in unseemly quarrels." Blair's next statement contains something stronger than a hint. "I will furnish all the troops you call for much sooner and in better order than these independent regiments can do, and thus avert a great amount of local ill feeling." (See entries for June 14 and August 24.)[157]

20: The Committee on Hospital Supplies and Havelocks makes its second report, including summaries from across Michigan. Ladies' Aid Societies from Kalamazoo, Atlas, Lansing, East Saginaw, Adrian, St. Clair, Port Huron, Farmington, Jonesville, Mt. Clemens, Concord, Albion, Detroit, Highland, and scattered individuals have sent varying amounts of flannel shirts, havelocks, sheets, pillowcases, drawers, towels, and socks, as well as food.

Separately, General George B. McClellan is appointed commander of the newly organized Army of the Potomac.[158]

In Kalamazoo, the Sixth Michigan musters into U.S. service for three years, with companies from Niles, St. Joseph, Schoolcraft, Dowagiac, Marshall, Saline, Allegan, Charlotte, and Albion. The unit will initially be deployed east but also serves south and west.[159] (See July 28, 1863.)

Meanwhile, the Confederate Congress recognizes Claiborne Jackson's government and authorizes the admission of Missouri to the Confederacy.[160]

21: Cameron, acting outside of Blair's authority, authorizes Colonel Thornton F. Brodhead* to recruit a Michigan cavalry regiment. This becomes the First Michigan Cavalry.[161] (See September 13.)

22: In Monroe, the 884 men of the Seventh Michigan muster into U.S. service; recruits are drawn from Port Huron, Mason, Jonesville, Monroe, Tuscola, Farmington, Lapeer, Pontiac, and Burr Oak. It will deploy and serve east.[162] (See July 5, 1865.)

24: Blair keeps his August 19 promise to update Cameron about deployments: the Sixth Michigan, 950 officers and men, will entrain in Kalamazoo for Detroit on the 29th and thence to Cleveland by steamer, by rail to Harrisburg via Pittsburg for a Washington arrival on September 1. Before departing, the Sixth will be given "uniforms (of blue), undershirts, drawers, forage-caps, stockings, and shoes, and with tents, cooking utensils, haversacks and canteens." Blair asks Cameron to provide them with arms and accouterments "immediately" on arriving in Washington; moreover, Blair wants Cameron to confirm this by telegraph before the Sixth leaves Michigan. The Seventh Michigan will depart from Monroe on September 2 by rail for Cleveland, and from there will take the same route to Washington as the Sixth. It is clothed and equipped similarly to the Sixth and presumably will need arms and accouterments on arrival in Washington, expected about September 5. The First Michigan (Detroit rendezvous) and the Fifth Michigan (Ann Arbor rendezvous) are now "rapidly concentrating" and will be sent to Washington as quickly as "indispensably necessary" clothing can be supplied; that clothing is under contract and suppliers are being pressed for delivery. The Eighth Michigan is being organized at Grand Rapids, and once filled, the Ninth Michigan will be formed. In the meantime, Colonel Backus will process the two independent units, Stockton's infantry and Brodhead's cavalry, both which are concentrating in Detroit. Backus will report to the War Department when these independent units will deploy.

Separately, mirroring concerns about disloyal persons and subversive organizations throughout the North, Secretary of State Seward asks Senator Chandler for suggestions on a Detroit-based person "to detect and arrest persons in the employment of the insurgents" there. In Michigan, questions of loyalty are about to flare. (See September 7.)[163]

26: Cameron replies to Blair's August 24 status report. "You can retain your men ten days in camp to fully uniform and equip them. Do not delay beyond that period." Meanwhile, in Detroit, Company C of the First USSS musters into U.S. service.[164] (See August 20, 1864.)

27: Zachariah Chandler writes Cameron with an unusual proposal. A "Colonel Elliott, member of the Canadian Parliament" [NB: no person named Elliott could be found in the membership of the First through Seventh Canadian Parliaments] wants to raise a regiment of Canadian cavalry "for the war against treason." Chandler endorses the idea and offers four reasons. Elliott "is a brave and experienced officer"; Elliott also favors "the closest union between the Canadas and the United States"; third, "It would satisfy England that hands-off was her best policy" [NB: Chandler is probably speculating that military cooperation between Canadians and the federal government would somehow discourage British intervention]; finally (and probably *closer* to Chandler's heart), he believes that establishing this liaison will eventually facilitate deploying colored troops: "The moment it is proven that blacks are used in the Southern Army to fight us, I propose to recruit a few regiments of sables in Canada to meet that enemy, and think this would be an opening wedge for that movement." An unnamed colleague of Chandler will introduce Elliott to Cameron.[165]

28: At Fort Wayne, 900 men of the Fifth Michigan muster into U.S. service for three years; recruits are drawn from Detroit, Mt. Clemens, East Saginaw, Owosso, Saginaw, Brighton, St. Clair, Pontiac, and Port Huron. It will deploy and serve east.[166] (See July 5, 1865.)

Federal forces occupy Fort Hatteras, North Carolina.

29: At Camp Denison, Columbus, Ohio, Company B, composed mainly of Michigan men, of the Forty-Seventh Ohio musters into U.S. service. After brief service in western Virginia, it will serve in the west and accompany Sherman to Atlanta, the sea, and the Carolinas Campaign.[167] (See August 11, 1865.)

30: General John C. Fremont issues, without Washington's authority, an emancipation proclamation for Missouri. (See September 2.) The *Lansing State Republican* approves, declaring that Fremont's proclamation "is of the right stamp, and possesses the genuine ring," adding "Secession will feel the blow struck by the gallant Fremont through every nerve and artery of its beastly form." The Democratic *East Saginaw Courier* understands things differently: "In matter of Fremont's they set themselves above the constitution, the laws, and even the President himself."[168]

September

2: Lincoln asks Fremont ("of your own motion") to conform his emancipation proclamation to the First Confiscation Act, which emancipates few. Lincoln is candid: "I think there is great danger . . . [that your proclamation] will alarm our Southern Union friends, and turn them against us—perhaps ruin our rather fair prospect for Kentucky." (See September 8.)[169]

3: Confederate General Gideon Pillow crosses the Mississippi into Kentucky with the goal of occupying Columbus, Kentucky.[170]

4: Canadian parliamentarian and British Army officer Colonel Arthur Rankin* is commissioned colonel of the First United States Lancers. (See entry for November 30 and December 9.)[171]

6: Union forces reoccupy Paducah, Kentucky.

7: Cameron asks Blair "What number of volunteer regiments can you have ready for marching orders on a few hours' notice, if required to meet an emergency?" He adds that, "It is desirable that organizations and equipment should progress as rapidly as possible, and in such manner as will enable the Government to use the forces actually mustered in." Blair replies that the Sixth Michigan deployed to Washington last week; the Seventh is en route; the Fifth, now fully uniformed, can march "in a few hours' notice"; the reorganized First numbers some 700, can also march. Likewise with Stockton's unit and the Eighth Michigan. "We are proceeding with the greatest dispatch," Blair promises, and also complains about cavalry recruiting. "The two new cavalry regiments have driven away recruits from the infantry badly." Separately, the Democratic ex-president Franklin Pierce arrives in Detroit, intending to visit his niece in East Saginaw; while in Detroit, he stays with his former secretary of the interior and now state Democratic leader Robert McClelland*. Although the trip is personal, Pierce will meet with other Michigan Democrats, including Lewis Cass. Republican allegations questioning Pierce's loyalty are about to ignite a firestorm. (See September 10 and 23.)[172]

Meanwhile, the War Department issues GO No. 73, initiating a series of moves against states sending minors into service.[173]

8: The Sixteenth Michigan musters into U.S. service at Detroit with 761 men; recruits and officers are drawn from Flint, Detroit, Ionia, East Saginaw, and Plymouth. It will deploy east.[174] (See July 18, 1865.)

Fremont replies to Lincoln and asks the president to make public his request to retract the emancipation order. (See September 11.)

9: At the Benton Barracks in St. Louis, a company of Michigan sharpshooters musters into U.S. service as Company D, Birge's Western Sharpshooters. Major John Piper of Battle Creek recruited his men and officers from Battle Creek, Hartford, Lawrence, Keeler, Watervliet, Benton Harbor, and St. Joseph. The unit serves west and will accompany Sherman to Atlanta, the sea, and the Carolinas Campaign. (See July 7, 1865.) Also in St. Louis today, Michiganders in Merrill's Horse muster into U.S. service. Michigan cavalrymen compose most of companies H and I, and are drawn from Battle Creek and vicinity.[175] (See January 1, 1863.)

10: Civil engineer and railroad man William P. Innes★ of Grand Rapids, inspired by Illinois's example in organizing an engineer regiment (Illinois had advertised for Michiganders), wires Cameron a question: "Will the War Department accept a regiment from Michigan on the same terms as Colonel [James W.] Wilson's of Chicago?" Cameron, probably mindful of Blair's earlier scolding about independent regiments (see August 19) and perhaps feeling the pressure that will produce GO 78 (see September 16), immediately contacts Blair with Innes's offer. "I have telegraphed [Innes] the matter would be referred to you, and if you deem it advisable for the interests of Government the organization may be made under your direction." Blair will meet with Innes and his group on September 12 to form the First Michigan Engineers and Mechanics Regiment. (See September 13 and October 29.)[176]

The *Free Press* defends Franklin Pierce against "a number of journals" who are attempting "to im-

peach his patriotism, and openly charge him with treason . . . or sympathy with treason." The sheet contends that in fact, Pierce has been speaking on behalf of the Union and for the war effort; in a dig at the *Tribune*, the *Free Press* concludes that it has no respect for those who "so flippantly and infamously charge treason and disloyalty upon political opponents without knowing or caring anything about the facts."[177]

Meanwhile, Confederates lose the Battle of Carnifex Ferry, western Virginia.

11: Lincoln orders Fremont to retract his emancipation order.

The Kentucky House demands Governor Magoffin to order Confederates to evacuate the state. Magoffin will veto this, but the House overrides. Magoffin eventually issues a proclamation.[178]

Separately, General Robert E. Lee begins the Cheat Mountain Campaign in western Virginia. His forces will lose a series of battles before withdrawing.

12: Cameron instructs Blair "to put in rapid march to [Washington] all organized regiments under your control." In a second wire, he asks Blair to have all Michigan sharpshooters [three companies] sent to Washington to report to Colonel Hiram Berdan. "Special uniforms furnished here," Cameron promises. The sharpshooters' companies, including the four from Michigan, will rendezvous at Weehawken, New Jersey, on September 24 before departing for Washington. (See entry for September 28.)[179]

13: Blair acknowledges Cameron's September 10 wire about Innes and an engineer regiment. "Finding that several companies have already been formed for this purpose," he notes, "I have cheerfully authorized the formation of the regiment and will assist in it to the utmost of my ability." In a second wire, Blair admits he is confused by Cameron's inexact wire from the previous day ordering all regiments to Washington. By "organized regiments" did the secretary mean to include all regiments, "whether full or part full, and also independent infantry and cavalry regiments raising within the State by direct instructions to colonels from the War Department?" (See entry for September 16.)[180]

Meanwhile, in Detroit, the First Michigan Cavalry musters into U.S. service with 1,144 men; recruits and officers are drawn from Gross Isle, Detroit, Ovid, Lapeer, Kalamazoo, and Almont. The unit's twelve companies will be deployed east and will reenlist as Veteran Volunteers in December 1863; postwar, the unit will have brief frontier service. They will be joined by Bridget Divers,[181] perhaps accompanying her husband, who later distinguishes herself by providing aid to soldiers, including first aid under fire. By war's end, 2,490 men will be enrolled, of whom 96 will be KIA, 40 MIA, 52 DOW, 58 died as POWs, 172 DOD, 2 drowned, 2 died accidentally, 1 killed by Indians, and 209 DFD. It will muster out in March 1866.[182]

14: Cameron instructs Blair to "Start to-day for Washington the First and Colonel Stockton's [Sixteenth Michigan] regiments." Blair is to use "such authority as may be necessary to fill these regiments from any men now mustered into service. Secure transportation and forward immediately. Answer what we may expect from Michigan."[183]

15: Blair replies to Cameron that the First Michigan and Stockton's unit leave tomorrow.[184]

16: Cameron pulls back from his recent urgency for rapid deployment to Washington, at least for Michigan. "We intend that you shall use your discretion in forwarding all regiments," he wires Blair, "and put them in such shape as to be serviceable."

Meanwhile, in Ann Arbor, 960 men of the reorganized, three-year iteration of the First Michigan, deploy to Virginia, except for two detachments. Recruits are drawn from Detroit, Manchester, Burr Oak, Ann Arbor, Jackson, and Sault Ste Marie. The unit will be deployed in the eastern theater.[185] (See July 9, 1865.)

The War Department issues GO No. 78, which instructs "All persons having received authority from the War Department to raise volunteer regiments" that "These troops will be organized, or reorganized, and prepared for service by the Governors of their respective States."[186]

17: William H. Seward receives an anonymous letter from Detroit regarding visiting ex-president Pierce: he and others "are traitors and are aiding and abetting secretly and covertly the leaders of the Southern rebellion."[187] (See September 23.) Separately, in Coldwater, Battery D of the First Michigan Light Artillery musters into U.S. service; recruits and officers are drawn from the vicinities of Coldwater and Union City. The unit will deploy west.[188] (See August 3, 1865.)

18: At Camp Webb (Chicago), the Michiganders of Company D of the Thirty-Seventh Illinois muster into U.S. service. The company serves west and musters out in May 1866. Total wartime enrollment was sixty-three Michiganders, including 2 KIA, 2 DOW, 2 DOD, and 3 DFD.[189]

19: The War Department issues GO No. 81, specifying allotment procedures.[190]

20: Federal forces are defeated at Lexington, Missouri. Surrendering forces include the Detroiters of Company A of the Twenty-Third Illinois. They will be paroled in October and serve the balance of the war in the east.[191] (See July 24, 1865.)

23: At Fort Wayne, the Eighth Michigan musters into U.S. service; recruits or officers are drawn from Flint, Detroit, Alma, Grand Rapids, Lansing, and Richland, among other towns. The unit will deploy east, and in December 1863, will reenlist as Veteran Volunteers.[192] (See August 3, 1865.)

In St. Louis and on instructions from the U.S. Sanitary Commission, Dr. John S. Newberry[193] meets with the Western Sanitary Commission, previously established by General John C. Fremont. The Western Sanitary Commission agrees to join (as its western branch) the U.S. Sanitary Commission. The Western will distribute supplies and provide nurses and doctors from western states to the western theater. Beside Michigan, the Western Sanitary Commission includes Ohio, Illinois, Wisconsin, Iowa, Kentucky, Indiana, Tennessee, Minnesota, and Missouri, with branches in Pittsburgh, Pennsylvania, and Buffalo, New York. (See August 1, 1863.)[194]

Meanwhile, the day's *New York Times* carries an undated excerpt from the Detroit *Tribune* asserting that while in Detroit, President Pierce "was closeted with a select circle who are *known to be doubtful in their loyalty*"; the *Tribune* claims that Pierce had delivered a speech to this "circle" whose attendees confided to others "who were invited but would not be contaminated by the foul conspiracy" that, "You ought to have heard Ex-President Pierce last night; he would have cured you of the idea of supporting this government in this damnable war." The *Tribune* then declared, "Our opinion is that Franklin Pierce is a prowling traitor spy."[195] (See September 25.)

24: The Eleventh Michigan organizes at White Pigeon with 1,000 men; recruits and officers are drawn from

White Pigeon, Centerville, Quincy, Sturgis, Burr Oak, Three Rivers, Morenci, Bronson, Coldwater, London, and Adrian. It will deploy west and serve through the Atlanta Campaign. By war's end, total enrollment will be 1,323, including 61 KIA, 31 DOW, 9 died as POWs, 178 DOD, and 265 DFD.[196] (See September 30, 1864.)

Throughout the war, Michigan newspapers print letters from soldier-correspondents, which provide at-home civilians with a glimpse of army life. Today, Detroiters see one such letter, this one from "J," a soldier with the Seventh Regiment. Writing from headquarters "Two miles from Poolsville [sic], Md.," "J" reports that the Seventh is brigaded with the Nineteenth and Twentieth Massachusetts regiments, and men from Berdan's Sharpshooters. "Poolsville is directly opposite Leesburg [Virginia, across the Potomac] where the rebels are congregated in large numbers, and it at that point on the Potomac at which it is expected they will attempt a crossing. At present [we] are under marching orders and then carry four day's [sic] cooked provisions in their haversacks, and are ready to march at a moment's notice." "J" expected a fight "within a very few days." The "monotony of camp life" gave him little to write, but "if our expectations are realized, it will be but a few days before we shall have been through scenes, the notation of which will be of interest to Michigan people."[197]

25: The *Free Press* reprints the *New York Times*'s September 23 piece with a comment: "there is not one word of truth in the [*Tribune's*] article." There was no meeting with Pierce, nor did the ex-president make a speech. The *Free Press* concludes, "The whole story is a deliberate manufacture of whole cloth, without a single circumstance having occurred to give it even the semblance of truth." Among those who almost certainly read today's *Free Press* are three North Branch (Lapeer County) antiwar Democrats, Dr. Guy S. Hopkins★, David C. Wattles★, and Isaiah Butler.★ (See October 5.)[198]

From Ann Arbor, the University of Michigan Board of Regents adopts a resolution lamenting the "the great scarcity of men possessed of suitable military education to drill and prepare our Volunteer Armies for camp life and the battle field and to lead them in action"; that the "present means of furnishing a thor-

ough military education whereby men may become masters of the art of war are entirely inadequate"; and that neglecting to provide military education is "not safe" to the government. The Regents declare, "That as soon as the State shall add to the University Fund the sum of $100,000 from which the University shall derive a permanent annual income of $7,000, the Board of Regents will establish in the University a Military School in which shall be taught Military Engineering and Tactics, Strategy, and the Art and Science of War."[199]

26: Echoing Lincoln's call, on September 20, Austin Blair proclaims that today should be a "a day of public humiliation, prayer, and fasting by the people" for Michigan.[200]

27: Blair informs Cameron that new Michigan regiments "are all nearly full"; however, new companies continue seeking Blair for permission to organize, which he cannot grant without the War Department increasing the number of U.S. authorized regiments. He asks Cameron how many new regiments Michigan might be asked to furnish, and over what time period. (See October 11.)[201]

28: Cameron authorizes a second regiment of USSS. Of the unit's eight original companies, one will be from Michigan.[202]

October

1: Chicago's Union Defense Committee, representing western interests, complains to Lincoln that western units are being used to fight the eastern war, and Washington has thereby failed to address threats in the west. Men "raised in New England, New York, New Jersey, Pennsylvania, Delaware, Maryland, Michigan, Wisconsin, Minnesota," and worse yet, "five-sixths of those raised in Ohio and Indiana" (and several detached Illinois companies) have been deployed in Maryland and Virginia. "The state of affairs in Kentucky and Missouri is such as to cause the greatest anxiety to every lover of the Union," but western units deployed west are "entirely inadequate to meet the enemy," and also lack "discipline and proper arms."

But what probably perked up Lincoln's ears is the potential political damage: "it would create a feeling throughout this section of country which might endanger the cause of the Union. It might be said with some show of justice that the East was strengthened at the expense of the West, even after Western troops had already been freely given to hold the line of the Potomac." Furthermore, "the West" understands this war quite differently than some in the "East": "an opinion prevails through the West, that aside from coast attacks, the importance of which all acknowledge, the true line of military operations, to strike at the heart of the insurrection is through the Valley of the Mississippi." (See October 12.)[203]

2: In Grand Rapids, the Second Michigan Cavalry musters into U.S. service with 1,163 men; recruits and officers are drawn from Detroit, Flint, Eaton Rapids, Pine Plains, Berlin, Lowell, Hillsdale, Kalamazoo, Port Huron, Niles, and Marshall. The unit's twelve companies will be deployed east and will reenlist as Veteran Volunteers in March 1864. By war's end, 2,139 men will be enrolled, of whom 39 will be KIA, 26 DOW, 12 died as POWs, 217 DOD, and 328 DFD.[204] (See November 1 and December 6; also, August 17, 1865.)[205]

5: Cameron asks Blair if he has "two regiments armed, uniformed, and equipped that can be prepared for marching orders to-day?" If so, "Get them ready and answer immediately." Separately, U.S. Senator Kinsley S. Bingham dies at his home at Green Oak.

In North Branch, Dr. Guy S. Hopkins decides to teach Michigan's Republican newspapers a lesson. He is frustrated at the baseless newspaper attacks on Franklin Pierce and Robert McClelland and angry that last month, he was assaulted on the street and his office ransacked; he believes Republicans perpetrated both acts. Hopkins's lesson takes the form of a hoax. He composes a letter filled with initials that are easily identified with the names of leading Michigan Democrats, references to a mysterious "league," and strong hints that it is engaged in subversive activities; finally, he signs the letter with bizarre symbols. The idea is straightforward: induce Michigan's Republican press to print the letter and later expose their gullibility.

Hopkins then mails the letter to a Mr. Mills, a name he randomly selected from a newspaper. Mills, a Democrat, forwards the letter to the *Detroit Free Press*'s editor, Henry N. Walker; Walker advises Mills to give it to William A. Howard, Detroit's postmaster, who in turn shares it with the editors of the *Tribune* and *Advertiser*. The letter, mislaid for several weeks,

is finally given to Acting U.S. District Attorney Alfred Russell.* (See November 8.)[206]

Separately, in Detroit, Company B, Second USSS, musters into U.S. service. It will deploy east, and on February 18, 1865, transfers to the Fifth Michigan, with which it will muster out.[207] (See July 5, 1865.)

7: Blair replies to Cameron's October 5 request for two regiments: Michigan has two units that can march in five days. However, "Neither of them are armed, there being no arms in the State"; one has equipment, and the other should also "unless the uniforms are delayed on the way." (See October 12.)[208]

8: Detroit Republicans invite Democrats to "unite without distinction of party in nominating municipal candidates" for the November 5 city elections.[209] (See October 24.)

9: In St. Louis, Howland's Engineers (also known as the Battle Creek Engineer Corps), originally recruited by E. P. Howland,[210] musters into U.S. service. It will serve briefly in Missouri before being deemed an "irregular organization" and ordered to disband on January 8, 1862. The unit's total enrollment was fifty-four.

11: ASW Scott answers Blair's September 27 request by authorizing five new regiments.[211]

12: ASW Scott replies to the October 1 letter from Chicago's Union Defense Committee and makes an important commitment. "The Department fully appreciates the force of the statements [the appeal] contains," Scott begins, "and begs to inform the Union Committee that the Governors of the various States west of Pennsylvania have been instructed to reserve their troops for service in Virginia, Kentucky, and Missouri, and that hereafter no troops from the Western States will be moved eastwards for service on the Potomac unless the exigencies of the times imperatively require it, of which the Department has no knowledge." (The "exigencies of the times" did require it. For example, see various entries in May and June, 1862.)[212] Separately, in response to Blair's statement that the two regiments requested by Cameron on October 7 will be delayed for lack of arms and in one case, equipment, ASW Scott replies that, "We have not arms and equipments on hand to furnish you now. We expect them any day. As soon as they arrive you shall be provided."[213]

13: In Chicago, Companies B and H, composed of

Michiganders, of the Forty-Fourth Illinois, muster into U.S. service. With officers from Coldwater and Kalamazoo, these companies serve west, accompany Sherman to Atlanta until being ordered to Texas.[214] (See September 25, 1865.)

14: Seward writes Blair (and other coastal and lakefront governors) about the possibility of waterborne attacks and urges them to fortify coastal defenses.[215]

15: At Fort Wayne, 913 men of the Ninth Michigan muster into U.S. service; recruits or officers were drawn from Detroit, Romeo, Niles, Jackson, Lyons, Linden, Owosso, Mt. Clemens, and Fowlerville. It will deploy and serve west.[216] (See February 10, 1864.)

21: Federals are defeated at Ball's Bluff, Virginia. Among the dead is sitting U.S. senator Edward D. Baker, and among the consequences will be the formation of the Joint Committee for the Conduct of the War.

22: Captain John McDermott, originally from Michigan but commissioned as captain of Company A in the "Mulligan Regiment of the State of Michigan," has (apparently) contacted the War Department with a request to raise an artillery battery that would be attached to the Twenty-Third. ASW Scott informs Blair and authorizes him "to form a battery of six guns for the purpose aforesaid, if in your discretion you should see proper so to do, with the distinct understanding, however, that said battery may at any time be detached from said regiment, if the wants of the service require it." But Scott is in error: Mulligan's Regiment is in fact the Twenty-Third Illinois (also nicknamed the "Irish Brigade"), and it is unclear what stake Blair might have in furnishing troops to Illinois.[217]

23: The War Department arranges to pay wages to POW families.[218]

24: In Detroit at the Democratic City Convention, eight resolutions are adopted, including one that implicitly rejects the October 8 Republican invitation to propose a Union slate of municipal candidates. It asserts that "the democratic party has ever been a Union party"; another resolution pledges Detroit Democrats "to a vigorous prosecution of the war"; another states the importance of a "speedy termination . . . with honor to the government." The convention also unanimously endorses William C. Duncan for mayor.[219]

Separately, Western Virginians ratify the acts of the Second Wheeling Convention, with 18,408 favoring statehood and 781 opposed.[220]

26: The War Department asks Blair to account for all troops furnished to date, including three-month regiments, and troops expected by December 1. State AG Robertson answers immediately. Michigan has contributed to date one three-month, a 780-man infantry regiment; for three-year service, ten infantry and one cavalry regiment, two companies of sharpshooters, and one battery, altogether comprising some 11,000 men. Currently organizing in state are two cavalry regiments, one infantry regiment, and one battery, altogether comprising 3,450 men. Just starting to organize are four infantry regiments, one lancer and one fusilier regiment, two companies of sharpshooters, and two artillery batteries.[221]

28: ASW Scott notifies the New York Arsenal that "Governor Blair of Michigan wants 3,000 arms. If the 2,500 arms in Moller's contract at $10, can be had, and meet your approval as suitable for service, buy them and send 500 rifles for flanking companies. They are wanted immediately. Do the best you can."[222]

29: First Michigan Engineers and Mechanics regiment is mustered into U.S. service; officered and recruited from Grand Rapids and vicinity, it will be deployed in the western theater and accompany Sherman to the sea.[223] (See September 22, 1865.)

30: Dr. G. P. Miller, an African American physician from Battle Creek, has read an October 14 letter from ASW Scott to General T. W. Sherman granting him discretion, in areas Lincoln deems in a state of insurrection, to employ slaves or freemen "in such services as they may be fitted for—either as ordinary employees, or if special circumstances seem to require it, in any other capacity . . . as you may deem most beneficial to the service"; however Scott admonishes Sherman that they are not to be armed for military service. Nevertheless, Dr. Miller sees an opening and asks Cameron for permission to recruit "from 5,000 to 10,000 freemen to report in sixty days to take any position that may be assigned us (sharpshooters preferred)." Miller asks for white officers if this unit is accepted, but if not accepted, he offers to "fight as guerillas" so long as the U.S. provides arms. Miller also notes one of Michigan's demographic realities: "A part of us are half-breed Indians and legal voters in the State of Michigan. As we are all anxious to fight for the maintenance of the Union and the preservation of the principles promulgated by President Lincoln, we are sure of success if allowed an opportunity. In the name of God, answer immediately." (See November 9.)[224]

November

1: In Grand Rapids, the Third Michigan Cavalry musters into U.S. service with 1,160 men; recruits and officers are drawn from Grand Rapids, Allegan, Detroit, Paw Paw, Ypsilanti, Jackson, Schoolcraft, Whitmore Lake, Fentonville, Tecumseh, St. Joseph, and Saginaw. The unit's twelve companies will be deployed west and will reenlist as Veteran Volunteers in January 1864. By war's end, 2,264 men will be enrolled, of whom 24 will be KIA, 9 DOW, 8 died as POWs, 333 DOD, and 319 DFD. It will muster out in March 1866.

Meanwhile, George B. McClellan replaces Winfield Scott as general-in-chief.[225]

2: Fremont is replaced by General David Hunter as commander of the Western Department.[226]

5: Local Elections: In Detroit, elections are held for municipal offices, notably mayor and aldermen. Democrat William C. Duncan is elected mayor over Republican H. P. Baldwin, 3,329 to 2,650, and the City Council remains solidly Democratic.[227]

6: At a scheduled meeting at the Woodward Avenue Methodist Church women gather to formally organize "The Soldiers' Aid Society of Detroit for Relief of the Sick and Wounded of the Federal Army" (soon shortened to the Ladies Aid Society of Detroit; but see August 8, 1863) and elect Isabella Graham Duffield as president. Committees of four women each are appointed from Detroit's Episcopal, Presbyterian, Methodist, Baptist, New Jerusalem, Roman Catholic, Unitarian, Congregational, and other Christian churches and the Jewish Synagogue. (See entry for November 12.)[228]

7: General Ulysses Grant defeats Confederates at Belmont, Missouri. In South Carolina, federals are victorious at the Battle of Port Royal.

8: DA Russell has asked Detroit's assistant city marshal (and police detective) Joseph P. Whiting to investigate "the treasonable sentiments of various individuals" in North Branch, including Guy S. Hopkins. Posing as "Richard Jenkins," the next day Whiting interviews the sheriff and other locals to learn "that it is the

common report that Isaiah Butler, David C. Wattles and Guy S. Hopkins with many other were secessionists, and openly avowed themselves as such." Other witnesses make allegations: Butler, Wattles, and Hopkins harassed a soldier on leave, shouting pro-Southern threats and cheering Jefferson Davis; the three men gave barroom speeches favoring secession and on another occasion raised a secessionist flag; according to Whiting, in conversation with Hopkins, the latter denounced the government "as unjust and tyrannical." All three men are described as influential in North Branch. This information is forwarded to Seward. (See November 20.)[229]

Captain Charles Wilkes, commanding the USS *San Jacinto*, boards the RMS *Trent* and seizes two Confederate diplomats and staff. (See December 18.) This provokes British protests, saber rattling, and military countermoves. Seward's letter of October 14 now assumes a new urgency.[230]

9: ASW Scott replies to Dr. G. P. Miller's October 30 request to recruit 5,000 to 10,000 black troops. He explains that, "the orders to General Sherman and other officers of the U.S. service authorize the arming of colored persons only in cases of great emergency and not under regular enrollment for military purposes." He thanks Miller for his "patriotic spirit and intelligence" but adds that, "upon reflection you will perceive that there are sufficient reasons for continuing the course thus pursued."[231]

12: The Ladies Aid Society of Detroit announces its formation and directly appeals to "the Detroit ladies" to help them carry it on. Women should not be discouraged by those "telling you there are enough of hospital supplies." Political differences must be transcended: "God does not designate who is to be the recipient when he says, 'It is more blessed to give than to receive.'" Women are urged to organize and produce mittens, nightcaps, flannel hospital shirts, blankets, and bed ticks; to send mustard, barley, and cocoa, "anything you would provide for your dear ones, were they invalids." "Women feel where men act," it declares, and urges recipients to ignore class distinctions: "The rich may make need a bed-sack or a hospital shirt as well as the poor." (See November 20.)[232]

18: The War Department begins to track each state's troop contributions. Blair is requested to provide the

War Department on the 10th, 20th, and last day of each month with a complete roster of all regiments being recruited in Michigan; this should include "a full report of the condition of the volunteer recruiting service in your State setting forth the number of complete regiments for duty, the number nearly completed and number in process of organization," as well as the names of commanders and arm of service. (See December 10 and January 10, 1862.)[233] Meanwhile, in Russellville, Kentucky, a Sovereignty Convention convenes, planned by secessionists to take the state out of the Union.[234]

Separately, in Detroit at Mrs. H. A. Perry's Metropolitan Theatre, John Wilkes Booth is scheduled to perform Shakespeare's *Richard III*, "to conclude with the laughable farce of Pleasant Neighbors."[235]

20: Isabella Graham Duffield resigns as president of the Ladies Aid Society. Miss Valeria Campbell* will assume her responsibilities as corresponding secretary.[236]

Meanwhile, the Kentucky Sovereignty Convention adopts an ordinance of secession and will appoint a provisional government allied with the Confederacy.[237]

Separately, on Seward's orders, Dr. Guy S. Hopkins is arrested in Detroit, on his way (he claims) to join the Union army. He is imprisoned in Fort Lafayette[238] in New York Harbor, "charged with treasonable correspondence with parties in the rebel States and with forwarding correspondence between such parties and their friends in Europe through Canada and with propagating treasonable sentiments in the region of his residence." (See November 21, below, and February 22, 1862.)[239]

21: Tavern owner Isaiah Butler is arrested in North Branch, Lapeer County, by order of William Seward and charged with "forwarding correspondence to and from the rebel States between said States and Canada and with propagating treasonable and secession doctrines in the neighborhood of his residence." He will be incarcerated in Fort Lafayette in New York Harbor, which is used throughout the Civil War as a prison. (See November 25, December 6, and February 22, 1862.)[240]

25: Cameron writes Blair to ask that Michigan recall any agents who might be purchasing arms on its behalf. "It is found by experience that competition by agents of States authorized to purchase arms in competition with agents of the Government is highly detrimental to the public service, as it advances prices both to the States and the United States, the loss of which may ultimately fall upon the General Government." This should remove "the present inducement for speculators to withhold arms from the service." Cameron pledges that U.S. arms "will be distributed to the troops of the several States as soon as received." However, Michigan has few, if any, purchasing agents.[241]

Separately, David C. Wattles of North Branch, Lapeer County, is arrested and will be incarcerated in Fort Lafayette. Authorities claim Wattles has "long been notoriously active in propagating disloyal sentiments at North Branch." (See February 22, 1862.) Despite this charge, Wattles is actually seeking a lieutenancy in the Eleventh Michigan Infantry. Later, national Democrats will list Wattles's arrest as one of the many that had no real basis.[242]

26: In Grand Rapids, Battery B of the First Michigan Light Artillery musters into U.S. service; recruits and officers are drawn from Grand Rapids and vicinity. The unit will deploy west and accompany Sherman through the Carolinas Campaign.[243]

27: The War Department approves the mustering of men who are "three quarters Indian blood." (But see July 6, 1862.)[244]

28: In Grand Rapids, Battery C of the First Michigan Light Artillery musters into U.S. service; recruits and officers are drawn from Grand Rapids and vicinity, Hillsdale, Detroit, and Jonesville. The unit will deploy west and accompany Sherman through his Atlanta march to the sea and Carolinas Campaign.[245]

30: The First United States Lancers (recruited in Canada) is organized at Detroit, Saginaw, and St. Johns. It will recruit through February 20, 1862. (See December 9.)[246]

Meanwhile, General Totten reports on federal fortifications around the U.S. and includes an assessment of Fort Wayne. Repair and construction are under Captain Charles E. Blunt*, who has spent some $900 "in renewing a length of 150 feet of the timber scarp revetment." The barracks are "unfinished, and the quarters destroyed by fire several years since have not been rebuilt." However, "The work can be prepared for its armament in a short time." An estimated

$100,000 is required to build a stone revetment for the current wooden scarp.[247]

December

1: Cameron makes his annual report to the War Department, including estimates of army strength. Michigan is credited with 781 three-month volunteers and 28,550 three-year volunteers, for an aggregate of 29,331 men. Michigan furnished 1.0 percent of the national total (77,875) of three-month volunteers and 4.45 percent of the national total (640,637) of three-year volunteers.[248]

Cameron's report also includes cheery statements for several western states. As of July, Kentucky and Missouri were among the states "threatened with rebellion"; but "the people of Kentucky early pronounced themselves, by an unequivocal declaration at the ballot-box, in favor of the Union"; in Missouri, "a loyal State government has been established by the people . . . and . . . in conjunction with troops from other portions of the country have forced the rebels to retire into the adjoining State." As for western Virginia, "The government established . . . by the loyal portion of her population is in successful operation."[249]

3: The War Department notifies Blair that no more cavalry regiments will be accepted into service; moreover, it declares that "a number" of cavalry already raised will be converted into "infantry or garrison artillery."[250]

Separately, the War Department issues GO No. 105, stripping governors of recruiting authority, to take effect on January 1, 1862. Under its provisions, Lieutenant Colonel Electus C. Backus will be appointed as the U.S. superintendent of recruiting for Michigan, headquartered in Detroit.[251]

Lincoln delivers his annual message and underscores Cameron's assessment of the situation with Kentucky, western Virginia, and Missouri.[252]

4: In a critical shift of opinion, Congress refuses to renew the Crittenden-Johnson Resolution (see entry for July 25), which had proclaimed that the sole object of the war was restoration of the Union and not to interfere with slavery in the seceded states.[253]

5: With the recent federal defeats at Ball's Bluff and Bull Run in mind, Zachariah Chandler offers the following resolution: "That a committee of three be appointed to inquire into the disasters of Bull Run and Edward's Ferry, with power to send for persons and papers." It seems to strike a chord. Kansas's senator James Lane wants to add the battles of Wilson's Creek and Lexington, and Iowa's Grimes wants to add the battles of Belmont and Big Bethel. Chandler's motion is the genesis of the Joint Committee on the Conduct of the War.[254]

6: Congressman Francis W. Kellogg is commissioned (by the War Department, not Blair) colonel of the Third Michigan Cavalry. The commission is largely honorary: just several weeks earlier, the Second Michigan Cavalry, also organized by Kellogg and which left Michigan on November 14, arrived at Benton Barracks in St. Louis, where Gordon Granger* (who was appointed the Second's colonel to date from September 1) assumed actual command. (See May 25, 1862.) Separately, US DA Russell writes Seward that "There exists in [Michigan] an extensive branch of the treasonable organization known as the Knights of the Golden Circle." Russell's chief evidence is the Hopkins letter. The next day, the *Detroit Tribune* publishes an editorial attacking ex-President Franklin Pierce's visit to Detroit: "There is little doubt but that ex-President Pierce's tour . . . is to foster division among the people, excite sedition, and to get up an organized treasonable opposition to the efforts of the Government to crush out rebellion." When Pierce was in Detroit, "he was closeted with a select circle who are known to be doubtful in their loyalty." The *Detroit Tribune* quotes one of those who listened to Pierce: "You ought to have heard ex-President Pierce last night; he would have cured you of the idea of supporting this Government in this d---nable war." (See December 10.)[255]

9: Colonel Backus is troubled by Canadian Colonel Rankin and his Michigan First Lancers, and so informs the War Department. He claims that foreign recruiting was the brainchild of Detroit lieutenant colonel James W. Tillman* and regards it as a "dangerous experiment" in which Tillman "has willfully endangered the peace of the United States and Great Britain." Backus presumes that "the Government does not desire to give Her Britannic Majesty a just cause of complaint."[256] And he has another worry. The auditor of the Detroit & Milwaukee (which also owns the Canadian railroad over which these recruits have been passed) has informed Backus that the rail passes (probably those issued by Michigan for free transportation for recruits) given these recruits are forged. "I have checked all passes in this State until I can adopt some system which will check this barefaced swindling." (See December 17.)

Meanwhile, in Marshall, Battery E of the First Michigan Light Artillery musters into U.S. service; recruits and officers are drawn from Grand Rapids, Marshall, and Adrian. The unit will deploy west and reenlist as Veteran Volunteers.[257] (See July 30, 1865.)

10: State AG Robertson reports Michigan's "Regiments and companies organized and in process of organization." (See State Military Affairs—1861.) Separately, in the Washington, D.C., office of General H. L. Stevens★, Michigan residents form the Michigan Soldiers' Relief Association of the District of Columbia, and elect James M. Edmunds★ as president. The Association's purpose is "To look after the sick and wounded in the hospitals and the general condition of the soldiers in camp; to see that the comforts and necessities which are constantly being made up and forwarded to this city by the families and friends of the soldiers reach the company or regiment desired, and to be a special means of communication between the people of Michigan and their gallant representatives in the army of the Potomac." Money is contributed to launch the group, subcommittees are formed, and John B. Bloss★, a storekeeper "of the General Land Office," is chosen to receive goods from Michigan. The association pledges to meet monthly. Throughout the war, the association, acting with the group Sons of Michigan, will hold annual banquets.[258] (See September 13, 1862.)

In Washington, the Joint Committee for the Conduct of the War is established. With Michigan senator Zachariah Chandler as one of two Senate representatives, the Committee will monitor military operations throughout the war. Meanwhile, Kentucky is formally admitted to the Confederacy. (See July 17, 1862.) Separately, in what is more of an attack on the *Detroit Tribune* than a defense of Franklin Pierce, the *Detroit Free Press* answers its competitor's attack on the former president. "We have no sympathy or respect whatever for treason-mongers or treason-sympathizers, and just as little for those in the present state of the country so flippantly and infamously charge treason and

disloyalty upon political opponents without knowing or caring anything about the facts."[259]

11: AG Thomas asks Blair, "How many regiments have you not provided with arms; and how many to take their field, except their arms?"[260]

17: AAG E. D. Townsend[261] answers Backus's December 9 letter about Canadian recruiting. "I am instructed to direct you not to muster into service any recruits who may have been imported from Canada for the purpose of filling up the regiments now organizing in your vicinity." Backus is also ordered "not to muster in the men of any regiment unless satisfied that all its recruits have been enlisted within the limits of the United States." (See December 21.)[262]

18: From Detroit, Lewis Cass wires Seward regarding the *Trent* Affair. He urges Seward to accept England's interpretation of international law and release Mason and Slidell. "The power to arrest rebel agents on board neutrals is of very little practical importance to us," he argues. (See next day's entry.)

19: Cass writes Seward with additional thoughts on resolving the *Trent* Affair. War with Great Britain is a bad idea, for "it would go far to prevent the restoration of the rebel States to the authority of the Constitution." Cass has carefully read the report of Captain Charles Wilkes (the commander of the USS *San Jacinto*) and is critical. Wilkes's arrest of the two Southerners was made without express orders; moreover, Wilkes practically concedes that he had no basis in international law to make the arrests. Cass is "amazed" at "the laudations bestowed upon Captain Wilkes for his courage in taking three or four unarmed men out of an unarmed vessel." He urges Seward to disregard concerns that rebel agents in Europe might persuade governments to recognize the Confederacy. "The question of recognition will be decided by the government there on views of their own interests and not from any representations which such men or any men indeed could make." Seward takes Cass's advice (he hears similar sentiments from others) and later profusely thanks him for this counsel.[263]

21: Colonel Arthur Rankin resigns as commander of the First Michigan Lancers. (See February 1, 1862.)[264]

23: Cameron wires Blair and notes that "Large numbers of foreign officers of military education and experience have tendered their services to the Government, which has to the extent of its ability availed itself of their offers." He now "respectfully recommends" that Blair do likewise.[265]

24: Congress passes an act to enable soldiers to allot pay, under which the president may appoint three allotment commissioners from each state. Eventually five allotment commissioners will serve in this role for Michigan: Frederick Hall* of Ionia and William Warner* of Detroit, William Phelps* of Detroit, Thomas D. Gilbert* of Grand Rapids, and James Geddes of Adrian (about whom no more is heard.) (See February 24, 1862.) Congress also appropriates $1,000,000 to finance "gun boats on the Western rivers."[266]

26: AG Thomas orders Captain Alfred Gibbs, USA*, to "Proceed with two companies to Fort Brady, Sault Sainte Marie, to guard the locks of the canal. Arms and two field pieces will be sent you immediately."[267]

Meanwhile, the Confederate diplomats seized from the *Trent* are released, and on New Year's Day board a British warship. The formal crisis with Britain, of no small concern to Michigan, now ends.

31: The year closes as the *Free Press* informs readers that yesterday "The Banks of New York, Boston and Philadelphia Suspended [Specie] Payment."[268]

Selected Legislation

Regular Session of 1861

These laws [Michigan's personal liberty laws] are right, and speak the sentiments of the people, and are, as I believe, in strict accordance with the constitution, and ought not to be repealed. Let them stand. This is no time for timid and vacillating counsels, when the cry of treason is ringing in our ears. . . . Michigan cannot recognize the right of a State to secede from this Union. We believe that the founders of our government designed it to be perpetual, and we cannot consent to have one star obliterated from the flag. For upwards of thirty years this question of the right of a State to secede has been agitated. It is time it was settled.

—GOVERNOR MOSES WISNER,
   VALEDICTORY SPEECH, JANUARY 1,
   1861[269]

Secession is revolution, and revolution, in the overt act, is treason, and must be treated as such.

—GOVERNOR AUSTIN BLAIR,
   INAUGURAL MESSAGE, JANUARY 2,
   1861[270]

No. 3: Joint Resolutions on the state of the Union

Whereas, "Certain citizens of the United States are at this time in open rebellion against the government, and by overt acts threaten its peace and harmony, and to compass its final overthrow"; therefore,

Resolved: "That the government of the United States is supreme, with full inherent powers of self-protection and defense."

Resolved: "That Michigan adheres to the government, as ordained by the constitution, and for sustaining it intact hereby pledges and tenders to the general government all its military power and material resources."

Resolved: "That concessions and compromise are not to be entertained or offered to traitors, while the rights and interests of Union-loving citizens should be regarded and respected in every place and under all circumstances."

Resolved: The governor is to send these resolves to Michigan's congressional delegation and other governors. Approved February 2, 1861.[271]

No. 185: An Act to amend an act entitled "an act to provide a military fund in aid of the uniformed volunteer militia," approved February 14, 1859.

Section 1: Appropriates $3,000 for 1861 (thereafter, annually appropriated) for a Military Fund, the proceeds of which are to be spent for military purposes and subject to the approval of the State Military Board.

Section 2: "All able-bodied, white male citizens, between the ages of eighteen and forty-five years, and not exempted by the laws of the United States or this State, shall be subject to military duty."

Section 10: Exempts from service those exempted from U.S. service and ministers, state court judges, legislators and officers, prison guards, commissioned officers of militia who have served for five years, and state and county officers, including public school teachers.

Section 11: Authorizes the governor, "In case of actual or threatened war against, insurrection in, or invasion of the State, or in case of actual rebellion in, or war against the United States, or in the case the President . . . shall make a requisition on the Governor, to "order out, by draft, voluntary enlistments, or otherwise, the whole, or so much of the militia of this State, as the public necessity demands . . . to suppress riots, and aid civil officers in the execution of the laws of this State or the United States." Authorizes the governor to "appoint the number by draft according to the population of the several counties of the State or otherwise. . . ." [This section also details mechanics of the draft.]

Section 12: Draftees who fail to appear, furnish a substitute, or have not paid the sheriff $25 within 24 hours "shall be deemed to be a soldier in actual service, absent without leave, and dealt with accordingly." Also authorizes county sheriffs to arrest those AWOL.

Section 16: Officers, NCOs, privates and musicians who uniform, arm and equip themselves shall possess these items exempt from civil process, including any levy to collect taxes; the horses of cavalrymen and light artillerymen are likewise exempt from civil process.

Section 17: "In case of any breach of the peace, tumults, riot or resistance of any process of this State, or apprehension of immediate danger thereof," the county sheriff, a city mayor, or recorder may "call for aid from any portion of the volunteer force"; requires the commanding officer contacted "to order out in aid of the civil authorities the military forces under his command; verbal orders will suffice; requires the commander to provide at least 24 rounds per soldier upon the call.

Section 19: "In case any officer, non-commissioned officer, musician or private, shall be wounded or disabled while in the service of the State, or in case of riot, tumult, breach of the peace, resistance of process, he shall be taken care of by the State, or whenever called in aid of the civil authorities of the county, he shall be taken care of and provided for at the expense of the county where such service shall have been rendered, until such disability ceases." Approved March 15, 1861.[272]

No. 251: An Act to provide a military force. [NB: Amended by Act No. 1, see Extra Session.]

Whereas, "Certain States have resolved to secede from the federal Union, have forcibly seized upon the arsenals, forts, custom houses, navy yards and other public property of the general government, and have willfully fired upon and insulted the flag of the United States, and are now in continued defiance of the federal laws, by which open rebellion and a state of war actually exists; *And whereas,* This State, as one of the loyal States of the Union, ought to be prepared to meet this public emergency, and to aid in sustaining the American Union and the federal laws and authority"; therefore,

Section 1: Empowers the governor to accept into state service the volunteer uniformed militia and in case their numbers are insufficient, "such of the enrolled militia as shall volunteer to be so mustered." This force will be organized as currently required by U.S. Army regulations and may not exceed twenty companies, or two regiments of ten companies each. The governor may commission their field officers. On the governor's orders, this force is "to be first used in case of actual hostilities, or to be transferred to the military service of the general government, whenever required by the President." Approved March 16, 1861.[273]

Extra Session, May 7, 1861

Gentlemen of the two Houses: We are just entering upon a war, the exact result of which no man can foresee. The sudden and splendid outburst of popular enthusiasm, which has illumined its commencement will shortly, in a great measure, disappear, and must be replaced by calm determination and resolute vigor. . . . He who went forth joyously singing the national anthem, will sometime be brought back in a bloody shroud. . . . This is to be no six weeks' campaign. . . . They who have taken the sword will perish by the sword, and this war, inaugurated to establish slaveholding despotism forever on this continent, will result in its total and speedy destruction.

—Austin Blair, Message to the Michigan Legislature, May 7, 1861[274]

[Senate Bill Introduced but not Passed]
A bill to provide for the punishment of certain offenses

against the public safety, and to define treason and sedition

Section 1: "That if any person, while any war, rebellion, or insurrection exists against the United States or this State, shall publish or cause to be published any seditious address, pamphlet, notice, letter, advertisement, picture, design, or any other printed engraved or lithographic matter, tending to bring into hatred or contempt the constitution and government of the United States, as lawfully established, or to excite unlawful opposition to the government of the United States or of this State," is liable to imprisonment for up to five years and a fine up to $10,000.[275]

No. 1: An Act to amend an act entitled "an act to provide a military force," approved March sixteenth, eighteen hundred and sixty-one, and to add several sections thereto.

Section 1: Authorizes the governor to accept up to one hundred companies not less than 78 nor more than 100 men each; organizes this force into one division of not more than two brigades, the whole divided into regiments of ten companies each; authorizes the governor to appoint general and field officers, the whole force "to be the first used in case of actual hostilities, or to be transferred to the military service of the general government whenever required by the president."

Section 2: The term of service shall be three years.

Section 15: Subjects Michigan soldiery to the U.S. Articles of War "provided that punishment by flogging or branding shall not in any case be inflicted."

Section 17: Authorizes the governor on necessity and whenever required to maintain existing regiments in U.S. service "to establish one or more recruiting offices."

Section 18: Authorizes the governor to appoint "three competent officers" to constitute a Military Contract Board: "no contract on behalf of this State, for equipment, clothing, rations or other supplies, or for labor or materials for the furnishing or providing for the troops" is valid without majority Board approval.

Section 20: In addition to the companies authorized in Section 1, the governor may recruit "a company of engineers, or sappers and miners," provided that this unit is accepted by the War Department.

Section 21: Empowers the governor "to purchase and distribute all necessary military stores, whether of subsistence, clothing, pay, medicine, field and camp equipage, arms, munitions and equipments. . . ." Approved May 10, 1861.[276]

No. 2: An Act to provide for the relief, by counties of the families of volunteers mustered from this State into the military service of the United States, or of this State.

Section 1: Requires the county Board of Supervisors at each June 1861 session "to make adequate provision for all requisite relief and support of the families of the commissioned and non-commissioned officers, musicians and privates, enlisted from their counties and mustered into the military service of the United States, or of this State." Authorizes counties to borrow money at a rate not to exceed 10 percent or issue bonds with maturities not exceeding one year, and to levy taxes for repayment.

Section 2: Requires the appropriate town official "to make diligent inquiry in regard to the necessities and relief required by the family of any such [officer or soldier] . . . in conducting such inquiries, it shall be his duty to consult with any voluntary committees of citizens who may have heretofore taken, or who shall hereafter take action upon the subject." Authorizes "temporary relief" not to exceed $15 per month per family. Where a soldier dies in service, his family may receive for one year after his death, "the same measure of relief herein provided for."

Section 3: Permits counties to establish a separate fund into which money not otherwise spent may be transferred for family relief; such a fund will be known as the Volunteers' Family Relief Fund; requires the county to establish such a fund whenever the county debt trades at an average discount of 10 percent for a six-month period.

Section 5: Any family aid afforded under this act "shall be and remain separate from, and independent of, the relief, temporary or otherwise, afforded to poor persons under existing laws." Approved May 10, 1861.[277]

No. 4: An Act to provide a tax for interest on the war loan.

Section 1: Imposes a tax in 1861 and 1862, in addition to other taxes "for the payment of the interest on the war loan of the State"; if taxes exceed the amount required for interest payments, the surplus will be applied to principal repayment. Approved May 10, 1861.[278]

No. 5: An Act authorizing a war loan.

Whereas, "Our country has reached a crisis unprecedented in its past history, and treason and civil war are raging within its borders; *And whereas,* Attempts are made, in large sections of the country, to break up and destroy the government, and it has become necessary for the several States to look to their own safety, as well as the defense and perpetuity of the Union and government of the nation"; therefore: **Section 1:** Directs the governor and treasurer "for the purpose of organizing the volunteer militia, repelling invasion, suppressing insurrection, or defending the State in time of war, to negotiate the contract for a loan or loans" as may be necessary for these purposes, not exceeding $1,000,000. This loan must be redeemable at the state's call and not to exceed in maturity twenty-five years with an interest rate not to exceed 7 percent, to be called the War Loan of the State of Michigan. Exempts bonds issued from all Michigan taxes, the proceeds to be used for the War Fund ("for no other purpose").

Section 6: To repay the bonds, in addition to existing taxes, a statewide tax levy is authorized commencing in 1861 equal to 1/16 of a mill on all property. The proceeds will constitute a sinking fund, and when collected will be segregated and applied to bond repayment.

Section 8: "The faith of the State is hereby pledged for the repayment of principal and interest of the bonds which may be issued under the provisions of this act." Approved May 10, 1861.[279]

State Affairs

AG Robertson's 1861 annual report claimed that 24,000 Michigan recruits had been or were then in service since the beginning of the war: 21,548 consisting of the First Michigan (three-month), the First through Fifteenth Michigan (three-year) and Stockton's independent infan-

try; the First through the Third Michigan Cavalry and the company-sized Chandler Horse Guards[280]; and six companies of sharpshooters, seven companies of attached or independent light artillery, the Lancer Regiment, and First Michigan Engineers. Robertson claimed 1,679 men enlisted in companies formed in Michigan but who had migrated to other states, and a "supposed" 773 men enlisted directly into other state regiments.[281]

By one estimate, the thirty-day First Michigan would prove fertile: from its original roster of 798 men, 154 would eventually become officers, serving in forty-one regiments, most of these from Michigan. These officers would be found in infantry, cavalry, and artillery units; their ranks included at least ten colonels and one major general.[282]

By the time AG Robertson reported on December 24, 1861, the distribution of Michigan regiments mirrored the breadth of the war: the state's infantry, artillery, and cavalry could be found in one or more locations in Maryland, western Virginia, Virginia, South Carolina, Kentucky, Missouri, and in the Washington defenses. A number of units remained organizing in Michigan and were encamped in Flint, Niles, Kalamazoo, Ypsilanti, Monroe, Detroit, and Coldwater.[283]

As of December 10, these in-state units included the Tenth (661 men in camp/Flint) Twelfth (805/Niles), Thirteenth (708/Kalamazoo), Fourteenth (no report/Ypsilanti), and Fifteenth (292/Monroe) infantry regiments; the First Regiment Engineers and Mechanics (1,000 men, under orders for Kentucky), the Lancer Regiment (500 men "at last report"/Detroit); and attached artillery companies with the First Engineers (45), the Second Cavalry (110), and the Third Cavalry (80). There were two more artillery companies and one sharpshooter company, about which there is no report. (No locations were reported for company-sized units. See update for January 10, 1862.)[284]

The War Department figures (which usually varied from state totals) for Michigan's 1861 contributions were (quota/furnished):

Three-month call of April 15, 1861: 780/781.
Three-year call of May 3 (confirmed by Congress August 6), July 22 and 25, 1861: 21,357/23,546.[285]

Costs, and the shifting of military and personnel costs between state, local, and federal governments, would become an issue as the war matured; at this point, the balance was chiefly between localities and states advancing funds and the federal government's glacial pace of reimbursements, essentially transferring costs to states and their taxpayers; in 1861 these were mostly state costs with federal expenditures imposed through the direct tax. Prompting this cost-shifting were the enormous expenses of mobilization and the federal government's inability to pay. In 1861, the best cost estimate to stand up five Michigan infantry regiments was $346,020. Costs included pay; rifled muskets; matching accouterments; wall, conical, and hospital tents; company desks; mess kits; 65 wagons for transportation; 260 horses for wagons, with harness to match; drums, fifes, and bugles; clothing and blankets; knapsacks; stationary; and camp and garrison equipage. These items plus heat and medical care for these units cost $135,956.65 each month. By comparison, artillery units were bargains: initial costs for two light artillery batteries were $50,560, with a modest monthly cash flow drain of $8,103.14 to heat, treat, and pay the 180 to 200 men that might compose two companies.[286]

For the fiscal year ending November 30, 1861, treasurer John Owen reported that total state disbursements amounted to $1,321,441.22 against receipts of $1,294,261.43, leaving an operating deficit of $27,179.79. These accounts were separate from the War Fund, created under the act of May 10, 1861. Of the $1,000,000 bonds authorized, Michigan had sold $449,100 in face value at 95 percent of par, in other words, realizing $426,631.50 exclusive of accrued interest. In his January 1862 annual message, Blair stated that the total amount Michigan had effectively advanced to the federal government was $539,428.91; when accounts were compiled, he estimated this figure would rise to approximately $600,000. However Michigan had received only $92,000 in reimbursement from the U.S. Treasury.[287]

For 1861, the War Bonds were the only war-connected debt outstanding. Total debt, including the War Bonds, was $2,836,264.24.[288]

1862

Key Events

January

2: Michigan legislature convenes. Blair delivers annual message.[1]

3: Lieutenant Colonel Joseph Rowe Smith* is appointed U.S. chief mustering and disbursing officer for Michigan, and is based in Detroit. (See June 11, 1864.) The War Department asks Blair to list the names and strengths of Michigan's two- and three-year as well as independent units.[2]

4: After seven ballots, the Michigan legislature elects Jacob M. Howard to the U.S. Senate. Blair challenged Howard for the nomination but lost on the final ballot, 49 to 9. (See January 5, 1865.)[3]

9: In Coldwater, Battery F of the First Michigan Light Artillery musters into U.S. service; recruits and officers are drawn from Coldwater, Three Rivers, and vicinity.[4] (See July 1, 1865.)

10: Michigan AAG DeGarmo Jones* updates the December 10, 1861, report on the status of Michigan units organizing: the Tenth (883 men in camp), Twelfth (900), Thirteenth (1,100); Fourteenth (700), and Fifteenth (600) infantry regiments; the Lancer Regiment (850); the artillery company with the First Engineers (45); the artillery company with the Second Cavalry (110); the artillery company with the Thirteenth Infantry (140); Captain Kin S. Dygert's* company of sharpshooters (110); Captain Floyd A. Willett's* company of sharpshooters (70); Captain Spencer J. Mather's* company of sharpshooters (50); Captain J. Brown Jr.'s company of sharpshooters (70).[5]

11: Simon Cameron resigns as secretary of war.

15: Edwin M. Stanton[6] replaces Simon Cameron as secretary of war. Like other Democratic sheets in Michigan, the *Free Press* is impressed and self-impressed. "The appointment of Edward M. Stanton in the place of Mr. Cameron, must be regarded as a tribute from Mr. Lincoln to the loyalty and sacrifices of the democratic party." The Republican *Lansing State Journal*, glad to see Simeon Cameron depart, is hopeful about the new secretary, as is the *Jackson Citizen*: "The appointment of Mr. Stanton gives universal satisfaction. . . . There does not seem to be a single exception."[7]

17: In Kalamazoo, the Thirteenth Michigan musters into U.S. service with 935 men; recruits and officers are drawn from Kalamazoo, Galesburg, Gun Plain, Battle Creek, Pewamo, Portage, Otsego, and Mattawan. The unit will deploy west and accompany Sherman to the sea. (See January 12, 1864.) Meanwhile, in Coldwater, Battery G of the First Michigan Light Artillery also musters into U.S. service; recruits and officers are drawn chiefly from Coldwater, Hillsdale, St. Joseph, Kalamazoo, and Branch County. (See August 6, 1865.) Meanwhile, in response to numerous allegations of improprieties in military contracting, the Michigan Senate adopts a resolution to "inquire into the military expenditures of the State" during 1861. (See March 20.)[8]

19: The Battle of Mill Springs (which the press in Michigan and elsewhere calls the Battle of Somerset) is fought in Kentucky: Federals defeat Confederates, who withdraw across the Cumberland River. Confederate momentum in eastern Kentucky is sapped and their line, which had run from the Cumberland Gap to Columbus, Kentucky, is broken. Both the *Cass County Republican* and the fiercely Democratic *East Saginaw Courier* agree: it is a "glorious victory."[9]

20: Michigan legislature adjourns.[10]

23: In the U.S. Senate, Jacob Howard presents Michigan's Joint Resolution No. 3 (see Selected Legislation—1862) asking for POW exchanges.[11]

27: Lincoln issues General War Order No. 1, decreeing that February 22, 1862, "be the day for a general movement of the Land and Naval forces of the United States against insurgent forces." Among the armies specified in the order are "The Army of the Potomac, The Army of Western Virginia, The Army near Munfordsville, [sic] Kentucky, and The Army and Flotilla at Cairo."[12]

30: Halleck gives U. S. Grant permission "to take and hold Fort Henry."[13]

31: Chapter 15: An Act to authorize the President of the United States in certain Cases to take Possession of Railroad and Telegraph Lines, and for other purposes, becomes law.[14] (See February 26.)

February

1: Stanton directs ASW Thomas A. Scott to Detroit "to examine into the condition of Michigan troops, and particularly the Rankin Lancers." Scott will arrive in Detroit by the evening of February 3.[15] (See March 20.)

6: In Flint, 997 men of the Tenth Michigan muster into U.S. service; recruits are drawn from Byron, Saginaw, Orion, Sanilac, Port Huron, Almont, Memphis, Pontiac, Flint, and Hillsdale. The unit will serve west and accompany Sherman to the sea.[16] (See February 6, 1864.)

Meanwhile, in Tennessee, Fort Henry surrenders to federal forces.

10: General George B. McClellan recommends to Stanton "that all authority heretofore given to raise corps, regiments, or independent companies other than through the Governors of the several States be revoked"; persons authorized to raise these independent units should be ordered to report "the numbers and condition of the troops raised by them, and that they be directed to stop recruiting." (See February 21.)[17]

12: The Thirteenth Michigan, 925 men, and 145 men of the Seventh Michigan Battery (Company G of the First Michigan Light Artillery, "Lanphere's Battery," commanded by Captain Charles H. Lanphere*) depart the state.[18]

13: The Fourteenth Michigan musters into U.S. service at Ypsilanti with 925 men; recruits and officers are drawn from Grand Rapids, East Saginaw, Detroit, Lansing, Monroe, Ypsilanti, Pontiac, and St. Johns. The unit will deploy west and accompany Sherman to the sea.[19] (See May 16, 1864.)

13–16: Grant's infantry attacks Fort Donelson (on the 13th); federal gunboats bombard the fort (14th), followed by battle (15th). On the 16th, Fort Donelson surrenders. "'Unconditional surrender' was the terms demanded of the rebels at Fort Donelson by Gen. Grant, and we like the words and accept them.

Let this be the proposition of the President, and no other," exults the *Lansing State Journal*. The Democratic *Grand Haven News* also exults, declaring that "the heroism displayed at the taking of Fort Henry, and the Spartan bravery and stoic endurance of our troops at Fort Donelson [have] full wiped out the stain upon our glorious escutcheon" of First Bull Run.[20]

14: Returns for Michigan's volunteer cavalry show three regiments (unidentified) all mounted, armed, and equipped, numbering 1,131, 1,173, and 1,134, or a total of 3,438 aggregate; a separate War Department accounting shows the aggregate number of Michigan horse troopers at 3,671, consisting of 3,510 enlisted men and 161 officers.[21]

21: The War Department issues General Order No. 18, which provides in part that "The Governors of States are legally the authorities for raising volunteer regiments and commissioning their officers. Accordingly, no independent organizations, as such, will be hereafter recognized in the U.S. service."[22]

22: Hopkins and Butler are released from Fort Lafayette after signing the following parole: "We, the undersigned, do solemnly promise on our word of honor that we will render no aid or comfort to the enemies in hostility to the Government of the United States." But David C. Wattles feels differently. "I am, and have always been, a loyal citizen. I have said or done nothing worthy the treatment I have received. . . . I therefore demand a trial or unconditional release." His imprisonment continues. (See April 9.)[23]

24: In Detroit, Michigan's allotment commissioners meet at the Biddle House. Within several days they depart to visit Michigan's deployed units in the eastern and western theaters, beginning with Washington and Kentucky.[24]

25: Buell's forces occupy Nashville, Tennessee; the Legal Tender Act becomes law.[25]

Meanwhile, Stanton warns newspaper editors and publishers in important cities against publishing "intelligence" about military operations. Violators are subject to arrest and newspapers to seizure.[26]

26: Stanton orders that the army "will take military possession of the telegraphic lines in the United States." Newspapers publishing unauthorized military news "will be excluded . . . from receiving information by telegraph or from transmitting their papers by railroad."[27]

27: The *Detroit Free Press* reprints an article from the Republican-leaning *Niles Inquirer* that claims, "We know, beyond the possibility of a doubt that there is a lodge of the Knights of the Golden Circle in this city, and that certain prominent democrats are members." The *Inquirer's* accusations end on a sensational note: one of this group members now serves as a Union soldier from Michigan, and he had "taken the horrid oath to wade to his knees in human blood to kill President Lincoln at the bid of Jefferson Davis." *Free Press* publisher Walker declares this last claim "shows that a man's gullibility must have the dilating powers of an anaconda to swallow such transparent humbug. Pshaw, you have been badly sold!" (See March 18.)[28]

28: Complying with a U.S. Senate request, Stanton accounts for recent state troop contributions. Michigan's contribution is 12,024. This presumably includes three residents promoted to volunteer general from the Regular Army and two promoted to general from civil life.[29]

March

2: The *Detroit Free Press* calls what it believes to be the bluff of Detroit's Republican sheets on the subject of disloyal organizations. "The opposition organs of this city pretend to know of the existence of a secret treasonable organization in the State of Michigan styled 'The Knights of the Golden Circle.' . . . The Republican papers of Detroit charge that such organizations do exist in Michigan." If so, then the *Free Press* demands that the Republican U.S. DA Alfred Russell and his U.S. marshal investigate and prosecute, or else face charges of dereliction.[30]

Confederates complete evacuation of Columbus, Kentucky. Federal troops occupy Columbus tomorrow.

4: In Detroit, Company I of the First USSS muster into U.S. service. It will deploy east. On December 23, 1864, it will transfer to the Fifth Michigan.[31] (See March 4, 1865.)

5: The state democratic convention convenes in Detroit's Young Men's Hall (see August 31, 1864), S. Dow Ellwood* presiding, and postpones nominations for state office. Resolutions include supporting the Federal government by any constitutional means to end the rebellion, and opposing ending the war until resistance ends; denouncing abolition as the moral equivalent of secession; approving Stanton's appointment and Lincoln's retraction of Fremont's emancipation measure; and denouncing Republican corruption. (See October 2 and 8.)[32]

In Niles, the Twelfth Michigan is mustered into U.S. service; recruits or officers were drawn from Niles, Cassopolis, St. Joseph, Buchanan, Albion, Lansing, Lawton, Berrien, and Porter. It will deploy and serve east. By war's end, total enrollment will be 2,357, including 29 KIA, 26 DOW, 17 died as POWs, 316 DOD, and 221 DFD. The Twelfth will be discharged in February, 1866.[33]

6: Lincoln introduces a resolution to Congress, "That the United States ought to cooperate with any State that may adopt gradual abolishment of slavery, giving to such State pecuniary aid, to be used by such State in its discretion, to compensate for the inconveniences, public and private, produced by such change of system." This the House will approve (97 to 36) on March 11 and the Senate (32 to 10) on April 2. (See July 12.)

Meanwhile, in Jackson, Battery H of the First Michigan Light Artillery musters in to U.S. service; recruits and officers are drawn from Spaulding, Port Huron, Detroit, and Pontiac. The unit deploys west and will accompany Sherman in the Atlanta Campaign.[34] (See July 22, 1865.)

7: State elections are held.

7–8: A federal victory at the Battle of Pea Ridge reestablishes control over Missouri and northern Arkansas.

8: Battle of Hampton Roads, the first day. The ironclad CSS *Virginia* (formerly USS *Merrimack*) destroys the wooden hulled *Cumberland* and *Congress*, and runs the *Minnesota* aground.

9: Battle of Hampton Roads, the second day: the federal ironclad *Monitor* engages the *Merrimack* but with indecisive results. Checkmated, the *Merrimack* returns to port. The federal blockade continues.

13: Congress amends the Articles of War: no soldier or sailor may return slaves to anyone claiming ownership. Meanwhile, the Eighth Michigan Battery (Company H of the First Michigan Light Artillery Regiment, "DeGolyer's Battery," commanded by Captain Samuel DeGolyer*, departs the state with 156 men. Colonel Kellogg resigns from command of the Second Michigan Cavalry.[35]

14: Federals capture New Madrid, Missouri, in the west and New Berne, North Carolina, in the east.

17: The Army of the Potomac boards steamers to commence the Peninsula Campaign.

18: The Detroit *Tribune*, seeking to refute Democratic denials of that party's connection with subversive organizations, publishes as genuine Dr. Hopkins's hoax letter. And it goes a step further, commenting that the "secret organizations referred to existed in Detroit, Ypsilanti, Jackson, Michigan Centre, Kalamazoo, Lapeer, North Branch, Almont, Lakeville, Utica, Mount Clemens, Emmett, and other towns in the interior of Michigan"; moreover, these organizations were active in Canada, at Port Sarnia, St. Mary's Windsor, Hamilton, Toronto, and other places. Franklin Pierce was on a "treasonable mission," and "One object of these SECRET DEMOCRATIC ORGANIZATIONS was and is to prevent enlistments. . . . Another object was to enlarge and extend their organization for *open resistance to the government*." (See March 26.)

The Twelfth Michigan, 1,000 men, departs the state.[36]

19: War Department AG Lorenzo Thomas[37] wires Blair asking for "an immediate telegraphic report of whole number of organized regiments, companies, or batteries, of cavalry, artillery, and infantry now mustered or ready to be mustered into U.S. service, but still within the limits of your State."[38] (See March 20.)

20: AG Robertson replies to yesterday's request from Thomas. There are presently three infantry regiments in state and no cavalry or artillery units. Of these units, those that have been mustered into U.S. service are fully armed, uniformed, and equipped, and have been ordered to St. Louis by General Henry Halleck. One complication is money: men have been unpaid for months and will move if they can be paid through January 31. The officers "are much in debt" and "have been led to believe that they would be paid before leaving the State." Although U.S. paymaster Major Joshua Howard* has been ordered to pay the men, he has no funds, and Blair is anxious for men to march. The one unit that has been paid left the previous day for St. Louis. "It is hoped that money will be immediately sent to Major Howard," Robertson states.[39]

Meanwhile, two Michigan units muster into U.S. service. In Monroe, the Fifteenth Michigan musters in with 869 men; recruits and officers are drawn from Monroe, Burr Oak, Detroit, Trenton, St. Clair, and Petersburg. The unit will deploy west and accompany Sherman to the sea.[40] (See May 4, 1864.) In Detroit, Company K of the First USSS musters in. It will deploy east, and on December 23, 1864, will transfer to the Fifth Michigan.[41]

Separately, over the protest of Governor Blair, the First United States Lancers is mustered out of service. During its brief stint, 683 men were enrolled, of whom 4 DOD, 1 DFD, and 29 deserted.[42]

Finally, in Lansing, the Senate Select Committee issues its report on corruption among Michigan's military contractors. It declares that "the military expenditures of the State during the past year have been conducted with ability and fidelity, and that strict economy has generally characterized every branch of the service."[43]

23: General Thomas J. "Stonewall" Jackson, CSA, commences his Valley Campaign with victory at the Battle of Kernstown.

26: In the U.S. Senate, Senator Milton Latham, a Democrat from California and friend of Franklin Pierce, introduces a resolution asking Seward to give the Senate any correspondence between him and Franklin Pierce, "having reference to a supposed conspiracy against the Government." When Senate President Hannibal Hamlin asks if there are any objections, Michigan senator Howard expresses the hope that no one will object to this. But Michigan's senior senator, Chandler, while not objecting, offers some comments.

Chandler acknowledges that the Hopkins letter was "a joke" and that when arrested, Hopkins was en route to enlist in the Union army; but he also declares (and implies that he has other information) that at the same time, the Knights of the Golden Circle had decided to infiltrate the Union army, placing men in every regiment, implying that perhaps Hopkins was one of these. Chandler is certain that "they did succeed in getting a large number of the worst traitors" into the army. Chandler concludes by declaring that he now has "more information than it is necessary for me to divulge at this time in reference to the matter."

Senator Howard, while supportive of Latham's resolution, professes not to know what Seward's correspondence will contain. But he asks Latham to amend the resolution to include government documents "relating to the organization and purposes of a secret combination known commonly as the Knights of the Golden Circle." Latham demurs and a slightly amended resolution is eventually adopted.[44] (See April 5.)

27: The Fifteenth Michigan, 869 men, departs the state.[45]

28: Detroit *Tribune* editor Barns writes Seward that "Circumstances have transpired which render it certain to my mind that there exists here and probably through every Northern State an organized treasonable association which is in sympathy and constant communication with similar associations in the rebel States and with the rebels." These disloyal persons belong to "a certain class of men uniformly known as Democratic sympathizers with the rebels," and Canada is the base of their operations and communication with Europe and the South, all of which is aided by "sympathizing friends along the borders of this frontier," from Detroit to Lake Huron. Barns asks not only that more detectives be assigned to Detroit, but that they be more reliable: the current U.S. marshal is often absent, and his backup consists of untrustworthy Democrats.[46]

April

3: The War Department issues GO No. 33 that halts all recruiting. (See May 19 and June 2.) AG Thomas notifies Blair that "Volunteer recruiting service will cease from this date." An unsigned note in Stanton's handwriting gives more details: officers on recruiting duty will return to their regiments, and governors will be notified "that no expenses of enlistment or recruiting will be paid unless it has been authorized by a previous call of this Department." (See May 1.)[47]

5: The *Free Press* editorializes on Franklin Pierce's innocence. "Will the papers in Michigan which have assailed him retract the slander, now that they *know* it is a slander? We fear they will not. The spring elections are to be carried."[48] (But see April 7.)

Siege of Yorktown, Virginia, begins.

6: Battle of Shiloh, first day.

7: State elections: Later, the *Free Press*, seeing Democratic victories in counties and municipalities, will comment that the results "could not be more gratifying." In Oakland, Washtenaw, Ingham, and Clinton Counties, Democratic boards of supervisors were elected "for the first time in years." It also reports "large gains" in Kent, Jackson, Calhoun, Cass, Kalamazoo, Macomb, Lapeer, and Shiawassee. "These returns show an extraordinary revolution going on in Michigan, a revolution that the lying and defamation of partisans and party organs cannot stop."

Battle of Shiloh, second day. Separately, federals capture Island No. 10. The *Free Press* header declares, "The Great Victory," while the headers for stories about Island No. 10 and McClellan's occupation of Yorktown describe "Bloodless Victories." The *Cass County Republican* agrees, with the headline "Great Victory in Western Tennessee." Still, few details about the battle have reached Michigan.[49]

9: The first news of the scale, casualties, and outcome of the Battle of Shiloh reaches Detroit. "A Great Battle on the Tennessee . . . Beauregard's Forces Utterly Routed . . . The Loss on Both Sides Very Heavy" are the *Free Press* headlines this morning. The news takes a day or so longer for sheets outside of Detroit. On the next day, the *Cass County Republican* has the headlines, "The Battle at Pittsburgh Landing . . . Total Route [*sic*] of the Enemy . . . Great Loss on Both Sides." When the news is received at Grand Haven the next day, business is suspended and crowds gather to hear the dispatches read publicly. "To reside in a place where there is no daily mail," the editor later laments, "is like placing us a century behind the times."[50]

Meanwhile, at Fort Lafayette, David C. Wattles signs a parole on similar terms to those Hopkins and Butler signed on February 22. (See that date.) Wattles is soon released. Meanwhile, although the elections are over, the *Lansing State Republican* continues to express concern about the KGC. "[Of t]he existence of this treasonable secret order of Knighthood there can no longer be any doubt," and its reach extends to the North, northwest, Canada, and the South. It laments that Michigan "is not without her share of this infamy," and that "Men, who Michigan has in former time, delighted to honor with high positions of trust, and who now claim to be leaders of the democratic party have . . . joined this secret band of traitors." It concludes that "The halter [death by hanging] would fail to do justice to them."[51]

10: As more of the Battle of Shiloh's particulars are received, joy in victory competes with news of casualties. In general, the army's medical resources are overwhelmed at the unprecedented scale of losses. The *Free Press* publishes an appeal, "Surgeons Wanted."[52]

11: Federals capture Fort Pulaski, Georgia.

12: News of Shiloh's casualties has moved from the general to the specific, as word of Michigan's losses reach home. In Detroit a large public meeting convenes in Detroit, chaired by Mayor William C. Duncan.* Several resolutions are passed, including one that declares, "It is the duty of the citizens of this State to provide for the wants of the sick and wounded soldiers of the Michigan troops now in the field; and that an efficient, reliable and organized system should be instituted to dispense the contributions of the people, through their own agents directly to our own disabled and suffering fellow citizens." An organization is formed called the Michigan Soldiers' Relief Committee (not to be confused with the Detroit/Michigan Ladies' Soldiers' Aid Society). One important difference is that men lead the committee, including state AG Robertson, Charles C. Trowbridge, Anthony Dudgeon, Henry A. Morrow*, William A. Butler*, and Lewis Cass. The meeting raises $1,385 and two fundraisers are appointed for each city ward.

Across Michigan, casualty lists begin to appear over the next month, and not just from Shiloh; other battles have been fought, including Yorktown and Island No. 10. The Twelfth Michigan reports twenty-six men killed, ninety-three wounded, and ninety-six missing; in Hillsdale, George Sanderson, "formerly of L. B. Baldy's Store and an orderly sergeant in an Indiana regiment," died of wounds in Cincinnati. Lists from the Fifteenth Michigan show that it entered the battle 800 strong and came out with 400.[53]

14: Stanton notifies Blair that the returns [of regiments and soldiers] made by many states are "imperfect"; he now asks for "a full and accurate statement of all the troops from your State which are now in the service of the General Government, together with a separate list of all not mustered into the service, and all used as home guards, &c?" The purpose is to allow Washington to make "adequate appropriations for payment and supply."[54]

16: The previous night, William A. Howard and Detroit doctor E. M. Clark left Detroit for an inspection tour of Michigan units at Yorktown. On this day, Austin Blair and AG Robertson leave for the Shiloh battle-field, accompanied by Colonel Pittman, Reuben N. Rice, and Detroit businessman and Common Council clerk Heman A. Lacey. "All the Michigan regiments in the department [of Mississippi] were visited," Robertson reports later, and notes that their health conditions "compare favorably" with those of other Northern troops. Blair will return to Michigan on May 3.[55]

Slavery is abolished in the District of Columbia. Meanwhile, the War Department issues GO No. 41, which requires U.S. paymasters to cooperate with "All agents appointed by the Governors of a State under its laws to obtain from its volunteer soldiers assignments of pay for the benefit of their families." The order also requires federal reimbursement to states for transporting soldiers on sick leave traveling to and from their units. Reimbursements are to be deducted from the soldier's pay.[56]

17: The Fourteenth Michigan, 925 men, departs the state.[57]

18: On the lower Mississippi approximately eighty airline miles south of New Orleans, federal gunboats bombard Fort Jackson and Fort St. Philip.

22: The Tenth Michigan, 997 men, departs the state.[58]

25: Federals occupy New Orleans.

May

1: Stanton rationalizes to General Halleck that the April 3 cessation of recruiting was only a ploy "for the purpose of compelling returns from the respective Governors" (see April 14). But "It is the design of the [War] Department to keep the force up to its present standard"; since all governors have responded with updates, Halleck may now "call upon the Governors of the respective States in your command for recruits to fill up the regiments now in the field." Today the War Department issues GO No. 49, returning recruiting authority to governors, but only for requisitions by field commanders to fill existing regiments.[59]

5: Federals are victorious at the Battle of Williamsburg, Virginia. Among federal regiments engaged, the Fifth Michigan ranked fifth in casualties suffered (144).[60]

9: In Detroit, the Stanton Guard, formed at the request of Lieutenant Colonel Joseph Rowe Smith, musters into U.S. service a single company designated for guard duty at Mackinac Island. Grover S. Wormer* commands.[61] (See May 14.)

Meanwhile, Confederates evacuate Norfolk, Virginia.

11: The *Merrimack* (CSS *Virginia*) is destroyed.

14: Docking at Mackinac Island, the steamer *Illinois* disembarks three high-ranking Confederate sympathizers: General William G. Harding, General Washington Barrows, and Judge Joseph C. Guild, all arrested earlier on orders from Tennessee military governor Andrew Johnson. Wormer's Stanton Guards will provide security.[62] (See September 9.)

17: Army surgeon-general Hammond asks Stanton for authority to halt "the interference of State agents and others who are not acting under the direction of this Bureau." State agents are destined to become a pillar of Michigan's war effort.[63]

19: As the April 3 suspension of recruiting was reversed, AG Thomas now asks Blair "how soon you can raise and organize three or more infantry regiments" to be armed and equipped and sent to Washington. Michigan AAG Frederick Morley* replies that Governor Blair and AG Robertson are absent at Pittsburgh Landing (Shiloh); however, Morley forwards Thomas's note to Blair.[64]

21: AG Thomas asks Blair to "Raise one regiment of infantry immediately" and to "Do everything in your power to urge enlistments." Blair need not worry about supplies because orders were issued to provide "clothing, arms, and equipments" before that unit will leave Michigan. (See May 24.)[65]

23: Stonewall Jackson is victorious at the Battle of Front Royal, Virginia.

24: AG Thomas offers Blair an incentive concerning the regiment requisitioned on May 21: if the unit is raised in thirty days, the officers will be paid from the commencement of service, that is, from the time they begin recruiting versus waiting for U.S. muster.[66]

25: General Nathaniel Banks retreats in confusion from Winchester, Virginia. An anxious Stanton telegraphs Blair that "Intelligence from various quarters leaves no doubt that the enemy in great force is advancing on Washington." He asks Blair (and other governors) to "forward immediately all the volunteer and militia force in your state." Separately, Lincoln "takes military possession of all railroads in the United States."[67]

Meanwhile, at Pittsburg Landing, Blair and AG Robertson finish their inspection tour. Just minutes before departing, the Second Michigan's Captain Russell A. Alger* informs them that the Second's commander Colonel Granger has been promoted to brigade command and the regiment is leaderless. Alger pitches Granger's recommendation for a replacement, an obscure commissary officer. The governor, hesitant but harried (the steamship's departure whistle has blown), finally agrees and orders AG Robertson to write the order on the spot: "General Orders No. 148: Captain Philip H. Sheridan, U.S. Army, is hereby appointed colonel of the 2d Regiment Michigan Cavalry."[68]

26: Stanton asks Blair to telegraph chief of ordnance General James Ripley and U.S. QMG Montgomery Meigs "the points where you desire arms and clothing to be placed for your new regiments to be raised under [the] recent call." Separately, the War Department wants to make certain that U.S. mustering officers are cooperating with state authorities: "Afford every assistance to the Governor of your State in raising the troops just called for," AG Thomas wires Colonel Backus.[69]

27: Washington is no longer threatened, and Stanton's wire to Pennsylvania governor Curtin ("General Banks is at Williamsport with his force in much better condition than was expected, and without having suffered any great loss.") is now generally known in Michigan. As Banks's emergency has passed, Stanton informs Blair what he has just told Curtin: that since the US can now "procure promptly" enough three-year troops, "you will please accept no more [men] for less term without special order."[70]

30: Stanton notifies Blair of an order that redeems the War Department's call for three-month volunteers during the recent emergency. All militia units and ninety-day troops who were (or will be) able to report to Washington by June 10 will be mustered into three-month U.S. service, and will be paid; 50,000 three-year men will be accepted under this call.[71] (See June 9.)

Elsewhere, Confederates evacuate Corinth, Mississippi; this severs the critical Memphis & Charleston Railroad.

31: AG Thomas authorizes Blair to raise one three-year cavalry regiment, to be readied by July 4. (See June 10.) In Virginia, the Battle of Fair Oaks begins; it ends the next day in a Federal victory. Among federal regiments engaged, the Third Michigan ranks fifth in casualties (169) and the Fifth Michigan ranks eighth (155).[72]

June

1: Blair commissions Darius Clark* colonel in the Michigan militia and orders him to New York City to act as the state military agent. (He will serve throughout the war. Clark had already been representing Michigan's sanitary interests, and will serve as state agent without pay.) Meanwhile, Jabez Fountain provides a list of thirty-seven Michigan soldier patients in Philadelphia's military hospitals.[73]

5: Confederates evacuate Fort Pillow in Tennessee.

6: Federal and Confederate fleets engage on the Mississippi River in front of Memphis. The Confederates are overmatched and Memphis surrenders.

Separately, War Department GO No. 60 formally retracts the discontinuation of volunteer recruiting established in GO No. 33, issued April 3, 1862.[74]

8: Confederates are victorious at the Battle of Cross Keys, Virginia.

9: Perhaps referring to Stanton's May 30 wire declaring that 50,000 three-year men would be accepted, AG Thomas asks Blair, "When will your regiments be ready? When will they be ready to march to Annapolis?" Separately, Confederates triumph at the Battle of Port Republic, Virginia.[75]

10: Reflecting the seasonality of recruiting in an agricultural state, Blair replies to Stanton in reference to the May 31 authorization to raise a cavalry regiment. Blair promises to "cheerfully undertake to raise the regiment" but warns Stanton that it cannot be done by July 1, and that recruiting is unlikely to end by August 1. "It is the worst season of the year to recruit in the West, and the drain has already been considerable," Blair states. He asks if Stanton can accommodate this timing.[76]

16: Confederates triumph at the Battle of Secessionville (James Island), South Carolina. Among federal units engaged, the Eighth Michigan ranks first in casualties suffered (184).[77]

18: Troop shortages deepen as casualties mount in both eastern and western theaters. "We are in pressing need of troops," AG Thomas writes Blair. "How many can you forward immediately?"[78]

21: In Washington, Mrs. Elmina Brainard* of Lapeer,

Michigan, who has been in Washington since March visiting hospitals as a freelance nurse, is hired as a "visiting and distributing agent" of the Michigan Soldiers' Relief Association of Washington and given charge of hospital visiting. She is a volunteer, although she is given $5 per week for expenses. (See September 23 and October 1.)[79] Meanwhile, back in Detroit, eight nuns from the Sisters of Charity[80] leave for Baltimore to serve as nurses in federal hospitals; they join five others already there. The absence of so many teaching sisters threatens to close several of Detroit's parochial schools.[81]

23: Stanton forwards Blair an "Order to Encourage Enlistments" that allows for a $2 bounty and an advance of one months' pay to volunteers upon muster.[82]

June 25–July 1: Seven Days' Campaign, Virginia.

June 25: Separately, Seward, reflecting the Lincoln administration's concerns about army losses, prepares to travel to New York to "rouse the popular feeling and raise troops to reinforce the wasting Army." Lincoln writes a letter making the case for a new levy (but not specifying numbers) that he hands to Seward "to use in his confidential intercourse with prominent men in the North."[83]

26: Farragut commences bombarding the Vicksburg, Mississippi, defenses. The Seven Days' Campaign Battle of Mechanicsville is a seeming Union victory.

27: Seven Days' Campaign: Confederates triumph at the Battle of Gaines's Mill. Among Federal units engaged, the Sixteenth Michigan ranks fifth in casualties suffered (214).[84]

28: By 6:00 a.m., Farragut's fleet had run the Vicksburg defenses, and incurred casualties of fifteen dead and thirty wounded. Back east, Seward is in New York with Lincoln's message as well as a letter (perhaps written by Seward) that he plans to circulate to loyal governors. The letter is cast as a petition[85] from the governors to Lincoln; citing "the reduced condition of our effective forces in the field," the governors would ask the president "at once [to] call upon the several States for such number of men as may be required to fill up all military organizations now in the field," that is, to direct recruits to old regiments. The governors would also declare, "All believe that the decisive moment is near at hand." Most loyal governors, including Michigan, will sign this petition. (See July 1.)[86]

29: At Seward's invitation, dinner is served at New York's Astor House to Morgan, Thurlow Weed, and Curtin in the evening. Seward broaches his scheme to the three men, and almost certainly shows them Lincoln's message as well as the draft petition. The response is favorable.[87]

In the Seven Days' Campaign, there is a stalemate between opposing sides at the Battle of Savage's Station.

30: Seward forwards to Stanton a copy of the governors' petition. Stanton replies, noting that Lincoln is away, tired and gone "to the country." But he thinks Seward's proposal is "all right" and promises that the president will answer when he returns tomorrow, July 1. At some point in late June 29 or today after receiving Stanton's approval, Seward circulates the draft petition to Blair and other governors.

Meanwhile, a draft circular dated today and bearing Lincoln's signature is distributed to loyal governors. Citing military successes in New Orleans and Corinth, the president declares that "there will soon be no formidable insurgent force except in Richmond." He notes that existing regiments are depleted, but not wishing to "hazard the misapprehension of our military condition and of groundless alarm by a call for troops by proclamation," he instead will only ask the governors for 150,000 more troops for existing regiments. Later, Seward wires Stanton with a request, perhaps prompted by his conversations with Curtin and Weed. "Will you authorize me to promise an advance to recruits of $25 of the $100 bounty?" he asks. "It is thought here and in Massachusetts that without such payment recruiting will be very difficult, and with it probably entirely successful."[88]

Meanwhile, on the eve of Lincoln's July 1, 1862, call, the War Department reports that Michigan has furnished 19,095 men currently in U.S. service. Using state returns, AG Robertson has compiled his own figures (based on quite different assumptions). Through July 1, Robertson will disclose that of men of all arms (including three-month units mustered out), Michigan has provided 24,281 recruits since the war began. In addition, he claims another 1,453 Michiganders who enlisted in units of other states, for a total of 25,784. Robertson notes that if one counted other units also mustered out (the First U.S.

Lancers and Hughes's [Chandler's] Horse Guards), Michigan's contribution has been "nearly twenty-seven thousand men."[89]

The Seven Days' Campaign Battle of Glendale is a federal tactical victory, but the aggregate campaign represents a humiliating failure for federal arms. In Michigan, the newspaper battles begin when the actual battles ended. Republican sheets are quick to blame McClellan and dismiss claims that the failure on the Peninsula was because Washington withheld troops from the general, and did so because McClellan is a Democrat. The *Advertiser and Tribune* dismisses Democratic claims as "purely political" while the Democratic *Grand Haven News* claims that in Detroit, news of the Union defeat "was hailed with open demonstrations of rejoicing, by certain extremists there, who can see no virtue in a war that has not for its main object the speedy abolition of slavery"; the *Michigan Argus* declares that McClellan's maneuvers during the Seven Days' was in fact "a wonderful feat" that "even Gen. McClellan's most determined slanderers are forced to applaud."[90]

July

1: At 4 p.m. Seward, still in New York, wires Stanton with good news and some advice about numbers. First, the governors have approved the petition, and Seward names them, including Blair. He also recommends that "the President make the order, and let both papers [i.e., the governors' petition and Lincoln's order, which is yet to be written] come out—to-morrow morning's papers if possible." But how many troops to call?

Lincoln returns, approves Seward's plan, and wants to increase the call from 150,000 to 200,000 men. But Seward, having consulted several governors, offers another suggestion. "No one proposes less than 200,000," he declares, "make it 300,000 if you wish. They say it may be 500,000 if the President desires." He reminds Stanton about the $25 bounty advance. By now, Stanton, is prepared on his own hook to grant this request; he issues an order that the $25 be paid in hand to recruits; it will be funded from a $9,000,000 account held by the U.S. adjutant general "for collecting, organizing, and drilling volunteers." And Lincoln now acts. "Fully concurring in the wisdom of the views expressed to me in so patriotic a manner by you," he opens his response to the governors and then declares, "I have decided to call into the service an additional force of 300,000 men. I suggest and recommend that the troops should be chiefly of infantry."(See July 7.) Under this call, Michigan will be requisitioned for 11,686 troops; it eventually provides 17,656.[91]

Separately, Stanton has taken a second look at the governors' petition and notices three missing names. "Did not the Governors of Massachusetts, Rhode Island, and Iowa respond favorably, and should not their names be subscribed to the petition?" he asks Seward. In Michigan, the petition, bearing the names of eighteen loyal governors (and in Kentucky, the president of the Military Board) including Austin Blair, will be published within a week.

Finally, Congress passes an income tax.[92]

In the Seven Days' Campaign, the Battle of Malvern Hill is a federal victory. Among federal units engaged, the Fourth Michigan is first ranked in casualties suffered (164).[93]

2: Lincoln calls for 300,000 troops.

3. To Blair, Lincoln rationalizes yesterday's call. "I should not want the half of 300,000 new troops if I could have them now," he claims, adding, "If I had 50,000 additional troops here now I believe I could substantially close the war in two weeks." He cites arithmetic. Fifty thousand new men each month must be netted against 20,000 in monthly losses: "The quicker you send the fewer you will have to send." Lincoln concludes, "The enemy having given up Corinth [Mississippi], it is not wonderful that he is thereby enabled to check us for a time at Richmond."[94]

Meanwhile, C. P. Buckingham is dispatched to Cleveland "to explain to gentlemen there"—but explain what? Most likely, what he told Governor Morgan the previous day: "The recruiting service, including supplies of quartermaster's and ordnance stores, subsistence expenses, and mustering of New York volunteers, will be placed entirely under your [the governor's] control." (See July 8.)[95]

4: In Cleveland, Ohio, Governor David Tod confers with governors Austin Blair, Salomon (Wisconsin), Morton, Temple (Kentucky), superintendent of military telegraphs Colonel Anson Stager, and the War Department's C. P. Buckingham to solicit support for Lincoln's troop call. Curtin, Morgan, and Seward were expected but did not attend. The meeting may deal with logistical matters raised by Lincoln's call. The governors tour the Soldiers' Aid Hospital at the depot, then return to their homes. The meeting attracts little notice in Michigan.[96] (See July 5.)

Confederate colonel John Hunt Morgan leading 876 horse troopers leaves Knoxville to begin what will (much) later be called the First Kentucky Raid. (See July 9.)[97]

5: AAG C. P. Buckingham wires Stanton from Cleveland regarding governors Tod, Morton, Blair, Salomon, and president of Kentucky's Military Board, J. B. Temple. "All feel right and will do their duty," he happily reports.[98]

7: AAG C.P. Buckingham informs Blair that "You are requested to raise as soon as practicable for the U.S. service, for three years or during the war, six regiments of volunteer infantry, being a part of your quota under the call of the President."(See July 12 and 15.) War Department GO No. 74 will help Blair's efforts: Federal premiums will be $2 for recruits entering new regiments; $3 for those entering old regiments; a month's advance pay for those entering volunteer or Regular units. Of the $100 Federal bounty Congress authorized, $25 will be paid as an advance.[99]

8: Two Republican sheets, the *Detroit Advertiser* and the *Detroit Daily Tribune*, merge to become the *Detroit Advertiser and Tribune*.[100]

Separately, the War Department issues GO No. 75 granting new authority for governors to assist in recruiting volunteer forces and providing for their subsistence. Governors are given exclusive control of units until federal muster; it also authorizes Federal QMs to "turn over stores to the State authorities to be issued by them."[101]

9: Morgan has reached Tompkinsville, Kentucky, and continues north toward Lebanon, Kentucky.

10: Washington decides to secretly subsidize a western propaganda campaign to encourage enlistments. ASW C. P. Wolcott writes to governors Blair, Morton, Tod, Salomon, and Kentucky's Temple that "You are hereby authorized to make a requisition on the Secretary of War for such sum as you may deem necessary (not to exceed $1,000), to be expended at your discretion in employing speakers, or in such other secret manner as you may deem advisable, for encouraging enlistments of volunteers."[102]

11: AAG C. P. Buckingham reminds Blair that under GO No. 75 (see July 8), the War Department and not the states will provide "arms, equipments, and all other supplies" for troops. Separately, General Henry Halleck relieves General George B. McClellan as general-in-chief of federal forces. (But see September 2.)[103]

12: In Detroit, a petition circulates calling for a War Meeting to raise recruits to meet Lincoln's call. Signed by 102 of Detroit's leading businesses or businessmen, local politicians, and civic leaders, it asks Detroit Mayor Duncan "to . . . call for a public mass meeting to be held on Tuesday, the 15th inst. at such hour as you shall think advisable." Mayor Duncan wastes no time. He issues a proclamation to Detroiters calling for a meeting to convene at 7:30 p.m. on the Campus Martius, "the object of which will be to facilitate enlistments in the service."[104]

In Ohio, reports circulate that John Hunt Morgan's cavalry nears Cincinnati. The next day, Lincoln will worriedly telegraph General Halleck "They are having a stampede in Kentucky. Please look into it."[105]

In Washington, Lincoln meets with border-state senators and congressmen in an effort to secure compensated emancipation. He believes that had they approved his March 6 resolution, "the war would now be substantially ended." But the way is still open: "Let the States which are in rebellion see definitely and certainly that in no event will the States you represent ever join their proposed Confederacy, and they cannot much longer maintain the contest," and adds, "But you cannot divest them of their hope to ultimately have you with them so long as you show a determination to perpetuate the institution within your own States." Lincoln emphasizes that "the mere friction and abrasion" of the war itself will doom slavery. And if the border states do nothing, "It will be gone, and you will have nothing valuable in lieu of it. Much of its value is gone already," he notes. "How much better for you and for your people to take the step which at once shortens the war and secures substantial compensation for that which is sure to be wholly lost in any other event!" He stresses that emancipation will be gradual, and that colonization remains an option. ("Room in South America . . . can

be obtained cheaply and in abundance.") The president emphasizes that if they reject his proposal, "this is not the end of it." He is under increasing pressure from others who (he implies) are pushing for immediate, uncompensated emancipation.[106]

13: Lincoln, on a carriage ride with secretaries Gideon Welles and William Seward, raises the subject of emancipation.[107] (See July 22.)

In the Battle of Murfreesboro, Tennessee, the Ninth Michigan suffers 137 casualties.[108]

14: Congress enacts Chapter 166, authorizing federal pensions for veterans with disabilities. In Washington, border-state governors reply to Lincoln's July 12 offer of compensated emancipation. A majority reject Lincoln's program, although a few border states accept.[109]

15: Morning: Blair issues a proclamation calling for troops under Lincoln's July 2 call. Alluding to recent reversals on the Peninsula, he declares that "Michigan has never faltered in her fidelity to the government and must not hesitate now in the hour of its severest trial." The call is made necessary "by the events of a sanguinary war. . . . Union armies, beset in every quarter by immense hordes of conscripts gathered by desperate traitors," need reinforcements. Blair calls for six new regiments in addition to the Seventeenth Infantry and Fourth Cavalry already recruiting. One regiment will be assigned to each of Michigan's six Congressional Districts. Blair touts current compensation for recruits and finders: $2 for introducing each volunteer to a new regiment, and $3 for an introduction to an existing regiment; he reviews dependent benefits and urges soldiers now in Michigan to return to the field.[110]

Meanwhile, the *Free Press* publishes an appeal, "To Arms!," reminding readers about this night's war meeting. It enthusiastically endorses the meeting, urging, "Let every man forget party and behold only his imperiled country. . . . The Federal Union must be preserved." Here recruiting begins for what will be the Twenty-Fourth Michigan.[111]

Evening: The war meeting convenes; scheduled speakers include Mayor Duncan, eighty-year-old Lewis Cass, state treasurer Owen, Eber B. Ward, Duncan Stewart, ex-congressman William A. Howard, Thomas N. McEntee*, and recorder Henry A. Morrow*. But serious trouble lurks. Earlier, rumors had circulated that hundreds of Irishmen had somehow been drafted and that this meeting's purpose was to enforce conscription. The crowd includes men variously described as friends or "pimps" for Jefferson Davis, "traitors," or "a few dozen secession sympathizing rowdies." It is later claimed that the troublemakers were expatriate Southerners who, residing in Windsor, Ontario, had crossed the river to disrupt the meeting. As the rally continues, catcalls and jeers grow in volume. McEntee's speech is drowned out by jeers, and Morrow takes the stand and spars with dissenters. "There is a mistaken feeling that this meeting is preliminary to a draft," he declares. "This meeting is for inducing men to volunteer and I for one am ready to go." But when Howard begins reading proposed resolutions, disrupters somehow mistake these as favoring a draft and they rush the speakers' platform. Pandemonium ensues; even the revered Lewis Cass is chased to his carriage. The Wayne County sheriff, six-foot four-inch Mark Flanigan★, and at least one deputy, both armed, intervene: for unclear reasons the crowd, now a mob, turns on Ward and Stewart, but under Flanigan's protection, both men withdraw to the nearby Russell House Hotel. The mob pursues them, demanding that Ward and Stewart be lynched, but at the hotel entrance stand Flanigan and his deputy, pistols drawn. The crowd soon disperses.[112]

16: Prompted by last night's melee, a meeting convenes in Detroit at the Michigan Exchange building. Detroit's Unionists, shamed, angry, and defiant, schedule another meeting for July 22. (See July 19.) At night, state AG Robertson and Henry Barns★, editor of the *Detroit Advertiser and Tribune*, leave for Jackson and meet with Blair to obtain authorization for a Detroit/Wayne County unit. The governor is unreceptive: it is difficult enough to raise the six regiments demanded on July 7.[113]

17: On the previous night, Sarah Louise Horton Blair★, the governor's wife, had listened to Robertson and Barns pitch the new regiment; this morning she brings her husband the newspapers, telling him that the war news is very bad and that the government needs help. She lobbies Blair to grant the men's request. Blair relents and authorizes the unit. (See July 26.)[114]

Separately, President Lincoln signs two important acts. First, Chapter 201, "An Act to amend the Act calling forth the Militia to execute the Laws of the Union, suppress Insurrections, and repel Invasions, approved February twenty-eight, seventeen hundred and ninety-five, and the Acts amendatory thereof, and for other purposes." Its provisions include authority to draft 100,000 men for nine-month terms; to enlist "persons of African descent" for "constructing entrenchments, or performing camp service, or any other labor, or any military or naval service for which they may be found competent"; moreover, slaves of disloyal masters are now "forever free." Second is Chapter 195, "An Act to suppress Insurrection, to punish Treason and Rebellion, to seize and confiscate the Property of Rebels, and for other purposes." Better known as the Second Confiscation Act, it imposes criminal penalties on aiders and abettors of the Confederacy, declares that slaves who escape, desert disloyal masters, or reside in places that are liberated from Confederate control are "forever free of their servitude, and not again held as slaves." It also prohibits the return of fugitives unless the claimant can demonstrate his loyalty.[115]

Separately, in the U.S. Senate, Michigan's Zachariah Chandler delivers a blistering attack on General George B. McClellan and furnishes military orders, reports, and testimony given the JCCW. Federal losses at First Bull Run and Ball's Bluff are blamed on army incompetence, while at the latter battle, he holds McClellan responsible for the debacle. Chandler scores McClellan's incompetence—and worse, he alleges—in the recent unsuccessful Peninsula Campaign, reserving special venom for the enormous casualties incurred by several Michigan regiments at Williamsburg and Fair Oaks. And who will criticize Chandler for speaking the truth? "There are two classes of men who are sure to denounce me, . . . and they are traitors and fools," adding later that "The traitors North are worse than the traitors South." In Michigan, reaction falls along partisan lines.[116] (See September 26.)

18: Confederates cross the Ohio River and raid Newburgh, Indiana.

19: Over 3,000 people have signed a petition encouraging mass participation in Detroit's upcoming July 22 war meeting. Referring to the failed July 15 meeting, the petition asks, "Shall a few pestilent sympathizers with treason neutralize your patriotic effort? Let an expression go forth which shall rebuke the traitors and vindicate the patriotism of the city."[117]

Separately, in Jackson a war meeting convenes in Jackson City Hall. Local politician G. Thompson Gridley* presides and declares that, "We want less party and more country." Another speaker urges enlistments and declares that "There is no nigger question; I feel easy about that. You know that." Governor Blair speaks and addresses the indifferent. "Many say, 'this war don't affect me or my business.' You remember reading in the papers a day or two since of a rebel raid on the town of Newburgh, Indiana. Let the enemy cross the Ohio river, and you can stop him till they get to Mackinaw? You can't do it."[118]

21: Pennsylvania Governor Curtin issues a proclamation calling for twenty-one new regiments for nine-month terms—a development that Lincoln first opposes and later embraces. (See July 26.)[119]

22: At 3:00 p.m., Detroit's war meeting convenes on Campus Martius. Vice presidents now include Detroit's leading Catholic and Episcopal clerics as well as Federal Judge Ross Wilkins. A report recommends that to meet Detroit's 500-man quota, it should pay a $50 bounty to unmarried volunteers accepted as privates or NCOs, and married volunteers should receive $100. Because the governor lacks legislative authority to pay these sums, Detroiters should finance these bounties, beginning with the city's Common Council. (See July 24.)

Speaker after speaker takes the lectern without incident. Although Lewis Cass will live for almost four more years, this occasion will mark his last public address: "his voice was too weak to be heard by but a small part of the vast multitude," but he posed a question: "Our fathers endured much in their struggle for independence, and shall we prove degenerate sons of those noble sires? It cannot be." Perhaps the most important speech was delivered by Henry Morrow, the man who would lead the Twenty-Fourth Michigan. This time, Morrow broadens his appeal: the issue is Southern ingratitude; Southerners had controlled the federal government for forty-nine of the past seventy-five years since the Constitution was adopted; now the North is a victim of Southern aggression. Morrow devotes considerable time to what the war is not: "I hear much upon the streets a great deal of very foolish and very unpatriotic talk. It is called by some 'a negro-war,' by some an 'abolition war,' by some a black republican war.' Gentlemen, all such phrases are untrue." But most of Morrow's remarks consist of patriotic sentiments and are received enthusiastically. Sheriff Flanigan also speaks, announcing that he will join Morrow in the new unit. "You do not want leaders to say, 'There's the enemy, boys; go in!' but leaders who will straighten themselves out like a yard of pump water, and say, '*Boys, come in.*'"[120]

Duncan Stewart, an object of last week's lynch mob, offers mostly patriotic words; in a nod to the (presumably) racist foreign-born, he adds, "Negroes are not employed upon my boats nor upon the dock, except in menial positions where Irishmen and Germans refuse to work." Prominent lawyer Halmor H. Emmons* expresses surprise that anyone could even employ black troops. ("What, call upon a negro to defend the hearthstone upon which you will not let him step?")

A letter from Catholic bishop Peter Paul Lefevre* is read, and while he cannot attend the meeting, he describes supporting the government as "a great end" and hopes that "all differences of opinion in relation to the manner of accomplishing it will be abandoned." The meeting concludes as individuals donate $5 and $10 bounties to volunteers from Detroit's ten wards.[121]

Separately, a war meeting convenes in Kalamazoo's courthouse. Resolutions ask that the state of Michigan provide a $50 bounty to each recruit and also to provide family aid "while regiments are being formed and before other means of support can be had." As the band punctuates the fundraising with the *Star Spangled Banner* and *Yankee Doodle*, men and businesses verbally pledge money. Three thousand dollars is raised.[122]

Meanwhile, to the south, Morgan's force leaves Kentucky for Tennessee. And at Haxall's Landing, Virginia, General John Dix, USA,[123] and General D.H. Hill, CSA, enter into what will become known as the Dix-Hill Cartel, establishing a system of prisoner exchanges for the army and navy. An early Michigan beneficiary is Orlando Willcox.[124] (See August 15.)

Finally, in Washington, Lincoln presents a first draft of his proposed Emancipation Proclamation to his cabinet; Seward advises that the president not issue it until a Union military victory.[125]

23: C. P. Buckingham[126] notifies all governors about "the large number of soldiers absent from the Army on sick-leave who are abundantly able to rejoin their regiments, but who are neglecting their duty"; fears of being charged with desertion have diminished and Buckingham asks for the governors' "vigorous co-operation . . . in finding out and sending men to join their comrades in the field." Buckingham recommends that "A system of committees appointed throughout your State from among the most reliable and influential of your citizens, who, acting under your official sanction, would be willing to give to their country a few weeks of time and labor, would be extremely useful in this matter, as well as in exerting a wholesome influence on the volunteer recruiting service."[127]

24: The Detroit Common Council conditionally accepts the July 22 war meeting's recommendation to pay bounties to meet the city's quota: it pledges $40,000, subject to authorization by the Michigan legislature. (See Selected Legislation—1863, No. 56.) The Council also affirms the war meeting's choice of individuals to distribute the money raised, including Major Lewis Cass, Jr., H. P. Baldwin, and Elon Farnsworth*. (See entry for August 26.)[128]

25: The War Department issues GO No. 88, which permits recruiting details from deployed regiments to return home.[129]

26: The first company of the Twenty-Fourth Michigan is completed.[130]

Separately, C. P. Buckingham clarifies with Blair any confusion resulting from a July 25 order to a Federal mustering officer in Pennsylvania authorizing induction of recruits for either a one-year or a nine-month term. Pennsylvania governor Curtin's proclamation set these terms, not the War Department. Washington believes that mustering in troops for these short terms is "inexpedient." (But see August 4.)[131]

28: Lincoln writes Blair and other governors, "It would be of great service here for us to know, as fully as you can tell, what progress is made and making in recruiting for old regiments in your State." He also wants to know when the new regiments (referring to those called in July) will be ready to leave. "This information is important to us in making calculations." The calculations that Lincoln is making almost certainly refer to the next call. (See July 29 and August 4.)[132]

29: Blair replies to the previous day's request from Lincoln on progress under the July call. "Very little can be done in recruiting old regiments until the new regiments are filled up, although every exertion is being made to do so," he explains. "The new regiments will commence to take the field about the 1st of August, or sooner if possible, and will all be in service in the field that month."[133]

August

4: President Lincoln calls for 300,000 troops to serve for nine months. (See August 14.) Simultaneously, the War Department issues GO No. 94, which says that the nine-month quota must be filled by August 15, and that any deficiency remaining after that date will be filled by a special draft on the militia. (See entry for August 9.) The Democratic *Michigan Argus* observes, "It is now that the Government is in earnest, that it begins, at last, to appreciate the magnitude of the work before it"; it will not politicize this call but declares, "THE SHIP IS NOW ON FIRE; PUT OUT THE FLAMES."[134]

Michigan's nine-month quota is 11,686, and it will furnish none of these: see August 23.[135]

5: Northern governors have flooded the War Department with requests that deployed soldiers return home to recruit, and C. P. Buckingham sends Blair a discouraging update. "Applications for men in the field to officer new regiments are so numerous that great inconvenience and injury to the service must ensue if all are granted. Some general rule will be adopted soon and made known," he promises. On another matter, Buckingham informs Blair "That if any State shall not by the 18th of August, furnish its quota of the additional 300,000 volunteers . . . the deficiency of volunteers in that state will also be made up by special draft from the militia."[136]

6: The War Department credits Michigan with furnishing 19,095 men, in seventeen infantry regiments, three cavalry regiments, and three companies of an artillery regiment, as of March 20, 1862; it claims that the last new unit was fielded on that date.[137]

Meanwhile, C. P. Buckingham notifies Wisconsin

governor Edward Salomon that Lincoln "declines to receive Indians or negroes as troops." (But see November 27, 1861.)[138]

7: The possibility of conscription spurs executive officers from five major Midwest railroads to petition Stanton to exempt critical railroad employees. (See August 8.) None of the signatories represented railroads that passed through Michigan; but all of them represented connections to Michigan, principally through the Michigan Central that linked Detroit, Jackson and Michigan City with the Illinois towns of Matteson and Joliet, and the Michigan Southern & Northern Indiana which linked Monroe and Adrian with Indiana towns Elkhart, La Porte and ultimately to Chicago.[139]

Separately, Buckingham instructs Blair on enrolling militia. If Michigan has not begun enrolling, it must commence "immediately. Take the names of all able-bodied citizens between eighteen and forty-five years if age by counties. If State laws do not provide officers, appoint them, and the United States will pay all reasonable expenses. The lists should contain age, occupation, and all important facts in each case." (See August 9.) The *Detroit Advertiser and Tribune* supports the new enrollment, arguing that it will more fairly apportion draft quotas.[140]

8: Stanton issues two orders. The first is, "Order Authorizing Arrests of Persons Discouraging Enlistments." The second order is, "The Recent Orders to Prevent the Evasion of Military Duty."[141]

Meanwhile, ASW (and, more helpfully, former Pennsylvania Railroad executive) Thomas A. Scott reports on his meeting with the presidents of several Ohio and Pennsylvania railroads and urges the War Department to exempt critical railroad employees.[142] (See next day's entry.)

9: Blair receives formal notice that Michigan's call under the August draft is 11,686 men. Also, the War Department issues GO No. 99, "Regulations for the Enrollment and Draft of 300,000 Volunteers." (See August 25.) GO 99 provides for states to conduct enrollment and supervise conscription, and also specifies certain exempt occupations.[143]

Separately, Senator Chandler asks AG Lorenzo Thomas, "Are the boys of the Michigan First (Bull Run prisoners) exchanged yet?" The senator had promised that it would done quickly, but he now discovers that many of the former prisoners, falsely believing that the exchanges had been done, are reenlisting into new regiments. On the matter of recruiting generally, Chandler adds that "Our quota is full and the blood of the people up. They were yesterday paying $10 for a chance to enter some of the regiments."[144]

Meanwhile, Jacob N. McCullough[145] of the Cleveland & Pittsburgh Railroad warns Stanton that "T. A. Scott's list of exemptions . . . is the only thing now that will prevent an utter demoralization of the entire railroad organization of the West." Trains run now "with the utmost difficulty" and "another week and it will be impossible so to do with anything like regularity and promptness, which is very necessary in moving troops successfully."[146]

Separately, Confederates are victorious at the Battle of Cedar Mountain.

11: The Twenty-Fourth Michigan is filled: 1,335 officers and men, including 428 from Detroit and most of the 907 others from Wayne County; these numbers include 324 foreign-born.[147]

13: C. P. Buckingham requests that Blair notify the War Department "as soon as possible how many volunteers are enlisted at 12 o'clock to-day under the call of July 2 for 300,000." If exact numbers are unavailable, an approximation will do. AG Robertson replies that Michigan has "eight regiments of infantry and one of cavalry enlisted to the maximum and a surplus."[148]

The War Department issues GO No. 104, which attempts to restrict foreign travel by anyone subject to draft; it also suspends habeas corpus for any person arrested for violating this order.

Confederate General E. Kirby Smith begins his march from Tennessee to invade Kentucky. (See August 16.)[149]

The *Grand Haven News* exemplifies attitudes about the draft. "Don't Wait! Tarry Not!" it advises, for "it is more than probable that this is the *last week for volunteering.*"

14: Under pressure from some governors, War Department GO No. 99 is amended to add "counties and subdivisions" to "municipalities and towns" as entities into which draft quotas may be divided. This reflects the fact that the subdivisions in some states included counties and unincorporated areas as well as towns.[150]

The War Department wires to all governors

Stanton's "Order Respecting Volunteers and Militia," which discusses recruiting, bounties, and the draft, and issues timetables respecting the last two topics. Provisions include that after tomorrow, bounties will only be paid to volunteers for old regiments, and will continue until September 1; of greater importance, if by September 1 volunteers have failed to fill old regiments, a special draft will be held for any deficiency.[151]

15: C. P. Buckingham telegraphs Blair that "Drafting will take place on Wednesday, September 3." (See August 16.) Meanwhile, in Detroit the Twenty-Fourth Michigan is mustered into U.S. service; recruits and officers are drawn from Detroit, Plymouth, and Livonia. It will deploy west and serve through the Atlanta Campaign. (See June 30, 1865).

Meanwhile, in Ypsilanti a meeting convenes to organize men over forty-five years of age (and thus exempt from the draft) to form "the Old State Guard" regiment. "Our own State, in the event of collision with Great Britain, would be directly exposed to frontier attack and to have its channels of trade and intercourse obstructed," a resolution declares. Diplomatic considerations may bar Michigan officials from organizing such a force, but private citizens are not so constrained. The *Free Press* approves.[152]

At Aiken's Landing, Virginia, AG USA Lorenzo Thomas receives Willcox under the Dix-Hill Cartel. Over the next ten days, exchanged Michigan officers will include colonels Thomas B. W. Stockton (Sixteenth) and W. W. Duffield (Ninth Michigan) and a number of officers from these units and the First, Fourth, and Fifth Michigan Infantry.[153]

16: War Department GO No. 108 confirms that the draft for nine-month militia [under the August 4 call] will occur on September 3 between 9:00 a.m. and 5:00 p.m., "and [be] continued from day to day, between the same hours, until completed."[154]

Confederate general E. Kirby Smith crosses the Cumberland Mountains from Tennessee and into Kentucky. (See August 21.)

17: In Minnesota, the Dakota War opens as Sioux braves attack white farmers. (See August 23.)[155]

18: Lincoln dines with hero Orland B. Willcox. Lincoln also meets with Governor Blair and Senator Chandler to confer on officer appointments.[156]

In Kentucky, Unionist James F. Robinson becomes governor, replacing secessionist Beriah Magoffin. E. Kirby Smith captures Barbourville, Kentucky.[157]

19: C. P. Buckingham wires Blair seeking information about the August call: first, how many new regiments have been organized under this call? Second, how many are full? Third, how many men are necessary to fill them, and finally, how many regiments [under this call] have been deployed? AG Robertson replies that "Ten infantry regiments and two cavalry regiments have been organized under the last call [July] for three years' men; [all] are full to the maximum. Have sent none to the field. Waiting for clothing and arms." (See August 20.) But AG Robertson's reply leaves ASW Peter Watson[158] puzzled. "Arms and equipment for seven infantry and one cavalry regiment have already arrived at Detroit. What does your telegram of to-day mean?" (See entry for August 20.)[159]

Amid recruiting pressure, an important administrative change occurs: Stanton wires the relevant governors that the Department of the Ohio has been redefined to include Ohio, Michigan, Indiana, Illinois, Wisconsin, and Kentucky east of the Tennessee River, which will include the Cumberland Gap and surrounding areas. Horatio G. Wright[160] will command the Department (see March 25, 1863).[161]

Separately, in Jackson the Twentieth Michigan musters in to U.S. service with 1,012 men; recruits and officers are drawn from Lansing, Ypsilanti, Battle Creek, Ann Arbor, Parma, Grass Lake, Eaton Rapids, Marshall, and Chelsea. It will deploy east and in March 1863, move west before returning east.[162] (See May 30, 1865.)

20: AG Robertson clarifies yesterday's wire to Watson. First, some clothing and arms for the seven infantry and one cavalry regiment have arrived, but not all. Two infantry regiments and one cavalry regiment are full, and clothing and arms have not even been ordered. "Can they be furnished?" Robertson asks. Also, "Blankets for three regiments are needed immediately, as the men are suffering for want of them."[163]

Meanwhile, AG Robertson wires Stanton with more information about unit readiness: the ten infantry regiments will be ready to move beginning August 25. "To what point will they be ordered?" he asks Stanton. (See August 21.) Because these units raised under the July 2 call are nearly full and surplus companies continue to report, AG Robertson orders the formation of the Twenty-Fifth and Twenty-Sixth Michigan regiments.[164]

Separately, in Detroit, Battery I of the First Michigan Light Artillery musters into U.S. service; recruits and officers are drawn from Hudson, Detroit, and Trenton. The unit deploys west and accompanies Sherman to Atlanta.[165] (See July 14, 1865.)

21: Stanton replies to AG Robertson. "General Halleck informs me that he has heretofore ordered the Michigan regiments forward to Washington"; Stanton affirms the order.[166]

Separately, Confederate general Braxton Bragg's army crosses the Tennessee River north of Chattanooga. (See August 27.)[167]

22: Lincoln writes to his "old friend" Horace Greeley ("whose heart I have always supposed to be right") in response to Greeley's "The Prayer of the Twenty Millions." "My paramount object in this struggle is to save the Union, and is not either to save or to destroy slavery," Lincoln declares. "If I could save the Union without freeing any slave I would do it, and if I could save it by freeing all the slaves I would do it; and if I could save it by freeing some and leaving others alone, I would also do that." The *Free Press*, unaware of Lincoln's plans for emancipation, declares of the president's letter, "This is the true ground."[168]

AAG Thomas M. Vincent[169] notifies Electus Backus that he may recruit minors between the ages of eighteen and twenty-one "upon the affidavit of the captain of the company offering them for muster that the parents or guardians consented to enlistment. Written consent is not required."[170]

Meanwhile, at the Twenty-Fourth's rendezvous at Camp Barns (located in Detroit at the Detroit Riding Park), two events unfold that illustrate something about political consensus in the Peninsula State. At a ceremony, Republican editor Henry Barns presents a sword to his brother, the regimental adjutant James J. Barns★; in a separate ceremony, Democratic publisher of the *Detroit Free Press* Henry N. Walker★ presents a sword to Company E's Lieutenant Malachi O'Donnell★, foreman of the *Free Press* compositors.[171]

23: Buckingham asks Blair "what preparations have been made in your State for the draft of militia, and whether [you] will be ready on the 3d of September to carry it into effect." (See entry for August 25.) Meanwhile, the allotment commission visits the Twenty-Fourth Michigan to enroll soldiers in the program. Separately, news of Minnesota's Dakota War reaches Detroit. "Frightful Depredations of the Indians in Minnesota," reads the *Detroit Free Press*; but the sheet also acknowledges the problem: "The troubles are said to originate in the failure of the government to pay the Indians their usual bounties." For weeks to come, Michigan newspapers will graphically and extensively cover the Dakota War, provoking a wave of white anxiety. (See September 3.)[172]

24: Stretching the rules to accommodate slow recruitment, AAG Vincent wires Colonel Backus to "Muster into service and pay the bounty, &c., to any volunteers who may have enlisted prior to the 23d instant, although they may not have reached the rendezvous or been mustered in by that date."[173]

25: Faced with the July and August calls and the possibility of a draft, Blair issues a proclamation requiring assessors in towns, and in larger cities in wards, "to make and complete a census of the male citizens between the ages of eighteen and forty-five." Assessors are to report to county clerks, who will deliver the returns by September 10. Also today, AG Robertson issues GO 168 containing instructions to execute the enrollment. (See September 10.)[174]

Blair also replies to Buckingham's August 23 question about preparations. "We have only commenced proceedings to draft, and cannot possibly be ready [to draft] before the 15th of September. Let us recruit for regiments until that time, and we will fill them all with the three years' volunteers." (See August 26.)[175]

26–September 1: Second Bull Run Campaign, Virginia. Among federal units during this campaign, the First Michigan is ranked tenth in casualties suffered (178).[176]

26: ASW Buckingham formally notifies Blair that Michigan's quota under the August call totals 11,686. He also answers Blair's question from yesterday about whether recruiting three-year volunteers will replace the nine-month militia quota. It will, and Buckingham explains why. For Michigan, the July and August call were equal at 11,686; "if your [three-year] volunteers for old and new regiments mustered in from July 2 to September 1 exceed this number [11,686 under the three years' July call], the excess may be deducted from the number drafted [under the August call]." In short, a total of 23,372 men furnished will eliminate the need to draft any militia under the August call. Buckingham also replies to Blair's inability to commence drafting by September 3: Blair may draft "as soon thereafter as possible, yourself taking the responsibility of extending the time."[177]

In Detroit, the Common Council, facing recruiting requirements under the August call, now repeats what it did on July 24: it pledges $20,000 for a bounty fund, subject to Michigan legislative approval. (See Selected Legislation—1863, No. 56.)[178]

Also meeting in Detroit is the Democratic State Committee. It invites "the republican organization to suspend party nominations in the coming [November] election . . . and to unite with the democracy in the nomination of a ticket." Democrats' intent is to unite an anti-Radical coalition of Democrats and conservative Republicans. (See September 15.)[179]

Separately, 1,000 men of the Eighteenth Michigan are mustered into U.S. service at Hillsdale; recruits and officers are drawn from Hillsdale, Hudson, Adrian, Tecumseh, Exeter, Jonesville, Dundee, and Monroe. The unit will deploy west and serve through the Atlanta Campaign. (See April 27, 1865.)[180]

27: Orland B. Willcox, released from Confederate captivity, returns to Detroit and is enthusiastically greeted: large crowds and a public procession march under triumphal arches among flag-draped buildings and enthusiastic crowds. At the Campus Martius, Willcox is received by much of Michigan's governing class, Democrat and Republican. Governor Blair delivers the keynote address, and careful listeners might have discerned criticism of the Lincoln administration's waging war "with a surpassing benevolence, to put down the rebellion and not harm the rebel." "Is there any longer doubt," he asked, "that this was a fatally mistaken policy?" Blair answers his own question, and demands, "Let us make war—actual, positive, annihilating war. And why should we not? Rebellion is a crime."

Willcox replies and offers insights into his captivity and life in the Confederacy.[181]

As this unfolds, 982 men of the Seventeenth Michigan deploy east. Recruits and officers are drawn from Jackson, Adrian, Manchester, Coldwater,

Kalamazoo, Ypsilanti, Detroit, Quincy, and Battle Creek.[182] (See May 12, 1864.)

AAG Buckingham delivers further details about extending the draft start date. Citing Stanton's authority, "in the present exigency of the country, the [War] Department cannot postpone the time fixed by the order hereof issued, but must leave the responsibility of any delay with those who make it; that if in any State the draft be not made at the time specified in the order of August 14 [15], it should be made as speedily thereafter as practicable." Meanwhile, Colonel Henry D. Terry*, in Detroit after the Peninsula Campaign, informs the War Department that the Seventeenth Michigan, armed and equipped and commanded by Colonel William H. Withington, leaves tonight; the Twenty-Fourth Michigan leaves the next night [but see August 29], and the Twentieth Michigan will leave September 1. "Every effort is being made to forward the balance of the troops," Terry promises.[183]

To the south, E. Kirby Smith, in concert with Bragg's proposed movements, advances toward central Kentucky.

28: Second Bull Run campaign opens with the Battle of Groveton.

Bragg begins the Confederate invasion of Kentucky: he intends to prevent Don Carlos Buell from taking Chattanooga and to "restore" Confederate sovereignty over Kentucky and Tennessee.[184]

29: E. Kirby Smith is halted by federals at Kingston, south of Richmond, Kentucky; the federals prepare Richmond for attack. Meanwhile, the War Department issues GO No. 121, "Order Concerning Supplies to Drafted Militia." Its requirements include that a lance corporal be appointed for every eight men and a lance sergeant for every sixteen men; these NCOs are tasked with making "reasonable contracts" for providing subsistence for the men. After arriving at rendezvous (and until accepted into Federal service), camp commanders are responsible for subsistence. This GO also famously requests recruits to bring their own blankets, as the government has none. Captain George W. Lee*, assistant U.S. quartermaster in Detroit, is charged with executing the GO.[185]

Meanwhile, two Michigan units muster into U.S. service. First, the Twenty-Second Michigan, recruited from the Fifth Congressional District, draws officers and recruits from Pontiac, Farmington, Shelby, Port Huron, Newport, New Baltimore, Mt. Clemens, Green Oak, Brighton, and Lexington. The unit will deploy west; it later accompanied Sherman to Atlanta. (See June 26, 1865.)

Second, in Detroit, the Fourth Michigan Cavalry musters into U.S. service with 1,233 men; recruits and officers are drawn from Detroit, Wellsville, Allegan, Paw Paw, Plymouth, Manchester, Adrian, Quincy, Dearborn, Jackson, Lapeer, and Niles. The unit's twelve companies will be deployed west and will accompany Sherman to Atlanta; later they will be involved in the capture of Jefferson Davis.[186] (See July 1, 1865.)

Separately, the Twenty-Fourth Michigan departs Detroit. The Twenty-Second will eventually include eleven-year-old drummer boy John Joseph Clem★.[187]

30: After the Battle of Richmond, Kentucky, Confederates occupy the town and the Federals retreat toward Louisville. Meanwhile, the Fifth Michigan Cavalry musters into U.S. service. (See December 4.)[188]

September

1–2: Confederates occupy Lexington, Kentucky.[189]

1: Second Bull Run campaign: Battle of Chantilly, Virginia.

2: Enormous casualties from the Second Bull Run battles prompt the Michigan Soldiers' Relief Association to send money to Washington; the Association dispatches to the front an additional agent and three doctors. Meanwhile, Detroit's mayor calls for an afternoon meeting to promote enlistments. The *Free Press* declares, "If there ever was a time when it was the duty of every one to lend his whole aid to sustain the government, it is now." In the immediate aftermath of Second Bull Run, Michigan sheets must rely on New York papers for casualty lists. As the *Free Press* notes, "Michigan has to mourn a great loss in killed and wounded, and prisoners, but how great, it will take days to determine with precision."[190]

Lincoln returns General George B. McClellan to command federal armies in Virginia and Washington.

3: The *Saginaw Valley Republican* reports that last week, many Bay City residents, worried about a local Indian uprising, were alarmed when hundreds of Indians gathered in woods across from the town. In fact, the Indians were peacefully traveling to seasonal hunting grounds. (See October 14.) Meanwhile, New England governors informally meet at Brown University's commencement. Discussed is unhappiness with McClellan, Lincoln's failure to emancipate, and other issues. Separately, Confederates occupy Frankfort, Kentucky.[191]

4: The Twenty-First Michigan is mustered into U.S. service at Ionia with 1,000 men; recruits and officers are drawn from Saranac, Ionia, Grand Rapids, Hastings, Greenville, Grand Haven, and Cannonsburg. It will deploy west and accompany Sherman to the sea.[192] (See April 27, 1865.)

The War Department abandons its time limits for recruiting for old regiments: "Recruiting for old regiments will continue, and advance pay and bounty will be paid until further orders."[193]

5: Concern about the Kentucky invasion spreads to Indiana. Indiana governor Morton declares martial law in the river counties and asks citizens to organize defenses. (See September 7.) Meanwhile, in Dowagiac, 995 men of the Nineteenth Michigan are mustered into U.S. service; recruits and officers are drawn from Coldwater, Allegan, Constantine, Sturgis, Kalamazoo, South Haven, and St. Joseph. It will deploy west and ultimately accompany Sherman to the sea.[194] (See June 10, 1865.)

Back east, Confederates continue crossing the Potomac.

6: In the first move toward the Altoona Conference, Pennsylvania's Governor Curtin suggests to Massachusetts's Governor John A. Andrew a meeting of loyal governors. (See September 13 and 14.) Curtin soon extends the invitation to other loyal governors. Separately, Confederate General Thomas J. "Stonewall" Jackson occupies Frederick, Maryland.

7: As Confederates advance through Kentucky, General Wright wires Governors Tod, Yates, Morton, and Austin Blair: "Don't remit your exertions in hastening forward your troops. Cincinnati is threatened, whether seriously or not I cannot confidently say, but we must be prepared." Wright declares that he must take the offensive in Kentucky to prevent Confederate recruiting, and that the blockade against General George W. Morgan[195] in the Cumberland must be lifted "or he may be starved out." In the east, the Army of the Potomac advances north of Washington to meet Confederate invaders. Stonewall Jackson at Frederick now stands between federal armies and Pennsylvania.

9: The remains of First Michigan Cavalry commander Thornton Brodhead, mortally wounded at Second Bull Run, arrive from Cleveland by boat at 9:00 a.m. The Detroit Light Guard escorts the body to Firemen's Hall, where it lies in state. Businesses close for the day.[196]

Separately, Wormer's Stanton Guards muster out of service. During its service, eighty-six men were enrolled, including three DFD and one deserted.[197]

10: Michigan reports its enrollment, ordered on August 25 (including the June state enrollment). The number of Michiganders reported to be subject to draft is 91,071. The number is almost certainly higher. Based on the 1860 census, the total population of the forty-two counties included was 715,595. At that time, the ratio of persons subject to draft (males between the ages of eighteen and forty-five less exemptions) was 1 to 7.857. However, in the recent enrollment, eighteen counties (with a total population of 35,415) did not return enrollments; based on the ratio, however, these counties are expected to produce 4,507 eligible men. AG Robertson believes that the true number of eligible males is 95,578.[198]

Separately, in Jackson, a meeting of conservative Republicans convenes to establish a new political party in Michigan, opposed to what it believes is the party drift toward Radicalism. (See September 16.) Meanwhile, at a schoolhouse in Ionia, teacher Julia Wheelock* learns that her brother Orville, a sergeant with the Eighth Michigan, was wounded at Chantilly, losing a limb. Julia immediately leaves to care for her brother, and begins one of the most remarkable nursing careers in Michigan's wartime history. Julia does not know that her brother died the previous day. (See October 1.)[199]

At Fort Mackinac, the three Tennessean POWs imprisoned since May 10 are transported to Johnson's Island (Ohio) in Lake Erie.[200]

10–11: Confederate General Henry Heth's forces reach Fort Mitchell several miles south of Covington, Kentucky.[201]

11: Confederates occupy Maysville, Kentucky, on the Ohio River—some fifty miles southeast of Cincinnati. Meanwhile, Confederates enter Hagerstown, Maryland.

12: Federals reoccupy Frederick, Maryland, as Jackson advances on Harper's Ferry.

13: The Twenty-Third Michigan musters into U.S. service at Saginaw with 983 men; recruits and officers are drawn from Detroit, St. Johns, East Saginaw, Flint, Vassar, Saginaw City, Bay City, Caledonia, and Houghton. It will deploy west and accompany Sherman to Atlanta before pursuing Hood to Tennessee.[202] (See June 28, 1865.) Meanwhile, in Washington, D.C., Henry J. Alvord* and other state agents meet to confront the limitations of single-state action in serving soldier patients hospitalized in Washington. State relief associations from Michigan, Maine, New Hampshire, Massachusetts, Rhode Island, Connecticut, New York, New Jersey, Pennsylvania, Ohio, Indiana, and Illinois discuss "mismanagement and bad treatment" of patients in some U.S. General Hospitals. They resolve to form a "Union Soldiers' Relief Association." A "gentleman from Michigan," probably H. J. Alvord, proposes another resolution, that a committee consisting of one representative from each state relief association "confer with the [U.S.] Surgeon General in relation to the abuses in some of the hospitals in Washington" and make suggestions to improve soldiers' diets. On September 16, this committee will meet with U.S. surgeon general William A. Hammond.[203] (See September 17.)

Separately, William K. Gibson departs as Austin Blair's military secretary. Eugene Pringle, also of Jackson, replaces him. Pringle will continue in service until March 10, 1865.

14: In south central Kentucky, Bragg occupies Glasgow. In Maryland, battle erupts at Boonsboro Gap, Crampton's Gap, and Turner's Gap. Among Federal units engaged at South Mountain, the Seventeenth Michigan is ranked third in casualties suffered (132).[204]

14–17: In Kentucky Bragg halts to besiege Munfordville and Woodsonville. Meanwhile, General Don Carlos Buell moves toward Bragg. (See September 20.)[205]

15: In Detroit, the Democratic State Committee meets. The Republicans have rejected its invitation to form a unity slate of candidates; but the Democrats are "still anxious and willing to co-operate with all men, without regard to former political combinations," by which is meant conservative Republicans. The committee calls for a convention on October 8. (See September 16 and October 2 and 8.)

Meanwhile, Jackson captures Harper's Ferry.

16: A "large and enthusiastic" (90 delegates) Union Conference Meeting convenes in Jackson. Similar to the People's Party[206] in Massachusetts, the Michigan iteration of the Union Party or the People's Union Party consists of conservative Republicans, some War Democrats, and Constitutional Union members and is best understood as an effort to oppose Radical Republicans. The Republican *Jackson Citizen*, seeing the threat to Republican votes by this group, dubs it the "Surprise Party" and declares it "uncalled for by any public necessity." (See September 18 and 24, October 2.)[207]

Meanwhile, Lee concentrates at Antietam.

17: Blair notifies Stanton that the Fourth Michigan Cavalry "is ready to march but it has no carbines, although the requisition was made on the Ordnance Department several weeks since." He asks Stanton to forward them "immediately" and requests Sharps carbines. ASW Watson replies for Stanton and news is not good. He has only 350 carbines for the Fourth. "They are sufficient for scouting and skirmishing," Watson notes, adding, "Their equipment is complete with either pistols and sabers, or with carbines and pistols." Meanwhile, AAG Thomas M. Vincent reports that under the summer of 1862 calls, Michigan has fielded 6,860 three-year troops. Recruits were assigned to seven infantry regiments, including two expected to deploy by the 20th, two deployed cavalry regiments (1,200 men each), and a battery stationed in Detroit.[208]

Meanwhile, in Washington, Michigan's Dr. Henry J. Alvord, having met with SG Hammond, reports on the meeting and the status of area military hospitals. Abuses in soldier diet, discipline, and burial are discussed.[209]

In Maryland, the federals are victorious at the Battle of Antietam. Among federal regiments engaged, the Seventh Michigan ranks sixth in casualties suffered (221).[210]

18: First reports of federal victory at Antietam are reported in Detroit, which the editors infer from a series of published dispatches from Washington and Harrisburg, Pennsylvania. The battle has not been named; the *Free Press* refers to the soon-to-be famous creek as the "Antitown Creek," but locates it at Sharpsburg, Maryland. No one reading this sheet can be assured by the headline, "Great Carnage on Both Sides." Over the next several weeks, individual obituaries and casualty lists will be printed in Michigan newspapers. Among the mortally wounded is General Israel Richardson. (See entry for November 11.)[211]

The Wayne County People's Union Party calls for a county convention of those "who are willing to unite in a cordial support of the National Administration in its efforts to suppress the rebellion and maintain the laws" by nominating "unconditional Union men—honest capable and faithful to the Constitution" as delegates to the October 8 state convention in Jackson. "Let every friend of the Union rally to its banner and assuming defensive armor against the wiles of the partisan, stand for the Government against all enemies."[212]

Confederate forces withdraw toward Virginia and will cross the Potomac the next day.

19: In Mississippi, the Battle of Iuka is fought, a federal victory.

20: Bragg marches north toward Bardstown at a midpoint south of Lexington and Louisville, hoping to join E. Kirby Smith. But Smith is not there.[213]

22: Lincoln issues the preliminary Emancipation Proclamation. Among other things, it holds that as of January 1, 1863, "all persons held as slaves within any State or designated part of a State," whose "people whereof shall then be in rebellion against the United States, shall be then, thenceforward, and forever free." For states returning to the Union, it offers the prospect of compensated, gradual emancipation, and encourages colonization by blacks ("with their consent, upon this continent or elsewhere"). (See January 1, 1863.)

The *Free Press* will recognize that "It is the beginning of a revolution" that "will henceforth color the war." It fears that the proclamation will weaken border-state loyalty; argues that Britain's textile industry is invested in American slavery, and thus because the proclamation threatens that industry, will increase hostility; and finally, asks questions that seem to involve Northern racial anxieties as much as the war: "What will become of the slaves? Are they to remain in the South until emancipated? Who believes it? Are they to come into the North to take the bread from white labor? Who will endure it? Are they to be admitted to citizenship? Who will submit to it? Are they to occupy as colonists the States from which their masters have been exterminated? Who will fight for such a result?" And yet the *Free Press*, one of the most racist sheets in the northwest, also declares, "the proclamation has been issued, it is now a fact and must be treated as such." The *East Saginaw Courier* declares the proclamation "will be disastrous in every respect"; however, it adds that, "we must abide by the policy unless the people of the loyal states put their seal of condemnation upon it at the ballot box in November."

Republican sheets have no doubts. The *Detroit Advertiser and Tribune* describes Lincoln's proclamation as "one of the most important acts in the history of any government"; it notes that "It does not invite the slaves to rise and cut their masters['] throats," nor does it "propose to put arms in their hands." Emancipation was the result of rebellion, and the rebels have only themselves to blame. "If any man chooses to save his slaves by obeying federal authority, an opportunity is given him to do so." It places the proclamation squarely in the spirit exemplified by Lincoln's August 22 [see that date] letter to Horace Greeley.

The *Cass County Republican* declares it to be "the grandest proclamation ever issued by man," which will eventually produce "nothing less than complete emancipation and the establishment of a Free Republic from the Atlantic to the Pacific, from the Lakes to the Gulf." The *Lansing State Republican* compares Lincoln's proclamation to that of the angel proclaiming the birth of Christ, and declares, "Ten thousand blessing upon the head of Abraham Lincoln," adding, "He has struck a blow at the very life of the rebellion." "Slavery is now to abolished, and the rebellion ended. Amen! Amen!"[214]

Meanwhile, the Twenty-Fifth Michigan musters into U.S. service with 896 men; officers and recruits are drawn from Schoolcraft, Marshall, Otisco, St. Joseph, Three Rivers, Galesburg, Lansing, Niles, Florence, Oshtemo, Holland, and Buchanan. The unit will deploy west and serve through the Atlanta Campaign and pursue Hood in Tennessee.[215] (See June 24, 1865.)

23: In an open letter to Michigan's wounded soldiers in Washington and Alexandria hospitals, the Michigan Soldiers' Relief Association of Washington confesses that it is "impossible for us, as we would desire, to pay daily visits to each hospital." But the Association has a plan. First, Michigan men in each hospital should form a Branch Soldiers' Relief Association for that facility; ambulatory Michiganders should assume the responsibility of daily patient visitation. Second, Branch members should report hospitalizations and especially deaths of Michigan patients. Third, contact information about the relatives of dangerously wounded or ill patients should be kept. Fourth, daily visits should include inquiries about patient needs, especially food and clothing. Finally, the information gathered and lists of wants should be given to the main organization.[216]

24: Altoona Conference. For several days in Altoona, Pennsylvania, governors from Ohio, Massachusetts, Pennsylvania, New Jersey, Illinois, Maine, Maryland, Wisconsin, New Hampshire, Iowa, Rhode Island, and West Virginia have been conferring. Michigan's Blair arrives only on this day, but in time to sign the address. (New York's Governor Morgan and Indiana's Oliver Morton do not attend, although an agent represents the Hoosier.)

Massachusetts's Andrew chairs the meeting; he also is tasked with writing its final resolutions—the Altoona Address—to submit to Lincoln. The Address supports the preliminary Emancipation Proclamation, reaffirms the Union's value, supports Lincoln and the use the power of states to help crush the rebellion unconditionally, and recommends a 100,000-man, one-year force. (See SAW.5.33–34 for greater detail on the address.) Among the governors and Morton's agent who are present, Maryland's Augustus Bradford will not sign. Some governors who are not present also decline to sign: New York's Morgan (citing his absence), New Jersey's Governor Charles Smith Olden (probably related to looming elections in his sharply divided state), Hamilton Gamble (slave state Missouri), J. B. Robinson (slave state Kentucky), and slave state Delaware's Burton.[217]

Reflecting later on the Altoona Address's significance, Austin Blair writes that it "at once made known to the people the vigorous policy recommended by the Governors, [and] it had some influence in restoring confidence in the ability of the government to sustain itself" in the midst of a brutal war. To Blair, the Address's crucial prop was its support of the preliminary Emancipation Proclamation. He believed that it "promoted enlistments in the states, and infused greater activity into the recruiting service [thereby] strengthen[ing] armies in the field."[218]

In Michigan, the **Republican State Convention** convenes in Detroit's Young Men's Hall and nominates Austin Blair for governor and Charles S. May* for lieutenant governor. Republicans reject a request from the People's Union Party asking for support. In his acceptance speech, Blair in absentia urges that Republicans "must maintain our organization," and while welcoming all those who support the Lincoln administration, declares that, "we cannot disband and desert the principles upon which the Administration, which we, and they support, stand."[219]

Foreshadowing next year's conscription, the War Department issues GO No. 140. It establishes the national position of provost marshal general and appoints Simeon Draper,[220] who is tasked with arresting deserters and disloyal persons, reporting treasonable practices, uncovering spies, and returning stolen or embezzled U.S. property. To assist Draper, special provost marshals are appointed in each state. Previous to Draper's appointment, a network of twenty-two "special provost marshals" had been appointed throughout many loyal states. In Michigan, John S. Newberry* serves as PM by prior appointment.[221]

Separately, Lincoln issues a proclamation suspending the writ of habeas corpus. The proclamation asserts that "disloyal persons are not adequately restrained by the ordinary processes of law" from obstructing enlistments and the draft. First, the trial "by courts-martial or military commission" is declared for all "rebels and insurgents, their agents and abettors, within the United States, and all persons discouraging volunteer enlistments, resisting militia drafts . . . guilty of disloyal practice, [or] affording aid and comfort to rebels." Second, habeas corpus is suspended to all arrestees "now or hereafter during the rebellion" who are detained in any "fort, camp, arsenal, [or] military prison" by military authority or by military tribunal or commission. The *Free Press*, shocked, notes in a full-page editorial, "Bolt follows bolt. One Presidential proclamation succeeds another—the first [emancipation] a folly. What shall we call the last?" It concludes, "We implore [Lincoln] not to suspend the constitution and the law."[222]

26: Blair joins his colleagues in Washington to present the Altoona Address to Lincoln. Governor Andrew reads it aloud, and in the discussion that follows, Iowa governor Samuel Kirkwood comments to Lincoln, "That in the opinion of our people George B. McClellan is unfit to command the Army of the Potomac." Kirkwood asks if Lincoln believes in McClellan's loyalty. Lincoln replies emphatically: "I have the same reason to believe in his loyalty that I have to believe in the loyalty of you gentlemen before me now." He knows that McClellan has "deficiencies," that "He is very cautious, and lacking in confidence in himself and his ability to win victories with the forces at his command." Lincoln adds a few more comments and closes with a question: "But if I remove him, some one must be put in his place, and who shall it be?" Austin Blair, much opposed to McClellan, asks, "Why not try another man, Mr. President?" Lincoln replies, "Oh, but I might lose an army by that." Nevertheless, Blair remembered that "the unanimous agreement of the loyal Governors to sustain the administration" was much welcomed by Lincoln.[223]

Separately, the Fourth Michigan Cavalry commanded by Colonel Robert H. G. Minty* leaves Michigan.[224]

The Detroit *Free Press* asserts that the Altoona Conference was really an abolitionist "conspiracy" to remove McClellan.[225]

Meanwhile, Buell's army arrives in Louisville.[226]

27: Tonight, Blair, still in Washington, joins in a serenade of General James Wadsworth, abolitionist general. "Men and means are provided in abundance [for victory]," Blair declared, "and if his advice were asked, he would say, send to France for a guillotine and chop off the heads of all incompetents and cowards"—probably a less-than-subtle reference to McClellan.[227]

29: In New York City's Astor House, a meeting of "former citizens of Michigan" convenes to establish the Michigan Soldiers' Aid Society of New York to "more systematically and effectively . . . furnish prompt and adequate aid to those of our State soldiers who may need our assistance." Resolutions passed include an appeal to women to provide nursing assistance; a plea to Michiganders back home to forward supplies to the Society; and the election of Colonel Darius Clark, Blair's military agent for New York City, as the group's president.[228]

October

1: The Michigan Soldiers' Relief Association in Washington hires Julia Wheelock as a "lady agent" for $5 weekly. Since arriving in Washington and learning of her brother's death, Wheelock has provided freelance nursing services in area hospitals. Now she joins Elmina Brainard at the Association. A later historian describes Wheelock's job: "She read and wrote letters, sat with the dying, brought in food sometimes in defiance of doctors' orders, listened sympathetically to all complaints, and in every conflict of authority or personality invariably took the side of the soldier patient." Wheelock is ordered to Alexandria, where she finds "fifteen Government hospitals occupying no less than twenty different buildings," not including Camp Convalescent ("Depot of Misery"), a Camp for Paroled Prisoners, the Fairfax Seminary, and soon the Twenty-Sixth Michigan's camp. All are within her circuit.[229]

2: The Union Convention (the relabeled Democratic Party) convenes at Jackson with 270 delegates (representing twenty-three counties), George A. Coe of Branch County presiding. The Convention adopts nine resolutions, including statements in support of the war; that the unity required to triumph over secession cannot be achieved by the Republican or Democratic Parties, and only by "a union of true patriots"; that the enemy must unconditionally submit to federal authority; that the party is devoted to "an energetic prosecution of the war, by the use of all means consistent with the laws and usages of civilized nations . . . the restoration of the Union, and the preservation of the constitution and government of the United States in all their former power and purity"; that the party has "confidence" in Lincoln "although we may, as individuals, differ as to the wisdom of [his] policies"; and that the party *will stand by the government.*" It endorses "a liberal provision for the families of soldiers," including those killed and disabled. The committee nominates a complete slate of state candidates, including former Republican Byron G. Stout* for governor, Henry H. Riley for lieutenant governor, and Charles C. Trowbridge* for treasurer. In the end, Democratic attempts to rebrand as a "Union" party will attract few Michigan Republicans.[230]

3: AG Robertson issues two GOs. The first lists county and quotas and deficiencies from each under the two summer calls. The aggregate quota is 21,372 men, and the counties have supplied 13,488 men, leaving a deficiency of 7,884. He also allows twenty days for these counties to cure the deficiency or face a draft. The GO appoints draft commissioners in the named counties, whose duties include superintending the draft and determining eligibility for exemptions. Blair also appoints county commissioners to oversee the draft. (See October 29 and January 29, 1863.)

In a circular issued today, the Michigan's Republican State Central Committee, like the Democrats yesterday, also uses bipartisan appeals: "While the Government is in peril, [the Republican party] neither *offers* nor *accepts* any party discussion. . . . The complications of the present enormous civil war, render the destruction of the Government almost certain, unless it be supported by the organized powers of the loyal people. The isolated fibers of the hemp cannot hood the ship in the storm."[231]

4: In Frankfort, Richard Hawes is inaugurated as Confederate governor of Kentucky. However, as federal forces approach, Confederates evacuate, and the inaugural ball is cancelled. Lincoln concludes his three-day visit to the Army of the Potomac and McClellan. Lincoln remains disappointed by his general. In Mississippi, the Battle of Corinth concludes, a federal victory.[232]

8: The **Democratic State Convention** opens in Detroit's Young Men's Hall, with 211 delegates. Lyman D. Norris* presides. A letter is read from the October 2 People's Union Convention urging Democrats to support a joint ticket. Resolutions passed today include a pledge that Democrats will support the government "to restore the Union as it was, and maintain the Constitution as it is"; a statement of adherence to the Crittenden Resolution (see July 25, 1861); a denunciation of "illegal and unconstitutional arrest[s]"; a reaffirmation of freedom of speech; and an expression of support for soldiers in the field. While Democrats refuse to merge with the People's Union Party, they nominate the same slate of candidates: Byron G. Stout for governor, H. H. Riley for lieutenant governor, and Charles C. Trowbridge for treasurer.

Separately, in Kentucky, Federals win the Battle of Perrysville.[233]

9: The War Department issues GO No. 154 permitting

commanding officers of Regular Army units to detail "one or more recruiting officers," who are "authorized to enlist, with their own consent, the requisite number of efficient volunteers to fill the ranks of their command to the legal standard." [NB: *In effect, these officers are authorized to poach volunteers from state volunteer units in the field.*][234]

11: The Sixth Michigan Cavalry musters into U.S. service with 1,229 men; officers and recruits are drawn from Grand Rapids, Lapeer, Burns, Ionia, Plainfield, Detroit, Caledonia, Pentwater, Thornapple, Saginaw, and Saranac. The unit will serve east throughout the war, followed by brief frontier service.[235] (See November 24, 1865.)

14: More stories of Indian massacres circulate, this time from Traverse City. The *Detroit Free Press* considers the tales "improbable." However, unlike Minnesota and Wisconsin, Michigan will in fact experience no uprisings, and thus no diversion of state resources from the war.[236]

20: Stanton forwards Blair a copy of Lincoln's order that "all persons who may have actually been drafted into the military service of the United States and who may claim exemption on account of alienage, will make application therefor directly to the Department of State or through their respective ministers or consuls."[237]

24: In the west, General William S. Rosecrans[238] replaces General Don Carlos Buell.[239]

29: AG Robertson issues GO No. 186 extending the draft to December 1, because the draft commissioners appointed October 3 "having from necessity required more time to make exemptions and complete the lists for carrying the draft into effect than was anticipated." (See November 29.) Blair also authorizes five new three-year regiments: under Colonel (and congressman) Francis W. Kellogg, the Seventh Cavalry; the Eighth Cavalry under Colonel John Stockton* of Mount Clemons; the Ninth Cavalry organized by Captain James I. David* of Trenton; the Twenty-Eighth Infantry under Colonel Edward Doyle* of Detroit; and the First Regiment Michigan Sharpshooters, officer not yet appointed. (Captain Charles V. DeLand* will be appointed to command the sharpshooters.) County draft commissioners are directed to channel enlistments into these units.[240]

Separately, Stanton authorizes Erasmus D.

Robinson* to raise one company for provost duty in Detroit, to be headquartered at the Detroit Barracks. On January 3, 1863, it musters into U.S. service.[241] (See May 9, 1865.)

31: C. P. Buckingham requests from all governors "as soon as possible," the number of men enrolled for the draft, the number actually drafted, the number of draft commissioners for administering the draft, the number of examining surgeons, the number of camps of rendezvous, the number of nine-month volunteers to take the place of draftees, and the number of draftees who have volunteered for three-year service.[242]

November

1: William Hammond* replaces Jabez Fountain as state QMG.[243]

4: Congressional and State Elections:

First District: *Fernando C. Beaman, Republican,* 13,400 (50.36); Ebenezer J. Penniman, Democrat, 13,208 (49.64)

Second District: *Charles Upson, Republican,* 14,147 (55.41); John W. Turner, Democrat, 11,385 (44.59)

Third District: *John W. Longyear, Republican,* 12,317 (51.79); Bradley F. Granger, Democrat, 11,467 (48.21)

Fourth District: *Francis W. Kellogg, Republican,* 10.013 (57.81); Thomas B. Church, Democrat, 7,308 (42.19)

Fifth District: *Augustus C. Baldwin, Democrat,* 10,696 (50.62); Ronald E. Trowbridge, Republican, 10,432 (49.38)

Sixth District: *John F. Driggs, Republican,* 7,879 (51.77); John Moore, Democrat, 7,340 (48.23)

NB: Nationally, the Democrats gained thirty-eight seats compared with 1860; in Michigan, they gained the Fifth District seat, and that by a very close margin.[244]

State Elections:

For Governor:

Austin Blair, Republican, 68,716, *52.5 percent*

Byron Stout, Democrat, 62,102, 47.5 percent[245]

Total votes cast (130,818) were 15 percent lower than in 1860, perhaps reflecting soldiers absent in service and reduced voter excitement in a year without a presidential contest. While Blair received 23,940 fewer votes than in 1860, his Democratic challenger received 4,951 fewer votes than his 1860 predecessor. In Detroit, aggregate votes for Democrats increased from 661 in 1861 to 775 in 1862.[246]

State House

Senate: 14 Democrats, 18 Republicans

House: 39 Democrats, 60 Republicans, 1 possible independent

NB: *In the Senate, Republicans lost 12 seats while Democrats gained 12, compared with 1860. In the House, based on 100 up for election (compared with only 83 seats in 1860), Republicans lost 12 seats while Democrats gained 12.*[247]

7: The election over, Lincoln removes George B. McClellan as commander of the Army of the Potomac. McClellan's performance has been subject to harsh rhetoric for almost a year, and Michigan reactions cover the spectrum. Not all Democratic newspapers jump into the fray. The *Michigan Argus* observes that McClellan's removal "elicits much discussion in political and general circles, and is both violently condemned and heartily approved." While the *Argus* doubts "either its necessity or propriety," it recognizes Lincoln's responsibility as commander-in-chief, and declares that "we will not censure until the new commander of the army of the Potomac has been thoroughly tried." The Republican *Lansing State Journal* is less circumspect. It applauds McClellan's removal and, speculating on the reasons for it, concludes that "He either lacks capacity, or he sympathizes with the rebels, or he feared a stern and relentless prosecution of the war would prevent a compromise with the rebels."[248]

11: In Pontiac, Major General Israel Richardson is buried today, his funeral including "an immense concourse of citizens."[249]

12: From Beaufort, South Carolina, Brigadier General Rufus Saxon reports to Stanton that First South Carolina (colored) has just returned from an expedition in Georgia; he wanted "to prove the fighting qualities of the negroes (which some have doubted)" and informs Stanton that "It is admitted upon all hands that the negroes fought with a coolness and bravery that would have done credit to veteran soldiers." Henry Barns of the *Advertiser and Tribune* will use Saxton's and similar reports to promote black enlistments in Michigan. (See February 2, 1863.)[250]

21: According to the War Department's "latest muster and payrolls," Michigan has provided four cavalry regiments totaling 4,051 men, five artillery companies totaling 679 men, and twenty-six infantry regiments totaling 22,190. The total number of Michiganders in service is 26,920. Between August 15 and November 21 the state had provided 1,705 men to old regiments. (See Military Affairs—1862.)[251]

22: War Department GO No. 193 orders the discharge from military custody of all those who have interfered with the draft, discouraged enlistments, or aided the enemy.

24: Buckingham asks Blair to "report by telegraph immediately" the number of three-year recruits enlisted since July 2 and the number of nine-month men drafted or volunteered.[252]

26: Blair notifies General Halleck that he can forward two cavalry regiments, one infantry regiment, and one artillery battery. "To which army do you want them sent?" Blair asks. Except for one of the cavalry regiments (it has pistols but needs sabers and rifles), all others are armed and equipped. Halleck replies that all three units should be sent to Washington "immediately."[253]

29: Blair issues a proclamation rescheduling the December 1 draft to December 30. He had hoped that volunteers would cure the deficiency, "but it will be impossible at the rate enlistments have been making for the last month or more"; in the thirty days remaining "unless the men are furnished by voluntary enlistment, they will be taken by the draft." Blair promulgates rules: first, through December 29, recruits will be received for new and existing regiments; however all enlistments must be for three years. From December 1 to 16, recruits will be permitted nine-month terms for old regiments only; finally, the much-delayed draft will occur December 30. "Less than four thousand men are now required to fill the entire quota of the State," Blair declares, "and I earnestly hope that they will be found to come forward cheerfully and *enlist for the war,* as all our troops thus far have done." (But there will be no draft in 1862—see January 29, 1863.)[254]

December

1: Lincoln sends his annual message to Congress.

4: The Fifth Michigan Cavalry, commanded by Colonel

Joseph T. Copeland,[255] departs Michigan with 1,144 men; recruits and officers in its twelve companies are drawn from Pontiac, Blendon, Detroit, Northville, Armada, Grand Haven, Bingham, Allegan, Ann Arbor, and Kalamazoo. The unit is deployed east, but postwar was sent briefly to the frontier.[256] (See June 23, 1865.)

6: Simeon Draper makes his annual report to Stanton. Before Draper took over, John S. Newberry was Michigan's PM, based in Detroit. Newberry remains and Draper has not made any additional PM appointments in Michigan. (See September 4.)[257]

The Sixth Michigan Cavalry, the authorization for which was obtained by Congressman Kellogg, leaves the state.[258]

11–13: The Battle of Fredericksburg is a Federal disaster. (See December 15.)

12: The Twenty-Sixth Michigan musters into U.S. service with 900 men; officers and recruits are drawn from Mt. Clemens, Grand Traverse, Pinckney, Muskegon, Arcadia, Hamburg, Franklin, Niles, Mason, Lowell, and Jackson. The unit will deploy east; their duties will include suppressing the New York City draft riots and Grant's Overland Campaign.[259] (See June 4, 1865.)

The Michigan Cavalry Brigade is formed, consisting of the Fifth, Sixth, and eventually, the Seventh Michigan cavalry regiments (see February 20, 1863). Later, the First Michigan Cavalry joins the brigade.[260]

15: The Army of the Potomac retreats across the Rappahannock following the disaster at Fredericksburg. The *Free Press* declares, "The Generals were competent, the army brave, but the administration at Washington lacked the energy to supply the necessities of our soldiers until too late to insure success." The Lansing *Republican* finds reason to hope. "We see no reason for discouragement in this result. . . . It cannot be expected that our armies should meet with *no reverses* and enjoy *uniform success*. Such is the fate of war."[261]

29: In Mississippi, the Battle of Chickasaw Bayou takes place.

31–January 3, 1863: Battle of Stone's River.

31: Tonight and through New Year's Day, Hillsdale College students and faculty, led by President Edmund Burke Fairfield*, celebrate the Final Emancipation Proclamation. Windows are illuminated to spell the word "Liberty"; the next day, "several hundred" will attend chapel services, with music from the college glee club, a sermon, and the singing of "We Are Coming Father Abraham, Six Hundred Thousand Strong."[262]

Separately, West Virginia is admitted to the Union.

Selected Legislation

Michigan, with more than a hundred thousand fighting men, had arms for hardly more than a thousand, and for military organization, she had next to none at all. . . . We were now to learn war; to create armies, arm and equip them for the field and send them forth to fight those against whom they had done no wrong and had never intended any, and who were bound by obligations the most solemn to keep peace towards them. The ordinary machinery of government had been found inadequate to meet the exigencies of our present rapidly changing affairs, and a frequent resort to the legislative power is rendered imperative.

—GOVERNOR AUSTIN BLAIR, ANNUAL MESSAGE, JANUARY 2, 1862[263]

Joint Resolution No. 1: Joint Resolution for the location and establishment of a naval station and dock yard within the State of Michigan.

Whereas, "The relations of the United States with foreign countries are such that we deem it important that prompt and ample measures be taken to provide adequate protection to the commerce of our western lakes, and to ensure the more perfect defense of our exposed frontier. . . . *Whereas,* The State of Michigan, almost entirely surrounded by navigable waters, the opposite shores of a large portion of which are held by a foreign government, thus exposed to incursions and invasions, by which the immense commerce of the northwest . . . [is] subject to capture and devastation. . . ." *Resolved,* Requests Michigan's congressional delegation to lobby for a naval station and dock yard at Grand Haven, "or such other suitable harbor on the eastern shore of Lake Michigan, [or the] western shore of Lake Huron." Approved January 9, 1862.[264]

No. 1: An Act relative to the direct tax imposed by the Congress of the United States.

Section 1: Authorizes the governor to notify the

U.S. Treasury Secretary "on or before the second Tuesday of February next" that Michigan intends to "assume and pay" the direct tax due under the [U.S.] act of August 6, 1861.[265]

Joint Resolution No. 2: Joint Resolution in regard to frauds upon the treasury of the United States.

Whereas, loyal persons "actuated by a patriotism that knows no limit, have thrown their fortunes and their lives into the great conflict which has been forced upon them; *And whereas*, It is charged that traitors, in the disguise of patriots, have plundered our treasury, destroyed our substance, and paralyzed our efforts, by a system of fraud and peculation." Asks Michigan's congressional delegation to lobby for legislation to make such corruption "a felony, punishable by imprisonment for years, or for life"; or if during the war, "like treason, by death upon the gallows." Approved January 11, 1862.[266]

Joint Resolution No. 3: Joint Resolution relative to exchange of prisoners.

Resolved, "with no prospect of an immediate termination of the war, and many of the citizens of this State in captivity, as prisoners of war, it is expedient that arrangements should be made for exchange of prisoners"; instructs Michigan's congressional delegation to lobby for a POW exchange cartel; *Resolved*, we "deem it not only expedient, but a dictate of humanity that all persons captured as privateers upon the high seas should be held and deemed to be prisoners of war, to be held and treated as such during the continuance of the existing contest (see SAW.2.121). *Resolved*, instructs Michigan's Congressional delegation "to urge the adoption of measures for the exchange of Orlando B. Wilcox [sic]." Approved January 13, 1862.[267]

Joint Resolution No. 4: Joint Resolution relating to the mode of raising revenues by Congress.

Whereas, by the Constitution, direct taxes must be distributed among the states "in proportion to their population, and not according to their wealth, and all such taxes must therefore bear with oppressive weight upon the west, as compared with the commercial and manufacturing States of the seaboard, vastly more wealthy in proportion to population than those of the west." *And whereas*, Congress

may also "levy and collect duties, imposts and excises as well as direct taxes." *And whereas*, justice demands that while Congress can collect a direct tax, that it also "make use of all other modes of taxation authorized under the Constitution, which have a tendency to more nearly apportion taxation among the States according to their wealth." *And whereas*, Michigan's Congressional delegation is requested to lobby in favor of a fairer tax system, that "will have a tendency to equalize the burdens of taxation upon the various sections of the country in proportion to their wealth." Approved January 15, 1862.[268]

Joint Resolution No. 5: Joint Resolution for the relief of Mrs. Isaac W. Ingersoll★.

Whereas, "Mrs. I.W. Ingersoll★, of Detroit, has incurred expenses in going to Charleston, South Carolina, for the purpose of relieving Michigan soldiers, held by the rebels as prisoners of war; therefore, "the State Board of Auditors be . . . authorized, to allow the said Mrs. I. W. Ingersoll an amount sufficient to pay her expenses to Charleston and back, and the amount paid by her in freight on articles sent for the relief of soldiers." Approved January 15, 1862.[269]

Joint Resolution No. 6: Joint Resolution relative to a grant of land by the government of the United States to endow a military school in the State of Michigan.

Whereas, the war "has shown the imperative necessity of greater facilities for the education of young men in the elements of military science, and the arts and strategy of war. . . . *And whereas*, The geographical position of Michigan admonishes us of the necessity of preparing for war, and to meet any sudden attacks; [and] *therefore:*" requests Michigan's congressional delegation to secure legislation "appropriating two hundred thousand acres of public lands to establish and endow a military school within this State." Approved January 15, 1862.[270] (See No. 211, approved March 20, 1863.)

No. 14: An Act to amend an act entitled "an act to provide for the relief by counties, of the families of volunteers mustered from this State into the military service of the United States, or of this State," approved May tenth, eighteen hundred and sixty-one, and to add certain sections thereto.

Section 1: Requires county supervisors hereafter "to

make adequate provision for all requisite relief and support of the families of the noncommissioned officers, musicians and privates, enlisted from counties" and in U.S. or state service. Authorizes supervisors to finance these distributions by borrowing money at a rate not to exceed 10 percent, through bonds or other securities, for a term not to exceed three years, and to finance debt service (and relief distributions) by taxing real and personal property.

Section 3: Requires supervisors "to afford such temporary relief as may be necessary for the support of such families not exceeding fifteen dollars per month to any one family, and not exceeding, in any case, to any family or person, the actual sum necessary, in connection with his, her or their other means of support, to relieve such family or person." [NB: *means testing*.] In the event of the soldier's death, his family is entitled to such relief for "one year and no longer."

Section 4: Requires supervisors to keep records of soldiers and their beneficiaries, including "the measure of relief that the particular family or persons, in [the supervisor's] opinion, require per week or month." The person seeking relief must provide this information under oath. False statements, or statements made "to procure a larger measure of relief than otherwise would be afforded shall forfeit all further relief."

Section 7: Authorizes the supervisors "to adopt and enforce such rules and regulations . . . as shall secure prompt relief to families and persons . . . as shall be just."

Section 8: This relief is independent and separate from "the relief, temporary or otherwise, afforded to poor persons under existing laws."

Section 9: Requires that those in U.S. service must actually be mustered into U.S. service if their families are to receive relief. Approved January 17, 1862. (See Military Affairs—1862.)[271]

Joint Resolution No. 7: Joint Resolution relating to the volunteer force enlisted into the service of the United States, or of this State.

Whereas, "No adequate means has been provided for obtaining the numerical volunteer force enlisted in the several counties of this State; *And whereas,* In the event of any future legislation being necessary upon the subject of relief for the families of volunteers, such information would be of great service to the legislature as well as to officers having duties to perform under existing laws providing for the relief of such families"; therefore, Michigan's adjutant general, before October 1, 1862, will forward counties a correct list of Michigan soldiers in U.S. or Michigan service from each county, listing "the name, date of enlistment, company, regiment, whether married or unmarried, also the number that have died in battle, or from sickness or wounds in battle, and the names of those that have been discharged, or have deserted." Updated lists will be transmitted each October 1 thereafter. Approved January 17, 1862.[272]

Joint Resolution No. 9: Joint Resolution relative to the frontier defences of this State.

Whereas, "The forts along our frontier, as [at] Detroit, Port Huron, Mackinac and Sault St. Mary's, are in a dismantled condition, and some of them are wholly without arms"; therefore, *Resolved,* "That the Governor be requested to call upon the General Government to place within this State such quantity of guns, and of suitable quality, as to provide Fort Wayne, Fort Gratiot, Fort Mackinac, and Fort Brady, with a full armament, and also to put them in the best defensive condition to meet any emergency which may occur." Approved January 17, 1862.[273]

Joint Resolution No. 10: Joint Resolution in relation to the sale and use of intoxicating liquors, as a beverage in the army.

Resolved, instructs Michigan's congressional delegation "to procure the passage of a stringent law prohibiting the sale or use of any intoxicating liquors, as a beverage, to the officers, soldiers or employees of the Government within the District of Columbia." Approved January 17, 1862.[274]

No. 16: An Act for the re-organization of the military forces of the State of Michigan. [NB: *After nine months of war, this act of 96 sections reformed Michigan's militia to improve it as a domestic peacekeeper and to better transform it into a Federal-ready force. Amended by No. 194, approved March 15, 1865. See Legislative Sessions—1865.*]

Section 1: Subjects to military duty "all able bodied, white male citizens between the ages of eighteen and forty-five years" not exempted by U.S. law.

The enrolled militia is not subject to military duty "except in case of war, rebellion, invasion, the prevention of invasion, the suppression of riots, tumults, and breaches of the peace, and to aid civil officers in the execution of the laws and the service of process." Here the enrolled militia may be called for active duty. Beside those exempt under U.S. law, the following are exempt under Michigan law: ministers, state court judges, legislators and legislative officers, honorably discharged commissioned militia officers who have served for six years, state and county officers (except notaries), and public school teachers.

Section 3: "In case of actual or threatened war against, insurrection in, or invasion of, the State, or in case of actual rebellion in, or war against, the United States, or in case the President shall make a requisition on the Governor of this State," the governor may draft militia "as the public necessity demands." The governor may deploy militia "to suppress riots, and to aid civil officers" in the execution of state or federal law, and to "appoint the number by draft, according to the population of the several counties of the State, or otherwise"; [NB: *This section also specifies procedures for drafting.*]

Section 19: Soldiers and officers wounded or disabled in state service "shall be taken care of and provided for at the expense of the State during such period of disability."

Section 31: Authorizes the governor to appoint a five-person State Military Board each to hold office for two years, and excludes the AG, IG, and QMG or any assistant from membership. The State Military Board shall also be "an advisory body" to the governor "on all the military interests of the State. They shall inspect and report . . . on all estimates and accounts of and for the State troops, and audit all claims and accounts, of a military character, against the State; and no contract on behalf of this State exceeding an expenditure of two hundred dollars for military purposes . . . shall be valid . . . until the same as been approved by said board." Authorizes the board "to prepare and promulgate all articles, rules and regulations for the government of state troops not inconsistent" with U.S. laws.

Section 34: Companies may elect their officers;

regimental field officers are elected by company officers; regimental adjutants and QMs are selected from the regimental first lieutenants ("as far as practicable") and sergeants; quartermaster sergeants and color sergeants are selected by the colonel. Also: when deployed, vacancies may be filled from the regiment's officers.

Section 44: "In case of any breach of the peace, tumults, riot, or violent resistance of any process of this State, or apprehension of immediate danger thereof," the county sheriff or city recorder may call for assistance upon the commanding officer of state troops.

Section 49: Any soldier wounded or disabled in service during any "riot, tumult, breach of the peace, resistance of process or whenever called in aid of the civil authorities . . . shall be taken care of and provided at the expense of the county where such service shall have been rendered . . . [and] . . . in case of death in consequence of such wounds, his widow and children, if any, shall receive such relief as the Board of State Auditors may determine to be just and reasonable."

Section 85: Requires the governor on necessity to establish recruiting offices to supply deficiencies in the ranks.

Section 93: To finance all expenses under this act, in 1862 the Auditor General will "apportion to the several counties of this State in proportion to the whole amount of real and personal property . . . a sum equal to fifteen cents for each person whom it shall appear . . . voted at the next preceding gubernatorial election for the office of Governor of this State." The proceeds shall be deposited into the State Military Fund. Approved January 18, 1862.[275]

Joint Resolution No. 12: Joint Resolution in reference to the rebellion.

Whereas, "The Government of the United States is engaged in putting down a causeless and wicked rebellion against its authority, inaugurated by ambitious men to obtain political power—a Government, the safety and perpetuity of which must ever rest upon the loyalty of its citizens and an adherence to the Constitution." *Resolved*, "That Michigan, loyal to herself and to the Federal Government, re-affirms her undying hostility to traitors, her abiding love for freedom, and her confidence in the wisdom and patriotism of the national administration." *Resolved*, "That the people of Michigan deem it the imperative duty of the government to speedily put down all insurrection against its authority and sovereignty, by the use of every constitutional means, and by the employment of [the] energy it possesses; that Michigan stands firm in her determination to sustain, by men and treasure, the Constitution and the Union, and claims that the burthen of loyal men should be lightened, as far as possible, by confiscating, to the largest extent, the property of all insurrectionists; and that as between the institution of slavery and the maintenance of the Federal Government, Michigan does not hesitate to say, that in such exigency, slavery should be swept from the land and our country maintained." Copies of this resolution are to be sent to the state's Congressional delegation. Approved January 18, 1862.[276]

Joint Resolution No. 13: Joint Resolution providing for the payment of the traveling expense of commissioners to secure the allotments of volunteers from the State of Michigan. Approved January 18, 1862.[277]

Joint Resolution No. 16: Joint Resolution relative to an armory in the north-west.

Resolved, "That there being now left in the country but one Government manufactory of arms, and that almost upon the sea-board, it is expedient and important that another should be established, at some point in the north-west, easily accessible from all parts of this great section of the country"; instructs Michigan's Congressional delegation "to secure the establishment of an armory, by the General Government, at some point in the northwestern States," and recommends Chicago as the best location. Approved January 18, 1862.[278]

State Affairs

From the beginning of the war to December 23, 1862, AG Robertson claimed Michigan contributed 45,569 men to service. These included 24,281 men deployed before July 1, 1862; 987 recruits for the Lancers and Hughes Horse Guards, who were mustered but were disbanded before deployment; 13,739 three-year recruits enlisted and deployed since July 1, 1862; 2,162[279] (this figure includes the

six Michiganders who volunteered for nine-month service) recruited through U.S. officer Electus Backus; and 4,400 troops still organizing in the state, representing three cavalry, two infantry, and one sharpshooter regiment, and two artillery batteries. Robertson estimated that 1,400 Michiganders have enlisted in other states' units, but did not include these figures in his calculation. Also not included were an estimated 400 Michiganders who may have enlisted in the Regular Army. The volunteer forces Robertson did include represented about one-third of the military-eligible population of the state.[280]

Between July 2 and December 31, 1862, Michigan furnished ten infantry regiments (the Seventeenth through the Twenty-Sixth, inclusive), three cavalry regiments (the Fourth through Sixth, inclusive), and Battery I of the First Michigan Light Artillery. Total strength at departure was 13,739 men. However, this figure only includes state enlistments. Under War Department GO No. 105 (see entry for December 3, 1861), general recruiting was transferred from governors to U.S. appointees (in Michigan, it was Lieutenant Colonel Electus Backus and his successor, Lieutenant Colonel James R. Smith). As of December 23, 1862, their efforts produced another 2,156 recruits; adding this figure to state enlistments gave Michigan a total credit of 15,895 men. Initial deployments of the "Summer of '62" units included Washington (seven units), Covington (three units), and Louisville, Kentucky (four units).[281]

Robertson also subtracted from Michigan's quota an estimated 4,400 Michiganders still organizing in state and a 101-man provost guard garrisoned at the Detroit barracks. According to Robinson, as of December 24, 1862, Michigan's deficit was "about" 2,970 men. Reportedly, Michigan recruited only six nine-month volunteers; the balance were for three years or the war. Those regiments still organizing were soon to be merged into the Twenty-Seventh and Twenty-Eighth Infantry, the Seventh, Eighth and Ninth Cavalry, and the Tenth and Eleventh Batteries.[282]

The War Department figures for Michigan's 1862 troop contributions were (quota/furnished):
Three-year call of July 1862: 11,686/17,656
Nine-Month call of August, 1862: 11,686/0[283]
By year-end 1862, Michigan's cost to implement the state draft was approximately $30,000, including $7,053 for enrollment and $8,450 to pay surgeons, commissioners, sheriffs, clerks, and so forth to process draftees. An estimated $15,000 remained outstanding.[284]

By the end of 1862, Blair had decided on a policy of not raising additional new regiments, and gave his reasons in his January 1863 annual message: "Notwithstanding the obvious advantages of enlistment in old regiments, it has been found impossible to fill up their ranks while new ones are raising in the State. The superior activity of new officers on the ground working for their commissions, with the ambition of the soldier for the non-commissioned offices of the company, have swept the great body of recruits into the new organizations. To get clear of this difficulty it is proposed to organize no more new regiments after the present are completed." This remained Blair's preference throughout his tenure.[285]

A list of major battles in which Michigan units had been engaged since 1861 illustrates its extensive deployment in the war's two main theaters. In the East, units fought at First Bull Run, Ball's Bluff, Hilton Head, Wilmington Island, James Island, New Bridge, Williamsburg, Fair Oaks, Chickahominy, Hanover Court House, Gaines's Mills, Malvern Hill, Winchester, Second Bull Run, South Mountain, Antietam, and Fredericksburg. In the west, Michiganders fought at Rich Mountain, Lexington, Fort Donelson, Shiloh, New Madrid, Corinth, Iuka, Perrysville, and Baton Rouge.[286]

The war's rapidly expanding scale and ferocity and increased exposure to camp illnesses were reflected in Michigan's casualties. Across forty-seven units of all arms, Michigan totaled 6,742 casualties. Categories included "Died in Action or of Wounds received there" (771), "Died of Disease, &c." (1,810), "Missing in Action" (370),[287] and "Discharged," most for disability (3,791). At this time, the five infantry regiments with the largest number of casualties were the Sixteenth (422), Eighth (406), Fourth (394), Sixth (389), and Third (384).[288]

Detroit was one of twenty-one main depots maintained by the federal government for the warehousing and purchase of war materiel. In the twelve months preceding June 30, 1862, 3,109 horses, 16 wagons, 10,440 greatcoats, 6,339 uniform coats, 10,795 pantaloons, 8,686 blankets, 284 shelter tents, 370 common tents, 100 wall tents, 2 Sibley tents, and 6 hospital tents were purchased there.[289]

Few of these supplies could be found in state arsenals. QMG Fountain's 1862 annual report noted that most ordnance owned or received by the state had been distributed to regiments "long since gone into the service of the United States." The brass cannon that remained were distributed to Detroit-based batteries, and also, given anxieties about Indian attacks in nearby Minnesota, to Ontonagon "for the purpose of protection against Indians." Fears of an in-state insurgency also placed pressure on the QMG's inventories. Most arms and ammunition on hand were distributed "to the northern and western parts of the State for the purpose of repelling any hostile demonstrations that might be made by Indians in those localities." Arms were also sent to student militias at Hillsdale College and the University of Michigan, the former supervised by Captain Henry E. Whipple* and the latter under Professor Henry P. Tappan.* Fountain was especially pleased with the colleges' military-training programs, "that we may in the future have competent, educated officers to command our men, without being obliged to allow West Point graduates to be placed in command of our regiments." Fountain believed that Michigan should educate its own officers rather than sending them to West Point, "a school of aristocracy, where republicanism is ignored, and from whence a few, educated at the national expense, have done honor to the nation, while many are in the command of the rebel army."[290]

Fountain also addressed the approximately $400,000 unappropriated funds from the War Loan, the bonds for which now sold at a premium. Based on what was spent, Michigan had sent twelve regiments to the war; he said the remaining funds should be used for "salaries of officers and clerks of the military department" and also for "transportation of sick and disabled soldiers, agents, surgeons, nurses, sanitary supplies, &c." as well as paying for a draft. Fountain had toured the Peninsula encampments in July 1862 and discovered that while the federal government was now supplying arms, ammunition, and equipment, it had failed to provide proper hospitals and diet. (These were field hospitals; Fountain found that soldiers in city hospitals were "well cared for.") He suggested that Michigan fill this void, and was attempting to do so by private contributions raised by organizations such as Detroit's Soldiers' Aid Society and channeled through the Washington-based Michigan Soldiers' Relief Association.[291]

For the twelve months preceding December 11, 1862, the Michigan Soldiers' Relief Association distributed to the state's soldiers in camps and hospitals in Washington, Georgetown, and Alexandria 370 containers of food and other items. The association also transshipped supplies from Michigan to units deployed in the field. During the same time period, it shipped 400 boxes, barrels, and packages, chiefly to the Peninsula. Aside from goods, its cash receipts were $2,166.13 and expenditures $2,066.86.[292]

In 1862, Fountain spent $5,000 transporting sick and wounded soldiers from distant hospitals to their homes, implementing a policy that Blair adopted after the Battle of Shiloh. The Detroit & Cleveland Navigation Company had been helpful here, offering passage to all soldiers without regard to means. For disabled soldiers, the company furnished free beds and meals during the journey. Fountain complained bitterly about the nonpayment by the army of wages due Michigan soldiers, the effect of which had been to force families to rely on the charity of neighbors. He insisted that Michigan's family aid program should convert from means-tested to a fixed entitlement, "so that [dependents] can demand it as a right and not as a charity." Moreover, the families of disabled soldiers should receive this pay during the time it might take to process their applications for back pay, bounty, and pensions, "instead of immediately casting them off as being no longer entitled to our regard." Fountain noted that for those soldiers still in service Michigan had established only one state agency, and that in New York City. Agent Colonel Darius Clark was badly underfunded, and Michigan's needs were filled by the Massachusetts-founded New England Soldiers' Relief Agency (see SAW.1.324), which had also been serving Michigan soldiers. The 1863 legislature would address several of these concerns. See Selected Legislation—1863, No. 31: An Act for the relief of sick, disabled and needy soldiers, passed February 18, 1863

For the fiscal year ending November 30, 1862, the State of Michigan's total receipts were $1,124,595.10, and total expenditures were $896,620.69, leaving a surplus of $200,794.62. Treasurer Owen sold an additional $150,539.94 in War Bonds, which increased the aggregate War Loan to $607,300. (These 7 percent bonds were due in 1886.) During the year, $40,072.99 from various sources was credited to the War Loan Sinking Fund: once paid in, this would reduce the aggregate loan to $567,227.01. Michigan's total debt by year end was $2,981,088.55.[293]

1863

Key Events

January

1: Lincoln issues the final Emancipation Proclamation. At the Lafayette Street African Methodist Church, Detroit's black community honors the day. The congregation sings, "Blow ye the Trumpet, Blow," while a committee adopts the following resolution: *Resolved*, "That we thank God for putting it into the heart of Abraham Lincoln, to proclaim liberty to the colored race; because it works benefit not only to four millions of colored men, but to five millions of white men, called at the South 'poor white trash' who have no education, and their masters, the slave-owners, are determined they shall have none, and they are, therefore, fit only for fillibustering [sic], and carrying out the cursed designs of their slavery propagandists at the South, and their vile supporters at the North. We believe that slavery makes labor disrespectable, and any country in this state, must necessarily remain under the curse of God, until such evils are removed. We hail the emancipation as a great good to mankind. We hail it with joyful acclamations, and shall only await the morrow to see more plainly and perfectly developed the idea and principles of the President. May God bless Abraham Lincoln and the people." (See entry for January 6.)[1]

Separately, a third company, designated Company L, joins the two Michigan companies of Merrill's Horse in the western theater; together, they become the Michigan Battalion. Company L was recruited from Battle Creek and vicinity.[2] (See September 19, 1865.)

3: Trouble in neighboring Indiana. Governor Morton wires Stanton that when the state legislature convenes, it will "pass a joint resolution acknowledging the Southern Confederacy and urging the States of the Northwest to dissolve all constitutional relations with the New England States." Also, Morton has heard that the Illinois legislature may do the same. Separately, the Battle of Stone's River concludes.[3]

4: Former governor and now commander of the Twenty-Second Michigan, Moses Wisner, dies from typhoid in Lexington, Kentucky.[4]

5: Jefferson Davis, reflecting on a recent Southern victory, predicts that northwestern states will separate from the eastern states: "Out of this victory is to come that dissatisfaction in the North West, which will rive the power of that section; and thus we see in the future the dawn—first separation of the North West from the Eastern States, the discord among them will paralyze the power of both;—then for us future peace and prosperity."[5]

6: A large cross-section of Detroit's black community convenes in the Baptist Church (Crogham Street) to celebrate emancipation. A letter is read from mining tycoon Charles A. Trowbridge* proposing to print 50,000 copies of the final Emancipation Proclamation to distribute to all Michigan regiments and Southern blacks. The cost is $350 and "the white people of our town" will contribute $250 if the black community contributes the remaining $100. The five resolutions passed at this day's church meeting include praise for Abraham Lincoln, "who, despite the opposition of the Border States, or the weak kneed of his northern friends, had the courage" to issue the Proclamation; that Detroit's black community is "ready when called up . . . to buckle on our armor in defence of Liberty"; and praise for U.S. attorney general Edward Bates, whose recent letter[6] to Treasury secretary Chase has "established the fact beyond the power of refutation, that birth on [American] soil always secures the right of citizenship."[7]

7: Michigan legislature convenes. Blair delivers his annual message, which concludes on a ringing note: "Only one thing stands between [peace] and us, and that is—slavery. All the blood and carnage of this terrible war, all the heart-rending casualties of battle and the end of bereavements occasioned by them have the same cause—slavery. . . . It must perish, for so it chose, struck dead by the resistless arm of its conquering antagonist, *Emancipation*. Let us rally round the government; the last great blow is striking."[8]

8: Radical Republican Zachariah Chandler is reelected to the United States Senate, 60 to 35 in the House and 18 to 14 in the Senate. The *Hillsdale Standard's* headline trumpets "The Victory Complete. Republicanism Triumphant in Michigan," while the *Detroit Advertiser and Tribune* declares that "Michigan sends him back to the Senate as her righteous and fiery protest against all this recusancy and treason." Democratic sheets are sullen, but the *Grand Haven News* probably spoke for most when it notified readers that "the Abolition Legislature" reelected Chandler and offered its opinion that "We would have greatly preferred to have had an honest man, and one that has had some brains thus honored."[9]

19–22: Ambrose Burnside, USA, commences the "Mud March."

20: Sensing change it deems unwelcome, the *Detroit Free Press* denounces Pennsylvania Congressman Thaddeus Stevens' (see *SAW*.3.68–69) proposed bill to enlist 150,000 black troops. "Following close on Mr. Lincoln's proclamation of emancipation [which the *Free Press* describes as a "stupendous failure"], it shows the inevitable drift of the radicals towards destruction."[10]

22: In Michigan's House, Republicans introduce (and the body adopts) a resolution that mourns the dead and the "appalling sacrifices of blood and treasure," and then declares, "we nevertheless rejoice that, through the mad and guilty act of the Southern conspirators, that wicked and barbarous institution of African slavery will receive its death blow." But Michigan's Democrats are unhappy with this insinuation of abolition as a war aim. Democrat Abner Pratt★ of Calhoun County introduces a series of substitute resolutions, one of which concerns the Emancipation Proclamation. The *Michigan Argus* insists that these resolutions "may be taken as defining the position of Democrats in the Legislature."[11] (For excerpts, see Legislative Session—1863.)

25: Major General Joseph Hooker relieves Burnside as commander of the Army of the Potomac.

27: Ten of twelve companies of the Seventh Michigan Cavalry are mustered into U.S. service; the remaining companies will be raised through May. Recruits and officers are drawn from Detroit, Niles, Royalton, East Saginaw, Eaton Rapids, Palmyra, Ross, Tecumseh, Grand Rapids, and Birch Run. The unit will serve east.[12] (See December 15, 1865.)

29: The state draft nears. AG Robertson's orders to county draft commissioners and sheriffs include detailed instructions for drawing names and processing draftees. In a public place, a wheel or a box similar to that used for drawing jurors will be placed, and the names of eligible males will be written on folded ballots. The commissioner (or delegate), blindfolded, will draw "the number of men to be drafted as the proper quota of each township or ward, after deducting the credits." Draftees will be personally served a draft notice (or one will be left at his last known residence) stating the place of rendezvous (the county seat) and time to appear (ten days from the date of drawing). At that time, the draftee may offer a substitute. The state's general rendezvous is the Detroit Barracks (commanded by Lieutenant Colonel John R. Smith), to which all draftees will be sent. The draft will commence within five days from the time that county draft commissioners receive these orders (thus, the draft will commence at slightly different times across the state), and volunteering may continue during that time. (See February 9.)[13]

February

1: Both the Twenty-Seventh Regiment at Port Huron and the Twenty-Eighth at Ypsilanti have insufficient recruits; the two units are consolidated at Ypsilanti into the Twenty-Seventh Michigan.[14]

2: The War Department reports that between August 15, 1862, and January 31, 1863, Michigan has furnished 2,194 recruits for old regiments.[15]

9: In Jackson County, the state draft begins under the supervision of draft commissioner Eugene Pringle, county sheriff Jacob K. Smalley★, and county clerk Daniel Upton★. After netting credits and quotas, drawings occur in only three towns: Liberty (eighteen drafted), Henrietta (eighteen drafted), and Waterloo (fifteen drafted). A contemporary notes that "Some of the drafted men, upon hearing that they were among those drawn, found out that the climate of Canada would prove congenial to their falling health, and immediately 'skedaddled,' preferring to live under a petticoat government just now." Several men arranged for substitutes ("generally" $100 per). See Military Affairs—1863.[16]

11: The **Democratic State Convention** convenes in Detroit. The 1862 statewide elections will be for associate Supreme Court (David Johnson* is nominated) and circuit court judgeships, and University of Michigan regents. However, the Democrats' resolutions also address national policies and include a statement that loyalty is to the Constitution and "not to any one man or officer." They state that Union flows from that Constitution, and when the latter's provisions are violated [NB: *such as suspension of habeas corpus*], it is as destructive as secession. They call for a convention of states to settle national differences, and denounce free speech suppression, arbitrary arrests, suspension of habeas corpus, and "the proposed taxation of the laboring white man to purchase the freedom and secure the elevation of the negro" [NB: *compensated emancipation*]. Many of these planks flow from a paper[17] submitted by prominent Democrat William V. Morrison*.[18]

Separately, census data submitted to the War Department disclose that Michigan has 164,007 white males between eighteen and forty-five years old, and 1,622 black males in the same age cohort. Of the latter, an estimated 324 would be available for military service.[19]

12: The **Republican State Convention** convenes in Detroit and nominates regents for the University of Michigan, and one statewide office on the ballot. Ten resolutions are adopted, including an endorsement of the Emancipation Proclamation ("That to deprive the rebel States and districts of 3,000,000 black laborers must diminish the number of white soldiers they can hereafter marshal against us, lessen the supplies of those already in the field, cripple the enemy, [and] diminish the hardships and dangers of loyal soldiers."); a denunciation of any compromise with rebels short of "unconditional surrender"; a carefully worded statement that the party will stand with the government and Constitution "against all sympathizers, croakers and grumblers" regardless of whether Lincoln's future acts are "the wisest possible or not"; implicitly comparing Republicans and Democrats by noting that not one Republican has served as "an armed traitor for Jefferson Davis' army"; and an invitation to patriotic citizens to join in the defense of the government.[20]

18: "An Act for the relief of sick, disabled and needy soldiers" becomes law, which among other things enables Blair to appoint state military agents. (See Selected Legislation—1863 and entry for March 14.)

20: The Michigan House tables a bill to repeal the state's personal liberty law. Separately, the first battalion of the Seventh Michigan Cavalry deploys east. Meanwhile, in Grand Rapids, Battery K of the First Michigan Light Artillery musters into U.S. service; recruits and officers are drawn from Detroit. The unit will serve in Tennessee.[21] (See July 22, 1865.)

25: Blair sends the legislature a February 22 wire from General William S. Rosecrans. He recommends "that all deserters should be returned to duty," and urges the Michigan legislature to enact a law "disenfranchising and disqualifying [deserters] from giving evidence . . . as for other infamous crimes." In his accompanying message, Blair endorses Rosecrans's recommendations and notes that "The court martial, in an organized and disciplined army, is adequate for this purpose." Blair also asserts that in Michigan, the case is different: "in a State far away from the field of operations, [a court martial] in a great measure fails. There is substantially in this State now no punishment for desertion." Meanwhile, in Lansing, Michigan's attorney general Albert Williams* issues an opinion that nothing in the state constitution prohibits soldiers deployed out of state from voting.[22] (See No. 21, Legislative Sessions—1864.)

Separately, Congress enacts Chapter 58, "An Act to provide a national Currency, secured by a Pledge of United States Stocks, and to provide for the Circulation and Redemption thereof," originally called the National Currency Act, now more commonly known as the first National Bank Act.[23] (See June 3, 1864.)

26: In Detroit, a man named William Faulkner is arrested and charged with two rapes: a nine-year-old white girl as she passed by his saloon to mail a letter, and a similarly aged black girl. Faulkner's racial status, a key fact in the events that follow, is unclear: he claims a Spanish Indian heritage; Detroit's black community (based on a contemporaneously published history) regards him as "to all intents a white man. . . . for he was a regular voter, and the journals of the city that understood his politics state that he voted the Democratic ticket." But certain elements of Detroit's white community (and the Democratic *Detroit Free Press*) believe that Faulkner is black. He is held in Detroit's city jail awaiting trial. (See March 6.)[24]

March

2: As the state draft continues in Michigan, Blair informs Stanton that "For the purpose of filling up the old regiments now in the field, I have required all the drafted men to go into them." Most draftees and substitutes are volunteering for three years, and Blair hints at their motives for choosing the longer term: "I have promised them the advance bounty of $25, allowed to volunteers, and the $4 premium." Stanton will agree to this higher amount, and promises to issue orders to Colonel Smith.[25]

3: Chapter 75, nicknamed the Enrollment Act, becomes law. It federalizes what had been state responsibilities of enrolling and drafting. It creates a federal bureaucracy for administering, regulating, and enforcing U.S. laws respecting conscription. While headquartered in Washington, it extends to every state capital and beyond. It creates the PMG, whose responsibilities also include arresting deserters and exposing spies. The Act permits commutation for $300 and substitution; it also establishes three enrollment categories: those legally exempt; a First Class of unmarried men aged twenty to forty-five, including married men aged twenty to thirty-five; and a Second Class of married men aged thirty-five to forty-five. (See SAW.5.35–37 for excerpts from this important law.)[26] (See March 17.)

Anticipating this act, the *Advertiser and Tribune* argued for its support: "In all sections of the country recruiting has almost ceased, and yet our old regiments are shrunk to mere skeletons," adding that "Now it is for the people to determine if conscription is too high a price to pay for the Union." The Republican *Jackson Citizen* finds the act "a necessary means of national defence in the future" and that "This law will prove itself to the salvation of the country." The *Free Press* comments that while it might have changed several provisions of the law, it is now the law and "must be obeyed by every good and loyal citizen until it is repealed or declared by the proper judicial tribunals unconstitutional." The Democratic *Grand Haven News* praises the act for allowing commutation for $300 and substitution, and declares "any attempt at resistance to a draft would be deprecated by all sober-minded citizens." But the Democratic *Michigan Argus* laments what the *News* found admirable: "Are the rich under no obligations to shed their blood to maintain the institutions which have enriched them? Or shall they shed only crocodile tears and treasury notes while the poor men go forth to save country?"[27]

Another act is passed today: Chapter 81, "An Act relating to Habeas Corpus, and regulating Judicial Proceedings in Certain Cases." It gives congressional sanction to Lincoln's right to suspend the writ of habeas corpus in certain cases. The *Advertiser and Tribune* defends the act. While conceding that mistaken arrests have been made, "No man in his senses pretends that the Government, in time of war, has not the authority to arrest bad men engaged in compassing its destruction."[28]

4–5: The Battle of Thompson's Station, Tennessee. Among federal regiments engaged, the Nineteenth Michigan ranks first in casualties suffered (457).[29]

4: The Chicago branch of the Western Sanitary Commission issues an appeal: "General Grant's army is in danger of scurvy. Rush forward anti-scorbutics." They are sent to auxiliaries in Detroit, Ann Arbor, Adrian, Battle Creek, Grand Rapids, Hillsdale, Jackson, and Kalamazoo, among other places. In response, Michigan will contribute (with other states) some 6,000 barrels of assorted vegetables to the Army of the Tennessee and the Army of the Cumberland via the Chicago branch.[30]

5: In Detroit, in the presence of "an immense crowd," the trial of the "Negro Faulkner" begins in City Hall in Recorder's Court; there is difficulty impaneling a jury as "there are but few persons who have [not] formed an opinion of the matter." Both alleged rape victims—one white and the other black—testify against Faulkner. The jury (alone) is taken to view the supposed crime scene while Faulkner is returned to jail. As he leaves the courthouse, a large crowd is waiting with "A perfect storm of hisses, curses and threats"; "a general rush" is made toward Faulkner, but is stopped by police. As Faulkner passes the German Protestant Church on Monroe Avenue, the crowd bursts through the escort and a hurled paving stone hits Faulkner's head, knocking him unconscious. Revolvers drawn, the police surround Faulkner until he revives and then continue toward the jail. Neighborhood women appear from windows and demand that their men "hang, shoot, butcher or kill" Faulkner. By now the crowd includes "respectable citizens . . . [who] . . . were among the foremost to set the law at defiance." The police manage to spirit Faulkner into the jail without further incident. (See March 6.)[31]

6: Faulkner's trial continues amid a tense atmosphere. Whites assault ("kicks, cuffs and blows") blacks in the vicinity of the Recorder's Court. The Provost Guard, with bayonets fixed, escort Faulkner from jail and fall in line around the courthouse. The waiting crowd shouts ("almost deafening") but there is no physical violence. After ten minutes' deliberation, the jury finds Faulkner guilty, and he is sentenced to life imprisonment. The crowd outside, now estimated as "thousands," follows the prisoner, continues screaming, and just as he nears the jail, rush the soldiers. Lieutenant Van Stan*orders his men in line and fires a blank volley; some soldiers fire again but directly into the crowd with live rounds. A twenty-four-year-old daguerreotype studio owner, Charles Langer, a German, is shot dead, and several of the mob are wounded. Faulkner is returned unharmed but the frenzied crowd, especially the Germans, start for Detroit's black neighborhoods, shouting, "Kill the niggers."

On Beaubien Street, a black-owned cooperage shop is surrounded and attacked by "bricks, paving stones and clubs." Some workers inside are armed and fire into the mob, wounding several attackers. The mob will not enter—it is certain death—but continues to hurl stones and finally, fires the building. Fleeing occupants are assaulted, including a black woman holding a baby who begs for mercy. (According to the Detroit Free Press, an unidentified white man rescued mother and child.) However, there is no mercy for the other occupants, who are beaten insensible as they exit the cooperage, and are left for dead; one eventually dies. Meanwhile the mob has fanned across the neighborhood (Lafayette Street between Beaubien and St. Antoine), looting houses and barns and then applying the torch. Pillage—including feather beds, furniture, and musical instruments—is piled in the streets and burned in huge bonfires. Firemen with trucks appear, but the mob prevents them from dousing fires in buildings inhabited by black people; the water is for white residences only. Some

twenty fires are set, and an estimated fifty buildings, most in the Third Ward, are destroyed. Buildings are burned on Larned and Brush Streets, and by nightfall, flames illuminate Detroit's skyline as the rioters move toward the city center. The white mob has become indiscriminate, attacking homes inhabited by blacks and whites. Fire bells now sound in the First and Sixth Wards. A black man carrying water to help extinguish one fire is chased through the streets, the mob yelling, "Nigger! Nigger!"

At some point, the mob moves to attack the A.M.E. Church on Lafayette Street near Beaubien. Officer Dennis K. Sullivan of the Detroit Police Department prevents the church from destruction by standing between the building and the mob. He also rescues several black men who are about to be beaten.

Around dusk acting mayor Francis B. Phelps[32] (Mayor William C. Duncan is in Lansing) mobilizes the Detroit Light Guard and the Lyon Guard, and also requests help from any Regular Army at Fort Wayne. He wires Ypsilanti for troops from the Twenty-Seventh Michigan. At 7:00 p.m., fifty men of the Detroit Light Guard are patrolling Third Ward neighborhoods; the Lyon Guard is assigned to protect the jail. By 9:00 p.m., Colonel Dorus Morton Fox* commanding five companies of the Twenty-Seventh arrives and is sent to disperse the crowds. Fifty Regulars from the Nineteenth U.S. Infantry arrive with two brass cannon.

By midnight, all is quiet. Destruction is widespread with twenty-two arrests, up to thirty-five buildings destroyed, and two hundred blacks made refugees. Given the mob's ferocity and destructiveness, deaths are surprisingly few: Charles Langer[33] and Joshua Boyd[34] from the cooperage. The number of wounded is unclear, but among the whites mentioned, most seem to have been shot by blacks defending the cooperage. Meanwhile, many blacks flee to Canada or the surrounding woods. (See March 7 and 11.)[35]

7: Detroit reckons with the riot's aftermath. Just after midnight, acting mayor Phelps issues another proclamation that for the next forty-eight hours closes all saloons after 7:00 p.m. In Detroit, a public meeting called by the Advertiser and Tribune convenes at the County Court House at 4:00 p.m. Called to order by D. B. Duffield* and led by alderman Edward C. Walker*, the meeting passes a resolution, "That this disgrace which has befallen our city should have been averted by a reasonable precaution on the part of police authorities." Charges are made that the police were too few and unarmed. The truth is that Detroit has no regular police force, and as the *Free Press* opined, "is as badly prepared to resist a riot as any city of her size can be."[36]

9: In Memphis, Major General Stephen A. Hurlbut orders chaplain Samuel W. Day* of the three-year Eighth Illinois "to repair to Chicago, Illinois and Detroit Michigan, for the purpose of collecting contributions in vegetable and other sanitary stores for the hospitals in this [Sixteenth Army Corps] Department." (See Military Affairs—1863.)[37]

10: Lincoln proclaims an amnesty under Section 26 of the March 3 Enrollment Act: AWOL soldiers who report to places designated by Lincoln by April 1 will forfeit pay but not face other punishment. Under this proclamation, wayward soldiers are to report to Lieutenant Colonel Smith at the Detroit Barracks.[38]

11: Reverend John A. Warren (who will later blame "*prejudice* and passion, brought on by the Democratic Free Press, the most reckless sheet that was ever issued from any press") and J. J. Byrd convene a meeting of Detroit African Americans at the A.M.E. Church on Lafayette Street. Resolutions are drafted decrying the riot, thanking Officer Dennis Sullivan and others who intervened, and declaring, "That as citizens we do not consider that we have laid ourselves liable to be censured as the instigators of these disturbances in this community, but on the contrary, have proved ourselves to be law-abiding and peaceable citizens."[39]

14: Blair appoints Luther B. Willard* as state military agent at Nashville and Benjamin Vernor* as state military agent at Detroit. Within several weeks, Blair will appoint Dr. Joseph Tunnicliffe, Jr.,* as state military agent in Washington. (See June 25, and State Military Affairs—1863.)[40]

17: Pursuant to Chapter 75, James B. Fry[41] is appointed U.S. provost marshal general, headquartered in Washington. (See April 21.) Separately, the Battle of Kelly's Ford, Virginia, is fought.[42]

23: Michigan legislature adjourns.[43]

25: Major General Ambrose E. Burnside relieves Horatio G. Wright as commander of the Department of the Ohio, which includes Michigan. (See December 11, 1863.)[44]

April

2: The War Department issues GO No. 86 pursuant to Sections 19 and 20 of the recent Enrollment Act. It requires that state units falling below "one-half the maximum number [of soldiers] required by law" must be consolidated and that any "supernumerary" officers be discharged. This helps fuel the nationwide "Fill Up the Old Regiments!" movement. Governor Blair had earlier objected to consolidation: "To abandon the old regiments which have fought with marked distinction through all the campaigns of the war, would be to disregard the first principles of military success, the pride of the soldier in his corps."[45]

6: Republicans sweep Michigan elections, including the University of Michigan's board of regents, also reelecting Judge James V. Campbell* to the state Supreme Court.[46]

7: A fleet commanded by flag officer Samuel Du Pont attacks Charleston, South Carolina.[47]

10: Eight companies of the Twenty-Seventh Michigan muster into U.S. service; officers and recruits are drawn from Lyons, Ontonagon, Houghton, Eagle Harbor, Greenfield, Springfield, Port Huron, Detroit, and East Saginaw. The unit initially deploys west but will enter the eastern theater for Grant's Overland Campaign.[48] (See July 26, 1865.)

11: In Coldwater, Battery L of the First Michigan Light Artillery musters into U.S. service; recruits and offices are drawn from the vicinities of Detroit, Hudson, and Coldwater. The unit deploys in Kentucky, Ohio, and Tennessee.[49] (See August 22, 1865.)

12: In Lebanon, Kentucky, Brigadier General Mahlon D. Manson orders the Eighteenth Michigan to surrender any blacks employed by the regiment. All but one worker was born in Kentucky, and the regiment reluctantly renders these men. Manson then demands surrender of the non-Kentuckian, and orders two Kentucky units into line to enforce his demand. But Colonel Charles C. Doolittle* of the Eighteenth orders his men to load muskets, fix bayonets, and form line of battle. "Come and take him," Doolittle dares Manson, who then sends for reinforcements from the Seventy-Ninth New York; its colonel reportedly answers, "I am not fighting Michigan men." Manson then wires Burnside, who declines to intervene. The Eighteenth spends the night sleeping on its arms. The black employee is not surrendered.[50]

13: General Ambrose Burnside, commanding the Department of the Ohio (which includes Michigan), issues GO No. 38. It declares (among other things) that "hereafter all persons found within our lines who commit acts for the benefit of the enemies of our country will be tried as spies or traitors, and if convicted, will suffer death." After a list of proscribed acts, Burnside adds the following: "The habit of declaring sympathies for the enemy will not be allowed in this Department. Persons committing such offenses will be at once arrested, with a view to being tried as above stated, or sent to beyond our lines and into the lines of their friends. It must be distinctly understood that treason, expressed or implied, will not be tolerated in this Department." See May 1 and 4–5.[51]

17: Benjamin H. Grierson raids Mississippi to distract attention from Grant's Vicksburg Campaign.

21: The War Department issues "Regulations for the government of the Bureau of the Provost-Marshal-General of the United States." These regulations give effect to the Enrollment Act. Federal officers, AAPMGs (often career soldiers), are assigned to each state; each state is divided into districts that parallel congressional districts; each district will conduct its own enrollment, and the draft will be based on these enrollments.[52] (See April 25.)

23: Major Bennett H. Hill* of the Second U.S. Artillery is assigned as acting assistant provost marshal for the State of Michigan. He serves until July 31, 1865.[53]

24: The War Department issues GO No. 100 (the "Lieber Code"), which establishes a law of war. Of particular importance to states are provisions regulating the declaration of martial law.[54]

25: PMG Fry instructs Major (and now AAPMG for Michigan) Bennett H. Hill (copied to Blair) that, when dealing with Blair, he must emphasize diplomacy as well as authority. Fry explains that "there is no law creating the position of provost-marshals for States," so Hill must act "in the name of the Provost-Marshal-General and as his assistant." He "will be exclusively under the orders of this department; yet, while the Governor of Michigan has no control over you, you will be required to acquaint yourself with his views and wishes, and give them

due weight in determining as to the best interests of the General Government, of which you are the representative. To this end you will use all proper means to gain and retain the confidence and good will of the Governor and his State officers. You will endeavor by all means in your power to secure for the execution of the enrollment act the aid and hearty co-operation of His Excellency the Governor and of the civil officers in his State, as also of the people." Aside from supervising enrolling officers, surgeons, draft commissioners, and others, Hill must also report on the "the localities, numbers and strength of the enemies of the Government, if there be any" and the "strength of military forces and of all enrolled, organized or partially organized parties friendly to the Government."[55]

The system takes hold quickly. Within ten days appointments are made for all six Michigan congressional districts, and rules published.[56]

28: The War Department issues GO No. 105, which establishes the Invalid Corps, later renamed the Veteran Reserve Corps. AAPMG Hill has authority over their recruitment. (See June 15.)[57]

May

1–5: Chancellorsville Campaign. Following the Union defeat, Michigan newspaper reaction centers on Army of the Potomac commander General Joseph Hooker. The *Free Press* partly bases its criticism along political lines: Hooker, the darling of Senator Zachariah Chandler, had performed as poorly as General McClellan, who the sheet believed had been maneuvered from office by Chandler with Hooker's help. The *Advertiser and Tribune* understood things differently, doubting that "any serious charge can be established either against [Hooker's] competency or his courage," and blaming the Eleventh Corps' German troops for the defeat.[58]

1: Ohio Congressman Clement L. Vallandigham speaks at "an immense mass-meeting" in Mt. Vernon, Ohio. Burnside's note-takers are in the audience.[59]

Meanwhile, the Battle of Port Gibson is fought, part of Grant's Vicksburg Campaign.

2: Recruited at Mt. Clemens, 1,117 men of the Eighth Cavalry muster into U.S. service; recruits and officers are drawn from Mt. Clemens, Marshall, Pontiac, East Bloomfield, Romeo, Prairie Ronde, Ray, St. Claire,

Detroit, and Coldwater. The unit deploys west.[60] (See September 28, 1865.)

PMG Fry recommends that the next draft should first fill any state deficiencies remaining from the 1862 calls, which total 87,103 among all states. Fry claims that Michigan's share of this deficiency is 4,288 men.[61]

3–4: In Virginia, the Second Battle of Fredericksburg and the Battle of Salem Church are fought, part of the Chancellorsville Campaign.

4–5: General Ambrose Burnside arrests Clement Vallandigham for violation of GO No. 38, issued April 13, 1863. (See entry for that date.) Over the past several weeks, Vallandigham has been a featured speaker at Peace Democrat rallies, where Burnside's agents have been monitoring him. With an antiwar speech given on May 1 at Mount Vernon, Ohio—including an obnoxious, Burnside-baiting denunciation of the general order—Vallandigham crosses the line. In the wee hours of May 5, he is arrested at his home in Dayton and imprisoned in Cincinnati. After a military trial, he will be exiled to the Confederacy.

In Michigan this creates enormous controversy, which Democratic newspapers and the *Free Press* in particular follow carefully, and from the editorialists' perspective, bitterly.[62] (See May 24.)

7: Stanton informs Blair that Hooker has failed at Chancellorsville "but there has been no serious disaster to the organization or efficiency of the army." It has recrossed the Rappahannock and returned its former positions. Stanton promises, "The Army of the Potomac will speedily resume offensive operations."[63]

8: Stanton reassures Burnside about Vallandigham's arrest, "In your determination to support the authority of the Government and suppress treason in your department, you may count on the firm support of the president." (But see May 16 and June 7.)[64]

12: The Eighth Michigan Cavalry deploys from Mt. Clemons for Kentucky.[65]

14: Fighting around Jackson, Mississippi, as Grant continues driving to Vicksburg.

16: The Military Commission finds Vallandigham guilty and sentences him to imprisonment at Fort Warren, Boston Harbor. Also, Vallandigham's writ for habeas corpus is denied. (See May 19.) Meanwhile, Grant fights at Champion Hill.[66]

18: Grant crosses the Big Black River to begin the siege of Vicksburg. The first attack occurs on the 19th.[67]

19: At Coldwater, at least ten companies of the Ninth Michigan Cavalry are mustered into U.S. service with 1,073 men; recruits and officers are drawn from Trenton, Columbia, Rome, Whitmore Lake, Monroe, Antwerp, New York City, Monguagon, Lapeer, Coldwater, Pokagon, and Detroit. The unit served west and joined Sherman's Atlanta Campaign, the march to the sea, and the Carolinas Campaign.[68] (See July 21, 1865.)

Lincoln commutes Vallandigham's sentence to banishment to the Confederacy. (See June 7.)

20: Austin Blair, in Washington, will visit Michigan units.[69] (See May 28.)

20–21: The Union League Convention opens in Cleveland, Ohio. Of 171 delegates, eleven are from Michigan. Although the league professes to be nonpartisan, it draws harsh criticism from Democrats. The *Grand Haven News* offers a quick description: "No-Party-Emancipation-High-Taxation, Centralization, Confiscation, Negro Equalization, Usurpation, Abolition, Administration-Party."[70]

22: The War Department issues GOs No. 143 and 144. The former establishes in the adjutant general's office a bureau "relating to the organization of colored troops." An officer will be assigned to head this effort, assisted by "three or more inspectors to supervise the organization of colored troops." Boards are established "to examine applicants for commissions to command colored troops." No one may recruit these troops without War Department authorization, and no authority will be given "to persons who have not been examined and passed by a board," nor may any person recruit more than one regiment. The War Department will establish depots and recruiting stations. NCOs may be recruited from "the best men of their [i.e., the colored troops'] number." GO No. 144 establishes rules for examining applicants "for commissions in regiments of colored troops." Applicants will be "subjected to fair but rigorous examination as to physical, mental and moral fitness to command troops." Requirements include "good moral character and standing in the community in which the applicant resided, or, if in the military service, on testimonials from his commanding officers."

No person rejected by the board can be reexamined.[71] (See July 24.)

23: Although there is no indication that Robert E. Lee's army has yet moved, Stanton, anticipating a spring offensive, asks General Halleck for a plan of contingency.[72]

26: In Detroit, A "Large and Enthusiastic Meeting" convenes at City Hall to protest the arrest of Clement L. Vallandigham. With Robert McClelland presiding, featured speakers include senior Democrats George V. N. Lothrop and Levi Bishop. Eight resolutions are adopted including a statement of loyalty to the Union and to sustain the war effort while simultaneously denouncing Vallandigham's trial as a "military and unwarrantable interference with the freedom of speech, and as illegal assertion of the supremacy of the military power over the civil power." Bishop's speech includes a reminder that Democrats too answered the call to arms and "today, the silent voice of the slain, on a hundred battle fields, PROCLAIMS THE LOYALTY OF THE DEMOCRATIC PARTY."

27: Federals begin attacking Port Hudson, Louisiana.

28: Blair, accompanied by the Sixteenth Michigan Cavalry, visits Colonel George Gray's* Sixth Michigan Cavalry near the Bull Run battlefield. Blair, mindful of the Chancellorsville defeat, says in an address to the troops "that the war should be prosecuted until the Union should be restored, and that, although we were not so fortunate as to have achieved a success at Fredericksburg, yet this disaster was counterbalanced by the triumph of our arms in the West." After a long day and a tour of the battlefield, Blair reviews the First Michigan Cavalry. When asked how "he bore the fatigue," Blair replied "that he got along first rate"; however, the reporter noted that "by his looks, he was considerably fagged, and will not feel much in the humor for visiting the Falls of the Potomac, as he proposes for tomorrow."[73]

30: Michigan's Blair visits General Joseph Hooker, who probably informs him that Confederates have stirred from the Rappahannock, although in what direction is unclear.[74]

PMG Fry cautions PMs from arresting deserters whose court convictions were uncertain.[75]

June

1: General Ambrose Burnside, commanding the Department of the Ohio, issues GO No. 84, closing the *Chicago Times* "On account of repeated expressions of disloyal and incendiary sentiments." Instantly controversial, the order takes on special significance for Michiganders and its Democrats as Wilbur F. Storey, former owner of the *Free Press*, now owns the *Chicago Times*. Lincoln avoids an extended controversy by revoking Burnside's order within several days. While the suppression infuriates Michigan's Democratic sheets, the Republican *Advertiser and Tribune* is almost as unhappy with Lincoln's revocation of GO No. 84. "It seems strange . . . that as Mr. Vallandigham was condemned . . . for promulgating the sentiments that the Chicago paper disseminated, that the latter should be permitted to go free of punishment, while the former was sent into the rebel lines."[76]

4: The War Department issues GO No. 163 establishing bounties for Regular and volunteer forces. All accepted recruits (or others responsible for their enlistment) will be paid a $2 premium; recruits will receive one month's advance pay and a $100 bounty, of which $25 will be paid in advance. However, black soldiers will be paid "ten dollars per month and one ration; three dollars of which monthly pay may be in clothing."[77]

5: Hooker, commanding the Army of the Potomac in Falmouth, Virginia, informs Lincoln that Lee's army has begun to move. Hooker is uncertain as to Confederate intentions, but reports indicate something like September 1862's Maryland Campaign. Meanwhile in Washington, the War Department instructs U.S. army commanders in Michigan to provide forces (if possible) on application by AAPMG Hill to enforce the Enrollment Act, principally duties related to guard, riot control, enrollment, delivery of draft notices, and conscription.[78]

7: Washington prepares to activate its defense of Pennsylvania from Lee's possible invasion. Meanwhile, Burnside reads General Jacob D. Cox[79] a letter from Stanton "which practically revoked the whole of his Order No. 38 by directing him not to arrest civilians or suppress newspapers without conferring first with the War Department."[80]

9: Federal enrollment under the Enrollment Act begins in Jackson (now the Third Congressional District); it has begun or will also begin in districts across the state. Jackson County's case is typical: an enrollment clerk is designated for each of the county's eighteen townships and one for each of the City of Jackson's four wards. The Third District PM, Captain Robert J. Barry*, formerly in Lansing but now in Jackson ("a more central location"), names James Monroe* of Marshall and George P. Sanford* of Lansing as Deputy PMs. (See June 15 and 24; for enrollment, see Military Affairs—1863.) Meanwhile, in Virginia, the Battle of Brandy Station is fought. None of Michigan's formidable cavalry units are engaged.[81]

11: From Alexandria, Tennessee, General John Hunt Morgan takes the first step in his raid of Indiana and Ohio. Morgan's superior, Army of Tennessee commander General Braxton Bragg, orders him to confine his operations to Kentucky and specifically forbids him to cross the Ohio River. However, Morgan has other ideas. (See June 17 and July 2.)[82]

14–15: In Virginia, the Battle of Second Winchester is fought.

15: Lee's advance element crosses the Potomac into Maryland. Separately, Lincoln issues a call for 100,000 six-month militia from the states of Maryland, West Virginia, Pennsylvania, and Ohio; 50,000 of these will be from Pennsylvania, and will be divided into forty-two infantry and five cavalry regiments and three artillery batteries. Stanton also wires Blair and other governors raising as probable Lee's invasion of Maryland, Pennsylvania, "and other states"; Stanton asks Blair, "Will you please inform me immediately what number, in answer to a special call of the President, you can raise and forward of militia or volunteers, without bounty, for six months, unless sooner discharged, and to be credited on the draft of your state?"

Blair immediately replies with bad news. "Have no organized militia, and no considerable number of militia could be furnished from this State for sixty days," adding, "I much prefer to furnish troops required from this state for three years." Other replies sent today include Illinois's Richard Yates, who can offer nothing because of threatened in-state insurrections; Iowa's governor is at Vicksburg, but an official replies that his state could raise "three or four six months regiments [that] could be ready in twenty days."[83]

Meanwhile, AAPMG Hill informs Fry that "Everything is being done possible by me to hasten the enrollment and creation of the Invalid Corps." Hill explains that part of the problem is Washington, as the PMs have not received the "prescribed blanks for the certificate of enrollment boards," and Dr. Charles Tripler[84] has no examination blanks. Hill has far better news on another topic: "There has been no trouble reported in making the enrollment."[85]

At a public meeting in Detroit, the Michigan branch of the Christian Commission is founded. Its management committee will eventually include Edward C. Walker, Henry P. Baldwin, and Rev. George W. Taylor*; the last-mentioned will serve as state agent. (See December 7.)[86]

17: In neighboring Indiana, Captain Thomas Henry Hines leads 62 of Morgan's men across the Ohio River into Perry County. His objective is to steal horses and hopefully "stir up" Copperhead sentiment in the Hoosier State. Both missions will fail: on June 19, Hines's forces are defeated at Leavenworth in Crawford County (Hines escapes), and the reports of willing Copperheads prove greatly exaggerated. (See July 8.)[87]

23: PMG Fry authorizes Congressman Francis W. Kellogg "to raise two additional Regiments of Volunteer Cavalry, and two Batteries of Artillery, to serve for three years," provided that they be complete within forty days. Blair continues to oppose recruiting for new rather than old regiments, but after the War Department's "direct and urgent" requests, makes an exception for Kellogg. This order is the genesis of the Tenth Michigan Cavalry and its future attached Thirteenth Battery, organized in Grand Rapids, in 1864. Under this authority, the Fourteenth Battery will be attached to the Eleventh Michigan Cavalry.[88]

Separately, General Rosecrans begins what will become the successful Tullahoma Campaign against Bragg.

24: The Third Congressional District enrollment begun June 9 is complete for Jackson City, although it continues in other district municipalities. (See July 22.) "[The] business is transacted in a most expeditious manner," notes a local Republican sheet.[89]

25: Hooker's army crosses the Potomac in pursuit of Lee. Meanwhile, from Washington, Blair's recent appointee as Washington's Michigan State military agent Dr. Joseph Tunnicliffe, Jr. files a report about Michigan men at Camp Convalescent in Alexandria, Virginia. He lists 102 names (which will be published in Michigan newspapers), and notes that some men have been hospitalized at that place since their original enlistment. He also identifies a problem (which he will expand on in his 1863 annual report) well known to hospitalized soldiers of every state: "A number of [soldiers] had floated about through different hospitals, without being mustered, until the authorities recognized them as deserters. Many of them had not been paid in a number of months, and appeared to have no knowledge as to how to proceed to get [their pay]." (See Military Affairs—1863.)[90]

Separately, expiring terms of service for 1861 volunteers present a looming manpower crisis for the army. In response, the War Department issues GO No. 191, which establishes rules for reenlisting men. Incentives include a new designation, "Veteran Volunteers," increased bounties and other compensation, chevrons to distinguish veterans from other soldiers, and thirty-day furloughs. Michigan has many units whose terms expire in 1864, and many of these will reorganize under GO No. 91, averting a manpower crisis.[91]

26: Confederates briefly occupy Gettysburg. Separately, Confederate naval raiders hijack the *Caleb Cushing* in Portland (Maine) Harbor.[92]

27: General George Meade relieves General Hooker of command of the Army of the Potomac. Meanwhile, the division of General Jubal Early, CSA, leaves Gettysburg for York.

28: Jubal Early occupies York. He demands clothing, especially 2,000 shoes, socks, and hats. He also demands $100,000. If Early's tribute is met, he will restrain his men from sacking the town. A citizens' committee works to comply with these demands. (See June 30.)[93]

Meanwhile, George Armstrong Custer* is promoted to brigadier general and assigned to the Cavalry Corps's Second Brigade of its Third Division. This is the Michigan Brigade, initially consisting of the First, Fifth, Sixth, and Seventh Michigan.[94]

30: General Willcox issues GO No. 5 for the district of Indiana and Michigan. "The peace of Indiana has lately been disturbed by violence, murder, and other acts contrary to law," he declares. These acts have caused "dread and mistrust—they divide and provoke hostility between neighbors," weaken courts, risk

martial law, and discourage enlistments. Willcox then turns to the GO's substance: although naming none, he inveighs against secret societies. No matter how well intentioned, "they are both dangerous and beyond the ordinary grasp of law; they are therefore declared to be hostile, and will be put down by all the military power of the District, if need be." He asks that all Union men join "to discontinue and peaceably break up such organizations within . . . the District." Many interpret this order as directed against Union Leagues as well as Knights of the Golden Circle. (See Military Affairs—1863.)[95]

Meanwhile, in Dearborn, Battery M of the First Michigan Light Artillery musters into U.S. service; recruits and officers are drawn from Detroit, Mt. Clemens, and Coldwater. The unit will deploy to Kentucky and Tennessee.[96] (See August 1, 1865.)

July

1: This morning advance federal and Confederate units find each other four miles west of Gettysburg.

2: Gettysburg's second day. Meanwhile, to the west, John Hunt Morgan crosses the Cumberland River from Tennessee into Kentucky. (See July 3.)[97]

3: Gettysburg's third day. Meanwhile, as news of the battle spreads, private and public aid efforts flood into Gettysburg. From Washington, the Michigan Soldiers' Relief Association will dispatch two agents: one remains for six weeks and the other for three months. Among federal regiments engaged, the Twenty-Fourth Michigan ranks first in casualties suffered (363). Among cavalry regiments engaged, the Seventh Michigan ranks first in casualties (100), the First Michigan Cavalry second (73), and the Fifth Michigan Cavalry fourth in casualties suffered (56).[98]

4: In the Ottawa village of Pentwater (Oceana County), a white man reportedly fluent in Chippewa, Captain Edwin V. Andress*, and Ottawa chief Pay-baw-me* recruit twenty-four Ottawa for Company K of the First Michigan Sharpshooters. Included in this batch of recruits are Garrett Gravaraet* and his father Henry G. Gravaraet. Of 109 original company members, Garrett recruits 30. Company K is destined to become the most famous Native American unit in the Army of the Potomac. (See Selected Summaries.)[99]

Separately, Vicksburg surrenders and Lee withdraws from Gettysburg. But on the morning of this day, the *Advertiser and Tribune* is apprised only that federal forces have held the line at the Peach Orchard against a determined Confederate assault—"The Enemy Repulsed at all Points"—after erroneously reporting the death of General Henry Baxter*, who had started the war as a captain in the Seventh Michigan. The *Free Press* headlines "Rumored Capture of Richmond," "Loss on Both Sides Severe in Officers," "The Greatest Battle of the Rebellion to be Fought in Pennsylvania," and "A Dispatch that Vicksburg Surrendered."[100]

Meanwhile, in Kentucky, as Confederate raider John Hunt Morgan continues his drive to the Ohio River, federal units confront him; in the ensuing action, the Twenty-Fifth Michigan suffers twenty-nine casualties.[101]

5: Vallandigham arrives in Halifax, Nova Scotia, via Bermuda. (See July 15.)

7: "Victory! Victory!" trumpets the *Advertiser and Tribune* as editorialists gain a better understanding of what happened at Gettysburg between July 1 and July 4. But it comes a price. "The great victory is not without its alloy," the *Free Press* notes. "Thousands of homes are filled with the sobs of mourning." In particular, it notes casualties of the Twenty-Fourth Michigan (which would suffer the highest number of casualties of any single federal regiment at Gettysburg) was, after the battle said to be reduced to 150 men from 496 officers and men at the start of the of three days' fight. Across Michigan during July and August, casualty reports will be published, long lists of regimental losses as well as individual obituaries. The Fourth Michigan, late at Gettysburg, lost more than half its men, including the colonel; ten men from Company M, First Michigan Cavalry, were lost. Captain Samuel Golyer is DOW incurred at Vicksburg, and Lieutenant Butler Brown is KIA at Gettysburg. The Twenty-Fourth Michigan's casualties spill onto two pages, as does a list of wounded reported by the Michigan's Washington state agent Tunnicliffe in area hospitals: the First, Fourth, and Sixteenth Michigan Infantry and the First, Fifth, Sixth, and Seventh Cavalry; in late July, casualties Michigan's cavalry incurred between June 30 and July 20 fill a column and a half.[102]

And then there is the Confederate surrender at Vicksburg. "Vicksburg Has Fallen!!," the *Hillsdale*

Standard informs its readers, while the *Advertiser and Tribune* offers fulsome praise for General Grant and observes, "The dark clouds that two weeks ago, obscured the future, have been suddenly dissipated, and bright hope illumines the whole horizon." But politics is never far off. The Democratic *Grand Haven News* also shares the happiness of victory and notes that the country sighs for "a peace constitutionally honorable, just and permanent," which hints at something less than unconditional surrender.[103]

Meanwhile, Gettysburg and Vicksburg spur relief efforts throughout Michigan. In Detroit, the Detroit Board of Trade raises $410 for the wounded and dispatches two members to Gettysburg to "look after the wounded" while the Common Council appropriates $1,000 to aid wounded soldiers and also sends a committee to Harrisburg, Pennsylvania; Valerie Campbell makes a public appeal for "materials, in money, [or] in work" for soldiers' aid; in Ann Arbor, the mayor leads a meeting in which $1,000 is raised, while the Ladies' Soldiers' Aid Society raised $100; Soldiers' Aid groups work in North Adams and Hillsdale, while in Grand Haven, the Ladies' Soldiers' Aid Society announces a "Patriotic Concert" for the benefit of "our brave and suffering soldiers in the army of the Union."[104]

In Dearborn, six companies of the First Michigan Sharpshooters muster into U.S. service; the remaining companies will muster later. Recruits and officers are drawn from Jackson, Battle Creek, Grand Haven, Reading, Albion, Lansing, Niles, Coldwater, Berrien Springs, and Chesaning. Noteworthy is Company K, which includes a large number of Native Americans. But their immediate service is to help defend against Morgan's raiders; afterward, the unit deploys east.[105] (See July 28, 1865.)

Meanwhile, Morgan has reached Garnettsville, Kentucky. Federal forces pursuing him are fifty miles behind.[106]

8: Port Hudson surrenders, restoring the Mississippi River to federal control. Among federal regiments engaged since the operations commenced on May 23, the Sixth Michigan ranks fifth in casualties suffered (149).[107]

Meanwhile, only six companies of the First Michigan Sharpshooters have been filled, and these leave Dearborn for Indianapolis. Meanwhile across the

Ohio River from Indiana, John Hunt Morgan reaches Brandenburg, Kentucky. He secures the town, captures two steamers, and crosses the river into Indiana.[108]

From Detroit, Senator Jacob M. Howard, responding to rumors that the Confederate vice president Alexander Stevens seeks to put a "proposition" before Lincoln, advises the president "not [to] suffer one of the rebel crew to approach you except as a prisoner & supplicant. They are going under & they see it. Show them no indulgence."[109]

9: Morgan reaches Corydon, Indiana. He is approximately 110 airline miles from Ohio near the Ohio-Indiana border.[110]

10: Morgan reaches Salem, Indiana, approximately 85 airline miles from Harrison, Ohio.[111]

11: Morgan reaches the outskirts of Vernon, Indiana. He is checked but continues east. Morgan is approximately 50 airline miles from Ohio.[112]

12: Mrs. Brainard and Mrs. P. P. Barnard leave for Gettysburg to deliver relief. The town of Gettysburg is overflowing with the wounded, POWs, local residents, and relief workers. "[We] were grateful for the privilege of sleeping on the floor," Brainard notes; the Association's supplies not having arrived, the two women approach the Christian Commission, which shares its own stores. She will remain on and off until October.[113]

Morgan is at Versailles, Indiana, approximately 30 airline miles from Ohio. Ohio governor Tod, at the "urgent solicitation" of Department of the Ohio commander Ambrose Burnside, calls out militia in Ohio's southern counties.[114]

13: Draft riots erupt in New York City (see SAW.2.225–241) with scattered antidraft activity in other locales across the north. Fry wires AAPMG Hill, asking for status reports on the situations in their states. (See July 14 and 15.)[115]

On this morning, Morgan crosses into Ohio; this evening, he reaches Cincinnati's outskirts. (See July 14.)[116]

14: New York's riots threaten to spill into Michigan. Detroit's PM Newberry gives Hill a disturbing report about potential violence in the city. "I have consulted with some of the leading men of this city and others of the same class have called on me at my office, in relation to the condition of this city and the mob

violence that is to be apprehended here." All agree: "there is existing here an organized armed body of men in this city to resist the draft." Many believe that there are 5,000 Detroiters bent on antidraft violence, but Newberry believes this is "an idle estimate." Instead, he offers a more realistic assessment. Detroit has ten wards, and "I do not believe there is to exceed an average of over 100 to 150 [troublemakers] in each ward, making, say, 1,500." He disbelieves claims that these men are organized but also concedes that "there is doubtless a large number of disaffected persons who have threatened violence and who would instantly join any attempted outbreak having for an object the obstruction or prevention of the draft." Newberry believes that two factors dispose Detroit to violence. First is the "successful violence" in New York City, which has forced postponement of the draft. But a second factor is local. "We had a negro riot [NB: *white riot*] here within the last few months that controlled the city fully, burning some thirty houses, and finally was quelled by the arrival of the Twenty-seventh Michigan Infantry. That mob violence is here now, but intensified a thousand fold." (See March 6.)

Newberry makes several recommendations to Hill. He suggests that "it would be the height of folly" to draft or enforce the draft now "without a strong military force to protect the office and papers"; indeed, Newberry flatly declares, "it could not be done." Even officers serving draft notices would be in danger. "The condition of things is more critical than they have been at any time during the war," he declares. "A strong force should be ordered to this city at once." (See July 15.)[117]

In Virginia, at the Battle of Falling Waters, the Sixth Michigan suffers seventy-nine casualties. This evening, Morgan's column reaches Williamsburg, Ohio, twenty-five miles east of Cincinnati.[118]

15: Complying with Fry's July 13 request, Hill forwards Newberry's report to Fry and includes an evaluation. Detroit has only one company of provost guards and a few members of the Invalid Corps. There are also 100 sharpshooter recruits at Dearborn, but they are needed to protect that arsenal. "There is no doubt but that there is among a portion of the population of this city a most bitter opposition to the Government, and it extends to other parts of the State." The previous night Hill spoke with Blair, who will return to Detroit in several days. Meanwhile, Hill has learned the same intelligence as Newberry, "and coming from the source they do, I must say that unless the present mob is put down most summarily [as] in New York the attempt to execute a draft here will lead to similar violence unless supported by a strong military force." (See July 18 and 21.)[119]

Separately, Vallandigham arrives in Niagara Falls. To the south, Morgan continues pushing east through southern Ohio. (See July 18.)[120]

16: Confronted by General William T. Sherman, Joseph Johnston, CSA, evacuates Jackson, Mississippi. In the fighting leading up to this point, among federal units engaged, the Second Michigan is ranked fifth in casualties suffered (59).[121]

18: AAPMG Hill recommends to Blair and Fry that Michigan regiments depleted by casualties return home to recruit. (See July 21.) Separately, back east in South Carolina, the siege of Charleston soon begins. Meanwhile, the War Department issues Circular 52, ruling that "Indians and half-breeds are not citizens of the United States, within the meaning of the enrollment act, unless they have been made citizens by act of Congress." In sum, they are exempt from enrollment.[122]

Finally, In South Carolina, the Fifty-Fourth Massachusetts (colored), assaults Battery Wagner in Charleston Harbor. The attack fails but establishes the regiment—and by inference, African Americans—as credible combatants. This heightens confidence in Henry Barns's efforts to recruit Michigan's first (and only) black regiment. (See July 24.)

19: At the Battle of Buffington Island, federal cavalry, gunboats, and local militia stop Morgan, and his command fragments. (See July 26.) Separately, PMG Fry establishes rules to determine alienage exemptions, no small matter in Detroit. The exemption turns on two issues: whether the claimant is the subject of a foreign government, and whether he has previously intended to become a citizen.[123]

21: Hill reports to Fry on antidraft activity in Michigan. The news is mostly good. At Blair's request, six companies of Michigan sharpshooters have returned to the state; the stated purpose is to recruit, but in fact they return as reinforcements against potential antidraft violence. Five of these companies have

been sent to protect Dearborn Arsenal, and another is garrisoned at Fort Wayne. The Invalid Corps will serve two Parrott guns at the Detroit Barracks, and "forty or fifty" cavalry recruits at Coldwater have been ordered to Detroit. "There has been a very excited state of feeling in the community for some days," Hill observes. Prominent war supporters, fearing attack on their homes, "have made preparation for their defense"; nevertheless, "I do not think there is ground for further apprehension." The reinforcements mentioned "will be fully adequate to put down any riot in the city." (See July 27.) As for returning depleted regiments to Michigan to recruit, Hill reports that Blair "highly approves" of the idea. Some of these units number fewer than 100 men, and Hill opines that "the more I reflect on the practical working of the draft the more I am convinced of the advisability of some such plan."[124]

22: Jackson County learns the results of the previous month's federal enrollment: 18,943 men of the First Class (between ages twenty and thirty-five and unmarried males between thirty-five and forty-five) and Second Class ("all others subject to military duty") were enrolled within the five counties comprising the Third Congressional District. For Jackson County, the number of First Class enrollees is 3,033, comprised of 3,005 whites and 28 blacks. The county's Second Class enrollment is 1,256 whites and 12 blacks. (See Military Affairs—1863.)[125]

24: Stanton informs Blair that Henry Barns (who had earlier appealed to Blair directly but was refused) has applied for permission to raise a colored infantry regiment in Michigan. The War Department "is very anxious that such regiments should be raised" and authorizes Blair to do just that—if Blair approves Barns's application. "It seems to me that there has been some misunderstanding upon this subject, and I am informed that you were under the impression that the department would not authorize it," Stanton explains. But the problem was not lack of will but of way: "Until suitable arrangements could be made for the organization of a bureau, it was not deemed advisable to raise such troops"; however, the bureau is now established (see May 22) and Stanton is enthusiastic. (See July 25.) Blair's earlier refusals of Barns's application is curious, as he had already declared, "I am utterly unable to see why it is not proper to use a rebel's sacred nigger. . . . I am entirely unable to see, too, why Sambo shouldn't be permitted to carry a musket."[126]

Separately Gettysburg resident David Wills[127] suggests to Pennsylvania governor Curtin of "the propriety and actual necessity of the purchase of a common burial ground for the dead, now only partially buried over miles of country around Gettysburg." Curtin approves Wills's plan. (See August 13.)[128]

25: The War Department's AAG C. W. Foster[129] formally authorizes Blair to raise a three-year regiment of colored men in Michigan. (The unit will be temporarily enumerated the First Michigan Colored Infantry.) But Foster's consent had discriminatory conditions: no bounty will be paid recruits; the pay is $10 monthly ($3 of which is a clothing allowance) and one ration daily. The names of proposed officers must be sent to the War Department and all men examined; an examination board now sits in Cincinnati and Washington. (See August 12.)[130]

26: John Hunt Morgan and most of his command are captured near Salineville, Ohio.[131]

27: Hill reports to Fry about Michigan affairs. Enrollment in the Fourth and Sixth Congressional Districts remains incomplete [NB: *These two districts encompass northern Michigan, including the UP*]. Hill recommends that drafting begin in the completed districts, without waiting for the Fourth and Sixth Districts. Yet clouds appear: "I have received reports from the provost-marshals of other districts that difficulty and trouble are apprehended when the draft is ordered, and the applications have been made to me for arms." Hill recommends starting the draft in the First District (which includes Detroit). If the draft can be completed there, "there will be but little trouble in other parts of the State." This would have the advantage of allowing Hill to better concentrate available forces as needed. (See August 8 and September 25.)[132]

John Hunt Morgan and several officers are imprisoned at the Ohio Penitentiary in Columbus.[133]

28: Commodore John C. Carter★, commander of the USS *Michigan*,[134] reports on his visit to Michigan. "The visit of this ship to Detroit . . . at this time was opportune. I found the people suffering under serious apprehensions of a riot in consequence of excitement in reference to the draft, probably brought about by unscrupulous newspapers predicting such riots."

He adds that the presence of the USS *Michigan* "did something towards overawing the refractory, and certainly did much to allay the apprehensions of an excited, doubting people. All fears in reference to the riot had subsided before I left."[135]

Separately, the Sixth Michigan becomes the Sixth Michigan Heavy Artillery.[136] (See August 20, 1865.)

August

1: Dr. John S. Newberry meets with Valeria Campbell of the Soldiers' Aid Society of Detroit. He suggests certain organizational improvements (which are accepted), and the Detroit society formally affiliates with the Western Sanitary Commission. (See September 23.)[137]

3: War Department GO No. 268 declares that the June 15 call for 100,000 six-month militia from Ohio, West Virginia, Maryland, and Pennsylvania is ended, and that no more enlistments will be made after today.[138]

5: AG Thomas sends Burnside Stanton's authorization "to raise and organize into regiments of ten companies each as many troops of African descent as you may be able to, with full authority to designate all officers for such regiments."[139]

7: AG Robertson issues GO No. 2, excerpting from Act No. 16, approved January 18, 1862. (See Selected Legislation—1862.) Under this order, infantry will be accepted as state troops. Robertson explains that the war demonstrates the need for a "well organized and equipped State Militia," not just to train soldiers and support the government" but also for the defense of a State itself, against foreign invasion or internal rebellion, and for the protection of the lives and property of its citizens." He elaborates Michigan's needs: "Although the State of Michigan, from its local position, has been in no danger of being invaded during the present rebellion, yet, in case of a foreign war, there would be no State in the Union more exposed, and it behooves every citizen of the State to encourage the preparation necessary to meet emergencies." As of December, only three companies will be raised. (See Military Affairs—1863.)[140]

8: AAPMG Hill informs Fry that "I have the honor to state that nothing worthy of being reported has occurred since my last report." Hill attributes this to the increased presence of troops and the "apprehensions among the more wealthy and influential of the opponents of the Government, in consequence of the extent to which the riots in New York were carried." However, if Fry orders a draft, Hill recommends "that the presence of a military force will be required when the draft is executed here." (See September 25.) The forces currently deployed include eight sharpshooter companies, fifty cavalry recruits with horses, a provost guard company, and an artillery section, served by Invalid Corps' recruits. Separately, Corresponding Secretary Valerie Campbell announces a change of name: henceforth, the Ladies' Aid or Soldiers' Aid Society will be called the Michigan Soldiers' Aid Society. She explains that "Our supplies come from various parts of the State, as far as the western shore of the lower peninsula, and the borders of Lake Superior. This being the case, it seems but fair to our contributors, that we should add to our designation the name of the State."[141]

12: AG Robertson notifies Henry Barns that he is now "authorized and empowered to raise and organize [a colored] regiment." (See August 18 and Military Affairs—1863.) Barns's task will be daunting: African American troops will be denied federal bounties until next summer, and presently, neither the state of Michigan nor any town or Detroit ward offers bounties for black troops. (See August 18.)[142]

13: National cemetery advocate David Wills sends a circular to Blair proposing a plan to establish a cemetery at Gettysburg.[143]

18: Henry Barns applies to Detroit's Common Council to offer a $50 bounty for colored troops. His application is referred to the Committee on Ways and Means, and will ultimately be denied. (But see September 11.)[144]

21: A newspaper war over Henry Barns's recruitment of colored troops erupts between the Detroit Free Press and Barns's Advertiser and Tribune. The (Democrat) Free Press claims that Barns's efforts are "plainly a game of plunder, for patronage, for commissions, for contracts. Neither the editor of the Advertiser nor the Negro men under him can be induced to go out of the state into the field of actual war." (See the 22nd.) Separately, Confederate irregular William C. Quantrill burns Lawrence, Kansas, and massacres some 150 men.[145]

22: The Advertiser answers yesterday's attack from the Free Press. Commenting on the recent return of arch-Democrat John S. Bagg* to the Free Press's editorial

pages, it declares that, "The association is congenial. The 'amalgamation,' Negro-hating, mob-inspiring copperhead character of the paper will, of course, become more intensified than ever." (See August 25 and September 25.)[146]

24: Vallandigham arrives in Windsor, Canada. From here he will campaign for governor of Ohio.[147]

25: The Free Press answers the Advertiser with a telling admission, but one buried in a litany of complaint: the Free Press is suspicious of Barns's motives in raising a black regiment; it is convinced that there are too few Wayne County blacks for many credits against the draft; it also believes that Barns's recent application to Detroit's city council for bounty payments for colored troops is hypocritical because the Advertiser had opposed the council funding commutation payments to draftees; nevertheless, the Free Press declares, "But it must not be understood . . . that we are opposed to granting a bounty of fifty dollars to all men, whether white or black, who will enlist or volunteer, and which the President will accept in lieu of drafted men. . . . If colored men enough can be found to fill the quota, let them be taken by all means." (But see October 29.)[148]

Separately, Lincoln proposes giving governors advance notice of upcoming drafts within their states.[149]

26: Reflecting on the victories at Vicksburg and Port Hudson, Lincoln writes to Illinois congressman James C. Conkling, "The Father of Waters again goes unvexed to the sea. Thanks to the great Northwest for it."[150]

27: Reflecting the experience gained from New York's draft riots, PMG Fry informs AAPMG Hill that hereafter, "You will in every case notify the Governor of your State in advance both by telegraph and mail, of the precise day upon which the draft will commence in each of the districts under your charge."[151] (See September 4.)

September

2: War Department AAG Vincent gives Blair a detailed statement (according to its records) of Michigan's draft quotas and credits through May 26, 1863:

Three-year troops

Quotas:

Under 1861 calls:	21,357
Under July 2, 1862, call:	11,686

Total three-years furnished: 40,368
Excess furnished over quota: 7,325

Nine-month troops:

Under August 2, 1862, call: quota: 11,686
Furnished: 0
Deficiency: 11,686

Detail of all furnished troops:

1861: sixteen infantry regiments (15,196); Mechanics and Engineer Regiment (851); Stanton Guards and provost guards (202); Brady (84);[152] four companies, First and Second USSS (Berdan's) (349); First, Second, and Third Michigan Cavalry (3,364); independent artillery batteries (1,745); and recruits for all arms (1861 and 1862: 2,435)

Three-year call in 1862: eleven infantry regiments (10,454); five cavalry regiments (5,688); and no artillery batteries. (See September 14.)[153]

3: AAG Vincent asks Blair to prepare "a quarterly return, or list, showing the number of volunteers" by their respective units that were mustered into U.S. service that quarter. The department wants to insure proper credit for recruits.[154]

4: PMG Fry orders AAPMG Hill to notify Blair "both by telegraph and mail" of dates when a draft will commence in their states. He also provides a form of notification.[155]

9: Federal troops occupy Chattanooga.

10: Federal troops occupy Little Rock, Arkansas.

11: The Wayne County Board of Supervisors approves a $100 bounty to all volunteers—including African Americans—whose enlistment reduces the county's draft quota. Bounties without regard to race will soon be offered in Kalamazoo, Ypsilanti, and by 1864, Detroit.[156]

14: AG Robertson disputes the War Department's September 2 calculation. He claims that Michigan is entitled to more credits than received thus far. (See September 21 and 22.)[157]

15: Under authority of Chapter 81 (March 3, 1863) Lincoln suspends the writ of habeas corpus throughout the United States in cases where "military, naval, and civil officers of the United States . . . hold persons under their command or in their custody, either as prisoners of war, spies, or aiders or abettors of the enemy, or officers, soldiers, or seamen, enrolled,

drafted, or mustered, or enlisted in or belonging to, the land or naval forces of the United States, or as deserters therefrom." The *Free Press* compares Lincoln to Napoleon III and questions the "necessity of such a suspension of this writ in Michigan," asking, "Can any one of our readers tell where the danger is which is now so pressing that such a proclamation must be sent throughout the land by telegraph? No one believes it."[158]

16: AG Robertson issues a General Order forbidding agents representing other states from recruiting in Michigan, excepting Regular Army (USA) recruiters. Michigan men who enlist in out-of-state regiments will, if drafted in Michigan, be deemed deserters. Citizens are requested to report all instances of agents recruiting for other states.

Perhaps not coincidentally on this morning, under the title "Caution to Colored Men," Henry Barns prints a notice in his *Advertiser and Tribune* "to caution the colored men of this city and State not to allow themselves to be deceived by false representations[,] high pay, etc., into enlisting in companies now being raised for regiments in other States." The notice adds that in Michigan, only Henry Barns has the authority authorize recruiting black men. Barns's notice angers some in Detroit's black community.[159]

Probably connected to these notices is a "Meeting of Colored Patriots" that convenes at Detroit's Lafayette Street Colored Church and hosts prominent African American leaders and Henry Barns. A Rhode Island recruiter attempts to enlist men for the Fourteenth (colored) Rhode Island Battery (see SAW.1.731), and argues with Barns about whether he had given him notice of his intention to recruit. He declares that, "Gov. Blair loves their color but would love to fill the quota better." As he speaks, black physician and activist Dr. Martin R. Delany* of Chatham, Ontario, reads Robertson's GO forbidding ex-state recruitment and Barns's "Caution to Colored Men." Delaney wonders aloud whether Michigan's intent is to "confine the negroes to the State regiments that their enlistment might save the heads of that number of white men who were now in fear of the draft." Delany also asks why, if Rhode Island is offering full citizenship, including the right to vote (see SAW.I, Rhode Island, for details on black male suffrage), a colored recruit should enlist in Michigan, a state that still forbids black suffrage? (Additionally, Rhode Island offers larger bounties than Michigan.) Delany turns to Barns and asks, "what rights were guaranteed to soldiers enlisting in this State—if after the war, those soldiers would be allowed the political rights of citizens?" Barns replies that "they would be allowed the same rights guaranteed by some *other* states," but Delany considers Barns's reply unsatisfactory: "[Delaney] did not come here to play upon words with any man." Barns is surprised that Delany would "charge upon the present generation this crime of depriving them of their rights." But Delany answered that he "[did] not see why the present generation was not equally to blame for allowing their rights to be withheld."

During the balance of the meeting various black speakers vent their frustration about Michigan, about Blair's longtime refusal to authorize colored regiments and that Robertson's GO was unfair; blacks owed it to themselves to affiliate with regiments that offer good discipline and bounties. And yet, local black leader George DeBaptiste* supports Barns. He had always considered Gov. Blair too vacillating, he never thought much of him, and did not now, but as he had finally allowed a regiment of colored citizens to be organized, he would recommend enlistment in it. (See October 23.)[160]

19–20: Battle of Chickamauga, Georgia. Shortly after the battle Michigan's state military agent in Nashville Luther B. Willard is on the field: "a thrill of horror stole over my senses as I picked up from the bloody field the dreadfully lacerated and mangled veterans . . . and beheld the bleeding and lifeless forms of my neighbors and friends." He will remain almost two weeks. Back in Michigan, casualty lists begin to appear in newspapers across the state. Among federal regiments engaged, the Twenty-Second Michigan is ranked first in casualties suffered (389).

First news of the federal defeat is published in Detroit on September 22.[161]

21: AAG Vincent updates PMG Fry with information about Michigan enlistments: credits are added to the state's manpower account that the September 2 statement did not reflect.

Furnished prior to May 26, 1863:

One company, Twenty-Third Illinois:	99
Two companies Merrill's Horse, Missouri:	164
Subtotal:	263

Volunteers:

February 8 to April 1, 1862:	412
April 1, 1862, to May 26, 1863	2,608
Total:	3,020
Of whom 2,435 were previously credited; net new recruits:	585
Adding net credit to above subtotal:	848
Add nine-month men (143) reduced to three-year standard:	36
Subtotal:	884
Furnished after May 26, 1863:	3,504
Men mustered August 29 to September 19, 1863:	727
Total credits:	4,231
Total additional credits converted to three-year standard:	5,115[162]

Separately, PMG Fry instructs Hill (copy to Blair) detailing approved compensations: for arresting deserters, $30; recruiters to receive $15 for each nonveteran and $25 for recruits with at least nine months' service; under GO No. 191 (1863) reenlisted veterans to receive premium and bounty totaling $402; for nonveteran recruits into old regiments, the premium and bounty total $302. This measure disadvantaged state agents and injured recruiting as recruiters now must be "persons deputized by the Provost-Marshal-General."[163]

22: AAG Vincent replies to AG Robertson's September 14 letter, which claims additional credits for Michigan and sends yesterday's information. The news is good. Michigan will be credited with an additional 5,115 men. However, Vincent excludes two of Robertson's claims. Federal rules forbid crediting the service of the Lancer Regiment and Chandler's Horse Guards. [NB: *Both units were never mustered into federal service and disbanded before leaving the state.*][164]

23: The Michigan Soldiers' Aid Society, now affiliated with the Western Sanitary Commission (see August 1), convenes a meeting in Kalamazoo with all other Michigan aid societies. The purpose is to discus ways of better coordinating statewide efforts. One result is that towns begin sending Detroit "headquarters" regular activity reports.[165]

25: Federal conscription nears for Michigan. PMG Fry notifies Blair that drafting will commence for 6,528 men of the First Class (see below, letter to AAPMG Hill). Fry assures Blair that these calculations are "impartial and claimed to be entirely correct"; however, "if an error should be discovered or pointed out in them it will be duly corrected."[166]

Fry instructs AAPMG Hill to order the Boards of Enrollment for all six congressional districts to commence drafting men of the First Class: In the First, 1,235 men; the Second, 1,198; the Third, 1,076; the Fourth, 892; the Fifth, 1,022; and the Sixth, 1,105. [NB: This draft is for existing deficiencies and should not be confused with the upcoming call of October 17.]

Hill is ordered to take personal charge of the draft, and boards should draft "immediately" after being so ordered. Other instructions include: draftees must receive legal notices, preferably delivered by enrolling officers whom Hill will deputize for the purpose. Hill will supervise the delivery of draftees to the district headquarters for examination and will make certain that each district headquarters has adequate inventories of "clothing, knapsacks, haversacks, canteens, blankets, knives, forks, spoons, tin cups, and tin plates" for issue to men selected. He will supervise arrests of deserters and draftees failing to report. He will also supervise the assignment of examining surgeons. (See October 3.)[167]

October

3: AAPMG Hill informs Blair "that the 26th day of this month has been fixed" for the federal draft in Michigan. However, volunteers who muster in on or before October 24 will be credited to Michigan's quota. (See entry for October 24.)[168]

14: Battle of Bristoe Station, Virginia.

17: Lincoln calls for 300,000 men, intended to replace losses from Gettysburg. It carries a large stick: states that fail to meet its quota will face a draft on January 5, 1864, that will not only include this quota but also dun states for any deficiencies remaining on prior calls. Michigan's quota under this call is 11,298 and is divided by district as follows: First District, 2,137; Second, 2,074; Third, 1,861; Fourth

1,545; Fifth, 1,768; and Sixth, 1,913. (See November 9.)[169]

23: Colonel Barns asks the War Department to pay a $15 premium to his black soldiers to equalize pay between white and black units. Meanwhile, the authority to recruit companies for the First Michigan (colored) has been conferred on persons across Michigan. For example, Colonel Emory M. Plimpton*, Detroit's assistant PM, is authorized to recruit a company in Berrien County, while Cassopolis resident Charles W. Clisbee has authorized black leader Thomas J. Martin to recruit in Dowagiac. (See December 14.)[170]

24: The draft for the First Congressional District is postponed until November 5. Volunteers between this day and November 5 will count against the quota. Municipal competition is intense; the *Detroit Free Press* comments, "Ward and town committees embarrass the efforts of the county committee by bidding against them and each other for men to fill up the quota of their respective wards and towns. The whole county can be cleared from the draft, if those interested will cheerfully co-operate with this [county] committee instead of embarrassing them."[171]

26: Grant reopens the Tennessee River to Chattanooga.

27: The federal draft begins in the Second, Third, Fourth, Fifth, and Sixth Congressional Districts. However, the UP will not be included nor, for now, will Wayne, Monroe, Lenawee, and Hillsdale Counties. (But see November 5.)[172]

Federals lift the siege of Chattanooga. Separately, in Chicago the Northwestern Soldiers' Fair opens. Michigan's contributions, organized by the Michigan Soldiers' Aid Society, include $1,806.81 in cash contributed by at least twenty-six institutions and individuals. Today, soldiers from the First Michigan Sharpshooters march in the opening parade and Michigan aid groups from Adrian, Ann Arbor, Kalamazoo, Jackson, Ypsilanti, Grand Haven, Pontiac, Marquette, Grand Rapids, and Detroit contribute fruit, decorative evergreens, Gettysburg relics, African-made cloth, tools manufactured by state prisoners, vases, paperweights, samples of gypsum, and other items.[173]

29: The *Free Press* publishes an anonymous letter attacking Colonel Barns and questioning his fitness to command the First Michigan Colored. "He does not possess one single quality for the position, [is] absolutely without military experience, of very doubtful integrity, mercenary, and selfish in all his instincts, over bearing, insolent, ungentlemanly and vulgar in his manner."[174]

31: Between January 1 and October 31, 1863, the War Department credits Michigan with 1,260 infantry, 3,210 cavalry, and 372 artillerymen mustered into U.S. service in new organizations. No nine- or six-month units were organized; however, the state did muster 143 infantrymen for nine-month service in other units. During the same period, Michigan sent 864 infantry, 335 cavalry and 138 artillerymen into existing regiments, all three-year recruits.[175]

November

3: Detroit's municipal elections. Democrat Kirkland C. Barker* is elected mayor.[176]

Austin Blair proclaims November 26 to be "a day of *Praise, Thanksgiving, and Prayer,*" asking Michiganders to remember especially those "dwelling in tents and in the open field, in arms gallantly defending our heritage of Liberty, our homes and property." He also offers another reason for being thankful: "The people of Michigan have been prospered in business during the year that is past beyond all previous example."[177]

4: According to War Department records, through August 6 Michigan has been credited with nine three-year cavalry regiments totaling 7,854 men. Michigan also has two regiments "now organizing for service:" the Tenth and Eleventh Michigan Cavalry, both expected to "completed in a very short time."[178]

5: The draft begins in the First Congressional District. PMG Fry informs Hill that "If a State furnishes her full quota of volunteers under the President's call of October 17, 1863 . . . the draft ordered for the 5th January, 1864, will not take place" in Michigan.[179]

6: PMG Fry informs Hill that he will do "everything in my power" to permit governors to summon home and detail for recruiting duty officers with priority to those regiments whose terms expire in 1864; where possible, entire regiments will return home to recruit under the governor's direction; next, any volunteers recruited will remain under Blair's control until redeployed; Blair is given flexibility in "the amount and mode of payment of premium for obtaining recruits for old regiments and the persons to whom

it is paid," as long as it does not exceed $25 for veterans and $15 for recruits. However, Fry asserts that he has no legal authority to declare exempt from the draft cities or towns that meet their quotas. Hill is instructed that, "Should the Governor desire to recommend recruiting agents under this scheme the Provost-Marshal-General directs that his wishes be consulted."[180]

8: Detroit military commander Lieutenant Colonel Joseph R. Smith (who has spies in Canada) alerts Ohio District commander general J. D. Cox to "definite information" that a rebel steamer in Montreal was "fitting out to attack Johnson's Island and release the rebel prisoners." Cox has asked Joshua Giddings,[181] now consul-general in Montreal, to investigate, and has also informed Ohio colonel William S. Pierson.[182] (See November 9.)[183]

9: Governor Blair issues a proclamation calling for volunteers under Lincoln's October 17 call. "This call is for soldiers to fill the ranks of the regiments in the field—those regiments which by long and gallant service have wasted their numbers in the same proportion that they have made a distinguished name both for themselves and the State. . . . The hopes of the rebellion are steadily perishing. . . . Fill up the ranks once more, and the next blast of the bugle for an advance will sound the knell of revolution and herald in the return of peace." Between Lincoln's October 17 call and December 31, 2,404 men will volunteer.[184]

Separately, AAPMG Hill reports to PMG Fry about the constant rumors from Canada concerning "rebel refugees'" intrigues; these reports are usually "so wild that I have not attached any importance to them." But Hill and Smith are receiving more creditable intelligence. A rebel agent recently traveled to Windsor and deposited bank orders worth $100,000; Confederate treasury secretary Christopher G. Memminger signed them and they are payable to one Henry Marvin; moreover, one W. M. Marvin bears a letter of reference from Confederate secretary of state Judah P. Benjamin. These bank orders are negotiable, and intelligence suggests that they will be used to purchase steamers in Montreal. "There are about 2,000 rebel refugees, escaped prisoners, and active rebel sympathizers, in Canada," he tells Fry. And recently there have also been suspicious arrivals in Toronto, including (Hill hears) John M. Jones and several Confederate naval officers. "That some project of magnitude is in contemplation I feel very certain, and I have communicated with the U.S. consul-general at Montreal." Hill updates his message to Fry: all the rebel refugees have left for Montreal, "and the information points more positively to Johnson's Island." Hill is sending an officer to the island to share details about the plot. (See next day's entry.)[185]

10: General Cox has received another disturbing report from Colonel Smith that two armed rebel steamers are being sent against Johnson's Island. He immediately wires Commissary of Prisoners William Hoffman with the news. "The report is very improbable," Cox opines, but he takes no chances. "I have ordered a detachment of infantry and a six-gun rifled battery to the island to-day." He notes that the steamer USS *Michigan* is somewhere on Lake Erie, and asks Hoffman, "Cannot the Navy Department send her to the assistance of Colonel Pierson?" (See next day's entry.)[186]

Separately, PMG Fry instructs Hill, "In filling the quota of volunteers called for by the President's proclamation of October 17, 1863, it is the desire of this Bureau that Governors of States from which troops are required shall take the leading part in the work." Any changes proposed by governors to federal recruiting practices will be immediately forwarded for Washington's approval. Fry's orders are clear: "You will also co-operate fully with the State authorities in carrying out whatever measures they may consider advisable to secure the filling of their quota." These measures will soon include federal permission to detail deployed troops for recruiting duty.[187]

11: Stanton warns Blair that British Ambassador Lord Lyons has notified the U.S. that "there is reason to believe that a plot is on foot by persons hostile to the United States, who have found an asylum in Canada, to invade the United States and destroy the city of Buffalo; that they propose to take possession of some of the steamboats on Lake Erie, to surprise Johnson's Island, and set free the prisoners of war confined there, and to proceed to attack Buffalo." Stanton also alerts Detroit mayor William C. Duncan and promises that "This Government will employ all the means in its power to suppress any hostile attack from Canada." Stanton quotes Canadian governor-general

Charles Stanley Monck[188] "that steam-boats should be watched, and any steam-boat or other vessel giving cause for suspicion by the numbers or character of the persons on board shall be arrested." In another wire, Stanton orders General Cox to "proceed immediately to Sandusky and take such measures for the security of the prisoners and the protection of the northern frontier of Ohio against invasion by rebels and their aiders and abettors from Canada." (See entry for next day.)[189]

12: Ohio prepares for the rebel raid warned of by Hill and Smith: batteries and troops are deployed to Sandusky. (See *SAW.5* entry for November 12, 1863.) Senator Chandler, following these events closely, informs Stanton that there is "Not a single gun larger than a 32-pounder on the lakes, and only four of them." These are at Erie but have no powder. "Please send heavy guns from Pittsburg instantly," he asks. In a second wire, Chandler promises that "Our fastest steamer will be sent to Cleveland," and he repeats his earlier request: "Send four guns of heavy caliber, with ammunition to Cleveland."[190]

Separately, the War Department furnishes Michigan's quota under Lincoln's October 17 call at 11,296.[191]

13: "All quiet at Johnson's Island this morning," Ohio's Governor Tod wires Stanton. "With the force we now have we have nothing to fear." General Cox agrees. His artillery and the volunteer militia have arrived. "I think I can answer for the safety of anything here in any emergency," he confidently declares to Stanton. "No further news of any hostile movements." (See next day's entry.)[192]

Meanwhile, Colonel Smith updates the War Department about the steps taken in response to reports of Confederate raiders massing in "some port of Canada or in Welland Canal for the purpose of attacking the guard at Johnson's Island," among other feared depredations. About ten days ago, Smith sent "special detectives" to Windsor to learn about any plans "from rebels and disaffected persons." Within a few days, "I became satisfied that there was an organization which would make us trouble unless precautions were taken." Smith consulted with Hill "and other influential persons" in Michigan and then notified Cox in Ohio and Peirson on Johnson's Island. Cox informed him that artillery and infantry were being sent to Sandusky. But in the last few days, the situation has become alarming. Smith has learned that the rebels in Windsor have disappeared, "gone to take possession of their vessels, the precise locality of which I could not ascertain." Two days earlier, more detectives were sent to follow some rebels and Smith now awaits their report. A consensus forms for preemptive action: Smith has consulted with Hill, AG Robertson, and Zachariah Chandler, and as a result the steamer *Forest Queen* is armed and sailing "to look around the lake for a day or two to ascertain the truth of rumors which had reached us that one or two hostile vessels were already in Lake Erie."

"This community [Detroit] was in a state of wild excitement at all the rumors," Smith continues, "and it was believed that the measure of sending a steamer with a few arms on board to make a reconnaissance would have the effect to allay the excitement, which has been happily effected." The *Forest Queen* is expected to return soon, and Smith will update his report.[193]

14: "We have no further information here," Cox reports to Stanton, adding that General John A. Dix is at Buffalo and General William T. H. Brooks[194] is at Erie. (See next day's entry.)

Meanwhile, Michigan's peace faction, however weak, is represented today by thirty-five University of Michigan students, who meet with the exiled Clement Vallandigham in Windsor, Ontario; a journalist present paraphrased a student addressing Vallandigham as mentioning "our sympathizing with him in his wrongs as a fellow citizen, and . . . our appreciation of him as a fearless and conscientious champion of constitutional rights." Vallandigham's lengthy reply, studded with literary, classical, and biblical allusions and a few lines of poetry, speaks about life, and the importance of principles, but says nothing about the events of the day.[195]

15: The Johnson's Island affair appears to wind down. Detroit (Colonel Smith?) wires Cox that "Rebels who left Windsor [Ontario] to join the raid are returning, saying that the plans are frustrated for the present, and will have to be postponed for a time." Cox concludes, "I regard this as ending the immediate danger, but will keep the force here as it is till the above is confirmed."[196]

Meanwhile, in Washington, military state agent Tunnicliffe has just returned from Michigan "to visit [the Detroit Barracks] and make a report as to locality, size, present condition, and the feasibility and probable expense that would be incurred" in converting these barracks to a U.S. General Hospital. (See next day's entry.)[197]

16: Stanton orders the Detroit Barracks ("and such additional buildings as are deemed necessary") be converted into a U.S. General Hospital. (See December 9.) Meanwhile, at Campbell's Station, Tennessee, four Michigan infantry regiments suffer casualties: the Seventeenth (73), the Twenty-Third (39), the Twentieth (37), and the Second (32).[198]

17: The Siege of Knoxville campaign begins. It will end on December 4; by the end of the campaign, among federal units engaged, the Second Michigan will rank first in casualties (93) and the Twenty-Seventh Michigan fourth (38).[199]

18: The Tenth Michigan Cavalry musters in to U.S. service; recruits and officers are drawn from Grand Rapids, Brooks, Franklin, Bay City, Eureka, Owosso, Ionia, Antrim, Bingham, Plainfield, and Marion. The unit deploys west, then to southwestern Virginia and North Carolina, later assisting in capturing Jefferson Davis.[200] (See November 11, 1865.)

19: At Gettysburg, a national cemetery is dedicated. The featured speakers are Edward Everett and President Lincoln. On the platform are governors Bradford (Maryland), Curtin (Pennsylvania), Morton (Indiana), Seymour (New York), Parker (New Jersey), and Brough (Ohio). Governor Blair does not attend. It is reported that to date, Michigan has forty-eight soldiers interred. (See December 17.)

The *Advertiser and Tribune* later praises Edward Everett's speech, observing that "wherever it goes [it] will nobly tell the story of those three heroic days at Gettysburg"; but the sheet confers its highest praise on Lincoln: "But he who wants to take in the very spirit of the day, catch the unstudied pathos that animates a sincere but simple-hearted man, will turn from the professed orator, to the brief speech of the President." In fact, in part because of its brevity, Lincoln's address is published in papers across Michigan.[201]

20: Sojourner Truth visits the First Michigan Colored at Camp Ward, rendezvous of the unit. She returns in two days to preach a sermon to the unit.[202]

21: The Great Western Sanitary Fair of Cincinnati opens.

23–25: The Battles of Chattanooga. Lookout Mountain

will be fought on the 24th and Missionary Ridge on the 25th.

23: At Detroit's Second Baptist Church, the black community rallies around Henry Barns. Speakers include Lewis Clarke, and resolutions are passed condemning the *Free Press* and endorsing and defending Henry Barns.[203]

26: General John Hunt Morgan and six of his officers escape from the Ohio State Penitentiary. Separately, General Meade, USA, commences the Mine Run Campaign.[204]

28: Blair appoints Rev. John B. Gilman* as Michigan state military agent with a mandate to establish an office in Louisville. Under his care are all Louisville hospitals; in Kentucky, hospitals in Lexington, Covington, and Camp Nelson; in Indiana, hospitals in Evansville, New Albany, Jeffersonville, Indianapolis, and Madison; and in Ohio, hospitals in Cincinnati and Camp Dennison.[205]

31: The War Department's Bureau for Colored Troops reports that as of today, Michigan's First Colored Infantry has recruited three companies.[206]

December

3: The Johnson's Island scare has prompted Stanton to assign General John G. Barnard "to make an examination of the lake coast, and report what temporary works are required to guard the lake shore from hostile invasion by rebels and pirates from Canada."[207]

Meanwhile, Fry informs Hill that quotas now can be apportioned by towns and wards within congressional districts and that municipal entities furnishing their quotas will be exempt from the draft scheduled for January 5, 1864; moreover, municipal entities will be credited for all volunteers furnished since the draft, such credits to be deducted against the quotas assigned under the October 17 call.[208]

7: In Detroit, the Ladies' Christian Commission is founded, with Jane W. Brent* serving as president.[209]

8: In an effort to fill ranks, the First Michigan Colored Infantry leaves Detroit on the Michigan Central Railroad for a recruiting tour through the state. Including a band and exhibiting close-order drill, over the next week the unit will visit Ypsilanti, Ann Arbor, Jackson, Kalamazoo, and Niles (with a sixteen-mile march to Cassopolis—see December 14).[210]

Meanwhile, Abraham Lincoln issues a Proclamation of Amnesty and Reconstruction. Recognizing that persons and states "heretofore engaged in rebellion" now wish "to resume their allegiance to the United States and re-inaugurate loyal State governments," Lincoln establishes the terms of resumption. The proclamation includes a specific loyalty oath, excludes certain high-ranking Confederate officials, and most importantly, declares how states may resume allegiance. First, 10 percent of the number of 1860 voters must take the loyalty oath; the state must guarantee a republican form of government and recognize the permanent abolition of slavery; and state measures wishing to "provide for [freed person's] education . . . will not be objected to by the national Executive." The proclamation creates a firestorm between conservative and Radical Republicans. (See July 2, 1864.) But Radical disdain is joined with Democrat suspicion. The *Free Press* believes that Lincoln's plan "places the power of the government in the hands of the Commander-in-chief. He who commands the armies will control the elections." The *East Saginaw Courier* agrees, declaring Lincoln's plan "a stupid whim" that included "conditions so debasing and exasperating that every sense of justice must revolt at the terms."

But the Republican *Cass County Republican* stands with Lincoln, believing it "will, we think, commend itself to the sober consideration of the country, and be very generally approved by earnestly loyal men everywhere."[211]

9: The War Department orders U.S. Quartermaster Lee in Detroit "to proceed . . . to convert the Detroit barracks into a general hospital."[212]

10: In Kalamazoo, 920 men of the Eleventh Michigan Cavalry muster in to U.S. service; recruits and officers are drawn from St. Claire, Albion, Lexington, Monroe, Battle Creek, Tecumseh, Adrian, Bolivia, Niles, Kalamazoo, and Hillsdale. The unit deploys west, then to southwest Virginia, and on to North Carolina.[213] (See September 22, 1865.)

11: General John G. Foster[214] relieves Burnside as commander of the Department of the Ohio. (See February 9, 1864.)[215]

14: The War Department declines Barns's October 23 request for a $15 premium for colored troops. It claims no legal authority to make these payments; however, "It is confidently expected that Congress will at a very early day by enactment place all who bear arms in the service of the country in the same footing as regards pay." Meanwhile, some 200 men of the First Michigan (colored) march ten miles through a "severe storm" to the town of Cassapolis. The weather prevented the usual drilling exhibition. The *Cass County Republican* notes that "The troops were a fine looking body of men, and seemed to be composed of the material of which soldiers are made."[216]

17: The Commissioners appointed by state governors to plan a Gettysburg cemetery meet at the Jones House in Harrisburg. David Wills presides. The Convention adopts five resolutions: first, Pennsylvania will hold title to the cemetery land in trust for states with soldiers buried within; second, a request will be made that the Pennsylvania legislature create a corporation with each participating state appointing one trustee (which shall be divided into three classes with staggered terms; after the initial cycle, each term is for three years); third, the projected cemetery cost is $63,500; fourth, states will divide this expense "according to representation in Congress"; and fifth, the costs of cemetery maintenance will be paid by a dedicated fund, the annual contributions to which are also determined by congressional representation. No agent represents Michigan at this meeting, but Blair sends a letter endorsing any "reasonable action of the Convention in reference to the completion of the [National] cemetery." Future U.S. Senator Thomas W. Ferry will become the state's first representative on the Board of Commissioners.[217]

By 1874, Michigan has 171 soldiers interred at Gettysburg.[218]

19: Blair calls an Extra Session of the Michigan legislature to convene at Lansing on January 19, 1864, to ask for authorization for state bounties.[219]

21: Michigan's entire congressional delegation appeals "To the People of the State of Michigan" on behalf of the Michigan Soldiers' Relief Association. Expressing "deep mortification and pain" that because of lagging donations the Association "will soon be compelled to wind up its affairs and disband," they ask that "liberal cash contributions" be sent to President James M. Edmunds. In addition, the *Advertiser and Tribune* prints excerpts from a soldier's letter that claims great differences between the Sanitary Commission and Michigan's efforts: the former refuses service

except by surgeon's order, but Michigan's efforts "are dispensed by its agents in person." (See Summaries.)[220]

22: U.S. Army Surgeon General Charles S. Tripler inspects the First Michigan Colored Regiment's barracks, amid accusations (led by Barns's *Advertiser*) that the federal government has provided substandard quarters. Tripler makes extensive recommendations: add tar paper to seal the walls; waterproof the roofs; plane the floor boards; replace stovepipes with brick flues; issue two blankets (instead of one) per soldier; replace ticks with bunk beds; and construct a mess hall.[221]

23: Congress passes a joint resolution declaring that after January 5, 1864, the $300 federal enlistment bounty no longer will be paid to veteran volunteers. After that date, only $100 federal bounty will be paid (but see January 4, 1865).[222]

28: Fry sends Hill important news about the next draft, now scheduled to begin on January 5, 1864: "It is the intention in making the next draft to give credit to each sub-district—that is, each town, county, or ward, as the case may be—for all its drafted men held to service under the late draft, whether they served in person, furnished substitutes, or paid commutation, and also give them credit for all volunteers they may have furnished since the draft, and which have not been credited on the draft." This letter represents an important political concession to governors: towns that have heretofore exceeded their quotas will be credited on an individual basis and may not be subject to the expected draft.[223]

31: In Detroit, temperatures suddenly fall from a reported 40 degrees to 20 below zero. Especially hard hit are the poor and, lending credence to complaints about the First Michigan Colored's barracks, its soldiers. By the next morning, twenty soldiers report with frostbite; two are in a "dying condition and apprehensions are entertained that others will suffer amputation of a limb." Soldiers are temporarily placed in private homes. Between December 1863 and March 1864, of 187 recorded desertions from Michigan, the First Michigan Colored account for 122 of these and at least 25 total deaths.[224]

Selected Legislation

One of the principal sources of encouragement to enlistments is the law for the relief of the families of the volunteers, when in destitute circumstances. In the main the law is well administered and productive of great good.

—ANNUAL MESSAGE OF GOVERNOR
AUSTIN BLAIR, JANUARY 7, 1863[225]

Excerpts of Michigan House Democratic Resolutions regarding the Final Emancipation Proclamation, introduced January 22, 1863.

Resolved, "That the emancipation proclamation of the President on the 1st of January, 1863, is unauthorized by the constitution and laws of the land, and is, as a war measure, not only unwise, but in its natural tendency of the most evil and pernicious consequences, being directly calculated, 1st, to forever alienate the loyal feelings of every Union man in the seceding States; 2d, to draw ultimately the border slave states out of the Union; 3d, to more effectually unite and exasperate the Southern people who are already arrayed in arms against us, and thus procrastinate the bloody intestine war that is now desolating the country and destroying the lives of our people; and, 4th, to excite insurrections and merciless massacres of innocent women and children by the blacks of the South."[226]

No. 14: An Act to legalize certain volunteer family relief orders in the county of Clinton, in this State.

Section 1: Validates Clinton County supervisors' good faith orders for family relief under the acts of May 10, 1861, or January 17, 1862; [NB: *presumably correcting technical noncompliance with the law*]. Approved January 29, 1863.[227]

No. 31: An Act for the relief of sick, disabled and needy soldiers.

Section 1: Appropriates $20,000 of the War Loan proceeds (approved May 10, 1861) for a "special fund" to be called the Soldiers' Relief Fund. **Section 2:** Authorizes the governor to "loan or donate, in his discretion" any amount of this Fund "to such sick, disabled and needy soldiers [as have been] mustered into the service of the United States, from the State of Michigan, for the purpose of effecting their recovery, or return home." **Section 3:** Authorizes the governor "to better effect the objects of this act to hire "one or more agents, whose duty shall be to visit the hospitals of the country, and other places where [Michigan soldiers] may be found, to look after their welfare, and loan or donate the moneys of said fund . . . for the purposes aforesaid." *Provided* that, the governor may appoint as many agents as he desires who are willing to serve without cost other than expenses. **Section 4:** Agents will "be subject to the control and instructions of the Governor; and the Governor may, in his discretion, discharge any agent appointed." Approved February 18, 1863.[228]

Joint Resolution No. 5: Joint Resolutions on the state of the Union.

Whereas, "The present rebellion threatens the peace and perpetuity of the Union of the States, and requires the united efforts of all patriotic and loyal citizens to sustain the Administration, to restore a permanent and honorable peace to the whole country; therefore,"

Resolved . . . "That we will sustain the National Administration with all the means in our power, in all its efforts to quell the present rebellion." . . . . *Resolved,* "That we unreservedly approve the proclamation of the President of the United States, issued on the first day of January, one thousand eight hundred and sixty-three, emancipating slaves in the insurgent States and districts of the Union, believing it to be an act of justice warranted by the constitution upon military necessity."

Resolved, "That while we lament the gallant dead who have given their lives for their country . . . we nevertheless rejoice that through the mad and guilty act of the southern conspirators, that wicked and barbarous institution of African slavery will receive its death-blow. . . ."

Resolved, "That we are unalterably opposed to any terms of compromise and accommodation with the rebels, while under arms, and acting in hostility to the government of the Union, and on this we express but one sentiment—unconditional submission and obedience to the laws and constitution of the Union." *Resolved,* requests the governor to send these resolutions to loyal governors and Michigan's congressional delegation. Approved, February 24, 1863.[229]

Joint Resolution No. 9: Joint Resolution to authorize the purchase of Lambert's "field tourniquets" for the use of Michigan soldiers, in the service of the United States.
Approved March 5, 1863.[230]

No. 51: An Act to authorize the payment of a State bounty to volunteers mustered from this State into the military service of the United States.

Section 1: Authorizes the governor to pay from the War Fund "such uniform bounty as he shall deem necessary, not exceeding fifty dollars to each volunteer, non-commissioned officer, musician or private, that may enlist and be mustered into the service of the United States" in any unit already mustered from Michigan and in U.S. military service, or now organizing in Michigan for U.S. service; *Provided,* No bounties will be paid to soldiers enlisted before this act's effective date. Approved March 6, 1863.[231]

No. 56: An Act to provide for paying or funding the bounty fund raised by the citizens of Detroit.

Section 1: A Detroit public meeting will be held this year and citizens asked to impose a tax or to issue bonds to finance the repayment, with interest, of monies advanced by various persons and associations under the authority of Common Council resolutions passed on July 24 and August 26, 1862 (see those dates), for the purpose of creating a fund to pay Detroiters' bounties who volunteered under the July and August [1862] calls. At these meetings, voters may reject taxes or bonds; but if they consent to either, the Common Council is authorized to levy taxes or issue bonds, to be called Volunteer Bounty Bonds, redeemable within four years with an interest rate not to exceed 7 percent.

Section 2: If voters approve bonds, the city may levy taxes for debt service.

Section 3: This authority is restricted to the fund-raised for bounties paid during the summer of 1862. Approved March 6, 1863.[232]

No. 67: An Act to legalize the action of townships, cities and counties, in raising bounties for volunteers.

Section 1: Validates the actions of towns, cities and counties that have raised taxes, borrowed money or issued bonds "for the purpose of paying bounties for volunteers in the military service of the United States." Approved March 7, 1863.[233]

No. 85: An Act to provide interest on the war loan.

Section 1: Appropriates from Michigan's treasury to the general fund for the years 1863 and 1864 the amount of $84,693 to pay interest on the war loan, if necessary; if not, the excess will be applied to principal repayment. Approved March 11, 1863.[234]

No. 109: An Act to amend an act entitled "an act to authorize a war loan," approved May 10th, 1861.

Section 1: Amends section 1 of the above act: Authorizes the governor and treasurer, "for the purpose of organizing the volunteer militia, repelling invasion, suppressing insurrection or defending the State in time of war," to borrow an amount not exceeding $1,250,000, with a term not to exceed 25 years and an interest rate not to exceed 7 percent, to be called the War Loan of the State of Michigan. These bonds are exempted from Michigan taxes, and bond proceeds will be deposited in the War Fund.

Section 3: The War Fund may pay bounties authorized by law "or for the relief of sick, disabled and needy soldiers," or for the purchase and distribution of "necessary military stores" including "subsistence, clothing, pay, medicines, field and camp equipage, arms, munitions, and equipments for such companies of the volunteer militia of this State as have been or will be mustered into" Michigan or U.S. service. Authorizes the governor to pay for "such necessary and proper expenses as have been in good faith, made" since April 16, 1861, "for the organization and subsistence of such companies as have been mustered" into Michigan or U.S. service. Approved March 14, 1863.[235]

Joint Resolution No. 15: Joint Resolution of thanks to the Michigan soldiers in the field.

Whereas, "The citizen soldiers of Michigan have responded cheerfully to their country's call, have never hesitated or faltered when duty prompted or danger threatened, and, by their indomitable fortitude under the fatigues and privations of war, their heroic bravery and brilliant achievement upon the battle field, have crowned themselves with glory, and given to Michigan imperishable renown; therefore, *Resolved . . .* That tendering to them the thanks of the State for their valuable services, we also assure them that while Michigan thus holds them forth as examples of emulation to the soldiers of other States, she is also proudly grateful to them for the renown which their noble deeds have shed upon her name, and claiming them for her own, she points to them with the feelings of maternal pride, and in the language of the noble Roman mother exclaims, 'these are my jewels.'" *Resolved*, The Governor will forward these resolutions to all deployed Michigan units. Approved March 14, 1863.[236]

No. 110: An Act to provide a tax for the expenses of the State government.

Section 1: Proposes a two mill per dollar tax on the "aggregate of real and personal estate" as taxable in Michigan. Approved March 14, 1863.[237]

No. 128: An Act to punish desertion, to prevent improper interference with the military, and to promote discipline therein.

Section 1: Deserters from Michigan or U.S. service shall, upon conviction, be imprisoned in the state penitentiary for up to two years. Authorizes sheriffs, deputy sheriffs, constables, city or village marshals to arrest deserters "wherever [they] may be found in this State" and to notify the state AG. [NB: *authorizes state law enforcement against federal deserters.*]

Section 2: Persons who, "during any war, rebellion or insurrection against the United States or against this State, shall maliciously and advisedly endeavor to seduce any person . . . by land or water, from his . . . duty of allegiance, or to incite or stir up any such person . . . to commit any act of mutiny, or to desert, shall upon conviction" be imprisoned in the state penitentiary for up to five years.

Section 3: If during any war, rebellion, or insurrection, any person "shall willfully and maliciously embezzle, steal, injure, destroy or secrete any arms or ammunition, or military stores or equipments" of the U.S. or Michigan, [or any soldier], or "shall willfully, and maliciously destroy, remove or injure any buildings, machinery or material used or intended to be used in the making, repairing or storing of any arms, ammunition or military stores or equipments" belonging to the U.S. or Michigan shall upon conviction be punished by imprisonment in the state penitentiary for up to five years. [NB: *Criminalizes sabotage as well as black marketeering in military stores.*]

Section 4: Persons who [during war or rebellion] "shall forcibly resist any military draft . . . or shall incite encourage or command" any other person(s) to resist the draft "or shall unlawfully and willfully dissuade, discourage or endeavor to hinder any other person . . . from volunteering, enlisting or mustering" into military service, "or shall forcibly resist, or attempt to resist such volunteering, enlisting or mustering" shall, upon conviction, be punished by imprisonment in the state penitentiary for up to one year and fined up to $500.

Section 5: Persons "who shall conceal or harbor any soldier or volunteer . . . knowing him to have deserted, and with intent to aid him in such desertion, or shall refuse to deliver him up to the orders of his commanding officer," shall, upon conviction "be imprisoned at hard labor" up to two years and fined up to $500.

Section 6: "Any person who has enlisted . . . and been sworn into service . . . or who shall offer himself as a substitute for a citizen of this State, duly drafted . . . [and who deserts]" shall, on conviction, be imprisoned in the state penitentiary up to one year and fined up to $1,000. Approved March 18, 1863.[238]

Joint Resolution No. 18: Joint Resolution on the state of the Union.

Whereas, "The existing rebellion, in its strength, extent and ferocity, in its baseness, enormity and wickedness, is without parallel in the history of mankind . . . . And whereas, The National Administration is the only legally constituted authority to direct the means and energies to be employed in the prosecution of the war. *And whereas*, The safety and perpetuity of the government can only be secured by the utter and complete overthrow of the rebellion, therefore, *Resolved*. . . . That to weaken the enemy by cutting off his supplies, taking away his means of support, stripping him of his property and depriving him of his slaves, is not less a duty than actually fighting him in the field . . . . [We] therefore approve the proclamation of the President, emancipating the slaves in the insurgent States, as a war measure eminently fit and proper, sanctioned by the usages of civilized warfare, and therefore warranted by the constitution; and emanating thus from the President, by virtue of his authority as Commander-in-Chief of the army, it becomes the duty of all good citizens at home, as well as soldiers in the field, to sustain and enforce it. *Resolved*, that we are unalterably opposed to any terms of compromise or accommodation with the rebels, while under arms and acting in hostility to the government. . . ." *Resolved*, that the governor send these resolutions to loyal governors and Michigan's congressional delegation. March 18, 1863.[239]

Joint Resolution No. 19: Joint Resolution to provide for a roll of honor to perpetuate the memory and noble deeds of Michigan soldiers, who have fallen in defense of our country.

[NB: *This resolution required the AG to prepare and keep "a roll of honor" containing the "name and age of every Michigan soldier who has fallen, or may fall in the service of his country during the present war, together with the rank, designation of company, residence, time and place of enlistment, time and place of mustering into service, also the time, place and manner he met his death, together with such remarks as may be appropriate, concerning the military career of the soldier." It should also include Michiganders who died in the service of other states, a "brief history" of Michigan units and company-sized units in other states' service. The AG will print up to 10,000 copies.*] Approved March 18, 1863.[240]

Joint Resolution No. 20: Joint Resolution relative to frauds against the government of the United States.

Whereas, "a vast amount of the treasure of the nation is necessarily being expended in the prosecution of the present struggle. . . . And *whereas* there are men destitute of every principle of honesty, and so lost to every impulse of patriotism, as to forget their obligations to their country and to humanity, and to engage in plundering the public treasury and in robbing our soldiers in the field. And *whereas*, Every contractor or public officer who is engaged in furnishing supplies, or who has in any way the care, custody, or control of public stores or funds, should be held to strict economy and rigid accountability," therefore, *Resolved*, that Michigan's congressional delegation should "use their influence for the passage of an act of Congress that shall more effectually provide for preventing and punishing frauds against the government." Approved March 18, 1863.[241]

No. 161: An Act to amend an act entitled "an act to amend an act entitled an act to provide for the relief, by counties, of the families of volunteers mustered from this State into the military service of the United States, or of this State, approved May tenth, eighteen hundred and sixty-one, and add certain sections thereto," approved January seventeenth, eighteen hundred and sixty-two, by adding thereto another section.

Section 1: [Amends Section 10 of act] Authorizes Detroit's Common Council to appoint a person "whose duty it shall be to afford such temporary relief as may be necessary for the support of such families as shall be entitled to relief under . . . this act [such benefit] not exceeding the sum of fifteen dollars per month, and not exceeding to any family or person the actual sum necessary, with his, her or their other means of support, to relieve such family or person." The appointee "shall discharge all the duties of all the aldermen of said city . . . [and the appointee] may give orders upon the county treasurer of his county, payable on to the person, or order, who is for the time being the head of the family to whom relief is afforded." Approved March 19, 1863.[242]

No. 173: An Act to amend an act entitled "an act to amend an act entitled an act to provide for the relief, by counties, of the families of volunteers mustered from this State into the military service of the United States, or of this State" approved May fourth, [sic, tenth] **eighteen hundred sixty-one, and to add certain sections thereto, approved January seventeenth, eighteen hundred sixty-two.** [NB: *For a joint resolution that clarifies this act, see Joint Resolution No. 5, enacted February 5, 1864.*]

Section 1: Amends the above act's sections one, three, and five [not included below] to read: Section 1: Requires county supervisors "to make adequate provision for all requisite relief and support of the families" of NCOs, musicians, and privates "enlisted or drafted from their counties, or as substitutes for persons so drafted and mustered into the military and naval service" of the U.S. or Michigan. Authorizes counties to borrow money and issue bonds for a term not exceeding three years and a rate not exceeding 10 percent. Taxes may be levied to finance this debt, Provided: "That the family of no person so drafted and furnishing a substitute shall receive any relief under the provisions of this act."

Section 3: Requires "the supervisor of each township, and each supervisor, alderman, or other officer representing any city or ward upon the board of supervisors of his county . . . to pay a soldier's family, in the event of his death" while in Michigan or U.S. family aid for up to two years "to the same measure of relief as his family would be entitled to receive if he had not deceased." Approved March 20, 1863.[243]

No. 211: An Act to establish a military school in connection with the Agricultural College.

Section 1: Establishes a new "course of instruction" on "military tactics and military engineering."

Section 3: That the State Board of Agriculture, with advice and consent of the governor and AG, will "procure, at the expense of the State, all such arms, accouterments, books and instruments, and appoint such additional professors and instructors as, in their discretion," are necessary to execute this act. Approved March 20, 1863.[244]

No. 220: An Act to allow the board of supervisors of the county of Wayne to issue bonds and create a sinking fund for the purpose of paying the indebtedness of said county, made on account of the volunteers' family relief fund.

Section 1: The board may borrow money and issue bonds at a rate not to exceed 7 percent for a term not to exceed twenty years, and may levy taxes to repay the borrowings and provide family relief.

Section 2: Authorizes the county Board of Supervisors at its 1864 meeting (or any year thereafter) "to provide for the establishment of a sinking fund sufficient to liquidate, at the proper time, such sums borrowed under the provisions of this act . . . ."; provided "That the money and interest accruing [in the sinking fund] shall not be applied to any other purpose than that of liquidating the debt incurred on account of the volunteers' family relief fund." Approved March 20, 1863.[245]

State Affairs

Between December 23, 1862, and December 31, 1863, 13,567 Michiganders mustered into U.S. service. By service branch, this number included 5,051 cavalrymen for the Seventh through Eleventh Regiments; 735 artillerymen for the Tenth and Eleventh Batteries; 865 for the Twenty-Seventh Michigan Infantry, and 469 men for the First Michigan Colored Regiment, which was still recruiting (see February 17, 1864). The Detroit PG enlisted 127 men, recruits for the First Michigan Cavalry added 306, 1,519 men volunteered for existing units through the U.S. superintendent of recruiting in Detroit, and 1,950 enlisted through district PMs throughout the state. Details on the state (545 men) and federal drafts (922 draftees and substitutes) are listed below.[246]

The Michigan state draft, intended to cure deficiencies from the August 1862 militia call, commenced after the first week in February (see February 9, 1863). Twenty counties had deficiencies and the number of draftees ranged from 7 (Tuscola County) and 8 (Calhoun) to the top five: St. Clair (178), Lapeer (158), Macomb (127), Genesee (76), and Monroe (74). A total of 1,278 men were drafted; of these, 710 (or substitutes) actually appeared at the Detroit Barracks; of these, 545 were sent to various deployed units. A few deserted, but U.S. officers discharged most of the 165 remaining for alienage, disability, or other causes. Inducted draftees were allowed the option of nine-month service, but Michigan authorities managed to persuade 430 men to serve for three years, leaving only 115 who chose the shorter period.[247]

Beginning around June 9 (see that date), a federal enrollment was conducted in each of Michigan's congressional districts as required by the federal March 3, 1863, Enrollment Act. This enrollment and not the Census of 1860 or any state enrollment provided the basis for quotas that year. Consistent with the Enrollment Act, Michigan's 120,264 military-eligible males (all able-bodied men aged twenty to forty-five years) were divided into two classes. The First Class totaled 80,038 and consisted of 79,052 whites and 986 blacks. The Second Class totaled 40,226 and consisted of 39,908 whites and 318 blacks. In making the enrollment, Michigan faced a problem that Massachusetts, for example, did not. AG Robertson would note, "The extent of our territory, and the difficulty of communication in some portions of it, with other causes, perhaps delayed the completion of the enrollment until the fall."[248]

To account for exemptions, the Enrollment Act stipulated that 50 percent of the required number would be added to the number of draftees. The total number of names drawn in Michigan was 6,383; of these, 261 actually presented at the general rendezvous at Grand Rapids; an additional 643 provided substitutes (of whom 43 deserted en route to the rendezvous), and 1,626 paid $300 commutation. Michigan thus furnished 861 men or 13.5 percent of the names drawn and paid $487,800 in cash fees, which was useful but not as important as men. Other draftees were exempted (or self-exempted by desertion) for various causes, the top five of which were physical disability (1,596), failure to report (1,069), alienage or nonresidency (384), only sons (210), and over or under age limits (204).[249]

Some of the enrollment coincided with the New York draft riots, creating considerable anxiety in AAPMG Hill. He remembered that Michigan's enrollment caused "a great deal of excitement and some apprehension . . . not only in the City [Detroit] but throughout the State." Hill obtained from the state arsenal two ten-pound Parrott rifles and horses from the QM, as well as VRC troops to serve these weapons. Fortunately, they were never used.[250]

By December 31, 1863, Michigan's federal draftees had been distributed to the following units: 518 men to the Second Michigan Cavalry, 259 to the Fourth Michigan Cavalry, 13 to the First Michigan Colored Infantry, and 1 transferred to the First Engineers and Mechanics. Forty-three had not yet reported and 33 had (thus far) deserted.[251]

After various adjustments, AG Robertson claimed that as of December 31, Michigan had furnished 53,749 men since the beginning of the war. This did not include Michiganders (estimated at "several hundred") enlisting in the Regular Army. Organizationally, as of December 31, Michigan had in service one engineer regiment, fourteen light artillery batteries, eleven cavalry regiments, a battalion in a Missouri regiment, twenty-seven regiments of infantry (including one serving as a heavy artillery battery), one sharpshooter regiment, and six sharpshooter companies. Michigan's role in many fierce engagements can be measured in casualties: for enlisted men between January 1 and October 31, 1863, 1,409 were killed in action or mortally wounded; 3,209 died of disease; 1,115

were missing in action and 7,305 had been discharged for disability. The total of 13,038 represented 24.25 percent of Michigan's deployed forces at year end.[252]

By year-end 1863, the Michigan's 1862 Militia Act (see No. 16) had failed to attract recruits into militia service. Only three units had been mustered: the Detroit Light Guard,[253] the Lyon Guard,[254] and the Detroit-based Scott Guard.[255]

Since 1862 Colonel Darius Clark had represented Michigan in New York City (see September 29, 1862); 1863 witnessed the expansion of the agent network to wherever Michigan troops were found.

War expenditures greatly stimulated Michigan's economy. In 1863, Detroit's U.S. QM George W. Lee reported that 223,236 tons of ordnance and substance were transported through Michigan, as were 55,008 troops. The following quantities of items were purchased: 16,725 horses, 9,152 tons of grain, and 11,547 tons of hay. Of 37,593 uniforms issued, 11,868 were made in Detroit. QM Lee also reported that the amount of rewards paid for apprehending deserters was $8,521.30 between January 1 and June 30 for 900 scofflaws; $9,455.17 was paid between July 1 and December 31, 1863, for 528. In 1863, the total amount of U.S. QM expenditures in Michigan was $2,278,500.[256]

The centralizing pressures of war impacted Michigan's private benevolence effort. The Detroit Ladies' Soldiers' Aid Society formally changed its name to the Michigan Soldiers' Aid Society (see August 8), which reflected the fact that many of the supplies the Society shipped had come from local aid associations across the state. Private benevolence had grown spontaneously into a statewide effort. But consolidation took more than a change of name. Probably during the summer of 1863, the indefatigable Dr. J. S. Newberry visited local aid societies across the state, including Saginaw, Flint, Ann Arbor, Jackson, and Kalamazoo. His objectives were to persuade local aid associations to continue (and expand) their conveyance of funds and supplies to the newly named Michigan Soldiers' Aid Society and to accept it as an auxiliary of the United States Sanitary Commission. According to Newberry, "everywhere the plan of bringing the activities and benevolence of the ladies of the State under a uniform system gave great satisfaction. . . ."[257]

In Washington, the Michigan Soldiers' Relief Fund's James M. Edmunds reported that for the twelve months preceding December 11, 1863, he distributed to Michigan soldiers in camps and hospitals in Washington, Georgetown, and Alexandria eighty-nine containers of food and other items. This represented a sharp decrease from the prior year, because Edmunds was able to compensate with supplies received from the United States Sanitary Commission. He estimated that since inception, his group had distributed over 60,000 items of clothing and a similar amount of "fruits, delicacies, &c." Edmunds and his agents, each of whom served for expenses only, visited Washington area hospitals weekly, but also traveled outside the District of Columbia when required: For example, after the Battle of Gettysburg, agents visited hospitalized soldiers in Annapolis, Baltimore, Harrisburg, York, Fort Monroe, and Gettysburg. Aside from goods, its cash receipts were $2,350.39 and expenditures $2,037.[258]

Edmunds explained that the decrease began after the appointment of state military agent Tunnicliffe. Edmunds speculated that "the people in Michigan had fallen into the error of supposing that the appropriation made by the Legislature [to support the military agents] . . . would obviate the necessity of further voluntary contributions." Another factor was that his effort had received large supplies from Detroit's Soldiers' Aid Society, but after its affiliation with the Western Sanitary Commission on August 1 (see that date), donations were sent to the west and not east to Washington.[259]

State military agent Dr. Joseph Tunnicliffe, Jr., was also in Washington. While Edmunds's association dealt mostly with food and clothing (there were exceptions—see Summary and note on Caleb Clark), Tunnicliffe spent considerable time negotiating the federal bureaucracy on soldiers' behalf. The most pressing issues were, first, obtaining pay for hospitalized Michigan soldiers. Wounded men were often sent from their units without descriptive lists, a requirement to be paid. The officers responsible for preparing these lists might be on the march or negligent, but the result was the same: destitution among soldiers and families. A second concern was the bureaucracy's use of "deserter" as a default classification whenever it was unable to track soldiers in hospitals or on furloughs. Men retrieved on the battlefield could be marked missing in action (after which they were not paid), or AWOL; men furloughed home or to hospitals whose illnesses extended beyond the furlough were declared deserters; it was a war in which the paperwork never caught up with events. The result was that many soldiers, grievously wounded or

ill, hospitalized for months, and honorably discharged for disability, might be arrested later for desertion and detained for weeks while the War Department's records were adjusted. (According to Tunnicliffe, three-quarters of the 80,000 men marked as deserters were unjustly classified.) Tunnicliffe was a physician, but in Washington, he functioned as a soldiers' "lawyer."

One of Tunnicliffe's deep concerns was about attempting to transfer sick and wounded Michigan men to Michigan hospitals from Washington facilities. The primary obstacle was that Michigan lacked a U.S. General Hospital. In fact, Blair's initial instructions to Tunnicliffe included lobbying Stanton "at every opportunity" to establish a Michigan U.S. General Hospital. Tunnicliffe was relentless, and the War Department finally granted his request to convert the Detroit Barracks into a U.S. general hospital. It would ultimately confer U.S. general hospital status on Detroit's Harper's Hospital. Other lobbyists included Michigan's congressional delegation, Blair, Dr. Charles S. Tripler, and Army surgeon general Joseph K. Barnes. (See November 15.)[260]

Tunnicliffe dealt with a myriad of other problems regarding which soldiers had little support other than state agents: obtaining back pay, lost furloughs, and passes; discharge examinations for men languishing in hospitals; and property left with hospital custodians following transfer or discharge. He arranged for the return of deceased soldiers to Michigan, connected soldiers who were left behind after their units deployed, traced missing allotment funds, and arranged transportation home for at least 450 furloughed soldiers. (Stanton would eventually provide transportation for all Michigan soldiers at government expense.) Tunnicliffe also cooperated with Edmonds in obtaining supplies from the U.S. Sanitary Commission's Frederick N. Knapp, and also to allow assistants Mrs. Brainard and Miss Wheelock to draw on supplies as necessary.[261]

Agent Luther B. Willard, military state agent, opened his office at 46 1/2 Cherry Street in Nashville. This space included several rooms for disabled soldiers and was also stocked with Michigan newspapers. Willard traveled weekly to hospitals and camps in "Nashville, Murfreesboro, Stevenson, Bridgeport, &c., ascertaining and ministering to the wants of those who are unable, by reason of severe illness" to visit his office. Willard provided soldiers the same general services as Tunnicliffe. He also reported receiving about thirty letters each day from relatives inquiring about the condition and whereabouts of sick and wounded soldiers; Willard then visited hospitals at Louisville, Cincinnati, Madison, New Albany, Jeffersonville, Camp Dennison, and Covington; he was able to answer about twenty inquiries per day. His visits also included giving assistance on fresh battlefields. (See September 19–20.) Until the November 28 appointment of Dr. J. B. Gilman, Willard covered Kentucky as well as Tennessee.[262]

State military agents outside of Michigan reported to Benjamin Vernor, also designated a military agent but based in Detroit. Because Vernor was also the vice president of the Detroit-based Michigan Soldiers' Relief Committee, he was able to better channel privately raised supplies to state agents elsewhere. In 1863, he received 400 shipments from 135 different Michigan communities, consisting of 331 boxes and 203 barrels.[263]

Finally, Chaplain Samuel Day's responsibilities extended throughout the upper Midwest, including the states of Michigan, Illinois, and Wisconsin. His task was to collect donated food (which chiefly seems to have been antiscorbutics) and send it to Chicago under the auspices of the Sanitary Commission at Chicago, which in turn would transship it to western military hospitals. In 1863 from Michigan, Day received 2,337 barrels of vegetables ("mostly potatoes and green apples"), 167 barrels of onions, and 29 barrels of "Best stock ale." Day also collected $3,137.55 in donations, which was spent acquiring another 3,336 barrels of vegetables. Day personally visited forty Michigan towns and cities in his drive for food and money; in addition, he received donations from thirty-four towns not visited. The aggregate weight of collections exceeded 500 tons. Day was impressed with Michigan's generosity and recommended posting a full-time agent in the state.[264]

As in other loyal states, 1863 witnessed the establishment and growth of a Union League Association in Michigan, which was certainly helped by Governor Blair's favor and James Edmunds's position as the national Union League's president. A state council was formed in April 1863, and helped by favorable coverage from Republican sheets, branches spread quickly across Michigan, to Dowagiac, Williamston, Wheatfield, Locke, LeRoy, and Detroit. Michigan's Democratic press discounted patriotic motives behind the Union League and understood it as "a secret organization for the purpose of carrying the next presidential election," believing it was an effort "to seduce democrats into the 'loyal league,' on which abolitionism now rests its hopes."[265]

Part of the Union League's outreach involved classifying every Michigan voter into one of four categories: "Union men, members of the League. Union men of Republican antecedents. Union men of Democratic antecedents. Copperheads." This list guided mailings of pro-Union propaganda to local newspapers as well as supplying pro-Union newspapers to select voters. After General Willcox's June 30 prohibition against secret societies (see that date), Union League activities temporarily ceased. However, Edmunds advised that Willcox's order did not cover the League and instructed Michigan groups "to proceed as if that Order had not been issued." By March 1864, Michigan's Union League professed 40,793 members organized into 360 "subordinate councils."[266]

The State of Michigan's receipts for FY 1863 (November 30), including the proceeds of bond sales, totaled $3,481,676.60. Subtracting bond sales of $2,080,310 left $1,401,366 in receipts "from the usual sources of revenue." Expenditures for ordinary state purposes were $1,047,245.52: this left Michigan with an operating surplus of $354,1221.08. The state spent $232,903.94 for "war purposes" during this period, continuing the shift towards federal assumption (and reimbursement to states) of state war expenses. In 1863 and for the balance of the war, Michigan's war expenses would be increasingly devoted to paying bounties.

At the end of FY 1863, state debt totaled $2,993,299.30.[267]

1864

Key Events

January

2: PMG Fry reports to Stanton that enlistments under the October 17, 1863, call "are, in the main, very encouraging as to the prospect of getting a large number of recruits by volunteer enlistments." His reports show that for the last three months of 1863 (partial for December), national enlistments total 42,429. Most states reveal a dramatic increase, which bolsters the argument that the draft may fail to produce men, but it does spur enlistments. But Michigan reveals only a slight increase: during the six months preceding the draft (January 1 to June 30, 1863), Michigan's voluntary enlistments were 4,606; but in the six months after orders for the draft began (June 30 to December 31, 1863), Michigan's enlistments were steady at 4,780 men.[1]

5: The draft scheduled for this day is deferred nationwide, "in consequence of the progress made in procuring volunteers." Separately, Lincoln, supported by Stanton and Fry, asks Congress to reconsider its joint resolution of December 23, 1863, and reauthorize the $300 enlistment bounty to veteran volunteers to February 1.[2]

Meanwhile at Camp Ward, the Colored Ladies' Aid Society presents the First Michigan Colored Regiment with its colors.[3]

Separately, in Jackson, the Fourteenth Michigan Battery musters into U.S. service; recruits and officers are drawn from Marshall, Kalamazoo, and Detroit. The unit deploys to Washington, D.C., and participates in defending the capital against Jubal Early's July 1864 raid.[4] (See July 1, 1865.)

6: PMG Fry notifies Michigan recruiters that "Recruits will be credited to the localities from which they received local bounties"; on the other hand, veterans reenlisting "will be credited to the localities to which the reenlistments and muster-in rolls show them as belonging." This furnishes reenlisting veterans with bounty-shopping opportunities.[5]

9: Major General Winfield Scott Hancock is assigned recruiting duty in thirteen states, including Michigan, to "fill up the old regiments of the Second Army Corps," to increase its strength to 50,000 men.[6]

11: In the U.S. Senate, Missouri's Senator John B. Henderson introduces a joint resolution to abolish slavery in the United States.[7]

12: The War Department creates the Northern Department, which includes the states of Michigan, Ohio, Illinois, and Indiana. (See January 20.)

Meanwhile, the Thirteenth Michigan, have successfully veteranized, returns to Kalamazoo for furlough. It will redeploy on April 20 and accompany Sherman to the sea.[8] (See July 25, 1865.)

14: PMG Fry notifies Hill that Congress has extended bounties (that were supposed to be discontinued after January 5) for several weeks: "Continue enlistments under regulations established prior to that date," he directs, "and keep up enthusiasm for recruiting. Inform Governor immediately."[9]

19: The Michigan legislature convenes in Extra Session. In Little Rock, Arkansas, the state constitutional convention votes to abolish slavery. (See March 18.)[10]

20: General Samuel P. Heintzelman[11] assumes command of the Northern Department, headquartered in Columbus, Ohio. (See October 1.)

Meanwhile, the Thirteenth Michigan Battery musters into U.S. service; recruits and officers are drawn from Detroit, Flint, and Grand Rapids.[12] (See July 1, 1865.)

25: After months of efforts by the Michigan Soldiers' Aid Society, the Soldiers' Home in Detroit opens. During its first month in operation, it admits 639 soldiers, serves 3,374 meals, and provides 740 lodgings. (See entry for June 30.)[13]

27: Michigan's House refers to the Senate a resolution denouncing AAPMG Hill. He has "by his arbitrary and insolent deportment towards those having business to transact at his office, rendered himself so odious to the people of this State, that his longer continuance in office would seriously impair the recruiting service in this State, and be too gross an outrage to be tolerated." The resolution asks that Michigan's Congressional delegation "make an earnest effort" to remove Hill.[14]

February

1: Lincoln calls for 500,000 three-year men with deficiencies drafted on March 10. (See March 14.)[15]

2: The War Department accounts for Michigan's contributions under earlier calls. For July 22 and 25, 1861 (500,000 call), the state has furnished (quotas in parenthesis) 23,546 (21,357) three-year men; for the July 1862 call, 17,656 (11,686) three-year men; and for the August 1862 call (11,686), it furnished no nine-month men (or very few; see Military Affairs—1862). As of this day, Michigan has furnished no six-month men.[16]

3: Sherman begins Meridian, Mississippi, Campaign. (See February 14.)

5: PMG Fry authorizes Blair to raise a company for the Fourth Michigan Cavalry and asks if he is interested in raising "some other companies to be formed into a regiment when complete?" (See February 8.)[17]

6: Michigan legislature adjourns. Meanwhile, the Tenth Michigan reenlists as Veteran Volunteers.[18] (See July 19, 1865.)

8: Blair replies to PMG Fry's February 5 note with his own question. "If you mean entire new companies, with officers, to be put into old regiments in the field, I do and would like to have such authority. Please answer." (See next day's entry.)[19]

9: Fry answers Blair's question. The PMG meant raising entirely new companies with officers; these may be assigned to existing regiments if there are vacancies; otherwise, they will be consolidated into new regiments. Meanwhile, at Richmond's Libby Prison, Colonel William B. McCreery* of the Twenty-First Michigan joins some 114 other Northern POWs to escape through a shaft some sixty feet long and eighteen inches wide, shortly to be known as the Great Libby Tunnel Escape. (See February 13 and 26.)[20]

10: The Ninth Michigan, having reenlisted enough Veteran Volunteers to qualify as a veteran unit, leaves Coldwater for what will become the Atlanta Campaign.[21] (See September 15, 1865.)

12: The U.S. Senate authorizes that the payment of bounties be extended until March 1, 1864. (See March 3.)[22]

13: Colonel McCreery reaches federal lines. From Fort

Magruder he wires his father Reuben, "I have made escape from 'Hell' (Libby Prison) and am again in God's country,—will be home soon."[23]

14: Sherman occupies Meridian, Mississippi.

16: An analysis comparing New York's enrollment rate with that of other states yields information about Michigan. According to this report, Michigan has 100,412 men between twenty and thirty-five years old and 45,493 men between thirty-five and forty-five years old. Thus, under the Enrollment Act's formula for determining men of the First Class most eligible for the draft (First Class = all enrolled men between twenty and thirty-five, and one-sixth of those between thirty-five and forty-five), Michigan's First Class is 107,994 men—all of whom should be enrolled. But only 79,985 men of the First Class are enrolled, which means that Michigan's ratio (actual enrollment to prospective enrollment) is 74 percent. The national ratio is 73.7 percent. Thus, Michigan appears slightly overenrolled.[24]

An accompanying analysis of the draft reveals that of 6,426 Michigan names drawn, 2,573 or 40 percent were actually held to service. Of the thirteen states listed, the average is 28.3 percent held to service, and Michigan is second-highest, behind Vermont with 40.2 percent.

On this day (or the 18th—the record is unclear) in Windsor, Ontario, Ohioan Clement Vallandigham meets with representatives of the Order of American Knights, shortly to be reorganized as the Order of the Sons of Liberty. Lately, Vallandigham agrees to become the new group's supreme commander. (See SAW.5.259.)[25]

17: The First Michigan Colored Infantry is mustered into U.S. service with 895 men. (See March 28.) Meanwhile, the Sixteenth Michigan, now veteranized, departs Saginaw for Virginia. (See March 28.)[26]

19: Because Michigan troops are now based in St. Louis, Blair asks Weston Flint,[27] Ohio's state military agent based in St. Louis, to also serve as Michigan's state agent. Flint's jurisdiction includes the hospital at Jefferson Barracks (some ten miles from St. Louis) as well as Paducah, Cairo, and Mound City.[28]

20: Battle of Olustee, Florida.

22: The national Republican Party's executive committee, to which Austin Blair belongs, calls for the national convention to convene in Baltimore on June

7. It invites "qualified voters, who desire the maintenance of the Union, the supremacy of the Constitution, and the complete suppression of the rebellion with the cause thereof [NB: *slavery*], by vigorous war and all apt and efficient means."[29]

24: The Battle of Buzzard Roost, Georgia begins, to end on February 27. By the end, the Tenth Michigan will suffer sixty-six casualties.[30]

Congress passes Chapter 13, the first amendment to the 1863 Enrollment Act. Its provisions include recognizing naval credits against draft quotas; exemptions for conscientious objectors; and that African American males must be included in federal enrollments, and providing for compensation to loyal masters whose slaves enlist in federal service.[31]

March

1: General Judson Kilpatrick's raid on Richmond fails.

2: Stanton responds to the request of Henry Wilson, chairman of the Senate's Committee on Military Affairs, for his views on raising troops. Stanton mentions that among others, "State Legislatures and Executives are earnestly requesting the continuance of bounties until the 1st of April."[32]

3: Stanton notifies governors (inexplicably, Blair is not listed) that Congress has authorized the payment of bounties until further notice.[33] Meanwhile, Congress amends the Enrollment Act to pardon any deserter who returns to his unit within sixty days.

4: The War Department issues GO No. 91, establishing naval recruiting stations and quotas for each station. The national naval quota is 12,000, of which Cairo, Illinois's (the station closest to Michigan), portion is 1,000. (See Legislative Sessions—1865, Joint Resolution No. 6.) Michigan's contribution will be at least 142 sailors and 2 Marines.[34] (See Selected Summaries.)

Separately, Fry notifies AAPMG Hill that the March 10 draft is suspended: "A subsequent day for commencing the draft will be in time to make all necessary preparations." He asks that Hill notify Blair. Meanwhile, Michigan's draft rendezvous is moved from Grand Rapids to Jackson, and is now commanded by Detroit's Colonel Grover S. Wormer.[35]

9: Ulysses S. Grant is appointed lieutenant general. Michigan's political factions are favorable to Grant's commission. The *Free Press* approvingly quotes the

New York World that "The secret military movements east and west, all having ended in disappointment and disaster, it is well to call upon someone with brains." The Democratic *Michigan Argus*'s approval is conditioned, not on Grant, but on Washington Republicans. "We trust that Gen. Grant will now be left to run the 'Armies of the United States,' and that he will not permit the know-nothing politicians in and around Washington to dictate military movements against his better knowledge and judgment."[36]

12: In Louisiana, the Red River Campaign begins. Separately, General Henry W. Halleck is relieved as general-in-chief of the army and reassigned as chief of staff under Grant.[37]

14: Lincoln calls for 200,000 men. This will be in addition to the February 1 call for 500,000 men. Under this call Michigan's quota will be 7,821, of which it will eventually furnish 7,344 men. (See June 10.)[38]

18: Arkansas voters ratify antislavery constitution.

25: Confederates unsuccessfully attack Paducah, Kentucky; the next day they are driven back.

28: The First Michigan Colored Infantry leaves Michigan for Annapolis and the Ninth Army Corps. (See April 12.)[39]

Separately, in Charleston, Illinois, an antiwar mob attacks federal troops stationed nearby.[40]

April

6: Maryland votes in favor of a constitutional convention to amend the constitution to abolish slavery. In Louisiana, a new constitution abolishes slavery. The *Advertiser and Tribune* asks, "Who would have predicted when Massachusetts troops, on their way to defend the national capital, were fired upon the inhabitants of Baltimore, on the anniversary of the battle of Lexington, that Maryland would within three years from the commission of that crime in the interest of slavery, thus range herself upon the side of freedom, or, still more extraordinary, that Baltimore herself would give 9,000 majority for immediate emancipation? Verily, the world does move."[41]

8: PMG Fry notifies Hill that "Lieutenant-General Grant directs that active measures be taken to get into the field all recruits, new organizations, and all old troops that can be spared. . . . Execute this order as soon as possible." Meanwhile, in Louisiana, the Battle of Sabine Crossroads is fought. Meanwhile, one Michigander with the Second USSS writes that his comrades "have great confidence in Gen. Grant" and that "Lincoln would get four votes where McClellan would get one."[42]

In Washington, the U.S. Senate passes a joint resolution abolishing slavery, 38 to 6, with Michigan senators Chandler and Howard voting approval.[43]

12: Henry Barns of the First Michigan Colored Infantry resigns as colonel and is replaced by Henry L. Chipman. (See May 23.)[44]

Separately, the Battle of Fort Pillow is fought, and in its sequel Confederates massacre surrendering black soldiers. The *Advertiser and Tribune* carries news of the massacre on April 16, and reaction is immediate. "Up until the time of surrender but few of our men had been killed; but insatiate as fiends, and blood-thirsty as devils incarnate, the Confederates commenced an indiscriminate butchery of both white and black soldiers, men who had thrown down their arms, and even the dead men were horribly mutilated. Children and negro women were murdered in cold blood"; in a related editorial, the sheet declares, "Their blood smokes to the skies—a prayer for vengeance which shall not be unanswered." The *Free Press*, while publishing straight news stories about the massacre, is at first doubtful ("The facts, when all obtained, will probably show that the garrison met with severe loss in trying to hold the fort against greatly superior forces"), then silent, and two weeks later, while acknowledging Confederate atrocities, blames the event on Washington, which "had known of [the fort's] exposed condition for weeks."

Meanwhile, in the U.S. Senate on April 16, Michigan's Jacob Howard introduces a resolution asking the Joint Committee on Conduct of the War "to inquire into the truth of the rumored slaughter of the Union troops after their surrender at the recent attack on Fort Pillow."[45]

15: In Windsor, Ontario, Vallandigham is formally inducted as the supreme commander of the Order of the Sons of Liberty. (See SAW.5.263.)

20: PMG Fry urges governors to accelerate the formation of heavy artillery units, which number 1,738 men each. These recruits will be credited against state draft quotas.[46]

21: In Washington, the governors of Ohio, Indiana, Illinois, Iowa, and in absentia, Wisconsin, meet with Lincoln to propose raising 85,000 hundred-day troops "for the approaching campaign." The next day, Lincoln accepts this proposal and directs Stanton to supervise. Blair is not present, nor does Michigan participate in this program.[47]

27: In Detroit on the Campus Martius, Colonel Henry A. Morrow accepts two new flags for the Twenty-Fourth Michigan.[48] Meanwhile, in Grand Rapids, Phineas C. Wright*, founder of the subversive Order of American Knights, is arrested on a lecture tour. He will be taken to Fort Lafayette, New York Harbor. Wright is never charged but is held until August 1, 1865.[49]

30: PMG Fry asks Blair, "Do you think it advisable to proceed to draft in the deficient sub-districts of your State, so that all of them shall thus be made to fill the quotas heretofore assigned?" Blair is en route to Washington and hopes to meet there with Fry. (See May 5 and May 9.)[50]

May

1: Congressman Kellogg and Governor Blair visit the White House, and finding Lincoln unavailable, leave cards. But the president still wants to meet although no reason is given. "If you and [Blair] please I will call and take you riding at half past 3," the president writes.[51]

4: In Virginia, the Army of the Potomac crosses the Rapidan. Meanwhile, the Fifteenth Michigan, having veteranized, arrives in Nashville after its home furlough.[52] (See September 1, 1865.)

Meanwhile, in Washington, the House passes a Radical measure, "A bill to guarantee to certain States whose governments have been usurped or overthrown, a republican form of government," known as the' Wade-Davis Reconstruction Bill, by a vote of 74 to 66. Among its terms are that states seeking readmission to the Union must have a republican form of government, at least 50 percent of white males must take a loyalty oath, and slaves must be immediately emancipated. Michigan's sole Democrat, Augustus C. Baldwin, votes against the measure, while Republicans Beaman, Kellogg, Upson, Longyear, and Driggs vote yes.[53]

5–7: Battle of the Wilderness.

5: Blair did not meet Fry in Washington, and the PMG repeats his April 30 question. But Blair has still not returned, and state AAG Colonel Frederick Morley promises an answer when the governor arrives.[54]

6: Tensions simmer between the Lincoln administration and Radical factions in the Republican Party. On this day, prominent Radicals issue "A Call to the Radical Men of the Nation," which proposes a convention in Cleveland, Ohio, for May 31. (Other Radicals will issue similar calls.) The purpose is to nominate John C. Fremont for president; Lincoln's policies are denounced as "imbecile and vacillating . . . being just weak enough to waste men and means to provoke the enemy, but not strong enough to conquer the rebellion." The Radicals demand "the immediate extinction of slavery throughout the whole United States by Congressional action, the absolute equality of all men before the law, without regard to race or color . . . [and reconstruction] as shall conform entirely to the policy of freedom for all, placing the political power alone in the hands of the loyal and executing with vigor the law for confiscating the property of rebels." Of sixty-two signatories, ten are from Michigan.[55] (See May 31.)

7: Sherman begins Atlanta Campaign.

8–21: Battles of Spotsylvania. On May 12, the Seventeenth Michigan, surrounded, loses almost 100 KIA and WIA and the same number as POWs. Afterward, the unit lacks sufficient troops to fight as a regiment. (See June 7, 1865.) Out of thirty-four federal infantry regiments considered, the Twenty-Seventh Michigan ranked fourth in losses (195), the Twenty-Sixth Michigan fifth (167), the First Michigan Sharpshooters seventh (162), and the Twentieth Michigan twenty-ninth (144).[56]

9: At Blair's behest, AG Robertson informs Fry that "he thinks it advisable, as soon as all the veterans are properly credited, to proceed with the draft in the deficient sub-districts of the State."[57]

10: Wounded men from Grant's campaign overwhelm existing medical facilities, and Tunnicliffe sends Mrs. Brainard, Miss Wheelock, three assistants, and twenty boxes of sanitary supplies to Fredericksburg.[58]

11: Confederate Cavalry General J. E. B. Stuart is killed at Yellow Tavern, the fatal shot supposedly fired by Private John E. Huff* late of Hiram Berdan's USSS and now with the Fifth Michigan Cavalry. The First Michigan Cavalry has the largest number of losses (48).[59]

12: News of Grant's enormous casualties has reached Michigan. AG Robertson wires Washington agent Tunnicliffe. "The Governor directs that you make every exertion to take care of the Michigan wounded soldiers. Employ sufficient assistance to do so, and use what money may be necessary. Should you need any number of assistants from the State, inform by telegraph." Tunnicliffe immediately meets with Surgeon General Joseph K. Barnes ("precisely the right man in the right place") and replies to Robertson. He updates the AG on his own efforts (see May 10) and those of other commissions; Tunnicliffe also forwards a message from Barnes: the Army will accept ten experienced surgeons equipped for ten days' field service. They are to report to Barnes's office, and transportation to hospitals near the front will be provided. In fact, thirty-three physicians will eventually be sent and distributed to hospitals at Fredericksburg, White House, and City Point. Heading the list is Dr. Alonzo B. Palmer*, professor of the theory and practice of medicine, and of pathology and materia medica at the University of Michigan. (See June 1.)[60]

14–15: Battle of Resaca, Georgia. Among federal units engaged, the Nineteenth Michigan ranks fourteenth in casualties suffered (80).[61]

16: The Fourteenth Michigan, having successfully veteranized and returned home for its furlough, deploys to Nashville, where it joins Sherman's Atlanta Campaign.[62] (See July 18, 1865.)

18: PMG Fry urges Hill to complete the revised enrollment "at the earliest possible day." Municipalities should be advised to strike from the rolls "all names improperly enrolled, because an excess of names increases the quota called for." Fry advises listing all eligible males "because the greater the number to be drawn from the less chance that any particular individual will be drawn."[63]

In Detroit's Merrill Hall, the **Republican State Convention** meets to select delegates for the National Convention in Baltimore. Hezekiah G. Wells* presides. Michigan will send a large delegation to Baltimore. Austin Blair will lead four at-large delegates (with four alternates); also sent are twelve regular delegates and twelve alternates. Five resolutions are passed, including a pledge to "sustain a just government and an honest administration without limit, notwithstanding any error of judgment"; a pledge to fight "until the last vestige of the rebellion is crushed out"; an endorsement of Lincoln's "honesty, integrity, patriotism and statesmanship"; a statement that Lincoln's reelection amounts to an endorsement of the Emancipation Proclamation; and instructions that delegates are to vote as a unit. Thanks are also offered to the serving military.[64] (See June 7.)

23: The First Michigan Colored Infantry is officially redesignated the One Hundred and Second United States Colored Troops. Meanwhile, in Virginia the battles of the North Anna River begin; these conclude on May 26. (See July 8, 1865.)[65]

25: In Georgia, General W.T. Sherman begins the New Hope Church Campaign; it ends on June 4.

28: Fight at Hawes's Shop, Virginia. The Fifth Michigan ranks second in casualties (50), and the Sixth Michigan Cavalry ranks fifth in casualties (33).[66]

30: U.S. AAG Thomas M. Vincent informs Blair that he "has made complete arrangements for the prompt muster-out and discharge of all regiments, detachments, and individuals of the volunteer forces whose terms may expire." However, he is concerned with controlling enlisted men after they have returned home but await discharge. Blair is told that the regimental officers are charged not only with preserving the rolls to enable muster-out (and final payment), but with controlling their men. Blair should report "neglectful officers" for discipline.[67]

31: The Cleveland Convention. An estimated 156 to 158 delegates are present, with a total attendance estimated at 350 to 400 Radicals assembled in Cleveland to adopt a party platform and make nominations for president and vice president. General John Cochrane[68] presides. Michigander C. C. Foote★ serves as one of nineteen vice presidents and serves on the resolutions committee; including Foote, twelve Michiganders serve as delegates. Thirteen resolutions are adopted, including that the rebellion "must be suppressed by force of arms and without compromise"; that the war has doomed slavery and "the Federal Constitution should be amended to prohibit its re-establishment, and to secure to all men absolute equality before the law"; and to amend the Constitution to provide direct election for vice presidents. The last two resolutions are the most controversial: control of reconstruction belongs to Congress (as opposed to the executive branch), and rebel lands should be confiscated and given to "soldiers and actual settlers [i.e., freed persons] as a

measure of justice." The Convention nominates John C. Fremont for president and General John Cochrane for vice president. The *Lansing State Republican* restates the conventioneers' hope: Fremont will either be embraced by the Republican National Convention in Baltimore (see June 7–8), or with a split electoral college, the House of Representatives would decide the election.[69] (See September 3.)

The *Free Press* ties Fremont's Radical candidacy to Lincoln: "There are none who will believe that the administration is conservative because the radicals say so—it is as destructively radical as the radicals themselves." But many of Michigan's Republican newspapers oppose Fremont's candidacy, believing it will divide the Republican vote and give victory to George B. McClellan or any other nominated Democrat. The *Jackson Citizen*, while sympathetic to many of the Convention's goals, criticizes Fremont for involving himself in politics and declares that "These nominations are not made in earnest." The *Hillsdale Standard* accuses Fremont of acting on intense personal animus against Lincoln, and compares the vindictiveness of his criticism with that of Peace Democrat Vallandigham. The *Advertiser and Tribune* declares that the Convention "does not bear any formidable proportions" and has attracted "the disaffected, the impracticable and the restless ambitious who are always ready to figure in any new movement."[70]

June

1–3: Battles of Cold Harbor. In cavalry action connected with the battles, the First Michigan Cavalry ranks second among horse troopers in losses (25).[71]

1: Five students from the University of Michigan's medical department arrive in Washington, are accepted by the Army as volunteer dressers, and are dispatched to City Point, Virginia, hospitals. Meanwhile, in the western theater, Stanton authorizes Dr. Robert C. Wood[72] to transfer home or to Northern hospitals individual cases of sick or wounded Michiganders if, after the Michigan state agent applies, a surgeon will certify that the patient cannot return to duty in six weeks. Michigan state agent in Louisville J. B. Gilman's mission now expands. (See Military Affairs—1864.) Finally, at the Battle of Bethesda Church, Virginia, the Twenty-Seventh Michigan is fourth ranked in casualties (74).[73]

7: The National Union (Republican) Convention. The convention, ex Ohio governor William Dennison president, convenes in Baltimore's Front Street Theater. National party executive committee member Blair leads sixteen Michigan delegates. Besides Blair, Michigan's other at-large delegates are Marsh Giddings*, Neil Gray*, and Charles W. Clisbee*; Michigan will have sixteen votes.

The Convention unanimously adopts eleven resolutions, including a pledge to win the war by military force and to bring "the punishment due to . . . Rebels and traitors arrayed against" government; a demand for "unconditional surrender"; and a declaration that "as Slavery was the cause, and now constitutes the strength, of this Rebellion," Republicans pledge to amend the Constitution "as shall terminate and forever prohibit the existence of Slavery" anywhere within U.S. jurisdiction. [*The reporter notes that here, "Tremendous applause, the delegates rising and waving their hats."*] There is an endorsement of Lincoln's presidency; thanks are offered to the Union military; a declaration states that "foreign immigration . . . should be fostered and encouraged"; and finally, French imperial schemes in Mexico are denounced.[74]

8: The National Union (Republican) Convention. Balloting takes place for president, and Lincoln is elected on the first ballot (484 to 22) with all Michiganders in support. The vote for vice president proceeds differently. The two principal candidates, current vice president Hannibal Hamlin and former Democrat Andrew Johnson of Tennessee, divide the convention, with Michigan casting its sixteen votes for Hamlin. Johnson prevails on the second ballot, however, with all Michiganders in support, although Michigan is the last state to endorse Johnson. The Republican National Committee is also reconstituted, with Marsh Giddings taking Austin Blair's seat.[75] (See July 7.)

Austin Blair, whose Radicalism had never abated, has mixed feelings about supporting Lincoln. Over the difficult summer ahead, Blair might regret supporting nominee Lincoln, but as a practical politician, he also believes that "any attempt now to substitute another candidate would result in disaster," a reference to other, more radical names floated to replace Lincoln. He wrote to Senator Chandler that "we shall forget all cause of discontent and shutting

our eyes to all faults" and advised, "Go in for Abraham with might & main."[76]

9: Although Michigan's federal draft begins on the tenth, it commences in the Third District on this day. Jackson County's deficiency is 39 men; 62 names are drawn. Drawings from other district counties are Eaton, 5; Ingham, 18; Calhoun, 32; and Washtenaw, 5. Many of the district's soldier-residents have already become Veteran Volunteers: 37 men from Jackson City's four wards and nineteen other towns, totaling 127 men.[77]

10: A draft begins in Michigan to fill deficiencies under the calls of October 17, 1863, and February 1 and March 14, 1864. (See Military Affairs—1864.) Separately, in Mississippi, the Battle of Brice Crossroads is fought.[78]

11: Colonel Joseph R. Smith resigns as the U.S. chief mustering and disbursing officer for Michigan.[79] Meanwhile, in Ontario, Canada, Clement Vallandigham meets with Confederate secret service chief Jacob Thompson. (See SAW.5.272.) Finally, in action at Trevilian Station, Virginia, the First Michigan Cavalry posts losses of 99, including 64 missing.[80]

14–15: Tonight, Vallandigham crosses the Detroit River and returns to the United States. In Hamilton County, Ohio, he appears at a district Democratic Party convention. He is chosen as a district delegate to attend the national convention in Chicago. (See SAW.5.273–274.) In Virginia, the Army of the Potomac crosses the James River.[81]

14: Congress equalizes black and white soldiers' pay.

15: In Detroit's City Hall, the **Democratic State Convention** meets to choose delegates for the Democratic National Convention in Chicago. Four at-large delegates are elected: John S. Barry, A. C. Baldwin, Alpheus Felch, and Nathan Barlow; also chosen are twelve district delegates and sixteen alternates. A resolution is adopted declaring that Michigan's Democratic Party "stands now, as ever heretofore, upon the platform of the Union, the Constitution and the supremacy of the laws."[82] (See August 29.)

Meanwhile, Congress passes Chapter 124, "An act making Appropriations for the Support of the Army for the Year ending the thirtieth of June, eighteen hundred and sixty-five, and for other purposes." It provides that African Americans enlisted and mustered under the call of October 17, 1863, shall receive the same bounty as whites, and that those men who were free on April 19, 1861, and serve in uniform will receive the same pay, bounty, and clothing allowances as whites.[83]

17–18: Petersburg is unsuccessfully attacked. Federals entrench for a siege. Five Michigan infantry regiments place in the top twenty-three in losses: the second-ranked Second (204 men), sixth-ranked Twenty-Seventh (128), tenth-ranked First Michigan Sharpshooters (156), seventeenth-ranked Fifth Michigan (92), and the twentieth-ranked Twentieth Michigan (69).[84]

19: USS *Kearsarge* sinks the CSS *Alabama* off the French coast.

20: At Noonday Creek, Georgia, the Fourth Michigan Cavalry loses forty-seven men in action.[85]

25: War Department Circular No. 24 reminds Boards of Enrollment that "their duties in regard to the correction of enrollments do not cease with its revision, as recently completed or now in progress. On the contrary, the revision and correction of these lists is a continuous duty to which the labors of all boards must be directed." It also includes an invitation to local communities to inspect enrollment lists and recommend changes.[86]

26: PMG Fry distributes Circular No. 25, which declares that "Persons not fit for military duty and not liable to draft from age or other causes" may be "personally represented in the Army." This creates the "Representative Recruit" (a voluntary form of substitution for those exempt from service). By war's end, 1,292 representative recruits enlist nationwide; Michigan's total is 15.[87]

27: In Georgia, the Battle of Kennesaw Mountain is fought.

30: This month, the Soldiers' Home in Detroit admitted 682 soldiers, served 7,414 meals, and provided 2,054 lodgings.[88]

July

2: In Washington, a showdown between moderate and Radical Republicans occurs over the Wade-Davis Bill, which the Senate passes, 18 to14. Michigan's Jacob A. Howard is absent, but Zachariah Chandler votes to support the bill.

Confederates reportedly move north in the Shenandoah Valley.[89]

3: Confederates occupy Martinsburg—about twenty-two airline miles from the Pennsylvania state line.

4: Congress passes Chapter 237, "An act further to regulate and provide for the enrolling and calling out the national forces and for other purposes." Its provisions include presidential authority to call men for one, two, or three years, with scaled bounties; repeal of the commutation clause; authority for states to send agents to recruit in "any of the former states declared to be in rebellion," except for Arkansas, Tennessee, and Louisiana. These recruits can be credited to the states under any call of the president.[90] (See July 21; regarding African Americans, see Selected Summaries.)

Meanwhile, Lincoln fails to sign the Wade-Davis Bill, thus pocket-vetoing the measure and for now ending Radical Reconstruction in favor of his own "10 Percent" plan.[91]

6: In retaliation for General David Hunter's depredations in the Shenandoah Valley, Confederate general John McCausland occupies Hagerstown and ransoms it for $20,000.[92]

Meanwhile, at City Point, Michigan Soldiers' Relief Agent Julia Wheelock is hospitalized with fever; she will be transferred to Washington for another five weeks of recovery.[93]

7: The **Republican State Convention** meets in Detroit and nominates Henry M. Crapo for governor. "I most fervently hope and fondly trust that our Constitution will be so amended as that slavery shall be blotted from the Republic forever," Crapo declares to cheering delegates. Resolutions adopted include calls for unconditional surrender and the "utter annihilation of this nefarious Rebellion"; and an affirmation of the June 7 national conventional resolutions, including a constitutional amendment to abolish slavery, an endorsement of black troops, an expression of gratitude to soldiers, and a denunciation of European attempts to establish a Mexican monarchy. It affirms the choice of Abraham Lincoln and Andrew Johnson, applauds Soldiers' Aid Societies and Christian and Sanitary Commissions, and endorses the Blair administration.[94]

At Petersburg, Virginia, the Seventieth New York, including Company C's Michiganders, musters out of service. At expiry, Company C's Michigan enrollment was 112, including 14 KIA, 3 DOW, 6 DOD, and 27 DFD.[95]

9: Battle of the Monocacy. Separately, the War Department issues GO No. 227 to facilitate recruiting in states formerly in rebellion.[96]

11: Confederate raiders menace Washington. They leave the next day.

14: In Mississippi, the Battle of Tupelo is fought.

18: Lincoln calls for 500,000 men and specifies that volunteers will be accepted for one-, two-, or three-year terms. A draft to cure any deficiency will be held on September 5. (See July 21.)[97]

19: The War Department notifies AAPMG Hill that under the previous day's call, Michigan's quota is 18,282 men. [NB: *Through credits, this quota will be reduced to 12,098 men.*][98]

20: In Georgia, the Battle of Peachtree Creek is fought.

21: Blair issues a proclamation in connection with Lincoln's July 18 call. He defends the new call ("eminently proper and necessary for the public service"), notes the rebellion's status ("it approaches final overthrow"), cites Southern war atrocities, and declares that while the quota is for 18,282 men, only "a little over 12,000" must still be recruited.

Although Chapter 237 allows recruiting in formerly insurgent states, Blair predicts this that few recruits will be raised under this program. Blair will consider appointing recruiting agents but towns must fund them, as "the State has no funds appropriated by law for this purpose." Regarding Chapter 237 recruits, Blair also declares that "No State bounty can be paid [because] the appropriation made for that purpose is exhausted." Blair notes progress: "Our troops are now led by tried and victorious Generals, leaving nothing to be desired in that direction. Conquering Union armies [are] in the very midst of the Confederacy, progressing steadily towards the final victory."[99]

22: In Georgia, the Battle of Atlanta is fought.

23: Blair informs Stanton that "I deem it necessary under the present call for troops from this State to raise and organize six or more regiments of infantry, and I hope you will give me the authority." Blair requests an answer "as soon as possible." (See July 26.)[100]

24: In Virginia, the Second Battle of Kernstown is fought.

26: PMG Fry approves Blair's July 23 request for six infantry regiments. In a second wire, Fry expands this authority to twenty infantry regiments: "The term of service will be for either one, two, or three years, as recruits may elect," the PMG instructs. The units must be mustered into U.S. service before September 5 to be credited against Michigan's quota; incomplete units will be consolidated. Authorization is given to reorganize the men of the Fourth Michigan Infantry into a reorganized, new Fourth; their terms are expiring and the unit will not reorganize as Veteran Volunteers. The new Fourth represents the First Congressional District, and is the first of Blair's proposed six regiments.[101]

28: In Georgia, the Battle of Ezra Church is fought.

29: Authorization is issued to reorganize the Third Michigan Regiment representing the Fourth Congressional District, and the new Thirty-First Michigan commanded by Congressman John F. Driggs, which represents the Sixth Congressional District; these are the second and third of the proposed six regiments. (The Thirty-First will later be redesignated the Twenty-Ninth, with which it consolidates.)[102]

30: Confederates enter Chambersburg, Pennsylvania, and demand tribute; unmet, the town is burned. In Virginia, the Battle of the Crater is fought. In the charge following the explosion, among twenty-one federal regiments ranked, the Twenty-Seventh Michigan is twelfth with eighty-five casualties.[103]

August

1: The War Department's solicitor William Whiting issues an opinion endorsing the legality of the "years of service" formula of quota and credit equalization.[104]

5: Battle of Mobile Bay.

Meanwhile, from Chattanooga, agent Luther B. Willard compiles a list of 186 hospitalized Michigan soldiers.[105]

6: The CSS *Tallahassee* slips through the federal blockade from Wilmington, North Carolina. (See August 26.)

9: PMG Fry informs Blair that "The authority to recruit civilized Indians for the First Michigan Sharpshooters is hereby renewed." This authority extends to recruiting two companies for the First Michigan Sharpshooters "and the one in service as requested." Meanwhile, authorization is given for the Twenty-Ninth Michigan, representing the Third Congressional District. This is the fourth unit organized under the July 18 call and will later be consolidated with the Twenty-Eighth Michigan. The training camp is established at Marshall and future Michigan congressman Edward S. Lacey* is appointed commandant.[106]

12: PMG Fry reminds Hill that except for recruiting in "states in rebellion," poaching by out-of-state recruiters is illegal and that he should "arrest recruiting officers and agents who may be found violating it."[107]

15: Authority is issued to organize the Twenty-Eighth Michigan (commanded in its Kalamazoo camp only by future congressman William B. Williams*), representing the Second District. It is the fifth unit organized under the July 18 call. This unit will later be consolidated with the Twenty-Ninth. (See October 26.)[108]

16: According to War Department intelligence, this day was designated by the subversive Order of the Sons of Liberty (or Order of American Knights) to commence military operations in Indiana, Ohio, Illinois, and Missouri to seize arsenals, assassinate federal military officers and state officials, and liberate Confederate POWs from camps across several states, including Johnson's Island. However, nothing happens. (See SAW.5.281.)

Meanwhile, from Washington, secretary H. J. Alvord of the Michigan Soldiers' Relief Association furnishes the names of Michiganders from the Second, Fifth, and Ninth Corps who are hospitalized at City Point. Alvord appeals for money, and hints at competition with other relief agencies: "Our citizens in Michigan contribute more than enough to provide amply for our soldiers, but unfortunately their contributions go into such channels that Michigan soldiers get but little benefit from them."[109]

18–19: In Virginia, the Battle of Weldon Railroad is fought.

20: Near Petersburg, Virginia, Company C, one of four Michigan companies recruited for Hiram Berdan's Sharpshooters, musters out of service. At this point, total enrollment has been 156, including 18 KIA, 5 DOW, 14 DOD, and 47 DFD.[110]

23: Seventy-nine Kalamazoo citizens sign a public petition requesting Mrs. John Potter and Miss Eliza Fisher of the Ladies' Soldiers' Aid Society of Kalamazoo to host a fair between September 20 and 23 "for the purpose of aiding the wounded and sick." The agricultural fairgrounds are proposed as the site. The Society accepts and declares that net proceeds will be equally distributed to the Michigan Soldiers' Relief

Society, the United States Christian Commission, and itself. The appeal is statewide: "We ask the people of Michigan, men and women, old and young, to bring or send to us, money or such articles of value as can be spared for this, a great national purpose." This event will be wartime Michigan's largest Sanitary Fair.[111]

24: Authority is issued to organize the Thirtieth Michigan [first version], representing the Fifth Congressional District. This is the sixth and last unit authorized under the July 18 call. Seven companies of this unit will later be distributed to Michigan's Third and Fourth Regiments.[112]

25: In Virginia, the Battle of Ream's Station is fought.

26: The CSS *Tallahassee* returns safely to Wilmington, North Carolina, after inflicting severe damage on East Coast shipping during the past month: twenty-six ships sunk or burned and seven captured.[113]

27: General Samuel P. Heintzelman, Northern Department commander, issues GO No. 53, which declares that "During the ensuing sixty days no firearms, powder or ammunition of any kind will be received, transported or delivered by any Railroad, Express or other forwarding company" within Ohio, Indiana, Illinois, and Michigan without a permit from his headquarters, or (for Michigan), issued by AAPMG Hill. "Dealers in these articles, or others having them in possession, will in no event be permitted to sell or deliver them during that time." All military commanders and PMs will help enforce this order, seizing "such articles as may be clandestinely sold, shipped or delivered, in evasion of it." GO No. 53 reflects Washington's fear of a subversive group insurgency.

29: Democratic National Convention, day 1. The Democratic National Convention convenes in Chicago's Amphitheater, presided over by New York's Governor Horatio Seymour. John F. Barry (who serves as one of twenty-three vice presidents) leads Michigan's delegation, which consists of four at-large delegates (A. C. Baldwin, Alpheus Felch, and Nathan Barlow), twelve district delegates, and a host of alternates. Altogether, Michigan will have eight votes.[114]

30: Democratic National Convention, day 2. This afternoon, six resolutions are adopted, including a pledge of fealty to the Constitution; a denunciation of federal military intervention in Kentucky, Maryland,

Delaware,[115] and Missouri; a declaration that the Democratic Party's object "is to preserve the Federal Union and rights of the States unimpaired," followed by a denunciation of Lincoln's suspension of habeas corpus, his violation of freedom of speech and press, and his violation of "the right of the people to bear arms in their defence." These transgressions are said to have been "calculated to prevent a restoration of the Union" and to defeat the idea that government derives its powers from the governed.

But the resolution that will prove the most controversial is the second, drafted by Vallandigham and representing the party's peace wing. It declares that "after four years of failure to restore the Union by the experiment of war . . . justice, humanity, liberty and the public welfare demand that immediate efforts be made for a cessation of hostilities with a view to an ultimate convention of the States [NB: *refers either to a convention called under Article V of the U.S. Constitution, or a convention calling for an Article V convention*], or other peaceable means, to the end that at the earliest practical moment, peace may be restored on the basis of the Federal Union of the States." In its call for an armistice and a convention of states, this resolution abandons unconditional surrender and the restoration of the Union as conditions of peace. (See September 8.) After debate, the resolutions are overwhelming approved viva voce.

The Convention next moves to nominations. The names of George B. McClellan and several others are put forward. But it is McClellan's nomination that leads to brief but contentious debate. Peace Democrat Benjamin G. Harris puts into the record McClellan's role in the arrest of Maryland legislators, while Alexander Long notes that McClellan was Lincoln's instrument in oppression.[116]

Back in Michigan, PMG Fry wires Hill, "Keep volunteering up as much as possible after the 5th of September, and let it be known that volunteers will be counted on the quotas of the present call up to the last practicable moment." Hill asks Fry if the draft might be postponed. (See September 6.)[117]

31: Democratic National Convention, day 3. George B. McClellan is nominated on the first ballot: with 151 votes needed to win, McClellan receives 202.5, against Connecticut Thomas H. Seymour's[118] 28.5 votes. Michigan casts all eight votes for McClellan.

On the first ballot, Kentucky's James Guthrie leads with 65.5 votes, including 1.5 votes from Michigan; in second place is Ohio Peace Democrat George H. Pendleton, who garners 6.5 Michigan votes. After the vote, several states switch votes to Pendleton, who is then nominated by acclamation. Michigan Democrats are reportedly in the prowar faction, favoring McClellan (believed to be prowar) but accepting Pendleton as a compromise with the peace faction.[119]

As the Democratic Convention ends, the *Advertiser and Tribune* begins a campaign against the "'Order of American Knights,' clearly showing the existence in our midst [of] this traitorous order, which can have no other object in view than the overthrow of the Government of the United States, and the inauguration of a reign of anarchy"; early Democratic victims of this campaign are Detroit Common Council president S. Dow Ellwood and one John T. Parker of Morenci. Ellwood is accused of possessing damning documents about the Order, while three dozen Sharps revolvers were seized en route to Parker.[120] (See October 8.)

Meanwhile, in Georgia, the Battle of Jonesborough begins. The Tenth Michigan is third ranked in casualties with ninety-six losses.[121]

September

1: The **Democratic State Convention** convenes in Detroit to ratify the results of the previous day's National Convention. Presidential nominee George B. McClellan speaks briefly, and the convention nominates former lieutenant governor (and late colonel of the Eighth Michigan) William M. Fenton for governor and Edwin H. Lothrop* for lieutenant governor. The principal resolution passed reaffirms the resolutions adopted by the previous day's Democratic National Convention at Chicago. The meeting closes "with three rousing cheers for Gen. McClellan." But there are no cheers from the *Advertiser and Tribune*, which asks about McClellan, "If he is a failure as a military man, can he succeed as statesman?"[122]

2: Sherman occupies Atlanta, Georgia. In Detroit, the first reports are published on the 3rd, which occasions public celebrations. The *Hillsdale Standard* will declare, "Victory upon Victory," noting first Farragut's closure of Mobile Bay and now Sherman's news. The *Ypsilanti Commercial* is more analytical.

"Atlanta is the territorial key of the Confederacy"; "Its capture is the forerunner of the dismemberment of the rebellion, and the hapless isolation of its component states." But war and politics are inseparable, and in a nearby announcement, the sheet announces a planned rally for September 15 under the headlines, "Liberty & Union! Lincoln and Johnson!! Grant, Sherman and Farragut!!! Rally Round the Flag!" The fiercely Democratic *Free Press* shares the Republicans' joy, but also subtly injects politics. It declares that "when Georgia asks for peace we hope that the Administration will be ready to grant it upon such terms as will make every Southern State eager to follow in her footsteps."[123]

3: Zachariah Chandler meets with Lincoln to propose a deal to mollify the Radical faction: conservative Montgomery Blair departs the cabinet in exchange for the support of Ohio's Senator Benjamin Wade and the crucial-to-win-Ohio Western Reserve constituency that he represents. (See September 21.)[124]

4: John Hunt Morgan is killed in Greenville, Tennessee.[125]

5: The draft scheduled for this day is postponed. See September 19. Meanwhile, Austin Blair is in Washington.[126]

6: Unaware of the previous day's delay, PMG Fry informs Hill that "No postponement of the draft is authorized," but that "volunteers will be accepted up until the latest possible moment." He offers Hill some advice: "We must now be raising men rapidly in every district, either by volunteering or drafting, and it may be well for you to make your arrangements to draft first in those districts and sub-districts which are not trying to fill their quotas, and thus give those who are raising volunteers as much time as possible."[127]

8: McClellan formally accepts the Democratic Party nomination for president, but in a move that stuns Peace Democrats, rejects Vallandigham's peace plank. (See August 30.) "The re-establishment of the Union in all its integrity is, and must continue to be, the indispensible condition for any settlement," he declares. And with undoubted sincere emotion, he adds, "I could not look in the face of my gallant comrades of the army and navy who survived so many bloody battles, and tell them that their labors and the sacrifices of so many of our slain and wounded brethren had been in vain; that we had abandoned

that Union for which we have so often periled our lives." For Michigan's Republican press, McClellan's rejection of the peace plank complicates efforts to tie him to the Democrat's peace wing. But the *Advertiser and Tribune* declares that McClellan's rejection is a only feint, "simply another attempt to befog the People and obscure the real purposes of the Democratic leaders, which is a disgraceful surrender of the National Cause. If Gen. McClellan is elected he will execute it."

Meanwhile, Ypsilanti African Americans gather in Follett Hall to celebrate Maryland's abolition of slavery.[128]

9: The *Free Press* publishes McClellan's full acceptance letter but elides the fissure between its party's peace and war factions. McClellan is pledged by the party platform to see "that at the earliest practical moment peace may be restored on the basis of the Federal Union of the States." Ann Arbor's *Michigan State Argus* understands McClellan's acceptance as that of an honest man: "Here is no double dealing, no ambiguous phrases to be construed both ways. . . . What patriot does not prefer the election of a man who speaks thus frankly, nobly, and with such dignity, in accepting so responsible a position?"[129]

But Republican sheets are not shy in exploiting these contradictions. The *Hillsdale Standard* declares that "it is evident that McClellan, wishes to be a consistant [sic] war man before election; and use the platform after election" to achieve the ends of Copperheads. The *Lansing State Republican* believes that by shifting to a war platform, McClellan will increase his vote; however it also notes that "Here, then, we have literally a house divided against itself; and we have high authority that such a house cannot stand long."[130]

12: PMG Fry orders Hill to "Commence the draft on Monday, the 19th instant, beginning as far as practicable in those deficient districts and sub-districts where there is the least volunteering going on. The quota of every sub-district under the present call must be filled and the draft will be continued until it is so filled by volunteering or drafting."[131]

13: Fry wires Hill with instructions that men, once drafted, cannot volunteer. (See the entry for the 14th.)[132]

Meanwhile, Stanton alerts Heintzelman that the draft is set to begin on September 19 in the Northern

Department. "You will please hold yourself in readiness to render any aid to the drafting officers that may be needed."[133]

14: Blair asks Stanton to reconsider the August 30 and September 13 orders prohibiting draftees from volunteering. "I recommend that they be allowed to volunteer for three years in the new regiments now organizing at any time before they are accepted under the draft, and that they receive the Government bounties." Blair argues that this revision "will insure the filling of the new regiments and give to the Government three[-year] in place of one[-]year men"; it would be "an act of justice to drafted men, and to a great extent will do away with much of the odium of the draft, which is important in this political crisis." Blair was in Washington the previous week and he reminds Stanton that he had agreed with this position. Stanton refers Blair's plea to Fry. (See next day's entry.)[134]

Meanwhile, Fry notifies mustering officers throughout the loyal states: VRC reenlistments will not be credited on the quota "of any State, district, or sub-district."[135]

15: PMG Fry notifies Blair that "The draft is ordered to commence in Michigan on Monday, the 19th of September." Fry also declines the previous day's request from Blair, arguing that allowing draftees to volunteer "would not be in accordance with law and regulations to recognize an enlistment on the part of a man after he is legally drafted for service, nor would it be legal or proper to allow him U.S. bounty." Fry reasons that if men could volunteer after being drafted, they would be less likely to volunteer before, "and the recruiting service would suffer." He repeats the rule that drafted men will be assigned to old regiments and not new ones: "This is the established law of the Department."[136]

17: Tonight, Canadian-based Confederate secret service agent Godfrey J. Hyams* clandestinely meets with AAPMG Hill and discloses a familiar plot: on September 19 from Detroit and Windsor, Ontario, Confederate agents led by John Yates Beall* will board the small passenger steamer *Philo Parsons*; once on Lake Erie, they will hijack the ship and then steam for Sandusky, Ohio, and Johnson's Island, where an estimated 3,000 Confederate-officer POWs are held. Next, while the *Philo Parsons* is underway, Confederate agent (and unremediated alcoholic) Charles H. Cole[137] will either have bribed the crew of the fifteen-gun USS *Michigan* (charged with defending Johnson's Island), or failing that, drug their officers at a party that he will sponsor. By the time the *Philo Parsons* arrives, they will be too intoxicated to resist. Once in possession of the *Michigan*, Confederates "would have control of the lakes for a couple of months, and would lay contributions on all lake cities." Hill believes Hyams.

Hill immediately wires the USS *Michigan*'s Captain John C. Carter. "It is reported to me that some of the officers and men of your steamer have been tampered with, and that a party of rebel refugees leave Windsor to-morrow with the expectation of getting possession of your steamer." (See September 18 and 19.)[138]

18: Carter acts on Hill's wire, but believes in his crew's loyalty. "Thanks for your dispatch. All ready. Cannot be true in relation to the officers or men." Meanwhile, this morning in Detroit, Bennett G. Burley* (in fact, an officer in the Confederate Navy) boards the *Philo Parsons* with a question for co-owner Walter O. Ashley*: en route to Sandusky, would he be willing to stop in Sandwich, Canada, to pick up a group of his friends? Ashley agrees.

On this night, Hyams again crosses the Detroit River to meet with Hill. New details emerge: Hyams believes that the *Philo Parsons*'s captain has been bribed, as has a USS *Michigan* officer named Eddy.[139]

19–20: The draft for deficiencies under the July 18 and earlier calls begins in Michigan. (See Military Affairs—1864 for annual totals.)[140]

19: At 6:00 a.m., Hill visits the *Philo Parsons* and is puzzled. "She was too small to be of any danger if taken by the persons, and after mature consideration I came to the conclusion that it would be better to let the steamer go, and place Captain Carter on his guard"; he now wires the captain with more specifics. "It is said that the parties will embark to-day at Malden [Canada] on board the Philo Parsons, and will seize either that steamer or another running from Kelley's Island," adding that he has been "assured" that the USS *Michigan*'s "officers and men have been bought by a man named [Charles H.] Cole." Their plan is this: "A few men to be introduced on board under the guise of friends of officers. An officer named Eddy to be drugged." Hill regards the matter as "serious." Carter replies with good news: "I have Cole, and fair prospect of bagging the party."

(In custody, Cole confesses, and at least six other men and a woman will also be arrested. See September 21.)[141]

Meanwhile, at 8:00 a.m. the *Philo Parsons* leaves Detroit with Burley and some forty passengers. The ship stops in Sandwich, Canada, and picks up three men, one of whom is mission leader Beall. Another stop is made at Amherstburg, Canada, and a group of "sixteen to twenty" men board. About 4:00 p.m., shortly after departing from Kelley's Island, Ohio, but before arriving at Sandusky, the Confederates, wielding revolvers and edged weapons, bloodlessly take control of the ship. They rob the captain, dump the cargo, and believing that the USS *Michigan* is now under Confederate control, slow down until nightfall—the time when Cole, presumably controlling the warship, would signal Beall. However, merely slowing down would still have the *Parsons* arrive too early, and the Confederates dock at Ohio's Middle Bass Island, some seven miles northwest of Kelley's Island. While at Middle Bass, the Confederates debark the civilians (securing a dubious promise that they will not communicate with authorities for twenty-four hours), load wood, and also hijack the *Island Queen*, a smaller passenger steamer, which is taken out and scuttled. (Confederates assume control only after a half-hour's fistfight with twenty-six federal soldiers aboard.)

As the *Philo Parsons* steams from Middle Bass, Ashley breaks his word and sails to Put-in-Bay, Ohio, where he contacts local militia led by John Brown, Jr., namesake of "Osawatomie" Brown; the men sail to Sandusky to alert the USS *Michigan*.

After nightfall the *Philo Parsons* finally arrives near Sandusky Harbor with the USS *Michigan* in view. Its Confederate crew awaits the prearranged signal, but none appears. After some hours, the Confederate raiders vote that the mission be aborted and that the *Parsons* return to Canada. At 4:00 a.m., it enters the Detroit River (Beall raises a Confederate flag) and drops the hijacked crew at Fighting Island, Canada. The *Parsons* is then scuttled and the Confederates, after destroying the ship's contents, go overboard. (For the Sandusky defendants, see *SAW*.5.284; for Michigan repercussions, see December 17.)[142]

Separately, in Virginia, the Third Battle of Winchester (Opequon) is fought. Among cavalry regiments engaged, the First and Fifth Michigan are first and second in losses, with casualties of thirty-nine and twenty-four, respectively.[143]

20: In Kalamazoo, the Michigan State Sanitary Fair opens on the state agricultural fairgrounds. (See September 23.) Separately, Pennsylvania governor Curtin poses to Stanton questions about soldiers voting in the field. (See September 30.)[144]

21: Zachariah Chandler's negotiations succeed: Fremont withdraws his candidacy and Lincoln unifies with his Radical faction: Montgomery Blair departs Lincoln's cabinet. The Lincoln-Johnson ticket is now the sole contender for Republican votes in Michigan and the nation. Polish Count Adam Gurowski, a well-informed State Department translator, notes, "The victory was exclusively won by Senator Chandler. He fought single-handed and earned the country's gratitude."[145]

22: In Kalamazoo, the Sanitary Fair has drawn an estimated "twenty-two or twenty-three thousand" people. The Fair's inauguration is on this day. The featured speakers are James B. Crippen* of Coldwater and Governor Blair. Its most compelling exhibit is the "Sanitary Hall," which displays the "torn and battle-scarred banners" carried by Michigan regiments and since replaced.[146] (See September 23.)

Separately, in Indianapolis, a federal military commission convenes to try Indianan Harrison H. Dodd and others for treason, claiming they were connected to the Sons of Liberty, the Order of the American Knights, or both. The charges include conspiracy against the USG, plots to seize the arsenals at Indianapolis and Columbus, Ohio, and release Confederate POWs at Camp Douglas (Illinois), Camp Morton (Indiana), Camp Chase (Ohio), and Johnson's Island.[147]

Finally, in Virginia, the Battle of Fisher's Hill is fought.

23: The Kalamazoo State Sanitary Fair closes. Gross revenues were $12,764.80, including $1,213.15 in ticket sales and $11,097.40 from the sales of donated goods. After expenses, sponsors distributed $2,900 each to the United States Christian Commission, Detroit's Michigan Soldiers' Relief Committee, and its sponsor, the Kalamazoo Ladies' Aid Society. Another $600 was sent to the Michigan Soldiers' Relief Association of Washington.[148]

27: Lieutenant General Ulysses S. Grant proposes rules for soldier voting.[149]

28: PMG Fry wires Hill to "Have every possible effort made to arrest promptly drafted men who fail to report as required"; he concludes with a question: "Are my orders to have such numbers of drafted men notified as will secure an examination by each board [of enrollment] of 120 men a day being [carried] out in all your districts? Answer."[150]

29: In Virginia, the Battle of Chaffin's Farm is fought.

30–October 1: The Battle of Peebles' Farm is fought.

30: Stanton forwards Blair Grant's answer to Curtin's questions about election procedures in the field: "A limited number [of election agents] accredited by State authorities or State committees will be allowed to go to each army." Grant suggests one agent for each army, which Stanton believes "is too small a number," and has so advised Grant. (See October 1.)[151]

Meanwhile, in Lansing Republican candidate for governor Henry Crapo speaks to a "Large and Enthusiastic Meeting." It is one of at least thirty-four speeches he will make across Michigan between September and November. This evening, he appeals to Union men of any party, defends Lincoln's initial response to secession, and charges Democrats with being a party of aristocrats, identical in belief with John C. Calhoun "and of slaveholders generally"; he asks for a Union majority "which should carry with them a moral power sufficient to sink the rebellion, and its cause, and its northern allies and supporters, beyond all hopes of resurrection." Crapo does not discuss Michigan issues.[152]

At Poplar Spring Church, Virginia, the Sixteenth Michigan loses forty-eight men. Separately, in Sturgis, the Eleventh Michigan musters out of service. However, Veteran Volunteers and new recruits will reorganize a "new" Eleventh Michigan.[153] (See March 18, 1865.)

October

1: General Joseph Hooker replaces Samuel Heintzelman as Northern Department commander. He will remain until the war's end.[154]

Separately, Grant clarifies his thinking on state election agents in the army. He had given Stanton only "general views" on limiting state election agents entering the army, but now declares that "Whatever orders you [Stanton] make on the subject will be cheerfully carried out." The War Department issues GO No. 265 regulating soldier voting.[155]

3: In Saginaw, the "new" Twenty-Ninth Michigan mustered into to U.S. service with 860 men; officers and recruits are drawn from Saginaw City, Vassar, Bay City, East Saginaw, Owosso, St. Charles, Flint, Burton, Ypsilanti, and Marquette. The unit will deploy west. By war's end, total enrollment will be 1,058, including 2 KIA, 4 DOW, 39 DOD, and 39 DFD.[156] (See September 6, 1865.)

4–7: In Syracuse, New York, a meeting of the National Convention of Colored Men adopts a constitution for the National Equal Rights League, which is dedicated to attaining black suffrage. It provides specifically that "Persons in the different States friendly to the purposes of this League may form State Leagues auxiliary to this, with such subordinate organizations as they may deep proper." It is chaired by Frederick Douglass, and four Michigan delegates are present: H. P. Harris and Henry F. Butler of Adrian and John D. Richards* and George H. Parker of Detroit.[157]

5: The Battle of Allatoona is fought in Georgia.

7: A U.S. naval raiding party captures the CSS *Florida* while it is docked in Bahia, Brazil. Separately, Harrison H. Dodd escapes custody.[158]

8: US JAG Holt reports on subversive organizations, including the Order of the Sons of Liberty ("OSL"), Knights of the Golden Circle, and the Order of American Knights. He locates one or more of these in Indiana, Illinois, Ohio, Kentucky, Missouri, Michigan, and New York. Holt estimates that the OSL numbers about 500,000 nationally; he also provides estimates by state: Indiana (75,000–125,000), Illinois (100,000–140,000), Ohio (80,000–108,000), Kentucky (40,000–70,000), and Missouri (20,000–40,000). Michigan and New York are each thought to host some 20,000 members. Holt believes that the OSL has eleven objectives: aiding and protecting federal deserters; discouraging enlistments and resisting the draft; circulating treasonable publications; communicating illicitly with and providing intelligence to the enemy; aiding and assisting with enemy recruiting within federal lines; providing the enemy with military supplies; aiding enemy raids and invasions; destroying government property; destroying private property and persecuting loyal citizens; committing assassination and murder; and finally, establishing a Northwestern Confederacy.[159]

Holt's report quickly reaches Michigan and initiates a newspaper dispute between Republican and Democratic sheets. Between this day and the November 8 election, Michigan's Republican press becomes aggressive on the subject of the Democratic platform. The *Hillsdale Standard*, in an editorial titled "Treason," denounces the peace plank as providing "aid and comfort" to the enemy; it singles out Michigan Democrats Levi Bishop and David Noble* as "traitors" who "have the brazen impudence to ask the loyal people of Hillsdale county to vote for them."

But the *Free Press* wonders. After noting Holt's allegation of 20,000 subversives in Michigan, it asks, "Is this true? Have we here in Michigan an association of twenty thousand men, capable of bearing arms, who are so unprincipled as to be willing not only to destroy the country, but bring fire and sword and desolation into every neighborhood?" It answers its own question—"simply ridiculous"—but notes that demonizing dissidents in this way has consequences of its own. "We reiterate and wish to impress the fact upon our opponents in Michigan, that the only danger of civil war and anarchy here . . . will come, if it comes at all, from those in power tramping upon the rights of the people of the North."[160]

12: Harper Hospital opens as a U.S. General Hospital. (See December 12, 1865.)[161]

12–13: Maryland abolishes slavery. (See SAW.4.442–443.)

14: Governor Blair instructs election commissioners appointed to administer voting by Michigan soldiers. They will first report to the state AG's office in Detroit to receive "poll books, blank forms, certificates, and instructions, together with copies of the law." Blair reminds them that while they carry preprinted ballots, "the act [No. 21, Legislative Sessions—1864] forbids them to attempt, in any manner, to influence or control the vote of any soldier." Eleven commissioners each are sent to the Army of the Potomac and the Army of the Cumberland, seven to the Army of the Gulf, eight to the Army of the Tennessee, and five to the Army of the Ohio. The commissioners are drawn from across the state, and each is assigned specific units. For example, Commissioner John C. Laird from Mendon is assigned to the Army of the Cumberland, Nineteenth Michigan, and Battery I of the First Michigan Light Artillery, now in the Third Division, Twentieth Army Corps. Commissioners are also dispatched to out-of-state units with large numbers of Michigan residents, as well as to hospitals in Annapolis, Baltimore, Philadelphia, York (Pennsylvania), St. Louis, Washington, Frederick (Maryland), and Detroit. (See November 8.)[162]

Meanwhile, in Adrian, the Michigan Fourth reorganizes and deploys to Tennessee and Texas. By its 1866 discharge, total enrollment will be 1,009, including 1 KIA, none DOW, no POWs, 119 DOD, and 51 DFD. The unit will muster out in May 1866.[163]

15: In Grand Rapids, 879 Third Michigan Infantry men reorganize as Veteran Volunteers and muster into U.S. service; it will deploy and serve west and south. By war's end, total enrollment will be 1,191, with no KIA or POW deaths, but 2 DOW, 78 DOD, and 32 DFD.[164]

16: With Lincoln and Michigan's elections looming, Blair instructs Michigan's agent Tunnicliffe to personally hand Stanton a note asking that "all Michigan soldiers, who are inmates of hospitals and camps of distribution, unfit for duty in the field [be] furloughed for twenty days each, and furnished gratuitous transportation to their houses and back, to enable [them] to vote at the ensuing Presidential election." The next day they meet and Blair's request is "promptly granted." (See November 2.)[165]

19: Confederates raid St. Albans, Vermont, and afterward escape north to British Canada. (See SAW.1.616.) Their treatment there will have certain Michigan repercussions. (See December 13.) In Virginia, the Battle of Cedar Creek is fought. The First Michigan Cavalry loses twenty-eight men.[166]

20: Michigan soldiers in Nashville hospitals who are "unfit for service" are furloughed home for the election. Meanwhile, in Detroit, the *Free Press* is deeply skeptical about the Holt Report.[167]

23: The Battle of Westport, Missouri.

25: Democratic gubernatorial candidate William Fenton speaks at an Ann Arbor barbecue and political rally, which the *Free Press* headlines as "The Largest Political Meeting Ever Held In The State." Fenton praises McClellan and implies that his removal was politically motivated: "They [i.e., Republicans] knew that if McClellan was allowed to succeed, he would be carried into the Presidential chair by a unanimous vote." He charges Lincoln with military failure, refusing three times to meet with Confederate peace commissioners, incurring "a frightful national debt, which mortgaged shops and farms, and yet his long fingers were sticking out, and his voice was stilling calling out, 'Give, give, give!'" As was the case with Crapo's September 30 speech, Fenton does not discuss Michigan issues.[168]

26: In Kalamazoo, 886 men of two understrength units, the Twenty-Eighth and the "old" Twenty-Ninth Michigan, merge into the Twenty-Eighth; officers and recruits are drawn from St. Joseph, Convis, Bellevue, Coldwater, Jackson, Allegan, Lansing, Decatur, Three Rivers, Galesburg, and Kalamo. The unit will deploy west until January 1865, when it joins Sherman's Carolina Campaign. By war's end, total enrollment will be 980, including 4 KIA, 3 DOW, 101 DOD, and 47 DFD. The unit will muster out in June, 1866.[169]

27: The CSS *Albemarle* is sunk off North Carolina's coast. Meanwhile, at Boydton Plank Road, Virginia, the Fifth Michigan is first ranked in losses with 121 casualties.[170]

31: On October 17, Major General George G. Meade submitted a list of Army of the Potomac soldiers who, after July 1, 1863, have "individually captured flags from the enemy . . . and who for their gallantry are recommended to the War Department as worthy to receive medals of honor." By October 31, Medal of Honor awardees included five Michigan men. Altogether, at least thirty-five Medals of Honor will be awarded to Michiganders.[171]

November

2: The Middle Department, Eighth Army Corps, issues GO No. 107, which issues twelve-day furloughs to Annapolis's Camp Parole's paroled men from certain states, including Michigan, who "desire to vote at the coming election." Furloughs are also granted to ambulatory patients in U.S. General Hospitals. The QM's department "will furnish free transportation to their homes and return."[172]

3: Hooker, concerned about Great Lakes security, writes Stanton, "Unless you can suggest some better mode of raising a regiment for service on the line from [the] foot of Lake Huron to [Fort] Malden, I recommend that authority be given the Governor of Michigan to raise a volunteer regiment for twelve months"; he adds that this force is "absolutely necessary and should be organized before the Detroit River is frozen over." AG Robertson believes a regiment can be recruited "at once, and that arms, accouterments, and clothing are now on hand for it. No lesser force can render the frontier of Michigan secure from the incursions of the disaffected in Canada." (See November 4.) Meanwhile, AAPMG Hill also has concerns about internal security. At around this time Hill communicates with Union Leagues in Michigan and assures himself that if trouble comes, he can mobilize 4,000 men in Detroit alone.[173]

4: Replying to Hooker, Stanton cannot "suggest some better mode" for Michigan's frontier protection; through AG Robertson, Stanton authorizes Blair to recruit a twelve-month regiment, as Hooker suggested. Hooker writes Blair, notes "the number of outlaws and sympathizers in Canada" and the "exposed condition of the frontier," and asks that only "experienced and capable officers" be commissioned; furthermore, the unit should deploy before the Detroit River freezes. Hooker then shifts subject: "In view of the election I have thought proper to order 200 drafted men here from Jackson, and shall send the little steamer in the Government employ, with a small detachment of men, up the river to-morrow as far as Port Huron, the men to go ashore and remain there until the polls are closed. These dispositions, I trust will prevent any irregularity at the polls at the points at which it is apprehended." [NB: *Hooker's concerns were mirrored across the U.S.-Canadian frontier.*][174]

From Ann Arbor, the Democratic sheet *Michigan Argus* endorses McClellan while disavowing any malice toward African Americans. "We are no admirer of the institution of slavery, no hater of the negro; and have no desire to the former perpetuated out of ill-will to the latter," it declared, adding, "We shall be glad to see its existence terminated whenever it can be done for the benefit of both master and slave"; however, it declares that "our rights as States and citizens" are held at the mercy of "Lincoln and his swarm of military subordinates,—to slaughter millions of white men, to pile up an untold debt . . . and all to confer a doubtful benefit upon the colored race." The sheet believes that "immediate, unconditional emancipation will sow the seeds of destruction in the black race."[175]

7: To deal with the frontier security issues, Blair authorizes the organization of the Thirtieth Michigan [second version], to train at Jackson. On December 10, it will move to Detroit, and on December 22, G. S. Wormer will be appointed colonel.[176] Separately, in Illinois, federal troops begin arresting suspects involved in the alleged Camp Douglas Conspiracy. It claims that the next day, Confederate agents and Northern sympathizers will raid Camp Douglas and free POWs held there.

Meanwhile, the *Free Press* makes it appeal to voters. It recognizes war weariness in many quarters and argues that "the people have had enough of Lincolnism, and that four years of civil, military and financial failure . . . is all that [the people] can or will endure." For those especially motivated by white supremacy, it adds, "The Union is the one condition of peace, says General MCCLELLAN. The negro is the only condition of peace, says ABRAHAM LINCOLN. The democratic candidate is for a white man's war, and white man's peace. The abolition candidate thrusts the white man's property, life, family and happiness into the rear rank, behind the negro. . . . All that is given to the negro in this war, is taken from the white man."[177]

8: Federal and State Elections:

For President (Eight Electoral Votes):

Abraham Lincoln/Andrew Johnson, Republican, 91,133; 55.1 percent

George B. McClellan/George Hunt Pendleton, Democrat, 74,146; 44.9 percent[178]

The soldiers' vote is 9,402 votes for Lincoln and 2,595 for McClellan. For governor, the vote is 9,612 for Republican Henry H. Crapo and 2,992 for Democrat William M. Fenton. Soldiers give Republicans a sweep of congressional offices and the state offices of lieutenant governor, secretary of state, state treasurer, auditor general, attorney general, and associate justice of the Michigan Supreme Court.[179]

For Congress (biographies of new members omitted):

First: *Fernando C. Beaman, Union, 17,906 (53.14)*; David A. Noble, Democrat, 15,790 (46.86)

Second: *Charles Upson, Union, 19,151 (60.43)*;

Nathaniel A. Balch, Democrat, 12,538 (39.57)

Third: *John W. Longyear, Union, 15,432 (54.74)*; David Johnson, Democrat, 12,758 (45.26)

Fourth: *Thomas W. Ferry, Union, 13,426 (58.94)*; Frederick Hall, Democrat, 9,355 (41.06)

Fifth: *Rowland E. Trowbridge, Union, 12,647 (51.44)*; Augustus C. Baldwin, Democrat, 11,937 (48.56)

Sixth: *John F. Driggs, Union, 12,490 (54.08)*; William Willard, Democrat, 10,604 (45.92)

Michigan's congressional delegation becomes exclusively Republican.

For Governor:

Henry Crapo, Union/Republican, 91,353, 55.2 percent

William H. Fenton, Democrat, 74,293, 44.9 percent[180]

State House

Senate: 11 Democrats, 21 Republicans

House: 27 Democrats, 73 Republicans[181]

16: Sherman begins March to the Sea

25: Confederate saboteurs attempt to set fire to New York City. (See SAW.2.270, 274.)

28: The War Department proposes to raise a new corps "to consist of not less than 20,000 infantry" of "able-bodied men who have served honorably not less than two years, and therefore not subject to draft." Two such corps will eventually be formed, the First and the Second, commanded by Major General Winfield Scott. On December 1, Circular No. 86 will set rules for enlistments and commissions for this Corps. A recruiting office is established in Jackson.

This results in two regiments known as the First and the Second Veteran Reserve Corps (VRC). Michigan sent 140 veterans to the First VRC and 172 to the Second VRC. Combined losses for the units were four DOD and twelve DFD.[182]

30: The Battle of Franklin, Tennessee.

December

5: Based on intelligence from his Canadian network, AAPMG Hill sends disturbing intelligence to David Thurston*, U.S. vice-consul general in Montreal. "I presume there is very little doubt that a great deal of trouble will be occasioned by the rebels in Canada this winter," Hill writes. "It is reported to me that the number has been largely increased of late by the disbandment in Kentucky of a rebel regiment, with directions for the officers and men to find their way to Canada." Hill has learned that when the Detroit River freezes, "a large force" divided into three units will cross the river with a mission "to plunder and destroy" Detroit. He emphasizes the major diplomatic and military consequences that might ensue. "The depredations already committed from Canada by rebels harbored there have been patiently borne by the people in the expectation that the Canadian authorities would adopt measures to prevent a recurrence of them." But if there should be a raid from Windsor, "the citizens will retaliate." Hill strongly recommends that the Canadian government "station a military force on this frontier of sufficient strength to check any outrages that the rebels may design to commit." (See December 10.)[183]

6: Lincoln delivers his annual message.

8: US QMG Montgomery Meigs issues GO No. 58, which cites reports of the "numbers of refugees lately within the limits of the British Provinces on our northern border [that] have removed with the intention of obtaining employment at the depots of military stores for the purpose of incendiarism." Depot commanders are forbidden to employ "persons who have at any time within the last six months been living in Canada as refugees from the disloyal states or as fugitives from the draft."[184]

10: Thurston forwards Seward AAPMG Hill's December 5 warnings and adds additional information. At present, there are a "great number" of rebels in Toronto, "assembled there because it is a good point from which to make their observations and attacks on any locality on the frontier of the United States." They have $3,000,000 on deposit; the money is used to provide subsistence to a pool of agents from which smaller parties are sent to raid the U.S. As an example, Thurston cites the November 25 New York City arson. Subversives begin with reconnaissance: "Parties of five or six are sent to the United States and directed to hire themselves out in different localities, in any kind of employment they can obtain, and while so employed to procure all the information of the neighborhood possible, of the people, their character, standing, and property and whether favorable or unfavorable to the Government of the United States." Orders follow, "to set fire to any property to which they can get access without being discovered; to steal,

to find out family secrets, and to do any and everything they can to injure the people and property of the loyal states." In Canada, the rebels manufacture "Every kind of instrument or invention calculated to destroy vessels, steam-boats or buildings, and carried across the border." (For example, Hill reports that bombs designed to resemble pieces of coal have been manufactured to blend with coal supplies used for steamships.) To facilitate their U.S. entry, rebel agents carry Canadian passports. Thurston also forwards Hill's December 5 letter to Canadian authorities.[185]

Meanwhile, Sherman arrives at Savannah's doorstep.

13: After raiding St. Albans (Vermont), Confederates escaped into British Canada, where they were arrested. On this day Montreal judge Charles J. Coursal claims lack of jurisdiction and releases the raiders. This decision shocks both U.S. and British Canadian opinion, embarrasses pro-Union Lord Monck, and presents a diplomatic crisis.[186] (See December 17.)

15–16: The Battle of Nashville.

17: Probably in response to cross-border raids into Michigan and Vermont, and perhaps in retaliation for Montreal judge Coursal's December 13 dismissal of charges against the St. Albans raiders, Lincoln issues an order that, except for immigrants arriving by sea, "no traveler shall be allowed to enter the United States from a foreign country without a passport."[187] (See December 21.)

19: Lincoln calls for 300,000 volunteers "to serve one, two, and three years." He seeks "to provide for casualties in the military and naval service of the United States." Deficiencies will be met by a draft, scheduled for February 15, 1865. Michigan's quota will be established at 10,026 (based on a federally conducted enrollment of 77,999), against which the state will furnish 7,842 men.[188] (See December 31.)

Separately, Fry notifies Wisconsin governor James Lewis (and Blair shortly afterward) "that all authority given to Governors of States to appoint Recruiting Agents [is] revoked" and that "The only persons authorized to enlist recruits are officers detailed on recruiting service by Special Orders from [the] War Department, and 2d Lieutenants appointed by Governors of States, and conditionally mustered into service." State agents may present recruits for enlistments but may not sign enlistment papers. (This changed the rule that had been established by GO No. 75, issued July 8, 1862.)[189]

21: DA Alfred Russell has just returned from Montreal with a mix of good and bad news for Seward. The good news is that British-Canadian public opinion, shocked by the December 13 judgment, has become favorable to the United States: "There is a total revolution of opinion in all Canada, caused by [Judge] Coursal's judgment." The Canadian government is promising to better control its previously lax passport system. But there is also bad news. Lincoln's December 17 order requiring passports from foreign nationals for U.S. entry has sparked complaints in Michigan. Thomas Swinyard*, manager of the Great Western Railway, lobbies Republicans Russell and H. H. Emmons and Democrat George V. N. Lothrop to somehow "cancel the passport system," which, if "promptly done," would support the growing "good feeling and cordiality" Russell has reported; Russell forwards this letter to Seward and adds that "I fully concur with the views of Mr. Swinyard, and so do prominent gentlemen here generally."[190] (See January 10, 1865.)

Separately, Sherman occupies Savannah, Georgia.

23: PMG Fry circulates instructions to Hill on calculating quotas, now complicated by the December 19 call that recruits for three unequal terms—one, two, or three years. Since the War Department does not credit a one-year enlistment as it does a three-year enlistment, Fry's instructions establish a formula to equalize quotas among different subdistricts (in most states, municipal entities within congressional districts) whose percentages of one-, two-, or three-year recruits will inevitably differ. Some statehouses, believing that they are in surplus, discover that under Fry's formula they no longer have credits to offset against the next call. In many states, a political firestorm ensues. (See SAW.5.335 for an example.)[191]

27: The War Department issues GO No. 305, which attempts to curtail bounty fraud, especially the influence of substitute brokers. The order requires that any bounty exceeding $20 due to a recruit be withheld and disbursed on the first regular payday after the recruit has mustered into his regiment. This measure is welcomed by the states.[192]

31: The War Department notifies Michigan that its quota under the call of December 19, revised to reflect cred-

its, totals 5,822, divided among the congressional districts as follows: First, 449; Second, 1,404; Third, 1,794; Fourth, 459; Fifth, 9; Sixth, 1,716. But unwelcome news lies ahead—see January 24 and February 4, 1865.[193]

Selected Legislation

The volunteer army of the United States is composed of the people of the United States. They have left their various occupations in civil life and taken up arms at the call of their country, not to become professional soldiers, but to defend their country and government from destruction and their homes and property from desecration and pillage. . . . If these volunteer citizen soldiers should not have a voice in the civil administration of the government for which they fight, then it would be well to inquire who is worthy of it.

—AUSTIN BLAIR, MESSAGE TO THE LEGISLATURE, JANUARY 19, 1864[194]

No. 1: An Act to provide for the preparation of the Soldiers' National Cemetery at Gettysburg, in the State of Pennsylvania.

Section 1: Appropriates $3,000 from the War Fund to pay Michigan's share for "preparing the grounds and furnishing the Soldiers' National Cemetery at Gettysburg." Approved February 3, 1864.[195]

Joint Resolution No. 2: Joint Resolution expressing confidence in the president, and nominating Abraham Lincoln for a second term.

Resolved, "That in the proclamation of amnesty recently put forth by the President of the United States, we recognize a great step towards the reconstruction of the Union upon sound and safe principles; and that in the author of that proclamation, we recognize the man who is pointed out to us as the instrument, in the hands of Providence, to conduct the nation to a happy issue out of these great trials and stupendous dangers." *Resolved*, "That in Abraham Lincoln we see a chief magistrate guided in his administration in the most trying period of our national history, by a clear head and a pure heart; and that as the Representatives of the people of Michigan, we recommend him to the nation as the people's candidate for another term, subject to the decision of the national convention." Approved February 4, 1864.[196]

No. 21: An Act to enable the qualified electors of this State, in the military service, to vote at certain elections, and to amend sections forty-five and sixty-one, of chapter six, of the compiled laws.

Section 1: "That every white male citizen or inhabitant of this State, of the age of twenty-one years, possessing the qualifications named in article seven, section one, of the constitution of the State of Michigan, in the military service of the United States or this State, in the Michigan regiments, companies or batteries, shall be entitled to vote at all of the elections authorized by law . . . and every such citizen or inhabitant shall thus be entitled . . . whether at the time of voting he shall be within the limits of this State or not."

Section 38: "This act shall continue in force during the present war, and no longer." Approved February 5, 1864. (But see January 28, 1865.)[197]

Joint Resolution No. 4: Joint Resolution relative to meetings of the enrollment boards.

Whereas, "a large number of the citizens of the State exempt from military duty under the [March 3, 1863 Enrollment Act], have been put to unnecessary expense and trouble by reason of being obliged to travel a great distance to, and sometimes compelled to remain a number of days at, the city or village in the congressional district fixed as the place for the sittings of the enrollment board"; *And Whereas,* "Our citizens might be saved much annoyance and expense if the meetings of the enrollment board, for the purpose of hearing claims for exemption, were held at the county towns of the counties in which applicants reside"; therefore, *Resolved,* "That our Senators and Representatives in Congress . . . are hereby requested to endeavor to procure an amendment to said [Enrollment Act], requiring the enrollment board to meet on certain days, at the county town of each county, for the purpose of hearing claims for exemption." Approved February 5, 1864.[198]

No. 22: An Act to provide for the interest on the war bounty loan.

Section 1: For 1864, levies on taxable property, in addition to existing taxes, the amount of $35,000; appropriates this money to pay the interest of the War Bounty Loan; if not required, the money will be used to purchase Michigan's outstanding, interest-bearing bonds. Approved February 5, 1864.[199]

No. 23: An Act authorizing the payment of bounties to volunteers in the service of the United States.

Section 1: Ratifies the prior acts of municipalities or counties in raising taxes or borrowing money (including bonds) "with the object and to the end of encouraging enlistments by paying bounties for volunteers in the military service of the United States, or with the object or end of procuring substitutes by persons who may have been or shall be drafted . . . or to encourage drafted men to enter into said service."

Section 4: Authorizes local voters to decide if bonds should be issued to finance bounties, or how much, if any repayment to make to individuals who previously advanced sums for bounties, to the maximum of $200 to each NCO, musician or private mustered into U.S. service and credited to that municipal entity's quota "on either of the last three calls of the President . . . or under the two calls of the President of the United States next preceding" January 20, 1864; authorizes tax levies to finance this debt.

Section 6: Authorizes municipal entities to levy taxes or borrow money to pay bounties not exceeding $100. Money may be borrowed for a term not to exceed five years at an interest rate of 7 percent.

Section 8: Authorizes the state to pay $100 bounty to enlisted persons joining U.S. land or naval forces who shall be credited to the Michigan's or any district therein under any call after January 1, 1864; however, this bounty will not be paid to any volunteer who was a resident of the state when enlisted but who is now credited to a different subdistrict other than where he enrolled or resided when enlisted. [NB: *This proviso was intended to reduce bounty shopping by fixing volunteers to the places where they lived or were enrolled at when enlisted.*] Approved February 5, 1864.[200]

No. 24: An Act authorizing a war bounty loan.

Section 1: Authorizes the governor and treasurer "for the purpose of paying a State bounty" to borrow $500,000 for a term not to exceed twenty-five years at an interest rate not to exceed 7 percent;

this loan is called the War Bounty Loan, and these bonds are exempt from state taxes, and proceeds are restricted to bounties.

Section 2: Denomination shall not be less than $500. Section 5: "The faith of the State is hereby pledged for the payment of principal and interest of the bonds." Approved February 5, 1864.[201]

No. 29: An Act to legalize the action of the township of York in reference to raising volunteers.

Whereas, at January 4, 1864, town meeting, a resolution was adopted by a vote of 53 to 6, appointing five named persons as "a committee to offer bounties and procure enlistments to fill the quota" of York "as they should deem best for the township."

Section 1: Legalizes these proceedings and allows York "to allow all proper charges of the aforementioned persons, for moneys paid or expenses incurred in the prosecution of their duties in enlisting men and paying bounties." Approved February 5, 1864.[202]

State Affairs

According to War Department records, under the three-year calls of October 17 (later merged into and augmented by the call of February 1, 1864), Michigan's quota was 19,553. Of this, it furnished 17,686 men with an additional 1,644 paying commutation, for a total of men and credits of 19,330.

For the 200,000-man, three-year call of March 14, 1864, Michigan's quota was 7,821, against which it furnished 7,344 men with an additional 323 paying commutation, thus totaling 7,667 credits.[203]

For the 500,000-man call of July 18, 1864, Michigan's quota was 12,098 men against which it furnished a total of 12,532, distributed as follows: 5,960 for one year, 57 for two years, 6,492 for three years, none for four years, and 23 men who paid commutation.[204]

For the 300,000-man call of December 19, 1864, Michigan's quota was 10,026, against which it furnished a total of 7,860, distributed as follows: 6,767 for one year, 41 for two years, 1,034 for three years, none for four years, and 18 who paid commutation.[205]

The War Department also furnished additional details: between October 1, 1863, and September 30, 1864, Michigan mustered in 21,838 volunteers. (This was 5.53

percent of a national total of 394,236.) The monthly detail between October 1, 1863, and December 31, was 5,731 men enlisted; in January 1864, 4,119; February, 4,076; March, 1,206; April, 840; May, 186; June, 96; July, 131; August, 2,935; and September, 1864, 4,062.[206]

In November 1864, the War Department provided more details about recruitment figures (although totals differ from those of the preceding paragraph). Between November 1, 1863, and October 31, 1864, Michigan sent 18,640 (5.1 percent of the national total of 366,459) men, who deployed for one-, two-, and three-year terms for existing or new units. Michigan was also credited with 5,197 reenlisted veterans furloughed and returned to the field, and 1,579 draftees actually forwarded to their units.[207]

For the period between November 1, 1863, and October 31, 1864, Michigan's three-year volunteers for new units were infantry (3,988 troops), cavalry (462), and artillery (126). Michigan furnished no two-year or six-month' troops to these branches.[208]

For the same period for existing units, Michigan furnished 7,662 three-year volunteers for infantry, 3,082 for cavalry, and 1,111 for artillery. For two-year terms, the state furnished 23, 14, and 3 volunteers for infantry, cavalry, and artillery, respectively. For one-year terms, Michigan sent 1,711, 885, and 288 for infantry, cavalry, and artillery, respectively. Including unassigned recruits (189) and late-reported musters (1,069), Michigan sent 20,711 men during this period.[209]

These are War Department records. The state AG, using his records and a different time period ("The Numbers Credited on each Term of Service, in each County of the State, from the 1st of January to the 31st of October, 1864"), had a different count: 20,041 volunteers; 1,956 men drafted (although it is unclear how many of these men actually served); 5,445 reenlisted Veteran Volunteers; and 430 naval enlistees. Michigan claimed 27,972 "total credits" with the following terms of service: 5,002 for one year, 39 for two years, and 22,931 for three years. Deducting 356 commuters from these credits left 27,616 credits. Michigan's aggregate count from the beginning of the war to November 1, 1864, was 81,365 men. (The total through 1863 was 53,749.) But if one added total commuters (1,982), the state's credits totaled 83,347. Commuters paid $594,600 into the U.S. Treasury.[210]

Under GO No. 191 (1863), the following units successfully reorganized as Veteran Volunteers: the First,

Second, and Third Cavalry; the First, Second, Fifth, Sixth (which served as Heavy Artillery), Eighth, Ninth, Tenth, Twelfth, Thirteenth, Fourteenth, Fifteenth, and Sixteenth Infantries; and Batteries B, C, and E, all of the First Michigan Light Artillery. In addition, Michigan soldiers from other units reenlisted, although not in numbers required to preserve their original units (reenlistments in parenthesis): Third (207), Fourth (129), Seventh (163) Infantries; various batteries of the First Michigan Light Artillery (157); and the Engineers and Mechanics (148). Under Michigan law (see Selected Legislation—1863, No. 51, and Selected Legislation—1864, No. 27), Veteran Volunteers reenlisting before February 5, 1864, were paid a state bounty of $50; subsequent reenlistments were paid $100.[211]

Casualties between November 1, 1863, and October 31, 1864, were as follows: (totals since April 1861 in parenthesis): 1,956 men KIA or died of wounds received in action (3,355); 2,778 died of disease (5,987); and 1,327 missing in action (2,442); 1,662 were transferred (0); 4,306 were discharged for disability (11,611); and 5,728 men were discharged to reenlist in another (or Veteran) regiment. Losses from all causes totaled 17,747 (30,785).[212] (See Selected Summaries.)

In his 1864 report, President Edmunds of the Washington-based Michigan Soldiers' Relief Association described four ways in which state associations differed from "the great Commissions" (i.e., the Sanitary and the Christian Commissions). First, state groups "feel a more direct and personal interest in the suffering men from their own State"; second, the money contributed by state residents is "given in direct aid to the soldiers, no portion being absorbed in salaries, as is the case with the Commissions"; third, "our agents seek out the suffering and place the aid directly in [the soldiers'] hands, whilst the Commissions only deal out their stores upon official requisitions of surgeons" or others in authority; finally, "Abuses and neglect in hospitals or camps are carefully sought out and exposed by our agents," and this reporting "is seldom or never performed by the Commissions, their systems and that of the officials being so nearly assimilated as to induce them to defend rather than expose the faults of each other." Nevertheless, in early 1864, Edmunds's Association nearly folded for want of funds; however, Michigan's congressional delegations lobbied on its behalf, and by year-end, the Association reported income of $5,552.53 and expenses of $5,188.49.[213]

In 1864, the Association received some thirty boxes, five barrels, and five kegs of "Shirts, drawers, socks, handkerchiefs, stimulants, and pickles." But it purchased most of what it distributed, including writing paper, 70 gallons of whiskey, 165 pounds of tobacco, and onions, herring, and butter. At this time, Washington, Alexandria, and Georgetown hospitals averaged some 1,000 patients from Michigan units; by year-end 1864, these decreased to 568. Facilities were visited regularly; agents were also dispatched to the hospital at Annapolis (where freed POWs were received), on the Rapidan, at Fredericksburg (where the "Michigan Soup House"[214] became famous), White House, and City Point.[215]

Michigan's state agency system was fully established by early 1864. Administering this network was straightforward: Governor Blair could (and often did) contact agents directly. But for mundane matters, agents reported to Benjamin Vernor, the state military agent headquartered in Detroit. As Vernor declared, "By the aid of our chain of agencies at Washington, New York, Louisville, Nashville and St. Louis, we can efficiently reach all the hospitals, and watch over the wants of our men."[216]

Vernor worked closely with (and was a vice president of) the Michigan Soldiers' Aid Society (not to be confused with its counterpart in Washington) under its indefatigable corresponding secretary, Valeria Campbell. The society was the largest private aid society in the state. Tracing its origins to the Ladies' Aid Society of Detroit (see November 6, 1861), it was now a branch of the Western U.S. Sanitary Commission. In part, Campbell's group was a shipping agency, receiving goods from local aid societies and individuals throughout the state and sending them via steamboat and rail to hospitals throughout the country. The scale was significant: of 1,219 boxes, barrels, and kegs, Louisville received 1,009, Chicago, 110, Cincinnati and Knoxville 40, Washington 35, with the balance going to Baltimore, Wheeling, York, and POWs in Richmond. Included in its primary responsibility was providing food, housing, and other "comforts" for soldiers in transit through Detroit, both deploying and returning, and to patients in Michigan's U.S. Hospitals: to St. Mary's and Harper's in Detroit, and to Grand Rapids, Jackson, Fort Wayne, and the Post Hospital at the Detroit Barracks. The society also provided supplies to soldiers of the First Michigan Colored Regiment.[217]

In 1864, the Society's operating expenses were $5,716.45, of which almost half ($2,565.64) was spent on the Soldiers' Home in Detroit. The Home, established in January 1864 at 81 Jefferson Street in a two-story building, functioned like a hotel with thirty regular beds and thirty more for emergencies. During its first eight months of operation, the Soldiers' Home fed 40,505 meals to 5,219 men and lodged 13,639.[218]

In his 1864 report, Washington's state military agent Tunnicliffe reported that in May 1864, state QMG Hammond sent him $5,000 "to be expended in the payment of State bounties to such of our gallant boys as were in the hospitals." One important development that eased Tunnicliffe's task occurred in Detroit, not Washington: the conversion of St. Mary's Hospital to a U.S. General Hospital and the opening of Harper Hospital. Permanently disabled soldiers could return to Michigan—"our gallant boys who have lost an arm, or a leg, or have been otherwise so seriously wounded that many months will elapse before restoration of health can be reasonably expected."

Mirroring the experience of the Washington Michigan Soldiers' Relief Association, Nashville state agent Luther B. Willard also reported that he received some supplies from private sources in Michigan but that most of what he distributed to "sick and needy" soldiers came gratis from the Christian Commission and Western Sanitary Commission, the latter based in St. Louis. Willard spent much of his time conducting soldiers to surgeons for discharges, lobbying officials for soldier furloughs and the Pay Office for back pay, and escorting soldiers to the railroad station for the trip home. Much of his 1864 report dealt with the poor treatment (with a few notable exceptions) of soldiers in hospitals. He blamed surgeons ("easy, fat places for lazy men who desire money which they cannot obtain in any other way"). Willard believed that soldiers languished for months as a result of doctors' incompetence and indifference. He was convinced that the failure to return wounded men home only increased mortality. There were about twenty hospitals in Willard's area, and together with his wife ("Her religion teaches her this duty") made frequent visits. Office expenses totaled $2,908.95, but this amount understates activity. Willard distributed goods and food to over 3,000 Michigan soldiers, gave writing materials and postage to 1,500, arranged furloughs for 1,000, and arranged to transfer 2,500 men to Northern hospitals. He obtained discharges for over 100 disabled soldiers. He answered over 3,000 letters of inquiry. Willard estimated that in the past year, he had traveled over 15,000 miles shuttling

around "all the hospitals and most of the regiments in this Department, where Michigan troops have been quartered."

But there was more to the Willards's responsibilities. Accompanying the uniformed army was another army of civilian contractors ("mechanics and laborers") estimated at 30,000 men, with an unnumbered share from Michigan. Willard helped solve their problems, which resembled those of soldiers: illness, hospitalization, and collecting pay.[219]

In 1864, Rev. Gilman, state agent in Louisville, reported that since January 1, 1864, 1,200 Michigan soldiers had been admitted to hospitals in that city and at New Albany and Jeffersonville, Indiana. He noted 74 deaths; by year-end, hospitalized Michiganders numbered about 500. After medical authorities began transferring north sick and wounded Michiganders (see June 1, 1864), Gilman began filing transfer applications, completing 252 by year end. Most were approved. Gilman also obtained 276 civilian passes to the front (application by the state agent was required), 41 requests for discharges, and 210 requests for Descriptive Lists, without which soldiers could not be paid. He received and answered 127 letters of inquiry about soldiers and wrote 157 letters for (presumably) disabled soldiers. Most of the supplies distributed by Gilman (including 500 shirts, 400 pair of drawers, and 250 pounds of tobacco) were obtained from the Sanitary Commission, with which he had good relations.[220]

In St. Louis, Weston Flint, the Ohio agent who doubled as Michigan's, reported (based on incomplete returns—numbers do not tally) that between March 1 and November 15, 1864, 226 men were admitted to St. Louis hospitals; 54 men had been transferred to other hospitals; 91 were returned to duty; 57 were furloughed; 24 were discharged; 20 had died; and 1 had deserted. Like other state agents, Flint spent considerable time obtaining Description Lists and back pay, which was given to the soldier without charging the 25 percent to 50 percent demanded by private agents.[221]

In 1864, Captain George W. Lee, U.S. quartermaster in Detroit, reported spending $1,669,603.78 on the following items: 188,075 tons of ordnance and subsistence supplies, 10,382 horses, 6,073 tons of grain, and 7,942 tons of hay. There were 73,384 troops transported through the state, and 21,384 uniforms were issued. Lee arrested 702 deserters and paid $19,450.10 in rewards.[222]

In his valedictory speech, Blair noted a decline in the

number of incarcerated convicts and acknowledged the war's influence: because of "the exceeding great demand both for soldiers and laborers," Blair "felt compelled" to "grant petitions [for release] more freely than heretofore." But he was satisfied. "Many of them are doing valiant service in the ranks of the country's defenders, some have died in battle, and others are supporting themselves by honest labor." And it turned out that the war had similarly affected the state reform school. In 1864, 87 boys were released, and two-thirds of these enlisted in the army. The board governing the reform school noted that if releases stopped and delinquents were freed only "as the law requires" the number of inmates might increase from 214 to around 300.[223]

The State of Michigan's receipts for FY 1864 (November 30), excluding the proceeds of bond sales, totaled $2,444,242.25. Expenditures were $2,004,194.98: this left Michigan with an operating surplus of $440,047.27. The state spent $823,216.75 for "war purposes" during this period, reflecting Michigan's assumption of personnel expenses in the form of bounties and increased debt service.

At the end of FY 1864, state debt totaled $3,541,149.80.[224]

1865

Key Events

January

2: PMG Fry's Circular No. 1 declares that quotas under the December 19 1864 call "must not be reduced except by actual enlistments in the Army, Navy, and Marine Corps." This causes great anxiety among the states. (See January 10.)[1]

4: Michigan's legislature convenes. Governor Blair delivers his valedictory message and Governor Henry H. Crapo delivers his inaugural address.[2]

5: Michigan's legislature reelects U.S. senator Jacob M. Howard 56 votes to 42 votes for Austin Blair, in his second attempt. (See January 4, 1862.)[3]

9: In Detroit, 995 men of the Thirtieth Michigan muster into U.S. service for twelve months; officers and recruits are drawn from Detroit, Chesterfield, Tecumseh, Eagle River, Muskegon, Hillsdale, Niles, Flint, and Bridgeport. The unit has a "special purpose" as described by the official history: "The confederate sympathizers and rebel refugees in Canada were becoming so outspoken in their sentiments and so bold in their actions that a raid was anticipated on the towns and cities on the Michigan side of the river," and "it was deemed expedient to organize a regiment of Michigan troops to prevent the occurrence of such an event." The Thirtieth will be posted on Mackinac Island.[4] (See June 30.)

10: PMG Fry's January 2 Circular No. 1 has reached most states, provoking consternation. Most states interpret the Circular as prohibiting them from offsetting quotas by prior surpluses. Fry is seen to have reneged on his promise to allow surpluses to offset quotas. Wisconsin's Governor James T. Lewis forcefully complains to Stanton.[5]

11: Trials for the Camp Douglas conspirators begin in Cincinnati.[6]

12: Regarding Circular No. 1 (see entry for January 2), Fry answers Minnesota governor Stephen Miller's concerns about whether it disallows surpluses. After a lengthy explanation of how the new formulation works, Fry confirms that surpluses will be allowed.[7]

13: Fort Fisher attacked.

15: Fort Fisher captured.

18: In Michigan's House, a committee of African American leaders personally appears to present a memorial signed by John D. Richards, Robert L. Cullen, and James D. Carter "asking that the constitution be so amended as to extend to them the right of suffrage." A vote is taken to offer the committee seats on the House floor, which passes, 75 to 15, along a party-line vote. The petition is then ordered printed.[8]

24: Despite the December 31, 1864 (see date), notice to Michigan, PMG Fry informs Hill that Michigan's revised quota under the December 19, 1864, call is 10,026, and reminds him of the new formula that accounts for years of service in determining credits: "This is the number required under the call after taking into account the credits to which the State is entitled by estimating the number of years of service furnished by one, two, and three years' men." (See February 4.) The *Detroit Advertiser and Tribune* complains that the quota is twice what was expected, but urges "the most active efforts to fill them at once."[9]

25–26: In Detroit, the Second Baptist Church on Croghan Street hosts a state Colored Men's Convention, which in turn establishes a State Equal Rights League as provided by the National Colored Men's Convention in Syracuse (see October 4–7, 1864). A letter to Michigan's legislature is authorized which asks that the state constitution be amended "so as to extend to us the rights of the elective franchise." The reasons advanced included this consideration: "in the progress of the great rebellion there has been found no traitors to your cause among the colored men of the country, but everywhere and always, as soldiers, as guides, and in many other capacities we have rendered valuable services to the government, and proven our fidelity to the Union cause, when called to assist the nation in her trial, to sustain republican government and institutions."[10] (See August 1 and September 12–13; for excerpts from the thirteen resolutions adopted, see Selected Summaries.)

28: The Michigan Supreme Court decides *Twitchell v. Blodgett*, which rules that Act No. 21 (see Selected Legislation—1864) is unconstitutional. But how should one count, if at all, the November 1864 soldiers' votes based on a statute now deemed unconstitutional? For state elections, each house will decide. (See February 23 and 24.)[11]

31: The Thirteenth Amendment passes the U.S. House. Michigan's Republican press is overjoyed. The *Advertiser and Tribune* declares that passage of the amendment "is one of the greatest events in the history of this government"; it lauds the Democrats who supported it, singling out for special praise Michigan's Augustus C. Baldwin. "For the Republic it is a proud day!" The *Hillsdale Standard* headlines it assessment, "Freedom's Victory," and the *Ypsilanti Commercial* declares, "The great deed is done. The grand event of the century. All hail to Free America."[12]

Democratic reception seems muted but accepting. The *Grand Haven News* simply carried this news, without immediate comment, while the *Free Press* declared that "If three-quarters of the States think it for the benefit of the whole . . . we will acquiesce" and that "We are willing, if such should be the Constitutional decision, to do everything to give the law a fair chance"; however, it then denounces those who "have been and are seeking social and political equality for this race. [Abolitionists'] indignant denials of the miscegenation and amalgamation designs were mere blinds" intended to pass the amendment.[13]

February

1: Although legally unnecessary, Abraham Lincoln signs the Thirteenth Amendment. It now proceeds to the states for ratification. Crapo is immediately alerted by wire and transmits the information to Michigan's House, along with a message, "[I] earnestly hope and recommend that Michigan may be the first to adopt and sanction this wise and humane action . . . to rid the nation of the disturbing and blighting institution of slavery."[14] (See next day's entry.)

Separately, in a letter distributed to AAPMGs

nationwide, Fry explains to southern New York's AAPMG Hincks why New York City's quota was raised from 4,433 on December 24, 1864, to 21,019 on January 24, 1865. The letter cites a number of factors, including the intentional manipulation of naval credits (hoarding them for Manhattan at the expense of other cities in the county), fraudulent and double-counted naval enlistments, and the fact that enrollments increased; however, Fry concludes with a surprise: "The President has ordered that 25 per centum of the quota in each district in the State be set aside until further orders." How this applies to Michigan will become clear on February 4. (See that date and February 6.)[15]

2: Crapo notifies Michigan's legislature that U.S. senator Howard and congressmen Driggs and Longyear have informed him that Congress has adopted the Thirteenth Amendment. "Permit me to call your attention to this important subject and recommend that the question of ratifying this action of Congress be considered at the earliest practicable moment," Crapo suggests to the legislators.

And Michigan's legislature complies. The House approves 56 to 12, and the Senate approves 21 to 2. By afternoon, Crapo signs the bill and Michigan formally approves the Thirteenth Amendment. (See Legislative Sessions—1865.) Of Michigan's eight Democratic senators, only three were present: one voted to ratify the amendment and two voted against; in the House, of twenty-four Democrats, twelve voted against ratification and three in favor. "It will be observed," the *Advertiser and Tribune* noted, "that a large number of Democrats were either absent or dodged."[16]

3: The Hampton Roads Conference.

4: AAPMG Hill, acting in accord with Fry's instructions, notifies AG Robertson that Michigan's quota is 10,026 (as opposed to the December 31, 1864, total of 5,822), calculated on the basis of "years of service" (Michigan owes 30,745 such years). It is divided among the Congressional districts as follows: First, 1,726; Second, 1,801; Third, 1,918; Fourth, 1,263; Fifth, 1,329; and Sixth, 1,986. This produces consternation in Lansing. (See February 6.)[17]

5–7: In Virginia, the Battle of Hatcher's Run is fought.

6: State complaints about draft policy have grown, and Lincoln appoints a three-man board "to examine into the proper quotas and credits of States and districts," under the December 19, 1864, call, and to correct any errors. Michigan is one of the states to be examined. A review completed February 16 finds that Fry's calculations are vindicated: based on Michigan total enrollment of 83,046, and excess years of 20,719, the state's quota should be 10,029, only three more than Fry's original determination of 10,026. The board will report to Lincoln that "We have carefully examined and proved the work done under this rule by the Provost-Marshal-General, and find that it has been done with fairness."[18]

Lincoln also orders Fry to begin drafting "as speedily as the same can be done after the 15th of this month."[19]

Crapo orders AG Robertson to send Stanton a detailed complaint about Fry's alleged mistreatment of Michigan, claiming "an enormous error in calculation." First, Michigan had a surplus after the July 1864 call, and thus has no deficiency to remedy under the December 19, 1864, call. "It is submitted that justice requires that a new and largely reduced quota shall be assigned to this State," Robertson insists.

The details are these: under the July 1864 call, Michigan's quota was 18,282; after adjusting the state's enrollment, the quota dropped to 15,760. Between the July call and December 31, 1864, Michigan enlisted 6,016 men for one year, 50 men for two years, and 10,121 men for three years, for a total of 16,187. Thus, before applying the "years of service" calculation, Michigan had a surplus of 427 men. However, after applying the "years of service" formula (e.g., one man enlisted for three years counts as three years of service, etc.), Michigan still produced a surplus credit for the call of July 1864 of 20,719 years of service. Fry now insists that instead of a surplus, Michigan owes 30,745 years of service, or an equal number of one-year men (or, under the formula, 10,248 men, which, when adjusted for unidentified credits, equals Fry's claim of 10,026).[20] (See February 6.)

11: In Michigan's House, a petition by Alfred Russell, James F. Joy, John Owen, and 130 other Detroiters is presented "asking the privilege of elective franchise for colored citizens."[21]

14: Fry, confident of his own work, replies to AG Robertson's February 6 complaint: "The quota of the State of Michigan is her equitable proportion of the 300,000 men called for by the President on the 19th of September, taking into account her enrollment as it stood on the 31st day of December, the amount of men heretofore furnished and the periods of their enlistment." First, Fry denies that the December 19 call is for any deficiencies—thus, Michigan's 20,719 surplus years of credit are inapplicable to that call; moreover, Fry declares that the first statement of Michigan's quota provided on December 31, 1864, was based on "incomplete data, and [has] been revised and corrected, which accounts for the difference alluded to in your [February 6] communication."[22]

17: Columbia, South Carolina, surrenders; at night, it will be burned.[23] (See February 21.)

21: Stanton notifies Governor Crapo that captured at Charleston were 200 artillery pieces and ammunition. However, Stanton claims that retreating Confederates burned "cotton warehouses, arsenals, quartermaster stores, railroad bridges, two iron-clads, and some vessels in the ship-yard."[24]

The War Department issues Circular 28, noting that a "general exchange of prisoners of war having been commenced, all payments to families of prisoners . . . will be suspended until further orders," in order to avoid "inadvertent double payments." (See October 23, 1861.)[25]

22: Wilmington, North Carolina, is captured.

23: *Twitchell v. Blodgett*'s ripples reach the Michigan Senate. After three votes, it refuses to consider applications to contest three seats, which, absent the soldiers' vote, would have gone to the November loser.[26]

24: Michigan's House votes not to seat ten Democrats who, but for the November soldiers' vote, would have won their seats.[27]

25: Congress passes Chapter 52, "An act to prevent officers of the Army and Navy, and other persons engaged in the military and naval service of the United States from interfering in elections in the States."[28]

March

4: Lincoln is inaugurated. Democratic newspapers are harshly critical of his inaugural address. Terming it an "abolition celebration," the *Grand Haven News* declared, is in fact proving "a wretched failure in every part of the country"; Lincoln's first inaugural was "the greatest calamity that ever befell this or any country," and the second is "the second event of precisely the same character!" The *Free Press* declares that the inaugural "contains not a single fact, result, or prediction," then comments, "His speech is more worthy of [a] puritanical hypocrite, than of an American Executive." Republican sheets note the improved state of affairs between Lincoln's First and Second Inaugurals and the Confederacy's pending collapse. The *Ypsilanti Commercial* perceived something deeper. "God bless Abraham Lincoln!" it declared. "His Inaugural is a sermon that ought to cause many a professed minister of the gospel to blush with shame at his neglect to recognize the mighty judgements [sic] and providences of God in this war visited upon us for the awful sin of oppression."[29]

Meanwhile, near Petersburg, Virginia, Company I of the First U.S. Sharpshooters musters out of service. At this point, total enrollment was 136 men, including 9 KIA, 18 DOD, and 26 DFD.[30]

8–10: Battle of Wyse Fork, North Carolina.

8: The **Republican State Convention** convenes in Detroit's Merrill Hall to nominate a Supreme Court justice (Isaac P. Christiancy) and two University of Michigan regents.[31]

10: The **Democratic State Convention** meets in Detroit. Although the Democrats differ with Christiancy politically, a resolution cites their "confidence in his ability, integrity and experience" and thus, it will not nominate a Democratic candidate. No resolutions on national issues are discussed.[32]

11: Lincoln issues his amnesty proclamation for army deserters.

16: Battle of Averasborough, North Carolina.

18: The reorganized Eleventh Michigan deploys from Jackson to Tennessee.[33] (See September 16.)

19–21: Battle of Bentonville, North Carolina. The Thirteenth Michigan is first in casualties (106), followed by the second-ranked Twenty-First Michigan (73) and the fifth-ranked Fourteenth Michigan (58).[34]

23: Michigan legislature adjourns.[35]

25: Confederates attack Fort Stedman, Petersburg, Virginia. In the meantime, Mobile, Alabama, is besieged.

27: Lincoln, Grant, and Sherman meet aboard the *River Queen*.

29: Grant begins Appomattox Campaign.

April

1: The Michigan Soldiers' Relief Association opens a "Home," that is, a hostel in Washington, D.C. It will operate until September 1.[36]

3: Republican Isaac P. Christiancy is elected to Michigan's Supreme Court. It is 1865's only state contest.[37]

Meanwhile, the news of Richmond's fall reaches Detroit. In Detroit, Mayor Barker orders businesses closed and bells rung; flags are raised at "nearly every store," and in the afternoon AG Robertson orders a 100-gun salute. At night, illuminations and fireworks light up Detroit's sky. In St. Joseph, the news arrives by hand-carried dispatch at around 9:00 p.m.; the hour proved no obstacle, as bells were rung and an impromptu meeting convened in front of the *Traveler*'s news office. More festivities would be held the next day. In Hillsdale, Grand Haven, and East Saginaw, the news is published on April 4 and 5. Hillsdale announces a "Grand Jubilee" for April 14, promising bonfires, illuminations, and music.[38]

9: Lee surrenders to Grant at Appomattox Court House. Referring to Grant's terms of surrender, the *East Saginaw Courier* declares, in an editorial titled "Magnanimity," that "We believe Gen. Grant acted wisely" and correctly predicts that "there will be no hesitation with the administration in confirming his act."[39]

10: Word of Lee's surrender at Appomattox reaches Detroit. On the Campus Martius, 200 guns are fired, a speakers' stand awaits, and repeated cheers go up for "Sherman, Grant, Sheridan, Meade, Wilcox [sic] and the brave boys of Michigan." "The City in a Blaze of Light," runs one headline of the *Free Press*, unable to contain its own enthusiasm. "What a flood of events has poured upon us during the last ten days!" the editors declare.

News of Lee's surrender reaches Ypsilanti in the morning. Rejoicing is spontaneous, with bells, cheers, and crowds gathering on Congress Street, which was soon closed. "People seemed to be at a loss how to make their joy known," the *Ypsilanti Commercial* noted, so "Everything that could make a noise was brought into requisition." As the *Jackson Citizen* was distributed throughout the area, spontaneous and joyful demonstrations break out in Manchester, Tecumseh, and Adrian, while in Jackson itself, the list of speakers featured Austin Blair.

The news reaches Ann Arbor just after 8:30 a.m.,

and when the surrender is announced from the telegraph wire, "the cheers for GRANT, and SHERIDAN, and the brave boys in blue, and victory, nearly took the roof of the building." The mayor immediately issued a proclamation recommending that businesses close and that "citizens join in an appropriate celebration of the event."[40]

12: Federals occupy Mobile, Alabama.

13: Meanwhile, the War Department notifies AAPMG Hill that "The Secretary of War directs that you discontinue the business of recruiting and drafting in all the districts of your State."[41]

14: In Washington, President Lincoln is shot while attending Ford's Theater. He dies at 7:22 a.m. the next day, and Andrew Johnson becomes the seventeenth president.

15: News of Lincoln's murder hits Detroit, and eventually the rest of Michigan, like a bombshell. This morning in a black-lined edition, the *Free Press* is no less dismayed than any Michigan Republican sheet. Under the head "The Dreadful News," the editorialist describes the act as "the atrocious deed of the bold and blood-thirsty assassins." Almost certainly speaking for most Michiganders, the *Free Press* notes the "gloom and pall" that hung over Detroit, and adds, "There is one universal feeling of detestation at the crime; one universal cry of vengeance on the perpetrators, and all those who have aided, abetted and counselled [sic] this most atrocious deed." In the coming days, the *Free Press* describes continuing shocks as more of the assassination's details become known. The *East Saginaw Courier*, one of Michigan's harshest Lincoln critics, declares "Not only Abraham Lincoln, the just and good man has fallen, but the President of a great Nation," and makes a concession probably unimaginable several days earlier: "Censure as we may some of the acts of the late Administration, we must make for Abraham Lincoln the highest record of honesty, firmness, justice and humanity ever written since the day of Washington."

In Jackson, the mayor issues a proclamation asking that businesses close. The city is draped in mourning, and church bells toll for an hour at 3:00 p.m. In Hillsdale, the news arrives just after 8:00 a.m. and the Village Board immediately issues a proclamation requesting the closure of businesses and tolling of bells for two hours. Shopkeepers redress their

windows that just last night "were glittering with illumination, in honor of the glad tidings of the few days past," and replaced them "with proper emblems of mourning." In Grand Haven, businesses close, flags are flown at half-mast from public buildings, and a mass meeting is scheduled for the next day. In Lansing, crowds gathered around the telegraph office, many disbelieving the news; a citizens' meeting asks that 1,000 copies of the news be printed and distributed, and that a meeting be held at 3:00 p.m. at the Statehouse. In Ann Arbor, the city is "immediately shrouded in gloom."

From Flint, Governor Henry Crapo issues a proclamation. "Michigan and the whole nation are in tears over this fearful tragedy," asking later that the "free and loyal men of Michigan stand firm in this hour of our country's peril."[42]

16: In Detroit at 3:00 p.m., "an immense gathering" convenes at the Campus Martius. Reflecting sentiment across Michigan, the memorial gathering is bipartisan. Meeting vice presidents include prominent Democrats George V. N. Lothrop, Robert McClelland, and Kirkland C. Barker, who are joined by Republicans Zachariah Chandler, Jacob M. Howard, and William A. Howard, among others.[43]

19: Eulogies on Lincoln are given in churches throughout Detroit.[44]

21: Orrin N. Giddings* replaces William Hammond as QMG.[45]

25: Andrew Johnson proclaims May 25 as the national day of mourning for Abraham Lincoln. Lincoln's funeral train en route to Illinois will not pass through Michigan. In Detroit, formal obsequies are held for Lincoln. An estimated 30,000 people come; the procession is two miles long. Senator Jacob M. Howard delivers the eulogy on the Campus Martius.[46]

27: The steamer *Sultana*, carrying some 2,100 soldiers and 200 civilians (six times the permitted number), blows up on the Mississippi River. Passengers include at least 243 Michigan ex-POWs; killed on the ship are 68 men of the Eighteenth Michigan and 1 man of the Twenty-First Michigan. (See June 8.)[47]

28: The War Department issues GO No. 77 ordering the honorable and immediate discharge of all federal POWs awaiting exchange, recruits in rendezvous awaiting assignments, and most soldier-patients in military hospitals. Work on military fortifications is halted and reductions required in transports and clerks. Meanwhile, a delegation of 500 Detroiters, escorted by bands from the Detroit Light Guard and the Detroit City Guard, travel to Cleveland to participate in Lincoln's funeral procession.[48]

29: The War Department notifies AAPMG Hill that "all recruits—drafted, substitutes, and volunteers— for old regiments remaining in rendezvous will be immediately mustered out and honorably discharged the service under your direction."[49]

Separately, Andrew Johnson modifies his April 25 proclamation that established May 25 as a day of national mourning for Lincoln. However, May 25 is also Ascension Day and Johnson reschedules the day of commemoration to June 1.[50]

May

4: Confederate general Richard Taylor surrenders forces in the Confederate Department of Alabama, Mississippi, and East Louisiana.

6: The War Department issues GO No. 82, mustering out volunteer regimental officers absent due to disability and leaves of absence.[51]

8: The War Department issues GO No. 83, mustering out all volunteer cavalry troopers whose terms expire before October 1, 1865.[52]

9: In Detroit, the Provost Guard musters out of service. Its total enrollment was 136, including 1 DOW, 1 DOD, 8 DFD, and 10 deserted.[53]

10: Johnson declares that "armed resistance to the authority of this Government in the said insurrectionary States may be regarded as virtually at an end."[54]

Separately, this day ends Jefferson Davis's presidency. At Irwinsville, Georgia, Lieutenant Colonel Benjamin D. Pritchard*, commanding the Fourth Michigan Cavalry, captures Davis and party.[55] Separately, Lambdin P. Milligan, whose execution is scheduled in nine days, files an appeal. A stay is granted and the case becomes known as *Ex Parte Milligan*.[56]

18: The War Department announces the muster out of "All volunteer organizations of white troops in General Sherman's army and the Army of the Potomac whose terms of service expire prior to October 1 next."[57]

23–24: The Grand Review in Washington of the Army of the Potomac (Twenty-third) and the Sherman's Army

(Twenty-fourth). Michigan attendees include Senator Chandler, Governor Crapo, David H. Jerome*, and Colonel Grosvenor.[58]

26: Confederate general Simon B. Buckner surrenders the Army of the Trans-Mississippi.

30: In Georgetown, DC, the Twentieth Michigan musters out of service; it will return to Michigan on June 4. By war's end, total enrollment was 1,183, including 72 KIA, 42 DOW, 21 died as POWs, 89 DOD, and 169 DFD.[59]

June

1: The national day of mourning for the death of Abraham Lincoln.[60]

3: Detroit organizes for Michigan's returning soldiers. This day's efforts are for the Twentieth Michigan, expected to arrive from Cleveland by boat the next day. To accommodate these men, superintendent of the Michigan Central Railroad R. N. Rice* has donated the use of the road's dock and nearby Central Depot. Meanwhile, citizens contribute "meat, bread, biscuit, eggs, [and] coffee" for the breakfast repast. (See June 4 and 6.)[61]

4: The Twentieth Michigan arrives in Detroit before proceeding to Jackson. Meanwhile, at Bailey's Cross Roads, Virginia, the Twenty-Sixth Michigan musters out of service; it will be discharged in Jackson on June 16. By war's end, total enrollment was 1,043, including 68 KIA, 40 DOW, 15 died as POWs, 135 DOD, and 150 DFD.[62]

6: At Detroit's Young Men's Hall, a second public meeting convenes to organize more receptions for returning soldiers. Organizers face the challenge: "Thus far, the attention our brave heroes who return from the wars have devolved upon a few, and they are entitled to great credit for the spirit and generosity exhibited," the *Detroit Free Press* remarks about organizers' efforts to date. "But there are many regiments coming home, and it is desirable to have a permanent organization with a fund at their disposal to give the welcome most appreciated by war-worn soldiers after a long and tiresome journey." Because Detroit serves as a rail and water transportation hub, soldiers from other states will also be arriving, and refreshments are planned. Permanent committees on reception and finance are formed; Rice's depot can hold some 1,000 men. Between June 4, 1865, and June 10, 1866,

19,510 Michigan and 3,506 Wisconsin soldiers will be refreshed at the welcoming committee's expense.[63]

Meanwhile, in Jackson at 3:00 p.m., the recently returned Twentieth Michigan leaves Camp Blair, marches down Main Street, stacks arms, and enters Union Hall, whose walls are draped with U.S. flags bearing the names of the unit's battles. Austin Blair makes the welcome speech. Like Detroit, Jackson will serve as a hub for returnees, and in the next twelve months will host 10,659 troops. Mary Blair, the wife of the ex-governor, takes charge of the reception efforts.[64]

7: In Detroit, the Seventeenth Michigan is discharged. By war's end, total enrollment was 1,224, including 84 KIA, 48 DOW, 54 died as POWs, 249 DOD, and 84 DFD.[65]

8: The Twenty-First Regiment musters out of service; it will return to Detroit for discharge on June 22. By war's end, total enrollment was 1,515, including 43 KIA, 29 DOW, 4 died as POWs, 279 DOD, and 198 DFD.[66]

10: The Nineteenth Michigan musters out of service; it will return to Detroit on June 13. By war's end, total enrollment was 1,206, including 54 KIA, 31 DOW, 7 died as POWs, 132 DOD, and 182 DFD.[67]

14: The War Department orders that all regimental colors from state units be given to state governors. Meanwhile, Governor Crapo issues a proclamation of welcome to returning Michigan troops. These men are "Citizen Soldiers" who, "In the hour of National danger and peril, when the safety—when the very existence—of your country was imperiled, you left your firesides, your homes and your families, to defend the Government and the Union. But the danger is now averted, the struggle is ended, and victory—absolute and complete victory—has perched upon your banners." Their achievement stands not only as a lesson to their country's enemies, "but to the world . . . that it is not necessary for men to be serfs and slaves in order to be soldiers, but that in the hands of free and enlightened citizens, enjoying the advantages of and blessings conferred by free institutions, the temple of Liberty will ever be safe, and its escutcheon forever unsullied."[68]

Meanwhile, in Detroit, Battery B of the First Michigan Artillery musters out of service. By war's end, 236 men were enrolled, of whom 24 DOD and 30 DFD.[69]

20: Detroit's own Twenty-Fourth Michigan arrives home. The unit will be discharged on June 30. By war's end, total enrollment was 2,104, including 125 KIA, 42 DOW, 28 died as POWs, 109 DOD, and 254 DFD.[70]

Also at a public meeting in Detroit, a resolution was adopted to erect a monument to the war's dead. A committee, including Judge Benjamin Franklin H. Witherell*, Henry Morrow, and Charles C. Trowbridge, is appointed to make recommendations. When matters are formalized at a July 20 meeting, AG Robertson, state treasurer Owen, Thomas W. Palmer, and James W. Tillman will join the committee. (See August 11.) In Washington, the Joint Committee for the Conduct of the War disbands.[71]

23: The Fifth Michigan Cavalry musters out of service. By war's end, total enrollment was 1,866, including 101 KIA, 24 DOW, 69 died as POWs, 109 DOD, and 196 DFD.

Meanwhile, Johnson rescinds the naval blockade of all southern ports.[72]

22: In Detroit, Battery C of the First Michigan Light Artillery musters out of service. By war's end, total enrollment was 226, including 2 KIA, 1 DOW, 27 DOD, and 30 DFD.[73]

24: In Salisbury, North Carolina, the Twenty-Fifth Michigan musters out of service; it will return to Jackson on July 2 for discharge. By war's end, total enrollment was 1,008, including 23 KIA, 17 DOW, 2 died as POWs, 126 DOD, and 157 DFD. Meanwhile, in Richmond, Virginia, the Detroiters of Company A join the rest of the Twenty-Third Illinois and muster out of service. By war's end, total enrollment was 199, including 4 KIA, 1 DOW, 1 DOD, 3 died as POWs, and 8 DFD.[74]

26: In Nashville, the Twenty-Second Michigan musters out of service; the unit arrives in Detroit in several days and on July 10 is discharged. By war's end, total enrollment was 1,679, including 47 KIA, 30 DOW, 77 died as POWs, 195 DOD, and 158 DFD.[75]

27: In Alexandria, the First New York Cavalry, including the Michiganders of Company K, musters out of service. By war's end, total enrolled Michiganders was 102, including 3 KIA, 1 DOW, 1 died as POW, 3 DOD, and 4 DFD.[76]

28: In Salisbury, North Carolina, the Twenty-Third Michigan is mustered out of service; it will return to Detroit, where on July 20 it will be discharged. By war's end, total enrollment was 1477, including 38 KIA, 21 DOW, 15 died as POWs, 214 DOD, and 150 DFD. In Jackson, Battery A of the First Michigan Light Artillery musters out of service. By war's end, total enrollment was 296, including 7 KIA, 3 DOW, 3 died as POWs, 10 DOD, and 25 DFD.[77]

30: The Thirtieth Michigan musters out of service. By war's end, total enrollment was 998, including 15 DOD and 2 DFD.[78]

July

1: In Nashville, the Fourth Michigan Cavalry musters out of service; it will return to Detroit on July 10 for discharge. By war's end, 2,006 men were enrolled of whom 30 were KIA, 15 DOW, 7 died as POWs, 283 DOD, and 230 DFD.

In Jackson, three artillery units muster out of service. Battery F of the First Michigan Light Artillery had by war's end 245 men enrolled, of whom 10 were KIA, 2 DOW, 10 DOD, and 41 DFD. The Thirteenth Michigan Battery had by war's end a total enrollment was 256, of whom 2 DOD and 29 DFD. And in the Fourteenth Battery by war's end, total enrollment was 221, 8 DOD, and 29 DFD.[79]

2: The Eighteenth Michigan arrives in Jackson; it will be discharged on July 4. By war's end, total enrollment was 1,308, including 8 KIA, 3 DOW, 12 died as POWs, 208 DOD, and 122 DFD.[80]

5: In Louisville, the Seventh Michigan musters out; it will return to Jackson and be dismissed on July 7. By war's end, total enrollment was 1,375, including 127 KIA, 56 DOW, 17 died as POWs, 147 DOD, and 344 DFD.

In Jeffersonville, Indiana, the Fifth Michigan also musters out. By war's end, total enrollment was 1,586, including 143 KIA, 63 DOW, 19 died as POWs, 94 DOD, and 269 DFD. Also mustering out with the Fifth are two sharpshooter units: first, the transferred men of Company B, Second USSS. By war's end, 152 were enrolled, including 9 KIA, 4 DOW, 19 DOD, 4 died as POWs, and 37 DFD. Company K of the First USSS also musters out. By war's end, 108 were enrolled, including 6 KIA, 5 DOW, 7 DOD, 1 died as a POW, and 19 DFD.[81]

7: Captain Christian Rath* from Jackson serves as the executioner for the Booth conspirators. He sews white canvas hoods (made from shelter tent halves) over the prisoners' heads and at 1:21 p.m., claps his hands three times, and the traps fall. "They bounded up like a ball attached to a rubber band," Rath remembered, "and then they settled down." Meanwhile, Michiganders serving in Birge's Western Sharpshooters muster out of service. By war's end, its total Michigan enrollment was 197, including 17 KIA, 2 DOW, 17 DOD, and 40 DFD.[82]

8: The Fifth Michigan returns to Detroit for discharge. Meanwhile, in Jeffersonville, Indiana, the Sixteenth Michigan musters out of service; it will return to Jackson on July 12. By war's end, its total enrollment was 2,194, including 173 KIA, 54 DOW, 8 died as POWs, 104 DOD, and 211 DFD.[83]

9: Jefferson, Indiana (or Louisville), the First Michigan musters out; it will return to Jackson for disbandment. By war's end, 1,884 men were enrolled of whom 130 are KIA, 39 DOW, 92 died as POWs, 76 DOD, and 303 DFD.[84]

14: In Detroit, Battery I of the First Michigan Light Artillery musters out of service. By war's end, total enrollment was 213, including 2 KIA, 2 DOW, 14 DOD, and 23 DFD.[85]

18: In Louisville, the Fourteenth Michigan musters out of service. It will return to Detroit on July 21. By war's end, total enrollment was 1,629, including 36 KIA, 17 DOW, 1 died as a POW, 163 DOD, and 155 DFD.[86]

19: In Louisville, the Tenth Michigan musters out of service; it will return to Jackson on July 22 and be dismissed on August 1. By war's end, total enrollment was 1,514, including 62 KIA, 23 DOW, 9 died as POWs, 86 DOD, and 178 DFD.[87]

21: In Concord, North Carolina, the Ninth Michigan Cavalry musters out of service and returns to Jackson on July 30. By war's end, total enrollment was 1,213, including 32 KIA, 8 DOW, 32 died as POWs, 110 DOD, and 59 DFD.[88]

22: In Jackson, Battery H of the First Michigan Light Artillery musters out of service. By war's end, total enrollment was 326, including 2 KIA, 1 DOW, 30 DOD, and 63 DFD. In Detroit, Battery K of the First Michigan Light Artillery musters out. By war's end, total enrollment was 199, including 1 KIA, 1 DOW, 8 DOD, and 7 DFD.[89]

25: In Louisville, the Thirteenth Michigan musters out of service. It will return to Jackson on July 27. By war's end, total enrollment was 2,092, including 47 KIA, 33 DOW, 7 died as POWs, 253 DOD, and 216 DFD.[90]

26: In Tennallytown (present-day Tenleytown, DC), the Twenty-Seventh Michigan musters out of service; it will be discharged in Detroit on July 29. By war's end, total enrollment was 1,897, including 134 KIA, 77 DOW, 40 died as POWs, 102 DOD, and 181 DFD. Official records also note 538 WIA and 130 MIA. The Twenty-Seventh is listed as one of Fox's "Fighting Three Hundred."[91]

28: In Washington, D.C., two units muster out of service: the Second Michigan, which had a total enrollment of 1,819, including 118 KIA, 100 DOW, 16 died as POWs, 109 DOD, and 208 DFD; and the First Michigan Sharpshooters, which had a total enrollment of 1,206, including 69 KIA, 42 DOW, 41 died as POWs, 62 DOD, and 98 DFD.[92]

30: In Jackson, Battery E of the First Michigan Light Artillery musters out of service. By war's end, total enrollment was 349, including 1 DOW, 3 DOD, and 48 DFD.[93]

August

1: There is a meeting in Detroit of the officers appointed to manage the Equal Rights League, which was established in January. Decisions made at the meeting, however, later generate dissension in Michigan's African American community. Some organizers of the January conference are excluded; the January constitution is replaced with another, to which the excluded members did not assent; delegates are elected to the National Equal Rights Convention, set to convene in Cleveland, for which the excluded members did not have an opportunity to vote. A state convention is called for September 12.[94] (See that date.)

Meanwhile, in Jackson, Battery M of the First Michigan Light Artillery musters out of service. By war's end, its total enrollment was 267, including 8 DOD and 7 DFD.[95]

3: In Detroit, the Eighth Michigan musters out of U.S. service. By war's end, total enrollment was 1,715, including 134 KIA, 87 DOW, 7 died as POWs, 181 DOD, and 278 DFD. In Jackson, Battery D of the First Michigan Light Artillery is discharged. By war's end, total enrollment was 314, including 1 KIA, 1 DOW, 35 DOD, and 53 DFD.[96]

6: In Jackson, Battery G of the First Michigan Light Artillery musters out of service. By war's end, total enrollment was 314, including 4 KIA, 1 DOW, 1 died in prison, 29 DOD, and 43 DFD.[97]

11: The Soldiers' Monument Committee reports that $50,000 will be necessary to build the memorial. The effort is statewide and includes prominent Michiganders representing thirty-eight counties as well as every principal city and most major towns across the state. The monument will be erected on the Campus Martius and designed by former Ann Arbor resident (now in Italy) Randolph Rogers*. The cornerstone will be laid on July 4, 1867, and dedicated on April 9, 1872, at a final cost of $70,185.91. Separately, in Little Rock, Arkansas, Company B of the Forty-Seventh Ohio musters out of service. By war's end, its total enrollment was 135, including 5 KIA, 4 DOW, 22 DOD, and 22 DFD.[98]

12–14: General Ulysses Grant visits Detroit. Mayor Barker and the Common Council have made special preparations and also welcome him "to his former home in this city to renew his previous friendships, and give our citizens the privilege and opportunity of congratulating him on the return of peace."[99]

17: In Macon, Georgia, the Second Michigan Cavalry musters out of service; it will be discharged in Jackson on August 26.[100]

20: The Sixth Michigan Heavy Artillery (formerly the Sixth Michigan Infantry) musters out of service. By war's end, 1,992 men were enrolled, of whom 45 were KIA, 25 DOW, 13 died as POWs, 432 DOD, and 327 DFD.[101]

22: In Jackson, Battery L of the First Michigan Light Artillery musters out of service. By war's end, total enrollment was 210, including 22 DOD, and 10 DFD.[102]

September

1: The Fifteenth Michigan arrives in Detroit for discharge. By war's end, total enrollment was 2,390, including 51 KIA, 24 DOW, 4 died as POWs, 182 DOD, and 286 DFD.[103]

6: In Murfreesboro, Tennessee, the Twenty-Ninth Michigan musters out of service; on September 12, it will be discharged in Detroit.[104]

12–13: In Detroit, the Colored Men's Convention convenes, for the purpose of severing any connection with the Michigan Equal Rights League (for "having failed to meet the object for which it was instituted") and to establish a new Michigan Equal Rights League. Vice presidents are appointed for Lenawee, Hillsdale, Washtenaw, Macomb, Kalamazoo, Jackson, Branch, Wayne, Calhoun, Eaton, Berrien, Cass, and Gratiot Counties. After some debate, resolutions adopted include a denunciation of President Johnson's version of reconstruction, especially its disenfranchisement of blacks. Dr. James Fields* of Adrian will lead the new organization and three delegates are chosen to attend the National Equal Rights Convention in Cleveland on October 19.[105]

15: In Chattanooga, the Ninth Michigan musters out of service; it will arrive in Jackson on September 27 and be dismissed. By war's end, its total enrollment was 1,947, including 14 KIA, 11 DOW, 271 DOD, and 208 DFD.[106]

16: In Nashville, the Eleventh Michigan (reorganized) musters out of service and will return to Jackson. By war's end, total enrollment was 1,017, including 50 DOD and 9 DFD.[107]

19: In Nashville, the Michigan Battalion, formerly with Merrill Horse, musters out of service. By war's end, its total enrollment was 527, including 3 KIA, 6 DOW, 49 DOD, and 59 DFD.[108]

22: In Nashville, two Michigan cavalry regiments muster out of service, the Eighth and Eleventh Michigan Cavalry. By war's end, the Eighth's total enrollment was 2,152, including 21 KIA, 8 DOW, 67 died as POWs, 88 DOD, and 197 DFD. The Eleventh's total enrollment was 1,375, 18 KIA, 5 DOW, 2 died as POWs, 22 DOD, and 55 DFD. Also in Nashville, the First Michigan Engineers and Mechanics muster out. By war's end, it had 2,920 men enrolled, of whom 2 were KIA, 4 DOW, 2 died as POWs, 280 DOD, and 279 DFD.[109]

25: At Fort Lavaca, Texas, the Forty-Fourth Illinois musters out of service, including its Michiganders in Companies B and H. By war's end, 215 Michiganders were enrolled, including 11 KIA, 6 DOW, 29 DOD, and 49 DFD.[110]

30: In Charleston, South Carolina, the One Hundred and First USCT, formerly the First Michigan Colored Regiment, musters out of service. By war's end, 1,673 men were enrolled, including 5 KIA, 7 DOW, 116 DOD, and 114 DFD.[111]

October

5: Five companies of the One Hundred and Second USCT, formerly the First Michigan (Colored), return to Detroit and are paid off and discharged. The balance arrive two days later and are discharged on October 17.[112]

19: In Cleveland, Ohio, the National Equal Rights League holds its first annual meeting. Detroit's John D. Richards is active at the convention, serving as its secretary and also on its executive committee. He successfully introduces a series of resolutions, including a demand that "in the reconstruction of the Southern States, justice demands that the Elective franchise be extended to men of color in those States"; that freed persons acquire property and seek educational opportunities; and that "the positions of teachers for our people in [the South] should be filled by persons of our own color."[113]

31: Michigan closes its state military agency in Washington. Soldiers needing assistance must hereafter apply to the United States Sanitary Commission.[114]

November

11: In Jackson, the Tenth Michigan Cavalry musters out of service. By war's end, total enrollment was 1,886, including 13 KIA, 12 DOW, 11 died as POWs, 121 DOD, and 80 DFD.[115]

24: The Sixth Michigan Cavalry musters out of service. By war's end, 1,838 men were enrolled, of whom 121 were KIA or DOW, 65 died as Andersonville POWs and another 42 in other prisons, 132 DOD, and 150 DFD.[116]

December

1: President Johnson restores the writ of habeas corpus in most loyal states and territories.

12: Harper U.S. General Hospital reverts to the Protestant Society on condition that it care for invalided Michigan soldiers. (See December 28.)[117]

15: Eligible recruits from the Seventh Michigan Cavalry are discharged. Casualties were 85 KIA or DOW and 258 DOD.[118]

18: The Thirteenth Amendment is ratified, accepted by twenty-seven of thirty-six states.

28: The U.S. Sanitary Commission's Michigan Branch donates $2,000 to Harper Hospital on condition that it provide care for the residents of the Soldiers' Home in Detroit.

Selected Legislation

The great conflict has had its useful lessons. Under the hard experience of the past four years, the relations sustained by the State and National governments towards each other have come to be more clearly understood and more accurately defined. We understand now the full meaning of that pernicious phrase "sovereign States," which had stealthily crept its way into so many public documents, political speeches and platforms, and finally into the common language of the people, until it came to teach and be understood to mean that there was no other sovereign in the country but the States, and whatever they decided to do, it was lawful to perform.

—AUSTIN BLAIR, VALEDICTORY SPEECH,
JANUARY 4, 1865[119]

I do not propose to discuss, at this place, the issues involved in the [November 1864] election, but simply to declare that the result plainly establishes the determination of the American people that slavery shall cease to exist, and that the authority of the government shall not be made subservient to the doctrine of State sovereignty and the right of secession. . . . I also suggest—as a further embodiment of the late expression of the popular will in our State—the propriety of your officially requesting our Senators and Representatives in Congress, to use their influence in favor of the adoption of the necessary measures for so amending the Constitution as forever to prohibit the existence of slavery within the limits of the national jurisdiction.

—HENRY H. CRAPO, INAUGURATION
SPEECH, JANUARY 4, 1865[120]

[NB: *Legislative measures designed to legalize local actions to raise taxes, borrow money, issue bonds to recruits, or to repay advances made by individuals for the same purpose are identified in the footnote to Act No. 160 below.*]

Joint Resolution No. 1: Joint Resolution asking the government of the United States for a grant of land, in aid of the construction of a harbor at the mouth of the Ontonagon River, on the south shore of Lake Superior.

Whereas, "The dignity and security of the nation demands that our lakes, on the northern frontier, should be put in a condition of 'armed defense,'

and that Lake Superior should, in this respect, be placed on an equal footing with the other lakes, as its commerce and mineral interests have become of equal national importance; *And whereas,* There is at present no safe harbor between Copper Harbor and [La] Point, on Lake Superior, where our steamers and sailing vessels can enter, a distance of one hundred and fifty miles." *Resolved:* Asks the congressional delegation to lobby for federal funding to build a harbor at the mouth of the Ontonagon River. Approved January 21, 1865.[121]

No. 5: Joint Resolution ratifying the proposed amendment to the constitution of the United States.

Whereas, "The Congress of the United States, after solemn and mature deliberations therein, has, by a vote of two-thirds of both houses, passed 'a joint resolution submitting to the legislatures of the several states, a proposition to amend the constitution of the United States,' which resolution is in the following words: That the following article be proposed to the legislatures of the several States, as an amendment to the constitution of the United States, which, when ratified by three-fourths of said legislatures, shall be valid to all intents and purposes, as a part of the constitution, namely:

Article XIII

'**Section 1:** Neither slavery nor involuntary servitude, except as a punishment for a crime, whereof the party shall have been duly convicted, shall exist within the United States, or any place subject to their jurisdiction.

Section 2: Congress shall have power to enforce this article by appropriate legislation.'" [End Amendment.]

"*And whereas.* American slavery, in its wickedness and infatuation, has added to its many other heinous sins, the crime of waging a causeless, cruel and bloody war for the avowed purpose of dividing and destroying the nation, whereby it has forfeited all right to further toleration, and has clearly demonstrated that its continuance is wholly incompatible with the safety and preservation of a free republican government, and that in order to form a more perfect union, establish justice, insure domestic tranquility, provide for the common defense, promote the general welfare, and secure the blessings of liberty to ourselves and our posterity, it has become necessary to utterly destroy this barbarous foe of civilization, humanity and religion; therefore[:] *Resolved* by the Senate and House of Representatives of the State of Michigan, That in the name and in behalf of the people of the State, we do hereby ratify, approve and assent to the said amendment. *Resolved*, That a copy of this assent and ratification be engrossed on parchment, and transmitted by His Excellency the Governor, to the United States, in Congress assembled." Approved, February 2, 1865.[122]

Joint Resolution No. 6: Joint Resolution instructing our Senators, and requesting our Representatives in Congress, to urge upon the general government the necessity of establishing a general naval recruiting and muster-in office for the State of Michigan.

Whereas, the president has called for 300,000 men; and whereas, Michigan citizens have "a deep interest in having the quota assigned to our State filled as speedily as possible." *And whereas*, "Many of our citizens, preferring the naval branch of the service, have made application at the recruiting offices located among us, and failing to find the proper officers to receive them, have been compelled to leave Michigan in order to be mustered into the naval service, and have been credited upon the quotas of other States. We therefore have been deprived of the advantages granted to our sister States, and compelled to furnish men by drafting, to fill the places of the men so lost," therefore, requests Michigan's congressional delegation "to secure the immediate establishment of a general naval recruiting and muster-in office for the State of Michigan . . . [to] . . . be located in the city of Detroit." Approved February 2, 1865.[123]

No. 27: An Act to provide for the payment of bounties to volunteers in the military and naval service of the United States.

Section 1: Authorizes the QMG to pay enlisted personnel actually mustered into U.S. army or naval service, "a uniform state bounty," to wit: first, $150 to volunteers enlisted and mustered to the credit against any quota of a Michigan military subdistrict[124] "under the last or future call of the President of the United States for troops"; second, to three-year volunteers, credited against quotas under the president's future calls, "the sum of two

hundred dollars in lieu of all other State bounties," subject to these conditions: the volunteer must be a state resident, produce a certificate from the PM or EO of his district that he is actually credited to the township or ward where he is enrolled, and if he is a state resident and not enrolled, he must produce his own affidavit and one from his town or ward supervisor that he is credited to that entity; and third, if a nonresident, prove by his own affidavit that he is in fact, a nonresident.[125]

Section 12: Prohibits counties, cities, or towns to "vote any tax, or sum of money, to raise, or pay, or to secure the payment of any sum of money, nor shall any such" entity "in any meeting of the electors therefor, or otherwise, pledge the faith or credit" of such entity "for the purpose of raising any sum of money for the payment of any bounty or gratuity, to induce any person to enlist in the military or naval service of the United States." [NB: *This was designed to eliminate bounty competition beyond the amounts permitted above.*] Approved February 4, 1865.[126]

No. 85: An Act authorizing a war bounty loan.

Section 1: Authorizes the governor on necessity to borrow up to $1,000,000 for state bounties, with a rate not exceeding 7 percent redeemable after twenty-five years.

Section 5: Pledges "the faith of the State" for repayment. Approved March 2, 1865.[127]

No. 86: An Act to legalize the action of certain townships, cities, and counties, in raising the bounties for volunteers.

Section 1: Legalizes municipal acts that have previously voted to raise taxes or borrow money, "or shall have directed a committee of citizens . . . to hire, advance or raise money" or "issued any bonds . . . with the object and to the end of encouraging enlistments by paying bounties to volunteers in the military or naval service of the United States, who enlisted and were mustered before" February 4, 1865, or shall have done the same to encourage procuring substitutes or encouraging draftees to enter the service themselves.

Section 2: Legalizes the payment or offers to pay bounties to draftees or to those procuring substitutes before February 4, 1865.

Section 3: Requires municipalities to raise taxes for

bonds issued or to be issued to those entering service before February 4, 1865. However: no bonds issued shall be valid unless voters approve. Approved March 2, 1865.[128]

No. 111: An Act to prevent the swindling of persons enlisting into the military or naval service of the United States, or of this State, and to make such offenses felony, and to punish the use of certain means to procure enlistments.

Section 1: "That any recruiting agent, or other person acting under the authority of this State or the general government, or any local municipality . . . who shall willingly defraud any person enlisting or having enlisted" of bounty or pay "shall be deemed guilty of a felony" and is liable to imprisonment for up to two years.

Section 2: "Whoever shall knowingly and willfully administer to any person any stupefying substance or drug, with intent, while such person is under the influence . . . to induce such person to enter" military service, is guilty of a felony and liable to imprisonment for up to two years.

Section 3: It is unlawful for any person "to induce or procure the enlistment" into military service "any person under arrest, charged with the commission of any offense punishable by imprisonment in the State prison, nor of any person recognized to appear before any court for trial for any offense punishable by imprisonment . . . unless such persons shall be discharged from such arrest, or allowed to go at large upon his own recognizance" by a judge's order. Violators will be guilty of a misdemeanor. Approved March 4, 1865.[129]

No. 118: An Act to provide means to complete and keep in repair the soldiers' national cemetery, at Gettysburg, Pennsylvania.

Section 1: Appropriates $2,500 from the War Fund to pay Michigan's proportion of the expenses of "completing and keeping in repair the soldiers' national cemetery, at Gettysburg." Approved March 8, 1865.[130]

No. 160: An Act to authorize the township board of the township of Coldwater, Branch County, to issue bonds for paying bounties to volunteers.

Section 1: Legalizes Coldwater's actions to raise money for bounties under the December 19, 1864, call.

Section 2: Bonds may be issued in maturities up to

five years at an interest rate not more than 7 percent, the aggregate amount of bonds not to exceed $4,000.

Section 3: Requires Coldwater to raise taxes by an amount equal to debt service. Approved March 14, 1865.[131]

No. 209: An Act to punish the recruiting of men for the volunteer service of other States.

Section 1: It is unlawful to "willfully and maliciously aid, with the design of preventing a resident of this State from being credited to the township or ward where he actually resides, to persuade or induce . . . any resident of this State to enlist in the military or naval forces of the United States for the purpose of being credited to the quota of any other State." Violators are liable to a fine up to $1,000 and up to one year imprisonment. Approved March 16, 1865.[132]

No. 228: An Act making appropriation for the soldiers' relief fund.

Section 1: Appropriates $5,000 "to be expended by the Governor . . . as may be necessary, in the payment of the arrears of the soldiers' relief fund."

Section 2: Appropriates $20,000 "for the relief of sick, disabled and needy soldiers." Approved March 18, 1865.[133]

No. 295: An Act to authorize a war bounty loan.

Section 1: Requires the governor and treasurer "whenever it shall become necessary for the purpose of paying a State bounty to borrow up to $500,000 with a maturity up to twenty-five years and a rate not to exceed 7 percent, to be known as the War Bounty Loan of the State of Michigan."

Section 5: "The faith of the State is hereby pledged" to repayment. Approved March 21, 1865.[134]

Joint Resolution No. 43: Joint Resolutions on the state of the Union.

Resolved, [the State of Michigan] "hereby re-affirm[s] the devotion of this Commonwealth to the Constitution and government of the United States, and the earnest determination of its people to do everything in their power, to support and sustain the national administration."

Resolved, "That as American slavery degrades man, and robs him of those sacred rights to life, liberty, and the pursuit of happiness . . . [and] as it has long shown itself an enemy to public peace, and inspired, caused, and is justly responsible for all the blood and tears, the crimes and horrors that cluster about this unholy rebellion . . . [the situation] imperatively demands the complete extirpation of this great wrong from every foot of the national soil; we therefore approve the measures adopted by the administration for its destruction . . . and heartily endorse the [Thirteenth] amendment."

Resolved, "That the wisdom, prudence, and faithful devotion to the preservation of the national life, that have characterized the administration of the general government of Abraham Lincoln, and of the State government of Austin Blair . . . merit our hearty approval." *Resolved*, "That we extend our sincere thanks to the soldiers of Michigan, and of the Union."

Resolved, "That the inhuman and barbarous treatment of our brave and suffering soldiers confined in rebel prisons, is shocking to humanity, contrary to the usages of modern warfare, and betrays a cruelty and baseness on the part of their captors."

Resolved, "That the thanks of the State are eminently due to its patriotic daughters, whose words of encouragement and gentle and sympathizing deeds of kindness and love, joined with their generous contributions of labor and means, through the instrumentality of aid societies and sanitary and Christian commissions, have cheered the hearts and contributed largely to the relief and comfort of our wounded soldiers." Approved March 21, 1865.[135]

Concurrent Resolution No. 13: Tenders official thanks to "the soldiers of Michigan, who promptly responded to the call of their country in its time of peril, and who, by their fortitude and soldierly bearing under the privations and hardships of a soldier's life. . . ."

Resolved, that the House Clerk send a copy of this resolution "to each of the regiments and batteries of Michigan soldiers now in the field." Approved March 21, 1865.[136]

Concurrent Resolution No. 14: *Whereas*, "The Hon. Austin Blair, whose valedictory message was delivered to this legislature on the fifth of January, eighteen hundred and sixty-five, has retired to private life. . . .

And whereas, Governor's Blair's administration has been marked by eminent ability, rare integrity, and unsurpassed success, as shown by the enlistments and organization into companies, regiments and batteries in the most perfect military order, of over eighty thousand men. . . ."

Therefore, Resolved (the Senate concurring) "That the thanks of the people of Michigan, through this legislature, are hereby cordially tendered to ex-Governor Blair, for the able and satisfactory manner in which he has, during his administration, of the last four years, been able to conduct the affairs of the government of the State." Approved March 21, 1865.[137]

Selected Summaries

Recruiting, Manpower, and Casualties

The War Department listed Michigan's aggregate wartime quotas as 95,007 men, against which it furnished 87,364, with 2,008 paying commutation; thus, Michigan's men/credits were 89,372. However, when reduced to a three-year standard, Michigan furnished only 80,111 men. Total men included 85,479 white troops, 489 sailors and marines, and 1,387 colored troops. (For unclear reasons, 9 men were left unaccounted for.) As of April 30, 1865, Michigan's enrollment was 75,248. (The War Department listed no Michigan Native American troops, although many served. See below.) Michigan's estimated deserters were between 5,935 and 6,525.[1]

Of 23 Northern states and the District of Columbia, Michigan forces comprised 2.3% of the Union army. By comparison, New York was top ranked with a contribution of 11.7%, followed by Pennsylvania (8.8%) and third-ranked Ohio with 8.2%. However, because these states were far more populous than Michigan, their higher contributions to Union manpower were inevitable. Perhaps more meaningful was the percentage of total population that served. Michigan's 11.8% exceeded New York's 11.6% and trailed Pennsylvania's 14.3% and Ohio's 13.4%. Among states of the Old Northwest, top-ranked Illinois was at 15.1%, followed by Indiana at 14.5%, Minnesota at 14.2%, Wisconsin equaling Michigan at 11.8%, with Iowa trailing with 11.3%.[2]

Michigan raised eleven cavalry regiments and two short-term cavalry companies; one light artillery regiment and eleven independent batteries; one engineer regiment; one sharpshooter regiment and eight sharpshooter companies, of which four joined Berdan's USSS; one three-month infantry unit and thirty three-year units, including one African American regiment and two companies for in-state deployment.

Michigan's quotas and men furnished under the calls issued during the war:

April 15, 1861, for three months: 780 quota with 781 furnished.

Combined three-year call of May 3, July 22, and July 25, 1861: 21,357 quota with 23,546 furnished.

July 1, 1862, for three years: a 11,686 quota with 17,656 furnished.

August 4, 1862, for nine months: 11,686 quota with 0 furnished. [NB: *Michigan chose to recruit three-year units and fill vacancies in existing units rather than recruit nine-month troops.*]

October 17, 1863, combined with the call of February 1, 1864, both for three-year troops: a 19,553 quota with 17,686 furnished and 1,644 paid commutations; aggregate credits, 19,330.

March 14, 1864, for three years: a 7,821 quota with 7,344 furnished and 323 paid commutations; total credits, 7,667.

One Hundred Days' Militia for service between April 23 and July 18, 1864: 0. [NB: *Michigan offered no 100-day troops.*]

Call of July 18, 1864, for one-, two-, three-, or four-year service: 12,098 quota with 5,960 men furnished for one year, 57 for two years, 6,492 for three years, and 0 for four years with 23 paying commutation. Aggregate furnished, 12,532.

Call of December 19, 1864, for one-, two-, three-, or four-year service: 10,026 quota with 6,767 sent for one year, 41 for two years, 1,034 for three years, and 0 for four years with eighteen paying commutations. Aggregate furnished, 7,860.[3]

By AG Robertson's count, Michigan's total credits were 92,729, consisting of 81,365 men enlisting from the war's start to November 1, 1864; 1,982 commuters; and 9,382 men enlisted or drafted between November 1, 1864, and the war's end. Subtracting commuters, he arrived at an aggregate of 90,747 actual enlistments. This figure includes reenlistments, of whom 5,545 were Veteran Volunteers. Robertson includes a county breakdown of enlistments and credits, which underscores the south Michigan skew of state population. The top five counties measured in recruits were Wayne (9,213), Lenawee (4,347), Kent (4,214), Washtenaw (4,084), and Calhoun,

(3,878). The bottom five were Manitou (10), Menominee (19), Chippewa (21), Delta (24), and Iosco (27).[4]

Robertson also provided a detailed listing of the nativities of Michigan's volunteers. His figures here differ from those of Dyer,[5] the War Department, and occasionally his own earlier calculations, but Robertson's numbers provide details about Michigan's force composition. Of 90,747 Michiganders who served, 88,941 were white, 1,661 were African American, and 145 were Native American. Of all soldiers, 67,468 were born in the United States. Principal domestic nativities included 21,517 born in Michigan; 31,137 in New York, New Jersey, or Pennsylvania; 9,506 in Ohio and Indiana; 2,847 in New England; 300 in Illinois and Wisconsin; and 166 in Kentucky and Tennessee. Blacks born in slave states numbered 956, and 217 were blacks born in free states.

Foreign-born soldiers included 8,886 from British Canada, including 441 black Canadians; 14,393 others were chiefly European, including England (3,761), Ireland (3,929), Scotland (763), Germany (4,872), France or its colonies, (380), Spain or Latin America (22), Scandinavia, (381), miscellaneous white (238), miscellaneous colored (47).[6]

According to Dyer, of the 87,364 Michiganders who served in all branches, 14,753 died from all causes, which were composed of killed or mortally wounded in battle, 4,448; died from disease, 8,269; died as POWs, 1,268; died from accidents, 339; and death from all other causes, 429. In 1888, William F. Fox published his study, *Regimental Losses in the Civil War*, which listed the top 300 federal regiments in terms of combat losses: KIA or DOW. Fox's list included Michigan units from across the state and which fought in every major theater of the war: the First, Fifth, and Sixth cavalries; the First Michigan Sharpshooters; and the First, Second, Third, Fourth, Fifth, Seventh, Eighth, Sixteenth, Seventeenth, Twentieth, Twenty-Fourth, and Twenty-Seventh infantries.[7]

Benjamin Apthrop Gould's 1869 study of United States Volunteers sampled 39,107 Michigan volunteers aged between 13 and "50 & over," including 3 soldiers aged 13 and 61 men over 50 years of age: 5,862 were between 18 and 19 years old; 450 soldiers were under age 18; 566 were aged 45 and older. The five largest entries were between the ages of 18 and 22, totaling 18,595 men; however, the 22,864 men older than 22 raised the mean age of enlistment to 25.52 years. Gould also classified 8,986 Michigan volunteers by occupation: 4,928 (54.8%) were in agriculture, 1,717 (19.1%) mechanics, 1,217 (13.5%) laborers, 175 (1.9%) commercial, 120 (1.3%) professionals, 50 (0.5%) printers, and 779 (8.6%) miscellaneous. It should be noted that Michigan's sample was the smallest of the fifteen states Gould examined.[8]

Gould also classified the education of 1,001 soldiers born in Michigan, Wisconsin, and Illinois but combined the three states:

None: 24
Slight: 8
Limited Common School: 656
Good Common School: 286
High School: 23
Collegiate: 4
Professional: 0[9]

Michigan in the United States Navy

Given Michigan's long coastline and important role in the Great Lakes maritime economy (see Introduction), it is unsurprising that some Michiganders might be predisposed to naval service, while others sought to satisfy service obligations; the historian's challenge is in determining how many actually served. AG Robertson's 1882 *Michigan in the War* noted a lack of information; he relied on the War Department figure of 598 men credited. He gave biographies of 55 men. Dyer's *Compendium*, published in 1908, put the figure at 498. Curiously, and without any comment, the *Record of Service of Michigan Volunteers in the Civil War*, authorized in 1903, listed only 144 Michigan officers and men (including two Marines) in naval service. It is unclear whether the *Record* vetted the War Department's 598-man list to distinguish "credits" from actual Michigan residents in naval service; this seems unlikely, as anecdotal evidence suggests a far higher number—23 from Jackson alone in August of 1864. On August 22, 1865, the *Detroit Advertiser and Tribune* published a list of 74 Michigan sailors who were due bounties; of these, only 1 was also listed in the *Record*.

Finally, it is also unclear how many Michigan African American served in the Navy. Unlike the army and USMC, the USN had from its 1798 inception *always* accepted African Americans as enlisted personnel. Unfortunately, the *Record* contains no information on how many (if any) black Michiganders served in the Civil War navy.[10]

Of the *Record*'s 144 men, 143 specified start dates; of

these, 8 officers and 1 enlisted man had served in the prewar navy; the officers included men of considerable blue-water experience, skills that were utilized in both the naval blockade of the South's coast as well as the riverine war fought in western and eastern theaters. Of the *Record's* 144 sailors, the service records of 111 identified vessels; this allows some idea as to the type of service Michiganders experienced.

Service has been divided into four categories: blockade enforcement, riverine duty, foreign seas duty, and Great Lakes service. Inferring a sailor's assignment from the vessel identified in the *Record's* biography (and excluding receiving ships) reveals that 31 of 111 Michigan sailors helped enforce the blockade, 70 served on the nation's river waterways, four were on foreign seas duty, and three sailed with the USS *Michigan*. In addition, at least three Michiganders sailed with Admiral David G. Farragut as part of his famed flotilla.[11]

African Americans in Michigan Units

While Michigan fielded only one colored unit, the First Michigan, Colored, later redesignated the One Hundred and Second, USCT, many black Michiganders served in other state and many United States units. It should also be noted that the First Michigan Colored and other black units recruited until war's end, and for the July 18 and December 19, 1864, calls, of the 2,480 men drafted, 1,022 were substitutes, of which approximately 24% or 245 men were black, thus relieving an equal number of white males from service. As for Michigan's black unit, the difficulty is in determining how many black men credited to Michigan were actual state residents at the time of enlistment. The *Record of Service of Michigan Volunteers in the Civil War* omits many African Americans who served in other state units, while listing others who when enlisted had probably never seen Michigan.[12]

For example, the *Record* omits at least 60 men who served in the famed Massachusetts Fifty-Fourth Infantry and 5 who served in the Fifth Massachusetts Cavalry. The Fourteenth Rhode Island Heavy Artillery recruited Michigan African Americans, although the number who might have enlisted is unclear. The *Record* does include 14 USCT units that contained a total of 70 black soldiers, 1 surgeon (probably white), and 1 chaplain, heritage unknown. Of the 70 black enlistees 17 were substitutes and 8 were draftees. All were enlisted in 1864–1865, with all but 2 joining after July 4, 1864.

This last date is significant. On July 4, 1864 (see date), Congress enacted Chapter 237, Section 3, which permitted governors to recruit in some formerly insurgent states. While Governor Blair announced (see July 21, 1864) that Michigan would neither appoint nor pay state agents, he also declared that "under proper regulations" he might "appoint such agents for the benefit of any counties, towns or sub-districts which may require it" so long as they paid the expense. And many Michigan cities and counties did so, including the counties of Lapeer and Branch, and the towns of Adrian, Ann Arbor, and Coldwater. Excluding the Rhode Island and Massachusetts units already noted, USCT units follow, with the total number men credited to Michigan/probable Michigan residents/men enlisted in the field. Additional information appears in notes.[13]

Third Cavalry, USCT, 16/0/16[14]
Fifth Heavy Artillery, USCT, 14/0/14[15]
Ninth Heavy Artillery, USCT, 3/0/3[16]
Thirteenth Artillery, USCT, 21/21/0[17]
Thirty-First Infantry, USCT, 1/0/1[18]
Thirty-Eighth Infantry, USCT, 6/6/0[19]
Forty-Ninth Infantry, USCT, 1/0/1[20]
Fifty-Third, Fifty-Fifth, and Sixty-First Infantry, USCT, each, 1/0/1
Fifty-Fourth, Fifty-Eighth, and One Hundred and Twenty-Third Infantries, USCT, each 1/Unknown/1[21]
Captain Powell's Colored Infantry, USCT, 4/0/4[22]

Native Americans and Michigan's Civil War

Company K of the First Michigan Sharpshooters became the most famous Native American unit in the Army of the Potomac. About 150 men, mostly Indians, passed through its ranks from the time it commenced recruiting (see July 4, 1863) until the unit's discharge on July 28, 1865. Although Company K boasted men from the Delaware, Huron, Oneida, and Potawatomi peoples, the majority were recruited in the Lower Peninsula from the Ottawa, Chippewa, and Ottawa-Ojibwa communities, with many residing in Mason and Oceana Counties.[23]

Company K's profile included men recruited in Pentwater (24), Isabella (23), Little Traverse (9), and Saginaw (7), with 6 claiming New York or Ontario residency. The balance were from towns and villages scattered throughout Michigan. Of the 114 Native American recruits disclosing occupations, the largest number were farmers (75), followed by laborers (23), hunters and trappers (11), along with sailors (2), fishermen (1), merchants (1), and in his own category, Second Lieutenant Garrett A. Gravaraet, a musician. As described in Gravaraet's biographical note (see July 4, 1863) after initial deployments confronting John Hunt Morgan in Cincinnati and guard duty at Camp Douglas in Illinois, Company K fought throughout Grant's Overland Campaign, its last major action being the disastrous Battle of the Crater. It was there that an officer from another regiment observed Company K members, "mortally wounded, and drawing their blouses over their faces, they chanted a death song and died—four of them in a group."[24]

An 1890 history of Oceana County describes the July 4, 1863, Pentwater recruitment meeting and its immediate aftermath. "Some of them never returned," the historian wrote about Oceana's Native Americans recruits, "but gave their lives to perpetuate the white man's government." This raises a question: why did these men fight? Hauptman, after considering the mistreatment and discrimination to which Michigan's Native Americans were subject, concluded that after decades of efforts to "resettle" them outside of their traditional lands (which had only lately become a "state"), the Michigan Ottawa had become "desperate" to retain what lands were granted them under the 1855 Treaty of Detroit. Because of vagaries in that pact and the pressure of new white settlement, "The Ottawa as well as their Ojibwa neighbors quickly saw that it would be necessary to readjust their treaties in order to guarantee them and their progeny a larger and more permanent landbase. Thus the Ottawa and Ojibwa enlisted in the Civil War in part in hopes of gaining the trust and leverage for a new treaty agreement." The fate of that aspiration exceeds the scope of this work.[25]

Finances

For the twelve months preceding November 30, 1864 (the end of Michigan's fiscal year), the state had received $2,444,242.25 in revenue and spent $2,004,194.98, leaving a cash balance for 1865 of $440,047.27. For the same twelve months, the War Fund account, through which the state paid its war-related expenses, spent $943,603.79, of which $120,387.04 represented an overdraft from

the prior year. Excluding this overdraft, Michigan spent $823,216.75. Total debt at the end of this fiscal year was $3,541,149.80; however, much of this represented prewar borrowings. However, a true statement of "Michigan's" debt would have to include the town and county borrowings, chiefly for bounties.[26]

Local governments and individuals financed bounties from the war's beginning. As is apparent from the legislation in this chapter, the state did not begin to pay bounties ($50) until 1863; in 1864, the bounty increased to $100, and in 1865, to $150. In 1864, the state capped local bounties at $200 in an effort to control soaring recruitment costs.[27]

These personnel costs shifted downstream from federal to state and state to local governments. In PMG Fry's 1866 report, within Michigan's six congressional districts (and excluding U.S. bounties) a total of $9,664,855 in bounties was paid: First District, $1,610,809; Second, $1,493,006; Third, $1,845,950; Fourth, $1,480,172; Fifth, $1,582, 518; and Sixth, $1,652,400. Fry's report suggests that Governor Blair's efforts to make bounties uniform by requiring documentation to match recruits with their places of enrollment probably had some success: for example, under the call of December 19, 1864, the average bounty paid ranged from $328 in the Second District to $400 in the Fourth District. This was not nearly as wide as in Ohio, where the average bounties under the same call ranged from $300 to $545. Fry's report also reveals local bounty inflation in Michigan: for example, in the First District, the bounty for 1863 averaged $100; under the calls of February 1 and March 14, 1864, it averaged $150; under the call of July 1864, $300; and under the call of December 19, 1864, $375.[28]

Family aid expenses totaled $3,591,248.12. For the war and by county, aid ranged from zero (Delta, Mackinac, and Manitou) to $8.80 (Alpena) to $547,200 (Wayne). By 1884, the United States had reimbursed Michigan $844,262.53 for its wartime expenses.[29]

Benevolence

The State

State benevolence had four main pillars: aid to families, state-paid bounties, allotment commissioners, and state agents in the field. Michigan's first family-aid law was passed in the Extra Session 1861 and amended in every session through 1864. These acts are summarized in the appropriate legislative sessions. Michigan addressed Congress's December 24, 1861, passage of an allotment bill on January 18, 1862, in Joint Resolution No. 13. This paid for the expenses of the state allotment commissioners tasked with marketing the program to soldiers and sometimes handling funds. (See Selected Legislation—1862.) Michigan's state agency program eventually produced six principal agents: Benjamin Vernor in Detroit; Dr. Joseph Tunnicliffe, Jr., who was joined in early 1865 by Rev. David Edmond Millard* in Washington; Luther B. Willard at Nashville; J. B. Gillman at Louisville; Weston Flint in St. Louis; and Darius Clark in New York City.

State benevolence also extended to other areas: the state paid for transportation and certain expenses for volunteer surgeons, nurses, and hospital supplies. (See Military Affairs—1862.) Michigan also paid for soldiers' transportation from camp to home front, an expense scandalously ignored by the War Department. On February 18, 1863, in response to Governor Blair's request, the legislature appropriated $20,000 to help return casualties to their homes. It authorized Blair to hire agents charged with visiting hospitals and identifying Michigan casualties eligible for return home. (This act will be found in Selected Legislation—1863.)

The state also provided for the machinery to provide transport, and process ballots during the 1864 elections. (See No. 21, passed February 5, 1864.) Postwar in 1867, the state began appropriating funds for the Soldiers' Home (the Detroit facility having been absorbed by Harper Hospital) and transferring management to the State Military Board. Ultimately, many of these disabled veterans were moved to National Homes when these supplanted state systems: to Dayton, Milwaukee, Wisconsin, Augusta, Maine (Togus), and Hampton, Virginia.[30]

The Hospital Network

Michigan, far from the front, was spared the burdens of Washington, Philadelphia, Baltimore, Louisville, and Nashville of accommodating sick and wounded men from many nearby encampments and battlefields. Instead, Michigan's hospital "network" was devoted chiefly to its own soldiers (and transients) and consisted of two U.S. General Hospitals located in Detroit: St. Mary's Hospital and Harper Hospital. (Two lesser facilities, the Marine Hospital and the Post Hospital at Fort Wayne, are discussed below.) Harper and St. Mary's provided for those ill or wounded in battle elsewhere, and then sent home to recover or die. Michigan was unexceptional in this regard: beginning in 1863 and in response to constituents' political pressure, governors everywhere began to lobby the War Department to provide home-state federally run or subsidized facilities for the return of their own citizen casualties. Harper Hospital opened in October 1864 (see October 12, 1864), and in common with many hastily erected U.S. General Hospitals, was built of wood: a contemporary engraving depicts the Harper compound as a two-story building flanked on each side by four long one-story wards (not visible were two smaller buildings in the rear). When first opened, Harper had some 200 beds, but that number quickly grew to 528. As noted in the entries, in December 1865, the War Department returned Harper to civilian control (on condition that it continue to treat military patients), and on January 1, 1866, Harper opened to the general public.

Harper continued to treat Michigan veterans, and as that population aged, it became a veterans' care facility. The Michigan branch of the Sanitary Commission turned over $2,000 for veterans' care, and as late as 1883, the hospital housed a dozen men requiring in-patient treatment. (Harper continues today as Harper University Hospital, part of the Wayne State University School of Medicine.)[31]

St. Mary's Hospital, founded in 1845, was administered by the Sisters of Charity (see June 21, 1862) and originally named St. Vincent's Hospital. The facility that served for the war was a masonry structure built in 1850 and contained 150 beds. It was St. Mary's that served as the main hospital before Harper's opened late in the war. Although a Catholic facility, it was nonsectarian in service. In 1949 St. Mary's became Detroit Memorial Hospital, which continues to provide care on the same site. Two other facilities deserve mention. The Marine Hospital, built in 1854 with a federal subsidy and maintained by local taxes, was devoted to civilian and military seamen. The second facility was the Post Hospital at Fort Wayne, which treated garrison patients.[32]

Private Benevolence

United States Sanitary Commission: Michigan

The origins of the Michigan Branch of the United States Sanitary Commission are detailed in this volume (see

April 22, 1861). Michigan women responded spontaneously to the needs of war at a time when state and federal quartermasters lacked some articles necessary to outfit soldiers. Michigan was fortunate in its early aid organizers Isabella Duffield and her married daughter, Isabella Graham Duffield Stewart: matriarch Isabella was born into New York City's upper echelons and quickly reestablished connections with New York City–based Mrs. Richard N. Blatchford and Mrs. George L. Schuyler, among the founders of what became the United States Sanitary Commission. Stewart also had contacts with her more recent acquaintance, Dorothy Dix; these connections helped Duffield rapidly organize.[33]

Michigan's location soon turned its benevolence west. Much of what it supplied by way of cash and supplies went to Chicago; from the war's beginnings, Michigan private aid trickled to state units in western Virginia, Kentucky, and Missouri. Once the Western Commission established its Western Central Office in Louisville, it began to receive packages from Michigan donors for shipment to Cleveland, Cincinnati, and Chicago, although most contributions were directed to the last-mentioned city.[34]

What began as "Ladies' Aid" soon became Detroit Aid and then the Michigan branch of the Western Sanitary Commission. (Shortly after this affiliation, the Michiganders politely informed the New York Central Women's Association that henceforth, its supplies would be directed west, not east.) This reflected the fact that Detroit quickly became not only a source of supplies but also a hub for other in-state organizations, which were also raising cash and forwarding supplies. By war's end, there were 358 local organizations located in 45 Michigan counties. Many shipments were prompted by a series of targeted efforts: the antiscorbutic campaigns of 1862, 1863, and 1864 and periodic pushes for hospital supplies, which included items readily available to nonmedical civilians, such as socks, slippers, books, and bedsheets.[35]

Among Michigan Soldiers' Aid Society's final projects was the Soldiers' Home in Detroit. The Home had grown from its opening on January 25, 1864 (see that date). Through October 31, 1864, it admitted 5,599 soldiers, served 42,785 meals, and provided 14,399 lodgings.[36]

Christian Commission

After it established a Michigan branch in June 1863 (see June 15, 1863), the Christian Commission was largely inactive in state for the balance of that year. The one exception was its efforts to provide relief after the Battle of Gettysburg. Several Michigan delegates were appointed in Philadelphia en route to the battlefield. Fundraising for Michigan's Christian Commission did not commence in earnest until Thanksgiving, 1863. From that point until the end of 1864, the Commission had raised $21,725.20 in Michigan. In addition, it received in-kind contributions estimated at $10,000 in value.

The Michigan branch described itself as ministering "both to the mental and spiritual, as well as the bodily wants of the army. It sends the living preacher, the bible, and the religious newspapers of all denominations, and all the time it is ministering to the temporal wants of the soldier, and working for the sick, wounded and dying. It searches for the wounded amid the thickets of the battlefield, and never leaves him till he is discharged from the hospital, or a prayer consigns him to a soldiers' grave." The Commission sought to differentiate itself from the more institutionally directed Sanitary Commission when it declared that "All that is given to the Commission is dispensed personally by these delegates, and placed by their own hands in the hands of the soldier—not handed over to be dispensed by officials of the Government, or salaried agents of the Commission."[37]

To deliver these highly personalized services, the Michigan branch appointed 57 delegates, of whom 35 were identified as reverends and 5 as professors. There was 1 physician, and the rest were laymen. These men followed the armies: 34 were assigned to the Army of the Potomac, 16 to the Army of the Cumberland, and 7 to the Army of the Mississippi. They hailed from Detroit, Adrian, Ypsilanti, Ann Arbor, and other places throughout the state.[38]

One scholar has described the relationship between the Christian Commission and the Sanitary Commission (and more particularly, the Michigan Soldiers' Aid Society) as "alternatively bitter and sweet." The two organizations competed for supplies and cash from the same donor base. While battlefield accounts often stress the cooperative spirit between these groups, especially during emergencies, administrators further from the action sometimes questioned their counterparts' *raison d'etre*; the Michigan branch of the Sanitary Commission complained that Christian Commission delegates were begging supplies from their agents, while many "Christians" believed rumors that "Sanitaries" were personally corrupt or that donations were skimmed for improper purposes. Some friction resulted from two different aid models: the "Christians'" delegates were unpaid volunteers, and coupled with their religious motives, may have enjoyed higher prestige among donors. In contrast, the Sanitary Commission operated more on a business model, and most of its agents were paid, leading some to conclude that it shared in the general corruption that sometimes characterized government-business relations during the war.[39]

The Michigan Christian Commission continued its operations after war's end. In Detroit, it converted a warehouse into a reception facility for returning soldiers. (See June 4, 1865.) Between June 4, 1865, and June 10, 1866, it provided for over 23,000 returning soldiers.[40]

Michigan Soldiers' Relief Association: Washington, D.C.

The Michigan Soldiers' Relief Association did not limit its relief to Michigan soldiers. "At the front, after a battle, there is no time for discrimination as to State or locality," the Association reported in December 1864. "The wounded must all be attended to and their sufferings and wants must be relieved." It was only later "so soon as the hurry and excitement incidental to battles is over [that] we turn our attention more particularly to the men from our own State." By 1865, on those battlefields and in hospitals were agents Julia Wheelock (who left in July 1864), Elmina Brainard, Mrs. Laura Plumb[41] from Ypsilanti; Mrs. Ann E. Gridley* and Mrs. T. S. Mahan* from Hillsdale; Mrs. Louise Johnson* of Oakland County; and two male agents, Caleb Clark* and Luke Howard.* The Association and presumably these agents were at pains to distinguish themselves from the Sanitary Commission. "Other organizations may and doubtless have done much in relieving the wants of our Union soldiers, but their relief is so diffused over a wide and almost measureless field that when it reaches an individual soldier it is so attenuated that its effects are but little more than the dew of evening upon the dry and parched earth." When the Association went "institutional" it was on behalf of ventures such as establishing a Michigan Soldiers' Home in Washington intended as a hostel for transient Michiganders.[42]

For the year ending 1864, the Association had revenues of $6,779.73 and expenses of $5,448.48. However, these figures understated actual economies: its full-time employees worked virtually gratis (including its executive staff), and despite efforts to differentiate itself from the "national commissions," the Association received enormous in-kind distributions from the Sanitary and Christian Commissions. However, as a reading of the Association's reports makes clear, its relations with the latter were especially close. "Their mode of relief is similar to our own, in that they usually distribute directly to the needy soldier without waiting for requisitions, and that a great majority of their delegates accept no pay for their benevolent work among soldiers of the Union," treasurer Zebina Moses* noted.[43]

In January 1864, excerpts from a soldier's letter contrasted the Sanitary Commission with the Association: the Sanitary required a surgeon's order before dispensing aid, but the Association's benefits "are dispensed by its agents in person." The writer had special praise for Brainard and Wheelock: "These ladies . . . visit the different hospitals, barracks and camps in and about the city, and give to those who are needy. Five days in the week, on foot, through cold and rain, sunshine and storm, these women may be seen on their errands of mercy."

The Association remained active until September 1866, when it ceased operations and forwarded its remaining cash balance ($1,000) to Harper Hospital in Detroit, for the benefit of disabled soldiers.[44]

Michigan's African Americans: The Struggle Continued

Michigan's African American community was acutely aware that the Thirteenth Amendment was a beginning and not an end. For African Americans, the period between the war's final months and Andrew Johnson's cruel presidential Reconstruction was an optimistic one: emancipation was a reality and the part played by African Americans in vanquishing the Confederacy was beyond cavil. During this time, Michigan's African American community held two 1865 conventions in Detroit. Excerpts from several resolutions adopted by the first convention follow:

Colored Men's Convention, Detroit, January 25–26, 1865
"Resolved. . . . We would most respectfully, yet most
    earnestly ask the administration, to use every honorable endeavor that they may, to have the rights of the
    country's patriots respected, especially in the matter
    of merit, pay and promotion."

"Resolved, That we assert our full confidence in the fundamental principles of this government, the Christian spirit of our age and the justice of our sons; and that we further believe the influence of humanity, justice and religion will ultimately triumph and accord us our just claims, and concede us equal rights under the broad shield of the constitution."

"Resolved, That should an attempt be made to reconstruct the Union with slavery, we should regard such a course as a flagrant violation of good faith on the part of the government, false to the brave colored men, who have fallen in its defense. . . ."

"Resolved, That we extend the right hand of fellowship to the Freedmen of the South . . . [and for them] it is imperatively necessary to acquire education."

"Resolved, That we congratulate the people of Michigan in having elected to the National Legislature, one unbroken front of Legislators upon the principle of human freedom. . . ."

"Resolved, That the members of our Legislature are entitled to our thanks . . . for their kindness towards and treatment to our delegates, lately sent to Lansing with a petition, praying for the exercise of the elective franchise."[45]

Notes

Michigan in 1860

1. EHM, 21–23.

2. *Michigan: A Guide to the Wolverine State, Compiled by workers of the Writers' Program of the Work Projects Administration in the State of Michigan* (New York: Oxford University Press, 1941), 18; PR8, 107.

3. AAC.61.469; MOG, II.397–398.

4. *Encyclopedia of the War of 1812*, 346–347.

5. The American Lock at St. Mary's Falls, completed in 1855, was meant to bypass the falls on the St. Marys River. Michigan operated the lock and financed repairs and improvements. Although generally frozen over between November and May, during the open months in 1860, 916 total passages were made, representing 403,657 gross tons of shipping ("the measure of the overall size of a ship") carrying 153,721 tons of total freight. This included 50,250 barrels of flour, 133,437 bushels of grain, 9,000 tons of copper, and 120,000 tons of iron ore. Activity increased during the war: in 1864, total ship passages were 1,411, representing 571,438 net tons, carrying 284,350 tons of freight. This included 33,937 barrels of flour, 143,560 bushels of grain, 5,331 tons of copper, and 213,753 tons of iron ore. *Illustrated History of the St. Mary's Falls Ship Canal* (no city, Chapman & Kirby, 1893), 2–5; *St. Mary's Falls, Canal, Michigan: Statistical Report of Lake Commerce Passing through Canals at Sault Ste. Marie Michigan and Ontario during the Season of 1921, with Supplementary Report of Commerce passing through the Detroit River* (Washington, DC: Government Printing Office, 1922), 18–19. *International Convention on Tonnage Measurement of Ships, 1969* (London: International Maritime Organization, 1983), 9.

6. MOG, II.392; *Governor's Inaugural Message to the Legislature of the State of Michigan, in Session, January 4, 1865* (Lansing, MI: John A. Kerr & Co., Printers to the State, 1865), 14; for legislation, see JR No. 1, passed January 9, 1862; JR No. 9, passed January 17, 1862; JR No. 1: passed January 21, 1865; and JR No. 34, passed March 21, 1865.

7. "Railways, April 1, 1861," in Taylor and Neu, *The American Railroad Network, 1861–1890*.

8. SAW.5.66–67.

9. Smith, *The Borderland in the Civil War*, 327.

10. PR8, 195; Minnesota's growth was not calculated.

11. MOG, II.394; *Governor's Inaugural January 4, 1865*, 12; MOG, II.395, 400–401; Rudolph Diepenbeck was based in New York City and George F. Veen Fleit in Detroit.

12. Henry M. Utley and Byron M. Cutcheon, *Michigan as a Province, Territory, and State, the Twenty-Sixth Member of the Federal Union* (no city, Publishing Society of Michigan, 1906), vol. II, 369; EHM, 21–23.

13. "United States and Canadian Railways, April 1, 1861," in Taylor and Neu, *The American Railroad Network, 1861–1890*; Mills, *History of Saginaw County, Michigan, Historical, Commercial, Biographical* (Saginaw, MI: Seemann & Peters, 1918), 722; PR8, 121, 230. (Michigan consisted of 56,242 square miles, Illinois 55,405, and Wisconsin 53,924.)

14. MOG, II, 502; MAP, III.414; PR8, 197, 169, 198–205. *1860 Population*, 249; Gould, 210–211.

15. PR8, 190, 176, 173; MAP, III.414.

16. PR8, 1860, 107.

17. MAP, III.101–105; Copper was a component of almost every electrical storage and transmission device of the day. See generally, George B. Prescott, *History, Theory, and Practice of the Electric Telegraph* (Boston: Ticknor and Fields, 1860).

18. MAP, III.400; *Michigan in the War*, 17–21.

19. *Report of the Commissioner of Internal Revenue on the Operations of the Internal Revenue System for the Year Ending June 30, 1863* (Washington, DC: Government Printing Office, 1864), 232.

20. The private's wage assumed in this example is $13 monthly, which did not become law until August 6, 1861. *Statistics*, 512. Except for farmhands, the Eighth Census lists wages per diem. In calculating the figures given in the text, daily wages were multiplied by 365; to calculate board, the average weekly figure of $2.31 was annualized.

21. *The Revised Constitution of the State of Michigan, adopted in Convention, August 15, 1850* (Lansing, MI: R. W. Ingals, State Printer, 1850); *Constitution of the State of Michigan, as adopted in convention, begun and held at the capital, in the city of Detroit, on Monday, the 11th day of May, A.D. 1835* (Detroit: Sheldon M'Knight, 1835). Hereafter, each charter will be referenced by the year of its adoption. 1850, Article IV, Sections 1, 2, 3 and 5; 1850, Article VII, Section 1; *Journal of the House of Representatives for the State of Michigan, 1861* (Lansing, MI: Hosmer & Kerr, Printers to the State, 1861), 4–5.

22. 1850, Article IV, Sections 34, 15.

23. 1850, Article VII, Section 1; permitting foreigners to vote before citizenship was unpopular with many national Whigs; nevertheless, after Michigan was admitted to the Union with this constitutional provision, Wisconsin followed with its own version. Joseph Shafer, "The Yankee and the Teuton in Wisconsin, V: Social Harmonies and Discords," *Wisconsin Magazine of History* VII, no. 2 (December 1923): 160–161; DWT, September 18, 1860.

24. Dillon et al., *Michigan Women in the Civil War*, 8; 1850, Article XVI, Section 5; as quoted, Roy E. Finkenbine, "A Beacon of Liberty in the Great Lakes: Race, Slavery, and the Law in Antebellum Michigan," in *The History of Michigan Law*, ed. Paul Finkel and Martin J. Hershock (Athens: Ohio University Press, 2006), 93–94.

25. John K. Mahan, *History of the Militia and the National Guard* (New York: MacMillan, 1983), 83.

26. 1850, Article V, Sections 1, 2, 4; for judges, see Article VI, Sections 2, 6, 13, 17; Article VIII, Section 1; Article XVII, Section 1; Article XVIII, Sections 7 and 8.

27. 1850, Article VI, Sections 26, 28, and 29; Article IV, Sections 39, 40, 42, 43, 44. Article VI, Section 30.

28. Constitution of the State of Michigan, [1850], Article XIV, Sections 3, 4, and 2 (Lansing: np, 1850).

29. David M. Katzman, "Black Slavery in Michigan," *Midcontinent American Studies Journal* 11, no. 12 (Fall 1970): 60, 61, 65.

30. For facts relating to Michigan's historic black population, see Blanch Coogan, "The Underground Railroad in Michigan," *Negro History Bulletin* 27, no. 5, Special Detroit Edition (February, 1964), 122–126; Katzman, "Black Slavery in Michigan," 65n13; McRae, *Negroes in Michigan during the Civil War*, 1–3; *Negro Population in the United States, 1790–1915*, 57; *Constitution of the State of Michigan, 1835 as adopted in convention begun and held at the capitol, in the City of Detroit, on Monday, the 11th day of May, A.D. 1835* (Detroit: Printed by Sheldon M'Knight, 1835), 13.

31. *Laws of the Territory of Michigan*, vol. II (Lansing, MI: W. S. George & Co., State Printers, 1874), 634–636; *Negro Population in the United States, 1790–1915*, 57; McRae asserts that enforcement was lax.

32. Chapter 1, "Of Marriage and the Solemnization Thereof," Section 5, *The Revised Statutes of the State of Michigan, passed at the Adjourned Session of 1837, and the Regular Session of 1838* (Detroit, MI: John S. Bagg, 1838), 333–334; Finkenbine, "A Beacon of Liberty in the Great Lakes: Race, Slavery, and the Law in Antebellum Michigan," 92, 86, 96–98. The antikidnapping sections in the 1827 law survived the 1838 revision in Section 17 of "Offenses against lives: Kidnapping and selling as slaves," Approved July 15, 1838, Revised Statutes, found in Stephen Middleton, *The Black Laws of the Old Northwest*, 356–357; *Encyclopedia of African American History, 1619–1895: From the Colonial Period to the Age of Frederick Douglass*, vol. 2, ed. Paul Finkelman (New York: Oxford University Press, 2006), 357; Jacque Voegeli, "The Northwest and the Race Issue, 1861–1862," *Mississippi Valley Historical Review* 50, no. 2 (September 1963): 236, 238, 240; DFP, December 10, 1861. CG, Senate, 37th Congress, 2nd Session, 1780.

33. Hanes Walton Jr., Sherman C. Puckett, and Donald R. Deskins, Jr., *The African American Electorate: A Statistical History*, vol. 1 (Thousand Oaks, CA: CQ Press, 2012), 153; FAC, 9.

34. *Acts of the Legislature of the State of Michigan, passed at the annual session of 1849* (Lansing, MI: Munger and Pattison, 1849), 362–363; *The Journal of the House of the Representatives*, 1849, 56; "Legislative Doings," HWS, January 16, 1849; *Acts of the Legislature of the State of Michigan, passed at the regular session of 1855* (Lansing, MI: Geo. W. Peck, 1855), 483–485; *Journal of the Senate of the State of Michigan*, 1855, 127, 97–98; Streeter, *Political Parties in Michigan*, 115–117; *Acts of the Legislature of the State of Michigan, passed at the annual session of 1850* (Lansing, MI: R. W. Ingalls, 1850), 463–464.

35. *Acts of the Legislature*, 1855, 413–415; Title XXXVIII, Chapter CCXLI, "The Protection of the Rights and Liberties of Persons Claimed as Fugitive Slaves," *The Compiled Laws of the State of Michigan, compiled and arranged under an Act of the Legislature, approved January 25, 1871*, James S. Dewey, compiler, vol. II (Lansing, MI: W. S. George, 1872), 2065–2067.

36. DFP, February 8, 1861.

37. MSSM, vols. IV and VI.

38. *The Proceedings of Black State Conventions*, vol. 1.

39. *Under the Oaks*, 35–50; Michael F. Holt, *The Rise and Fall of the American Whig Party: Jacksonian Politics and the Onset of the Civil War* (New York: Oxford University Press, 1999), 861–862; JC, July 4, 1854.

40. Martin H. Hershock, "Copperheads and Radicals: Michigan Partisan Politics during the Civil War Era, 1860–1865," MHR 18, no. 1 (Spring, 1992): 30–31; *Historical Statistics of the United States, Millennial Edition, vol. 5: Governance and International Relations* (New York: Cambridge University Press, 2006), 5:186–188; For brief biographies of George H. Pendleton and Clement Vallandigham, see SAW.5.65–67; for Horatio Seymour and Fernando Wood, see SAW.2.86–87 and SAW.2.89–91.

41. Dubin, Parsons, and Beach, *United States Congressional Districts and Data*, 67.

42. See SAW.5.61–62.

43. See SAW.3.58–60.

44. See SAW.5.75–76.

45. Allan G. Bogue, *The Earnest Men: Republicans of the Civil War Senate* (Ithaca: Cornell University Press, 2009), 104–105.

46. For Benjamin Butler, see SAW.1.47.

47. BD.807; *Under the Oaks*, 22, 40–41, 121, as quoted, 62; *Early Michigan History*, 164–165; Wilmer Carlyle Harris, *Public Life of Zachariah Chandler*, 24, as quoted, 43, 48, 57; Bogue, *Earnest Men*, 96, 104–105; CG, Thirty-Seventh Congress, 2nd Session, 16–17, 32; Tap, *Over Lincoln's Shoulder*, 24, 30, 60–61, 122–126, 26; *Appleton's Cyclopaedia of American Biography*, I.574–575.

48. BD.657; SJ.37.1.20–21; EHM, 99–100; *Biographical Directory of Governors*, 747; MacPherson, 63, 64, 65, 195–196; William McDaid, "Kinsley S. Bingham and the Republican Ideology of Antislavery, 1847–1855," *Michigan Historical Review* 16, no. 2 (Fall 1990): 45–47, 50–51, 61–62, 64–65, 70; Bingham's views of ter-

ritorial slavery can be found in "Speech of Hon. Kinsley S. Bingham, of Michigan, Delivered in the House of Representatives of the U. States, August 7, 1848," (Washington, DC: J. and G. S. Gideon, Printers, 1848).

49. BD.1284; SJ.37.3.25; SJ.38.1.21–22; SJ.38.2.17–18; Bogue, *Earnest Men*, 39, 133, 97, 104–105; EHM, 357–358.

50. BD.797; *Appleton's Biography*, I.551–553; *In Memoriam. General Lewis Cass* (Detroit: Free Press Printing House, 1866), 207; David M. Potter, *The Impending Crisis*, 57; see SAW.6.285–286 for Cass and Fort Sumter.

51. March 4, 1861, to March 3, 1863; BD.162–163. Only standing committee assignments for the first session are listed. These may be found in HJ.37.1.38–41; subsequent sessions may be found at HJ.37.2, 36–37, and HJ.37.3, 46.

52. BD.1145; YC, November 11, 1882; PH, 224–225, 226, 229; *Journal of the Executive Proceedings of the Senate of the United States of America, from March 4, 1871 to March 3, 1873, inclusive*, vol. XVIII (Washington, DC: Government Printing Office, 1901), 188; *History of Washtenaw County Michigan* (Chicago: Chas. C. Chapman, 1881), 110, 226, 230, 254–255, 910, 1315.

53. BD.626; *Under the Oaks*, 44, 77; *Portraits and Biographies of the Governors of Michigan and of the Presidents of the United States* (no location, Chapman Bros., 1885), 201–202; EHM, 82–83; WE, October 5, 1882.

54. BD.1366; Walter Romig, *Michigan Place Names: The History of the Founding and Naming of More than Five Thousand Past and Present Michigan Communities* (Detroit: Wayne State University Press, 1986), 300; CIB, 161; Thomas, *History of Alabama and Dictionary of Alabama Biography* (Chicago: S. J. Clarke Publishing Company, 1921), 4 vols., vol. I, 348; MIW, 628, 569, 614, 571.

55. SAW.5.228.

56. March 4, 1863, to March 3, 1865; BD.166–167. Only standing committee assignments for the first session are listed. For the Thirty-Eighth Congress these may be found in HJ.38.1, 39–43, and for the second session, HJ.38.2, 32.

57. BD.2077; Rev. Henry P. Collin, *A Twentieth Century History and Biographical Record of Branch County, Michigan* (New York: Lewis Publishing Company, 1906), 348–350; KG, September 11, 1885.

58. BD.1467; Samuel W. Durant, *History of Ingham and Eaton Counties, Michigan, with Illustrations and Biographical Sketches of their Prominent Men and Pioneers* (Philadelphia: D. W. Ensign & Co., 1880), 373; DFP, March 12, 1873.

59. SAW.5.77.

60. BD.601; Dell, *Lincoln and the War Democrats*, 401, 283, 285, 286; PH, 590; DFP, January 22, 1903.

61. BD.982–983; James Cooke Mills, *History of Saginaw County, Michigan* (Saginaw, MI: Seemann & Peters, 1918), 430, 700; MIW, 482.

62. SAW.1.247–248.

63. BD.664; "Biographical Sketch," MOG, II, 417–421; *Presidential Elections, 1798–2008: County, State, and National Mapping of Election Data*, ed. by Hanes Walton, Donald Deskins Jr., and Sherman Puckett (Ann Arbor: University of Michigan Press, 2010), Table 18.1; 139, 161; *DeLand's History of Jackson County*, 275; as quoted in Greeley, *Proceedings of the First Three Republican National Conventions*, 157–158; NYT, August 7, 1894; FAC, 19; see also Stephen D. Engle, *Gathering to Save a Nation: Lincoln & the Union's War Governors* (Chapel Hill: University of North Carolina Press, 2016), 28–29, 143–144.

64. *Portrait and Biographical Album of Ingham and Livingston Counties, Michigan*, 149–150; BD, 748–749.

65. *Portrait and Biographical Record of Kalamazoo, Allegan and Van Buren Counties, Michigan, containing Biographical Sketches of Prominent and Representative Citizens* (Chicago: Chapman Bros., 1892), 1112–1115; Dyer, 1264; CIB, 147–148; *History of Kalamazoo County, Michigan* (Philadelphia: Everts & Abbott, 1889), 18, 174, 228, 227; DFP, July 15, 1883.

66. DFP, March 21, 1887; Belle McKinney Hays Swope, *History of the Families of McKinney-Brady-Quigley* (Newville, PA: Franklin Repository Printery, 1905), 190; Friend Palmer, *Early Days in Detroit, Papers written by General Friend Palmer of Detroit, being his personal reminiscences of important events and descriptions of the city for over eighty years* (Detroit: Hunt & June, 1906), 182; Walter F. Clowes, *The Detroit Light Guard: A Complete Record of this Organization from its Foundation to the Present Day* (Detroit: John F. Eby & Company, 1900), 22–23.

67. *The Flags of Michigan*, compiled by Jno. Robertson, Adjutant General (Lansing, MI: W. S. George & Co., State Printers, 1877), 5.

68. Frederick Phisterer, *Statistical Record of the Armies of the United States* (New York: Charles Scribner's Sons, reprint, 2009), 44–45.

69. Farmer, *History of Detroit*, 306; Taylor, *Old Slow Town*, 59.

70. DFP, December 3, 1863.

71. Craig Hutchison and Kimberly Rising, *Dearborn Michigan* (Charleston, SC: Arcadia Publishing, 2003), 15–22 John T. Blois, *Gazetteer of the State of Michigan in three parts, containing a General View of the State, and etc.* (Detroit: Sydney L. Rood & Co., 1839), 269–270.

72. Farmer, *History of Detroit*, 226, 962, 228; Taylor, *Old Slow Town*, 25.

73. Silas Farmer, *History of Detroit and Wayne County, and Early Michigan: A Chronological Cyclopedia of the Past and Present* (Detroit: Silas Farmer & Co., 1890), 225–226; James Conway and David F. Jamroz, *Detroit's Historic Fort Wayne* (Charleston, SC: Arcadia Publishing, 2007), 24; *Annual Report of the Adjutant General, Military Department, Michigan, December 31, 1861* (State of Michigan, 1861), 42–43; hereafter, AG.61.

74. U.S. War Department, *Circular No. 4, Surgeon General's Of-*

fice, Washington, December 5, 1870 (Washington, DC: Government Printing Office), 120–123.

75. U.S. War Department, Circular No. 4, December 5, 1870, 132–133; Dwight H. Kelton, Annals of Fort Mackinac (Detroit: Detroit Free Press Printing Co., Carter Edition, 1892), 171, 186–187.

76. U.S. War Department, Circular No. 4, December 5, 1870, 124–125.

77. Comparable western states were Ohio at 58.54, Indiana at 39.93, Illinois at 30.90, Wisconsin at 14.39, Iowa at 12.26, and Minnesota at 2.08.

78. Population, 1860, 237–247; PR8, 121, 131.

79. Population, 1860, 237–247; Statistics, xviii; PR8, 130–131.

80. Southern counties include Monroe, Lenawee, Hillsdale, Branch, St. Joseph, Cass, Berrien, Van Buren, Kalamazoo, Calhoun, Jackson, Washtenaw, Wayne, Allegan, Barry, Eaton, Ingham, Livingston, Oakland, Macomb, and St. Claire. The next tier north consisted of Ottawa, Kent, Ionia, Clinton, Shiawassee, Genesee, and Lapeer Counties. County population figures may be found in PR8, 264–265.

81. Population of the United States in 1860, 230–235; OR.III.5.622–623. Fry's count of males and females for Michigan differs slightly from the figures used above.

82. Like African Americans, Indians were not at first eligible for military service. For example, in sparsely populated Cheboygan County, 109 men were originally part of the enrollment for Michigan's 1862 draft; however, 72 were subsequently exempted, mostly on the grounds of being Indians, which left only 37 men "for the wheel." MIW, 36.

83. Population of the United States in 1860, 230–236.

84. Lawrence M. Hauptman states that Michigan's 1861 Native American population totaled 7,755 people in seventy-two bands. For additional information, see Lawrence M. Hauptman, Between Two Fires: American Indians in the Civil War (New York: Free Press, 1995), 127.

85. Population of the United States in 1860, 237–247.

86. Statistics, li; Report of the Superintendent of the Census for December 1, 1852 to which is appended the Report for December 1, 1851 (Washington, DC: Robert Armstrong, Printer, 1853), 13–15, 16–17.

87. Statistics, liii–liv.

88. Floyd Benjamin Streeter, Political Parties in Michigan, 1837–1860: An Historical Study of Political Issues and Parties in Michigan from the Admission of the State to the Civil War (Lansing, MI: Michigan Historical Commission, 1918), 180–182; Humphrey J. Desmond, The Know Nothing Party. A Sketch (Washington, DC: New Century Press, 1906), 61, 69, 113; Tyler Anbinder, Nativism and Slavery, 128.

89. Christina A. Zieglar-McPherson, Selling America: Immigration Promotion and the Settlement of the American Continent (Santa Barbara, CA: ABC-Clio, 2017), 21; DWT, April 3, 1860.

90. DWT, reprint, May 1, 1860, from the DFP, April 17, 1860.

Key Events: 1860

1. SAW.4.756.

2. MA, February 6, 1860; LSJ, February 7, 1860; DWT, February 7, 1860; the DFP, February 7, 1860, was less welcoming.

3. LSR, February 14, 1860.

4. The others are Benjamin Follett, Fidus Livermore, John G. Parkhurst, Philo Wilson, Franklin Muzzy, Alex F. Bell, Augustus C. Baldwin, and William S. Bancroft.

5. DFP, February 23, 1860; Murat Halstead, A History of the National Political Conventions (Columbus, OH: Follett, Foster and Company, 1860), 17.

6. DWT, February 28 [sic; February 23], 1860; see also DWT, February 28, 1860.

7. The Civil War–era Detroit Free Press, founded as a weekly in 1831, became a daily in 1835—the first in the Michigan Territory. It was purchased by staunch Democrat John S. Bagg in 1836. Thereafter and through the Civil War, the Free Press remained a Democratic sheet, the organ of Michigan's Democracy, the state's largest circulating paper and one with few peers in its hatred of abolitionists and its racist treatment of all people and things African American. In 1853, Storey assumed control of the paper and intensified these biases. He also introduced major innovations. He expanded the page size from seven columns to eight, brought out a Sunday edition, stopped publishing on Mondays, and soon brought out a weekly and a triweekly edition. In 1856, circulation for all editions was 18,100. In 1860, it was 45,619. Under Storey's editorial control, the Free Press's racism was coupled with opposition to anti-Catholic nativists, and anti-immigrant Know-Nothings. He fought the prohibition of alcohol and coeducation at the University of Michigan. Despite its principles, Storey's Free Press was also sensationalist sheet.

On June 5, 1861, Henry N. Walker replaced Storey as the Free Press's editor and co-owner. His Free Press (a regime that lasted until 1872) pledged from the beginning to maintain "the absolute right of free discussion" and promised to do this "without pandering to the vulgar appetite for abuse and scandal or violating the rules of strictest propriety." Some things did not change, however. The sheet would be "thoroughly democratic" in party, but of greater interest to close students of Michigan's Civil War was the sheet's commitment to support the war effort. The South had behaved unconstitutionally, and "In such a contest the North will stand as one man until the rebellion is crushed out, and the traitors and conspirators punished." Angelo, On Guard, 3, 24, 47, 52, 59, 63–71; DFP, June 5, 1861; Frank Boles, "Michigan Newspapers: A Two-Hundred Year Review," Michigan Historical Review 36, no. 1 (Spring 2010): 36, 37, 39–41, 45–46.

8. DFP, February 23, 1860.

9. DFP, March 2, 1860.

10. Halstead, *National Political Conventions*, 23.

11. Halstead, *National Political Conventions*, 24; John G. Parkhurst, *Official Proceedings of the Democratic National Convention* (Cleveland: Nevins' Print, Plain Dealer Job Office, 1860), 20–21; as quoted, Hershock, "Copperheads and Radicals," 32–33.

12. Halstead, *National Political Conventions*, 43–44.

13. Halstead, *National Political Conventions*, 55.

14. See Parkhurst, *Official Proceedings*, 52, as Halstead's Michigan vote tally is erroneous. See also *SAW*.6.265–268 for a summary of these events; Parkhurst, 53–55.

15. Parkhurst, *Official Proceedings*, 66, 74–77.

16. Parkhurst, *Official Proceedings*; *DWT*, May 8, 1860.

17. Parkhurst, *Official Proceedings*, 78–89; *LSR*, May 9, 1860. Several of the Michigan delegates who appeared in Chicago were not mentioned in *LSR*'s account; see Greeley, *Proceedings*, 151; Erastus Hussey was among these delegates.

18. A daily summary of the Bolters' convention, then referred to the as "Democratic Constitutional Convention," can be found in *SAW*.6.267–268.

19. Halstead, *National Political Conventions*, 104–105.

20. Greeley, *Official Proceedings*, 9, 28, 32–33, 37.

21. Greeley, *Republican National Conventions*, 79–83; No. 4 was intended to assure Southerners that Republicans did not intend to abolish slavery within states where it existed; No. 7 repudiated Dred Scott, which potentially opened territory to slavery; and No. 8 called for abolishing and/or preventing *any* territorial slavery, and thus opposed Douglas's Freeport Doctrine.

22. *SAW*.1.221.

23. *DWT*, May 22, 29, 1860; the Seward-Greeley antagonism was prominent in antebellum New York politics. See Walter Stahr, *Seward: Lincoln's Indispensable Man* (New York: Simon & Schuster, 2012), 150–151, 190–191, 194–195.

24. Greeley, *Republican National Conventions*, 107–108; 113, 114–115, 124–125, 143–145; Hershock, "Copperheads and Radicals," 34–35; *HS*, May 22, 1860; *LSR*, May 23, 1860; *MAP*, III.423–425.

25. *MAP*, III.427; *KG*, June 8, 15, 1860.

26. *DWT*, June 12, 1860.

27. *SAW*.6.269.

28. *SAW*.6.269; Parkhurst, *Official Proceedings*, 93, 161.

29. *CCR*, June 28, 1860.

30. Parkhurst, *Official Proceedings*, 161, 168.

31. Halstead, *National Political Conventions*, 217–231.

32. *DWT*, June 26, 1860.

33. *AG*, June 25, 1860.

34. *DFP*, June 29, 1860.

35. *DFP*, July 3, 1860; See Hershock, "Copperheads and Radicals," 33.

36. *LSR*, July 25, 1860.

37. *DWT*, July 10, 1860.

38. *DWT*, July 31, 1860.

39. *KG*, August 3, 1860.

40. *DWT*, August 7, 1860; *MA*, August 3, 1860.

41. *DFP*, July 31, 1860; *DWT*, August 7, 1860.

42. *SAW*.5.68.

43. *LSJ*, August 15, 1860; *DWT*, August 14, 1860.

44. *SAW*.5.62–65.

45. *DWT*, August 14, 1860.

46. *LSR*, August 22, 1860; *DWT*, August 21, 1860; *KG*, August 17, 1860.

47. *DWT*, August 21, 1860; *ESC*, August 23, 1860; *KG*, August 24, 1860.

48. *KG*, August 24, 1860; *DWT*, September 4, 1860; Oran W. Rowland, *A History of Van Buren County*, 245, 166, 265–264.

49. *GHN*, September 12, 1860.

50. *DFP*, August 29, 1860. *The First Call of the Civil War: Personal Recollections of Michigan's Response, A Paper Read by Gen. W. H. Withington before Edward Pomeroy Post, G.A.R. at Jackson Michigan, in 1897*. The Detroit Light Guard, the Jackson Greys, the Steuben Guard, and the Ypsilanti Light Guard numbered among the first companies of the First Michigan; the Adrian Guard and the Hudson Artillery numbered among the first companies of the Second Michigan; the Union Guard and the Curtenius Guard numbered among the first companies of the Seventh Michigan; the Coldwater Light Artillery formed Battery A of the First Michigan Light Artillery.

51. *DWT*, September 11, 1860.

52. *DWT*, September 11, 1860; *DFP*, September 5, 1860; *NYT*, September 5, 1860.

53. *LSJ*, September 12, 19, 1860; *DWT*, August 21, 1860.

54. *KG*, September 14, 1860.

55. *CCR*, September 13, 1860; *DWT*, September 18, 1860.

56. *DWT*, October 2, 1860.

57. *DWT*, September 25, 1860.

58. *DWT*, October 2, 1860.

59. *DDT*, September 24, 1860.

60. *DFP*, September 28, 30, 1861; *DFP*, October 28, 1861; August 20, 1861; see also *DFP*, July 9, 1861; *LSJ*, July 24, 1861; Dillon et al., *Michigan Women in the Civil War*, 116–117.

61. *DFP*, October 6, 1860.

62. The Battle Creek "State Convention of Colored Men" was preceded by at least two local conventions that chose delegates for the October meeting. The first convention was on July 6 in Lansing (see July 6) and consisted of "the colored citizens of Ingham County." Chaired by N. Turner, speeches were made by T. Wilson, William Butcher, and T.J. Brown. On August 23, another convention representing African Americans in Muskegon and Ottawa counties (see August 23) met in Grand Haven in the house of L. Thompson. H.G. Smith,

a prominent Grand Haven fruit grower, presided over this meeting, with A.G. DeBlain as secretary. Smith was chosen as delegate to Battle Creek. LSR, July 25, 1860; GHN, September 12, 1860; GHN, October 15, 1862.

63. *Michigan Manual of Freedmen's Progress*, compiled by Francis H. Warren (Detroit: Freedmen's Progress Commission, 1915), 35; see letter, Martin to editor, CCR, November 1, 1860.

64. DWT, October 16, 1860.

65. DFP, October 16, 1860; see DWT, October 22, 1860 for criticism of Douglas's speech and questions about crowd size.

66. CQ, 282, 335.

67. Dubin, *Congressional Elections*, 187.

68. CQ, 509.

69. Dubin, 99.

70. DWT, November 13, 1860; HS, November 13, 1860; CCR, November 8, 1860.

71. ESC, November 8, 1860; DFP comment reprinted in MA, November 9, 1860; KG, November 16, 1860.

72. If newspaper editorialists were faithful reflections of Michigan public opinion, there was little hope that Congress would solve national divisions over Secession Winter. William A. Howard joined his colleagues, fellow Republicans Francis Kellogg and DeWitt Clinton Leach in voting *against* the resolution authorizing the Committee of Thirty-Three. When it was approved 145 to 38, the five-member Michigan House delegation chose Howard to represent Michigan on the committee. Howard's votes on Committee propositions will be found in the text; but Michigan newspapers were gloomy. The *Lansing State Journal* bitterly parodied the proceedings; the *East Saginaw Courier* was pessimistic but knew who to blame: "conservatism in [Congress] is powerless to contend against the ultraism of black republicans and fire eaters who are joined hand in hand in their efforts to prevent a settlement of the difficulties . . ." No Michiganders sat on the Senate Committee of Thirteen; but hope was faint. The *Cass County Republican* blamed "the cotton oligarchy" and supine Northern Democrats. "One thing is certain," the *East Saginaw Courier* observed, a modification of the extreme views of both parties must take place or a Dissolution of the Union is certain." CG, House, Thirty-Sixth Congress, 2nd Session, 6–7; PH.52, 70; ESC, December 27, 1860; CCR, January 3, 1861.

73. PH, 53. For Howard's votes on the Committee's propositions, see entries for February 27 and 28, and March 1, 1861.

74. *General Lewis Cass, 1782–1866* (privately printed, 1916), 34–35; MAP, 431; Assistant Secretary of State William Henry Trescot recalled Cass's handling of the secession crisis as a member of Buchanan's cabinet: "Gen. Cass stood I think by himself. From the beginning he believed Lincoln's election certain and the dissolution of the Union inevitable. Not

recognizing any right in a State to secede except as a revolutionary right, he would have resisted the right at the commencement and as the sworn officer of the U.S. have done his utmost to preserve its integrity. That he believed to be his duty." *Narrative and Letter of William Henry Trescot concerning the negotiations between South Carolina and President Buchanan in December, 1860*, contributed by Gaillard Hunt, reprint from the *American Historical Review* XIII, no. 3, April, 1908: 532–533; see SAW.6 for Fort Sumter chronology, November 1860 to April 1861.

75. *A Compilation of the Messages and Papers of the President*, vol. 5, 655.

76. NYT, December 19, 1860; PH, 79.

77. SAW.6.303–304.

78. Maine's Governor Washburn, Massachusetts's Andrew, Pennsylvania's Curtin, and Ohio's Dennison only were invited to meet with Morgan. Vermont and Rhode Island repealed or modified their personal liberty laws; not so Maine or Massachusetts. See *New York Herald*, December 24, 1861; Engle, *Gathering to Save a Nation*, 26–27; William B. Hesseltine, *Lincoln and the War Governors* (New York: Alfred B. Knopf, 1955), 107–108.

79. See SAW.6.303–304; "Declaration of Independence of South Carolina, Done in Convention, December 24, 1860," as quoted in *The Tribune Almanac for 1861*, 35, contained in *The Tribune Almanac for the years 1838 to 1868, inclusive* (New York: New York Tribune, 1868), vol. II.

80. ALP, Bingham to Lincoln, December 26, 1860.

81. PH, 70–72.

82. ESC, November 8, 1860; the proclamation was issued on October 9.

83. SAW.5.323.

84. PH, 28; Warner, *Generals in Gray*, 89–90.

85. DFP, November 14, 1860.

86. No 169, contained in *Acts of the Legislature of the State of Michigan passed at the regular session of 1859, with an appendix* (Lansing, MI: Homer & Kerr, Printers to the State, 1859), 469–471. See the following for details and context of Michigan's militia unpreparedness: Utley and Cutcheon, *Michigan as a Province*, vol. III, 411–412; also notes to August 28, 1860, and April 24, 1861, infra.

87. MOG, II. 397; Charles Lanman, *The Red Book of Michigan*, 147.

88. OR.III.1.1.

89. These figures illustrate the "paper army" that was the antebellum state militia. OR.III.1.900–901; for ordnance inventories, see 902–905; 899.

90. Auditors Report in *Joint Documents of the State of Michigan for the year 1860* (Lansing, MI: Hosmer & Kerr, 1861).

Key Events: 1861

1. HS, January 1, 1861; DFP, January 1, 1861; SJT, January 2, 1861; as quoted, George May, "Ann Arbor and the Civil War," 243.

2. Document No. 2, Legislature, 1861, "Governor's Inaugural Message" (State of Michigan), 18, 24.

3. OR.III.3.28–29.

4. Frank Moore, Rebellion Record, "Documents and Narratives," vol. 1, 17.

5. A Compilation, vol. 5, 655; see SAW.6.10 for excerpts; May, Ann Arbor, 243; LSR, January 16, 1861; PH, 80.

6. SAW.6.316–317.

7. DFP, April 19, 1861.

8. PH, 57–59.

9. OR.III.1.49.

10. CG, Senate, Thirty-Sixth Congress, 2nd Session, January 21, 1861, 489; OR.III.1.43, 48.

11. JMH, 1861, 258–260, 341.

12. JMS, 1861, 197–199; DFP, January 26, 1861.

13. JMH, 1861, 356–357.

14. JMS, 1861, 248–254.

15. JMS, 1861, 273.

16. May, Michigan and the Civil War Years, 1860–1866, 5.

17. See SAW.6.19–20 for excerpts.

18. NYT, March 8, 1861; DFP, February 8, 1861.

19. JMH, 1861, 526–540.

20. PH, 5.

21. Zachariah Chandler: An Outline Sketch of His Life and Public Services (Detroit: Detroit Post and Tribune Company, Publishers, 1880), 190; Public Life of Zachariah Chandler, vol. 2, 53–54; Chandler's letter was entered into the CG, Senate, 36th Congress, 2nd Session, 1,247; the letter, which had appeared in the DFP, was introduced by Kentucky senator Powell as evidence that Republicans were determined to sabotage the Peace Conference.

22. MOG, II.442.

23. CG, Senate, 36th Congress, 2nd Session, 1247.

24. NYT, February 22, 1861.

25. See SAW.6.44–45.

26. SAW.5.69.

27. PH, 58–59; CG, Thirty-Sixth Congress, 2nd session, 1,247; Bogue, Earnest Men, 47.

28. PH, 62–63; excerpts, SAW.5.14–15.

29. SAL.12.251. PH, 59–60.

30. PH, 60–62.

31. SAL.12.251. MacPherson, 59–60.

32. "The tree of liberty must be refreshed from time to time with the blood of patriots & tyrants," Letter, Thomas Jefferson to Colonel William Smith, November 13, 1787, The Writings of Thomas Jefferson, ed. H. A. Washington, vol. 2 (New York: Cambridge University Press, 2011), 318–319.

33. CG, Thirty-Sixth Congress, 2nd Session, 1370–1372.

34. DFP, March 5 and 8, 1861; MA, March 6, 1861; CCR, March 7, 1861; ESC, March 7, 1861.

35. LSR, March 6, 1861; WES, March 6, 1861.

36. AG.62.4.

37. MPL.63.53.

38. Annual Report of the Adjutant General, Military Department, Michigan, December 24, 1861, published as Document No. 8 (State of Michigan), 2; hereafter, AG.61.

39. Journal of the Senate of the State of Michigan, Extra-Session, 1861 (Lansing: John A. Kerr & Company), 11.

40. DFP, April 13, 1861. As quoted, Frankenbine, The History of Michigan Law, 98.

41. DFP, April 13, 1861; the Hillsdale Democrat's editorial was reprinted in the HS, April 16, 1861.

42. OR.III.1.67–69; George S. May, Michigan and the Civil War Years, 1860–1866: A Wartime Chronicle (Lansing: Published by the Michigan Civil War Centennial Observance Committee, 1964), 96; see SAW.5.15–16 for excerpts from the 1795 Militia Act. The 1795 Act repealed the 1792 Militia Act but not the Act of May 8, 1792, which stipulated that only white males could serve.

43. DFP, April 16, 1861.

44. DFP, April 17, 1861; Deland's History of Jackson County, Michigan, embracing a Concise Review of its Early Settlement, Industrial Development and Present Conditions, together with Interesting Reminiscences, compiled by Colonel Charles V. Deland (No city: B. F. Bowen, Publisher, 1903), 161–162; Rosentreter, Grand Rapids and the Civil War, 7–8; Ray Lennard, Lenawee County and the Civil War, 31; May, "Ann Arbor," 248–249; SJT, April 17, 1861.

45. "Proclamation by the Governor Calling for a Regiment of Volunteers," DFP, April 17, 1861; MIW, 232, 48, 233; Withington, First Call, 17. Withington states that a total of $81,020 was collected. FAC, 21.

46. DFP, April 17, 1861.

47. Michael O. Smith, "Raising a Black Regiment in Michigan: Adversity and Triumph," Michigan Historical Review 16, no. 2 (Fall, 1990): 25–26.

48. DFP, April 19, 1861.

49. OR.III.1.75.

50. DFP, April 18, 1861.

51. OR.III.1.78. Initially, Austin Blair and Michigan's congressional delegation were its chief lobbyists, and first among equals was Zachariah Chandler. See April 20. LSR, April 17, 1861.

52. SAW.6.26–27.

53. CCR, April 25, 1861.

54. OR.III.1.120. Blair's offer is not found in the OR but is inferred from Cameron's April 26 response. AG.61.38; May, "Ann Arbor," 250; the evidence suggests that only $2,550 was actually paid.

55. ORN.II.3.98; also, OR.III.89–90.

56. LSR, April 23, 24, 1861.

57. OR.III.I.97; KG, April 26, 1861.

58. DFP, April 20, 1861; see photograph, Richard Bak, *A Distant Thunder: Michigan in the Civil War* (Ann Arbor, MI: Huron River Press, 2004), 24; DFP, May 17, 1872.

59. HS, April 23, 1861; GHN, April 24, 1861; DFP, April 20, 1860.

60. OR.III.I.97.

61. From the DDT, April 22, 1861; ESC, April 25, 1861.

62. As quoted in DFP, April 25, 1861; Harriet M. Dilla, *The Politics of Michigan, 1865–1878* (New York: Columbia University, Longmans, Green & Co., Agents, 1912), 23.

63. Frank Moore's *Rebellion Record*, vol. 1, 310; OR.III.1.107; Judith E. Harper, *Women During the Civil War: An Encyclopedia* (New York: Routledge, 2004), 116–118.

64. LSR, April 24, 1861.

65. MIW, 166; the First Michigan produced ten future colonels, among whom were several brigadiers. MAP, 442; DFP, April 24, 1861.

66. ESC, April 25, 1861.

67. MIW, 187–188; CCR, April 25, 1861.

68. OR.III.I.120.

69. See SAW.5.16; MA, May 3, 1861.

70. OR.III.I.129. The idea of two-year units would soon be dropped in favor of three-year volunteer units. See May 3.

71. AG.61.38.

72. AG.61.4; ROS.1.1.

73. PH, 5.

74. OR.I.51.i.339. This is the first of three iterations of what will later be called the Anaconda Plan; see SAW.5.17.331; for the third iteration, see OR.I.51.i.387.

75. OR.III.145–146; 148–149.

76. CPD, May 4, 1861; CML, May 4, 1861, for Blair's speech; another version can be found in the CH, May 4, 1861; DFP, May 7, 1861; see *Gathering to Save a Nation*, 70–73.

77. DFP, May 7, 1861.

78. OR.III.1.151–154; 154–157.

79. OR.III.167–170.

80. *Michigan Legislative Manual and Official Directory for the years 1899–1900*, 182. This source incorrectly lists May 2.

81. *Lincoln Day by Day, A Chronology: 1809–1865*, edited by Earl Schenck Miers (Washington, DC: Lincoln Sesquicentennial Commission, 1960), vol. III, 40; DFP, May 9, 1861.

82. JMS, Extra Session, 1861, 13, 16, 33.

83. *Michigan Legislative Manual and Official Directory for the years 1899–1900*, compiled by Justus S. Stearns (Lansing, MI: Robert Smith Printing Co., State Printers and Binders, 1899), 182–183; "Certificate," MPL.63.53, gives the adjournment date as May 11.

84. See SAW.1.129.

85. DFP, May 11, 1861.

86. OR.III.1.187. Cameron's response does not appear in the OR and is quoted in MAP, vol. III, 444; FAC, Illustration No. 5.

87. DFP, August 20, 1861; Dillon et al., *Michigan Women in the Civil War*, 116–117.

88. Virgil A. Lewis, *History of West Virginia, in two parts* (Philadelphia: Hubbard Brothers, 1889), 347–352, 355.

89. Welcher, II, 126; AG.61.38; as quoted in Frances McTeer and Minnie Dubbs Millbrook, "For Loved Ones Far Away," in Dillon et al., *Michigan Women in the Civil War*, 114–115; FAC, 33; On May 14, official War Department orders for the First Michigan's deployment are received, see OR.III.1.200.

90. OR.III.I.204.

91. As quoted in *The First Call of the Civil War: Personal Recollections of Michigan's Response, A Paper Read by Gen. W. H. Withington before Edward Pomeroy Post, G.A.R. at Jackson, Michigan, in 1897*, 19–20.

92. NYTr, May 18, 1861; DNI, May 18, 1861; Withington, *The First Call*, 21. Jack Dempsey, author of *Michigan and the Civil War*, notes that this might have been the time Lincoln declared, "Thank God for Michigan!" The source for this anecdote is unclear but it remains part of the state's tradition. Dempsey, 160n43.

93. SAW.2.343.

94. PH, 8; OR.III.1.217.

95. MIW, 221. Cameron's note was attached as an exhibit.

96. OR.I.51.i.387; *Annual Report of the Adjutant General of the State of Michigan for the year 1862* (Lansing: John A. Kerr & Co., Printers to the State, 1862), 4; hereafter, AG.62.

97. OR.III.1.227–228.

98. SAW.3.304–305.

99. OR.III.1.228.

100. OR.III.1.229.

101. Withington, *First Call*, 21–22.

102. OR.I.52.i.146–147.

103. AG.61.4; ROS.2.17; MIW, 41.

104. OR.I.52.i.147–148.

105. OR.III.I.246.

106. AG.61.189; Bak, *A Distant Thunder*, 97–98.

107. ROS.45.115.

108. PH, 5.

109. ROS.3.3.

110. MIW, 221–222.

111. Lewis, *History of West Virginia*, 357–359.

112. OR.III.I.269.

113. OR.III.I.271.

114. OR.III.I.282–283. Walbridge's June 20 letter to Cameron quotes Blair. Chandler to Lincoln, June 15, ALP.

115. SAW.2.334–335.

116. Captain C.A. Stevens, *Berdan's United States Sharpshooters in the Army of the Potomac, 1861–1865* (Dayton, OH: The Press of Morningside Bookshop, 1972, reprint, 1892), 3–4. Michiganders included Company C under Captain Benjamin Duesler, Company I under Captain A. M. Willett, and Company K under Captain S. J. Mather. A summary of Michigan's role in Berdan's unit can be found at ROS.45.103–106.

117. ROS.45.47–48; *Report of the Adjutant General of the State of Illinois*, vol. I (Springfield, IL: Baker, Bailhache & Co., Printers, 1867), 479–480.

118. OR.III.I.276.

119. Lewis, *History of West Virginia*, 362.

120. ROS.4.1–3.

121. OR.III.I.282–283.

122. OR.III.I.284, 286–287.

123. PH, 5.

124. DFP, June 30, 1861; Dillon et al., *Michigan Women in the Civil War*, 118n17; a postwar account of Michigan women may be found in L. P. Brockett and Mary C. Vaughn, *Woman's Work in the Civil War: Record of Heroism, Patriotism and Patience* (Philadelphia: Zeigler, McCurdy & Co., 1867), 593–595.

125. *The Collected Works of Abraham Lincoln*, IV.438–439.

126. OR.III.I.327.

127. DFP, July 18, 1861; CCR, August 8, 1861; as quoted, Engle, *Gathering to Save a Nation*, 91.

128. OR.I.2.314.

129. OR.III.I.339.

130. OR.I.II.314–315, 405.

131. DFP, July 23, 1861; LSR, July 25, 1861; CCR, July 25, 1861; ESC, July 25, 1861.

132. SAL.12. 268–271 or excerpts in SAW.5.19–20.

133. ROS.45.75; *Illinois Adjutant General*, vol. 1, 652–653.

134. SAW.5.365–366.

135. SAW.2.66.

136. NR, July 26, 1861; WES, July 26, 1861.

137. SAW.5.324–325.

138. OR.III.I.351; SAL, vol. 12, 274; Horace Greeley, *American Conflict*, 568; CG, 37th Congress, 1st Session, July 26, 1861, 257–265; OR.III.1.349.

139. PH, 286.

140. Welcher, *Union Army*, II, 127, 154.

141. SAL.12.276; chapter 21 left to the tight-fisted Treasury Secretary Salmon P. Chase the responsibility for administering reimbursements. From 1861 to 1884, Michigan received $844,262.53 in federal reimbursements. Kyle S. Sinisi, *Sacred Debts*, 9–16, 19–20, 23, 185.

142. SAL.12.281–282; while the act limited militia service in some respects, it also imposed fines and/or imprisonment for defaulting soldiers and expanded the authority of U.S. marshals to enforce state law in their districts.

143. As quoted in *MIW*, 110.

144. SAL.12.284; see SAW.5.20–21 for excerpts.

145. OR.III.1.380–384. However, in his 1862 report, AG Robertson disagreed, stating that under the August 3 statute, Michigan owed 19,500 men. Michigan recruited sixteen infantry and three cavalry regiments, one engineer regiment, eight batteries, six sharpshooter companies, and one cavalry squadron. Combined with miscellaneous contributions, this equaled (by Robertson's count) 23,501 men. AG.62.7.

146. OR.III.1.455. This will be reported to McClellan on August 26.

147. SAL, vol. 12, 292–313; 315–316; see SAW.5.21 for excerpts

148. SAL, vol. 12, 326, 319; see SAW.5.21 for excerpted; SAL-C, 173–174.

149. Lewis, *History of West Virginia*, 373.

150. Dyer, *A Compendium*, 1281.

151. OR.III.1.391. GO No. 45 was intended to ease recruitment in states with large foreign-born populations.

152. ROS.45.193.

153. ROS.45.127.

154. OR.III.1.406–407. Recall that on May 11, Blair had requested that Michigan regiments be brigaded, which Cameron had refused on May 21.

155. OR.III.1.408–409.

156. OR.III.1.425–426.

157. OR.III.1.428.

158. DFP, August 20, 1861.

159. ROS.6.1, 3.

160. See SAW.6.61.

161. MIW, 553; Dyer, 1269.

162. ROS.7.1.

163. OR.III.I.450–451; as quoted, Klement, "Hopkins Hoax," 8.

164. OR.III.I.456; ROS.44.120; MIW, 747.

165. OR.III.I.457–458.

166. ROS.5.1–4.

167. ROS.45.139; Reid, *Ohio in the War*, 291–295.

168. LSR, September 4, 1861; ESC, September 24, 1861.

169. *Lincoln: Speeches and Writings*, 266–267.

170. OR.I.4.180.

171. CIB, 138.

172. OR.III.1.490. Blair suggests that cavalry volunteering is more popular with prospective recruits than infantry. Klement, "Franklin Pierce and the Treason Charges of 1861–1862," *The Historian* 23, no. 4 (August, 1961): 439–440.

173. OR.III.1.489, 490, 491.

174. ROS.16.1–3.

175. ROS.44.164–165; ROS.45.1–2; MIW, 740.

176. Innes telegram as quoted in Hoffman, *My Brave Mechanics*, 4; OR.III.I.497; see ROS.1.ix

177. DFP, September 10, 1861.

178. PH, 8.

179. OR.III.I.501; Stevens, *Berdan's United States Sharpshooters, 1861–1865*, 4.

180. OR.III.I.508.

181. Elizabeth D. Leonard describes Bridget Divers as "an Irish immigrant of modest social origins" who joined the First Michigan while in her early twenties. Nicknamed "Irish Biddy" and "Michigan Bridget," various admiring soldier accounts attest to her services. These included a behind-the-lines mission to recover the body of a company captain, cheering on troops during battle, and dispensing first aid under fire. Little is known about her before the war and there are suggestions that postwar she traveled west with a frontier-bound army detachment. Leonard, *All the Daring of a Soldier*, 121–125.

182. ROS.31.1–5.

183. OR.III.I.513. Today Cameron also wires a number of governors to start all regiments for Washington.

184. OR.III.I.516.

185. OR.III.I.521; MIW, 174, 774; ROS.1.2, 3.

186. GO No. 71 had applied to New York. OR.III.I.518–519. This GO ended what had been virtual anarchy in many states. But see the Andrew-Butler controversy, SAW.1, Massachusetts

187. OR.2.2.1246.

188. ROS.42.65.

189. *Illinois AG Report*, vol. 1, 90; ROS.45.67.

190. OR.III.1.527–528.

191. ROS.45.47.

192. ROS.8.1–3; MIW, 118.

193. SAW.5.376.

194. Dr. J. S. Newberry, Sanitary Commission No. 96, *The U.S. Sanitary Commission in the Valley of the Mississippi, during the War of the Rebellion* (Cleveland: Fairbanks, Benedict & Co., Printers, 1871), 18; his biographical note is at SAW.5.376.

195. NYT, September 23, 1861.

196. ROS.11.1–3.

197. DFP, September 24, 1861.

198. DFP, September 25, 1861.

199. *Proceedings of the Board of Regents*, 967–968; the regents later vote to send the resolution to the governor, president of the state Senate, and speaker of the state House. In his January 2, 1862, annual message, Governor Blair recommended that the legislature fund this request. *Annual Message of the Governors of Michigan*, vol. II, 450; University of Michigan students' experience during the war is discussed in Julie Mujic, "Ours is the Harder Lot: Student Patriotism at the University of Michigan during the Civil War," in *The Midwestern Homefront during the Civil War*, eds. Ginette Aley and J. L. Anderson (Carbondale: Southern Illinois University Press, 2013).

200. ESC, September 24, 1861.

201. OR.III.I.544. The OR does not contain a reply. Perhaps Cameron's October 5 message was related to Blair's question.

202. Stevens, *Berdan's United States Sharpshooters*, 1861–1865, 4–5; Company B was recruited in Michigan and led by Captain Andrew B. Stuart.

203. OR.III.I.549–550; the writers conceded that their views may not be militarily sound, but are simply conveying public sentiment.

204. ROS.32.1–4.

205. MIW, 614.

206. OR.III.I.563; Klement, "Hopkins Hoax," 5; OR.2.2.1247–1251; DFP, March 9, 1862.

207. ROS.44.107; MIW, 747.

208. OR.III.I.567.

209. Hershock, "Copperheads and Radicals," 48.

210. Sometime in August 1861, Edwin P. Howland, "formerly a Professor of Natural Sciences in an academy in Wheeling West Virginia," arrived in Battle Creek to recruit an engineer corps. He had earlier written to General John Fremont and obtained a captain's commission and authority to recruit a fifty-man unit. While based in Missouri, Howland's unit constructed a "portable observatory sixty feet high." See letters, DFP, October 5, 1861; CCR, November 28, 1861.

211. OR.III.I.572. There were two conditions: the term must be for three years or the war and officer appointments could be revoked for incompetence.

212. OR.III.I.573.

213. OR.III.I.574.

214. ROS.45.95.

215. OR.III.I.575–576.

216. ROS.9.1–3.

217. OR.III.I.587; *Report of the Adjutant General of the State of Illinois*, ed. J. W. Vance, vol. 2, 245, 276.

218. *General Orders Affecting Volunteers*, 42.

219. DFP, October 25, 1861.

220. Robert M. Bastress, *The West Virginia State Constitution: A Reference Guide* (Westport, CT: Greenwood Publishing Group, 1995), 10.

221. OR.III.I.598–599.

222. OR.III.I.603.

223. ROS.1.43.ix–xiv; Rosentreter, *Grand Rapids and the Civil War*, 57–70.

224. OR.III.I.609–610. Scott's message to Sherman appears at OR.I.VI.176. Scott referenced similar orders that were issued to Benjamin Butler, see OR.III.I.243.

225. ROS.33.1–4; *Michigan in the War*, 473.

226. Welcher, *Union Army*, II, 154.

227. DFP, November 5, 6, 7, 1861; *Biographies of Mayors*, 106.

228. *The City of Detroit Michigan, 1701–1922*, edited by Clarence M. Burton (Cleveland: S. J. Clarke Publishing Company,

1922), vol. II, 1099; *Red Book of Michigan*, 202; Dillon et al., *Michigan Women in the Civil War*, 127 n38.

229. OR.2.21252–1253; *Johnston's Detroit City Directory and Advertising Gazetteer of Michigan*, 303; Klement, "Hopkins Hoax," 6; Wattles later described his "secession flag" as "an old shirt which he had used in straining blackberry juice for wine making which he on the occasion exhibited as a secession flag," *Hand-book of the Democracy for 1863 & '64*, 15.

230. DFP, November 17, 1861.

231. OR.III.I.626.

232. DFP, November 12, 1861; Dillon, *Michigan Women in the Civil War*, 128.

233. OR.III.1.656–657.

234. PH, 8; Berry Craig, *Kentucky Confederates: Secession, Civil War, and the Jackson Purchase* (Lexington: University Press of Kentucky, 2014), 157–158.

235. DFP, November 17, 1861.

236. Dillon, *Michigan Women in the Civil War*, 129–130; see also *The U.S. Sanitary Commission in the Valley of the Mississippi*, 242, and *Funeral Address and Memorial Notices of Mrs. Isabella Graham Duffield, of Detroit, Mich.* (Detroit: Wm. Graham's Steam Presses, 1872), 19.

237. PH, 8; Craig, *Kentucky Confederates*, 157–159.

238. SAW.2.48, and generally.

239. OR.II.2.1244–1245; Klement, "The Hopkins Hoax," 6.

240. OR.II.2.1245–1246; despite the claims of disloyalty, Butler's son served in Thornton Brodhead's First Michigan Cavalry. After being released from prison, Butler went south to visit his son, who had been wounded and had his leg amputated after the Battle of Winchester. DFP, April 20, 1862.

241. OR.III.1.676. Massachusetts and New York had major purchasing agents abroad, as did the city of Philadelphia, and other, lesser efforts were pursued in many states.

242. OR.II.2.1246, 1254; Klement, "Hopkins Hoax," 7; *Hand-Book for the Democracy* (no publisher, no date), 15.

243. MIW, 747; ROS.42.27–28.

244. OR.III.1.679.

245. ROS.42.46; MIW, 747.

246. Dyer, 1275; HS, November 26, 1861; LSR, December 25, 1861.

247. OR.III.I.685.

248. OR.III.1.699.

249. OR.III.1.701–702.

250. OR.III.1.724.

251. GO, 1861, 55.

252. OR.III.1.718.

253. *Annual Register*, 1862, 277. The vote was 76 in favor of tabling the resolution and 65 opposed, and presumably for affirmation.

254. CG, 37th Congress, 2nd Session, 16–17. A more detailed discussion of the Committee's origins may be found in Bruce Tap, *Over Lincoln's Shoulder*.

255. Kellogg resigned on March 13, 1862. MIW, 614; CIB, 161. Cullum, *Biographical Register*, vol. II (1868), 133; MIW, 615. 629; Frank B. Woodward, FAC (Detroit: Wayne State University Press, 1999), 54–55; OR.II.2.1253–1254.

256. Backus was concerned about violating British neutrality laws. The British proclamation of neutrality may be found in DFP, May 28, 1861.

257. OR.III.1.734. Backus's concerns were justified. Rankin sought to recruit 1,600 Lancers for U.S. service, but his request for British Army leave was refused. The Toronto *Leader* editorialized against his activities, but Rankin insisted that Queen Victoria's May 13, 1861 proclamation (see date), applied to governments, not individuals, and he was free to do what he wished. His government did not agree and the day after the *Leader's* editorial, Rankin was arrested for violating the Foreign Enlistment Act. The matter was debated in Canada's Parliament, and word soon reached British prime minister Lord John Russell, who then asked British ambassador Lord Lyons to raise the matter with Seward. Seward directed U.S. Ambassador to Britain Charles F. Adams to assure Russell that it had not authorized any such recruitment. Robin W. Winks, *Canada and the United States: The Civil War Years* (Montreal: McGill–Queen's University Press, 1988), 189–190. See December 21. ROS.42.87–88.

258. WES, December 11, 1861; February 24, 1862; Lanman, *The Red Book of Michigan*, 197. The Association was originally self-financing through membership dues, but was soon sustained by private contributions from Michigan. See also Zebina Moses, *The Sons of Michigan and the Michigan State Association of Washington, D.C., from December 1862, to December, 1912* (Washington, DC?, n.p., 1912), 4–17.

259. SAL-C, Chapter 5, 222; OR.II.2.1256.

260. OR.III.1.737.

261. SAW.5.327.

262. OR.III.1.750.

263. OR.II.2.1130, 1131–1132; Frank B. Woodford, *Lewis Cass: The Last Jeffersonian* (London: Octagon Books, 1973), 339.

264. CIB, 138; AG.62.5.

265. OR.III.1.756.

266. SAL.12.331; "Allotment Commissioners," DFP, February 7, 8, 1862; see DFP, March 23, June 21, August 24, September 18, 1862, for reports of allotments.

267. OR.III.1.760.

268. DFP, December 31, 1861.

269. MOG, vol. II, 412–413.

270. Document No. 2, Legislature, 1861, 18, 24.

271. PL.61.

272. *Legislature*, 1861 (Lansing, MI: John A. Kerr & Co., Printers to the State, 1861), 298–304, hereafter, MPL.61.

273. MPL.61.527.

274. Blair's speech was prescient in many respects, and paid tribute to Southern fighters: "I do not underestimate the gallantry of Southern men, and they will find it a grave error that they have under-estimated ours. The sectional pride and bitter remembrance of previous taunts, which enter into this contest will make its battles fierce and bloody."

275. JMS, Extra Session, May 8, 1861, 13; DFP, May 11, 1861.

276. MPL.61.595–602.

277. MPL.61.602–604. This act would be amended in important ways. See Legislative Session—1862 and No. 14: approved January 17, 1862; Legislative Session—1863 and No. 161, approved March 19, 1863, and No. 173, approved March 20, 1863.

278. MPL.61.605.

279. MPL.61.605–608; this act would be amended during the war as financial exigencies presented. See No. 25, approved January 18, 1862, and No. 109, approved March 14, 1863.

280. Chandler's Horse Guards was a cavalry battalion organized by Major William C. Hughes at Coldwater on September 19, 1861. Four companies mustered in, "but on account of some irregularities in its organization, was disbanded before leaving the State." MIW, 744–745. According to Dyer at 1275, it mustered out on November 22, 1861. Three decades later, Congress recommended that Hughes should be compensated for his services. Report No. 3504, found in *The Reports of Committees of the House of Representatives for the Second Session of the Fifty-First Congress, 1890–'91, with Index, in Six Volumes* (Washington, DC: Government Printing Office, 1891).

281. AG.61, "Consolidated Abstract." With the advent of conscription, out-of-state enlistees were rarely credited to a state's quota.

282. FAC, 51.

283. AG.61, "Consolidated Abstract."

284. OR.III.I.736.

285. OR.III.4.1264.

286. AG.61.46.

287. "Annual Report of the State Treasurer—1861," contained in Appendix, AG.62; 450.

288. Appendix, AG.62; *Message of the Governors*, vol. II, 448.

Key Events: 1862

1. *Michigan Legislative Manual and Official Directory for the years 1899–1900*, 182.

2. *Biographical Register*, vol. I (1868), 250; OR.III.I.777. There is some overlap in the tenures of Smith and his predecessor, Lieutenant Colonel Electus Backus. The latter was on sick leave between March 8 and September 24, 1861; he was on duty between September 24 and March 6, 1862, after which he again took sick leave until his death on June 7, 1862. *Biographical Register*, vol. I (1891), 336.

3. *Under the Oaks*, 122–123. On the first ballot, Howard had 21 votes and Blair 20. Other candidates this year were Hezekiah Wells, Henry Waldron, and Isaac Christiancy.

4. ROS.42.110–111.

5. OR.III.I.787–788.

6. SAW.3.304.

7. DFP, January 15, 1862; KG, January 17, 1862; LSJ, January 29, 1862; JC, January 29, 1862.

8. ROS.13.1–3; ROS.42.129; *Documents accompanying the Journal of the Senate of the State of Michigan, 1863*, 1.

9. CCR, January 25, 1862; ESC, January 28, 1862.

10. *Michigan Legislative Manual and Official Directory for the years 1899–1900*, 182.

11. OR.IV.3.211.

12. *Collected Works*, vol. 5, 111–112.

13. OR.I.7.121.

14. SAL.12.334–335; for excerpts, see SAW.5.24–25.

15. OR.III.1.876–877; DFP, February 4, 1862.

16. ROS.9.1–3.

17. OR.III.1.885.

18. AG.62.5.

19. ROS.13.1–3.

20. LSJ, February 26, 1862; GHN, February 26, 1862.

21. OR.III.I.911, 913.

22. OR.III.1.898.

23. OR.II.2.1263. DFP, April 20, 1862.

24. DFP, February 27, 1862.

25. See SAL.12.345–348 for the Legal Tender Act or SAW.5.25 for excerpts.

26. OR.III.1.899.

27. OR.III.1.899.

28. DFP, February 27, 1862.

29. OR.III.1.906–907. During conscription, state AGs and the War Department clashed over differing accounts of troop contributions, a critical number in determining draft quotas.

30. DFP, March 2, 1862.

31. ROS.44.136.

32. DFP, March 6, 1862; KG, March 7, 1862; AAC.62.585.

33. ROS.12.1–3.

34. PH, 209; ROS.42.151–152.

35. AG.62.5.

36. As quoted, Klement, "Hopkins Hoax," 12; see also, DFP, March 19, 1862, which reprints the *Tribune's* charges and answers them; AG.62.5.

37. SAW.5.ii

38. OR.III.1.933.

39. OR.III.I.936. Robertson does not specify particular regiments.

40. ROS.15.1–3.

41. ROS.44.147.

42. Dyer, 1275; AG.62.5; ROS.45.149.

43. *Documents of the Senate of Michigan*, 7; during at least half of the war's first year, much of the equipping and arming of troops fell to the states, who had no more experience doing this than the War Department had in supplying an army of hundreds of thousands. It seems few states were exempt from charges of fraud in contracting. Brooks Brothers is probably most famous example. See SAW.2.110. See generally, Mark R. Wilson, *The Business of Civil War: Military Mobilization and the State, 1861–1865* (Baltimore: Johns Hopkins University Press, 2006), 5–33. Real or perceived government fraud and contractor cronyism is grist for partisan mills, and Michigan was no exception. For example, see DFP, November 6, 1861, and a response from the Fourteenth Michigan's QM, published on November 27.

44. CG, 37th Congress, 2nd Session, 1370–1371; for the Democrats' answer to Chandler's implications, see DFP, March 27, 1862.

45. AG.62.5.

46. OR.II.2.275–276.

47. OR.III.2.2–3.

48. DFP, April 5, 1862.

49. DFP, April 10, 1861; CCR, April 10, 1862.

50. DFP, April 9, 1862; CCR, April 10, 1862; GHN, April 16, 1862.

51. OR.II.2.1267; Wattles's arrest would be remembered long after the war; see a one-page defense of Wattles in John Marshall's *American Bastille: A History of the Illegal Arrests and Imprisonment of American Citizens during the Late Civil War* (Philadelphia, 1884), 558; LSR, April 9, 1862.

52. DFP, April 10, 1862.

53. DFP, April 13, 1862. The Relief Committee dispatched agents to Michigan units in Tennessee and Virginia, and accompanied Governor Blair on several western inspection tours. After Gettysburg, the Committee sent four agents, including two doctors, to the battlefield. Robert Spiro, *History of the Michigan Soldiers' Aid Society, 1861–1865*, PhD diss., University of Michigan, 1959, 28–29. See Selected Summaries for additional information. DFP, April 27, 1862; LSR, April 30, 1862; HS, May 27, 1862, DFP, April 17, 18, 29, 1862; JC, April 23, 1862; CCR, May 8, 1862.

54. OR.III.2.16.

55. DFP, April 17, 29, 1862; KG, June 6, 1862; Blair collecting allotments, LSJ, June 4, 1862.

56. OR.III.2.19.

57. AG.62.5.

58. AG.62.5.

59. OR.III.2.28, 29.

60. RL, 428.

61. ROS.45.229; AG.62.5; Dyer, 1293; "Tennessee Prisoners at Fort Mackinac," *Wisconsin Magazine of History* 4, no. 2 (December 1920): 220.

62. Dwight H. Kelton, *Annals of Fort Mackinac* (Detroit: Island Edition, Detroit Free Press, 1884), 61; see OR.3.IV.537.

63. OR.III.2.41; see SAW.5.25 for details.

64. OR.III.2.44, 45.

65. OR.III.2.61; Thomas's message reflected the deteriorating military situation near Washington.

66. OR.III.2.69.

67. OR.III.2.69–70.

68. MIW, 615. Sheridan refers to this appointment in his memoirs and believed that his chief qualification was his outsider status: he knew no one in the unit and was thus uninvolved in the factionalism then dividing the Second. However FAC understands the matter differently, 54–55; *Personal Memoirs of P. H. Sheridan, General U.S. Army, in Two Volumes* (London: Chatto & Windus, Piccadilly, 1888), vol. I, 140–141.

69. OR.III.2.75, 82.

70. OR.III.2.86.

71. OR.III.2.98–99.

72. OR.III.2.101; Fox, RL, 429.

73. *Public Acts and Joint and Concurrent Resolutions of the Legislature of the State of Michigan passed at the Regular Session of 1879, with an Appendix* (Lansing: W. S. George & Co., State Printers, 1879), 315–316; DFP, June 17, 14, 1862.

74. OR.III.2.109.

75. OR.III.2.114.

76. OR.III.2.142–143.

77. RL, 429.

78. OR.III.2.163.

79. Dillon et al., *Michigan Women in the War*, 68; "Official Report of James M. Edmonds, President, Michigan Soldiers' Relief Association at Washington, D.C., January 19, 1864," in AG.63.477; "Report of Mrs. E. Brainard, General Visiting Agent of the Michigan Soldiers' Relief Association," in *Second Annual Report of the Michigan Soldiers' Relief Association for 1863* (no place, date, or year), 7–8, found in Bentley Historical Library, University of Michigan.

80. By 1861, the Sisters of Charity was a fixture in Detroit's Catholic community, and when needed, the larger community, such as during an 1833 cholera epidemic, when they managed the Wayne County Poorhouse. In 1844, the Sisters established a parish free school, which evolved into the Trinity Parish School. In 1851, they assumed management of St. Vincent's Catholic Female Orphan Asylum, and in 1860, St. Joseph's retreat, which under Church auspices cared for the mentally ill. In 1845, the Sisters established Detroit's first hospital. Initially called St. Vincent's, it later became St. Mary's. (Until the 1880s, St. Mary's was the only Detroit hospital to accept patients with communicable illness.) In around 1850, a brick, 150-bed hospital replaced the original wooden structure. This was the St. Mary's during the Civil War that eventually became a U.S. General Hos-

pital. By 1861, the Sisters of Charity (and other, mostly Catholic female orders) offered something in short supply: skilled nurses. Farmer, *History of Detroit and Wayne County and Early Michigan: A Chronological Encyclopedia*, 648, 721, 651, 656, 653; Patricia Ibbotson, *Detroit's Hospitals, Healers and Helpers*, [Illustration], 11.

81. DFP, June 21, 1862. The sisters were from Detroit's St. Mary's Hospital and Trinity Parish School. On July 14, 1862, William Hammond, U.S. Army surgeon general, issued Circular No. 7, which appointed Dorothy Dix as "Superintendent of Women Nurses" and placed all nurses under her supervision. It also provided for Sisters of Charity, but exempted them from Dix's control. *The Army Surgeon's Manual, for the use of Medical Officers, Cadets, Chaplains, containing the Regulations of the Medical Department, all General Orders from the War Department, and Circulars from the Surgeon-General's Office, from January 1st, 1861 to July 1st, 1864* (New York: Bailliere Brothers, 1864), 103–104.

82. OR.III.2.171. Pressure from the governors for greater enlistment incentives persuaded Congress to permit this order.

83. OR.III.2.178; Frederick Seward, *Seward at Washington as Senator and Secretary of State: A Memoir of his Life, with Selections from his Letters, 1861–1872* (New York: Derby & Miller, 1891), 100–101. The text of Lincoln's letter is in *Seward*; the quoted material is taken from Seward's autobiography, coauthored with his son Frederick, who served as his father's aide. In Seward's autobiography, the letter is dated June 28; in the OR, June 30; the former is probably accurate.

84. RL, 430.

85. Robertson provides a different version of this petition, which is cast as a letter from Pennsylvania's Governor Curtin and New York's Governor Morgan to Blair. It is dated June 30, marked "Private and Confidential," and concludes with a request to the Michigan governor: "Shall we add your name to the memorial?" This wire may be found at MIW, 384.

86. OR.III.2.180. See also the internal communications between Stanton and Seward, 181–182. Accurately dating this letter is problematic but important to properly sequence the numerous back-channel communications that made it possible. The OR offers a "signed" letter dated June 28; the *New York Times* (and other sheets) released a text of the governors' letter (and its acceptance by Lincoln) dated July 1. The events actually unfolded as follows: after the draft letter was circulated, beginning June 29 or 30, governors' replies began to arrive: by the evening of June 30, Berry, Buckingham, Olden (who immediately traveled to New York to meet with Seward), Blair, Johnson, Tod, Pierpont, Gamble, and the Kentucky Military Board members John B. Temple and George T. Wood, and Indiana Governor Morton (the last-mentioned was away, but apparently telegraphed his concurrence that evening); no telegrams were required from Morgan and Curtin, both of whom were in New York. On July 1, Washburn, Bradford, and Solomon concurred,

with Andrew consenting on July 2. Seward's case was strengthened when the Seven Days' casualties became known. *Seward*, 100–107; "Important from Washington," NYT, July 2, 1862; OR.III.2.187.

87. OR.III.2.181.

88. OR.III.2.181–182.

89. OR.III.2.183–184; AG.62.6–7.

90. DAT, reprinted in CCR, July 3, 1862; GHN, July 9, 1862; MA, July 11, 1862; see also JC, July 16, 1862.

91. OR.III.2.187–188.

92. OR.III.2.187–188; CCR, July 10, 1862; *Seward*, 107; SAL.12.432–489; see SAW.5.27 for excerpts.

93. RL, 430.

94. OR.III.2.200–201.

95. OR.III.2.200, 199, 205.

96. CDE, July 8, 1862; Engle, *Gathering to Save a Nation*, 186.

97. Lowell H. Harrison, *The Civil War in Kentucky* (Lexington: University Press of Kentucky, 1975), 36; Steven E. Woodworth and Kenneth J. Winkle, *Atlas of the Civil War* (New York: Oxford University Press, 2004), 128–129.

98. OR.III.2.205.

99. OR.III.2.208; a Congressional resolution authorized GO No. 74 on June 21, 1862.

100. Farmer, *History of Detroit and Michigan*, 226.

101. OR.III.210–211.

102. OR.III.2.213.

103. OR.III.2.217–218; GO 75 may be found at OR.III.2.210–211. Such federalization served efficiency by centralizing procurement, and reducing competition for the same goods.

104. DFP, July 13, 1862.

105. OR.I.16.i.735, 738.

106. PH, 215–217.

107. Gideon Welles, "The History of Emancipation," 842.

108. RL, 430.

109. SAL12.566–569; see SAW.5.28 for excerpts; MacPherson, *Political History*, 217–218; see SAW.5.28 for summaries.

110. See Taylor, *Old Slow Town*, 78–82 for a narrative account of this meeting; JC, July 16, 1862; KG, July 18, 1862. It was understood, Robertson reported later, that "each Regiment should depend upon its own District for men to fill it."

111. DFP, July 15, 1862; O. B. Curtis, *History of the Twenty-Fourth Michigan of the Iron Brigade, known as the Detroit and Wayne County Regiment* (Detroit: Winn & Hammond, 1891), 24; FAC, 93.

112. Curtis, *History of the Twenty-Fourth Michigan*, 25–26; OR.III.5.905; DFP and DAT, as quoted in *History of the Twenty-Fourth Michigan*, 25; FAC, 63–64.

113. Robert B. Ross and George B. Catlin, *Landmarks of Detroit: A History of the City*, revised by Clarence W. Burton (Detroit: Evening News Association, 1898), 423; comparing the list of

vice presidents of the failed July 15 meeting with that of the successful July 22 meeting suggests that promoters broadened the base of supporters: the July 22 meeting vice presidents would include prominent clerics: Episcopal reverend S. A. McCoskry and Catholic bishop Peter Paul Lefevre. Moreover, the speeches given on July 22 added a new theme absent from those delivered on July 15: the war was not for abolition, and blacks would never become soldiers.

114. Curtis, *History of the Twenty-Fourth Michigan*, 29.

115. SAL.12.432–489; see *SAW*.5.29 for excerpts.

116. CG, 3286–3392; *Public Life of Chandler*, 60; see for Democratic reaction see DFP, July 30, 1862; for Republican, see LSJ, July 30, 1862, and DAT, August 8, 1862.

117. Curtis, *History of the Twenty-Fourth Michigan*, 29.

118. JC, July 23, 1862.

119. *SAW*.3.158.

120. The Twenty-Fourth's regimental history includes the stirring remarks; however, other remarks, especially those disparaging African-Americans, do not appear; these can be found in contemporary newspaper accounts.

121. DFP, July 23, 1862.

122. KG, July 25, 1862.

123. *SAW*.2.324.

124. OR.II.4.265–268.

125. Mark Neely, Jr., "Colonization and the Myth That People Prepared the People for Emancipation," in *Lincoln's Proclamation: Emancipation Reconsidered*, ed. William A. Blair and Karen Fisher Younger, 45–46 (Chapel Hill: University of North Carolina Press, 2009), *Collected Works*, vol. 5, 336–337.

126. *SAW*.5.328.

127. OR.III.2.247–248.

128. Farmer, *The History of Detroit and Michigan* (Detroit: Silas Farmer & Co., 1889), 311.

129. OR.I.16.i.751.

130. This was Captain John Cullen's Company E. *SAW* focuses on the Twenty-Fourth not because its prominence overshadowed other Michigan regiments but because its regimental history and other sources offer unusual detail on its recruitment. Soon after the July 22 War Meeting, Morrow, Flanigan, Lieutenant Governor Henry T. Backus, and prominent civic and religious leaders swept Wayne County on a recruiting blitz whose itinerary illustrates the work involved in recruiting. On July 26, meetings were held in Detroit and Springwells; on July 28, Blair, Senator Howard, and others spoke in Detroit, July 30 in Detroit again, July 31 in Wayne, August 1 in Livonia Center, August 2 in Redford Center and Grosse Point, August 4 in Detroit, August 5 in Plymouth, August 6 at Pike's Peak August 7 at Dearborn, August 8 at Belleville, August 9 at Flat Rock and Trenton, and August 11 at a meeting at Wyandotte. These meetings were often elaborately staged events with bands, refreshments, and

considerable ceremony. Curtis, *History of the Twenty-Fourth Michigan*, 34–37.

131. OR.III.2.255. Washington scolds Curtin but declares that it will accept the short-term troops; however, the state must bear the recruiting costs.

132. OR.III.2.265.

133. OR.III.2.283–284.

134. OR.III.2.291–292. MA, August 8, 1862.

135. OR.III.2.291.

136. OR.III.2.295–296.

137. OR.III.2.314.

138. OR.III.2.314.

139. OR.III.2.315. See map, "Railways, April 1, 1861" in *The American Railroad Network 1861–1890*.

140. OR.III.2.317–318; DAT, August 8, 1862.

141. OR.III.2.321–322. For further elaboration of Stanton's second order, see OR.III.2.348–349, and for excerpts, *SAW*.5.30.

142. OR.III.2.323.

143. OR.III.2.342; see *SAW*.5.31 for excerpts.

144. OR.II.4.361.

145. *SAW*.5.394.

146. OR.III.2.337.

147. FAC, 93.

148. OR.III.2.374, 378.

149. OR.III.2.370; Harrison, *The Civil War in Kentucky*, 41; GHN, August 13, 1862.

150. OR.III.2.381.

151. OR.III.2.380–381; see *SAW*.5.32 for excerpts; DFP, August 23, 1862.

152. OR.III.2.389. Current War Department rules were as follows: no new units could be organized after August 15; afterward, unfilled new units would be consolidated, and if there remained any deficiency, a draft would be ordered. AG.62.12–13; ROS.24.1–3; the casualty figures appear in ROS as given, but readers should note that the ROS inexplicably provides a competing set of numbers, as does Orson Blair Curtis in *History of the Twenty Fourth Michigan*, 381; DFP, August 17, 1862.

153. OR.II.4.394–395, 437–447.

154. OR.III.2.397.

155. Gregory Michno, *Dakota Dawn: The Decisive First Week of the Sioux Uprising, August, 1862* (El Dorado Hills, CA: Savas, Beatie, 2011), 49–51.

156. *Collected Works of Abraham Lincoln*, vol. 5, 381; *Inside Lincoln's Cabinet: The Civil War Diaries of Salmon P. Chase*, edited by David Donald (New York: Longmans, Green and Co., 1954), 114.

157. Harrison, *The Civil War in Kentucky*, 41.

158. *SAW*.5.325–326.

159. OR.III.2.412; 419.

160. *SAW*.1.129.

161. OR.I.16.ii.374–375.

162. ROS.20.1–8.

163. OR.III.2.420.

164. OR.III.2.420; AG.62.8–9.

165. ROS.42.175–176.

166. OR.III.2.432.

167. OR.III.2.432.

168. OR.III.2.433–434; DFP, August 29, 1862.

169. SAW.5.327.

170. OR.III.2.434. The War Department will soon have reason to regret this ruling.

171. Curtis, *History of the Twenty-Fourth Michigan*, 37–39.

172. OR.III.2.440; Curtis, *History of the Twenty-Fourth Michigan*, 38.

173. OR.III.2.451.

174. HS, September 2, 1862; The remoteness of the Upper Peninsula was evident in its constituent counties' tardiness in making the required enrollment returns. As December 24, 1862, some had still not been received. However, Robertson said that in most UP counties, "the full quota has already been furnished, while in others it is too small to warrant a resort to the draft, especially while our relations with the Indian tribes are at all precarious." AG.62.19–20. Under the "Summer of '62" quotas, the UP had furnished three companies, and Robertson was confident that they would fill any deficiencies.

175. OR.III.2.456.

176. RL, 431.

177. OR.III.2.466.

178. Farmer, *The History of Detroit and Michigan*, 311. The sequel proved that the money raised in July was sufficient, and on July 21, 1863, the Council ordered the refunding of $40,226.25 to the citizens who had contributed the cash after the War Meeting one year earlier.

179. DFP, September 15, 1862; Hershock, "Copperheads and Radicals," 53.

180. ROS.18.1–2.

181. DFP, August 27, 28, 1862; Farmer, *History of Detroit and Michigan*, 307.

182. ROS.17.1–3.

183. OR.III.2.474.

184. Harrison, *The Civil War in Kentucky*, 42.

185. OR.III.2.482–484; Farmer, *History of Detroit and Michigan*, 307.

186. ROS.22.1–4; ROS.34.1–5; *Michigan in the War*, 484.

187. AG.62.10.

188. OR.I.16.I.3; ROS.35.1.

189. OR.I.16.I.3.

190. DFP, September 2, 1862; for casualties see DFP, September 2, 3, 5, and 7, 1862 (reprinted from *New York Tribune*).

191. *Saginaw Valley Republican*, September 3, 1862, reprinted, DFP, September 11, 1862; SAW.1.286–287.

192. ROS.21.1–3.

193. OR.III.2.512.

194. William Dudley Foulke, *Life of Oliver P. Morton, including his important speeches* (Indianapolis: Bowen-Merrill Company, 1899), vol. I, 190; ROS.19.1–2.

195. SAW.5.400.

196. DFP, September 10, 11, 1862.

197. ROS.45.229; official records conflict about the Guards' muster-out date, with MIW giving September 25; based on newspaper reports, the ROS is probably correct, see DFP, September 16, 1862.

198. AG.62.21–22. The top five of forty-two counties reporting by number of draft-eligible men were Wayne County (10,106), Lenawee (5,477), Oakland (4,932), Washtenaw (4,895), and Calhoun (4,003) counties; those with the fewest were Emmet (25), Mason (35), and Cheboygan, 37.

199. Francis Davis McTeer, "In Bonnet and Shawl: Adventures of a Michigan Relief Agent during the Civil War," contained in Dillon et al., *Michigan Women in the Civil War*, 66.

200. "Tennessean Prisoners at Fort Mackinac," *Wisconsin Magazine of History*, 4, no. 2 (December 1920), 220–221.

201. OR.I.16.I.3.

202. ROS.23.1–3.

203. WES, September 15, 1862.

204. Harrison, *The Civil War in Kentucky*, 43.

205. Harrison, *The Civil War in Kentucky*, 43–44.

206. SAW.1.289.

207. DFP, September 17, 1862; Dell, *Lincoln and the War Democrats*, 176; JC, September 17, 1862.

208. OR.III.2.562, 565.

209. WES, September 26, 1862.

210. RL, 432.

211. DFP, September 18, 1862; JC, September 24, October 1, 1862; KG, September 19, 1862.

212. DAT, September 23, 1860.

213. Harrison, *The Civil War in Kentucky*, 46.

214. DFP, September 24, 1862; ESC, September 30, 1862; CCR, September 25, 1862; LSR, October 1, 1862; DAT, September 25, 1862.

215. ROS.25.1–3.

216. DAT, October 2, 1862.

217. NYH, September 25, 27, 1862; DAT, September 26, 1862; Engle, *Gathering to Save a Nation*, 229–230.

218. OR.III.2.582–584; as quoted Harris, *Lincoln and the Union Governors*, 76–77; Engle, *Gathering to Save a Nation*, 231–232.

219. JC, October 1, 1861.

220. SAW.2.340–341.

221. OR.III.2.937.

222. OR.III.2.587. DFP, September 28, 1862.

223. Egle, *Life of Curtin*, 321–322; Engle, *Gathering to Save a Nation*, 234; as quoted, Harris, *Lincoln and the Union Governors*, 77.

224. *MIW*, 639.

225. DFP, September 26, 1862.

226. Harrison, *The Civil War in Kentucky*, 46.

227. DFP, September 30, 1862; NYH, September 28, 1862, published Blair's remarks in full.

228. DFP, October 8, 1862. Other men involved in the society included H. H. Riley, J. T. Montross, G. W. Thomas, D. C. Langley, George E. Jarvis, W. C. Stevens, W. W. Davis, C. T. Gilbert, and G. C. Gibbs. NYT, September 20, 1862.

229. Dillon et al., *Michigan Women in the War*, 68, 73; "Report of Miss Julia Wheelock," contained in *Second Annual Report of the Michigan Soldiers' Relief Association for 1863* (no place, date, or year), 11; found in Bentley Historical Library, University of Michigan.

230. DFP, October 4, 1862; Hershock, "Copperheads and Radicals," 54.

231. *Michigan Reports*, 301; KG, October 10, 1862; CCR, October 23, 1862; for a list of quotas and county commissioners and surgeons, see DFP, October 5, Hershock, "Copperheads and Radicals," 56.

232. As quoted in Lewis Collins, *History of Kentucky, Revised, Enlarged four-fold, and brought down to the year 1874, by his son, Richard H. Collins* (Covington, KY: Collins & Co., 1874), vol. I, 113; Harrison, *The Civil War in Kentucky*, 48–49.

233. DFP, October 9, 1862.

234. OR.III.2.654.

235. ROS.36.1–12.

236. DFP, October 14, 1862.

237. OR.III.2.960.

238. SAW.5.365–366.

239. OR.I.16.ii.642.

240. AG.62.17.

241. ROS.45.209.

242. OR.III.2.705–706, 707.

243. "Military Officers of the State," *Annual Report of the Adjutant General of the State of Michigan, for the year 1863* (Lansing, MI: John A. Kerr & Co., Printers to the State, 1864), no page.

244. *Congressional Elections*, 194; Hershock, "Copperheads and Radicals," 57n 49.

245. CQ, 509.

246. Hershock, "Copperheads and Radicals," 57n49.

247. Dubin, 99; Hershock, "Copperheads and Radicals," 57n 49.

248. MA, November 14, 1862; LSJ, November 19, 1862; also see DFP, November 11, 1862.

249. DFP, November 12, 1861.

250. OR.I.14.189–190; McRrae, *Negroes in Michigan in the Civil War*, 31.

251. OR.III.2.859–861.

252. OR.III.2.865.

253. OR.III.2.880.

254. AG.62.17–18.

255. SAW.3.387–388.

256. Dyer, 1271; AG.62.10.

257. OR.III.2.937.

258. Dyer, 1272, AG.62.10.

259. ROS.26.1–3.

260. *Michigan in the War*, 573.

261. DFP, December 19, 1862; *Lansing State Republican*, December 24, 1862.

262. DAT, January 7, 1863.

263. MOG, vol. II, 446.

264. *Acts of the Legislature of the State of Michigan, passed at the Extra Session of 1862, with an Appendix* (Lansing, MI: John A. Kerr & Co., Printers to the State, 1863), 59–60; hereafter, MPL.62. This call was renewed in 1865—see JR 34, in MPL.65.802–803.

265. MPL.62.1–2.

266. MPL.62.60–61.

267. MPL.62.61.

268. MPL.62.62–63. See Article I, Section 8 and Section 9 of the United States Constitution for background. Congress responded with the income tax, which began in 1861 and was replaced in 1862. Income taxes were not properly "constitutionalized" until adoption of the Sixteenth Amendment in 1913.

269. MPL.62.64.

270. MPL.62.63–64. See Section 4 of the Morrill Land Grant Act, July 2, 1862, which required that "military tactics" be taught at Land Grant colleges. SAL.12.503–505.

271. MPL.62.14–18. For soldiers discharged for disability, this law was imperfect: family aid ceased after discharge. Processing times to collect U.S. pensions meant long gaps with no revenue. See AG.63.458–459.

272. MPL.62.64–65.

273. MPL.62.66.

274. MPL.62.66–67. Recreational and not medical usage was banned.

275. MPL.62.20–48.

276. MPL.62.67–68.

277. MPL.62.68–69.

278. MPL.62.72.

279. The War Department recalculated this number for the period between August 15, 1862, and January 31, 1863, to arrive at 2,194 volunteers for old regiments. OR.III.3.36.

280. AG.62.23.

281. AG.62.11.

282. AG.62.18–19, 24.

283. OR.III.4.1265.

284. QMG.62.18.

285. *Governor's Message*, January 7, 1863, 17.

286. AG.62.25.

287. Since this report was filed, 36 who returned to their units reduced the number of men missing. AG.63.436.

288. AG.62, Supplement, 308.

289. OR.III.2.810–813. Comparing these figures with those of New York City, Philadelphia, and Cincinnati illustrates that Detroit's industry was its future, not its present.

290. *Annual Report of the Quartermaster General of the State of Michigan for the year 1862* (Lansing: John A. Kerr & Co., Printers to the State, 1862), 3–4, 6–7, hereafter QMG.62.

291. QMG.62.11–13.

292. "Official Report of James M. Edmonds, President, Michigan Soldiers' Relief Association at Washington, D.C., January 19, 1864," in AG.63.477.

293. "State Treasurer's Annual Report—1862," in Appendix, MPL.63, 469–471.

Key Events: 1863

1. DAT, January 3, 1860; the Final Emancipation Proclamation may be found in McRae, *Negroes in Michigan during the Civil War*, 27. For other Republican newspaper reactions, see DAT, January 5, 1863; Democratic sheets were mostly negative, see DFP, January 4, 1863; ESC, January 6, 1863.

2. ROS.45.1; MIW, 740.

3. OR.III.3.4.

4. DFP, January 10, 1863.

5. *The Papers of Jefferson Davis*, vol. 9, January to September, 1863, edited by Lynda Lasswell Crist (Baton Rouge: Louisiana State University Press, 1997), 12.

6. *Opinion of Attorney General Bates on Citizenship* (Washington, DC: Government Printing Office, 1862), 15–16; comment from some Michigan Democratic sheets was profoundly racist but raised a question probably of concern to many Michigan whites—that Bates's opinion opened the door for desegregated public schools and an end to states laws excluding blacks. DFP, January 4, 1863, reprinted in ESC, January 6, 1863; DFP, January 8, 1863.

7. As quoted in McRae, *Negroes in Michigan during the Civil War*, 28–29.

8. *Michigan Legislative Manual and Official Directory for the years 1899–1900*, 183; HDN, January 13, 1863.

9. Wilmer C. Harris, *Public Life of Zachariah Chandler, 1851–1875* (Michigan Historical Commission, 1917), 69; HS, January 13, 1863; DAT, January 10, 1863; GHN, January 14, 1863.

10. DFP, January 20, 1863.

11. DFP, January 24, 1863, where this debate may be followed; MA, January 30, 1863.

12. ROS.37.1–8.

13. Contained in *Michigan Advance Reports*, 302–303.

14. AG.64.6.

15. OR.III.3.36.

16. JC, February 18, 1863.

17. See John Perry Pritchett, "Michigan Democracy in the Civil War," in *Michigan History Magazine* XI (1927), 92–109. Too long to be adequately summarized here, Morrison's paper objected to New England's dominance and Lincoln's civil rights violations. He posited a Calhoun-type states' rights theory and claimed that emancipation would produce political and social equality with blacks.

18. As quoted in AAC.63.645; also see DFP, February 12, 1863.

19. OR.III.3.43–45. These figures were probably prepared in advance of raising colored regiments. The estimation of eligible black males was based on applying the same recruiting discount that experience had proved was the case for white males.

20. JC, February 18, 1863.

21. DFP, February 21, 1863.

22. MOG, II, 478; DFP, March 1, 1863; for a legislative history see David S. Inbody, *The Soldier Vote: War, Politics and the Ballot in America* (New York: Palgrave MacMillan, 2016), 36–38.

23. SAL, vol. 13, 665–682; see SAW.5.35 for excerpts.

24. FAC, 64–65; Anonymous, *A Thrilling Narrative from the Lips of the Sufferers of the Late Detroit Riot, March 6, 1863, with the Hair Breadth Escapes of Men, Women and Children, and Destruction of Colored Men's Property, Not Less than $15,000* (Detroit: Published by the Author, 1863), 1; The *Detroit Free Press*'s headline was "Trial of the Negro Faulkner," DFP, March 6, 1863.

25. OR.III.3.58. These sums were promised to volunteers, not draftees.

26. OR.III.3.88–93.

27. DAT, February 25, 1863; JC, March 4, 1863; DFP, March 5, 1863; GHN, March 4, 1863; MA, March 13, 1863.

28. OR.III.3.755–758; see SAW.5.37 for excerpts; DAT, March 6, 1863.

29. RL, 435; losses included 345 taken prisoner.

30. Newberry, *The U.S. Sanitary Commission in the Valley of the Mississippi*, 222. Two slightly different versions of this message were sent. *The United States Sanitary Commission: A Sketch of its Purposes and its Work, compiled from documents and private papers* (Boston: Little Brown and Company, 1863), 185.

31. For accounts of the trial and subsequent riots, see DFP, March 6, 7, 8, 1861; DAT, March 9, 1863; a recent narrative account is Taylor, *Old Slow Town*, 93–106. Faulkner's racial status was ambiguous, see DAT, March 9, 1863.

32. Between 1860 and 1863, Francis B. Phelps, a furrier, was alderman for Detroit's Fourth Ward, and in 1862 and 1863 was president of the Board of Alderman. Detroit's municipal charter provided that if the mayor were absent, the Board's president automatically became acting mayor; with Mayor Duncan away, Phelps was in control during the riot, perhaps an unfortunate

choice. Woodford opines that during the violence, Phelps "appeared paralyzed by indecision." Given the red flags from the previous day, security was inadequate; on the 6th, the riot had been ongoing for almost seven hours before Phelps wired for troops. *History of Detroit and Michigan*, 144, 137; FAC, 67.

33. DFP, March 8, 1863.

34. DFP, March 14, 1863.

35. This account is drawn from DAT, March 9, 1863; DFP, March 6, 8, 1863, and FAC, 63–70; AG.63.446; Anonymous, *A Thrilling Narrative* is a compilation of first-hand accounts by black victims of the mob. The mob is depicted as largely "Dutch" (i.e., German) and Irish men. The *Narrative's* editor blamed the city for not suppressing the riot earlier, concluding that "Detroit is a Democratic city, and being in the majority, of course, it was in harmony with [the rioters'] feelings." The Democratic *Free Press* blamed the Germans; the Republican *Advertiser and Tribune* blamed the Irish. An excellent recent account is Paul Taylor, *Old Slow Town*, 93–105; all twenty-two arrestees were white.

36. DAT, March 9, 1863; DFP, March 10, 1863.

37. "Report of Chaplain Samuel Day, in reference to Sanitary Supplies," in AG.63.479.

38. *General Orders of the War Department, embracing the years 1861, 1862 & 1863*, ed. Thomas M. O'Brien and Oliver Diefendorf (New York: Derby & Miller, 1864), vol. II, 61; No. 58, March 10, 1863. This can also be found at OR.III.3.60–62; see SAL.12.731–737 for Enrollment Act.

39. As quoted, *Old Slow Town*, 100; Anonymous, "A Thrilling Narrative," 18–19.

40. AG.63.494, 499.

41. SAW.5.329–330.

42. OR.III.3.74.

43. *Michigan Legislative Manual and Official Directory for the years 1899–1900*, 283; DFP, March 27, 1890.

44. Welcher, *Union Army*, vol. II, 129.

45. OR.III.3.112–113. The influence of GO No. 86 should not be overemphasized: the most important factor in filling up old regiments was the benefits of associating veterans with inexperienced soldiers. Objections to consolidating Michigan's "old regiments" were expressed before and after the general order and the statute on which it was based. See ESC, January 13, 1863; see also GHN, April 29, 1863.

46. JC, April 22, 1863.

47. See SAW.6.495–496 for details.

48. ROS.27.1–3.

49. ROS.42.202–205.

50. FAC, 76–77. This anecdote is contained in a letter from Private David Lane, serving with the Seventeenth Michigan.

51. *The Trial of Hon. Clement L. Vallandigham, by a Military Commission: and the proceedings under his application for a Writ of Ha-*beas Corpus from the Circuit Court of the United States for the Southern District of Ohio* (Cincinnati: Rickey and Carroll, 1863), 7. Burnside's inartfully drawn GO, which left undefined "treason" or "sympathies" but implied a death penalty and specified banishment for either, was catnip to able defenders (which Pugh and Pendleton surely were) and guaranteed partisan martyrdom to any pacifist or peace Democrat unlucky (or, depending on the political use to which such an event might be put, fortunate) enough to be ensnared in its application.

52. OR.III.3.125–146. These far-reaching regulations (which also listed thirty-nine separate administrative forms) contained much more, and together with the March 3 enrollment act, are required reading for those seeking to understand the shift from state to federal control of the conscription process.

53. OR.III.5.889.

54. OR.III.3.148–164; excerpts pertaining to martial law, see SAW.5.38. Francis Leiber wrote the code, see SAW.2.365.

55. OR.III.3.167–169; The OR contains only the full letter to the provost marshal for New York, but notes that a "similar" letter was sent to Hill.

56. DFP, May 6, 1863; subsequent changes, DFP, May 30, 1863.

57. OR.III.3.170–172.

58. DFP, May 8, 1863; DAT, May 8, 1863.

59. James Laird Vallandigham, *A Life of Clement L. Vallandigham*, 248–249, 252–253; SAW.5 details Vallandigham's wartime activities.

60. ROS.38.1–4.

61. OR.III.3.185–186.

62. Wiley, *The United States*, 265; DFP, May 6, 14, 17, 20, 21, 1863; the DFP, May 22, 1863, sharply denounced the denial of Vallandigam's habeas corpus writ; see ESC, May 19, 1863, reprint of undated *Chicago Times* article; ESC, May 26, 1863; GHN, May 27, 1863.

63. OR.I.25.ii.437–438.

64. OR.I.23.ii.319.

65. AG.64.6.

66. *Decision of Judge Leavitt, of Ohio, in the Vallandigham Habeas Corpus Case* (Philadelphia: Printed for Gratuitous Distribution, 1863).

67. AG.64.6.

68. Dyer, *A Compendium*, 1274; ROS.39.1–4.

69. DFP, May 22, 1863.

70. CL, May 21, 1863; Guy James Gibson, *Lincoln's League: The Union League Movement during the Civil War* (Urbana: University of Illinois Press, 1957), 106. See CCR, May 14, 1863; GHN, August 26, 1863.

71. OR.III.3.215. See also GO No. 144 at OR.III.3.216.

72. OR.I.25.ii.514.

73. DFP, May 29, 1863; Blair's remarks are the reporter's

paraphrase. One Michigan cavalryman's recollection of Blair on this or another visit to the front may be found in J. H. Kidd, *Personal Recollections of a Cavalryman, with Custer's Michigan Cavalry Brigade in the Civil War* (Ionia, MI: Sentinel Printing Co., 1908), 105.

74. WES, June 1, 1863.

75. The date and contents of the circular are inferred from Fry to A. W. Bolenius, OR.III.244–245.

76. "General Burnside's Order No. 84, Suppressing the Chicago Times, and its History" (Boston: Printed by Prentiss and Deland, 1864?), 1; see DFP, June 9, 1863; GHN, June 10, 1863; ESC, June 16, 1863; undated DAT, reprinted DFP, June 9.

77. OR.III.3.250–252; OR.III.3.320.

78. OR.I.27.i.30; OR.III.3.320.

79. SAW.5.353–354.

80. See SAW.5.222 and n.93, at 421 for background on Cox's note.

81. JC, June 10, 3, 1863.

82. Basil W. Duke, *History of Morgan's Cavalry* (n.p., UK: Leonaur Publishing, 2010), 331, 325–328.

83. OR.I.27.iii.144; 60, 162; OR.III.3.360–361; OR.I.27.iii.137–139, 140, 142–144, 145; 141.

84. SAW.5.452–453.

85. OR.III.3.367.

86. Moss, *Annals of the United States Christian Commission*, 348–349.

87. For Hines's raid, see William H. H. Terrell, *Indiana in the War of the Rebellion* (Indiana Historical Society, 1960, reprint, 1869), 204–208. The words quoted are Duke's, see 343–344; a biographical note about Thomas Henry Hines appears in the Indiana chapter.

88. AG.63.8–9.

89. JC, June 24, 1863.

90. DFP, June 29, 1863.

91. OR.III.3.414–416; MIW, 747–748.

92. OR.I.27.iii.347–348.

93. Coddington, *Gettysburg Campaign*, 168–169.

94. Eicher and Eicher, *Civil War High Command*, 196.

95. "General Order No. 5," DSS, July 1, 1863.

96. ROS.42.220.

97. Duke, *History*, 331.

98. "Official Report of James M. Edmonds," contained in AG.63.478; RL, 439, 440.

99. Hauptman, *Between Two Fires*, 133–134; 130; Herek, *First Michigan Sharpshooters*, 35–36.

100. DAT, July 4, 1863; DFP, July 4, 1863.

101. RL, 440.

102. DAT, July 4 and July 7; see July 13 for Michigan soldiers in Philadelphia hospitals; DFP, July 10, 18, 31, 1863; *Michigan at Gettysburg. July 1st, 2nd and 3rd, 1863. June 12, 1889. Proceedings In-cident to the Dedication of the Michigan Monuments upon the Battlefield of Gettysburg, June 12, 1889* (Detroit: Winn & Hammond, 1889), 124; HS, July 21, 28, August 18, 1863; LSR, July 29, 1863; CCR, August 13, 1863.

103. HS, July 7, 1865; DAT, July 8, 1863; GHN, July 15, 1863.

104. DFP, July 18, 8, 9, 10, 7, 1863; MA, July 17, 1863; HS, July 28, 1863; GHN, September 2, 1863.

105. ROS.44.1–3; see DFP, July 7, 1863.

106. Duke, *History*, 342.

107. RL, 438.

108. Duke, *History*, 343–344; AG.64.6.

109. ALP, Jacob Howard to Abraham Lincoln, July 8, 1863.

110. Duke, *History*, 347.

111. Duke, *History*, 347–348.

112. OR.III.3.483; Terrell, *Indiana in the War*, 188–189.

113. "Report of Mrs. E. Brainard, General Visiting Agent of the Michigan Soldiers' Relief Association," in *Second Annual Report of the Michigan Soldiers' Relief Association for 1863* (no place, date, or year), 7–11; see also Barnard letter, HS, August 11, 1863.

114. CPD, July 13, 1863.

115. Fry's request to AAPMGs does not appear in the OR and is inferred from Hill's July 18 message to Fry, at OR.III.3.551–552.

116. Duke, *History*, 350–353. As quoted in Duke, 351.

117. OR.III.3.488.

118. RL, 440; Duke, *History*, 354.

119. OR.III.3.488–489.

120. Porter, *Political History*, 177–178; Duke, *History*, 354–355.

121. RL, 440.

122. OR.III.3.552. This letter is not found in the OR but is inferred from the July 21 message of Hill to Fry, at OR.III.3.551–552. The implication is that two objectives would be met: refilling old units while providing additional security for the draft; as quoted, Duke, *History*, 355–357; OR.III.3.535–536.

123. Duke, 360–362; map, 352; OR.III.3.545.

124. OR.III.3.551–552.

125. JC, July 22, 1863. The county's second-class enrollment is a close estimate, because the source used for this entry was only partially legible.

126. MIW, 488; see also OR.III.3.564; Smith, "Black Regiment," 29; As quoted, Randal Maurice Jelks, *African Americans in the Furniture City: The Struggle for Civil Rights in Grand Rapids* (Urbana: University of Illinois Press, 2009), 12; historian Richard M. Reid observed that "It speaks to the nature of mid-nineteenth-century politics that someone such as Blair, who was active in founding the Republican Party and who has been described as a Radical Republican, would think nothing of using the racist language of his day." Richard M. Reid, *African Canadians in Union Blue: Volunteering for the Cause in the Civil War* (Vancouver: UBC Press, 2014), 106.

127. SAW.3.388.

128. Bartlett, *The Soldiers National Cemetery at Gettysburg*, 1–3. See SAW.3.221.

129. SAW.5.327–328.

130. MIW, 488–489; Foster's authorization was also conditioned upon compliance with War Department GO No. 110 (1863), and GOs Nos. 143 and 144 (1863). No. 110 may be found at OR.III.3.175–176; for GOs 143 and 144, see OR.III.3.215–216.

131. Duke, *History*, 362–365.

132. OR.III.3.577–578.

133. David Tod, *Annual Message*, January 4, 1864, 5.

134. USS *Michigan* was an iron-plated-hull, twin-paddle-wheel naval vessel built in 1844 and launched from Erie, Pennsylvania. It displaced 600 tons with a draft of ten feet. It was 168 feet long with the main deck beam 27 feet across. The *Michigan*'s entire service career was spent on the Great Lakes until it was decommissioned in 1928. FAC, 286.

135. As quoted in Bradley A. Rogers, *Guardian of the Great Lakes: The U.S. Paddle Frigate Michigan* (Ann Arbor: University of Michigan Press, 1996), 84.

136. Dyer, *History*, 161.

137. Dr. J. S. Newberry, Sanitary Commission No. 96, *The U.S. Sanitary Commission in the Valley of the Mississippi, during the War of the Rebellion* (Cleveland: Fairbanks, Benedict & Co., Printers, 1871), 113.

138. OR.III.3.611.

139. OR.III.3.630.

140. AG.63.339–444. Robertson attributed few enlistments to the cost of uniforms, which the volunteer had to pay. He recommended that the state furnish uniforms, as it did arms, equipment, and transportation.

141. OR.III.3.639; "Circular of the Michigan Soldiers' Aid Society," *The Sanitary Reporter*, Volume I, No. 9, September 15, 1863.

142. MIW, 489; Smith, "Black Regiment," 30–31.

143. Egle, *Life of Curtin*, 149.

144. JCC, 140; MA, August 21, 1863; Smith, "Black Regiment," 31; DFP, August, 25, 1862.

145. As quoted in McRae, *Negroes in Michigan during the Civil War*, 43.

146. As quoted in McRae, *Negroes in Michigan during the Civil War*, 43.

147. James Laird Vallandigham, *Life of Clement L. Vallandigham*, 348.

148. DFP, August 25, 1863.

149. OR.III.3.721. Providing notice of upcoming drafts was a reform that followed the New York draft riots. See SAW.2.214–215.

150. OR.III.3.733.

151. OR.III.3.727.

152. Brady's Independent Company of Sharpshooters was organized in Detroit on February 3, 1862, and later attached to the Sixteenth Michigan.

153. OR.III.3.761–762.

154. OR.III.3.765.

155. OR.III.3.767.

156. DFP, September 11, 12, 1863; Smith, "Black Regiments," 32.

157. OR.III.3.832. This letter is inferred from AAG Vincent's September 22 reply.

158. OR.III.3.817–818. This was circulated in War Department GO No. 315 (September 17, 1863); DFP, September 17, 1863.

159. Robertson's authority for issuing this GO is unclear. Michigan would not outlaw other states to recruit in the state until March 16, 1865; see No. 209 in Legislative Sessions—1865; DAT, September 16, 1863, reprinted DFP, September 17.

160. DFP, September 17, 1863. For another version of this meeting (drawn from Barns's *Advertiser and Tribune* of August 7, 1863), see also McRae's account, *Negroes in Michigan during the Civil War*, 44–45.

161. "Official Report of Luther B. Willard, State Military Agent, at Nashville," contained in AG.63.494; RL, 441; DFP, September 27, October 3, 1863, CCR, October 8, 1863; HDS, October 13, 1863; MA, October 23, 1863 DAT, September 22, 1863.

162. OR.III.3.825. Vincent identifies these units (number of recruits in parenthesis) as having received men since May 26, 1863: Ninth Cavalry (1,053); First Sharpshooters (874); Eleventh Battery (150); Twelfth Battery (119); Companies M and L, Seventh Cavalry (173); and miscellaneous recruits, including Invalid Corps, through August 28, 1863 (1,135).

163. OR.III.3.826–829.

164. OR.III.3.832; Robertson later estimated the total credits due Michigan, fully adjusted under the three-year standard, as 9,518 men. AG.63.14.

165. *History of the Michigan Soldiers' Aid Society, 1861–1865* by Robert Spiro, PhD diss., University of Michigan, 1959, 38–39.

166. OR.III.3.838–839.

167. OR.III.3.775–776.

168. DFP, October 4, 1863.

169. OR.III.3.892, as contained in GO 340, October 19, 1863. AG.63.17. Quotas were not (yet) netted against enlistments.

170. McRae, *Negroes in Michigan's Civil War*, 51; CCR, October 15, 1863.

171. DFP, October 24, 1863.

172. AG.63.14.

173. On October 24, Grant established the famous "cracker line" supplying the starving federals with food. *History of the North-Western Soldiers' Fair, Held in Chicago, The last week of October and the first week of November, including a list of donations and names*

of donors, *Treasurer's Report*, &c. (Chicago: Dunlop, Sewell & Spalding, 1864), 15, 16, 178–181, 7, 183, 59–60.

174. As quoted (and sourced), McRae, *Negroes in Michigan's Civil War*, 52; the *Free Press* also accused Barns of defrauding his own men—see DFP, November 18, 1863.

175. OR.III.3.1079–1080.

176. DFP, November 4, 4, 1863.

177. DAT, November 24, 1863.

178. OR.III.3.991.

179. OR.III.3.996.

180. OR.III.3.1004. This letter incorporated another that Fry had sent to Massachusetts militia general R. A. Pierce, which can be found on p. 928.

181. SAW.5.351–352.

182. SAW.5.432–433.

183. OR.III.3.1012–1013. See also OR.II.VI.491; AG.63.462. What Smith probably did not know was that over the summer, Confederate Secretary of the Navy Stephen Mallory had sent twenty-seven naval officers and forty "trustworthy" petty officers to Canada "to organize an expedition and cooperate with Army officers and attempt to release the Confederate prisoners on Johnson's Island in Lake Erie." In his report, Mallory lamented that substantial sums of money had been invested in this scheme (which, in his opinion, was "one of the best-planned enterprises of the present war"); it might have succeeded had not the British authorities alerted the United States. ONR.II.2, 599–600.

184. As quoted in MIW, 47; also, May, *A Wartime Chronicle*, 52; AG.63.17.

185. OR.III.3.1008.

186. OR.III.3.1012–1013.

187. OR.III.3.1012; this order temporarily reversed the federalization of recruiting. Washington was persuaded that recruiting was more productive when managed by states. While the War Department did not cede legal authority, as a practical matter, the effect was the same. In 1864, too many veteran regiments were scheduled for extinction; this was a real military emergency, and the Lincoln administration would not insist on prerogatives over productivity.

188. SAW.5.433.

189. OR.III.3.1013–1015. These threats provoked a crisis along the northern frontier. Stanton also alerted Department of the East Commander John Dix, the mayors of Erie, Detroit, Milwaukee, Chicago, Ogdensburg, Oswego, Lewiston, and Rochester, and the governors of Indiana, Illinois, Michigan, and New York.

190. OR.III.3.1019.

191. OR.III.3.1018.

192. OR.III.3.1033.

193. OR.III.3.1031–1032.

194. SAW.3.379–380.

195. OR.III.3.1036; as quoted, *The Making of the University of Michigan, 1817–1992*, ed. Margaret Steneck and Nicholas Steneck (Ann Arbor: University of Michigan, Bentley Historical Library, 1994) 60–61; Rev. James L. Vallandigham, *A Life of Clement Vallandigham* (Baltimore: Turnbull Brothers, 1872), 336–345.

196. OR.III.3.1043.

197. "Official Report of Dr. Joseph Tunnicliffe, Jr.," contained in AG.63.486.

198. "Official Report of Dr. Joseph Tunnicliffe, Jr.," contained in AG.63.486; RL, 442.

199. RL, 442.

200. Dyer, *History*, 1275; ROS.40.1–18.

201. NYT, November 20, 1863; DFP, November 21, 25, 1863; DAT, November 23, 1863; LSR, November 25, 1863; CCR, December 03, 1863.

202. DFP, November 22, 1863; McRae, *Negroes in Michigan's Civil War*, 53.

203. Smith, "Black Regiment," 33–34; DFP, November 24, 1863.

204. Duke, *History*, 386.

205. "Official Report of Dr. J.B. Gilman, State Military Agent, at Louisville, Ky.," contained in AG.64.884.

206. OR.III.3.1113.

207. OR.III.3.1118.

208. OR.III.3.1116; see also SAW.2.224.

209. Moss, *Annals of the Christian Commission*, 348–349.

210. McRae, *Negroes in Michigan during the Civil War*, 54–58.

211. *Abraham Lincoln Political Writings and Speeches*, ed. Terence Ball (New York: Cambridge University Press, 2013), 197–200; DFP, December 15, 1863; ESC, December 30, 1863; CCR, December 17, 1863.

212. "Official Report of Dr. Joseph Tunnicliffe, Jr.," in AG.63.486.

213. MIW, 747; ROS.41.1–4.

214. SAW.5.435–436.

215. Welcher, *Union Army*, II, 129.

216. McRae, *Negroes in Michigan's Civil War*, 51. This letter also references bond issues for privately financing First Michigan Colored bounties as "questionable transactions." These bonds were apparently issued to enlisted men, but (the claim was) were repurchased at sharp discounts by speculators. The *Detroit Free Press* did its best to blame Barns, who later denied responsibility. At a meeting in November (led by such luminaries as Underground Railroad conductor George DeBaptiste, local cleric Reverend Madison Lightfoot, and white abolitionist Gerritt Smith), Detroit's black community closed ranks around Barns and condemned the *Free Press* as "an ancient and persistent enemy of the colored man." DFP, November 18, 1863, and April 18,

1864; McRae, *Negroes in Michigan's Civil War*, 53; CCR, December 17, 1863.

217. Bartlett, *Soldiers' National Cemetery at Gettysburg*, to the [Pennsylvania] Legislature (Indianapolis: W. R. Holloway, State Printer, 1865), 583–585; "Proceedings," 3–5, in *Reports of the Heads of Departments, transmitted to the Governor of Pennsylvania, in pursuance of law, for the year ending November 30, 1863* (Harrisburg: Singerly & Myers, State Printers, 1864), vol. II.

218. Bartlett, *The Soldiers' National Cemetery at Gettysburg*, 20.

219. DFP, December 19, 1863.

220. "To the People of the State of Michigan," in *Second Annual Report of the Michigan Soldiers' Relief Association for 1863* (no place, date, or year), 11; DAT, January 4, 1864.

221. McRae, *Michigan Negroes during the Civil War*, 58.

222. OR.III.4.4; see OR.III.3.1189.

223. OR.III.3.1195.

224. DFP, January 4, 1864; Smith, "Black Regiment," 34–35.

225. *Governor's Message*, January 7, 1863, 18; Blair also notes that a few local officials administer the program "without humanity but with positive cruelty." He lobbies the legislature to allow recipients the right of appeal.

226. MA, January 30, 1863.

227. *Acts of the Legislature of the State of Michigan, passed at the Regular Session of 1863, with an appendix* (Lansing: John A. Kerr & Co., Printers to the State, 1863), 12–13; hereafter, MPL.63; for other actions involving ratification of municipal or individual acts relating to recruitment, see No. 36, MPL.63.32–33; No. 80, MPL.63.122–123; No. 201, MPL.63.352–353; No. 169, MPL.63.307; regarding No. 169, because the calendar of tax receipts did not always correlate with the timing of bounty payments, other funds might be used as a form of "bridge financing."

228. MPL.63.29–30.

229. MPL.63.434–435.

230. MPL.63.438; Lambert's Tourniquet was enormously popular during the Civil War; for a description see Surgeon General T. Longmore, *Gunshot Injuries: Their History, Characteristic Features, Complications, and General Treatment* (London: Longmans, Green and Co., 1877), 304–306.

231. MPL.63.60–61; No. 51 was amended by No. 27, approved February 5, 1864 (MPL.64.64) for re-enlistees.

232. MPL.63.66–67.

233. MPL.63.92–95.

234. MPL.63.106.

235. MPL.63.166–168.

236. MPL.63.442. When asked to show her jewels, Cornelia, mother of ill-fated land reformers Tiberius and Gaius Gracchi, instead presented her two sons.

237. MPL.63.168–169.

238. MPL.63.187–189.

239. MPL.63.443–445.

240. MPL.63.445–447.

241. MPL.63.447–448.

242. MPL.63.295–296.

243. MPL.63.317–319; see 1864 clarifications in JR 5, at MPL.64.142–143. There had been complaints that some supervisors were unfairly denying relief or harassing qualified families seeking relief. However, although JR 5 provided relief, it continued to allow counties to deny relief if the volunteer had been credited to another county or state.

244. MPL.63.364.

245. MPL.63.373.

246. AG.63.18.

247. AG.63.7–8. County information can be found at *Michigan in the War*, 42.

248. AG.63.11–13. This table contains a detail by district.

249. AG.63.15. This table was current only through December 31, 1863. It also contains a detail by district.

250. As quoted in Robert E. Mitchell, "The Organizational Performance of Michigan's Adjutant General and the Federal Provost Marshal in Recruiting Michigan's Boys in Blue," in *Michigan Historical Review* 28, no. 2 (Fall, 2002): 138.

251. AG.63.14–15.

252. AG.63.19, 439.

253. The Detroit Light Guard was organized in 1855; by 1863, approximately 305 men were on its rolls, with 56 currently serving as commissioned officers in U.S. service and 14 serving in the ranks. It had volunteered its services to Blair on April 17, 1861, and went into the three-months' iteration of the First Michigan as Company A. On March 6, 1863, it had helped quell Detroit's race riot. (See that date.) On July 18, 1863, the Light Guard had 47 officers and men, a number that grew to 79 by that December.

254. The Lyon Guard was organized on October 3, 1861, and was accepted into state service on July 28, 1863. It had 40 officers and men on its rolls. The Guard also performed patrol duty during the March 6, 1863, riot. By December 1863, it had 43 current members. To this date, the Guard had sent into U.S. service 14 members as commissioned officers and one enlisted.

255. The Scott Guard was organized in 1841 and through 1863 had counted 468 men on its rolls. It mustered into state service on September 13, 1863, and then had 41 active members; by year end, it had 47 members. The Scott Guard offered its services to Blair on April 17, 1861, was accepted, and soon formed Company A of the Second Michigan. To date, the Guard had sent 58 men into active service, 17 as commissioned officers; AG.63.444–447.

256. AG.63.500–501.

257. "The Sanitary Commission in Michigan—Letter of Professor Andrews, and Circular of the Michigan Soldiers' Aid

Society, *The Sanitary Reporter*, vol. I, no. 9 (September 15, 1863), 67.

258. "Official Report of James M. Edmonds, President, Michigan Soldiers' Relief Association at Washington, D.C., January 19, 1864," in AG.63.477.

259. *Second Annual Report of the Michigan Soldiers' Relief Association for 1863* (no place, date, or year), 2; found in Bentley Historical Library, University of Michigan.

260. "Official Report of Dr. Joseph Tunnicliffe, Jr.," in AG.63.482–492. Tunnicliffe compared his constant importuning of the War Department to one where the "woman 'married the man to be rid of him.'"

261. "Official Report of Dr. Joseph Tunnicliffe, Jr.," in AG.63.482–492.

262. "Official Report of Luther B. Willard, State Military Agent, at Nashville," in AG.63.493–497; for examples of other Willard reports, see DFP, January 30, June 26, July 3, August 20, and August 25, 1863.

263. "Official Report of Benjamin Vernor, State Military Agent at Detroit, Michigan," in AG.63.497–500, 498. Vernor provided a sample list of contents: "shirts, drawers, socks, handkerchiefs, canned and dried fruits, wines, jellies, pickles of all kinds, spices, books, papers, pins, needles, thread, sheets, quilts, pillow cases, bed sacks, pads, bandages, lint. . . ."

264. "Official Report of Samuel Day," in AG.63.479–481.

265. *Dark Lanterns*, 48; Republican newspapers: HDN, March 3, April 28, July 21, December 22, 1863; JC, April 22, 1863; CCR, April 2, 1863; LSJ, April 8, September 2, 1863. Democratic newspapers: MA, September 4, 1863; ESC, November 25, 1863; DFP, March 15, 24, 25, April 4, 15, 21, 23, 28, 1863.

266. As quoted in Gibson, *Lincoln's League*, 286–288. Gibson notes that Edmunds asserted that the League was not a secret society of the type covered by Willcox's order: it "did not discourage enlistments or threaten to disturb the peace since it was not a political or secret society in the sense intended."

267. "Treasurer's Annual Report—1863, November 30, 1863," contained in Appendix to MPL.64.

Key Events: 1864

1. OR.III.4.5–6, 3.

2. OR.III.4.103, 4–6; OR.III.5.635. On January 4, 1864 Stanton wrote Lincoln with three reasons to extend the bounty to February 1. First, the public preferred volunteering rather than conscription, and bounties encouraged volunteering. The second was economy—veteran volunteers ("who have become inured to service") were thus a "cheaper force than raw recruits or drafted men without bounty." Stanton's implication was that there was no need to pay for training a force of veteran volunteers. Finally, he cautioned that veteran reenlistments would be "checked" unless Congress reversed its December 23, 1863,

resolution. Note that the December resolution did not suspend the $100 federal bounty instituted in 1861.

3. McRae, *Negroes in Michigan during the Civil War*, 59.

4. ROS.42.255.

5. OR.III.4.9. This rule allowed volunteers to "bounty shop" before enlisting; credit was established which locality paid the bounty rather than actual residency.

6. OR.III.4.16.

7. CG, 38th Congress, first session, January 11, 1864, 145.

8. Welcher, *Union Army*, II, 120; ROS.13.3.

9. OR.III.4.26.

10. *Michigan Legislative Manual and Official Directory for the years 1899–1900*, 183.

11. SAW.5.439–440.

12. Welcher, *Union Army*, II, 120; ROS.42.237.

13. Spiro, *History of the Michigan Soldiers' Aid Society, 1861–1865*, 322.

14. JMS, January 27, 1864, 89–90. The status of this resolution was unclear. That portion of the resolution asking that the Congressional delegation lobby for Hill's removal states, "the Senate concurring"; on the other hand, the measure was sent to the Committee on Federal Relations and does not appear in the official printings of joint or concurrent resolutions. See also Robert E. Mitchell, "The Organizational Performance of Michigan's Adjutant General and the Federal Provost Marshal in Recruiting Michigan's Boys in Blue," in MHR 28, no. 2 (Fall, 2002), 139.

15. Contained in GO No. 35, February 1, 1864, OR.III.4.59.

16. OR.III.4.72–74.

17. OR.III.4.79.

18. *Michigan Legislative Manual and Official Directory for the years 1899–1900*, 183.

19. OR.III.4.87.

20. DFP, February 25, 1864; OR.III.4.891; FAC, 184–185. After several retakes, the next morning's roll call turned up 115 men missing. Willard W. Glazier, *The Capture, the Prison Pen and the Escape, being a complete History of Prison Life in the South, principally at Richmond, Danville, Macon, Savannah, Charleston, Columbia, Belle Isle, Millin, Salisbury and Andersonville* (Hartford, CT: H. E. Goodwin, Publisher, 1869), 86–87.

21. ROS.9.2.

22. OR.III.4.28.

23. MIW, 419.

24. OR.III.4.111.

25. OR.III.4.112.

26. MIW, 489; AG.64.7; ROS.16.4.

27. SAW.5.430.

28. AG.64.886. In his year-end report, Flint explains what prompted Blair to retain him: the Third Michigan Cavalry was in St. Louis, many of whose troopers were hospitalized; how-

ever, Dyer (at 1270–1271) and Robertson (636) place the Third Cavalry elsewhere at that time.

29. *Proceedings of the National Union Convention*, 175; HS, May 10, 1864.

30. RL, 444.

31. OR.III.4.128–133; for excerpts, see SAW.5.42–43.

32. OR.III.4.148.

33. OR.III.4.150.

34. Distant official ports of enlistment could obscure the question of an enlistee's actual residence, which mattered for credits against state draft quotas. To which state did a sailor belong? A commission created under the act of July 4, 1864, would address this matter. GO No. 91, March 4, 1864, OR.III.4.151–152; count derived from ROS.45.315–324.

35. OR.III.4.154; see SAW.5.43.

36. DFP, March 9, 1864; MA, March 18, 1864.

37. OR.IV.172.

38. SAW.5.43 for excerpts from this call.

39. MIW, 490.

40. DFP, March 31, 1864.

41. SAW.4.426, 443; DAT, April 9, 1864.

42. LSR, April 13, 1862.

43. CG, 38th Congress, 1st session, June 8, 1864, 1490; the debate may be found on pp. 1479–1490.

44. Smith, "Black Regiment," 39; MIW, 796.

45. The *Advertiser and Tribune* had been editorializing about Confederate treatment of black troops, see DAT, August 3, 1863; DAT, April 16, 1864; DFP, April 14, 16, 28, 1864; CG, 38th Congress, 1st session, 1673.

46. OR.III.4.237.

47. OR.III.4.240, 237–238; OR.III.4.238; AG.64.54–55.

48. Farmer, *History of Detroit*, 308.

49. Frank Klement, *The Copperheads in the Middle West* (Chicago: University of the Chicago Press, 1960), 181. John A. Marshall, *American Bastille*, 231. Identified in the OR as "P. C. Wright," he figured prominently in JAG Holt's report on various subversive groups, which may be found in OR.II.7.930–931.

50. OR.III.4.251.

51. *Collected Works of Abraham Lincoln*, vol. 7, 326.

52. ROS.15.2.

53. *Journal of the House of Representatives*, 623, 625; Wade Davis may be found in *Federal Laws of the Reconstruction: Principal Congressional Acts and Resolutions, Presidential Proclamations, Speeches and Orders, and Other Legislative and Military Documents, 1862–1875*, compiled by Frederick E. Hosen (Jefferson, NC: MacFarland & Company, 2010), 15–20.

54. OR.III.4.265.

55. PH, 410–411.

56. ROS.17.3; RL, 446.

57. OR.III.4.280.

58. AG.64.861–862.

59. FAC, 167–169.

60. AG.64.862–863.

61. RL, 448.

62. ROS.14.2.

63. OR.III.4.385–386.

64. JC, May 25, 1864; *Hillsdale Standard*, May 24, 1864; Murphy, *Proceedings, National Union Convention*, 91.

65. Jonathan Sutherland, *African-Americans at War: An Encyclopedia* (Santa Barbara, CA: ABC-CLIO, 2004), 297.

66. RL, 449.

67. OR.III.4.415–416.

68. SAW.2.339–340; NYT, June 3, 1864; CML, May 31, 1864.

69. CML, June 1, 1864; LSR, June 8, 1864; NYT, June 3, 1864.

70. DFP, June 2, 1864; LSR, June 8, 1864; JC, June 8, 1864; HS, June 14, 1864; DAT, June 1, 1864.

71. RL, 450.

72. SAW.2.343.

73. AG.64.864. The citizens of Ann Arbor apparently furnished their expenses. RL, 449.

74. *Presidential Election, 1864. Proceedings of the National Union Convention held in Baltimore, Md., June 7 and 8th, 1864, reported by D. F. Murphy* (New York: Baker & Godwin, Printers, 1864), 3, 91.

75. *Proceedings of the National Union Convention held in Baltimore, Md., June 7 and 8th, 1864, reported by D. F. Murphy* (New York: Baker & Godwin, Printers, 1864), 3, 31, 57–58, 66, 73, 76, 91.

76. As quoted, Engle, *Gathering to Save a Nation*, 418.

77. JC, June 15, 1864.

78. AG.64.14.

79. *Biographical Register*, vol. I (1868), 250.

80. RL, 450.

81. ODS, June 16, 1864; Porter, *Ohio Politics*, 194–195.

82. DFP, June 16, 1864; *Official Proceedings of Democratic National Convention*, 18–19.

83. SAL 13.126–130. See also Circular No. 60 from the War Department, dated August 1, 1864, OR.III.4.564–565.

84. RL, 451.

85. RL, 452.

86. OR.4.452. Circular No. 24 also repeats the categories of those persons whose names will be stricken: aliens, nonresidents, minors, and persons with obvious physical disabilities.

87. OR.III.4.452–453; OR.III.5.927–928.

88. Spiro, *History of the Michigan Soldiers' Aid Society, 1861–1865*, 337.

89. JMS, 726; OR.I.27.ii.11; OR.I.37.i.175.

90. OR.III.4.472–474.

91. One of the few positive features of the commutation clause was that it set a ceiling on bounties; its repeal coupled with the shrinking pool of eligible males led to unprecedented

municipal competition and soaring bounties. Now poorer communities had a double burden: inability to compete for bounties prompted their male residents to enlist in wealthier towns; thus, poorer towns lost men to meet their own quotas.

92. Scharf, *History of Maryland*, 285–286. See *SAW*.4.433–434.

93. "Report of Miss Julia Wheelock," in *Third Annual Report of the Michigan Soldiers' Relief Association for 1864*, 21. The reports of agents Brainard, Wheelock, Mahan, Gridley, and Johnson all followed Grant's army.

94. JC, July 13, 1864.

95. ROS.45.115.

96. OR.4.484–486; see *SAW*.5.46 for excerpts.

97. OR.III.4.1002–1003; 515–516, 518–519. On July 19, Fry notified all AAPMGs of state quotas "under the enrollment recently completed, without regard to any excess or deficiency the State may have on former calls." By Fry's accounting, Michigan's quota under this call was for 12,098 men; it eventually furnished 12,509.

98. OR.III.4.519.

99. AG.64.10–12.

100. OR.III.4.541.

101. OR.III.4.551; AG.64.12; the Fourth will not reorganize as a veteran volunteer unit; those volunteers reenlisting are assigned to the First Michigan. *MIW*, 231.

102. AG.64.12.

103. RL, 454.

104. OR.III.4.566; see *SAW*.5.46 for details.

105. DAT, August 12, 1864.

106. OR.III.4.598; AG.64.13.

107. OR.III.4.613–614.

108. AG.64.13.

109. *The Trials for Treason at Indianapolis*, 24, 90, 92, 114, 130, 282, 285; DFP, August 20, 1864.

110. ROS.44.106.

111. "Report of Messrs. H. G. Wells, S. W. Walker, and John Potter, Executive Committee, Michigan State Sanitary Fair," contained in AG.64.905–906.

112. AG.64.13.

113. ONR.I.3.701–704.

114. *Official Proceedings of the Democratic National Convention*, 3, 18–19.

115. See *SAW*.4 for electoral interference in Maryland and Delaware.

116. *Official Proceedings of the Democratic National Convention*, 27, 29–40.

117. OR.III.4.647, 698; Hill's letter is inferred from Fry's September 6 response.

118. *SAW*.1.123.

119. *Official Proceedings of the Democratic National Convention*, 43, 46, 55–56; Hershock, "Copperheads and Radicals," 62–63.

120. DAT, August 31, 1864; HS, September 6, 1864, reprinting undated *DAT* article. On September 1, the *DFP* prints Dow's defense.

121. RL, 455.

122. DFP, September 2, 1864; DAT, September 1, 1864.

123. DFP, September 3, 5, 1864; HS, September 6, 1864; YC, September 9, 1864.

124. Thomas Harry Williams, *Lincoln and the Radicals* (Madison: University of Wisconsin Press, 1941), 329; for important correspondence, see Winfred A. Harbison, "Zachariah Chandler's Part in the Reelection of Abraham Lincoln," *Mississippi Valley Historical Review* 22, no. 2 (September 1935), 271–276.

125. Duke, *History*, 539–540.

126. DNR, September 5, 1864.

127. OR.III.4.698.

128. *The Civil War Papers of George B. McClellan*, edited by Stephen Sears, 595–596; Porter, *Ohio Politics*, 196–197; DAT, September 8 [9?], 1864; YC, December 16, 1864.

129. DFP, September 9, 1864; MSA, September 16, 1864.

130. HS, September 13, 1864; LSR, September 21, 1864.

131. OR.III.4.710.

132. This message is inferred from Blair to Fry at OR.III.4.719.

133. OR.III.4.715.

134. OR.III.4.719.

135. OR.III.4.719.

136. OR.III.4.725–726.

137. *SAW*.5.450.

138. The most recent narrative treatment of the *Philo Parsons* hijacking and its sequel may be found in Taylor, *Old Slow Town*, 168–173; MIW, 145–154; FAC, "The Cruise of the Philo Parsons," 137–147, and in the OR. Because the raiders' object was Johnson's Island in Ohio, part of the story may be found in *SAW*.5, beginning with September 19, 1864.

139. MIW, 151; built and launched from Algonac, Michigan, in 1861, the *Parsons* was a side-wheeler and originally displaced 221 tons, measuring 135 feet long and 20 feet wide with an 8-foot draft. The *Parsons* met its end while berthed in the Chicago River during the Great Fire of 1871. FAC, 387.

140. AG.64.14. Sources conflict on whether the draft began on the 19th or the 20th.

141. *Michigan in the War*, 151; OR.II.7.842; OR.II.7.902. A report on Cole's activities will be found at OR.II.7.906.

142. MIW, 152; FAC, 144–146; Amanda Foreman, *A World on Fire*, 681–682.

143. RL, 456.

144. "Report of Messrs. H. G. Wells, S. W. Walker, and John Potter, Executive Committee, Michigan State Sanitary Fair," contained in AG.64.904.

145. NYT, September 23, 1864; Alexander, 92–93; there was no Republican majority behind Fremont's candidacy, and it

ended through Chandler's efforts and September's military victories. By Detroit Post and Tribune, *Zachariah Chandler: An Outline Sketch of His Life and Public Services* (Detroit: Post and Tribune Company, Publishers, 1880), 271–276; Adam Gurowski, *Diary: 1863–'64 –'65* (Washington, DC: W. H. & O .H. Morrison, 1866), 359.

146. DFP, September 24, 1864; "Report of Messrs. H. G. Wells, S. W. Walker, and John Potter, Executive Committee, Michigan State Sanitary Fair," contained in AG.64.908.

147. Benn Pitman, ed., *The Trials for Treason at Indianapolis disclosing the plans for establishing a North-Western Confederacy* (Cincinnati: Moore, Wilstach & Baldwin, 1865), 9, 17–19.

148. "Report of Messrs. H. G. Wells, S. W. Walker, and John Potter, Executive Committee, Michigan State Sanitary Fair," contained in AG.64.905, 909–910.

149. OR.I.42.ii.1045–1046; see SAW.5.47 for excerpts.

150. OR.III.4.747–748.

151. OR.III.4.750. In GO No. 265, issued on October 1, 1864, the War Department established "Regulations in Respect to the Distribution of Election Tickets and Proxies in the Army."

152. Lewis, *Lumberman from Flint*, 158; LSJ, October 5, 1864.

153. RL, 456; ROS.11.2.

154. Welcher, *Union Army*, II, 120.

155. OR.III.4.751–752; for excerpts of GO No. 265, see SAW.5.47–48.

156. ROS.29.1–2.

157. *Proceedings of the National Convention of Colored Men, held in the City of Syracuse, N.Y., October 4, 5, 6, and 7, 1864* (Boston: J. S. Rock and Geo. L. Ruffin, 1864), 6, 36–39; *The African American Electorate: A Statistical History*, ed. Hanes Walton, Jr., Sherman C. Puckett, and Donald R. Deskins, Jr. (Los Angeles: Sage Publications, 2012), 200–201, 36–39.

158. ORN.2.1.252; *Trials for Treason at Indianapolis*, 50.

159. OR.II.7.930–953; see 935 regarding Michigan. Holt's allegations were controversial from the moment they were made. See Frank L. Klement, who made his case against Holt's report in *Dark Lanterns: Secret Political Societies, Conspiracies and Treason Trials in the Civil War* (Baton Rouge: Louisiana State University Press, 1984), see chapter 5, "The Holt Report on Secret Societies," 136–150; see also Klement's *The Copperheads in the Middle West* (Chicago: University of Chicago Press, 1960), 202–205. Recent scholarship has revisited the issue of subversive organizations, arguing that "Copperhead" strength was real and represented a threat to Lincoln's war policies. See Jennifer L. Weber, *Copperheads: The Rise and Fall of Lincoln's Opposition in the North* (New York: Oxford University Press, 2006).

160. HS, October 18, 1864; DFP, October 20, 1864.

161. *The History of Detroit and Michigan or Metropolis Illustrated: A Chronology of the Past and Present*, 2nd ed. (Detroit: Silas Farmer & Co., 1889), 658.

162. "Army Vote," in AG.64.911–921.

163. ROS.4.2–3.

164. ROS.3.3–4.

165. AG.64.860–861.

166. RL, 457.

167. AG.64.879; DFP, October 20, 1864.

168. DFP, October 27, 1864.

169. ROS.27.2.

170. RL, 457.

171. OR.III.4.814–818. Robert P. Broadwater, *Civil War Medal of Honor Recipients: A Complete Illustrated Record* (Jefferson, NC: McFarland & Company, 2007), 297–299.

172. OR.I.43.ii.530–531.

173. OR.III.4.918. The "line" between Lake Huron and Fort Malden is effectually a land bridge divided by the St. Clair River. As summarized in Robert E. Mitchell, "The Organizational Performance of Michigan's Adjutant General and the Federal Provost Marshal in Recruiting Michigan's Boys in Blue," in *Michigan Historical Review* 28, no. 2 (Fall, 2002): 139–140.

174. OR.III.4.919.

175. KG, November 4, 1864.

176. AG.64.47.

177. DFP, November 7, 1864.

178. CQ, 283, 336.

179. John Henry Benton, *Voting in the Field: A Forgotten Chapter of the Civil War* (Boston: W. B. Clarke Co., 1915), 101. The figures used by Blodgett were taken from Greeley's *American Conflict*, vol. 2, 672. In his 1864 *Report*, AG Robertson detailed voting results by presidential elector, which gave slightly different totals: 9,402 for Lincoln's eight electors and between 2,920 and 2,985 for the eight McClellan electors. AG.64.924. State totals are taken from AG.64.925–932.

180. CQ, 509.

181. Dubin, *Congressional Elections*, 99.

182. OR.I.42.iii.728–729; OR.III.4.969; DFP, December 1, 17, 1864; ROS.45.239, 253; MA, December 16, 1864.

183. OR.III.4.998.

184. OR.III.4.989.

185. OR.III.4.996–997. Thurston was correct about explosives intended to resemble coal; see *The Civil War Naval Encyclopedia*, ed. Spencer C. Tucker (Santa Barbara, CA: ABC-CLIO, LLC, 2011), 118–119.

186. See Robin W. Winks, *The Civil War Years: Canada and the United States* (Montreal: McGill–Queen's University Press, 1998), chapter 14, "Testing Canadian Neutrality: The St. Albans Raid and Its Aftermath," 295–336; NYT, December 13, 1864.

187. OR.III.4.1020.

188. OR.III.4.1002–1003; the quotas appear as a footnote to War Department GO No. 302, issued December 21, 1864; AG.64.62.

189. Lewis quotes from this letter at OR.III.4.1041; a complete copy of this letter may be found in *Report of the Adjutant & Inspector General of the State of Vermont, from Oct. 1, 1864 to Oct. 1, 1865* (Montpelier, VT: Walton's Steam Printing Establishment, 1865), Appendix B, 6–7.

190. OR.III.4.1003; see DFP, December 23, 1864, January 4, 5, 10, 28, 1865, also endorsing rescinding Lincoln's order. The *Free Press* gave its reasons: "The practical operation of this order now to be enforced, is to seriously affect the intercourse and obstruct the business relations now existing between the people of Canada and the United States." Mayor Barker complained about the system in his January "Message to the Common Council," JCC, 1865, 226–227.

191. OR.III.4.1008–1009; this formula was changed on January 24, 1865. See OR.III.4.1073–1075.

192. OR.III.4.1015–1017.

193. OR.III.4.1143.

194. MOG, II, 483–484.

195. *Acts of the Legislature of the State of Michigan, passed at the Extra Session of 1864, with an Appendix* (Lansing: John A. Kerr & Co., Printers to the State, 1864), 1–2; hereafter, MPL.64.

196. MPL.64.140. This resolution should be seen in the context of the battle between Lincoln and the Radicals over the Wade-Davis Bill and the simmering dispute, which would soon publicly erupt over Radical efforts to deny Lincoln a second term. See SAW.5.260.

197. MPL.64.40–52.

198. MPL.64.141–142.

199. MPL.64.52.

200. MPL.64.53–59.

201. MPL.64.59–61.

202. MPL.64.65–66.

203. OR.III.4.1265.

204. OR.III.4.1266.

205. OR.III.4.1267.

206. OR.III.4.751. The variations in the flow of volunteers were produced by the threat of conscription and the demands of seasonal employment (e.g., planting and harvesting cycles), among other factors.

207. OR.III.4.813.

208. OR.III.4.936.

209. OR.III.4.937.

210. AG.64.15–17. The AG report provides details by county. Robertson acknowledged that, for a variety of reasons, AAPMG Hill had a slightly different set of figures, which are also presented in the report. These provide details by county and may be found at AG.64.17–44. A recapitulation of Hill's numbers (which agree with Robertson's in some respects) shows, for the period of September 19, 1863, through October 31, 1864: one-year quota, 20,251; three-year quota, 15,674; army enlistments, 24,729; reenlistments, 5,545; naval enlistments, 430; commuters, 1,982; total draftees, 2,499; and credits for 5,002 one-year recruits; 39 two-year; and 30,206 three-year, for a total credit of 35,247. The AG's *Report* also contains a table for "Approximate Number of Troops," which classifies Michigan's total contributions by credits from January 1 to October 31, 1864 (27,972); enlistments before January 1, 1864 (49,793); additional enlistments before January 1, 1864, but not credited in the 1863 *Report* (2,026); and the aggregate through October 31, 1864: 79,791. This aggregate and the 83,347 figure above differ because the "Approximate" tables excluded three-month recruits, residents in other states, and some 2,000 soldiers whose residency could not be determined.

211. *Annual Report of the Adjutant General of the State of Michigan, for the year 1864* (Lansing, MI: John A. Kerr & Co., Printers to the State, 1865), 6–7. In what might be an error, Robertson identifies eleven men from the Thirteenth, already identified as a successfully reenlisted unit, as reenlisted in insufficient numbers to preserve the unit.

212. AG.64.842.

213. AG.64.844–845. The editor has numbered Edmunds's reasons.

214. Michigan Soup House, a project of the Washington-based Michigan Soldiers' Relief, and managed by Brainard and Wheelock, was an all-hours relief station open to wounded men collected at Fredericksburg. A month after the Overland Campaign commenced, it was reported that "Every ambulance train was halted there" as Wheelock and Brainard ("the untiring lady agents of the association") served "soup, tea, and coffee . . . of the best quality, [which] were distributed to all wounded soldiers freely, without regard to locality or State." MA, June 10, 1864, reprint of undated *Washington Chronicle* article. See also YC June 24, 1864, with an account from Michigan educational pioneer Joseph Estabrook, then serving with the Christian Commission.

215. AG.64.843–852.

216. "Official Report of Benj. Vernor, State Military Agent, at Detroit, November 25, 1864," in AG.64.893–894.

217. "Official Report of Miss Valeria Campbell, Corresponding Secretary Michigan Soldiers' Aid Society," in AG.64.894–900. For a list of articles furnished, see AG.64.899–900.

218. Frank B. Woodford and Philip Parker Mason, *Harper of Detroit: The Origin and Growth of a Great Metropolitan Hospital* (Detroit: Wayne State University Press, 1964), 108; AG.64.901.

219. AG.64.865–883.

220. AG.64.884–886.

221. "Official Report of Weston Flint, State Military Agent, at St. Louis, Mo., December 1, 1864," in AG.64.886–892.

222. "Statement," in AG.64, Appendix.

223. MOG, II, 499–500.

224. MOG, II, 496–498.

Key Events: 1865

1. OR.III.4.1035, 1040–1042.

2. "Michigan Legislative Manual and Official Directory for the years 1899–1900," 183.

3. *Under the Oaks*, 123.

4. ROS.30.1–2; Dyer, *Compendium*, 1293.

5. OR.III.4.10-40-1042.

6. CDE, January 12, 1865; G. R. Tredway, *Democratic Opposition to the Lincoln Administration in Indiana* (Indianapolis: Indiana Historical Bureau, 1973), 247–248.

7. Clarification in letter to Minnesota governor Stephen Miller, OR.III.41045–1048; the OR does not disclose if the clarification was circulated to all governors.

8. *Journal of the Michigan House of Representatives*, 158–165; 221; interestingly, the black leaders refused the House's invitation to be seated: "the gentlemen giving as a reason that they were highly respectable, Christian gentlemen, and they feared that the evil communications of this body might seriously impair their usefulness."

9. OR.III.4.1073–1075. This letter, which was sent to AAPMGs in all states still subject to the draft (without Iowa, Connecticut, Minnesota, Tennessee, Oregon, and California), contained detailed instructions for calculating quotas now that one-, two-, and three-year enlistments were being made. These instructions are omitted here but should be read by close students of the process through which quotas were calculated. DAT, January 31, February 1, 1865.

10. DFP, January 26, 27, 1865; while the *Free Press* accurately summarized the convention's official output, its characterizations of the delegates and other proceedings were crude and viciously racist even by its low standards; the next day, the convention expelled the *Free Press* reporter.

11. *Twitchell vs. Blodgett*, 13 Michigan, 127. Twitchell, a Washtenaw candidate for prosecuting attorney, was elected by counting the soldiers' vote; without the soldiers' vote, his competitor Blodgett would have won. The county rejected the soldiers' vote, arguing that it was unconstitutional. Three judges issued three separate opinions: two concurred in its unconstitutionality and one dissented. Josiah Henry Benton, *Voting in the Field: A Forgotten Chapter in the Civil War* (Boston: Privately Printed, 1915), 101. Benton traces the legislative history of No. 21.

12. DAT, February 2, 1865; HS, February 7, 1865; YC, February 3, 1865.

13. GHN, February 8, 1865; DFP, February 3, 1865.

14. MOG, II, 549–550.

15. OR.III.4.1092–1096.

16. MOG, II, 550; DAT, February 4, 1865; DFP, February 4, 1865; see LSJ, February 8, 1865 for extensive coverage of the proceedings.

17. OR.III.4.1143.

18. OR.III.4.1138; 1177–1178. This letter should be consulted for a statement of the formula by which years of service was applied to districts. The board's quota per district is almost identical to Fry's February 4 detail to Robertson. (See that date.) The district breakdowns were as follows:

	Total Enrollment	By Years of Service	Quota to Be Furnished
First	11,392	3,816	1,050
Second	12,308	2,388	1,714
Third	13,083	1,500	2,168
Fourth	11,436	1,742	1,751
Fifth	12,921	505	2,467

19. OR.III.4.1134. For Delafield, see SAW.2.347.

20. OR.III.4.1142–1143.

21. JMH, 619.

22. OR.III.4.1171–1172. Fry also included an explanation about the circumstances of the December 19 1864 call: it sought to raise men, not credits, because only men can shoulder a rifle. (Applying a surplus from previous calls would only reduce the number of men; some surpluses were permitted, but in limited circumstances.) This new rule altered the system by which states had been meeting quotas since mid-1863, and by early 1865 Fry was in a political maelstrom. He later blamed "the people" for not comprehending what the law required.

23. SAW.6.568.

24. OR.I.47.ii.526; Stanton was already blame shifting for the fire.

25. *Annual Report of the Adjutant-General of the State of Connecticut for the year ending March 31, 1866* (Hartford: A. N. Clark & Co., State Printers, 1866), 233.

26. May, *A Wartime Chronicle*, 72. By voting to seat the "winners" the Senate ignores *Twitchell v. Blodgett* and by implication, the Michigan Supreme Court.

27. May, *A Wartime Chronicle*, 72. Michigan's House joins the Senate.

28. OR.III.4.1204–1205.

29. GHN, March 8, 1865; DFP, March 6, 1865; DAT, reprinted, HDN, March 7, 1865; YC, March 10, 1865.

30. ROS.44.106.

31. LSJ, March 15, 1865; DFP, March 9, 1865.

32. DFP, March 11, 1865.

33. ROS.11.107.

34. RL, 460.

35. *Michigan Legislative Manual and Official Directory for the years 1899–1900*, 183.

36. MIW, 125.

37. AAC.65.568.

38. DFP, April 4, 9, 10, 1865; SJT, April 8, 1865; Hillsdale, April 4, 11, 1865; GHN, April 5, 1865; ESC, April 5, 1865.

39. ESC, April 12, 1865.

40. DFP, April, 11, 1865; YC, April 14, 1865; JC, April 11, 1865; MA, April 14, 1865.

41. OR.III.4.1263.

42. DFP, April 15, 16, 17, 1865; ESC, April 19, 1865; GHN, April 19, 1865. MA, April 21, 1865; Republican newspapers also issued black-lined editions eulogizing Lincoln. JCP, April 17, 1865; HDN, April 18, 1865; LSR, April 19, 1865; YC, April 22, 1865; SJT, April 22, 1865.

43. DFP, April 16, 1865; Farmer, History of Detroit and Michigan, 309–310.

44. Farmer, History of Detroit and Michigan, 310.

45. Michigan in the War, 5.

46. OR.III.4.1275; Farmer, History of Detroit and Michigan, 968. See Bak, A Distant Thunder, 198, for a photograph of the memorial service.

47. Heidler and Heidler, Encyclopedia of the American Civil War, 1901–1902; Chester D. Barry, Loss of the Sultana and Reminiscences of Survivors: History of a Disaster, where over One Thousand Five Hundred were Lost, most of them being exchanged prisoners of war on their way home after privation and suffering from one to twenty-three months in Cahaba and Andersonville Prisons (Lansing, MI: Darius D. Thorp, 1892), 7, 393–397, 418. A hand count of Berry's lists provided in this source produced the numbers given above; however, it is believed that Michigan casualties were far higher. George S. May stated that "many" of the Michiganders counted by the editor "were killed or drowned." May, A Wartime Chronicle, 78; ROS.18.4; ROS.21.3.

48. OR.III.4.1280–1281. Exceptions for patients were veteran volunteers, veterans of the First Army Corps, and members of the Veteran Reserve Corps. William T. Coggeshall, The Journeys of Abraham Lincoln; from Springfield to Washington, 1861, as president-elect; and Washington to Springfield, 1865, as president martyred (Columbus, OH: Ohio State Journal, 1865), 227.

49. OR.III.4.1282.

50. OR.III.4.1281.

51. OR.III.5.5.

52. OR.III.5.11–12.

53. ROS.45.208.

54. OR.III.5.18.

55. Michigan troopers' role is recounted in FAC, 229–243. After Davis was taken into custody, one Michigander summarily "appropriated" Davis's horse for his own use; an aide objected. "How dare you insult the President in this manner?" The trooper replied, "President, hell. What's he president of?" As quoted in FAC, 242.

56. A Source-Book of Military Law and War-Time Legislation, prepared by the War Department Committee on Education and Special Training (St. Paul, MN: West Publishing Company, 1919), 123.

57. OR.III.5.25. The troops were mustered out in the order of the call under which they enlisted. First were troops recruited under the call of July 2, 1862, and who enlisted prior to October 1, 1862; next were three-year recruits for old regiments enlisted during these dates; last were one-year men for new or old units who enlisted before October 1, 1864.

58. JCP, May 30, 1865.

59. ROS.20.8.

60. OR.III.4.1275, 1281.

61. DFP, June 5, 1865; FAC, 206.

62. DFP, June 4, 1865; MIW, 410; ROS.26.3.

63. DFP, June 6, 1865; MIW, 85–86.

64. JCP, June 7, 1865; MIW, 86.

65. ROS.17.3.

66. ROS.21.2.

67. ROS.19.2.

68. OR.III.5.54; MIW, 73–74.

69. ROS.42.28; MIW, 747.

70. ROS.24.3.

71. MIW, 447, 109–110.

72. Dyer, 161; ROS.35.5; OR.III.5.105–106.

73. ROS.42.46.

74. ROS.25.3.

75. ROS.22.15–16.

76. ROS.45.127; William H. Beach, The First New York (Lincoln) Cavalry, From April 19, 1861 to July 7, 1865 (New York: The Lincoln Cavalry Association, 1902), 536.

77. ROS.23.3; ROS.41.3.

78. ROS.30.2.

79. ROS.35.4; ROS.42.111; MIW, 532; ROS.237.

80. ROS.18.2.

81. ROS.7.2–3; ROS.44.106; MIW, 747.

82. As quoted in Richard Bak, A Distant Thunder, 200; ROS.44.165.

83. ROS.5.3; ROS.16.4.

84. ROS.1.3.

85. ROS.42.176.

86. ROS.14.3.

87. ROS.9.2.

88. ROS.39.4.

89. ROS.42.152; ROS.42.190.

90. ROS.13.3.

91. ROS.27.3.

92. ROS.2.16; MIW, 748; ROS.45.1–3.

93. ROS.42.88.

94. Proceedings of the Colored Men's Convention of the State of Michigan, Held in the City of Detroit, Tuesday and Wednesday, Sept. 12th and 13th, '65 (Adrian, MI: Adrian Times Office, 1865), 5, 6–11.

95. ROS.42.220.

96. ROS.8.2–3; ROS.42.65.

97. ROS.42.129.

98. MIW, 111–112; Farmer, History of Detroit and Wayne County, 312; ROS.5.139.

99. DFP, August 11, 13, 1865; Grant probably had mixed memories of his Detroit posting: he proved popular with his men but had difficulty coping with his wife Julia's absence (she removed to St. Louis to give birth to their son); his drinking problem revived but was soon controlled thanks to counseling from his Detroit pastor, Dr. George Taylor. He slipped on the ice in front of Zachariah Chandler's house, sued, and won, but during the trial, Chandler suggested that Grant might have slipped from drunkenness, and perhaps persuaded, the jury awarded him six cents. Ron Chernow, Grant, 65–69.

100. ROS.32.3.

101. Dyer, Compendium, 161; ROS.20.1–3.

102. ROS.42.205.

103. ROS.15.2.

104. ROS.29.2.

105. Proceedings of the Colored Men's Convention (Adrian, MI: Adrian Times Office, 1865), 6–8, 13.

106. ROS.9.3.

107. Dyer, 1286; ROS.11.107.

108. ROS.45.2.

109. ROS.38.4.

110. ROS.45.95.

111. ROS.46.4.

112. MIW, 491–492; McRae, 75–76.

113. First Annual Meeting of the National Equal Rights League, held in Cleveland, Ohio, October 19, 20th and 21st, 1865 (Philadelphia, E. C. Markley & Son, 1865), 9, 29, 20.

114. May, A Wartime Chronicle, 90.

115. MIW, 747; ROS.40.18; ROS.41.4.

116. Dyer, Compendium, 161, 1273–1274; ROS.36.12.

117. The History of Detroit and Michigan or Metropolis Illustrated: A Chronology of the Past and Present, 2nd ed. (Silas Farmer & Co., 1889), 658–659. The next month, Harper will open to the general public.

118. Dyer, Compendium, 161.

119. MOG, II, 508.

120. Governors Inaugural Message to the Legislature of the State of Michigan, in Session, January 4, 1865 (Lansing, MI: John A. Kerr & Co., Printers to the State, 1865), 33–34.

121. Found in 38th Congress, 2d Session, House of Representatives, Misc. Documents No. 26, The Miscellaneous Documents of the House of Representatives, printed during the Second Session of the Thirty-Eighth Congress, 1864-'65, in Three Volumes (Washington, DC: Government Printing Office, 1865), vol. I.

122. MPL.65.777–778.

123. MPL.65.779.

124. The phrase "Military sub-district" appears in Michigan legislation for the first time, and seems to refer to the sub-districts within congressional districts that were drawn by the AAPMG or the district PMs.

125. This was an effort to ensure that the volunteers were actually credited to the towns or wards in which they were enrolled and that paid the bounty. By requiring documentation (that functioned as verification of identity and address), the intent was to avoid fraud and also reduce cases where a volunteer might attempt to collect a state and municipal bounty in excess of the newly authorized limit of $100. See Section 3.

126. Acts of the Legislature of the State of Michigan, passed at the Regular Session of 1865, with an Appendix (Lansing: John A. Kerr & Co., Printers to the State, 1865), 29–34; hereafter, MPL.65.

127. MPL.65.139–140.

128. MPL.65.140–145.

129. MPL.65.179–180. This law did not appear to preclude judges from offering certain offenders a choice between incarceration or military service.

130. MPL.65.188.

131. MPL.65.269. Similar acts during this session include No. 161 (Oakland County and Pontiac wards), March 14; No. 163 (Shiawassee, Genesee, and Tuscola Counties), March 14, 1865; No. 173 (Marcellus, in Cass County), March 14, 1865; No. 201 (several townships of Kalamazoo County), March 16, 1865; No. 217 (several townships, cities and wards in the county of Jackson), March 18, 1865; No. 219 (townships and cities of the county of Washtenaw), March 18, 1865; No. 231 (township of Clinton, Macomb County), March 18, 1865; No. 271 (certain townships in Clinton County), March 20, 1865; No. 329 (Nankin in Wayne County, and Delta in Eaton County), March 21, 1865; No. 358 (certain towns in Cass County), March 21, 1865.

132. MPL.65.350.

133. MPL.65.467–468.

134. MPL.65.641–643.

135. MPL.65.810–811.

136. MPL.65.817–818.

137. MPL.65.818–819.

Selected Summaries

1. OR.III.4.1269–1270; Robertson's Michigan in the War count varies from the War Department's. Robertson claims 90,119 total men, which Fry later modified to 90,048; when reduced to a three-year standard, the figure was 80,865. MIW, 72; OR.III.5.729; As summarized in Robert E. Mitchell, "The Organizational Performance of Michigan's Adjutant General and the Federal Provost Marshal in Recruiting Michigan's Boys in Blue," Michigan Historical Review 28, no. 2 (Fall, 2002): 152.

2. Richard F. Selcer, Civil War America: 1850 to 1875, Alma-

nacs of American Life series (New York: Infobase Publishing, 2006), 231.

3. OR.III.4.1264–1267; Dyer, *Compendium*, 1269–1293.

4. *MIW*, 65–68.

5. Dyer, *Compendium*.

6. *MIW*, 69–70.

7. Dyer, *Compendium*, 12; RL, 3.

8. Gould, *Investigations*, 49, 53, 210, 53. Based on Gould's study, the mean ages of enlistment were very close: for Ohio, it was 25.4936; Indiana, 24.7100; Illinois, 25.9369; and for Wisconsin and Iowa, 26.1571. For total enlisted men (1,012,273) surveyed, the mean age at enlistment was 25.8362.

9. Gould, *Investigations*, 570.

10. *MIW*, 993; Dyer, *Compendium*, 11; ROS.46.iv; LSR, August 24, 1864; DAT, August 22, 1865; *Oxford Companion to American Military History*, ed. John Whiteclay Chambers, II (New York: Oxford University Press, 1999), 8.

11. Thirty-three listings specified no vessels; most of these men had enlisted in February or March, 1865. Ship battle itineraries were found in the *Dictionary of American Naval Fighting Ships*, ed. James L. Mooney (Washington, DC: Naval Historical Center, Department of the Navy).

12. ROS.46; Phisterer, *Statistical Record*, 8–9; Smith, "Black Regiment," 38.

13. HS, August 2, 1864; LSR, August 10, 1864; DFP, August 9, 10, 11, 20, 1864.

14. ROS.46.115; all recruits enlisted in Vicksburg, Mississippi, August, 1864.

15. ROS.46.116; all recruits enlisted in Vicksburg, Mississippi, August, 1864.

16. ROS.46.116–117; all recruits enlisted in (almost certainly) Decatur, Tennessee; see Dyer, *Compendium*, 1722.

17. ROS.46.117–118; all recruits enlisted or drafted in Michigan, March-April, 1865.

18. ROS.46.118; substitute, enlisted July, 1864.

19. ROS.46.118–119; five enlistees were substitute and one was drafted; mustered in March, 1865.

20. ROS.46.119.

21. ROS.46.119–120.

22. ROS.46.120; little is known about this unit; Dyer's *Compendium* has no listing.

23. The editor wishes to acknowledge his debt to Lawrence Hauptman's *Between Two Fires* and in particular, chapter 7, "Sharpshooters in the Army of the Potomac: the Ottawa," 125–144, on which this section is largely based. Dyer, *Compendium*, 1280–1281.

24. Hauptman, *Between Two Fires*, 130; as quoted, 143.

25. Hauptman, *Between Two Fires*, 131–133; L. M. Hartwick and W. H. Tuller, *Oceana Pioneers and Business Men of To-Day: History, Biography, Statistics and Humorous Incidents* (Pentwater, MI: Pentwater News Steam Print, 1890), 45–46.

26. "State Treasurer's Annual Report—1864," in Appendix to MPL.65.

27. As summarized in Robert E. Mitchell, "The Organizational Performance of Michigan's Adjutant General and the Federal Provost Marshal in Recruiting Michigan's Boys in Blue," *Michigan Historical Review* 28, no. 2 (Fall, 2002): 128.

28. OR.III.5.746–747; *MIW*, states gives the county bounty figure at $8,157,748.70.

29. *Sacred Debts*, 185; *MIW*, 120–121.

30. *MIW*, 105–106. The plural "Homes" is used by Robertson to include the national system as well as Harper.

31. FAC, 211–212; "Harper Hospital" [illustration] in *History of Detroit and Michigan*, 658.

32. *History of Detroit and Michigan*, 653, 923–924.

33. *The U.S. Sanitary Commission in the Valley of the Mississippi*, 242–243; a contemporary put the relationships between Duffield and her New York connections this way: it "did not result from old acquaintance, but led to its renewal, and also to the discovery that this Sanitary Commission work had brought together the children of old associates in charitable enterprises." The elder Duffield's mother had helped found New York's first orphan asylum with the mothers of both Mrs. Schuyler and Mrs. Blatchford.

34. *The U.S. Sanitary Commission in the Valley of the Mississippi*, 244–245; Spiro, *History of the Michigan Soldiers' Aid Society, 1861–1865*, 83.

35. Spiro, *History of the Michigan Soldiers' Aid Society, 1861–1865*, 38–39, 84; for antiscorbutic campaigns, see 105–106, 213, 224–248; 345, 360–384; for hospital supplies, see 107–108.

36. Spiro, *History of the Michigan Soldiers' Aid Society*, 339.

37. Christian Commission report for 1864, contained in *MIW*, 128–130.

38. Christian Commission report for 1864, contained in *MIW*, 128–130.

39. Spiro, *History of the Michigan Soldiers' Aid Society, 1861–1865*, 31–33.

40. FAC, 206. Annual national Christian Commission reports also contain some information about Michigan units in the field. See *United States Christian Commission, for the Army and Navy. First Annual Report* (Philadelphia, np, February 1863), 17–18, 21, 38–39; *United States Christian Commission, for the Army and Navy, For the Year 1863. Second Annual Report* (Philadelphia, np, April, 1864), 74, 89, 119–120, 224–225, 253; also see vii for list of Michigan members; *United States Christian Commission, for the Army and Navy. For the Year 1864. Third Annual Report* (Philadelphia, np, April 1865), 286, 293; *United States Christian Commission, for the Army and Navy. For the Year 1865, Fourth Annual Report* (Philadelphia, np, March 1866), ix, 153–154, 183–184.

41. Several letters of Mrs. Laura Plumb can be found in the Bentley Historical Library at the University of Michigan.

42. "Report of the Executive Committee," contained in the *Third Annual Report of the Michigan Soldiers' Relief Association* for 1864, 2–6.

43. "Treasurer's Report," contained in the *Third Annual Report of the Michigan Soldiers' Relief Association* for 1864, 11.

44. *MIW*, 126; DAT, January 4, 1863.

45. DFP, January 26, 1865.

Bibliography

Articles

Baldwin, Augustus C., "Oakland County—Its Bench and Bar Prior to 1840," in *Collections and Researches made by the Michigan Pioneer and Historical Society*, vol. XXXI (Lansing, MI: Wynkoop Hallenbeck Crawford Co., 1902).

Boles, Frank, "Michigan Newspapers: A Two-Hundred Year Review," *Michigan Historical Review* 36, no. 1 (Spring 2010): 36, 37, 39–41, 45–46.

"Captain Eber B. Ward's Fortress: An Untold Chapter of Civil War Times in Detroit," *Detroit Monthly* 1, no. 3 (May, 1901): 20–21.

Cavaioli, Frank, "Randolph Rogers and the Columbus Doors," *Italian Americana*, 17, no. 1 (Winter 1999).

Coogan, Blanch, "The Underground Railroad in Michigan," *Negro History Bulletin* 27, no. 5, Special Detroit Edition (February 1964).

Fennimore, Jean Jay, "Austin Blair: Pioneer Lawyer, 1818–1844," MHM 48 (March 1964): 1–17.

Fennimore, Jean Jay, "Austin Blair: Political Idealist, 1845–1860," MHM 48 (June 1964): 130–166.

Fennimore, Jean Jay, "Austin Blair: Civil War Governor, 1861–1862," MHM 49 (September 1965): 193–227.

Fennimore, Jean Jay, "Austin Blair: Civil War Governor, 1863–1864," MHM 49 (December 1965): 344–369.

Fesler, Mayo, "Secret Political Societies in the North during the Civil War," *Indiana Magazine of History* XIV, no. 3 (September 1918): 224–241.

Freund, Lawrence S., "Prisoners of State," *New York History Review* 11, no. 1 (New York History Review Press, 2017): 89–93.

Freund, Lawrence S., "The Wright Brothers of Rome," *New York History Review*, January 7, 2018 (online).

Gridley, Charles V., "Mrs. Ann Eliza Gridley," *Historical Collections and Researches made by the Michigan Pioneer and Historical Society*, Vol. XXXVII (Lansing: Wynkoop, Hallenbeck, Crawford Co., 1909–1910), 693–695.

Harbison, Winfred A., "Zachariah Chandler's Part in the Reelection of Abraham Lincoln," *Mississippi Valley Historical Review* 22, no. 2 (September 1935): 271–276.

Hershock, Martin H., "Copperheads and Radicals: Michigan Partisan Politics during the Civil War Era, 1860–1865," MHR 18, no. 1 (Spring 1992): 30–31.

Jerome, Lucy B., "Some Grand Old Women," *The World To-Day* (July 1911), 885–889.

Katzman, David M., "Black Slavery in Michigan," *Midcontinent American Studies Journal* 11, no. 12 (Fall 1970): 60, 61, 65.

Klement, Frank, "Franklin Pierce and the Treason Charges of 1861–1862," *The Historian* 23, no. 4 (August 1961): 439–440.

Klement, Frank, "The Hopkins Hoax and Golden Circle Rumors in Michigan, 1861–1862," *Michigan History* 47, no. 1 (March 1963).

"Lives of the Founders and Builders of Hillsdale College," *The Advance: A Magazine of Academic History and Current College Event* [Hillsdale College] 2, no. 19.

Magazine of Western History, ed. William W. Williams (Cleveland, np, 1886) 4 (May 1886–October 1886).

May, George S., "Ann Arbor and the Coming of the Civil War," *Michigan History* 36 (September 1862).

McDaid, William, "Kinsely S. Bingham and the Republican Ideology of Antislavery, 1847–1855," *Michigan Historical Review* 16, no. 2 (Fall 1990).

Mitchell, Robert E., "The Organizational Performance of Michigan's Adjutant General and the Federal Provost Marshal in Recruiting Michigan's Boys in Blue," in MHR 28, no. 2 (Fall 2002): 139.

"News from the Alumni and Former Students," *Meadville Theological School Quarterly Bulletin*, Volume II (October 1907), no. 1, 21.

Pritchett, John Perry, "Michigan Democracy in the Civil War," in *Michigan History Magazine* XI (1927): 92–109.

Shafter, Joseph, "The Yankee and the Teuton in Wisconsin, V: Social Harmonies and Discords," *Wisconsin Magazine of History* VII, no. 2 (December 1923).

Smith, Michael O., "Raising a Black Regiment in Michigan: Adversity and Triumph," *Michigan Historical Review* 16, no. 2 (Fall 1990): 25–26.

Stocking, William, "Prominent Newspaper Men in Michigan," in *Michigan Historical Collections*, vol. XXXIX, 1915 (Lansing: Michigan Historical Commission, 1915).

"Tennessee Prisoners at Fort Mackinac," *Wisconsin Magazine of History* 4, no. 2 (December 1920): 220–221.

[Trescott, William Henry], "Narrative and Letter of William Henry Trescot concerning the negotiations between South Carolina and President Buchanan in December, 1860," contributed by Gaillard Hunt, reprint from the *American Historical Review* XIII, no. 3 (April 1908).

Voegeli Jacque, "The Northwest and the Race Issue, 1861–1862," *Mississippi Valley Historical Review* 50, no. 2 (September 1963).

Welles, Gideon, "History of Emancipation," *Galaxy* 14 (December 1872), 843.

Wells, H. G., "Law and the Legal Profession," *Report of the Pioneer Society of the State of Michigan*, vol. III (Lansing: Robert Smith Printing, 1903), 137.

Primary Sources and Official Documents

Abraham Lincoln Papers at the Library of Congress.

Abraham Lincoln Political Writings and Speeches, ed. Terence Ball (New York: Cambridge University Press, 2013).

Acts of the Legislature of the State of Michigan, passed at the annual session of 1849 (Lansing: Munger and Pattison, 1849).

Acts of the Legislature of the State of Michigan, passed at the annual session of 1850 (Lansing: R. W. Ingalls, 1850).

Acts of the Legislature of the State of Michigan, passed at the regular session of 1855 (Lansing: Geo. W. Peck, 1855).

Acts of the Legislature of the State of Michigan passed at the regular session of 1859, with an Appendix (Lansing: Homer & Kerr, Printers to the State, 1859).

Acts of the Legislature of the State of Michigan, passed at the Regular and Extra Sessions of 1861, with an Appendix (Lansing: John A. Kerr & Co., Printers to the State, 1861).

Acts of the Legislature of the State of Michigan, passed at the Extra Session of 1862, with an Appendix (Lansing: John A. Kerr & Co., Printers to the State, 1863).

Acts of the Legislature of the State of Michigan, passed at the Regular Session of 1863, with an Appendix (Lansing: John A. Kerr & Co., Printers to the State, 1863).

Acts of the Legislature of the State of Michigan, passed at the Extra Session of 1864, with an Appendix (Lansing: John A. Kerr & Co., Printers to the State, 1864).

Acts of the Legislature of the State of Michigan, passed at the Regular Session of 1865, with an Appendix (Lansing: John A. Kerr & Co., Printers to the State, 1865).

Acts of the Legislature of the State of Michigan, passed at the Regular Session of 1869, vol. I (Lansing: W. S. George & Co., 1869).

The American Annual Cyclopaedia and Register of Important Events of the year 1861, vol. I, cited hereafter as *Annual Register, 1861* (New York: D. Appleton & Company, 1864).

The American Annual Cyclopaedia and Register of Important Events of the year 1862 (New York: D. Appleton & Company, 1868), vol. II, cited hereafter as *Annual Register, 1862*.

The American Annual Cyclopaedia and Register of Important Events of the year 1863 (New York: D. Appleton & Company, 1869), vol. III, cited hereafter as *Annual Register, 1863*.

The American Annual Cyclopaedia and Register of Important Events of the year 1864 (New York: D. Appleton & Company, 1870), vol. IV, cited hereafter as *Annual Register, 1864*.

The American Annual Cyclopaedia and Register of Important Events of the year 1865 (New York: D. Appleton & Company, 1869), vol. V, cited hereafter as *Annual Register, 1865*.

Annual Report of the Adjutant-General of the State of Connecticut for the year ending March 31, 1866 (Hartford: A. N. Clark & Co., State Printers, 1866), 233.

Annual Report of the Adjutant General of the State of Michigan, For the Year 1861 (Lansing: John A. Kerry & Co., Printers to the State, 1861).

Annual Report of the Adjutant General of the State of Michigan, For the Year 1862 (Lansing: John A. Kerry & Co., Printers to the State, 1862).

Annual Report of the Adjutant General of the State of Michigan, For the Year 1863 (Lansing: John A. Kerry & Co., Printers to the State, 1864).

— "Official Report of James M. Edmonds, President, Michigan Soldiers' Relief Association at Washington, D.C., January 19, 1864."

— "Report of Chaplain Samuel Day."

— "Official Report of Luther B. Willard, State Military Agent, at Nashville."

— "Official Report of Dr. Joseph Tunnicliffe, Jr."

— "Official Report of Benjamin Vernor, State Military Agent at Detroit, Michigan."

— "Official Report of Miss Valeria Campbell, Corresponding Secretary Michigan Soldiers' Aid Society."

Annual Report of the Adjutant General of the State of Michigan, For the Year 1864 (Lansing: John A. Kerry & Co., Printers to the State, 1865).

— "Official Report of Dr. J.B. Gilman, State Military Agent, at Louisville, Ky."

— "Report of Messrs. H. G. Wells, S. W. Walker, and John Potter, Executive Committee, Michigan State Sanitary Fair."

— "Official Report of Benj. Vernor, State Military Agent, at Detroit."

— "Official Report of Weston Flint, State Military Agent, at St. Louis, Mo."

Annual Report of the Adjutant General of the State of Michigan, For the Years 1865–6 (Lansing: John A. Kerry & Co., Printers to the State, 1866), 3 vols.

Annual Report of the Chief of Engineers to the Secretary of War for the Year 1874, In Two Parts, Part I (Washington, DC: Government Printing Office, 1874).

Annual Report of the Quartermaster General of the State of Michigan for the Year 1862 (Lansing: John A. Kerr & Co., Printers to the State, 1862).

Annual Report of the State Treasurer of the State of Michigan, for the Year 1861 (Lansing: John A. Kerr, Printers to the State, 1861).

Anonymous, *A Thrilling Narrative from the Lips of the Sufferers of the Late Detroit Riot, March 6, 1863, with the Hair Breadth Escapes* of Men, Women and Children, and Destruction of Colored Men's Property, Not Less than $15,000 (Detroit: Published by the Author, 1863).

The Army Surgeon's Manual, for the use of Medical Officers, Cadets, Chaplains, containing the Regulations of the Medical Department, all General Orders from the War Department, and Circulars from the Surgeon-General's Office, from January 1st, 1861 to July 1st, 1864 (New York: Bailliere Brothers, 1864).

Bartlett, John Russell, The Soldiers' National Cemetery at Gettysburg, with the Proceedings at its Consecration; at the Laying of the Corner-Stone of the Monument, and its Dedication (Providence, RI: Printed by the Providence Press Company for the Board of Commissioners of the Soldiers' National Cemetery, 1874).

Blair, Austin, Governor's Message to the Legislature [Extra Session], January 2, 1862 [Lansing: 1862].

—Governor's Message to the Legislature of the State of Michigan, in Session, January 7, 1863 (Lansing: John A. Kerr & Co., Printer to the State, 1863).

—Governors Inaugural Message to the Legislature of the State of Michigan, in Session, January 4, 1865 (Lansing: John A. Kerr & Co., Printers to the State, 1865).

Blois, John T., Gazetteer of the State of Michigan in three parts, containing a General View of the State, and etc. (Detroit: Sydney L. Rood & Co., 1839).

Boyd's [1860] Washington and Georgetown Directory, containing a Business Directory of Washington, Georgetown, and Alexandria, Congressional and Department Directory, and an Appendix of much useful information (Washington, DC: Taylor and Maury, 1860).

Charles F. Clark's Annual Directory of the Inhabitants, Incorporated Companies, Business Firms, etc., of the City of Detroit for 1864–'5, compiled by Charles F. Clark (Detroit: Published by Charles F. Clark, 1864).

Charles F. Clark's Annual Directory of the Inhabitants, Incorporated Companies, Business Firms, etc., of the City of Detroit for 1866–'7, compiled by Charles F. Clark (Detroit: Published by Charles F. Clark, 1866).

The Civil War Papers of George B. McClellan: Selected Correspondence, ed. Stephen Sears (New York: Da Capo Press, 1992).

Collected Works of Abraham Lincoln, ed. Roy P. Basler (Springfield, IL: Abraham Lincoln Association, 1953–55), 9 vols.

A Compilation of the Messages and Papers of the Presidents, ed. James D. Richardson (Washington, DC: Government Printing Office, 1899–1911), 10 vols.

The Compiled Laws of the State of Michigan, compiled and arranged under an Act of the Legislature, approved January 25, 1871, James S. Dewey, compiler, vol. II (Lansing: W. S. George, 1872).

Complete Works of Abraham Lincoln, ed. John G. Nicolay and John Hay (New York: No place, Lincoln Memorial University, 1894), 12 vols.

Concord Massachusetts: Births, Marriages, and Deaths, 1635–1850 (Boston: Printed by the Town, Thomas Todd, Printer).

The Congressional Globe.

Congressional Quarterly Guide to U.S. Elections, 2nd ed. (Washington: Congressional Quarterly, 1985).

Constitution of the State of Michigan, 1835 as adopted in convention begun and held at the capitol, in the City of Detroit, on Monday, the 11th day of May, A.D. 1835 (Detroit: Printed by Sheldon M'Knight, 1835).

Constitution of the State of Michigan [1850] (Lansing, 1850).

A Daily Journal for the use of Attorneys, Bankers and Business Men of Michigan, 1867 (Detroit: Wm. A. Throop & Co., nd).

Decision of Judge Leavitt, of Ohio, in the Vallandigham Habeas Corpus Case (Philadelphia: Printed for Gratuitous Distribution, 1863).

Detroit City Directory for 1879, compiled and published by J. W. Weeks & Co. (Detroit: J. W. Weeks & Co., 1879).

Documents Accompanying the Journal of the House of Representatives of the State of Michigan, at the Biennial Session of 1861 (Lansing: John A. Kerr & Co., 1861).

Documents Accompanying the Journal of the House of Representatives of the State of Michigan, at the Biennial Session of 1863 (Lansing: John A. Kerr & Co., 1863).

Documents Accompanying the Journal of the House of Representatives of the State of Michigan, at the Biennial Session of 1865 (Lansing: John A. Kerr & Co., 1865).

Dubin, Michael J., Party Affiliations in the State Legislatures: A Year-by-Year Summary, 1796–2006 (Jefferson, NC: McFarland & Company, 2007).

Dubin, Michael J. United States Congressional Elections, 1788–1997: The Official Results of the Elections of the 1st through 105th Congresses (Jefferson, NC: McFarland & Company, 1998), cited as Dubin, Congressional Elections.

Dubin, Michael J., United States Gubernatorial Elections, 1776–1860: The Official Results by State and County (Jefferson, NC: McFarland & Company, 2003), cited as Dubin, Gubernatorial Elections.

Dubin, Michael J., Stanley Parsons, William W. Beach, United States Congressional Districts and Data, 1843–1883 (New York: Greenwood Press, 1986).

Dyer, Frederick H., A Compendium of the War of the Rebellion (Dayton, OH: Press of Morningside Bookshop, 1978, reprint, 1908).

The 1863–1864 Diary of Captain James Penfield, 5th New York Volunteer Cavalry, Company H, ed. James Allen Penfield (Penfield Foundation, 1999).

Federal Laws of the Reconstruction: Principal Congressional Acts and Resolutions, Presidential Proclamations, Speeches and Orders, and Other Legislative and Military Documents, 1862–1875, compiled by Frederick E. Hosen (Jefferson, NC: MacFarland & Company, 2010).

First Annual Meeting of the National Equal Rights League, held in Cleveland, Ohio, October 19, 20th and 21st, 1865 (Philadelphia: E. C. Markley & Son, 1865), 9, 29, 20.

The First Call of the Civil War: Personal Recollections of Michigan's Response, A Paper Read by Gen. W. H. Withington before Edward Pomeroy Post, G.A.R. at Jackson Michigan, in 1897 (nd, np, np).

Fuller, George N., *Messages of the Governors of Michigan* (Lansing: Michigan Historical Commission, 1926), 4 vols.

Funeral Address and Memorial Notices of Mrs. Isabella Graham Duffield, of Detroit, Mich. (Detroit: Wm. Graham's Steam Presses, 1872).

"General Burnside's Order no. 84, Suppressing the Chicago Times, and its History" (Boston: Printed by Prentiss and Deland, 1864?).

General Orders Affecting the Volunteer Force, Adjutant General's Office, 1861 (Washington, DC: Government Printing Office, 1862).

General Orders Affecting the Volunteer Force, Adjutant General's Office, 1863 (Washington, DC: Government Printing Office, 1864).

General Orders of the War Department, embracing the years 1861, 1862 & 1863, edited by Thomas M O'Brien and Oliver Diefendorf (New York: Derby & Miller, 1864).

"General Pritchard is Dead," The AGZ, November 30, 1907, article In *Civil War Officers Union, Benjamin D. Pritchard, Excerpts from newspapers and other sources, from the files of the Lincoln Financial Foundation Collection.*

Gould, Benjamin Apthorp, *Investigations in the Military and Anthropological Statistics of American Soldiers* (New York: Arno Press, 1979, [reprint of vol. 2, 1869]).

Greeley, Horace, *Proceedings of the First Three Republican National Conventions Of 1856, 1860, and 1864, including proceedings of the antecedent national convention held at Pittsburg, in February, 1856, as reported by Horace Greeley* (Minneapolis: Charles W. Johnson, 1893).

Gurowski, Adam, *Diary: 1863–'64–'65* (Washington, DC: W. H. & O. H. Morrison, 1866).

Halstead, Murat, *A History of the National Political Conventions* (Columbus, OH: Follett, Foster and Company, 1860).

Hand-Book for the Democracy for 1863 & '64 (New York: Society for the Diffusion of Political Knowledge, 1863).

Indian Affairs. Laws and Treaties, vol. II, Treaties, compiled and edited by Charles J. Kappler (Washington, DC: Government Printing Office, 1904).

Inside Lincoln's Cabinet: The Civil War Diaries of Salmon P. Chase, ed. David Donald (New York: Longmans, Green and Co., 1954).

Internal Revenue Commissioner, *Report of the Commissioner of Internal Revenue on the Operations of the Internal Revenue System for the Year Ending June 30, 1863* (Washington, DC: Government Printing Office, 1864).

International Convention on Tonnage Measurement of Ships, 1969 (London: International Maritime Organization, 1983),

Johnston's Detroit City Directory and Advertising Gazetteer of Michigan (Detroit: Fisher, Fleming & Co., 1857).

Johnston's Detroit City Directory and Advertising Gazetteer of Michigan, with an Appendix Carefully Revised (Detroit: James Dale Johnston & Co., 1861).

Joint Documents of the State of Michigan for the year 1860 (Lansing: Hosmer & Kerr, 1861).

Joint Documents of the State of Michigan for the Year 1862 (Lansing: John A. Kerr & Co., Printers to the State, 1863).

Joint Documents of the State of Michigan for the Year 1864 (Lansing: John A. Kerr & Co., Printers to the State, 1865).

Journal of the Executive Proceedings of the Senate of the United States of America, from March 4, 1871 to March 3, 1873, inclusive, vol. XVIII (Washington, DC: Government Printing Office, 1901).

Journal of the House of Representatives of the State of Michigan. 1849. Printed by virtue of the Legislature under the supervision of A. W. Hovey, Clerk of the House of Representatives (Lansing: Munger and Pattison, Printers to the State, 1849).

Journal of the House of Representatives for the State of Michigan. 1861. Edward W. Barber, Clerk of the House of Representatives (Lansing: Hosmer & Kerr, Printers to the State, 1861), Parts I and II.

Journal of the House of Representatives for the State of Michigan. Extra Session, 1864. Edward W. Barber, Clerk of the House of Representatives (Lansing: John A. Kerr & Co., Printers to the State, 1864).

Journal of the House of Representatives for the State of Michigan. 1865. Nelson B. Jones, Clerk of the House of Representatives (Lansing: John A. Kerr & Co., Printers to the State, 1865), Parts I and II.

Journal of the House of Representatives of the State of Michigan, 1893, in Three Volumes, vol. I (Lansing, Michigan: Robert Smith & Co., State Printers, 1893).

Journal of the Senate of the State of Michigan. 1855. Printed by virtue of an Act of the Legislature under the supervision and direction of I. W. Wilder, Secretary of the Senate (Lansing: Hosmer & Kerr, Printers to the State, 1861).

Journal of the Senate of the State of Michigan. 1861. Printed by virtue of an Act of the Legislature under the supervision of Aaron B. Turner, Secretary of the Senate (Lansing: Hosmer & Fitch, Printers to the State, 1861).

Journal of the Senate of the State of Michigan, Extra-Session, 1861 (Lansing: John A. Kerr & Company, 1861).

Journal of the Senate of the State of Michigan. Extra Session of 1862. Printed by virtue of an Act of the Legislature under the supervision of

William A. Bryce, Secretary of the Senate (Lansing: John A. Kerr, Printers to the State, 1855).

Journal of the Senate of the State of Michigan. 1863. Printed by virtue of an Act of the Legislature under the supervision of William A. Bryce, Secretary of the Senate.

Journal of the Senate of the State of Michigan. Extra Session, 1864. Printed by virtue of an Act of the Legislature under the supervision of William A. Bryce, Secretary of the Senate (Lansing: John A. Kerr & Co., Printers to the State, 1864).

Journal of the Senate of the State of Michigan. 1865. Printed by virtue of an Act of the Legislature under the supervision of Thomas H. Glenn, Secretary of the Senate (Lansing: John A. Kerr & Co., Printers to the State, 1865).

Kennedy, Jos. C.G., Superintendent, Preliminary Report on The Eighth Census, 1860 (Washington, DC: Government Printing Office, 1862).

Laws of the Territory of Michigan, vol. II (Lansing: W. S. George & Co., State Printers, 1874).

Lincoln: Speeches and Writings: 1859–1865 (New York: Library of America, 1989).

Memorial Addresses, Fifty-Ninth Congress Second Session, Senate of the United States, February 23, 1907, House of Representatives, February 24, 1907 (Washington, DC: Government Printing Office, 1907).

Memorial Addresses on the Life and Character of Alpheus S. Williams (A Representative from Michigan) delivered to the House of Representatives and in the Senate, Forty-Fifth Congress, Third Session, Published by Order of Congress (Washington, DC: Government Printing Office, 1880).

Michigan at Gettysburg. July 1st, 2nd and 3rd, 1863. June 12, 1889. Proceedings Incident to the Dedication of the Michigan Monuments upon the Battlefield of Gettysburg, June 12, 1889 (Detroit: Winn & Hammond, 1889).

Michigan in the War, compiled by Jno. Robertson, Adjutant General (Lansing: W. S. George & Co., State Printers and Binders, 1880).

Michigan Legislative Manual and Official Directory for the years 1899–1900, compiled by Justus S. Stearns (Lansing: Robert Smith Printing Co., State Printers and Binders, 1899).

Michigan Reports. Reports of Cases heard and decided by The Supreme Court of Michigan from November 13, 1862, to October 24, 1863, Thomas M. Cooley, Reporter. Vol. VII, Being vol. XI of Series (Ann Arbor: Published by the Reporter, 1863).

Michigan Reports. Reports of Cases heard and decided by The Supreme Court of Michigan from October 18, 1864, to November 11, 1865, Elijah W. Meddaugh, Reporter, Vol. I, Being Volume XIII of the Series (Detroit: Wm. A. Throop & Co., 1866).

Michigan Soldiers' Relief Association: Second Annual Report of the Michigan Soldiers' Relief Association, for 1863, December 21, 1863 [Washington? The Association].

— "Report of Mrs. E. Brainard, General Visiting Agent of the Michigan Soldiers' Relief Association."

— "Report of Miss Julia Wheelock."

Third Annual Report of the Michigan Soldiers' Relief Association, for 1864, December 12, 1863 [Washington? The Association].

— Report of Miss Julia Wheelock.

Michigan State Gazetteer for 1867–'8, compiled by Chapin & Brother (Detroit: Detroit Post Company, 1867).

The Miscellaneous Documents of the House of Representatives, printed during the first session of the Thirty-Sixth Congress, 1859–'60, in Seven Volumes (Washington, DC: Thomas H. Ford, Printer, 1869).

Moss, Rev. Lemuel, Annals of the United States Christian Commission (Philadelphia: J. B. Lippincott & Co., 1868).

Narratives of the Sufferings of Lewis and Milton Clarke (Boston: Bela Marsh, 1846).

Negro Population in the United States, 1790–1915 (New York: Arno Press, 1968).

Newberry, Dr. J. S., Sanitary Commission no. 96, The U.S. Sanitary Commission in the Valley of the Mississippi, during the War of the Rebellion (Cleveland: Fairbanks, Benedict & Co., Printers, 1871).

W. A. Norton's Directory of Dowagiac, Cassopolis, and LaGrange, Pokagon, Silver Creek and Wayne Townships, comp. Willard A. Norton (St. Joseph, MI: A. B. Morse Co., 1899).

"My Experience as a Prisoner of War, and Escape from Libby Prison," a paper read before the Commandery of the State of Michigan, Military Order of the Loyal Legion of the U.S. (Detroit: Winn & Hammond, 1893).

Obituary Notice of Maj.-Gen. Samuel P. Heintzelman, first commander of the Third Army Corps, by Maj.-Gen. John C. Robinson, U.S.A. (New York: Published for the Third Army Corps Union, 1881).

Official Gazette of the United States Patent Office, vol. 10, no. 6, August 8, 1876 (Washington, DC: Government Printing Office, 1877).

Official Proceedings of the Democratic National Convention, held in 1864 at Chicago (Chicago: Times Steam Book and Job Printing House, 1864).

Opinion of Attorney General Bates on Citizenship (Washington, DC: Government Printing Office, 1862).

The Papers of Jefferson Davis, vol. 9, January to September, 1863, edited by Lynda Lasswell Crist (Baton Rouge: Louisiana State University Press, 1971–2015), 14 vols.

Parkhurst, John G., Official Proceedings of the Democratic National Convention (Cleveland: Nevins' Print, Plain Dealer Job Office, 1860).

The People v. John McKinney, in Michigan Reports. Reports of Cases heard and decided in the Supreme Court of Michigan from the beginning of April Term, 1862, to November 13, 1862, Thomas M. Cooley, reporter, vol. VI (Chicago: Callaghan & Co., 1880).

Personal Memoirs of P. H. Sheridan, General U.S. Army, in Two Volumes (London: Chatto & Windus, Piccadilly, 1888), 2 vols.

Phisterer, Frederick, *Statistical Record of the Armies of the United States* (New York: Charles Scribner's Sons, reprint, 2009).

Polk's Jackson City and County Directory, 1900–1901 (Detroit: R.L. Polk & Co., 1900).

The Political History of the United States of America during The Great Rebellion, ed. Edward McPherson, 2nd ed. (Washington, DC: Philip & Solomons, 1865).

Presidential Election, 1864. Proceedings of the National Union Convention held in Baltimore, Md., June 7 and 8th, 1864, reported by D. F. Murphy (New York: Baker & Godwin, Printers, 1864).

Presidential Elections, 1798–2008: County, State, and National Mapping of Election Data, ed. Hanes Walton, Donald Deskins Jr., and Sherman Puckett (Ann Arbor: University of Michigan Press, 2010).

The Proceedings of Black State Conventions, 1865–1900, ed. Philip S. Foner and George E. Walker (Philadelphia: Temple University Press, 1986), 2 vols.

Proceedings of the Colored Men's Convention of the State of Michigan, Held in the City of Detroit, Tuesday and Wednesday, Sept. 12th and 13th, '65 (Adrian, MI: Adrian Times Office, 1865).

Proceedings of the National Convention of Colored Men, held in the City of Syracuse, N.Y., October 4, 5, 6, and 7, 1864 (Boston: J. S. Rock and Geo. L. Ruffin, 1864).

Public Acts and Joint and Concurrent Resolutions of the Legislature of the State of Michigan passed at the Regular Session of 1879, with an Appendix (Lansing: W. S. George & Co., State Printers, 1879).

The Rebellion Record: A Diary of American Events, edited by Frank Moore (New York: Arno Press, 1977, reprint), 12 vols.

Record of Service of Michigan Volunteers in the Civil War, 1861–1865, Published by authority of the Senate and House of Representatives of the Michigan Legislature, under the direction of Brig. Gen. Geo. H. Brown, Adjutant General (Kalamazoo: Ihling Bros. & Everard, 1900–), 46 vols.

The Reports of Committees of the House of Representatives for the Second Session of the Fifty-First Congress, 1890–'91, with Index, in Six Volumes (Washington, DC: Government Printing Office, 1891).

Report of the Adjutant General of the State of Illinois, vol. II, Containing Reports for the Years, 1861–1866 (Springfield, IL: Phillips Bros., State Printers, 1901), 9 vols.

Report of the Adjutant & Inspector General of the State of Vermont, from Oct. 1, 1864 to Oct. 1, 1865 (Montpelier, VT: Walton's Steam Printing Establishment, 1865).

Report of the Adjutant General of the State of Illinois (Springfield, IL: Baker, Bailhache & Co., Printers, 1867), 8 vols.

Reports of the Heads of Departments, transmitted to the Governor of Pennsylvania, in pursuance of law, for the year ending November 30, 1863 (Harrisburg, PA: Singerly & Myers, State Printers, 1864), 2 vols.

The Revised Constitution of the State of Michigan, adopted in Convention, August 15, 1850 (Lansing: R. W. Ingals, State Printer, 1850).

The Revised Statutes of the State of Michigan, passed at the Adjourned Session of 1837, and the Regular Session of 1838 (Detroit, MI: John S. Bagg, 1838).

Sanitary Commission in the Valley of the Mississippi, during the War of the Rebellion, The United States Sanitary Commission: A Sketch of its Purposes and its Work, compiled from documents and private papers (Boston: Little Brown and Company, 1863).

Sanitary Commission in the Valley of the Mississippi, during the War of the Rebellion, United States Sanitary Commission Bulletin, vol. III, nos. 25 to 40 (New York: 1866).

The Sanitary Reporter, Volume I, No. 9, September 15, 1863.

Soldiers' National Cemetery at Gettysburg, to the [Indiana] Legislature (Indianapolis: W. R. Holloway, State Printer, 1865).

A Source-Book of Military Law and War-Time Legislation, prepared by the War Department Committee on Education and Special Training (St. Paul, MN: West Publishing Company, 1919).

"Speech of Hon. Kinsley S. Bingham, of Michigan, Delivered in the House of Representatives of the U. States, August 7, 1848" (Washington, DC: J. and G. S. Gideon, Printers, 1848).

State of Michigan Gazetteer and Business Directory for 1856–7. Complete in One Volume (Detroit: Huntington Lee & James Sutherland, 1856).

Statistics, Report of the Superintendent of the Census for December 1, 1852 to which is appended the Report for December 1, 1851 (Washington, DC: Robert Armstrong, Printer, 1853).

The Statutes at Large of the Provisional Government of the Confederate States of America, ed. James M. Matthews (Richmond, VA: R. M. Smith, Printer to Congress, 1864).

Stowe, Harriet Beecher, *A Key to Uncle Tom's Cabin: Presenting the Original Facts and Documents Upon which the Story is Founded* (London: Sampson Low, Son, & Co., 1853).

Stowe, Harriet Beecher, *Uncle Tom's Cabin: A Tale of Life Among the Lowly* (London: George Routledge & Co., 1852).

Telegraph and Telephone Age (New York, March 16, 1915), no. 6, Thirty-Third Year.

Tod, David, *Annual Message to the Governor of Ohio, to the Fifty-Sixth General Assembly, at the regular session commencing January 4, 1864* (Columbus: Richard Nevins, State Printer, 1864).

The Trial of Hon. Clement L. Vallandigham, by a Military Commission: and the proceedings under his application for a Writ of Habeas Corpus from the Circuit Court of the United States for the Southern District of Ohio (Cincinnati: Rickey and Carroll, 1863).

The Trials for Treason at Indianapolis disclosing the plans for establishing a North-Western Confederacy, ed. Benn Pitman (Cincinnati: Moore, Wilstach & Baldwin, 1865).University of Michigan Regents' Proceedings with Appendixes and Index (Ann Arbor: Published by the University, October 1915).

U.S. Census, Population of the United States in 1860; compiled from the Original Returns of the Eighth Census, under direction of the Secretary of the Interior, Joseph C. G. Kennedy (Washington, DC: Government Printing Office, 1864).

U.S. Census, Statistics of the United States (including Mortality, Property, &c) in 1860. Compiled from Original Returns and Being the Final Exhibit of the Eighth Census (Washington DC: Government Printing Office, 1866).

U.S. Congress, The Miscellaneous Documents of the House of Representatives, printed during the Second Session of the Thirty-Eighth Congress, 1864–'65, in Three Volumes (Washington, DC: Government Printing Office, 1865).

U.S. Congress, Journal of the House of Representatives of the United States: being the First Session of the Thirty-Seventh Congress, begun and held at the City of Washington, July 4, 1861 (Washington, DC: Government Printing Office, 1861).

U.S. Congress, Journal of the House of Representatives of the United States: being the Second Session of the Thirty-Seventh Congress, begun and held at the City of Washington, December 2, 1861 (Washington, DC: Government Printing Office, 1862).

U.S. Congress, Journal of the House of Representatives of the United States: being the Third Session of the Thirty-Seventh Congress, begun and held at the City of Washington, December 1, 1862 (Washington, DC: Government Printing Office, 1863).

U.S. Congress, Journal of the Senate of the United States of America, being the First Session of the Thirty-Seventh Congress, begun and held at the City of Washington, July 4, 1861 (Washington, DC: Government Printing Office, 1861).

U.S. Congress, Journal of the Senate of the United States of America, being the First Session of the Thirty-Eighth Congress, begun and held at the City of Washington, December 7, 1863 (Washington, DC: Government Printing Office, 1863).

U.S. Congress, "Report to accompany bill H.R. 7617," Forty-Eighth Congress, Second Session, Report no. 1307.

U.S. Congress, The Statutes at Large of the United States of America, from November 1903 to March, 1905; Concurrent Resolutions of the Two Houses of Congress, and Recent Treaties, Conventions, and Executive Proclamations, Vol. XXXIII (Washington, DC: Government Printing Office, 1905).

U.S. Congress, By Authority of Congress: The Statutes at Large, Treaties, and Proclamations of the United States of America. From December 5, 1859, to March 3, 1863, ed. George P. Sanger (Boston: Little, Brown and Company, 1863), vol. XIII.

U.S. Congress, By Authority of Congress: The Statutes at Large Treaties, and Proclamations of the United States of America. From December 1863 to December 1865, ed. George P. Sanger (Boston: Little, Brown and Company, 1866), vol. XIII.

United States Christian Commission, for the Army and Navy. First Annual Report (Philadelphia, np, February 1863).

United States Christian Commission, for the Army and Navy. For the Year 1863. Second Annual Report (Philadelphia, np, April 1864).

United States Christian Commission, for the Army and Navy. For the Year 1864. Third Annual Report (Philadelphia, np, April 1865).

United States Christian Commission, for the Army and Navy. For the Year 1865, Fourth Annual Report (Philadelphia, np, March 1866).

U.S. War Department. Circular No. 4: War Department, Surgeon General's Office, Washington, December 5, 1870 (Washington, DC: Government Printing Office).

U.S. War Department. The War of the Rebellion: A Compilation of the Official Records of the Union and Confederate Armies, 70 vols. in 128 parts (Washington, DC: Government Printing Office, 1880–1901).

U.S. War Department. The War of the Rebellion: Official Records of the Union and Confederate Navies in the War of Rebellion (Washington, DC: Government Printing Office, 1896).

United States Sanitary Commission, Dr. J. S. Newberry, Sanitary Commission No. 96, The U.S. Sanitary Commission in the Valley of the Mississippi, during the War of the Rebellion (Cleveland: Fairbanks, Benedict & Co., Printers, 1871).

The Universalist Register, Giving Statistics of the Church, Nov. 1, 1881, with the Usual Astronomical Tables, and a Counting House Almanac for 1882, ed. Mrs. C. L. F. Skinner (Boston: Universalist Publishing House, 1882).

Williams, George Washington, A History of Negro Troops in the War of the Rebellion, 1861–1865, preceded by a Review of the Military Services of Negroes in Ancient and Modern Times (New York: Harper & Brothers, 1888).

The Writings of Thomas Jefferson, ed. H. A. Washington, vol. 2 (New York: Cambridge University Press, 2011).

Secondary Sources

The African American Electorate: A Statistical History, ed. Hanes Walton Jr., Sherman C. Puckett, and Donald R. Deskins Jr. (Los Angeles: Sage Publications, 2012).

Africana: The Encyclopedia of the African and African American Experience, ed. Henry Louis Gates and Kwame Anthony Appiah (New York: Oxford University Press, 1999), 5 vols.

American Biographical History of Eminent and Self-Made Men, with Portrait Illustrations on Steel, Michigan Volume (Cincinnati: Western Biographical Publishing Co., 1878).

America's Successful Men of Affairs: An Encyclopedia of Contemporaneous Biography, ed. Henry Hall (New York: New York Tribune, 1896), 2 vols.

Anbinder, Tyler, Nativism and Slavery: The Northern Know Nothings and the Politics of the 1850s (New York: Oxford University Press, 1994).

Angelo, Frank, On Guard: A History of the Detroit Free Press (Detroit: Detroit Free Press, 1981).

An Indispensible Liberty: The Fight for Free Speech in Nineteenth Century America, ed. Mary M. Cronin (Carbondale: Southern Illinois University Press, 2016).

Appleton's Cyclopaedia of American Biography, ed. James Grant Wilson and John Fiske (New York: D. Appleton and Company, 1888), 6 vols.

Asante, Molefi Kete, 100 Greatest Americans: A Biographical Encyclopedia (Amherst, NY: Prometheus Books, 2002).

The Association of the Graduates of the United States Military Academy at West Point, New York, June 12th 1890 (Saginaw, MI: Evening News Printing and Binding House, 1890).

Bak, Richard, A Distant Thunder: Michigan in the Civil War (Ann Arbor: Huron River Press, 2004).

Barry, Chester D., Loss of the Sultana and Reminiscences of Survivors: History of a Disaster, where over One Thousand Five Hundred were Lost, most of them being exchanged prisoners of war on their way home after privation and suffering from one to two-three months in Cahaba and Andersonville Prisons (Lansing, MI: Darius D. Thorp, 1892).

Bastress, Robert M. The West Virginia State Constitution: A Reference Guide (Westport, CT: Greenwood Publishing, 1995).

Baxter, Albert, History of the City of Grand Rapids, Michigan (With an Appendix—History of Lowell, Michigan) (Grand Rapids: Munsell & Company, 1891).

Beach, William H., The First New York (Lincoln) Cavalry, From April 19, 1861 to July 7, 1865 (New York: Lincoln Cavalry Association, 1902).

Beall, John Yates, Memoir of John Yates Beall: His Life; Trial; Correspondence; Diary; including the account of the Raid on Lake Erie, [ed. Daniel B. Lucas] (Montreal: John Lovell, 1865).

Bell, Andrew McIlwaine, Mosquito Soldiers: Malaria, Yellow Fever, and the Course of the American Civil War (Baton Rouge: Louisiana State University Press, 2010).

Bench and Bar of Michigan: A Volume of History and Biography, ed. George Irving Reed (Chicago: Century Publishing Company, 1897).

Bennett, Charles W., Historical Sketches of the Ninth Michigan Infantry (General Thomas' Headquarters Guards) with an Account of the Battle of Murfreesboro, Tennessee, Sunday, July 13, 1862 (Coldwater, MI: Daily Courier Print, 1913).

Benton, John Henry Benton, Voting in the Field: A Forgotten Chapter of the Civil War (Boston: W. B. Clarke Co., 1915).

Bertera, Martin N., and Kim Crawford, The Fourth Michigan Infantry in the Civil War (Michigan State University Press, 2010).

Biographical Dictionary of American Mayors, 1820–1980, ed. Melvin G. Holli and Peter d'A. Jones,(Westport, CT: Greenwood Press, 1981).

Biographical Directory of the Governors of the United States, 1789–1978, ed. Robert Sobel and John Raimo (Westport, CT: Meckler Books, 1978).

Biographical Directory of the United States Congress, 1774–2005 (Washington, DC: Government Printing Office, 2005). Cited hereafter as BD, followed by the page number.

Biographical Record: Biographical Sketches of Leading Citizens of Oakland County, Michigan (Chicago: Biographical Publishing Company, 1903).

Biographical Sketches of the Leading Men of Chicago (Chicago: Wilson & St. Clair, 1868).

Bishop, Levi, The Poetical Works of Levi Bishop, 3rd ed., with a sketch of the author (Detroit: E. B. Smith & Co., 1876).

Bogue, Allan G., The Earnest Men: Republicans of the Civil War Senate (Ithaca, NY: Cornell University Press, 2009).

Bokross, Dan, The Battle of Raymond: The Untold Turning Point of the American Civil War (Raleigh, NC: LuLu Press, 2007).

Broadwater, Robert P., Civil War Medal of Honor Recipients: A Complete Illustrated Record (Jefferson, NC: McFarland & Company, 2007).

Brockett, L. P., and Mary C. Vaughn, Woman's Work in the Civil War: Record of Heroism, Patriotism and Patience (Philadelphia: Zeigler, McCurdy & Co., 1867).

Brown, Thomas J., Dorothea Dix: New England Reformer (Cambridge, MA: Harvard University Press, 1998).

Bulkley, John McClelland, History of Monroe County Michigan: A Narrative Account of its Historical Progress, its People, and its Principal Interests (Chicago: Lewis Publishing Company, 1913).

Burr, C. B., M.D., Medical History of Michigan, Michigan State Medical Society (Minneapolis: Bruce Publishing Company, 1930), 2 vols.

Carstens, Patrick Richard, and Timothy L. Sanford, The Republic of Canada Almost (Bloomington, IN: Xlibris Corporation, 2013).

Catalogue of the Sigma Phi with Thesaurus (Printed for the Society, 1891).

Chardavoyne, David Gardner, The United States District Court for the Eastern District of Michigan: People, Law, and Politics (Detroit: Wayne State University Press, 2012).

Chase, Theodore R., Michigan University Book, 1844–1880 (Detroit: Richmond, Backus & Co., 1881).

Chernow, Ron, Grant (New York: Penguin Press, 2017).

Chipman, Bert Lee, The Chipman Family: A Genealogy of the Chipmans in America, 1631–1920 (Winston-Salem, NC: Bert L. Chipman, Publisher, 1920).

The City of Detroit, Michigan, 1701–1922, ed. Clarence Burton (Detroit: S. J. Clarke Publishing Company, 1922), 5 vols.

The Civil War Naval Encyclopedia, ed. Spencer C. Tucker (Santa Barbara, CA: ABC-CLIO, LLC, 2011).

Clarke, Richard H., Lives of the Deceased Bishops of the Catholic Church in the United States (New York: P. O'Shea, Publisher, 1872), 2 vols.

Clowes, Walter F., The Detroit Light Guard: A Complete Record of this Organization from its Foundation to the Present Day (Detroit: John F. Eby & Company, 1900).

Coddington, Edwin B., The Gettysburg Campaign: A Study in Command (New York: Charles Scribner's Sons, 1984).

Coggeshall, William T., The Journeys of Abraham Lincoln; from Springfield to Washington, 1861, as president-elect; and Washington to Springfield, 1865, as president martyred (Columbus: Ohio State Journal, 1865).

Collin, Rev. Henry P., A Twentieth Century History and Biographical Record of Branch County, Michigan (New York: Lewis Publishing Company, 1906), 348–350.

Collins, Lewis, History of Kentucky, Revised, Enlarged four-fold, and brought down to the year 1874, by his son, Richard H. Collins (Covington, KY: Collins & Co., 1874).

Compendium of History and Biography of the City of Detroit and Wayne County, Michigan (Chicago: Henry Taylor & Co., 1909).

Compendium of History and Biography of Kalamazoo County, Mich., Illustrated, ed. David Fisher and Frank Little (Chicago: A. W. Bowen & Co., no date).

Conable, F. W., History of the Genesee Annual Conference of the Methodist Episcopal Church, from its organization by Bishops Asbury and M'Kendree in 1810 to the year 1884 (New York: Phillips & Hunt, 1885).

Conway, James, and David F. Jamroz, Detroit's Historic Fort Wayne (Charleston, SC: Arcadia Publishing, 2007).

Coolidge, Orville W., A Twentieth Century History of Berrien County Michigan (Chicago: Lewis Publishing Company, 1906).

Craig, Berry, Kentucky Confederates: Secession, Civil War, and the Jackson Purchase (Lexington: University Press of Kentucky, 2014), 157–158.

Cullum, Bvt. Maj.-Gen. George W., Biographical Register of the Officers and Graduates of the U.S. Military Academy at West Point, New York, 2nd ed. (Boston: Houghton, Mifflin and Company, 1868), cited hereafter as Biographical Register (2nd), 2 vols., volume and page number indicated.

Cullum, Bvt. Maj.-Gen. George W., Biographical Register of the Officers and Graduates of the U.S. Military Academy at West Point, New York, 3rd ed. (Boston: Houghton, Mifflin and Company, 1891), cited hereafter as Biographical Register (3rd), 2 vols., volume and page number indicated.

Cullum, Bvt. Maj.-Gen. George W., Biographical Register of the Officers and Graduates of the U.S. Military Academy at West Point, New York, Supplement (New York: James Miller, Publisher, 1879).

Curtis, O. B., History of the Twenty-Fourth Michigan of the Iron Brigade, known as the Detroit and Wayne County Regiment (Detroit: Winn & Hammond, 1891).

Cyclopedia of Michigan: Historical and Biographical, comprising a Synopsis of General History of the State with Biographical Sketches of Men who have in their various spheres contributed towards its development (New York: Western Publishing and Engraving Co., 1900).

Deland's History of Jackson County, Michigan, embracing a Concise Review of its Early Settlement, Industrial Development and Present Conditions, together with Interesting Reminiscences, compiled by Colonel Charles V. Deland (No city: B. F. Bowen, Publisher, 1903).

Dell, Christopher, Lincoln and the War Democrats: The Grand Erosion of Conservative Tradition (Rutherford, NJ: Farleigh Dickinson University Press, 1975).

Dempsey, Jack, Michigan and the Civil War: A Great and Bloody Sacrifice (Charleston, SC: History Press, 2011).

Desmond, Humphrey J., The Know Nothing Party. A Sketch (Washington: New Century Press, 1906).

Detroit in History and Commerce, Published under the direction of the Merchants' and Manufacturers' Exchange and Sanction of the Detroit Board of Trade (Detroit: Rogers & Thorpe, 1891).

Dictionary of American Naval Fighting Ships, ed. by James L. Mooney (Washington, DC: Naval Historical Center, Department of the Navy, 1959–1991), 9 vols.

Dictionary of Canadian Biography (Toronto: University of Toronto, 1965–), 12 vols.

Dilla, Harriet M., The Politics of Michigan, 1865–1878 (New York: Columbia University, Longmans, Green & Co., Agents, 1912).

Dillon, Ruby, Minnie Dubbs Millbrook, Virginia Everham, and Frances Davis McTeer, Michigan Women in the Civil War (Lansing, MI: Michigan Civil War Centennial Observance Commission, 1963).

Duke, Basil W., History of Morgan's Cavalry (London, UK: Leonaur Publishing, 2010).

Durant, Samuel W., History of Ingham and Eaton Counties, Michigan, with Illustrations and Biographical Sketches of their Prominent Men and Pioneers (Philadelphia: D. W. Ensign & Co., 1880).

Dwight, Benjamin W., The History of the Descendants of John Dwight, of Dedham, Mass. (New York: John F. Trow & Son, Printers, 1874), 2 vols.

Early History of Michigan with Biographies of State Officers, Members of Congress, Judges and Legislators (Lansing: Thorp & Godfrey, 1888).

Eddy, T. M., The Patriotism of Illinois, A Record of the Civil and

Military History in the War for the Union with a History of the Campaigns in which Illinois Soldiers have been Conspicuous (Chicago: Clarke & Co., Publishers, 1866), 2 vols.

Edmonds, S. Emma E. *Nurse and Spy in the Union Army: The Adventures and Experiences of a Woman in Hospitals, Camps, and Battlefields* (Hartford, CT: W. S. Williams & Co., 1865, reprint, Applewood Books).

Egle, William H., *Life and Times of Andrew Gregg Curtin* (Philadelphia: Thompson Publishing Company, 1896).

Eicher, John, and David Eicher, *Civil War High Commands* (Stanford, CA: Stanford University Press, 2001).

1830–1877 History of Calhoun County, Michigan, with Illustrations descriptive of its scenery, palatial residences, public buildings, fine blocks, and important manufactories (Philadelphia: L. H. Everts, 1877).

Eldredge, Robert F., *Past and Present of Macomb County Michigan* (Chicago: S. J. Clarke Publishing Co., 1905).

Emerson, Edward Waldo, *Emerson in Concord: A Memoir* (New York: Houghton, Mifflin and Company, 1890).

Encyclopedia of African American History, 1619–1895: From the Colonial Period to the Age of Frederick Douglass, vol. 2, ed. Paul Finkelman (New York: Oxford University Press, 2006), 3 vols.

Encyclopedia of the American Civil War: A Political, Social, and Military History, ed. David S. Heidler and Jeanne T. Heidler (New York: W.W. Norton & Company, 2002).

The Encyclopedia of the War of 1812: A Political, Social and Military History, edited by Spencer C. Tucker (Santa Barbara, CA: ABC-CLIO, LLC, 2012).

Engle, Stephen D., *Gathering to Save a Nation: Lincoln & the Union's War Governors* (Chapel Hill: University of North Carolina Press, 2016).

An Episcopal Dictionary of the Church: A User Friendly Reference for Episcopalians, ed. Don S. Armentrout and Robert Boak Slocum (New York: Church Publishing, 2000).

Farmer, Silas, *The History of Detroit and Michigan or The Metropolis Illustrated: A Chronological Encyclopedia of the Past and Present including a full record Territorial days in Michigan and the annals of Wayne County* (Detroit: Silas Farmer & Co., 1889).

Farmer, Silas, *History of Detroit and Wayne County, and Early Michigan: A Chronological Cyclopedia of the Past and Present* (Detroit: Silas Farmer & Co., 1890).

Farmer, Silas, *The Michigan Book: A State Cyclopedia, with Sectional County Maps Alphabetically Arranged* (Detroit: Silas Farmer & Co., 1911).

Fehrenbacher, Don E., *Slavery, Law & Politics: The Dred Scott Case in Historical Perspective* (New York: Oxford University Press, 1981, abridged edition).

Fisher, Ernest B., ed., *Grand Rapids and Kent County Michigan: Historical Account of their Progress from First Settlement to the Present Time* (Chicago: Robert O. Law Company, 1918), 2 vols.

Fitch, John, *Annals of the Army of the Cumberland: comprising the Biographies, Descriptions of Departments, Accounts of Expeditions, Skirmishers, and Battles* (Philadelphia: J. B. Lippincott & Co., 1864).

The Flags of Michigan, compiled by Jno. Robertson, Adjutant General (Lansing: W. S. George & Co., State Printers, 1877).

Foote, Abram William Foote, *Foote Family, comprising the Genealogy and History of Nathaniel Foote of Wethersfield, Conn.* (Rutland, VT: Marble City Press, 1907).

Foreman, Amanda, *A World On Fire: Britain's Crucial Role in the American Civil War* (New York: Random House, 2012).

Formisano, Ronald P., *The Birth of Mass Political Parties: Michigan, 1827–1861* (Princeton: Princeton University Press, 1971).

Foulke, William Dudley, *Life of Oliver P. Morton, including his important speeches* (Indianapolis—Kansas City: Bowen-Merrill Company, 1899), 2 vols.

Fox, Col. Dorus M. Fox, *History of Political Parties, National Reminiscences, and the Tippecanoe Movement* (Des Moines: Col. Dorus M. Fox, Publisher, 1895).

Fox, William A, *Regimental Losses of the American Civil War, 1861–1865* (Dayton, OH: Morningside House, 1985, reprint, 1898).

Frieze, Henry S., *Memorial of Alonzo Benjamin Palmer, M.D., LL.D.* (Cambridge: Riverside Press, 1890).

Funeral Address and Memorial Notices of Mrs. Isabella Graham Duffield, of Detroit, Mich. (Detroit: Wm. Graham's Steam Presses, 1872).

Gardner, Washington, *History of Calhoun County, Michigan; a Narrative Account of its Historical Progress, its People, and its Principal Interests* (Chicago: Lewis Publishing Company, 1913).

A Genealogy of the Descendants of Alexander Alford, an early settler of Windsor, Conn. and Northampton, Mass., compiled by Samuel Morgan Alvord (Webster, NY: A.D. Andrews, 1908).

Genealogy of the Whittelsey–Whittlesey Family, compiled by Charles Barney Whittelesey (Hartford, CT: Press of the Case, Lockwood & Brainard Company, 1898).

General Biographical Catalogue of Auburn Theological Seminary, 1818–1919 (Auburn, NY: Auburn Seminary Press, 1918).

General History of the State of Michigan, with Biographical Sketches, Portrait Engravings, and numerous Illustrations, compiled by Charles Richard Tuttle (Detroit: R. D. S. Tyler & Co., 1874.

General Lewis Cass, 1782–1866 (Privately Printed, 1916).

Gibson, Guy James, *Lincoln's League: The Union League Movement during the Civil War* (Urbana, IL, 1957).

Glazier, Willard W., *The Capture, the Prison Pen and the Escape, being a complete History of Prison Life in the South, principally at Richmond, Danville, Macon, Savannah, Charleston, Columbia,*

Belle Isle, Millin, Salisbury and Andersonville (Hartford, CT: H. E. Goodwin, Publisher, 1869).

Goss, Dwight, History of Grand Rapids and its Industries (Chicago: C. F. Cooper & Co., Publishers, 1906).

Greeley, Horace, The American Conflict: A History of the Great Rebellion in the United States of America, 1860–'64: Its Causes, Incidents and Results: Intended to Exhibit especially its Moral and Political Phases, with the Drift and Progress of American Opinion respecting Human Slavery from 1776 to the close of the War for the Union (Hartford, CT: O. D. Case & Company, 1866), 2 vols.

Hannings, Bud, Every Day of the Civil War: A Chronological Encyclopedia (Jefferson, NC: MacFarland & Co., 2012).

Harper, Judith E., Women During the Civil War: An Encyclopedia (New York: Routledge, 2004).

Harris, Wilmer Carlyle, Public Life of Zachariah Chandler, 1851–1875 (Chicago: Privately Distributed, University of Chicago Libraries, 1917), 2 vols.

Harrison, Lowell H., The Civil War in Kentucky (Lexington: University Press of Kentucky, 1975).

Hartwick, L. M., and W. H. Tuller, Oceana Pioneers and Business Men of To-Day: History, Biography, Statistics and Humorous Incidents (Pentwater, MI: Pentwater News Steam Print, 1890).

Hatch, Thom, The Custer Companion: A Comprehensive Guide to the Life of George Armstrong Custer and the Plains Indians Wars (Mechanicsburg, PA: Stackpole Books, 2002).

Hauptman, Lawrence M., Between Two Fires: American Indians in the Civil War (New York: Free Press, 1995).

Hayden, Jabez Haskell, Records of the Connecticut Line of the Hayden Family (Windsor Locks, CT: Case, Lockwood & Brainard, 1888).

Headley, John W. Headley, Confederate Operations in Canada and New York (no city, Neale Publishing Company, 1906).

Herek, Raymond J., These Men Have Seen Hard Service: The First Michigan Sharpshooters in the Civil War (Detroit: Wayne State University Press, 1998).

Hesseltine, William B., Lincoln and the War Governors (New York: Alfred B. Knopf, 1955).

Hinsdale, Burke A., History of the University of Michigan, with Biographical Sketches of Regents and Members of the University Senate from 1837 to 1906, edited by Isaac N. Demmon (Ann Arbor: Published by the University, 1906).

Historical Statistics of the United States, Millennial Edition, volume 5, Governance and International Relations (New York: Cambridge University Press, 2006), 5 vols.

History of Bay County Michigan and its Representative Citizens, ed. and compiled by Captain Augustus H. Gansser (Chicago: Richmond & Arnold, 1905).

History of Bay County, Michigan, with Illustrations and Biographical Sketches of some of its Prominent Men and Pioneers (Chicago: H. H. Page, 1883).

History of Branch County, Michigan, with Illustrations and Biographical Sketches of Prominent Men and Pioneers (Philadelphia: Everts & Abbott, 1879).

History of Cass County, Michigan, with Illustrations and Biographical Sketches of some of its Prominent Men and Pioneers (Chicago: Waterman, Watkins & Co., 1882).

History of Hillsdale County, Michigan, with Illustrations and Biographical Sketches of its prominent Men and Pioneers (Philadelphia: Everts & Abbott, 1879).

History of Jackson County, Michigan (Chicago: Inter-State Publishing Co., 1881).

History of Kalamazoo County, Michigan (Philadelphia: Everts & Abbott, 1889).

History of Livingston County, Michigan: With Illustrations and Biographical Sketches of its Prominent Men and Pioneers (Philadelphia: Everts & Abbott, 1880).

History of Macomb County Michigan (Chicago: M. A. Leeson & Co., 1882).

History of Lapeer County Michigan, with Illustrations and Biographical Sketches of some of its Prominent Men and Pioneers (Chicago: H. R. Page & Co., 1884).

History of Mendocino and Lake Counties, California, with Biographical Sketches of the Leading Men and Women of the Counties who have been identified with their Growth and Development from Early Days to the Present (Los Angeles: Historic Record Company, 1914).

The History of Michigan Law, ed. Paul Finkel and Martin J. Hershock (Athens: Ohio University Press, 2006).

History of Saginaw County, Michigan: Historical, Commercial, Biographical, Profusely Illustrated with Portraits of Early Pioneers, Rare Pictures and Scenes of Olden Times, and Portraits of Representative Citizens of Today (Saginaw: Seemann & Peters, 1918).

History of the Great Lakes, Illustrated (Chicago: J. H. Beers, 1899), 2 vols.

History of the Michigan Soldiers' Aid Society, 1861–1865, by Robert Spiro, PhD diss., University of Michigan, 1959.

History of Washtenaw County Michigan, together with sketches of its Cities, Villages, and Townships (Chicago: Chas. C. Chapman, 1881), 2 vols.

Hoffman, Mark, "My Brave Mechanics": The First Michigan Engineers and Their Civil War (Detroit: Wayne State University Press, 2007).

Holt, Michael F., The Rise and Fall of the American Whig Party: Jacksonian Politics and the Onset of the Civil War (New York: Oxford University Press, 1999).

Howard, Heman, The Howard Genealogy: Descendants of John Howard of Bridgewater, Massachusetts from 1643 to 1903 (Brockton, MA: Standard Printing Company, 1903).

Hunt, Roger D., Colonels in Blue: Michigan, Ohio, and West Virginia (Jefferson, NC: McFarland & Company, 2011).

Hunt, Roger D., & Jack Brown, *Brevet Brigadier Generals in Blue* (Gaithersburg, MD: Olde Soldier Books, 1990).

Hutchison, Craig, and Kimberly Rising, *Dearborn Michigan* (Charleston, SC: Arcadia Publishing, 2003).

Ibbotson, Patricia, *Detroit's Hospitals, Healers and Helpers* (Charleston, SC: Arcadia Publishing, 2004).

Illustrated History of the St. Mary's Falls Ship Canal (no city, Chapman & Kirby, 1893).

Inbody, David S., *The Soldier Vote: War, Politics and the Ballot in America* (New York: Palgrave MacMillan, 2016).

Jelks, Randal Maurice. *African Americans in the Furniture City: The Struggle for Civil Rights in Grand Rapids* (Urbana: University of Illinois Press, 2009).

Keirns, Aaron J., and Nathan J. Keirns, *Honoring the Veterans of Licking County, Ohio: An Illustrated History of Licking County's Military Heritage* (Howard, OH: Little River Publishing, 2009).

Kelton, Dwight H. *Annals of Fort Mackinac* (Detroit: Detroit Free Press Printing Co., Carter Edition, 1892).

Kidd, J. H., *Personal Recollections of a Cavalryman, with Custer's Michigan Cavalry Brigade in the Civil War* (Ionia, MI: Sentinel Printing Co., 1908).

Klement, Frank, L., *The Copperheads in the Middle West* (Chicago: University of Chicago Press, 1960), 202–205.

Klement, Frank L., *Dark Lanterns: Secret Political Societies, Conspiracies and Treason Trials in the Civil War* (Baton Rouge: Louisiana State University Press, 1984).

Knapp, John I., and R. I. Bonner, *Illustrated History and Biographical Record of Lenawee County, Mich, containing an Accurate Epitomized History from the First Settlement in 1824 to the Present Time* (Adrian, MI: Times Printing Company, 1903).

Landmarks of Wayne County, New York, illustrated, ed. George W. Cowles (Syracuse: D. Mason & Company, 1895).

Lanman, Charles, *The Red Book of Michigan; A Civil, Military and Biographical History* (Detroit: E. B. Smith & Company, 1871).

Lennard, Ray, *Lenawee County and the Civil War* (np, History Press, 2016).

Leonard, Elizabeth D., *All the Daring of the Soldier: Women of the Civil War Armies* (New York: W. W. Norton & Company, 1999).

Lewis, Martin Deming, *Lumberman from Flint: The Michigan Career of Henry H. Crapo, 1855–1869* (Detroit: Wayne State University Press, 1958).

Lewis, Virgil A., *History of West Virginia, in two parts* (Philadelphia: Hubbard Brothers, 1889).

Life and Public Services of Martin R. Delany, Sub-Assistant Commissioner Bureau Relief of Refugees, Freedmen, and of Abandoned Lands, and Late Major 104th U.S. Colored Troops (Boston: Lee and Shepard, 1883).

Lincoln Day by Day, A Chronology: 1809–1865, ed. Earl Schenck Miers (Washington, DC: Lincoln Sesquicentennial Commission, 1960), 3 vols.

Lincoln's Proclamation: Emancipation Reconsidered, ed. William A. Blair & Karen Fisher Younger (Chapel Hill: University of North Carolina Press, 2009).

List of Army Officers of the United States from 1779–1900: Embracing a Register of all Appointments by the President of the United States in the Volunteer Service during the Civil War, and of Volunteer Officers in the Service of the United States, June 1, 1900, compiled by Colonel Wm. H. Powell (New York: Hamersley & Co., 1900).

Longmore, Surgeon-General T., *Gunshot Injuries: Their History, Characteristic Features, Complications, and General Treatment* (London: Longmans, Green and Co., 1877).

Mabee, Carlton, *Sojourner Truth, Slave, Prophet, Legend* (New York: New York University Press, 1993).

McRae, Norman, *Negroes in Michigan during the Civil War* (Lansing: Michigan Civil War Centennial Observance Commission, 1966).

Mahan, John K., *History of the Militia and the National Guard* (New York: MacMillan Publishing Company, 1983).

The Making of the University of Michigan, 1817–1992, ed. Margaret Steneck and Nicholas Steneck (Ann Arbor: University of Michigan, Bentley Historical Library, 1994).

Marshall, John, *American Bastille: A History of the Illegal Arrests and Imprisonment of American Citizens during the Late Civil War* (Philadelphia: Thomas W. Hartley & Co., 1884).

Martin, Jay C., *General Henry Baxter, 7th Michigan Volunteer Infantry, A Biography* (Jefferson, NC: McFarland & Co., 2016).

Massachusetts Soldiers, Sailors, and Marines in the Civil War (Norwood, MA: Norwood Press, 1931), 9 vols.

May, George S., *Michigan and the Civil War Years, 1860–1866: A Wartime Chronicle* (Lansing: Michigan Civil War Centennial Observance Committee, 1964).

Memoirs of Lucas County and the City of Toledo, From the Earliest Historical Times down to the Present, including a Genealogical and Biographical Record of Representative Families, ed. Harvey Scribner (Madison, WI: Western Historical Association, 1910).

In Memoriam. General Lewis Cass (Detroit, MI: Free Press Printing House, 1866).

Men of Progress, embracing the Biographical Sketches of Representative Michigan Men with an Outline History of the State (Detroit: Evening News Association, 1900).

Men of the Century, An Historical Work: Giving Portraits and Sketches of Eminent Citizens of the United States, ed. Charles Morris (Philadelphia: L. R. Hamersly & Co., 1896).

Michigan Biographical Dictionary, 2008–2009 ed., ed. Caryn Hannan (St. Claire Shores, MI: Somerset Publishers, 2008).

Michigan Manual of Freedmen's Progress, compiled by Francis H. Warren (Detroit: Freedmen's Progress Commission, 1915).

Michno, Gregory, *Dakota Dawn: The Decisive First Week of the Sioux Uprising, August, 1862* (El Dorado, CA: Savas Beatie, 2011).

Middleton, Stephen, *Black Laws of the Old Northwest: A Documentary History* (Westport, CT: Greenwood Press, 1993).

The Midwestern Homefront during the Civil War, ed. Ginette Aley and J. L. Anderson (Carbondale: Southern Illinois University Press, 2013).

Miller, Richard F., ed., *States At War: A Reference Guide for Connecticut, Maine, Massachusetts, New Hampshire, Rhode Island and Vermont in the Civil War*, vol. I (Hanover, NH: UPNE, 2013).

Miller, Richard F., ed., *States At War: A Reference Guide for New York in the Civil War*, vol. 2 (Hanover, NH: UPNE, 2014).

Miller, Richard F., ed., *States At War: A Reference Guide for Pennsylvania in the Civil War*, vol. 3 (Hanover, NH: UPNE, 2014).

Miller, Richard F., ed., *States At War: A Reference Guide for Delaware, Maryland and New Jersey in the Civil War*, vol. 4 (Hanover, NH: UPNE, 2015).

Miller, Richard F., ed., *States At War: A Reference Guide for Ohio in the Civil War*, vol. 5 (Hanover, NH: UPNE, 2015).

Miller, Richard F., ed., *States At War: A Reference Guide for South Carolina in the Civil War*, vol. 6 (Hanover, NH: UPNE, 2018).

Mills, James Cooke, *History of Saginaw County, Michigan, Historical, Commercial, Biographical* (Saginaw: Seemann & Peters, 1918).

Moore, Charles, *History of Michigan, Illustrated* (Chicago: Lewis Publishing Company, 1915), 4 vols.

Moseley, Edward H., and Paul C. Clark, Jr., *The A to Z of the United States-Mexican War* (Plymouth, UK: Scarecrow Press, 1997).

Moses, Zebina, *The Sons of Michigan and the Michigan State Association of Washington, D.C., from December 1862, to December, 1912* (Washington?, n.p., 1912).

Moses, Zebina, *Historical Sketches of John Moses, of Plymouth, a Settler of 1633 to 1640; John Moses, of Windsor and Simsbury, a Settler Prior to 1647; and John Moses, of Portsmouth, a Settler Prior to 1640, also A Genealogical Record of some of their descendants* (Hartford, CT: Press of The Case, Lockwood & Brainard Company, 1890).

Muckenhoupt, Margaret, *Dorothea Dix: Advocate for Mental Health Care* (New York: Oxford University Press, 2003).

Mull, Carol E., *The Underground Railroad in Michigan* (Jefferson, NC: McFarland & Company, 2010).

Murdock, Eugene Converse. *One Million Men: The Civil War Draft in the North* (Madison: State Historical Society of Wisconsin, 1971).

Murdock, Eugene Converse, *Patriotism Limited, 1862–1865: The Civil War Draft and the Bounty System* (Kent, OH: Kent State University Press, 1967).

Officers of the Army and Navy (Volunteer) who served in the Civil War, ed. Lieutenant Colonel William H. Powell (Philadelphia: L. R. Hamersly & Co., 1893).

Owen, Thomas McAdory, *History of Alabama and Dictionary of Alabama Biography* (Chicago: S. J. Clarke Publishing Company, 1921), 4 vols.

Oxford Companion to American Military History, ed. John Whiteclay Chambers II (New York: Oxford University Press, 1999).

Palmer, Friend, *Early Days in Detroit, Papers written by General Friend Palmer of Detroit, being his personal reminiscences of important events and descriptions of the city for over eighty years* (Detroit: Hunt & June, 1906).

Pioneer Collections. *Report of the Pioneer Society of the State of Michigan, together with Reports of County, Town, and District Pioneer Societies* (Lansing: W. S. George & Co., Printers and Binders, 1874–1929), 40 vols.

Porter, George H., *Ohio Politics in the Civil War Period* (New York, 1911).

Portrait and Biographical Album of Ingham and Livingston Counties, Michigan (Chicago: Chapman Brothers, 1891).

Portrait and Biographical Album of Ionia and Montcalm Counties, Mich. Containing Full Page Portraits and Biographical Sketches of Prominent and Representative Citizens of the County Together with Portraits and Biographies of all the Presidents of the United States and Governors of the State (Chicago: Chapman Brothers, 1891).

Portrait and Biographical Record of Muskegon and Ottawa Counties, Michigan. Containing Biographical Sketches of Prominent and Representative Citizens, and of the Presidents of the United States (Chicago: Biographical Publishing, 1893).

Portrait and Biographical Album of Oakland County, Michigan (Chicago: Chapman Brothers, 1891).

Portrait and Biographical Album of Polk County, Iowa, containing Full page Portraits and Biographical Sketches of Prominent Representative Citizens of the County (Chicago: Lake City Publishing Co., 1890).

Portrait and Biographical Album of St. Joseph County, Michigan. Containing Full Page Portraits and Biographical Sketches of Prominent and Representative Citizens of the County, together with Biographies of all the Governors of the State, and of the Presidents of the United States (Chicago: Chapman Brothers, 1889).

Portrait and Biographical Record of Kalamazoo, Allegan and Van Buren Counties, Michigan, containing Biographical Sketches of Prominent and Representative Citizens (Chicago: Chapman Bros., 1892).

Portrait and Biographical Record of Saginaw and Bay Counties, Michigan, containing Biographical Sketches of Prominent and Representative Citizens, together with Biographies of all the Governors of the State, and of the Presidents of the United States (Chicago: Biographical Publishing Co., 1892).

Portraits and Biographies of the Governors of Michigan and of the Presidents of the United States (Chicago: Chapman Bros., 1885).

Potter, David, *The Impending Crisis: American Before the Civil War, 1848–1861* (New York: Harper Perennial, 2011).

Prescott, George B., *History, Theory, and Practice of the Electric Telegraph* (Boston: Ticknor and Fields, 1860).

Proceedings of the twenty-first Annual Meeting of the Michigan State Bar Association, Battle Creek, Michigan, July 6 and 7, 1911 (Grand Rapids, MI: West Michigan Printing, no date).

Raney, William Francis, *The Diplomatic and Military Activities in Canada, 1861–1865, as Affected by the American Civil War*, PhD diss., University of Wisconsin, 1918.

Reid, Richard M., *African Canadians in Union Blue: Volunteering for the Cause in the Civil War* (Vancouver, UBC Press, 2014), 106.

Reid, Whitelaw, *Ohio in the War: Her Statesmen, Generals, and Soldiers* (Cincinnati: Robert Clarke Company, 1895), 2 vols.

Report of the Annual Meeting of the Wisconsin State Bar Association held at the City of Milwaukee, February 17 and 18, 1903 (Madison, WI: Taylor and Gleason, 1903).

Rogers, Bradley A., *Guardian of the Great Lakes: The U.S. Paddle Frigate Michigan* (Ann Arbor: University of Michigan Press, 1996).

Romig, Walter, *Michigan Place Names: The History of the Founding and Naming of More than Five Thousand Past and Present Michigan Communities* (Detroit: Wayne State University Press, 1986).

Rosentreter, Roger L., *Grand Rapids and the Civil War* (Charleston, SC: History Press, 2018).

Ross, Robert B., *The Early Bench and Bar of Detroit: From 1805 to the end of 1850* (Detroit: Richard P. Joy and Clarence M. Burton, 1907).

Ross, Robert B., and George B. Catlin, *Landmarks of Detroit: A History of the City*, revised by Clarence W. Burton (Detroit: Evening News Association, 1898).

Ross, Robert B., and George B. Catlin, *Landmarks of Wayne County and Detroit* (Detroit: Evening News Association, 1898).

Rowland, Oran W., *A History of Van Buren County, Michigan: A Narrative Account of its Historical Progress, its People and its Principal Interests* (Chicago: Lewis Publishing Company, 1912), 2 vols.

Rusk, Jerrold G., *A Statistical History of the American Electorate* (Washington, DC: CQ Press, 2001).

Scharf, J. Thomas, *History of Maryland, from the Earliest Period to the Present Day* (Hatboro, PA: Tradition Press, 1879), 3 vols.

Schenck, John S., *History of Ionia and Montcalm Counties Michigan, with Illustrations and Biographical Sketches of their Prominent Men and Pioneers* (Philadelphia: D. W. Ensign & Co., 1881).

Schmutz, John F., *The Battle of the Crater: A Complete History* (Jefferson, NC: McFarland & Company, 2009).

Scott, Robert Garth, ed., *Forgotten Valor: The Memoirs, Journals, & Civil War Letters of Orlando B. Willcox* (Kent, OH: Kent State University Press, 1999).

Selcer, Richard F., *Civil War America: 1850 to 1875*, Almanacs of American Life series (New York: Infobase Publishing, 2006).

Seventy-Fifth Anniversary, General College of Oberlin College, 1833–1908, Including an Account of the Principal Events in the History of the College, with Illustrations of the College Buildings (Oberlin, OH: April 1, 1909).

Seward, Frederick, *Seward at Washington as Senator and Secretary of State: A Memoir of his Life, with Selections from his Letters, 1861–1872* (New York: Derby & Miller, 1891).

Shannon, B. Clay, *Still Casting Shadows: A Shared Mosaic of U.S. History*, vol. I, 1620–1913 (Lincoln, NE: iUniverse, 2006), 1 vol.

Sinisi, Kyle S., *Sacred Debts: State Civil War Claims and American Federalism, 1861–1880* (New York: Fordham University Press, 2003).

Smith, Edward Conrad, *The Borderland in the Civil War* (New York: MacMillan Company, 1927).

Snodgrass, Mary Ellen, *The Underground Railroad: An Encyclopedia of People, Places, and Operations*, vols. 1 and 2 (New York: Routledge, 2008).

Society of the Army of Cumberland Nineteenth Reunion, Chicago, Illinois (Cincinnati: Robert Clarke & Co., 1889).

Society of the Army of the Cumberland: Twenty-Seventh Reunion, Columbus Ohio, 1897, Published by Order of the Society (Cincinnati: Robert Clarke Company, 1898).

Spiro, Robert, *History of the Michigan Soldiers' Aid Society, 1861–1865*, PhD diss., University of Michigan, 1959.

St. Mary's Falls Canal, Michigan: Statistical Report of Lake Commerce Passing through Canals at Sault Ste. Marie Michigan and Ontario during the Season of 1921, with Supplementary Report of Commerce passing through the Detroit River (Washington, DC: Government Printing Office, 1922).

Stahr, Walter, *Seward: Lincoln's Indispensable Man* (New York: Simon & Schuster, 2012).

Steers, Edward, Jr., *The Lincoln Assassination Encyclopedia* (New York: Harper Perennial, 2010).

Stevens, Capt. C. A., *Berdan's United States Sharpshooters in the Army of the Potomac, 1861–1865* (Dayton, OH: Morningside Bookshop, 1972, reprint, 1892).

[Stewart, Morse], *Memorial of Mrs. Morse Stewart*, ed. by her husband, Morse Stewart, M.D. (Morse Stewart, 1889).

Streeter, Floyd Benjamin, *Political Parties in Michigan, 1837–1860: An Historical Study of Political Issues and Parties in Michigan from the Admission of the State to the Civil War* (Lansing: Michigan Historical Commission, 1918).

Sutherland, Jonathan, *African-Americans at War: An Encyclopedia* (Santa Barbara, CA: ABC-CLIO, 2004).

Swope, Belle McKinney Hays, *History of the Families of McKinney-Brady-Quigley* (Newville, PA: Franklin Repository Printery, 1905).

Tap, Bruce, *Over Lincoln's Shoulder: The Committee on the Conduct of the War* (Lawrence: University Press of Kansas, 1998).

Taylor, George Rogers, and Irene D. Neu, *The American Railroad Network, 1861–1890* (Chicago: University of Illinois Press, 2003).

Taylor, Paul, *"Old Slow Town": Detroit during the Civil War* (Detroit: Wayne State University Press, 2013).

Terrell, William H. H., *Indiana in the War of the Rebellion* (1869; repr., Indianapolis: Indiana Historical Society, 1960).

Thirty-Eighth Annual Reunion of the Association of Graduates of the United States Military Academy at West Point, New York, June 13, 1907 (Saginaw, MI: Seemann & Peters, 1907).

Transactions of the Grand Lodge, of Free and Accepted Masons of the State of Michigan (Grand Lodge F & A.M. Michigan, 1895).

Tredway, G. R., *Democratic Opposition to the Lincoln Administration in Indiana* (Indianapolis: Indiana Historical Bureau, 1973).

Trowbridge, Francis Bacon, *The Trowbridge Genealogy: History of the Trowbridge Family in America* (New Haven, CT: Printed for the Compiler, 1908).

Twice Told Tales of Michigan and Her Soldiers in the Civil War, ed. Minnie Dubbs Millbrook (Lansing: Michigan Civil War Centennial Observance Commission).

Under the Oaks: Commemorating the Fiftieth Anniversary of the Founding of the Republican Party, at Jackson, Michigan, July 6, 1854, ed. William Stocking (Detroit: Detroit Tribune, 1904).

Utley, Henry M., and Byron M. Cutcheon, *Michigan as a Province, Territory, and State, the Twenty-Sixth Member of the Federal Union* (New York: Publishing Society of Michigan, 1906), 4 vols.

Vallandigham, James Laird, *A Life of Clement L. Vallandigham, By His Brother* (Baltimore: Turnbull Brothers, 1872).

Vogel, Virgil J., *Indian Names in Michigan* (Ann Arbor: University of Michigan Press, 2005).

Walton, Hanes Jr., Sherman C. Puckett, and Donald R. Deskins Jr., *The African American Electorate: A Statistical History*, vol. 1 (Thousand Oaks, CA: CQ Press, 2012).

Warner, Ezra J., *Generals in Blue: Lives of the Union Commanders* (Baton Rouge: Louisiana State Press, 1999).

Warner, Ezra J., *Generals in Gray: Lives of the Confederate Commanders* (Baton Rouge: Louisiana State Press, 2008).

Wayne County Historical and Pioneer Society, *Chronography of Notable Events in the History of the Northwest Territory and Wayne County*, compiled by Fred. Carlisle (Detroit: O. S. Gulley, Bornman & Co., 1890).

Weber, Jennifer L., *Copperheads: The Rise and Fall of Lincoln's Opposition in the North* (New York: Oxford University Press, 2006).

Welcher, Frank J., *The Union Army, 1861–1865: Organization and Operations*, vols. I and II, *The Eastern Theater* (Indianapolis: Indiana University Press, 1993).

Welles, Albert, *History of the Welles Family in England and Normandy* (New York: Albert Welles, 1876).

Wert, Jeffry D., *Cavalryman of the Lost Cause: A Biography of J. E. B. Stuart* (New York: Simon & Schuster, 2008).

West Virginia Biographical Dictionary (St. Clair Shores, MI: Somerset Publishers, 1990).

Wheelock, Julia, S., *The Boys in White: The Experiences of a Hospital Agent in and around Washington* (New York: 1870).

The United States, ed. Edwin Wiley and Irving E. Rines (New York: American Educational Alliance, 1909), 6 vols.

Williams, Thomas Harry, *Lincoln and the Radicals* (Madison: University of Wisconsin Press, 1941).

Wilson, Mark R., *The Business of Civil War: Military Mobilization and the State, 1861–1865* (Baltimore: Johns Hopkins, 2006).

Winks, Robin W., *Canada and the United States: The Civil War Years* (Montreal: McGill–Queen's University Press, 1988).

Witteman, Barbara, *Dorothy Dix, Social Reformer* (Mankato, MN: Bridgestone Books, 2003).

Women and War: A Historical Encyclopedia from Antiquity to the Present, ed. Bernard A. Cook (Santa Barbara, CA: ABC-CLIO, 2006).

Woodford, Frank B., *Father Abraham's Children: Michigan Episodes in the Civil War* (Detroit: Wayne State University Press, 1999).

Woodford, Frank B., *Lewis Cass: The Last Jeffersonian* (London: Octagon Books, 1973).

Woodworth, Steven E., and Kenneth J. Winkle, *Atlas of the Civil War* (New York: Oxford University Press, 2004).

[WPA], *Michigan: A Guide to the Wolverine State, Compiled by workers of the Writers' Program of the Work Projects Administration in the State of Michigan* (New York: Oxford University Press, 1941).

Zachariah Chandler: An Outline Sketch of His Life and Public Services (Detroit: Detroit Post and Tribune Company, Publishers, 1880).

Zieglar-McPherson, Christina A., *Selling America: Immigration Promotion and the Settlement of the American Continent* (Santa Barbara, CA: ABC-Clio, 2017).

Index

Note: An asterisk [*] following a page number indicates a biographical entry. Locations for cities and counties can be found on the map at pages 4–5.

African American population, 75; American Party, 75; African American convention, 81, 82; Republican activities, 83; African American convention, 83; Burge's Western Sharpshooters, Company D, 106; Merrill's Horse, Companies H and I, 106; Dr. G.P. Miller, 110–11; Thirteenth Infantry, 120; Twentieth Infantry, 135; Sixteenth Infantry, 137; Merrill's Horse, Company L, 153; Western Sanitary Commission auxiliary, 156; First Michigan Sharpshooters, 164; Eleventh Cavalry, 175

Battles/Campaigns

Brady, Hugh, 7, 74

Bragg, Braxton, 136; invades Kentucky, 137; occupies Glasgow, Kentucky, 139; 140; orders to Morgan, 162

Brainard, Charles, 11

Brainard, Elmina, 11*; agent for Relief Association, 127; Wheelock joins, 143; to Gettysburg, 165; Washington activities, 183, 231; to Fredericksburg, 189

Branch County, map; 37th Congress, Second Congressional District, 63; First Regiment Light Artillery, Battery G, 120; 143; representation, Michigan Equal Rights League, 219; recruiting, **Chapter 237**, 227; 236n80

Brandenburg, Kentucky, 165

Brattleboro (Vermont) Academy, 65

Break-of-Day Base Ball Club (Jackson), 82

Breckenridge, John C., nominated, 81; 82, 84; Michigan election results, 1860, 84

Brent, Thomas, Lee, 11

Brent, Winifred Lee, 11

Brent, Jane W., 11*; Detroit Ladies' Christian Commission, founded and president, 175; Christian Commission, 230–31

Bridge, Henry P., 11–12*; 92

Bridgeport, Michigan, Thirtieth Infantry [second version], 210

Bridgeport, Tennessee, hospitals, 183

Brighton, Michigan, 36; Fifth Infantry, 105; Twenty-Second Infantry, 138

Bristol County (Massachusetts) Mutual Fire Insurance Company, 70

Brodhead, Thornton F., 12*; Cameron authorizes First Michigan Cavalry, 104; Detroit burial, 139; 243; 240

Bronson, Michigan, Eleventh Infantry, 108

Brookfield, Massachusetts, 17

Brooklyn, New York, 13, 23, 25, 74

Brooks Brothers (New York City), 245n43

Brooks, Michigan, Tenth Cavalry, 174

Brooks, William T. H., 174

Brough, John, Gettysburg cemetery dedication, 174

Brown, Butler, 164

Brown, John, 16, 77, 198

Brown, John Jr., *Philo Parsons*, 198

Brown, John Jr., sharpshooters, 120

Brown, T.J., 237n62

Brown University, 30, 138

Bryan, William Jennings, 51

Buckingham, Catharinus P., 6; visit to Cleveland, 129; 133; military service, racial restrictions, 133–34; draft, 135, 136, 137, 144, 145

Buckingham, William A., governors' petition, 1862 call, 246n86

Buchanan, James Jr., 11, 47, 64, 66; 1860 message, 66–67; 79;

83, 85; national day of fasting, and message to Congress, 87; 88, 90

Buchanan, Michigan, 36; Twelfth Infantry, 122; Twenty-Fifth Infantry, 141

Buckland, D.C., delegate to Chicago, 79

Buckner, Simon B., surrenders, 215

Buell, Don Carlos, 121, 137, 139, 142; Rosecrans replaces, 144

Buffalo Bill's Wild West Show, 37

Buffalo, New York, 13, 29, 70; Western Sanitary Commission, 107; rumors of rebel attack, 173, 174

Buhl, Christian H., 12*, 76, 92

Burley, [postwar, Burleigh] Bennett G., 12*; *Philo Parsons*, 197–98

Burlington, Vermont, 18, 72

Burns, Anthony, 50

Burnside, Ambrose E., 24, 41, 154; relieves Wright, 158; surrendering black employee incident, 159; GO No. 38, 159, 160; arrests Vallandigham, 160; implications, 251n51; GO No. 84, closes *Chicago Times*, 161; Stanton letter, 161; Morgan, 165; Stanton authorizes black troops, 167

Burns, Michigan, Sixth Cavalry, 144

Burr, Aaron, 71

Burr Oak, Michigan, Seventh Michigan, 104; First Michigan, 107; Eleventh Infantry, 108; Fifteenth Infantry, 123

Burton, Michigan, Twenty-Ninth Infantry, 199

Burton, William, Altoona Address, 141

Butcher, William, 237n62

Butler, Benjamin, 64

Butler County, Pennsylvania, 12

Butler, Henry F., National Equal Rights League, 199

Butler, Isaiah, 13*; 108; investigated, 111; arrested, 112; released, 121; 124; 243n240

Butler, William A., 13*; Relief Committee, 125

Butternuts, New York, 45

Byrd, J.J., Faulkner riot aftermath, 158

Byron, Michigan, Tenth Michigan, 121

Byron, New York, 39

Cairo, Illinois, 56, 96; **GO No. 1**, 120; **GO No. 91**, Naval recruitment stations, 187

Caleb Cushing, 163

Caledonia, Michigan, Twenty-Third Infantry, musters, 139; Sixth Cavalry, 144

Calhoun County, map; 27, 32; 37th Congress, Third Congressional District, 63; Democratic election gains, 124; 154; militia draft deficiency, 181; draft, 191; representation, Michigan Equal Rights League, 219; troop contribution, 225–26; 236n80; draft eligible men, 248n198

Calhoun, John C., 199; arguments recycled, 250n17

California, 9, 13, 20, 28, 40, 49, 50, 81, 123

Gamble, Hamilton R., 102; Altoona Address, 141; governors' petition, 1862 call, 246n86

Garnettesville, Kentucky, Morgan, 164

Garrison, William Lloyd, 44

Genesee County, map; 20, 28; Thirty-Seventh Congress, Fourth Congressional District, 63; militia draft deficiency, 181; 236n80; state laws supporting bounties, pay, family aid, 263n131

Geneva, New York, 25

Georgetown, D.C., 151; camps in, 183; Michigan hospital aid to, 207; 215

Georgetown, Michigan, 10, 93, 99

Georgia, 9, 28, 66, 78; secedes, 88; 145, 170, 187, 189, 193, 195, 199

Germans, homesteading, 56–57; Michigan settlement, 75, 76; Anti-Know Nothing Party, 75; in Detroit, 76; Faulkner riot involvement, 157; blamed for Chancellorsville defeat, 159

German Protestant Church (Detroit), 156

German States, 75; nativity of Michigan force, 226

Gettysburg, 38; dedication of national cemetery, 174; Michigan agent hospital visits, 183; No. 1: Soldiers' National Cemetery at Gettysburg (1864), 204; **No. 118** (1865), 222

Gettysburg Commission, 21, 167, 168; meeting of cemetery commissioners, 176

Gibbs, Alfred, 22*, 115

Gibbs, C.C., Michigan New York Aid Society, 249n228

Gibson, William K., 22*; status report, 100; resigns, 139

Giddings, Joshua, 172

Giddings, Marsh, 22–23*; National Union (Republican) Convention, replaces Blair, 191

Giddings, Orrin N., 23*, 26; replaces Hammond, QMG, 214

Gilbert, C.T., Michigan New York Aid Society, 249n228

Gilbert, Thomas D., 23*; 115

Gilman, John Briggs, 23*; appointed, hospitals, camps covered, 175, 184; 190; 1864 summary, 208; 229

"The Girl I Left Behind Me," 97

Gladwin County, map; 37th Congress, Fourth Congressional District, 63

Glasgow, Kentucky, 139

Glasgow, Scotland, 12

Glasgow, University (Scotland), 24

Gould, Benjamin Apthorp, 226; see 264n8 for ages of enlistments.

"Government Kitchen," state relief during war, 14

Grain, 57

Granby, Massachusetts, 21

Grand Army of the Republic, 7

Grand Haven city, map; 13, 21, 23; rail, 56, 57; African Americans meet, 82; Republican activities, 83; pro-war meeting, 94; reaction to Shiloh, 124; Twenty-First Infan-

try, 138; Fifth Cavalry, 145–46; contribute, Northwestern Soldiers' Fair, 171; Soldiers' Aid Society, fundraising Gettysburg, 164; First Michigan Sharpshooters, 164; Richmond's fall, 213; Lincoln's assassination, 214

Grand Haven News, 13; Fort Henry, 121; reaction to Seven Days', 128; Chandler's re-election, 154; Enrollment Act, 156; Union League Convention, 160; Vicksburg, 164; Thirteenth Amendment, 211; Lincoln inaugurated, 212–13

Grand Rapids, city, map; 7, 11, 23, 24, 27, 28, 33, 34, 42–43, 45, 67, 68; size, 74; foreign immigration, 75; American Party, 75; Republican activities, Wide Awakes, 83; Third Infantry musters, 99; women, supplies sent, 100; 103; Eighth Infantry organizes, 104; Innes, 106; Eighth Infantry, 107; Second Cavalry, musters, 109; First Michigan Engineers, 110; Third Cavalry, musters, 111; First Regiment Light Artillery, Batteries B and C muster, 112; First Regiment Light Artillery, Battery E, 114; Fourteenth Infantry, 121; reaction to Shiloh, 124; Twenty-First Infantry, 138; Sixth Cavalry, 144; Seventh Cavalry, 154; First Regiment Light Artillery, Battery K, 155; Western Sanitary Commission auxiliary, 156; Battery M (Thirteenth Battery), 162; contribute, Northwestern Soldiers' Fair, 171; Tenth Cavalry, 174; draft rendezvous, 182; draft rendezvous to Jackson, 187; P.C. Wright arrested, 188; Third Infantry, Veteran Volunteers, 200; private aid to patients at 207

Grand Rapids & Northern Railroad, 28

Grand Rapids, Draft Rendezvous, 25

Grand Rapids Enquirer, 42

Grand Review, Washington, 1865, 215

Grand River bands, Ottawa and Chippewa, 35

Grand River Times, 46

Grand Traverse, city, Twenty-Sixth Infantry, 146

Grand Traverse County, map; 37th Congress, Fourth Congressional District, 63

Grand Trunk Railroad, 57

Granger, Bradley, 67*; 82; 1860 election result, 84; 86; election result, 144

Granger, Gordon, 23*; colonel, Second Cavalry, 113; brigade, 126

Granson Street, Jackson, 82

Grant, Ulysses S., mentioned, 9, 15, 20, 23, 31, 33; in Detroit, 43, 73; meets Truth, 45; 47, 50, 64, 67, 70; Robertson dinner, 72; Belmont, 111; attacks Forts Henry and Donelson, 121; 146; 156, 159, 160; praised, 164; reopens Tennessee River, 171; appointed lieutenant general, 187; accelerates troops, 187; 196; *River Queen*, conference, Appomattox Campaign, 213; Appomattox Court House, 213; 214; visits Detroit, 218; "cracker line," 253–54n173; Detroit background, Julia Dent Grant, 263n99

Grass Lake, Michigan, Twentieth Infantry, 135

Hartranft, John, 37

Harvard Law School, 12, 30, 39, 46

Harvard Medical School, 17

Hastings, Michigan, Twenty-First Infantry, 138

Hawes, Richard, 143

Haxall's Landing, Virginia, 132

Hayden, Henry A., 26*; 92

Hayes, Rutherford B., 44, 68

Headley, John W., 27

Heidelberg University (Germany), 34

Heintzelman, Samuel P., 50; commands Northern Department, 185; prohibits firearms, 194; draft to commence, 196–97; relieves, 199

Helena, Arkansas, 27

Henderson, John B., U.S. Senate resolution to abolish, 185

Henrietta, Michigan, draft, 154

Heth, Henry, 139

H.H. Crapo, 71

Highland, Michigan, Ladies' Aid Society, 104

Hill, Bennett J., 26*; AAPMG instructions on state relations, 159; **Enrollment Act** enforcement, 161; accelerates enrollment, 162; Michigan anti-draft sentiment, report from Newberry, 165, 167; report, 165–66; troops for enforcement, depleted regiments recruit, 166; reports Michigan affairs, 167; status report, draft enforcement, 167–68; draft dates, 169; notice of draft, and supervisory duty, 171; draft set, 171; if quotas filled, 172; rebel activities reports, 172–74; governors to lead recruitment, 173; plans to thwart rebel attack, 173–74; apportioning quotas, 175, 176; 182; bounties extended, 185; legislators denounce, 185–86; draft suspended, 187; troop acceleration, 187; from Fry, enrollment, 189; Michigan quotas, July call, 193; illegal recruiting, 194; licensing firearms, 194; draft postponement, 195; disputes draft postponement, 196; draft to commence, 196; VRC enlistments, 197; meets Hyams, *Philo Parsons*, 197–98; arresting draft evaders, 199; internal security, Union Leagues, 201; alert on rebels in Canada, 202–3; from Fry, new quota calculations, 204; Michigan quota, 210; from Fry, New York City draft fraud, 211; recalculates Michigan quota, 211; Order to cease drafting and recruiting, 214; Order discharging recruits and draftees in rendezvous, 215; complaints about Hill, referred to Committee on Federal Relations 256n14; 1864 AG Report, draft and enlistments, Hill and Robertson compared, 260n210

Hill, Daniel Harvey, 132

Hillsdale city, *map*; 18, 24, 46; pro-war meeting, 94; 100; Second Cavalry, 109; First Regiment Light Artillery, Battery G, 120; Tenth Michigan, 121; Eighteenth Infantry, musters, 137; Western Sanitary Commission auxiliary, 156; Soldiers' Aid Society, fundraising Gettysburg, 164; Eleventh Cavalry, 175; Thirtieth Infantry [second version], 210; Richmond's fall, 213; Lincoln's assassination, 214; 231

Hillsdale College, 20, 30, 49; celebrates emancipation, 146; arms to student militia, 151

Hillsdale County, *map*; Thirty-Seventh Congress, Second Congressional District, 63; delayed October 1863 draft, 171; 200; representation, Michigan Equal Rights League, 219; 236n80

Hillsdale Democrat, reaction to Fort Sumter, 91; 94

Hillsdale Standard, endorses Lincoln, 80; on election results, 84; on secession, 87; Chandler's re-election, 154; Vicksburg, 164; Cleveland Convention, 190; Atlanta victory, 195; McClellan's acceptance, 196; Holt Report, 200; **Thirteenth Amendment**, 21

Hincks, Edward, 211

Hinesburg, Vermont, 27

Hines, Thomas Henry, Hines raid, 162

Hiram College, 37

Historical Society of Michigan, 46

Hoffman, William, 173

Holland, Michigan, Twenty-Fifth Infantry, 141

Holly, Michigan, 71

Holmes, Andrew Hunter, 73

Holt, Joseph, 6; secretary of war, 86, 87, 88; Holt Report on subversive organizations, 199–200; skepticism, 200

Hood, John Bell, 139, 141

Hooker, Joseph, 64; relieves Burnside, 154; Chancellorsville, 159; with Blair, 161; Confederate movement, 161; pursues Lee, 162; relieves Heintzelman, 199; to Stanton, incursions, 201; urges new regiment, 201

Hopkins, Guy S., 26*; 47, 108; hoax letter, 109; investigated, 111; arrested, Detroit, 112; KGC, 113; released, 121; controversy, 123; 124

Horseheads, New York, 44

Hot Springs, Arkansas, 33, 36

Houghton County, *map*; 58; Thirty-Seventh Congress, Fourth Congressional District, 63; foreign immigration, 75

Houghton city, foreign immigration, 75; Twenty-Third Infantry, musters, 139; Twenty-Seventh Infantry, 158

Howard, Jacob M., 21, 34, 61, 63; 65–66*; 70, 82, 83, 85; elected senate, 120; presents Joint Resolution 1, 122; Pierce debate, 123–24; advises Lincoln, peace negotiations, 165; supports abolition resolution, 188; resolution, Fort Pillow massacre, 188; Wade-Davis Bill, dispute, 192; re-elected, 210; **Thirteenth Amendment**, notice to Crapo, 211; speaker, Lincoln mourning, 214; eulogizes, 214; Twenty-Fourth recruiting, 247n130

Howard, Joshua, 26–27*; paymaster, 123

Howard, Luke, 14*; Michigan Soldiers' Relief Association of the District of Columbia, 231

ment, 82; 83; pro-war rally, 91–92; Second Infantry, 95; women, supplies sent, 100; 103; First Michigan, 107; Ninth Infantry, 110; Third Cavalry, 111; subversive organizations, 123; pro-war rally, 132; rail linkages, 134; Twentieth Infantry, musters, 135; Sixteenth Infantry, 137; Fourth Cavalry, 138; conservative Republicans meet, 139; 140; Union Party (Democratic Party) convenes, 143; Twenty-Sixth Infantry, 146; Western Sanitary Commission auxiliary, 156; Federal **Enrollment** (Act of March 3, 1863), commences, finishes, 162; First Michigan Sharpshooters, 164; contribute, Northwestern Soldiers' Fair, 171; First Michigan Colored Infantry recruitment tour, 175; Newberry visit, 182; Fourteenth Independent Battery, musters, 185; draft rendezvous to Jackson, 187; Twenty-Eighth Infantry, 201; camp, Thirtieth Michigan, 202; recruiting camp, VRC, 202; private aid to patients at 207; Eleventh Regiment departs, 213; Appomattox Court House surrender, celebration, 213; Lincoln's assassination, 214; Twentieth Infantry, 215; Twenty-Fifth Infantry, 216; Battery A, First Michigan Light Artillery, Battery F, First Michigan Light Artillery, Thirteenth Michigan Battery, Fourteenth Battery, Eighteenth Infantry, Tenth Infantry, Ninth Cavalry, Battery H, First Michigan Light Artillery, 217; Thirteenth Infantry, 217–18; Battery E, Battery M, Battery D, Battery G, First Michigan Light Artillery, Battery L, First Michigan Light Artillery, 218; representation, Michigan Equal Rights League, 219; Eleventh Michigan, 219

Jackson City Hall, 63, 132

Jackson County, *map*; 22, 25; Thirty-Seventh Congress, First Congressional District, 63; 70; Democratic election gains, 124; draft begins, 154–55; Federal **Enrollment Act** (March 3, 1863), commences, 161–62; conscription results, 166; draft, 191; 236n80; state laws supporting bounties, pay, family aid, 263n131

Jackson County Bar Association, 25, 52

Jackson Guard Band, 82

Jackson Hall (Michigan), 52, 91

Jackson (Michigan) *Patriot*, founding, 41

Jackson, Mississippi, Vicksburg campaign, 160; Sherman v. Johnston, 166

Jackson, Thomas J. ("Stonewall"), 123, 126, 138–39; captures Harper's Ferry, 140

James Island, South Carolina, 127

Jarvis, George E., Michigan New York Aid Society, 249n228

Jay Treaty, 1794, 60

J.B. Crippen & Co., 15

Jefferies, N.L., 6

Jefferson Avenue, Detroit, 94

Jefferson Barracks Hospital, St. Louis, Missouri, 186

Jefferson City, Missouri, 90

Jefferson County, West Virginia, 9

Jefferson Medical College (Pennsylvania), 45

Jefferson Street (Detroit), Soldiers' Home, 208

Jefferson, Thomas, 90

Jeffersonville, Indiana, rail, 56; State Agent Gilman, hospitals, 175 Michigan agent visits hospitals, 184; 208; Fifth Michigan, Sixteenth Infantry, 217

Jenkins, Richard, alias, 111

Jerome, Arizona, 32

Jerome, David H., 28*; Grand Review, 215

Jewish synagogue, Detroit, 111

Johnny: The True Story of a Civil War Legend, 15

Johnny Shiloh, 15

Johnson, Andrew, 8, 42, 43, 64, 66, 67, 68, 70, 71; military governor, 126; National Union (Republican) Convention, 191; Michigan endorses, 192; 196; election, 202; becomes seventeenth president, 214; proclamation, day of mourning, 214; reschedules, 215; declares hostilities over, national day of mourning, 215; Michigan Equal Rights League denounces, 219; restores habeas corpus, 219; presidential reconstruction, 231; governors' petition, 1862 call, 246n86

Johnson, David, 28–29*; 155; election loss, 202

Johnson, Herschel V., Michigan election results, 1860, 84

Johnson, Louise, 29*; Michigan Soldiers' Relief Association of the District of Columbia, 231

Johnson's Island, 9, 26, 43; Tennessean POWs transported to, 139; Johnson's Island attack warning, 172–73; rebel steamers, 173; Smith report, 173–74; attempt to liberate, 194; *Philo Parsons*, 197–98; plot to free prisoners, 198

Johnston, Joseph, 166

Johnstown, New York, 14

Joliet, Illinois, rail linkages, 134

Jones, DeGarmo, 29*; regiment status, 120

Jones House, Harrisburg, 176

Jones, John M., 173

Jonesville, Michigan, 9, 100; Ladies' Aid Society, 104; Seventh Michigan, 104; Eighteenth Infantry, 137

Joy, James F., signs equal suffrage petition, 212 and 261n8

Joy & Porter, 46

Kalamazoo city, *map*; 23, 29, 38, 42, 46, 47, 50; Under the Oaks, 63; 68, 71; size, 74; American Party, 75; Douglas Club formed, badges, 82; 83; Ladies' Aid Society, 104; Sixth Infantry, 104; First Cavalry, 106; Second Cavalry, 109; Forty-Fourth Illinois, 110; 118; Thirteenth Infantry, musters, 120; First Regiment Light Artillery, Battery G, 120; subversive organizations, 123; war rally, bounties and family aid, 132; Sixteenth Infantry, 137; Nineteenth Infantry, 138; Fifth Cavalry, 145–46; Western Sanitary

draft riots, 182; credits, 182; summary, 181–82; October 17, 1863, 171

—1864: Lincoln's 500,000 call, February 1, draft, March 10, 186; quota status, 186; comparison, New York and Michigan, and definition, "First Class," 186; draft suspended, draft rendezvous to Jackson, Wormer commands, 187; statewide draft commences, 191; draft postponed, 196; draft to commence, 197; Lincoln call, 203; summary, 206–7; 1864 AG Report, draft and enlistments, Hill and Robertson compared, 260n210; February 1, 1864, 186; March 14, 1864, 187; July 18, 1864, 193; December 19, 1864, 203; see years of service calculation by Michigan congressional district, 261n18, 22

—1865: **Circular No. 1** controversy, 210; surpluses allowed, 210; 25% quota reduction, 211; quota study commission, 211–12; Michigan quota confirmed, Lincoln orders draft, 212; Order to cease drafting and recruiting, 214; Order discharging recruits and draftees in rendezvous, 215

Michigan Economy, generally, 1861, 56–58; 1862 summary, 152; 1863 summary, 182; effect of passport system on, 204; *Free Press* on passport enforcement, 260n190; 1864 military spending, 208; agricultural production, ranked, 57; average wages, army wages, 58; basis, 233n20; Banks and banking, ranked, 58; manufacturing, ranked, 57–58; wartime, 151; Occupations, 57; Overall values, 56; revenue through Lock, 56; state homesteading, 56–57, 76; tax contributions to war, 58

Michigan elections, See Act No 21 (1864), 205 and *Twitchell v. Blodgett*, 211; presidential, 1856, 75–76; presidential, 1860, 84; November, 1860, 84; March, 1862, 122, 124; November, 1862, 144–45 and analysis; April, 1863: 158;November, 1864, federal and state, and analysis, 202

Michigan Exchange, 84, 92, 131

Michigan Family Aid: Michigan and local family aid, 58, 93, 94, 95; legislation, 117; in Kalamazoo, 132; Democrats endorse, 143; see **No. 14**: to provide for the relief by counties of the families of volunteers mustered from this State into the military service of the United States, or of this State, 147–48; **Joint Resolution No. 7**: 148; **No. 16**: for the re-organization of the military forces of the State of Michigan, 148–46; Blair message, 177; **No. 14**: to legalize certain volunteer family relief orders in the county of Clinton, 177; **Joint Resolution No. 20**: relative to frauds against the government of the United States, 180; **No. 161**: 180; **No. 173**, 180–81; **No. 211**: An Act to establish a military school, 181; **No. 220**: to allow Wayne County to issue bonds for the volunteers' relief fund, 181; **No. 228** (1865), 222; summary, family aid, 228–29

Michigan Federal Enrollment (Act of March 3, 1863), commences, Jackson, 161–62

Michigan, finances, Volunteer Bounty Bonds, 178; War Bounty Bonds, 205, 206, 222; War Fund, state agents, disability 177; bounties, 178; funding Gettysburg cemetery, 204; War Loan/Bonds, 151, 152; War Loan Sinking Fund, 152

—1860: 86

—1861: Financing the war, 92, 93; indemnity act, 102; amounts due, 1861, 119; Twenty Millions' tax and Michigan assessment, 102; family aid bonds, 117; debt service, 117–18; War Loan of the State of Michigan, 118; summary, 118–19; Treasurer's report, 119; unit stand up costs, 119

—1862: **No. 1**: direct taxes imposed by the Congress of the United States, 146–47; stand up costs, 150; War Loan, financing troops, 151; effect of non-payment of soldiers' wages, 152; 1862 summary, revenues, debt, expenses, 152

—1863: **No. 85**: to pay interest on the war loan, 178; **No. 5**: authorizing a war loan, 118; **No. 110**: to provide a tax for the expenses of the State government, 179; 1863 summary, 183, 184

—1864: **No. 22**: to pay interest on the war bounty loan, 205; **No. 23**: authorizing the payment of bounties to volunteers in the service of the United States, 205; **No. 24**: authorizing a war bounty loan, 205–6; 1864 summary, 209

—1865: **No. 85**, 221; **No. 86**, 221–22; **No. 295**, 222; summary, and U.S. reimbursement, 228

Michigan forts, 55

Michigan, franchise restrictions, 59; popular vote fails, 61

Michigan Free Soil party, mentioned biographies, 27, 41, 50, 65, 67, 70; Free Soil, 9, 14, 67; 1848 Buffalo Convention, 27; 50, 70; free soil Democrats, 63, 65; Van Buren-Adams ticket, 67; Blair and, 70

Michigan, geography, 55–56; protection of lake commerce, 146

Michigan, governor, constitutional powers, 59

Michigan House, attitude towards Peace Conference, 88; re-elects Howard, 210; Judiciary Committee, refuses liberty law repeal, 89

Michigan, immigration, commissioners, 57; by country, county, city, 75; generally, 75–76; Office of Foreign Immigration, 76

Michigan, interracial marriage banned, 61

Michigan in the War, 72, 226

Michigan Invasion, subversion, concerns, 56, 60, 73, 110; troops to locks, 115; Old State Guard, formed, 135; **Joint Resolution No. 6**: to endow and military school in the State of Michigan, 147; **Joint Resolution No. 9**: relative to the frontier defences of this State, 148; distribution of arms to frontier, 151; **GO No. 2**, troops to resist invasion, 167; fears of rebel attacks, 172–73; Lake Erie survey, 175; *Philo Parsons*, 197–98; Hooker, incursions, 201; fear attack on Detroit, from Canada, 202–3; QMG **GO No. 58**,

Mishawaka, Michigan, 41

Missaukee County, *map*; Thirty-Seventh Congress, Fourth Congressional District, 63

Mississippi, 38, 66, 78, 80; secession, 88; Iuka, 140; Corinth, 143; Chickasaw Bayou, 146; Grierson raid, 159; Tupelo, 193

Mississippi River, 30, 56, 88; free navigation promised, 89; strategic value, 96; 105, 127; federal control, 164

Mississippi River Valley, 56, 96, 109

Mississippi Valley, 25

Missouri, 50, 61, 67, 89; secession, 90; 98, 99; clash at Carthage, 100; pro-Union convention, 102; Confederates fund Missouri militia, 103; Confederacy accepts, 104; Fremont emancipates, 105; Western Sanitary Commission, 107; 108, 109, 113; Michigan deployments, 118; Pea Ridge, 122; subversive activities, 194; military intervention, 194–95; Holt Report on subversive organizations, 199–200; Michigan aid to forces, 230

Mr. Mills (Hopkins hoax), 109

Mobile, Alabama, 68; besieged, 213; occupied, 214

Moller's contract, 110

Monck, Charles Stanley, Fourth Viscount Monck, 12; warns U.S., rebel attacks, 173; release of raiders, crisis, U.S.-Canadian relations, 203

Monguagon, Michigan, Ninth Cavalry, 160

Monroe city, *map*; 14, 15, 25, 31, 34, 39, 50; rail, 56, 57; size, 74; Republican activities, Wide Awakes, 83; 100; women, supplies sent, 100; Seventh Infantry, musters, 104; 118; Fourteenth Infantry, 121; Fifteenth Infantry musters, 123; rail linkages, 134; Eighteenth Infantry, 137; Ninth Cavalry, 160; Eleventh Cavalry, 175

Monroe County, *map*; 45; Thirty-Seventh Congress, Second Congressional District, 63; delayed October 1863 draft, 171; militia draft deficiency, 181; 236n80

"Monroe Fair Oaks" farm, 25

Monroe, James, 32–33*; deputy provost marshal, 162

Monroe Street (Detroit), 156

Montague City, Massachusetts, 7

Montcalm County, *map*; Thirty-Seventh Congress, Third Congressional District, 63

Monterrey, battle of (Mexico), 33

Montgomery, Alabama, 88, 89, 93

Monthly Hesperian, 8

Montmorency County, *map*; Thirty-Seventh Congress, Fourth Congressional District, 63

Montreal, Canada, 18, 37, 39, 43, 172, 202–3, 204

Montrose, J.T., Michigan New York Aid Society, 249n228

Moore, Frank, 17

Moore, John, 144

Morenci, Michigan, Eleventh Infantry, 108

Morgan, Edwin D., governors' meeting, 85; 96; Astor House meeting, 128; meets Buckingham, 129; Altoona Conference, 141; 238n78; approach to Blair, Lincoln 1862 call, 246n85

Morgan, George W., 138

Morgan, John Hunt, 16, 24, 32, 41, 52; launches first raid, 129; approaches Cincinnati, 130; raids Indiana, 132; moves into Tennessee, 132; Great Raid, 162; Hines raid, 162; crosses Cumberland River, 163; in Kentucky, 164; crosses to Indiana, Ohio, 165; Buffington Island, 166; POW, Salinesville, Ohio Penitentiary, 167; escape, 175; death, 196; 228

Morley, Frederick, 33*; 126; to Fry, 188

Morrill Tariff Act, 88

Morrison, William V., 33*; 155; arguments, 250n17

Morrow, Henry, 33*; Relief Committee, 125; speaks, July 1862 rally, 130–31; speech, 132; accepts flags, 188; monument committee, 216

Morton, Oliver P., 96, 98; attends Cleveland meeting, 129; western propaganda campaign, 129–30; Kentucky invasion, 138; Altoona Conference, 141; rogue legislature, 154; Gettysburg cemetery dedication, 174; governors' petition, 1862 call, 246n86; Twenty-Fourth recruiting, 247n130

Moses, Zebina, 24; 33*; Michigan Soldiers' Relief Association of the District of Columbia, 231

Mount Clemens, *map*; 40, 43; American Party, 75; war meeting, 94; Ladies' Aid Society, 104; Fifth Infantry, 105; Ninth Infantry, 110; subversive organizations, 123; Twenty-Second Infantry, 138; 144; Twenty-Sixth Infantry, 146; Eighth Cavalry, musters, 159–60; First Michigan Light Artillery, Battery M, 163

Mt. Morris, New York, 31

Mt. Vernon, Ohio, Vallandigham speech, 159, 160

Muhlenberg, Rev. William A., 13

Mulligan, James A., 31; 110

Munfordville, Kentucky, army near, GO No. 1, 120; 139

Murfreesboro, Tennessee, hospitals, 183; Twenty-Ninth Infantry, 218

Murphy, William Walton, 34*; Delegate to Chicago, 79

Muskegon, Michigan, 45; African Americans, Battle Creek Convention, 82; 99; Twenty-Sixth Infantry, 146; Thirtieth Infantry [second version], 210

"My Experience as a Prisoner of War, and Escape from Libby Prison", 31

Mystery, 17

Nankin, Michigan, state laws supporting bounties, pay, family aid, 263n131

Napoleon III, 169

Ninth Upper Canadian Military District, 37

Noble, David A., 34*; accused of treason, 200; election loss, 202

Normal School (Indiana County, Pennsylvania), 20

Norris, Lyman D., 34*; presides, Democratic State Convention, 143

North Adams, Michigan, Soldiers' Aid Society, fundraising Gettysburg, 164

North Branch, map; 13, 26, 47, 108, 109; disloyal persons, 111; 112; subversive organizations, 123

North Carolina, 28; secedes, 98; Michigan deployments, 174, 175

Northern Department, 39

Northampton Association, 44

North Star, 17

North Vernon, Indiana, 24

Northville, Michigan, war meeting, 94; Fifth Cavalry, 145–46

Northern Pacific Railroad, 24

Northwestern Confederacy, Holt Report, 200

Northwestern Conference, 23

Northwest Ordinance, 60

Northwest sectionalism, 153

Northwest Territory, 66

Norwich, New York, 20

Nullification Crisis, 66

Oakland County, map; 41, 44; Thirty-Seventh Congress, Fourth Congressional District, 63; 69; foreign immigration, 75; Democratic election gains, 124; 231; 236n80; draft eligible men, 248n198; state laws supporting bounties, pay, family aid, 263n131

Oberlin College, 15, 20, 21, 49

Oberlin Seminary, 49

Oceana County, map; 35; Thirty-Seventh Congress, Third Congressional District, 63; Native American population, 75; Pentwater, 163; Native American recruiting, 227, 228

Odd Fellows' Literary Magazine, 8

O'Donnell, Malachi J., 35*; sword presentation, 136

Ogdensburg, New York, Stanton alerts rebel plot, 254n189

Ogemaw County, map; 37th Congress, Fourth Congressional District, 63

Ohio, 18, 20, 29, 36, 41, 43, 46, 55, 56, 57; southern population, 61; 74, 75, 89; governor, 96, 98; riverine war, 102–3; Western Sanitary Commission, 107; 108; railroads, 134; Department of the Ohio, 135; state agents, 139; Altoona Conference, 138–42; 158, 162; six month militia call, 162; Morgan approaches, enters, 165; six-month call ended, 167; Vallandigham, governor, 168; fears rebel attacks, 173; in Northern Department, 185; 100-day troops, 188; subversive activities, 194; firearms banned, 194; Peace

Democrats, 195; Holt Report on subversive organizations, 199–200; comparative, manpower contribution and percentages, 225; nativity of Michigan force, 226; mean age at enlistment, 264n8

Ohio River, 14, 56, 75, 89, 96; Morgan Raid, 132; 162; Hines raid, 162; Morgan, 164, 165

Ohio River Valley, 56

Ohio Third Volunteers (War of 1812), 66

Ojibwa language, 23; tour, 37

Ojibwa people, 228

Old Northwest, 56, 57, 74, 225

Olean, New York, 21

Olden, Charles Smith, Altoona Address, 141; governors' petition, 1862 call, 246n86

Olivet College, 29

Omaha, Nebraska, 31

One Hundred and Thirtieth New York Infantry, 22

Oneida Castle, New York, 35

Oneida people, 227

Onondaga County, New York, 69

Ontario (Canada), 37, 191; Native American troop contribution, 227

Ontonagon County, map; 58; Thirty-Seventh Congress, Fourth Congressional District, 63; Indian attacks feared, 151; Twenty-Seventh Infantry, 158

Ontonagon River, 56; **Joint Resolution No. 1** (1865), 220

Orange, New Jersey, 24

Oregon, 74, 81

Order of American Knights ("OAK"), 52–53; Vallandigham meets with, 186; Order of the Sons of Liberty, supreme commander, 186; P.C. Wright arrested, 188; uprising, 194; Indianapolis trial, 198; Holt Report on subversive organizations, 199–200

Orion, Michigan, Tenth Michigan, 121

Osage Indian Agency, 16

Osceola County, map; Thirty-Seventh Congress, Fourth Congressional District, 63

Oscoda County, map; Thirty-Seventh Congress, Fourth Congressional District, 63

Oshtemo, Michigan, Twenty-Fifth Infantry, 141

Ossining, New York, 44

Oswego, New York, 70; Stanton alerts rebel plot, 254n189

"O Tanenbaum, O Tanenbaum," 11

Otisco, Michigan, Twenty-Fifth Infantry, 141

Otsego, Michigan, Thirteenth Infantry, 120

Otsego County, map; Thirty-Seventh Congress, Fourth Congressional District, 63

Ottawa County, map; Thirty-Seventh Congress, Third Congressional District, 63; 74; African Americans, 82; 236n80

Ottawa people, 35; Pentwater village, recruiting, 163, 227

Rhode Island, 18, 89, 129; state agents, 139; Altoona Conference, 138–42; Michigan recruiting, 169; repeal personal liberty law, 238n78

Rice, Reuben N., 37*; visits Shiloh, 125; returning soldiers, 215

Richards, Fannie, 37–38

Richards, John D., 37–38*; National Equal Rights League, 199; equal suffrage petition, 210 and 261n8; role at National Equal Rights League Convention, 219

Richardson, Israel B., 38*; Second Regiment, 95; First Bull Run, 101; mortally wounded, 140; burial, 145

Richard III, 112

Richfield, New York, 35, 36

Richland, Michigan, 22–23, 30; Eighth Infantry, 107

Richmond, Kentucky, 137

Richmond, New York, 41

Richmond, Virginia, 9, 12, 16, 80, 81, 128, 129, 186; private aid to Michigan POWs, 207; fall, 213; Twenty-Third Illinois, 216

Riddle, Albert G., 64

Riley, Henry H., 38*, 77, 78; nominated, 143; Michigan New York Aid Society, 249n228

Ripley, James W., 6, 126

Ripley, Roswell S., 28

Rittenhouse Academy (Washington, DC), 33

River Queen, conference, 213

Riverside, California, 22

Robertson, John, 27, 29, 71, 72*; appointed AG, 91; 92; lobbies Chandler, 93; established headquarters, 94; advises status, Union Defence Committee, 96; replies Cameron, 97; 99; updates War Department, 110; status of Michigan units, 114; 1861 Report, 118–19; 123; Relief Committee, and visits Shiloh, 125; visits Shiloh, promotes Sheridan, 126; lobbies Blair for regiment, 131; status report, 134, 135; units forward, 136; 139; disputes figures, 169 and reply; bans out of state recruiters, 169; criticized, black recruitment meeting, 170; 181–82; to Fry, approves draft, 189; dispatches doctors, 189; incursions, 201; Michigan quota recalculated, 211; complains about Fry, 212; Fry defends, 212; Richmond's fall, 213; monument committee, 216; summaries, Michigan recruiting, manpower, casualties, 225–28; 226; approach to Blair, Lincoln 1862 call, 246n85; Upper Peninsula recruiting, 248n174; 1864 AG Report, draft and enlistments, Hill and Robertson compared, 260n210

Robinson, Erasmus D., 38*; Detroit provost guard, 144

Robinson, John B., Altoona Address, 141

Robinson, James F., 135

Rochester, Michigan, women, supplies sent, 100

Rochester, New York, 15, 20, 22, 36, 39, 48, 51, 52, 67; Stanton alerts mayor, rebel plot, 254n189

Rogers, Randolph, 38*; Soldiers' and Sailors' Monument, 218

Rome, New York, 52

Rome, Michigan, Ninth Cavalry, 160

Romeo, Michigan, 24, 34; Ninth Infantry, 110; Eighth Cavalry, 159–60

Romeyn, James W., 38–39*; 82

Roscommon County, map; Thirty-Seventh Congress, Fourth Congressional District, 63

Rosecrans, William, 15, 101; replaces Buell, 144; wire to Blair, 155

Ross, Michigan, Seventh Cavalry, 154

Royalton, Michigan, Seventh Cavalry, 154

RMS Trent, seizure, 111

Ruggles, George D., 6

Russell, Alfred, 39*; Hopkins hoax, 109; investigating disloyal persons, 111; reports disloyalty, 113; KGC controversy, 122; report to Seward, 204; lobbied to loosen Free Press on passport enforcement, 260n190; passport system, 204; signs equal suffrage petition, 212

Russell Avenue, Detroit, 73

Russell House Hotel (Detroit), 83, 131

Russell, William (Lord Russell), 12; proclamation of neutrality, Foreign Enlistment Act, 243n257

Russell, Massachusetts, 10

Russellville, Kentucky, secession, 112

Rutgers College (New Jersey), 46

Saginaw city, map; 17, 28, 57; Fifth Infantry, 105; Third Cavalry, 111; First United States Lancers, organized, 112; Tenth Michigan, 121; Twenty-Third Infantry, musters, 139; Sixth Cavalry, 144; Newberry visit, 182; Sixteenth Infantry departs, 186; Twenty-Ninth Infantry, musters, 199; Native American troop contribution, 227

Saginaw County, map; Thirty-Seventh Congress, Fourth Congressional District, 63; 82

Saginaw Daily Express, 17

Saginaw Morning Herald, 17

Saginaw Valley, 69

Saginaw Valley Republican, Indian scare, 138

St. Albans, Vermont, raid, 200, 203

St. Antoine Street (Detroit), Falkner riot, 157

St. Charles, Michigan, Twenty-Ninth Infantry, 199

St. Clair, Arthur, 60

St. Clair city, map; 52; women, supplies sent, 100; Ladies' Aid Society, 104; Fifth Infantry, 105; Fifteenth Infantry, 123; Eighth Cavalry, 159–60; Eleventh Cavalry, 175

St. Clair County, map; 28; Thirty-Seventh Congress, Fourth Congressional District, 63; 74; immigration, 75; militia draft deficiency, 181; 236n80

St. Clair, J.J., Delegate to Chicago, 79

St. Clair River, 52, 55, 73; land bridge, 259n173

St. Johns, Michigan, First United States Lancers, organized, 112; Fourteenth Infantry, 121; Twenty-Third Infantry, musters, 139

St. Joseph city, *map*; 92; Sixth Infantry, 104; Burge's Western Sharpshooters, Company D, 106; Third Cavalry, 111; First Regiment Light Artillery, Battery G, 120; Twelfth Infantry, 122; Nineteenth Infantry, 138; Twenty-Fifth Infantry, 141; Twenty-Eighth Infantry, 201; Richmond's fall, 213

St. Joseph County, *map*; 38, 41, 52; Thirty-Seventh Congress, Second Congressional District, 63; 68; 236n80

St. Joseph's retreat, 245n80

St. Joseph Traveler, on secession, 87; 92; Richmond's fall, 213

Saint Louis, Missouri, 17, 29, 34, 36, 52–53, 97, 102; Michigan units muster, 106; Newberry, 107; 109, 123; Michigan troops, 186; hospitals, soldier voting, 200; Michigan agency, 207; headquarters, "Western," 208; Weston Flint, services to hospitals, 208

St. Louis Times, 34

St. Mary's Falls, American Lock, 56; annual shipping, 233n5

St. Mary's Hospital, Detroit, U.S. General Hospital, private aid to patients, 207, 208; history, wartime service, 229, 245n80, 246n81

St. Marys River, 55; 233n5

St. Mary's Windsor, Canada, subversive organizations, 123

St. Vincent's Catholic Female Orphan Asylum (Detroit), 245n80

St. Vincent's Hospital, 229

Salem, Indiana, 165

Saline, *map*; 39; Sixth Infantry, 104

Salinesville, Ohio, 167

Salisbury, North Carolina, Twenty-Fifth Infantry, 216; Twenty-Third Michigan, 216–17

Salisbury, Vermont, 41

Salomon, Edward, attends Cleveland meeting, 129; military service, racial restrictions, 133–34; governors' petition, 1862 call, 246n86

Sanderson, George, casualty, 125

Sandusky, Ohio, 173–74; *Philo Parsons*, 197–98; Harbor, 198

Sandwich, Canada, *Philo Parsons*, 197–98

Sanford, George P., 39*; deputy provost marshal, 162

San Francisco, California, 31, 40

San Jose, California, 31

Sandisfield, Massachusetts, 30

Sangerfield, New York, 28

Sanilac County, *map*; Thirty-Seventh Congress, Fourth Congressional District, 63; Tenth Michigan, 121

Santa Fe, New Mexico, 23

Saranac, Michigan, 99; Twenty-First Infantry, 138; Sixth Cavalry, 144

Saulk band (Black Hawk War), 66

Sault Ste. Marie, city, *map*; 39; First Michigan, 107; 115; **Joint Resolution No. 9**, 148

Sault Ste. Marie River, 74

Savannah, Georgia, 203

Savannah privateers, 50

Saxon, Rufus, 145

Saybrook, Connecticut, 51

Scandinavia, nativity of Michigan force, 226

Schoolcraft city, 30; Underground Railroad, 61; Sixth Infantry, 104; Third Cavalry, 111; Twenty-Fifth Infantry, 141

Schoolcraft County, *map*; Thirty-Seventh Congress, Fourth Congressional District, 63

Schuyler, Mrs. George L, 19, 230

Scipio, New York, 27, 36

Scotland, Michigan settlement, 75; nativity of Michigan force, 226

Scott, Thomas A., 6; controls rails, telegraphs, 98; authorizes regiments, 109; African American troops, 111; inspection to Michigan, 121; railroad negotiations, 134

Scott, Winfield, 12, 50, 70; western strategy, 95, 96; Anaconda Plan, 98, 240n240; replies to governors, 98–99; replaced, 111

Scranton, Pennsylvania, 33

Secession Winter (1860–1861), 56, 62

Second Baptist Church (Detroit), 92

Seminole War(s), 7; 26, 38, 39, 50

Seneca County, New York, 42, 48

Seneca Falls, New York, 33

Seneca (New York) Observer, 38

Seventieth New York Infantry, Company C, 99; musters out, 192

Seventh Connecticut Infantry, 10

Seventy-Ninth New York, 158–59

Seward, William H., 44, 66, 70, 77, 79; nominated, 80; Detroit, Lansing, Kalamazoo speeches, 83; disloyalty in Michigan, 104–5; Pierce controversy, 107; warns Blair maritime threats, 110; report to, disloyal persons, 111; orders Michigan arrests, 112; disloyalty, 113; Cass advises, 114; demand for Pierce documents, 123; background July troop call, 127–29; Astor House meeting, 128; 129; emancipation, 130; advises Lincoln emancipation, 133; from Thurston, rebels in Canada, 203; Russell report, 204; British neutrality, 243n257; governors' petition, 1862 call, 246n86

Seymour, Horatio, Gettysburg cemetery dedication, 174; Democratic National Convention, 194

Seymour, Thomas H., Democratic National Convention, 195

Shaftsbury, Vermont, 65

Sharpsburg, Maryland, 140

Vernor, Benjamin, 45*; Blair appoints, stationed Detroit, 158; activities, 184, 207; 229

Vernor, James, 45

Vernor's Ginger Ale, 45

Versailles, Indiana, 165

Veteran Volunteers, 98, 107, 109, 111, 114; 1864 summary, 206–7

Vevay, Switzerland, 43

Vicksburg, Mississippi, 88; federal bombardment, 127

Vincennes, Indiana, rail, 56

Vincent, Thomas M., 6, 136; status report, 140; volunteers' status, 169; status, Michigan credits, recruiter compensation and bounties, 170; to Blair, discharging regiments, 190

Virginia, 13, 27, 32, 55; resolution to Michigan, 88; state convention, 93; secedes, 98; 107, 108, 109; Michigan deployments, 118, 138, 140, 174, 175; 158, 162, 165; credit dispute, 169 and reply, 170; 186, 188, 190; 192, 198, 199; Michigan Relief Association/Committee, 11, 14, 18; dispatched agents, 245n53

Wabash River, 56, 89

Wacousta, Michigan, 44

Wade, Benjamin, 64, 83; Ohio Western Reserve constituency, 196

Wadsworth, James, 142

Walbridge, Hiram, 45–46*; lobbying for Blair, 99, 100

Walbridge, David S., 46*; 78

Waldron, Henry, 46*, 82, 83; Corwin Amendment, 90; pro-war speaker, 94

Wales, Michigan settlement, 75

Walker, Charles, I., 46*, 92

Walker, Edward C., 46*; chairs post-Faulkner riot meeting, 158; Christian Commission, 162

Walker, Henry N., 46–47*; Hopkins hoax, 109; sword presentation, 136; 236n7

Walton, New York, 40

Ward, Eber, 47*, 72; speaks, July 1862 rally, 130; threatened, 131

Warner, William, 47*, 115

War of 1812, 7, 26, 40, 48; Michigan experience, 55; 71, 73–74

Warren, Rev. John A., Faulkner riot aftermath, 158

Warrenton, Virginia, 33

Washburn, Israel, 85, 238n78; governors' petition, 1862 call, 246n86

Washington, D.C., 7, 10, 11, 26, 27, 33, 39, 43, 49, 51, 56; abolition of slavery in, 62, 65, 75, 85; Peace Conference, 88; 93, 96, 98, 100; military division, 102; Michigan District of Columbia Soldiers' Relief founded, 114; Sons of Michigan, 114; allotment commissioners, deploy, 121; threatened, 126; 138; General Hospitals, 139, 141, 207;

140; Michigan benevolence, 151–52; Tunnicliffe state agent, 158; 161; officer examination board, 167; hospitals in, 183; Early raid, 185; Michigan agency, 207; private aid to, 207; Michigan Soldiers' opens "Home," 213; Grand Review, 215; Second Michigan, First Michigan Sharpshooters, 218

Washington, D.C., defenses, 25; Michigan deployments, 118, 150; 190; 192; Early's Washington Raid, 193; hospitals, soldier voting, 200; 225; hospitals, 229

Washington, George, 90

Washtenaw County, map; 9, 34; Thirty-Seventh Congress, First Congressional District, 63; African American population and foreign immigration, 75; Democratic election gains, 124; draft, 191; representation, Michigan Equal Rights League, 219; troop contribution, 225; 236n80; draft; state laws supporting bounties, pay, family aid, 263n131 eligible men, 248n198

Waterloo, Michigan, draft, 154

Waterloo, New York, 10, 38

Waterloo (New York) Observer, 51

Watertown Freeman, 8

Watertown, New York, 8

Waterville, New York, 34

Watervliet, Michigan, Burge's Western Sharpshooters, Company D, 106

Watson, Peter H., 6; 135; to Blair, 140

Wattles, David C., 47*; 108; investigated, 111; arrested, 112; refuses parole, 121; accepts parole, 124

Wayne, Anthony, 73

Wayne County, map; 12, 48; Thirty-Seventh Congress, First Congressional District, 63; African American population, 75; 131; Twenty-Fourth Infantry, 134; Michigan People's Union Party, 140; black recruits, 168; colored volunteer bounties, 169; delayed October 1863 draft, 171; **No. 220:** An Act to allow the county of Wayne to issue bonds for the purpose of paying the indebtedness of said county, made on the account of the volunteers' relief fund, 181; representation, Michigan Equal Rights League, 219; troop contribution, 225; summary, family aid, 228; 236n80; Twenty-Fourth recruiting, 247n130; state laws supporting bounties, pay, family aid, 263n131

Wayne County Poorhouse, 246–46n80

Wayne County Savings Bank, 20

Wayne County Sheriff, 21, 26

Wayne County (New York) Whig, 33

Wayne State University School of Medicine, 229

"We Are Coming Father Abraham," 20, 146

Webber, Jacob, 47*; 82

Webster, Daniel, 48

Weed, Thurlow, 85; Astor House meeting, 128

Welland Canal, Ontario, rebel attacks, 173

Welles, Gideon, emancipation, 130

Wells, Hezekiah G., 47*; Republican State Convention, 189–90

Wellsville, Michigan, Fourth Cavalry, 138

West Bloomfield, New Jersey, 32

West Bloomfield, New York, 32

Western District of New York College of Physicians and Surgeons, 35

Western Reserve College (Ohio), 23

Western Sanitary Commission, 107; Chicago branch appeal, Michigan response, 156; affiliates with Detroit Ladies' Soldiers' Aid, 167; 183, 207; headquartered, St. Louis, 208; Central Office, and generally, 230; Michigan Branch, 13, 19; affiliates with Western Sanitary Commission, 107; donates to Harper, continuing care, 219

Western World, 52

Westmoreland, New York, 31

West Point, United States Military Academy at, 7; 11, 15, 16, 22, 23, 25, 26, 38, 39, 40, 50; suspicion of, 64, 151; Visiting Board, 71; 98

West Virginia, 26, 29, 97, 99; formed, 100; 105; Carnifax Ferry, 106; 113; Michigan deployments, 118; 120; Altoona Conference, 138–42; admitted to union, 146; six month militia call, 162; six-month call ended, 167; Michigan aid to forces, 230

Wexford County, map; Thirty-Seventh Congress, Fourth Congressional District, 63

Wheatfield, Michigan, Union League Association, 184

Wheeler, Joseph, 32

Wheeling Conventions (Western Virginia), First, 97; Second, 99; "Ordinance," 100; Kanawha, State of, 103

Wheeling, West Virginia, 97, 99; private aid to, 207

Wheelock, Julia Susan, 48–49*; nursing, 139; Washington Association hires, 143; Washington activities, 183, 231; to Fredericksburg, 189; fever, 192

Wheelock, Orville, 139

Whigs, 63; immigrant voting, 233n23

Whipple, Francis, 49

Whipple, Henry E., 49*; 151

White House, Virginia, Michigan surgeons to, 189; Michigan hospital aid to, 207

White Pigeon, Indiana, 57

White Pigeon, Michigan, 9, 51; Chandler Horse Guard, musters, 103; Eleventh Infantry organizes, 107

Whiting, Joseph P., investigating disloyal persons, 111

Whiting, William, draft legality, 193

Whitmore Lake, Michigan, Third Cavalry, 111; Ninth Cavalry, 160

Whittlesey, Henry Martyn, 49*; 82, 92

Wilberforce, Ohio, 18

Wide Awakes, 82

Wilkes, Charles, 111, 114

Wilkins, Ross, 49*; pro-war meeting, 94; July 22 1862 war meeting, 132

Wilkins, William D., 11; 49–50*; 92

Willard, Electa L., 48

Willard, Luther B., 48*; Blair appoints, deployed, 158; Chickamauga, 170; 1863 responsibilities, 183–84; wounded, Chattanooga hospitals, 193; reports, 1864, 208; civilian workforce, 208; 229

Willard, William, election loss, 202

Willcox, Eben, 50

Willcox, Orlando, 38, 50*, 82, 92; First Michigan, 95, 97; First Bull Run, POW, 101; release, 132, 135; with Lincoln, Blair, Chandler, 135; Detroit celebration, 137; POW, 147; banning subversive organizations, 163, 213

Willett, A.M., First USSS, 241n116

Willett, Floyd A., First USSS, 50*

William Phelps & Company, 36

Williams, Albert, 50–51*; soldier voting, 155

Williams, Alpheus S., 11, 19; staff, 36, 49, 50; 51*; 82, 92; speaks pro-war meeting, 94; appointed brigadier, 94; commands Fort Wayne, 99; Cameron authorizes to muster, 103; 104

Williamsburg, Ohio, 165

Williams College (Massachusetts), 15, 34, 65

Williamsport, Virginia, 126

Williamston, Michigan, Union League Association, 184

Williamstown, Massachusetts, 34

Williams, William B., 51*; commands Twenty-Ninth Infantry, 194

Williston, Vermont, 49

Wills, David, Gettysburg cemetery, 167; to Blair, 168; meeting of cemetery commissioners, 176

Wilmington, Delaware, 66

Wilmington, North Carolina, 193, 194; captured, 212

Wilmot Proviso, 62, 65, 66

Wilson, Henry, bounty extension permanent, 187

Wilson, James W., 106

Wilson, T., 237n62

Wilson Township, Ohio, 37

Winchester, Virginia, 126

Windsor, Ontario, 9, 131; Vallandigham, 168; rebel activities, 172–73, 174; 186, 188; *Philo Parsons*, 197; rebel activities, 203

Winkler, Flanders, Smith, Bottom & Vilas, 22

Wisconsin, 55, 56, 57, 89; governor, 96; Western Sanitary Commission, 107; 108, 129; Department of the Ohio, 135; Altoona Conference, 138–42; Dakota War reaction, 144; 184; Charleston, Illinois, antiwar mob, 187; comparative manpower contribution and percentages, 225; nativity and comparative education of Michigan force, 226; mean age at enlistment, 264n8

Wisconsin River, 89; 233n23

Wisner, Moses, 51*; 55; on immigration, 57; Under the Oaks, 63; 70, 83, 85; valedictory speech, 86, 87, 115; personal liberty law, 115; death, 153

Witherell, Benjamin F.H., 48*; monument committee, 216

Witherell, James, 48

Withington, William H., 48*; 92; 137

Wolcott, Christopher P., 6; western propaganda campaign, 129–30

Wood, Benjamin, 53

Wood, Fernando, 53

Wood, George T., Kentucky Military Board, governors' petition, 1862 call, 246n86

Wood, James C., 51–52*; 91

Wood, Obadiah C., 52*; forms black militia, 91

Wood, Robert C., 98, 190

Woodbury, Dwight Avery, 52*; 88, 92

Woodsonville, Kentucky, 139

Woodstock, Vermont, 20

Worcester, Massachusetts, 18, 38

World's Columbian Exposition at Chicago, 35

Wormer, Grover S., 52*; commands Stanton Guard, 125' Mackinac Island, 126; muster out, 139; commands Jackson rendezvous, 187; commands Thirtieth Infantry, 202

Worthington, Massachusetts, 67

Wright, Horatio G., commander Department of the Ohio, 135; wires Blair, 138; Burnside relives, 158

Wright, Phineas C., 52–53*; arrested, Grand Rapids, 188

Wyandotte, Michigan, 52; Twenty-Fourth recruiting, 247n130

Yale College, 19, 34, 36, 46, 51

Yale Law School, 10, 19, 51, 68

Yankee Doodle, 132

Yates, Richard, 96, 98, 99, 138; Stanton requests troops, Yates replies, 162

Yellow Fever Plot, 27

York, Michigan, **No. 29:** An Act to legalize the action of the township of York in reference to raising volunteers, 206

York, Pennsylvania, 163; Michigan agent hospital visits, 183; hospitals, soldier voting, 200; private aid to, 207

Ypsilanti, *map*; 18, 19, 25, 34, 43; Underground Railroad, 61; size, 74; Second Infantry, 95; Republican mass meeting, 82, 83; Third Cavalry, 111, 118; Fourteenth Infantry, musters, 121; subversive organizations, 123; Old State Guard, formed, 135; Twentieth Infantry, 135; Sixteenth Infantry, 137; Twenty-Eighth Infantry, 154; 157; colored soldiers' bounties, 169; contribute, Northwestern Soldiers' Fair, 171; First Michigan Colored Infantry recruitment tour, 175; victory rally, 196; African Americans celebrate Maryland's abolition, 196; Appomattox Court House, 213; Christian Commission delegates, 230–31

Ypsilanti Commercial, Atlanta victory, 195–96; Twenty-Ninth Infantry, 199; Thirteenth Amendment, 211; Lincoln inaugurated, 213; Appomattox Court House, 213, 231

Zanesville, Ohio, 66